D1298880

[redacted]

[redacted]

European Marketing Data and Statistics 1993

Euromonitor Plc, 87-88 Turnmill Street, London EC1M 5QU

MERCER UNIVERSITY MAIN LIBRARY

EUROPEAN MARKETING DATA AND STATISTICS 1993

First published 1964
Twenty-eighth edition 1993

Researched and published by

EUROMONITOR
87-88 Turnmill Street
London EC1M 5QU
Great Britain

Telephone: (071) 251 8024
Telex: 262433
Fax: (071) 608 3149

European Marketing Data and Statistics 1993

A CIP catalogue record for this book
is available from the British Library

ISBN: 0 86338 457 9

ISSN: 0071-2930

© Euromonitor Plc 1993

This document is strictly copyright. Reproduction in any form whatsoever is prohibited and libraries should not permit photocopying without prior arrangement.

Printed in Great Britain

Distributed exclusively in North America by
Gale Research Company, Penobscot Building, Detroit, Michigan 48226

Ref
HA
1107
.E87
1993

CONTENTS

Continued...

Continued...

Continued...

Continued...

Continued...

Continued...

Continued...

Continued...

LIST OF CHARTS

FOREWORD

European Marketing Data and Statistics is a compendium of statistical information on the countries of Western and Eastern Europe. Published annually, it provides a wealth of detailed and up-to-date statistical information relevant to international market planning. The information is regularly updated and held on an international database of market information comprising 24 subject areas.

Published annually since the late 1960s, **European Marketing Data and Statistics**, or EMDAS, is now in its 28th edition. Data sections have been thoroughly revised for this new edition, and improved graphics have been included. Several sections have been expanded, to include completely new tables.

The data coverage includes a considerable number of fourteen- and fifteen-year trendings, which permit the analysis of socio-economic trends over a longer time span as a basis for forecasting. The inclusion of figures from the most recent complete year (in this edition 1991) for key parameters ensures that up-to-date information is available for analysis.

In addition to reporting on major European countries, the country coverage also includes smaller European countries and principalities. Although the availability of statistical information on these countries is limited and they are minor markets, it assists in building up a more comprehensive picture of the total European market and will be of interest to academic users.

The data are presented in spreadsheet form and a number of extrapolated tables have been included, together with graphs, marketing maps and diagrams.

Readers requiring guidance on further sources of information are referred to *European Directory of Marketing Information Sources* (Euromonitor 1990) and *European Directory of Non-Official Statistical Sources* (2nd edition, Euromonitor 1993) for more comprehensive listings.

The handbook contains a full alphabetical index, and there is also a guide to sources used in the compilation. The introduction includes an overview of the European market.

A companion volume of marketing data, *International Marketing Data and Statistics* (IMDAS) is also available. Country coverage in IMDAS 1993 provides a comprehensive world-wide context and there are unique regional consolidations (which also bring in comparisons with some European data from this volume). International data are provided in the same format for ease of comparison with the European figures presented in this volume.

User comments are welcomed concerning the databases in **European Marketing Data and Statistics**. Also, whilst the editors have made every effort to ensure accuracy Euromonitor cannot accept responsibility for any errors which may have occurred.

INTRODUCTION : THE EUROPEAN MARKET - AN OVERVIEW

In the last few years the entire post-war structure of Europe, and the political and economic divisions which emerged in the years after 1945, have witnessed tremendous change. In their place a newly formed and significantly united Europe is beginning to emerge, in which many of the confrontational positions underlying the whole historical division into East and West have become irrelevant.

The first element in this process of change has been the formation of the European Community's Single Market, which will go into force in January 1993 regardless of the doubts being expressed in various national quarters about the more far-reaching Maastricht Treaty on political and economic union. The Single Market has been widely perceived as permitting a large-scale deregulation of European business, and its impact on efficiency and free competition will be incalculable.

The second and equally important development has been the radical restructuring, during the late 1980s and early 1990s, of East European societies. The very rapid transition of these societies from the constraints of their communist ideologies has outstripped all but the most optimistic expectations. The introduction of multi-party politics and the opening of their economies to the principles of capitalism have attracted vast sums of Western investment capital, as producers see not only the potential for selling into a much larger consumer market in the East, but also for manufacturing within that market, with a view to re-exporting to the West.

The unification of Germany, which formally took place in October 1990, was perhaps the most obvious sign of the shift towards market forces and more liberal governments which has swept through the East of the continent. The opening up of the former Eastern Bloc countries has far-reaching implications for the collection of marketing data, and already during the compilation of this edition of **European Marketing Data and Statistics** the benefits have begun to filter through, in the form of more reliable data and better access to official information for countries where research has previously been difficult to come by. It seems likely that this trend will continue as these countries become more geared up to the collection and processing of consumer marketing data, and this will be reflected in future editions of this volume.

The third major factor which appears particularly significant in the early 1990s has been the virtual eclipse of EFTA, the European Free Trade Association. Of its members, Switzerland, Austria, Finland, Sweden and most recently Norway have all been making approaches to the Community with a view to full membership, and most have declared themselves interested in joining the proposed European Economic Area (EEA), the organisation through which Brussels plans to interact with all its traditional trade partners in the medium term. All the EFTA countries have been carefully aligning not only their production and trading standards but also their financial markets with the standards now being laid down by Brussels. By the end of the 1990s, it appears virtually certain that all EFTA members (except, perhaps, Iceland) will be full members of the EC.

1. Opportunities and Risks in Eastern Europe

The extraordinary rate of Eastern Europe's transition to capitalism notwithstanding, the region has not been without its problems since the abolition of communist rule in the late 1980s. In most countries, the abolition of price controls and the winding-down of state subsidies have caused a drastic escalation of the inflation rate, and considerable hardship has been experienced in many parts of the region as the unfamiliar forces of the marketplace have driven up the prices of those basic goods which were in short supply. The shortages were exacerbated by two further factors: firstly, the actual decline in the output of goods, as inefficient factories were forced to close by the forces of the marketplace, and secondly, the sudden disappearance of the state distribution mechanisms. In the former USSR, for example, it was claimed that vast amounts of food were left rotting in the fields because there was no longer a central authority to co-ordinate the harvest or to distribute and market the products.

It goes without saying that the closure of inefficient enterprises has caused massive unemployment, and that high rates of inflation have brought about an extremely rapid depreciation in the values of all Eastern European currencies - so much so, indeed, that nowadays most countries conduct their foreign trade in Deutsche Marks or in US dollars. The effective price of essential imports has risen accordingly. Yet despite all these hardships, there have been few indications that any significant sector of the public wants to turn back the clock. In Hungary, in Poland, in the former Czechoslovakia and in the new Federal German Länder, entrepreneurial skills have sprung up with unexpected speed to fill the vacuum left in the marketplace by the disappearing state. Each of these countries has implemented a privatisation programme, aimed at returning large parts of the old nationalised industries to the private sector, and many Western companies have found unique opportunities in the East.

The early months of 1993 will find the region still searching for any kind of political cohesion, and there will be attendant risks for all investors interested in the Eastern market. In the former Soviet Union, which has now splintered into 15 constituent republics, factional infighting and inter-regional feuding have marred the transition to multi-party democracy as the first flush of independence has worn off. In what used to be Yugoslavia, a brutal civil war has been the first result of the political deregulation which characterised the early 1990s. Even the former Czechoslovakia has taken the decision to split, albeit cordially, into its two constituent states, the Czech Republic and the Slovak Republic.

In some countries, voters' reaction to their new-found freedoms has been cautious. Bulgaria and Romania used their first free elections to re-elect the same small political cliques which had ruled them under the banner of their respective communist parties; the same happened in Serbia, and in several states of the former Soviet Union.

2. The Single European Market

For most observers, the triumphant arrival of the Single European Market in January 1993 will have been deeply overshadowed by the currency crisis of late 1992 and by the difficulties which it placed in the way of the Maastricht Treaty on economic and political union. Indeed, by October 1992 it was becoming fashionable to query whether the Single Market could function without Maastricht. Yet this is to miss the point: they are two (or rather, three) different entities.

The Single European Market has three main aims, none of which is essentially intended to broach the subject of either political or economic union. By demolishing the protective trade arrangements which have been erected by the 12 EC member states since the Second World War, and by establishing a set of pan-European manufacturing standards to facilitate cross-border trade, the Single Market aims to improve efficiency and to enhance the potential for cross-border co-operation. It aims to back up these opportunities by guaranteeing the right to freedom of movement, as well as freedom of employment and residence.

The Single Market does, however, hand certain national powers to the European Commission, in that it empowers Brussels to enforce its free-market rules across national frontiers. These have not, so far, aroused serious concern, since they are clearly intended for the protection of the consumer and the private investor.

3. The Maastricht Agreement and the 1992 Currency Crisis

The Maastricht Agreement of December 1991, like the Single European Market, has its basic origins in the Treaty of Rome in 1957. There, however, the similarities end. Maastricht envisages a considerable increase in the amount of power to be exercised by Brussels, to the extent that its critics have been able to accuse it of "Euro-federalism": the centralisation of all major strategic decisions, with only minor decisions being taken by regional bodies. Brussels has attempted to counter the Euro-sceptics' fears of continual Euro-interference, by endorsing the principle of "subsidiarity", by which it means that each policy decision in a united Europe will be taken by the smallest and most local body that is competent to consider it, rather than being taken consistently at the top.

Much the most contentious issue surrounding the Maastricht Agreement, however, is the proposal that the 12 European Community members, together with any new members who might have joined in the meantime, should share some sort of a common currency - or, at the very least, that their currencies should be permanently locked together in a fixed parity relationship. This is, by definition, a federal issue of the highest order, because no common European currency could be managed without a common European central bank implementing a common European fiscal policy.

The currency crisis of late 1992 dealt a particularly serious blow to the pro-Maastricht sentiment in many countries, because it highlighted the extent to which EC members were likely to resist moves towards a central fiscal policy. Germany, facing the prospect of rising inflation after its successful union with the East, had taken a unilateral decision to break the rules of the Exchange Rate Mechanism (ERM) within the European Monetary System, by opting to raise its interest rates to high levels in order to choke off its excessive demand. Under ERM regulations, it was obliged to bring them down again if its currency became too strong - as it very rapidly did. As the Deutsche Mark soared, the German government then sought to deflect international criticism by claiming that the fault lay in other countries' weakness rather than in its own excessive strength. Italy and Spain were obliged to devalue, while the UK withdrew "temporarily" from the ERM and allowed its currency to fall on market forces, and while Sweden resorted to interest rates of 500% in an attempt to bolster the kronor. Germany did, however, intervene to stop the French franc from falling excessively far.

The rights or wrongs of the 1992 currency crisis were still being debated at the time of writing this introduction, but the issue appeared to underline the inability of the ERM mechanism - as it stood - to enforce exchange rate stability in the face of determined opposition from any one member country. Full monetary or political union would inevitably imply the demand that all members should place their complete trust in the "European-mindedness" of their fellows. It appears to be this confidence which has been damaged by Germany's independent line.

4. Population Development

With a total population of almost 851 million in 1991, including some 290 million citizens of the former Soviet Union, the continent of Europe represents the world's second largest group of consumers. Practically all of them enjoy above-average standards of living when judged by world standards; most have longer life-spans and lower mortality rates than the global norm; none have to cope with a tropical climate; and in all but a handful of smaller countries there is a significant degree of industrial economy offering the opportunity of rising above the level of agricultural self-sufficiency.

There, however, the similarities end. Beside the relatively prosperous and industrialised countries of the north-west, including most of the European Community and all the member states of the European Free Trade Association, there are substantial populations in the east and the south whose way of life is still very distinct from those of their north-western counterparts, and whose priorities as consumers do not necessarily follow the north-western trend at all.

There are, for instance, at least 60 million Muslims in the region (excluding citizens of the former USSR), mostly in Turkey and Yugoslavia, for whom many of the cultural traditions of the north-west are still relatively unfamiliar. In large areas of Greece, Cyprus or Malta, life for many people goes on without any need for the ubiquitous microprocessor technology, and large numbers of the population spend their whole lives in the village where they grew up. Nor is there any real prospect that this will change in the foreseeable future.

The European population as a whole is growing by only about 0.5 per cent a year, a figure which is well below the world average of 1.8 per cent and which generally reflects its affluence and increasing sophistication. Growth is at its lowest in Germany (especially the Eastern half), and in Hungary, which recorded negative rates between 1977 and 1991; in Turkey and Albania, on the other hand, populations increased by up to 30 per cent during the same period. In the republics of the former Soviet Union, virtually all of the increase has been among the non-Russian and especially the Muslim peoples of the southern Republics, and for the first time since the October Revolution ethnic Russians now comprise less than half the population.

If we leave aside the Muslim states and those countries where contraception is still either illegal or unobtainable, we perceive a series of successive swings in the birth rate, most of which reflect the economic and social fortunes of their respective populations. The most notable, and of course the most completely documented, was the baby boom which occurred immediately after the end of the Second World War and during the early 1950s and 1960s; but other booms have occurred due to political factors (as, for example, in Albania or Romania, where premiums have at times been awarded to the parents of large families).

In most of Europe the baby boom ended in the late 1960s, and the recession-struck 1970s saw a noticeable drop in the numbers of pregnancies whose effects are already becoming increasingly apparent. In a few countries the effect is already so severe as to merit careful consideration by anyone looking at the future growth of their markets.

According to estimates from the European Commission, for example, the numbers of EC residents aged 15 to 25 are set to fall by 15 per cent between 1980 and 1995, bringing the cumulative fall since 1985 to 25 per cent - the worst effects being felt in Western Germany and in Scandinavia (down by some 35 per cent over the ten-year period).

For the Netherlands, the United Kingdom, Luxembourg and Belgium, too, the shortfall in the high-consuming 15-25 age band will be of the order of 20 per cent by the time 1995 arrives. Spain, Portugal and Italy can expect a steep relative decline in the younger age band of 5-14, reflecting the earlier onset of the decline in the birth rate.

For some countries (Germany, Sweden, Denmark and Austria) the problem may prove even more acute in the long run. Labour shortages are already pushing up wage rates in Scandinavia, and the signs are that Germany's dependency ratio (the ratio of over-65s to persons of working age) will exceed 1:1 by the year 2030.

In the shorter term, of course, the news is far from bad. The 25-45 age group whose numbers will be increasing in the first half of the 1990s are among the most affluent consumers of all, having formed family units and started to consume household goods in large quantities as they reach the peak of their personal earnings potential. By the year 2000 they will be starting to consume more leisure goods and more health care goods and services.

It is no coincidence that Greece, Portugal, Spain and the Republic of Ireland, as the poorest and most devoutly Catholic (i.e. anti- contraception) countries in Western Europe, were the least affected by the relative dearth of births in the 1970s - or that they will accordingly record some of the biggest overall population growths in 1985-1995 (6.82 per cent for Portugal, 6.67 per cent for Greece, and 4.15 per cent for Spain).

Nonetheless, the advent of economic prosperity in southern Europe during 1986-1990 resulted in a very severe drop in marriage rates, coinciding with a correspondingly large increase in divorce rates. The legalisation of abortion (and, in France, the approval of the so-called "abortion pill") represent a major departure from Vatican doctrine in Catholic countries - excepting, of course, Ireland, where all divorce, abortion and contraception is illegal.

Generally speaking, couples tend to postpone the start of a family during times of either great hardship or relative affluence - the first for obvious reasons, the second because a life of greater social sophistication encourages it. Certainly, most West European couples are bearing their first children at a later age than, say, thirty years ago; French statistics show, for example, that the average age rose by nearly five years between the mid-1950s and the mid-1980s, and the trend holds true for all countries except Ireland, Greece and Portugal. The trend has if anything been more marked in eastern Europe, where the average childbearing age has risen since the late 1980s, but this may change in the near future if sociologists' predictions are confirmed.

Males account for about 51.3 per cent of all live births, compared with the female proportion of 48.7 per cent. In most European countries, males outnumber females up to the age of about 50, and thereafter females start to predominate. But with the improving standards of health care in most countries the balance of the sexes is lasting later into life than was hitherto the case - all of which means that the absolute numbers of men aged 60 or more are rising somewhat faster than the numbers of women - a factor which is bound to prove of significance in marketing terms as the century progresses.

During the 1970s and 1980s, paradoxically, this increasingly healthy and long-lived European population of elderly people was being encouraged to retire from its working careers at an ever earlier age. On the one hand this simply reflected a growing view in society that it was unacceptable for the elderly to have to work as long as was hitherto the case; on the other the pressures of unemployment also militated in favour of an earlier retirement which would allow employers to concentrate job opportunities at the lower end of the age scale. By the early 1990s, however, there was a growing feeling that the trend toward early retirement could go into reverse, as the falling numbers of younger people, together with real shortages of labour (especially in the northern part of the continent), have threatened to push up the wage/price spiral to perhaps unsustainable levels.

5. Households

The relatively affluent spell of the last 20 years has been accompanied, predictably, by a steady increase in the numbers of households and a corresponding reduction in their size. Among members of the EC the average household size has shrunk from 2.8 persons in 1977 to 2.5 in 1991, and the decline may be expected to continue during the 1990s; in the EFTA group, where family sizes are already relatively small because of a much earlier devolution of the family unit, the recent decline has been slower, and in Eastern Europe the typical household has remained stable at around 3.6 persons.

In the smaller countries discussed in this handbook the average has actually increased - Turkey, for example, afflicted by a population explosion and a difficult economic climate, has seen the average household rise from 5.3 persons in 1977 to 5.6 in 1991. Among its more developed European neighbours, Ireland too has been only barely able to keep its households increasing at a fast enough rate to match the growth of the population; with an average 3.84 members (1991), it has by far the largest household units in the northern continent.

One factor behind the overall growth in European households has been the sharp increase in the numbers of divorced and separated people. Single-member households of all types have been increasing sharply in number since the mid-1960s (except in Spain and in Ireland), and the numbers of single-parent family units have more than doubled in practically all countries. One-person households are most common in Norway, in Western Germany, in Finland and in Denmark; they are least common in the southern states (Turkey, Albania, Malta, Cyprus, Spain and Gibraltar); the United Kingdom, with 25 per cent single-member households in 1987, is in the middle range as far as Europe is concerned.

Generally speaking, European populations are still moving towards the major conurbations as jobs disappear on the land, and as improved communications make it easier to move away from the family home. There is evidence that the trend towards the large cities has all but stopped in Switzerland, Austria and some of the northern states; but France, Greece, Spain and Portugal are already experiencing some depopulation of rural districts, while in Italy the depopulation of the southern *Mezzogiorno* has become a major political issue.

6. Living Standards

European housing standards, while not yet on a par with those of the United States, are on the whole reasonably comfortable. Table 1604 shows that around 82 per cent of all dwellings have an indoor shower or bath of some description, with the major exceptions being in Poland, Portugal and the former Yugoslavia. Some 88 per cent have their own toilet, and in most countries at least 90 per cent have a direct water supply - the major exceptions being the three countries listed above.

Typically, European households spend about a fifth of their disposable incomes on housing, rates and water supply, and another 4-7 per cent on domestic fuels. Relatively few households own the premises in which they live, and in many countries the price of building land, especially in the urban areas, has long since risen beyond the reach of many people. The UK, with 58 per cent home ownership, tops the league of strongly industrialised European countries, with Italy (55 per cent ownership) and France (51 per cent) also all well ahead of the bottom runners, Luxembourg and the Netherlands (about 32 per cent).

Among the non-socialist countries of Europe, owner-occupation tends to be most common among either the very wealthy countries or the very poor, where land is inexpensive and where populations do not migrate much from one region to another. Greece, for example, has 86 per cent owner-occupiers, while Portugal has 70 per cent, Ireland has 60 per cent and Spain has 58 per cent - about the same as the UK.

7. Consumer Demand

Private consumption, as Table 0314 shows, typically accounts for between 50 and 60 per cent of gross domestic product in European countries, and in the non-socialist economies direct expenditure through the retail sector has usually accounted for about two-thirds of this amount - the remainder going in rents, services, insurances and the like. Governments have always sought to boost private consumption when times were good and to restrain it, through high interest rates and other measures, when excessive purchasing threatened to push inflation too high. As such the moods of the consumer have become more important than ever in the calculations of finance ministers - who are often prevented by huge budget deficits from stimulating their economies with old-fashioned centralised spending.

In Britain, the frantic consumer boom occasioned by the 1988 tax concessions has been dampened down by the effects of recession in the early 1990s, with the high interest rate strategy adopted by the government exerting a lasting effect on consumer borrowing. In Italy, on the other hand, consumption levels are still on the increase, while in Germany the reunification with the East seems to have occasioned, belatedly, a consumer revival which reversed the somewhat disappointing trends of the late 1980s. In Spain and Portugal, both of which experienced a major surge in consumption after joining the Common Market in 1986, consumption has now been cut back by governments fearing a growing trade deficit and rising inflation: both have taken specific action to curb borrowing for consumer durables.

In Sweden and in Norway, too, governments have been trying to damp down the booming rate of private consumption - which shows every sign of engendering a return to high wage settlements and ensuing inflationary cycles unless something is done to prevent overheating.

In most of Europe, the rapid increase in numbers of households has been the main motive power behind sales of many household goods, especially durables. But in the next 15-20 years it seems likely that falling population levels among the 20-30 age group, together with rising costs, will have eroded the housing market, and durables manufacturers will have no option but to step up the rate of product innovation if they hope to achieve more than merely replacement sales.

Generally speaking, the experience of the minor markets in recent years has confirmed what one would expect: that consumer demand for certain items (notably food) rises disproportionately during the early stages of an economic revival, but that it tends to level off beyond a certain point of affluence as the purchasing of consumer goods, including durables, takes over. This is what we would expect to see happening in Spain and Portugal over the next ten to fifteen years.

Typically, as Tables 1102 and 1103 show, the European household spends about 20 per cent of its budget on buying foodstuffs (though the UK is a clear exception, spending not much more than half of this amount). In the less developed countries of the Mediterranean, of Eastern Europe and of Ireland, food accounts for a much larger proportion - sometimes as high as 45 per cent - and there is no immediate probability, in these slow-moving economies, of a major change here. Beverages tend to absorb 3-5 per cent of the household budget, depending on the very widely varying levels of indirect taxation on these products; in highly-taxed Ireland, for example, more than 13 per cent of the budget goes on alcoholic and non-alcoholic drinks.

In the West at least, clothing and footwear typically account for between 5 and 9 per cent of all outgoings, but in poorer countries the proportion may in fact be higher - despite the fact that in some low-wage areas (Turkey, most of Greece, Portugal and parts of Italy), a significant proportion of clothing and footwear is either home-made or manufactured locally at very low cost.

The remaining, less absolutely central areas of consumption (household goods and services, leisure, transport and personal goods) are, inevitably, those which are most vulnerable to short-term cancellation or postponement, and as such they serve as valuable indicators of the strength of the economy and its perceived prospects.

GUIDE TO USING THIS HANDBOOK

1. Scope of the Handbook

European Marketing Data and Statistics (EMDAS) is a statistical yearbook of business and marketing information. This edition features over 420 pages of up-to-date and detailed marketing statistics on 24 principal subject areas. These statistics are stored on a database of international marketing information and regularly updated by Euromonitor's research team.

The sections of EMDAS cover a wide variety of marketing topics, ranging from socio-economic trends and background information through to key consumer marketing parameters. The sections on economic indicators, communications, finance and banking, labour force, automotives and the environment all include additional data for this edition. Data covering energy, transport, industrial output and agricultural resources are included, as well as sections on service industries such as tourism and retailing.

In EMDAS 1993, each statistical tabulation presents pan-European comparative information, either in the form of trendings from 1977 to 1990, 1991 or 1992, or with single-year data for the latest year available. All the countries are listed down the left-hand column, presented in three economic entities (EC, EFTA, Eastern Europe) and "others". (Until data on individual republics becomes more plentiful, this book will continue to refer to the outdated entities of the USSR and Yugoslavia.) Where appropriate, regional totals and averages are included.

Where data is in values, units have been generally been left in national currencies. However the spreadsheets on which the data is stored facilitate calculations in US dollars. These are calculated only for the latest year available (usually 1990 and 1991) as fluctuations in exchange rates and contrasts in rates of inflation render year-on-year conversions meaningless.

In addition, calculations have been made where deemed appropriate to show European market shares by country, growth rates over a thirteen- or fourteen-year period, and per capita data. These permit easy cross-comparisons between countries, regions and markets.

Using EMDAS 1993 is easy. Whatever topic is of interest, you simply look up the tables (using the contents or index) and the table will show the relevant data for all countries. The heading shows the relevant section, title summary and title of the table, and unit. A guide to the sources used in the compilation of the data appears at the foot of the table, while any relevant notes are gathered together at the end of each section.

The aim of EMDAS is to locate in one handbook the essential statistical information relevant to European market planning. The handbook will save the busy marketeer or researcher hours of time trawling through statistics from many sources and provides a wealth of hard-to-get information drawn from the many reports and studies compiled by Euromonitor over the last 2-3 years - many based on trade interviews and original extrapolations. Business users and librarians will find the handbook especially useful.

2. Subject Coverage

EMDAS 1993 is presented in 24 separate sections or "databases" which have all been specially compiled for Euromonitor. The subjects have been selected as those most appropriate for strategic planning and European market analysis, covering both background marketing parameters and detailed consumer market information. The 24 databases are discussed below.

01 Marketing Geography

This database features maps for each of the major European markets, showing standard and marketing regions, and arranged by economic grouping. Also included is a summary of basic data (political conditions, languages, etc) for each country covered, and some key facts and figures. Several of the maps have been redrawn this year to reflect the changes in Eastern Europe.

02 Demographic Trends and Forecasts

This database features 23 statistical compilations covering population trends, vital statistics, urbanisation, demographic analysis by age and sex, and population forecasts. Much of the data is in thirteen-year trends, forming a basis for forecasting and projections.

03 Economic Indicators

This database features 16 tables of key economic data, again with several thirteen-year trend tables. The main economic indicators are all covered, including GDP, GNP, inflation, money supply, public and private consumption, government finance and exchange rates.

04 Finance and Banking

This enlarged section features nine tabulations mainly showing data from 1980-1991 and covering bank assets, liabilities, claims and interest rates, as well as information on credit card holders and accepting outlets, and usership of personal financial services.

05 External Trade by Destination and Commodity

This section includes ten tables which give a cohesive and structured trade overview covering total imports and exports and external trade breakdowns by origin/destination and commodity.

06 Labour Force Indicators

This database covers the key employment indicators including numbers employed, unemployed and hours of work. The structure of the economically active population by industry sector, age group and status is included for latest years available.

07 Industrial Resources and Output

This section provides key industrial indices for a 14-year period and includes output tables covering major industrial materials.

08 Energy Resources and Output

This section consists of 13 tables on energy supply and demand. Coverage extends to household energy consumption with several tables trended over 11 or 13 years.

09 Defence

Tables in this section give key data on defence spending and personnel.

10 Environmental Data

This section includes seven tables covering various environmental factors. New data have been included this year on industrial and municipal waste generation, as well as on recycling rates.

11 Consumer Expenditure Patterns

The presentation of this section comprises total consumer spending, a consolidated breakdown by product sector, and a series of tables analysing each major consumer sector. New 1991 data and estimates have been included and all the data are presented in 15-year trends with growth rates and 1991 dollar comparisons.

12 Retailing and Retail Distribution

This section has drawn on Euromonitor's extensive European retail research in recent years, with 21 tables covering retail sales and channels and breakdowns for different retail sectors.

13 Advertising Patterns and Media Access

This section includes a broad range of data on advertising expenditure and the media, organised into 11 tables.

14 Consumer Market Sizes

Per capita consumption and retail market sizes are included in 18 tables for 1991. The information for the EC and EFTA countries is drawn from Euromonitor's market information database, which forms the basis for the companion volume *Consumer Europe* (9th edition, Euromonitor 1993).

15 Consumer Prices and Costs

Trends in consumer prices and selected European living costs are included in five tables of data.

16 Housing and Household Facilities

This section comprises nine tables of comparative statistics on households. Data on housing stock and household composition are included together with available data on household ownership of selected consumer durables.

17 Health and Living Standards

This database comprises four tables covering major health indicators (including a table on reported AIDS cases).

18 Literacy and Education

A range of literacy and educational statistics are included in this six-table section.

19 Agricultural Resources

This section presents key data on land use and output of various agricultural products. There are ten tables on the database, mostly including figures for 1990.

20 Communications

This seven-table section features information on postal services and telecommunications. It has been expanded this year to include more data on fax and cellular radio systems.

21 Automotives

This 11-table database covers the circulation, manufacture and sales of cars, commercial vehicles and two-wheelers, and includes a new table on consumption of petrol, both leaded and unleaded.

22 Transport Infrastructure

This 16-table database covers major movements in terms of the road, rail, air and shipping transport sectors.

23 Tourism and Travel

This database consists of 10 tabulations covering tourism values and movements, tourist accommodation and its usage. New for 1993 is an analysis of holidaying habits across Europe.

24 Cultural Indicators

This section includes six tables covering available data on libraries, museums, book publishing and cinemas.

3. Data Coverage

Each of the statistical compilations is presented in one of four data periods:

(1) A 15-year trend table from 1977-1991, with data for each country drawn from the same consistent source. In some cases, intermediary years have been excluded for reasons of space, mainly 1978/79 and/or 1981/82.

(2) A different period trend, eg 1980-1991 (12-year trend) or a recent period (eg 1981-1988 or 1982-1989) where only certain periods are available.

(3) Latest year available, with the years differing between countries. These are used where the information is drawn from occasional studies, eg a census, or where statistical offices vary in the speed of publishing statistics.

(4) A single year, eg 1991, where space does not permit trends or where an interactive range of information is provided (eg imports by origin, usage of GDP, etc).

The statistics in this volume are as available during the compilation period (June-August 1992). Figures for 1991 (in some cases provisional or estimates) have been included where possible. However consolidations across Europe tend to take time and much of the data is for 1990. Various one-off surveys cover earlier years only.

4. Country Coverage

This edition of EMDAS includes a total of 32 countries in both Western and Eastern Europe. These are grouped into four economic entities, as follows:

EC (EUROPEAN COMMUNITY)

Belgium
Denmark
France
Germany: East
Germany: West
Greece
Ireland
Italy
Luxembourg
Netherlands
Portugal
Spain
United Kingdom

Note: Figures for the former East and West Germanies have been arranged consecutively, although for back data referring to the two countries separate rows of data have been included.

EFTA (EUROPEAN FREE TRADE ASSOCIATION)

Austria
Finland
Iceland
Liechtenstein
Norway
Sweden
Switzerland

EASTERN EUROPE

Albania
Bulgaria
Former Czechoslovakia
Hungary
Poland
Romania
Former USSR
Former Yugoslavia

Note: This book continues to refer to the former countries of the USSR and Yugoslavia, as statistics for individual republics are not yet available in large measure.

OTHERS

Cyprus
Gibraltar
Malta
Monaco
Turkey

5. Sources

European Marketing Data and Statistics is based on an extensive and on-going programme of research into European markets and industries. A Europe-wide network of market analysts and researchers work to pull together available data on socio-economic patterns, market conditions and trends, living standards and background information relevant to business, export and market planning.

The principal sources used in the compilation of EMDAS are as follows:

- International and European organisations, such as the United Nations, OECD, and the International Monetary Fund.
- National statistical offices in each country.
- Pan-European and national trade and industry associations.
- Industry study groups and unofficial research publishers.
- Euromonitor's own research publications, including one-off reports and statistical compilations.
- Original research specially commissioned for the handbook, including consumer research, trade interviews and retail surveys.

A guide to the main sources used in the compilation of each table is included at the foot of each table. For reasons of space the main sources are only briefly cited; in some cases, many different reports and publications are used in the preparation of just one table. For example, we may have extracted data from publications by the national statistical offices for all the countries covered in order to compile one table. In other cases, statistical compilations are from secondary sources which have in turn used many different sources.

A brief guide to the main sources used in each of the 24 databases follows.

01 Marketing Geography

Information mainly drawn from the business press, data from the yearbooks of the national statistical offices and various informal studies on the countries covered.

02 Demographic Trends and Forecasts

Drawn mainly from the statistical yearbooks of the national statistical offices supplemented with UN data and population forecasts.

03 Economic Indicators

The principal international sources are the World Bank and the International Monetary Fund (IMF). National statistical offices (yearbooks, national accounts) and economic bulletins by leading banks are also used.

04 Finance and Banking

The major source of comparative financial data is the IMF's *International Financial Statistics*.

05 External Trade by Destination and Commodity

The IMF, OECD and Eurostat (the Statistical Office of the European Community) track external trade flows in some detail. National statistical yearbooks are also utilised.

06 Labour Force Indicators

The primary international source is the International Labour Office, which publishes both a statistical yearbook and quarterly bulletins.

07 Industrial Resources and Output

Mainly drawn from UN and OECD publications, as well as associations covering various industry sectors.

08 Energy Resources and Output

This compilation draws mainly on the UN and the OECD.

09 Defence

Sources include the International Monetary Fund, the CIA and the International Institute of Strategic Studies.

10 Environmental Data

Drawn largely from OECD sources.

11 Consumer Expenditure Patterns

Drawn from the national accounts of each country (generally published by the national statistical offices). Euromonitor estimates have been used to reach levels of consolidation.

12 Retailing and Retail Distribution

Drawn from a wide number of Euromonitor's own surveys and market reports on European retailing including *European Directory of Retailers and Wholesalers* (Euromonitor 1988), *Retail Trade International* (Euromonitor 1991), and *World Retail Directory* (Euromonitor 1991) and also original research. Primary sources include retail trade censuses (various countries) by national statistical offices, retail trade associations, major retailers, etc.

13 Advertising Patterns and Media Access

Drawn from various media study groups, advertising associations and agents in various countries.

14 Consumer Market Sizes

Drawn from Euromonitor's consumer market database; primary sources include trade associations and industry leaders in all countries.

15 Consumer Prices and Costs

Mainly from the International Monetary Fund and the OECD; living costs from the International Labour Office and the Confederation of British Industry (CBI).

16 Households and Household Facilities

Compiled from various publications from national statistical offices, UN publications and incorporating Euromonitor estimates and calculations.

17 Health and Living Standards

The main sources are the World Health Organisation (yearbooks, various publications) and the OECD.

18 Literacy and Education

The main source is UNESCO with data from national statistical offices incorporated as available.

19 Agricultural Resources

Mainly based on the publications of the Food and Agricultural Organisation of the United Nations (FAO).

20 Communications

Mainly based on UN data.

21 Automotives

Drawn from various motor trades organisations and compilations from the same.

22 Transport Infrastructure

Based on various UN publications: other sources include the International Civil Aviation Authority, the International Road Federation, the Union Internationale des Chemins de Fer and Lloyd's Register of Shipping.

23 Tourism and Travel

A compilation drawn from the World Tourism Organisation, OECD and Euromonitor's own research.

24 Cultural Indicators

Mainly drawn from the UN, UNESCO and national statistical offices.

6. List of Abbreviations

BLEU	Belgo-Luxembourg Economic Union
CMEA	Council for Mutual Economic Assistance
EC	European Community
EFTA	European Free Trade Association
FAO	Food and Agricultural Organisation of the United Nations
GATT	General Agreement on Tariffs and Trade
IBRD	International Bank for Reconstruction and Development (World Bank)
ICAO	International Civil Aviation Organisation
ILO	International Labour Office
IMF	International Monetary Fund
IRF	International Road Federation
ITU	International Telecommunication Union (a UN agency)
OECD	Organisation for Economic Co-operation and Development
UIC	Union Internationale des Chemins de Fer
UN	United Nations
UN ECE	United Nations Economic Commission for Europe
UNESCO	United Nations Educational, Scientific and Cultural Organisation
WHO	World Health Organisation
WTO	World Tourism Organisation
EAP	Economically active population
GDP	Gross domestic product
GNP	Gross national product
LPG	Liquefied petroleum gases
SITC	Standard International Trade Classification
gWh	gigawatt-hours
hl	hectolitre
kg	kilogramme
km	kilometre
km2	square kilometre
kWh	kilowatt-hours
m2	square metre
m3	cubic metre
MW	megawatts
TJ	terajoules
0	denotes less than 0.5 where no fraction given

7. European Map

KEY EUROPEAN MARKET INFORMATION SOURCES

1. Introduction

This section identifies the major information sources for researching the European market. The listings are not intended as exhaustive; rather, we aim to list some of the main international and national organisations publishing statistics and locate some of the principal European libraries.

Readers are referred to several other Euromonitor publications for further information on European sources:

European Directory of Marketing Information Sources (Euromonitor 1991)

This handbook presents information on official sources including further detail on national statistical offices, together with listings of market research companies, online databases, trade associations, trade journals, and general business contacts for the major countries of Western Europe.

Consumer Europe 1993 (9th edition, Euromonitor 1993)

Primarily a handbook of consumer market data, this annual publication lists the major trade associations and trade journals publishing information on consumer markets across Western Europe.

European Directory of Non-official Statistical Sources (2nd edition, Euromonitor 1993)

This directory lists statistical information published by unofficial and semi-official organisations across Europe.

European Advertising, Marketing and Media Data (2nd edition, Euromonitor 1992)

This handbook examines advertising expenditure patterns, media availability and basic consumer marketing parameters across Europe and provides, in addition, an extensive directory section with details of the leading agency and media operators, advertisers and useful sources for further information.

2. Official Pan-European and International Organisations

Association of European Chambers of Commerce and Industry (EUROCHAMBRES)
Address: Rue Archimède 5, B-1040 Brussels, Belgium
Telephone: (02) 231 0715
Fax: (02) 230 0038

Benelux Economic Union (L'Union Economique Benelux)
Address: Sécretariat Général, Rue de la Régence 39, B-1000 Brussels, Belgium
Telephone: (02) 519 3811
Fax: (02) 513 4206
Publications: Benelux Review (quarterly), *Benelux Info* (irregular), *Benelux Textes de Base*

Council of Europe
Address: BP 431, R6, F-67006 Strasbourg Cedex, France
Telephone: 88412000
Fax: 88412780
Telex: 870943
Obtaining publications: from sales agents; the UK agent is HMSO, and copies of publications can be ordered from HMSO bookshops. (London: 49 High Holborn, WC1V 6HB for callers only, PO Box 276, London SW8 5DT for mail order.)
Guides to publications: *Catalogue of publications* (available from Publicity Department (P9D), HMSO Books, St Crispins, Duke Street, Norwich NR3 1PD)
Contact points: all information about publications can be obtained from the Council of Europe Publications Section at the address above or from sales agents

European Community
Address: Office for Official Publications of the European Community, BP 103, 2 rue Mercier, L-2985 Luxembourg-Ville
Telephone: 499281
Fax: 488573
Telex: 1324 PUBOF LU
Publisher of statistical series: main statistical series are published by Eurostat (qv). Publisher as above for other publications shown below
Obtaining publications: publications are either priced, free, or for limited distribution; free publications may be obtained from the issuing institutions or, if published by the Information Offices, from those offices. The UK Information Offices are in London (8 Storey's Gate, London SW1P 3AT, telephone (071) 973 1992), Belfast (Windsor House, 9/15 Bedford Street, telephone (0232) 40708), Cardiff (4 Cathedral Road, Cardiff CF1 9SG, telephone (0222) 371631) and Edinburgh (9 Alva Street, Edinburgh EH2 4PH, telephone (031) 225 2058). Priced publications are obtainable from sales offices; UK sales offices are HMSO, and, as sub-agent, Alan Armstrong Ltd., 2 Arkwright Road, Reading RG2 0SQ, telephone (0734) 751769
Guides to publications: *Annual Catalogue of Publications*, with quarterly updates. *The European Community as a publisher* (annual). Catalogues are available from sales offices. All catalogues are free of charge
Contact points: Information Offices and Sales Offices

European Free Trade Association (EFTA)
Address: 9-11 rue de Varembe, CH-1211 Geneva 20, Switzerland
Telephone: (022) 749 1111
Fax: (022) 733 9291
Obtaining publications: as above; UK distributors are Gothard House Publications Ltd, Gothard House, Henley-on-Thames, Oxon RG9 1AJ
Guides to publications: no catalogue is published, but each edition of the quarterly *EFTA bulletin* carries a list of publications currently available. The bulletin is distributed free of charge and published in English, French, German and Scandinavian editions
Contact points: EFTA, Press and Information Service, at address above

Eurostat (Statistical Office of the European Community)
Address: BP 1907, rue Alcide de Gasperi, L-2929 Luxembourg-Ville
Telephone: 43011
Telex: 3423 COMEUR LU
Publisher of statistical series: Office for Official Publications of the European Community
Obtaining publications: directly from the Office for Official Publications of the European Community, L-2985 Luxembourg-Ville, 2 rue Mercier, or through sales and subscription offices in individual countries; in the UK these are HMSO and, as sub-agent, Alan Armstrong Ltd, 2 Arkwright Road, Reading RG2 0SG, telephone (0743) 751769
Guides to publications: regular information on publications given in *Eurostat news* (quarterly); *Catalogue of Eurostat publications* (annual, free from sales and subscription offices. Eurostat publications are also included in the catalogues of the European Community (qv)
Contact points: Eurostat at main address

Food and Agricultural Organisation of the United Nations
Address: Via delle Terme di Caracalla, I-00100 Rome, Italy
Telephone: (06) 5797-1
Fax: (06) 5797-3152
Telex: 610181 FOODAGRI I
Obtaining publications: from sales agents (HMSO in the UK) or from the Distribution and Sales Section of the FAO at the address above for countries without agents
Guides to publications: FAO books in print (annual catalogue of FAO publications in English); *List of documents*, listing publications in all languages expected to be of reasonably lasting nature

General Agreement on Tariffs and Trade (GATT)
Address: Centre William Rappard, 154 rue de Lausanne, CH-1211 Geneva 21, Switzerland
Telephone: (022) 739 5208
Fax: (022) 731 4206
Telex: 412324 GATT CH
Guides to publications: GATT publications are included in the general *Catalogue of United Nations publications* (see main United Nations entry)

International Bank for Reconstruction and Development - IBRD (World Bank)
Address: 1818 H St NW, Washington, DC 20433, USA
Telephone: (202) 473 7561
Fax: (202) 473 8347
Telex: 248423
Obtaining publications: Publications Sales Unit, Dept E, above address
Guides to publications: World Bank Catalog of Publications

International Civil Aviation Organisation (ICAO)
Address: 1000 Sherbrooke Street West, Suite 400, Montreal, Quebec, Canada H3A 2R2
Telephone: (514) 285 8219
Telex: 24513
Obtaining publications: from the Document Sales Unit at the above address or from several addresses abroad (United Kingdom: Civil Aviation Authority., Printing and Publications Services, Greville House, 37 Gratton Road, Cheltenham, Gloucestershire GL50 2BN)

International Energy Agency
Address: 2 rue André-Pascal, F-75775 Paris Cedex 16, France
Telephone: (1) 45248200
Telex: 620160 OCDE F
Fax: (1) 45248500
Publications: Energy policies and programmes of IEA countries (annual), *Annual oil market report, Quarterly oil and gas statistics, Annual oil and gas statistics, Energy prices and taxes* (quarterly)
Notes: IEA is an autonomous body within the framework of OECD; for details on obtaining publications, etc see OECD entry

International Labour Office (ILO)
Address: 4 route des Morillons, CH-1211 Geneva 22, Switzerland
Telephone: (022) 799 6111
Fax: (022) 798 8685
Telex: 415647 ILO CH
Obtaining publications: from International Labour Office Publications at the above address or from branch offices in ca. 40 countries
Guides to publications: ILO Publications (quarterly in English, French, Spanish, German, Russian, Arabic and Chinese)

International Monetary Fund (IMF)
Address: 700 19th St NW, Suite 100, Washington DC 20431, USA
Telephone: (202) 623 7430
Fax: (202) 623 4661
Telex: (RCA) 248331 IMF UR
Obtaining publications: from address above. In the UK the publications maybe obtained from HMSO or Microinfo Ltd, telephone (0420) 86848
Guides to publications: IMF publications are included in the general *Catalogue of United Nations publications* (see United Nations entry); there is also a publications brochure available from the above address

International Telecommunication Union (ITU)
Address: Place des Nations, 1211 Geneva 20, Switzerland
Telephone: (022) 730 511
Fax: (022) 733 7256
Telex: 421000
Guides to publications: List of publications (twice a year)

Nordic Statistical Secretariat
Address: Postbox 2550, DK-2100 Copenhagen O, Denmark
Telephone: 31298222
Publisher of statistical series: publishes jointly *Yearbook of Nordic Statistics* with the Nordic Council of Ministers
Obtaining publications: through distributors: Denmark: Svensk-norsk boqimport, Postbox 1022, DK-1022 Copenhagen K; Finland: Government Printing Centre, Postbox 516, SF-00101 Helsinki 10; Norway: Universitets-forlaget, Avd. for offentlige publikasjoner, Postboks 8134 Dep., Oslo 1; Sweden: Liber distribution, Forlagsorder, S-16289 Stockholm; Iceland: Nordisk Rads delegation, Albingi, IS-Reykjavik
Contact points: Nordic Statistical Secretariat, as above

OECD
Address: 2 rue André-Pascal, F-75775 Paris Cedex 16, France
Telephone: (1) 45248200/
45248167)
Fax: (1) 45248500
Telex: 620160 OCDE F
Obtaining publications: all orders should be addressed to OECD Publications Services at the main address above
Guides to publications: OECD publications (annual catalogue) and quarterly supplements, Just out. News from OECD: monthly bulletin also lists publications appearing during the current month and is available regularly free on request
Contact points: Publications Office

United Nations
Address: Palais des Nations, CH-1211 Geneva 10, Switzerland
Telephone: (022) 734 6011 or 731 0211
Fax: (022) 740 0931
Telex: 289696
Obtaining publications: can be bought directly from the Sales Section in Geneva or from worldwide bookshops, agents or distributors (a list is available from the Sales Section, Geneva at the above address). The UK agent is HMSO, POB 276, London SW8 5DT (trade and mail orders only) or 49 High Holborn, London WC1V 6HB (callers only) and other HMSO bookshops
Guides to publications: *Catalogue of UN publications* (annual, free, lists all publications currently in print of UN bodies and affiliated agencies whose publications are sold by the UN Sales Section. *UNDOC: current index (United Nations Documents Index)* is issued ten times a year and gives comprehensive coverage of UN documentation, on a subscription basis
Contact points: Publishing Division/Sales Section at the Geneva address

United Nations Conference on Trade and Development (UNCTAD)
Address: Palais des Nations, CH-1211 Geneva 10, Switzerland
Telephone: (022) 734 6011/ 731 0211
Fax: (022) 733 9879
Telex: 289696 CH
Obtaining publications: most UNCTAD documents are first issued as mimeographed documents, some of which are later reissued in printed form and become sales publications. Sales publications are obtained from the usual UN Sales Sections or agents (see main UN entry); occasional copies of mimeographed UNCTAD documents may be obtained from the UNCTAD Editorial Section at the address above (stocks permitting), quoting the document number. Subscription orders for mimeographed documents should be send directly to the Geneva Sales Section. The complete output of UNCTAD is also available on microfiche from UN Sales Sections
Guides to publications: UNCTAD sales publications are included in the general *Catalogue of United Nations publications*. There is also an annual *Guide to UNCTAD publications* which contains entries in English, French and Spanish and is available from the UNCTAD Reference Unit, Conference Affairs Service, at the above address

United Nations Educational, Scientific and Cultural Organisation (UNESCO)
Address: 7 place de Fontenoy, F-75700 Paris, France
Telephone: (1) 45681000
Fax: (1) 45671690
Telex: 204461
Guides to publications: UNESCO publications are included in the general *Catalogue of United Nations publications* (see main UN entry)

World Health Organisation (WHO)
Address: Avenue Appia, CH-1211 Geneva 27, Switzerland
Telephone: (022) 791 2111
Fax: (022) 788 0401
Telex: 415416
Obtaining publications: Direct from WHO or HMSO in the UK
Guides to publications: *Catalogue of publications* (free)

World Tourism Organisation (WTO)
Address: Capitan Haya 42, E-28020 Madrid, Spain
Telephone: (91) 279 2804/5107
Telex: 42188 OMT E
Guides to publications: *Publications catalogue* (annual, free)

3. National Statistical Offices

ALBANIA

Drejtoria & Statistikës (State Planning Commission)
Address: Tirana
Publisher of statistical series: N.I.S.H. Shtypshkronjave Mihal Duri (Mihal Duri State Printing House), Tirana
Obtaining publications: from state printing house above

AUSTRIA

Österreichisches Statistisches Zentralamt (Austrian Central Statistical Office)
Address: Hintere Zollamtsstrasse 2b, Postfach 9000, A-1033 Vienna
Telephone: (01) 71128-0
Fax: (01) 71128-7728
Telex: 0132600
Obtaining publications: orders to be sent to Österreichisches Statistisches Zentralamt, Informationsabteilung (address as above) or to Österreichischen Staatsdruckerei, Rennweg 12a, A-1037 Vienna, telephone (01) 787631-39
Guides to publications: *Publikationsangebot* (half-yearly list of publications); there is also a booklet in English. *The Austrian Central Statistical Office,* published in 1978, which describes the history, legal basis, organisation etc
Contact points: for enquiries and advice contact the Central Information Service (Informationsabteilung) at the address given above

BELGIUM

Institut National de Statistique
Address: Rue de Louvain 44, B-1000 Brussels
Telephone: (02) 513 1304
Obtaining publications: from the above address; also on sale to callers at Place Albert 1er, 8e étage, B-6000 Charleroi, telephone (071) 328707 and Quai Marcellis 30, B-4020 Liège, telephone (041) 428070. Dutch language versions are on sale at Leuvenseweg 44, B-1000 Brussels, telephone (02) 513 9650; Rubenslei 2, B-2018 Antwerp, telephone (03) 231 1920; Coupure Rechts 620, B-9000 Ghent, telephone (091) 253273
Guides to publications: *L'Institut National de Statistique,* (free); *Rapport des activités de l'Institut National de Statistique* (annual, free); *Catalogue des publications de l'Institut National de Statistique* plus monthly updatings (free)

BULGARIA

National Statistical Institute
Address: 6th September Str., Sofia
Telephone: (2) 883057
Fax: (2) 877825
Telex: 25496
Obtaining publications: From above address

CYPRUS

Department of Statistics and Research
Address: Byron Avenue No. 13, Nicosia 162
Telephone: (02) 402349
Fax: (02) 456712
Telex: 3399
Obtaining publications: from the Government Printing Office, Michael Karaoli Street, Nicosia; telephone (02) 402202, telex 3399 MINFIN CY
Guides to publications: Publications of the Department of Statistics and Research (priced); *Price list of recent publications of the Department of Statistics and Research* (free)

The former CZECHOSLOVAKIA

Federalini Statisticky Urad (Federal Statistical Office)
Address: Sokolovska 142, 18000 Prague 8, Czech Republic
Telephone: (2) 814
Telex: 121197

Czech Statistical Office
Address: Sokolovska 142, 18613 Prague 8, Czech Republic
Telephone: (2) 684 6203
Fax: (2) 683 0139
Obtaining publications: From above address, small fee payable

Slovak Statistical Office
Address: Mileticova 3, 82467 Bratislava, Slovak Republic
Telephone: (7) 201 8201
Fax: (7) 214601
Obtaining publications: From above address, small fee payable

DENMARK

Danmarks Statistik
Address: Sejrogade 11, DK-2100 Copenhagen O
Telephone: 31298222
Fax: 31184801
Telex: 16236 DASTAT DK
Guides to publications: Vejviser i statistikken (Guide to the statistics); also annual report and work programme published each January, including information on scheduled new statistics and changes in current statistical series (free). There is also an annual list of publications in English, *Publications issued by Danmarks Statistik in 19..*
Contact points: for individual service for non-published statistics, and for general enquiries contact the Service Division. For individual monthly and quarterly data on exports/imports of particular commodities/groups and supply statistics (production plus imports minus exports) contact the External Trade Division

FINLAND

Tilastokeskus (Central Statistical Office of Finland)
Address: PO Box 504, Annankatu 44, SF-00101 Helsinki 10
Telephone: (90) 1734-1
Fax: (90) 1734-2279
Telex: 122656 TIKES SF
Obtaining publications: as above, or from Government Printing Centre, PO Box 516, SF-00101 Helsinki; also on sale at Government Printing Centre bookshops at Annankatu 44, Helsinki and Etelaesplanadi 4, Helsinki
Guides to publications: A catalogue, *Government statistics*, is published monthly and annually
Contact points: for enquiries contact the Central Statistical Office Library, telephone (90) 1734-220, telex 122656

FRANCE

INSEE (Institut National de la Statistique et des Etudes Economiques)
Address: 18 boulevard Adolphe Pinard, F-75675 Paris Cedex 14
Telephone: (1) 45401212
Telex: 204924 INSEEGD F
Obtaining publications: from INSEE at the above address, or if in France from the Observatoires Economiques Régionaux (Regional Economic Observatories), whose addresses appear in the INSEE catalogue; a network of 22 covers the whole of France
Guides to publications: a detailed catalogue of publications is published annually. As well as the publications it gives details of all the functions and services of INSEE
Contact points: INSEE Direction Générale at the above address or, if in France, the nearest regional economic observatory

GERMANY

Statistisches Bundesamt
Address: Gustav-Stresemann-Ring 11, W-6200 Wiesbaden 1
Telephone: (0611) 751
Fax: (0611) 753425
Telex: 4186511 STB D
Also offices in Berlin and Düsseldorf: Zweigestelle Berlin, Kurfürstenstrasse 87, W-1000 Berlin 30; telephone (030) 260030; fax (030) 26003-734. Aussenstelle Düsseldorf, Hüttenstrasse 5a, W-4000 Düsseldorf 1; telephone (0211) 38411-0; fax (0211) 38411-28
Publisher of statistical series: Verlag Metzler-Poeschel, Kernerstrasse43, W-7000 Stuttgart 10
Obtaining publications: from booksellers or direct from the publishers Verlag Metzler-Poeschel, Delivery: Messrs Herman Leins, Holzwiesenstr. 2, Postfach 7, W-7408 Kusterdingen. Telephone: (07071) 33046, fax (07071) 33653

Guides to publications: *Veröffentlichungsverzeichnis. Stand 1. Januar 19..* (annual list of publications, also available in English and French versions); *Das Arbeitsgebiet der Bundesstatistik* (much more detailed survey of the work of the Federal Statistical Office and guide to publications, also available in abridged English version; English version entitled *Survey of German Federal Statistics*). In addition, all new publications are announced weekly in the *Bundesanzeiger* (Federal Advertiser), and in *Statistischer Wochendienst* (Information on statistics weekly), and monthly in *Wirtschaft und Statistik* (Economics and Statistics)
Contact points: Allgemeiner Auskunftsdienst (General Information Service)

GIBRALTAR

Statistical Department
Address: Government Secretariat, Gibraltar
Telephone: 70071
Telex: 2223

GREECE

National Statistical Service of Greece
Address: 14-16 Lycourgou Street, 10552 Athens
Telephone: (01) 323 3748
Fax: (01) 322 2205
Telex: 216734

HUNGARY

Kozponti Statisztikai Hivatal (Hungarian Central Statistical Office)
Address: Keleti Karoly u. 5-7, H-1024 Budapest
Telephone: (01) 202 4011/4881/4490
Fax: (01) 155 9085
Telex: 224308
Obtaining publications: From PO Box 51, H-1525 Budapest. Most publications contain English headings and notes

ICELAND

Statistical Bureau of Iceland
Address: Hagstofa Islands, Hverfisgata 8-10, IS-150 Reykjavik
Telephone: (91) 26699

IRELAND

Central Statistics Office
Address: St Stephen's Green House, Earlsfort Terrace, Dublin 2
Telephone: (01) 767531
Fax: (01) 682221
Obtaining publications: Personal purchases: Government Publications Sales Office, Sun Alliance House, Molesworth Street, Dublin 2; telephone (01) 710309. Trade and postal sales: Government Publications Office, Trade and Postal Sales, Bishop Street, Dublin 8; telephone (01) 781666, fax (01) 780645
Guides to publications: Publication guide (annually) gives titles and descriptions of contents of publications and details of contact points for individual topics
Contact points: there are two Statistical Divisions; for general information and information on economy and finance, agriculture, tourism, trade (imports/exports) and transport contact the main address as given above. For information on building and construction, demography, distribution and services, household budget, industry, labour and prices contact Central Statistics Office, Ardee Road, Rathmines, Dublin 6; telephone (01) 977144, fax (01) 972360

ITALY

Istituto Centrale di Statistica (Istat)
Address: Via Cesare Balbo 16, I-00100 Rome
Telephone: (06) 4673 2384
Fax: (06) 464797
Telex: 610338 ISTAT I
Publisher of statistical series: as above
Obtaining publications: from address above
Guides to publications: *Catalogo 19..* (annual catalogue of publications with summaries of content)
Contact points: Centro Diffusione-Liberia Stat, Via Cesare Balbo 11a, I-00184 Rome; telephone (06) 482 7666

LIECHTENSTEIN

Presse- und Informationsamt der Fürstlichen Regierung
Address: Regierungsgebäude, 9490 Vaduz
Telephone: 66111
Telex: 889290

LUXEMBOURG

Service Central de la Statistique et des Etudes Economiques (STATEC)
Address: Boîte Postale 304 (19-21 boulevard Royal), L-2013 Luxembourg-Ville
Telephone: 47942-92/47942-76
Fax: 46428-9
Publisher of statistical series: STATEC
Obtaining publications: STATEC
Guides to publications: *Répertoire analytique des publications du STATEC du 19e siècle à ce jour* (annual); *Liste des publications du STATEC*

MALTA

Central Office of Statistics
Address: Auberge d'Italie, Merchants Street, Valletta
Telephone: 224597
Telex: 1800

MONACO

Direction du Tourisme et des Congrès
Address: Centre de Presse de la Principauté, Monte Carlo
Telephone: 304227
Notes: Monaco's external trade figures are included in those of France and are obtainable from INSEE (see France)

NETHERLANDS

Centraal Bureau voor de Statistiek (Netherlands Central Bureau of Statistics)
Address: Prinses Beatrixlaan 428, PO Box 959, NL-2270 AZ Voorburg
Telephone: (070) 369 4341
Fax: (070) 387 7429
Telex: 32692 CBS NL
(There is also an office at Kloosterweg 1, PO Box 4481, NL-6401 CZ Heerlen; telephone (045) 736666, fax (045) 727440), telex 56724 CBS HR NL
Publisher of statistical series: Staatsuitgeverij, Christoffel Plantijnstraat 2, PO Box 20014, NL-2500 EA The Hague; telephone (070) 378 9911
Obtaining publications: from publisher
Guides to publications: *Systematic list of publications* (last English edition 1988). Annual Dutch edition, *Systematisch overzicht van de cbs-publikaties*, plus monthly updates of new publications
Contact points: most subject fields covered at both offices, but Heerlen is the main base for foreign trade statistics, family and personal surveys, income and consumption, and Voorburg is the main base for agricultural statistics, prices, national accounts, population statistics and labour and wage statistics

NORWAY

Statistisk Sentralbyrå (Central Bureau of Statistics)
Address: Skippergata 15, PO Box 8131 Dep, N-0033 Oslo 1
Telephone: (02) 864500
Fax: (02) 864973
Telex: 11202
Obtaining publications: Universitetsforlaget, Division for Publications, PO Box 2977, Toyen, N-0608 Oslo 6, and overseas representatives. Subscriptions to weekly and monthly bulletins should be sent to the Central Bureau of Statistics
Guides to publications: *Publications* (free annual brochure in English describing main series of publications); *Veiviser i norsk statistikk/Guide to Norwegian statistics* (free survey of official Norwegian statistics arranged by subject in Norwegian and English). There is also a historical survey in *Catalogue of Norwegian statistics and other publications published by the Central Bureau of Statistics 1828-1976*

POLAND

Glowny Urzad Statystyczny (Central Statistical Office)
Address: Al. Niepodlegosci 208, 00-925 Warsaw
Telephone: (22) 2532411
Fax: (22) 251525
Telex: 814581
Obtaining publications: Statistical Publishing Establishment, Room 2421B from the above address; telephone (022) 253241 ext 210, fax (022) 251526. Most publications are in Polish

PORTUGAL

Instituto Nacional de Estatistica
Address: Avenida Antonio Jose de Almeida, P-1078 Lisbon CODEX
Telephone: (1) 847 0050
Fax: (1) 808093
Telex: 43719 PCDINE P
Obtaining publications: Imprensa Nacional - Casa da Moeda, R D Francisco Manuel de Melo 5, P-1000 Lisbon
Guides to publications: current price lists available
Contact points: INE, Servico de Documentaçao at address above

ROMANIA

Comisia Nationala Pentru Statistica (National Statistics Commission)
Address: Str. Stavropoleos 6, Sector 3, Bucharest
Telephone: (0) 154253
Fax: (0) 145560
Telex: 11153

SPAIN

Instituto Nacional de Estadistica (INE)
Address: Paseo de la Castellana 183, E-28071 Madrid
Telephone: (91) 583 9100/583 9438
Fax: (91) 279 2713
Obtaining publications: Instituto Nacional de Estadistica, Paseo de la Castellana 183, E-28046 Madrid, or Libreria Lines-Chiel, Plaza Virgen del Romero 6, E-28027 Madrid
Guides to publications: *Publicaciones en existencia* (annual list of publications available); *Catalogo de la biblioteca del Instituto Nacional de Estadistica: Tomo I. Obras cientificas. Tomo II. Publicaciones estadisticas* (catalogue of the INE Library); *Catalogo descriptivo de las publicaciones estadisticas* (descriptive catalogue of statistical publications)
Contact points: main INE address. For enquiries from abroad there is a Servicio de Relaciones Internacionales

SWEDEN

Statistiska Centralbyrån (Statistics Sweden)
Address: Karlavagen 100, S-11581 Stockholm
Telephone: (08) 783 4335
Fax: (08) 783 4899
Telex: (54) 5261 SWESTAT S
Obtaining publications: Statistics Sweden, Distribution, Box 902, S-70189 Örebrö; telephone (019) 140320, telex 73170 SWESTAT S
Guides to publications: *Farska fakta och sorterade siffror* (free annual publications catalogue with summaries of contents, in Swedish only); *Arets tryck* (free annual list of the previous year's publications, with English introduction and titles translated into English)
Contact points: Information Service for postal or telephone enquiries on Swedish statistics or general enquiries on the SCB and its work; Distribution Section (at Orebo address) for information about publications

SWITZERLAND

Bundesamt für Statistik/Office Fédéral de la Statistique (Federal Statistical Office)
Address: Hallwylstrasse 15, CH-3003 Bern
Telephone: (031) 618660/619111
Fax: (031) 617856
Telex: 32526 SLBBE CH
Guides to publications: *Verzeichnis der Veröffentlichungen/Liste des publications,* Publikationsverzeichnis/Liste des publications

TURKEY

Economic Research Department
Address: Necatibey Caddesi 114, Ankara
Telephone: (4) 117 6440
Fax: (4) 1253387
Telex: 46347
Guides to publications: subscriptions card available

The former UNION OF SOVIET SOCIALIST REPUBLICS

Central Administration of Statistics
Address: ul. Kirova 39, 103450 Moscow, Russia
Telephone: (095) 207 4630
Contact points: Collets, Subscription Import Dept, Dennington Estate, Wellingborough, Northants NN8 2QT; telephone (0933) 224357

Georgian National Encyclopaedia
Address: Tblisi, Georgia

Kazakh Soviet Encyclopaedia
Address: Alma Ata, Kazakhstan

State Committee of Kirghizia
Address: 720084 Bishkek, Kirghizia

Latvian Ministry of Culture
Address: Riga, Latvia

Ministry of Culture and Education of the Republic of Lithuania
Address: Vilnius, Lithuania

Academy of Sciences of Turkmenistan
Address: Askhabad, Turkmenistan

State Committee of the Ukraine for Statistics
Address: Kiev, Ukraine

State Committee of Uzbekistan on Publishing
Address: 700000 Tashkent, Uzbekistan

UNITED KINGDOM

Central Statistical Office
The CSO is the major collector of government statistics and also co-ordinates the Government Statistical Service, which embraces the statistics divisions of all major departments, and the Office of Population Censuses and Surveys, plus the CSO itself
Address: Information Branch (Press, Publications and Publicity), Room 65C/3, Government Offices, Great George Street, London SW1P 3AQ
Telephone: (071) 270 6363/6364
Publisher of statistical series: HMSO; some publications are published by individual Government departments - these are indicated where appropriate
Obtaining publications: HMSO publications are obtainable from HMSO Publications Centre, PO Box 276, London SW8 5DT (mail and telephone orders only), telephone (071) 873 9090 (orders), (071) 873 0011 (general enquiries), telex 297138. Also from HMSO bookshops in London, Birmingham, Bristol, Manchester, Edinburgh and Belfast (postal orders and counter service, except for London, which is counter service only; London area postal orders should be sent to the HMSO Publications Centre at the address above).

In many other large towns there is a bookseller who is an HMSO agent (for name of nearest agent ring HMSO general enquiries number above or consult Yellow Pages).
Departmental publications are obtained from the departments and details are given with individual publications below
Guides to publications: *Government statistics: a brief guide to sources* (free annual booklet, obtainable from the CSO at address above); *Guide to official statistics* (this is a substantial guide to official and significant non-official sources, arranged by topic with a keyword index); *HMSO publishes the CSO* (free CSO publications catalogue); *HMSO Books: guide to publications and services* (free brochure). Full HMSO catalogues are also available on subscription, including: *Daily list*; *Monthly catalogue*; *Annual catalogue*; *Consolidated indexes* (five-yearly indexes of HMSO publications). There are also free sectional lists updated at regular intervals, which are catalogues based on the divisions of responsibility between departments. Most HMSO titles are also listed on Prestel (Prestel number 50040) on the day of publication with details displayed for one week, and can be ordered via Prestel (further details from Bibliographic Services Manager, HMSO Books, 51 Nine Elms Lane, London SW8 5DR). Quarterly microfiche listings of all HMSO publications are also available on subscription, and online access to HMSO's bibliographic database is available. Non-official guides include the following: *Directory of British official publications: a guide to sources*, 2nd ed, Mansell Publishing, 1984; *Catalogue of British official publications not published by HMSO*, published by Chadwyck-Healey of Cambridge every two months; *Reviews of United Kingdom statistical sources*, a series published by Pergamon Press covering statistics in various subject areas
Contact points: for general publications and order enquiries see under heading for obtaining publications. For free HMSO catalogues/information leaflets contact HMSO Books, Publicity Department, St Crispins, Duke Street, Norwich NR3 1PD, telephone (0603) 622211 ext 6498. For enquiries on statistics, departmental responsibilities and contact points are listed in *Government statistics: a brief guide to sources*; in case of difficulty in finding the right contact telephone or write to the CSO at the main address given above or at, Cardiff Road, Newport, Gwent NP9 1XG, telephone (0633) 812973, telex 497121, fax (0633) 812599

The former **YUGOSLAVIA**

Savezni Zavod za Statistiku (Federal Statistical Office)
Address: Kneza Milosa 20, 11000 Belgrade, Serbia
Telephone: (011) 681744
Fax: (011) 681995/642368
Telex: 11317

Republicki zavod za statistiku Bosne in Hercegovine (Republican Statistical Office of Bosnia-Herzegovina)
Address: JNA 54, 71000 Sarajevo, Bosnia-Herzegovina
Telephone: (071) 213966
Telex: 41344

Republicki zavod za statistiku (Republican Statistical Office of Croatia)
Address: Ilica 3, 41000 Zagreb, Croatia
Telephone: (041) 424422
Telex: 21130

Republicki zavod za statistiku Makedonije (Republican Statistical Office of Macedonia)
Address: Skopje
Telephone: (091) 236311

Republicki zavod za statistiku Crne Gore (Republican Statistical Office of Montenegro)
Address: IV Proleterske 2, 81000 Titograd, Montenegro
Telephone: (081) 41206

Republicki zavod za statistiku Srbije (Republican Statistical Office of Serbia)
Address: Milana Rakisa 5, 11000 Belgrade, Serbia
Telephone: (011) 412922
Telex: 11957

Zavod republike Slovenije za statistiko (Republican Statistical Office of Slovenia)
Address: Vorzarski pot 12, 61000 Ljubljana, Slovenia
Telephone: (061) 155322
Fax: (061) 216932
Telex: 31105

4. Major Business Libraries

ALBANIA

National Library
Address: Tirana
Telephone: (42) 5887
Stock: over 800,000 volumes

AUSTRIA

Ministerialbibliothek des Bundesministeriums für Finanzen (Library of the Ministry of Finance)
Address: Himmelpfortgasse 4, A-1015 Vienna
Telephone: (01) 51433/1247
Stock: covers economy, law, administration, taxes and customs, banking relating to Austria and Germany. Material in German. 270,000 books, 550 journals, Austrian company annual reports, Austrian company directories, trade journals and statistics

Österreichische Nationalbibliothek
Address: Josefsplatz 1, A-1015 Vienna
Telephone: (01) 525255/524686
Telex: 12624 OENB A
Stock: includes all publications published or printed in Austria, and literature published abroad concerning Austria or written by Austrian authors. 2,490,000 volumes of printed books and 10,475 current periodicals

Österreichisches Statistisches Zentralamt Bibliothek
Address: Hintere Zollamtsstrasse 2b, PO Box 9000, A-1033 Vienna
Telephone: (01) 71128/7800/7804
Fax: (01) 71128/7728
Telex: 132600
Stock: stocks official statistics of Austria and other countries. 170,000 volumes and microfiche

Universitätsbibliothek Graz
Address: Universitätsplatz 3, A-8010 Graz
Telephone: (0316) 3803100
Telex: 311662 UBGRZ
Stock: general collections, particularly scientific. Stock mainly in German and English with international and European coverage. 1,107,774 books, 4,148 journals, 50 national and international newspapers, annual reports for European countries, German and Austrian company and trade directories, international statistics

Wiener Stadt- und Landesbibliothek
Address: Rathaus, 4. Stiege, 1. Stock, Zimmer 333, A-1082 Vienna
Telephone: (01) 42800/42809

Zentrale Verwaltungsbibliothek und Dokumentation für Wirtschaft und Technik, Vertragsbibliothek der Europäischen Gemeinschaften
Address: Stubenring 1, A-1011 Vienna
Telephone: (01) 711 0054-81
Stock: covers the EC and trade and commerce. Material mainly in German. 165,000 volumes, 360 journals, Austrian official statistics

BELGIUM

Antwerp University Library
Address: St.-Ignatius University Faculties, Prinsstraat 9, B-2000 Antwerp
Telephone: (03) 2316660/69
Telex: 33599 UFSIA B
Stock: 435,000 volumes, including periodicals, 3,600 current periodicals and annuals. Collections related to the four university faculties (Philosophy and letters, Law, Political and social sciences, Applied economic sciences), particularly strong in applied economic sciences, including marketing and business information

Bibliotheek voor Hedendaagse Dokumentatie
Address: Parklaan 2, B-2700 Sint Niklaas
Telephone: (03) 776 5063
Fax: (03) 778 0785
Stock: private and independent library on social, economic and political matters with a special collection on science, technology and industry. Stock is international in coverage and 80% in English. 120,000 books, 4,100 journals and newspapers, 400 trade journals, 2,000 annual reports, company and trade directories, and audio-visual material

Bibliothèque Fonds Quetelet (Central Library of the Ministry of Foreign Affairs)
Address: Rue de l'Industrie 6, B-1040 Brussels
Telephone: (02) 511 1930
Stock: covers economic and social sciences. 700,000 volumes, 7,000 journals

Bibliothèque Royale Albert I
Address: Boulevard de l'Empereur 4, B-1000 Brussels
Telephone: (02) 519 5357
Stock: all publications produced in Belgium and Belgian and foreign publications in all fields of knowledge. Section on official documents includes publications of the UN and some of its agencies, the European Community, the OECD, Council of Europe and Benelux. National official publications are held in the general reading room

Institut National de Statistique, Service des Renseignements et de la Documentation Générale
Address: Rue de Louvain 44, B-1000 Brussels
Telephone: (02) 513 9650
Stock: all Belgian official statistical publications. Material in French and Dutch

Rijksuniversitair Centrum Antwerpen-Bibliotheek (RUCA)
Address: Middelheimlaan 1, B-2020 Antwerp
Telephone: (03) 218 0790
Fax: (03) 218 0652
Stock: about 70,000 volumes on general, business, industrial and transport economics, foreign trade, management, accountancy; special collection covering the Third World. Material in Dutch, English, French and German. 100 trade journals, 1,000 other periodicals, company and trade directories on Benelux and Germany, national and European statistical publications; national and international financial newspapers (last 5 years)

BULGARIA

Central Scientific & Engineering Library
Address: 50 Nassar Boul., Sofia
Telephone: (2) 702935
Fax: (2) 710157
Telex: 22404
Stock: includes books, scientific reports, periodicals, company reference boooks and patents

Centre for Scientific, Technical and Economic Information
Address: V. Lenin 125, 1113 Sofia
Stock: collections on industry and agriculture

Cyril and Methodius National Library
Address: 11 Vassil Levski Boul., 1504 Sofia
Telephone: (2) 882811
Fax: (2) 881600
Telex: 22432
Stock: largest public scientific library in Bulgaria with over 2.5 million volumes; serves as the national bibliographic and information centre. Stock includes over 1.6 million books and periodicals

Sofia City and District State Archives
Address: Ul. Vitosa 2, 1000 Sofia
Stock: ca. 340,000 dossiers

Sofia University Library
Address: Boul. Ruski 15, 1504 Sofia
Telephone: (2) 443719
Stock: ca. 1.3 million volumes

CYPRUS

American Center Library
Address: 33B Homer Avenue, Nicosia
Stock: lending and reference library with ca. 6,000 volumes

British Council Library
Address: PO Box 5654, Museum St 3, Nicosia
Telephone: (02) 442152
Telex: 3911
Stock: ca. 25,000 volumes and periodicals

The former CZECHOSLOVAKIA

Central Economic Library of the Czech Republic
Address: Ustredni Ekonomicka Knihovna, Churchillovo nam 4, 13000 Prague 3, Czech Republic
Telephone: (2) 2365324
Stock: range of economic literature

Central Economic Library of the Slovak Republic
Address: Ustredna Ekonomicka Knihovna, Palisady 22, 81480 Bratislava, Slovak Republic
Telephone: (7) 316023
Stock: range of economic literature

Centre of Scientific, Technical and Economic Information
Address: UVTEI, Konvikska 5, 11000 Prague, Czech Republic
Telephone: (2) 264994
Stock: literature covering technical information, economics, education and publishing

Knihovny Fakult a Ustavu Univerzity Karlovy (Charles University Libraries)
Address: Ovocny trh 5,11636 Prague 1, Czech Republic
Stock: 2.7 million volumes, including ca. 10,000 periodicals

Statni Knihovna Ceske Socialisticke Republiky (State Library of the Czech Socialist Party)
Address: Klementinum 190, 11001 Prague 1, Czech Republic
Telephone: (2) 266541
Telex: 121207
Stock: central Czech research library with ca. 5.5 million volumes; collection of microfilms. Incorporates the Central Economic Library with 780,000 volumes

Statni Technicka Knihovna (State Technical Library)
Address: dr Vacka 5, 11000 Prague, Czech Republic
Telephone: (2) 264670
Stock: includes over 500,000 items of trade literature, 4,000 periodicals, microfiche and microfilm collections

DENMARK

Danmarks Statistik
Address: The Library, Sejrogade 11, Postboks 2550, DK-2100 Copenhagen
Telephone: 31298222
Fax: 31184801
Telex: 16236
Stock: covers official statistics from all countries and from the most important international organisations. 185,000 books

Gentofte Kommunebibliotek (Municipal Library of Gentofte, County Library, County of Copenhagen)
Address: Ahlmanns Alle 6, DK-2900 Hellerup
Telephone: 31627500
Telex: 19887
Stock: book collection of approximately 700,000 volumes, including a good collection of economic literature

Handelshojskolens Bibliotek (Copenhagen School of Economics and Business Administration Library)
Address: Rosenörns Alle 31, DK-1970 Copenhagen C
Telephone: 31396677
Stock: covers accounting, advertising, banking and finance, computer science, foreign trade, law, marketing, statistics etc. Over 200,000 volumes and 3,000 periodicals

Handelshojskolens Bibliotek - Århus (Library of the Århus Business School)
Address: Fuglesangsallé 4, DK-8210 Århus V
Telephone: 86155588
Fax: 86159339
Stock: covers marketing, foreign trade, management, economics, statistics and company information. Material in Danish and English, international in coverage but with the emphasis on Europe. 140,000 books, 800 journals, company reports, statistics, EC publications

Kongelige Bibliotek, Det (The Royal Library)
Address: Postboks 2149, DK-1016 Copenhagen K
Telephone: 33930111
Fax: 33329846
Telex: 15009
Stock: Danish national library, university library and principal research library for the humanities, social sciences and theology. Collections include all literature printed or published in Denmark as well as foreign literature about Denmark. The Office of International Publications has collections from the EC, UN, GATT, ILO, NATO, OECD, UNESCO and the Council of Europe

FINLAND

Central Statistical Office (Library of Statistics)
Address: POB 504, SF-00101 Helsinki
Telephone: (90) 1734-2220
Fax: (90) 1734-2279
Teletex: 1002111 TILASTO SF
Stock: Finnish and foreign national statistics and statistics from international organisations; collection of Old Russian statistics 1847-1917. Material mostly in Finnish, Swedish, English, French, Spanish, Italian, German, Russian. 220,000 volumes, 1,300 Finnish periodicals, 3,500 foreign periodicals, annual reports of Finnish companies, 29,000 microfiches

Helsingin Kauppakorkeakoulun Kirjasto (Helsinki School of Economics Library)
Address: Runeberginkatu 22-24, SF-00100 Helsinki
Telephone: (90) 4313425
Fax: (90) 4313539
Telex: 122220 ECON SF
Stock: the library is the national resource centre for economics and business sciences. 240,000 books, 1,600 periodicals, company and trade directories, company reports, dissertations and statistics. International in coverage with an emphasis on the English language

FRANCE

Bibliothèque de la Direction Générale de l'INSEE
Address: 18 boulevard Adolphe Pinard, F-75675 Paris Cedex 14
Telephone: (1) 45401212
Telex: 204924 INSEE F
Stock: this is the library of the national statistical service. There are 12,000 linear metres of statistical and economic material and related subjects

Bibliothèque Nationale et Universitaire de Strasbourg
Address: 5 rue du Maréchal Joffre, BP 1029/F, F-67070 Strasbourg Cedex
Telephone: 88360068
Stock: covers all disciplines

Centre d'Enseignement Supérieur des Affaires
Address: 1 rue de la Libération, F-78350 Jouy-en-Josas
Telephone: 39568000
Telex: 697942
Stock: about 45,000 volumes and 480 current periodicals

Centre Georges Pompidou, Bibliothèque Publique d'Information
Address: rue Beaubourg, F-75191 Paris Cedex 04
Telephone: (1) 47741233
Telex: 212726 CNACGP F
Stock: about 360,000 volumes covering all disciplines, and about 2,100 current periodicals, of which about 30% are foreign. Relevant sections include business management, industry, statistics, official publications, demography, economics, as well as a reference section containing directories etc

Chambre de Commerce et d'Industrie, Centre de Documentation/Bibliothèque
Address: Palais de la Bourse, La Canebière, PO Box 1856, F-13222 Marseille
Telephone: 91919151
Fax: 91914225
Telex: 410091
Stock: covers law, marine transport, economics, management, commerce and finance. Material mainly in French, relating to France and Africa. 120,000 books, several hundred journals, French company reports, market research reports, company and trade directories, statistical publications

Chambre de Commerce et d'Industrie de Marseille, Centre International d'Information
Address: 2 Rue Henri Barbusse, F-13241 Marseille Cedex 01
Telephone: 91393357
Fax: 91393360
Telex: 441247 COMERIM
Stock: covers international trade. 2,500 books, 590 journals, newspapers, annual reports, market research reports, company and trade directories, statistical publications

Cours des Comptes, Bibliothèque (Library of the Audit Office)
Address: 13 rue Cambon, F-75100 Paris
Telephone: (1) 42989714
Stock: about 50,000 volumes and 700 periodicals on finance, law and economics

Université de Paris IX-Dauphine Bibliothèque
Address: Place du Maréchal de Lattre de Tassigny, F-75775 Paris Cedex 16
Telephone: (1) 45051410
Stock: covers economics, management, mathematics, data processing and social sciences. Material in French and English. 90,000 books, 2,000 journals, national and international newspapers, French company reports, company and trade directories, statistical publications, audiovisual material and computer programs

GERMANY

Akadämie der Wissenschaften Hauptbibliothek
Address: 8 Unter den Linden, Postfach 1313, O-1086 Berlin
Telephone: (2) 207 0487
Telex: 114535
Stock: Academy of Science of the former GDR with approximately 320,000 books and 3,800 periodicals

Deutsche Bibliothek
Address: Zeppelinallee 4-8, W-6000 Frankfurt am Main
Telephone: (069) 75661
Fax: (069) 7566476
Telex: 416643 DEUBI
Stock: stocks all post-war material published in Germany, German language material published abroad, all translations of German works and all material about Germany printed abroad. 3 million books, 66,500 journals, 370 newspapers

Handelskammer Hamburg Commerzbibliothek (Library of the Hamburg Chamber of Commerce)
Address: Adolphsplatz, Börse, W-2000 Hamburg 11
Telephone: (040) 36138-373
Telex: 211250 HKHMB D
Stock: about 160,000 books on economics, politics, German law, business administration, sociology, history (especially of Hamburg), annual reports of firms, especially German ones, anniversary books of firms, about 400 journals and all German statistical office publications, microfiches, video tapes. Material in German, French and English

Ifo-Institut für Wirtschaftsforschung Bibliothek (Ifo Institute for Economic Research)
Address: Poschingerstrasse 5, Postfach 860460, W-8000 Munich
Telephone: (089) 92240
Fax: (089) 985369
Telex: 522269
Stock: covers the national and international economy, industry, agriculture, technology, transportation, construction, labour market, the environment, trade and distribution. Special collections on developing countries and Japan. Material mainly in German and English, international in coverage. 100,000 books, 1,300 journals, 1,500 statistical publications, German annual reports

Informationszentrum Sozialwissenschaften
Address: Lennestrasse 30, W-5300 Bonn 1
Telephone: (0228) 22810
Stock: central information and documentation centre for social sciences in West Germany, and national focal point for ECSSID (European Co-operation in Social Science Information and Documentation). Coverage includes sociology of industry and trade and economics

Institut für Arbeitsmarkt- und Berufsforschung (Institute for Labour Market and Occupational Research)
Regensburgerstrasse 104, W-8500 Nuremberg
Telephone: (0911) 171
Stock: main subjects covered: labour market and occupational research, economics, industrial relations, labour market policy. Computerised database contains 3,800 documents

Institut für Seeverkehrswirtschaft und -Logistik, Bibliothek (Library of the Institute of Shipping Economics)
Address: Am Dom 5A, W-2800 Bremen
Telephone: (0421) 36805-0
Stock: covers shipping, sea ports, seaborne trade

Institut für Weltwirtschaft Kiel, Bibliothek (Central National Library of Economics)
Address: Düsternbrooker Weg 120, Postfach 4309, W-2300 Kiel 1
Telephone: (0431) 884436
Fax: (0431) 85853
Telex: 292479 WELTWD

Stock: covers international economics, statistics and business administration. Material is in all languages and international in coverage. 800,000 books, 19,000 journals, comprehensive international statistical collection, international company information, small collections for the most important countries of market research reports, stockbroker reports, trade journals and company and trade directories

Institut für Wirtschaftsforschung-Hamburg (HWWA), Bibliothek (Institute of Economic Research)
Address: Neuer Jungfernstieg 21, W-2000 Hamburg 36
Telephone: (040) 3562219
Fax: (040) 351900
Telex: 211458 HWWA D
Stock: the HWWA Library is one of the largest specialised libraries for economic and social sciences. Collections on national and international statistical material are especially extensive, as well as the stocks of branches and product oriented periodicals, address books of firms and branches and special volumes. Total of 600,000 volumes including 280,000 annual reports of companies; annual addition: 20,000 volumes; 80 newspapers, 3,500 magazines and reviews, 9,000 yearbooks, 3,500 annual reports of companies, microforms

Osteuropa-Institut München, Bibliothek
Address: Scheinerstrasse 11, W-8000 Munich 80
Telephone: (089) 983821/987341
Stock: covers the economics, history and law of Eastern Europe. 140,000 volumes, 600 journals, newspapers, statistical publications and company information

Rheinisch-Westfälisches Institut für Wirtschaftsforschung, Bibliothek
Address: Hohenzollernstrasse 1/3, W-4300 Essen 1
Telephone: (0201) 233171
Fax: (0201) 238668
Stock: covers economics. Material mainly in German, covering Germany, Europe and the USA. 58,000 books, 300 journals, statistical publications and German company information

Staatsbibliothek Preussischer Kulturbesitz (State Library of the Prussian Cultural Foundation)
Address: Potsdamer Strasse 33, Postfach 1407, W-1000 Berlin 30
Telephone: (030) 2661
Fax: (030) 2662814
Telex: 183160 STAAB D
Stock: general coverage with special collections on Eastern Europe, Orient, East Asia and official publications. 4 million volumes, 600 newspapers, 30,000 journals, 850,000 microforms

Statistisches Bundesamt, Bibliothek (Library of the Federal Statistical Office of the Federal Republic of Germany)
Address: Gustav-Stresemann-Ring 11, Postfach 5528, W-6200 Wiesbaden 1
Telephone: (0611) 751/752475
Fax: (0611) 753425
Telex: 4186511 STBD
Stock: national and international statistical publications, covering economic and social life. 396,000 volumes

GIBRALTAR

Gibraltar Library Service
Address: 308 Main Street, Gibraltar
Telephone: 78000
Stock: ca. 30,000 volumes

GREECE

American Library
Address: 22 Massalias St, GR-10680 Athens
Telephone: (01) 363 7740/8114
Fax: (01) 364 2986
Stock: covers social sciences, arts and humanities, international relations, technology. Material mainly in English. 12,000 books, 160 journals, newspapers, statistical publications

Athens Graduate School of Economics and Business Sciences
Address: 76 Patission Street, GR-10434 Athens
Telephone: (01) 823 7361/7345, (01) 822 1456
Telex: 225363 ASOE GR
Stock: 50,000 titles and 450 current periodicals on economics, business, mathematics, statistics, econometrics, operational research, business administration and law. Includes serial publications of the national statistical organisation and international organisations (EC, OECD, UN, ILO and IMF)

ESYE (National Statistical Service of Greece Library)
Address: 14-16 Lycourgou, (3rd Floor), GR-10552 Athens
Telephone: (01) 324 1102
Fax: (01) 322205
Telex: 216734
Stock: covers statistical data, statistical theory, demography, economics. Material mainly in Greek. 4,500 - 5,000 volumes and ca. 2,000 statistical series including all Greek statistical publications, those from several foreign countries and international organisations; 160 journals mainly on statistics and demography, 5 local newspapers, microforms

National Library of Greece
Address: 32 Panepistimiou Street, Athens
Telephone: (01) 361 4413
Stock: aims to cover every field of knowledge

HUNGARY

Budapesti Kozgazdasagtudomanyi Egyetem Konyvtara (Central Library of Budapest University of Economics)
Address: Zsil u. 2, H-1093 Budapest
Telephone: (01) 111 7023
Fax: (01) 117 4539
Telex: 224186

Kozponti Statisztikai Hivatal Konyvtar es Dokumentacios Szolgalat (Library and Documentation Service of the Central Statistical Office)
Address: Keleti Karoly u. 5, H-1024 Budapest
Telephone: (01) 202 0092
Fax: (01) 115 9095
Telex: 224308
Stock: exchange centre for official statistical publications; ca. 580,000 books and periodicals

Marx Karoly Kozgazdasagtudomanyi Egyetem Kozponti Konyvtara (Central Library of the Karl Marx University of Economic Sciences)
Address: Zsil u. 2, H-1093 Budapest
Telephone: (01) 117 5827
Telex: 224186
Stock: ca. 530,000 volumes

Orszaggyulesi Konyvtar (Library of the Hungarian Parliament)
Address: Kossuth Lajos-ter 1-3, H-1357 Budapest
Telephone: (01) 112 0600
Telex: 227463
Stock: 600,000 volumes; UN depository library

Orszagos Muszaki Informacios Kozpont es Konyvtar (National Technical Information Centre and Library)
Address: Muzeum u. 17, H-1428 Budapest
Telephone: (01) 138 2300
Fax: (01) 138 4074
Telex: 224944
Stock: ca. 450,000 volumes and 6,000 current periodicals

Orszagos Szechenyi Konyvtar (National Szechenyi Library)
Address: Budavari Palota F-epulet, H-1827 Budapest
Telephone: (01) 556167
Telex: 224226
Stock: ca. 2.4 million books and periodicals and ca. 4 million manuscripts, maps, prints, microfilms etc

ICELAND

Landsbokasafn Islands (National Library of Iceland)
Address: Reykjavik
Stock: ca. 380,000 volumes

IRELAND

Central Statistics Office Library
Address: St Stephen's Green House, Earlsfort Terrace, Dublin 2
Telephone: (01) 767531 ext 116/152
Fax: (01) 682221
Stock: statistics on demography, agriculture, industry, economics, finance, distribution and tourism. 1,500 books, Irish, EC and OECD statistics, Irish company reports

Dublin Public Libraries, Business Information Centre
Address: ILAC, Henry Street, Dublin 1
Telephone: (01) 733996
Fax: (01) 721451
Telex: 33287
Stock: general coverage of business. Material in English with wide international coverage. 15,000 books, 300 journals, national and international newspapers, Irish and some UK trade journals, Irish and some international statistics, company and trade directories, annual reports and press cuttings for Irish companies, some market research and stockbrokers' reports

Economic and Social Research Institute
Address: 4 Burlington Road, Dublin 4
Telephone: (01) 760115
Stock: Holdings of about 45,000 items cover economics, sociology, statistics, social psychology and include books, periodicals, annual reports etc of national and international origin

James Hardiman Library
Address: University College, Galway
Telephone: (091) 24411
Telex: 28831 UNIG EI
Stock: about 200,000 volumes covering arts, commerce, law, medicine, science and engineering

Trinity College Library Information Service
Address: Trinity College Library, College Street, Dublin 2
Telephone: (01) 772941
Telex: 25442 TCD EI
Stock: access to entire College library, which includes British and Irish copyright intake. Official publications: Irish, British, EC and the majority of UN publications. Many well known indexing services and a worldwide range of company directories

University College Dublin Library
Address: Belfield, Dublin 4
Telephone: (01) 693244
Telex: 93207
Stock: about 750,000 books and pamphlets and 8,000 current periodical titles. Holdings include an extensive collection of books and periodicals on business studies, including annual reports of Irish companies, McCarthy's Information Service (Industry section and small Irish company section), Extel UK listed companies service, collection of UCD MBS/MBA theses

ITALY

Biblioteca Nazionale Braidense
Address: Via Brera 28, I-20121 Milan
Telephone: (02) 808345
Fax: (02) 7202 3910
Stock: general stock covering all disciplines. Material mainly in Italian. Ca. 1 million volumes, local and main national newspapers, microforms of catalogues and newspapers

Biblioteca Nazionale Centrale di Firenze
Address: Piazza Cavalleggeri 1, I-50122 Florence
Telephone: (055) 244441/42/43
Stock: large general collection including section on economic sciences and separate periodicals room. Subject catalogue with 30,000 main headings

Biblioteca Nazionale Centrale Vittorio Emanuele II
Address: Viale Castro Pretorio 105, I-00185 Rome
Telephone: (06) 4989
Stock: the library is a general one, but with a bias towards the humanities and literature; it is a copyright library, receiving all Italian publications by legal deposit. Holds about 4 million volumes, including books, periodicals and newspapers

Biblioteca Nazionale Vittorio Emanuele III
Address: Palazzo Reale, I-80100 Naples
Telephone: (081) 402842
Stock: economic and business material contained in "Sezione Moderna"

LUXEMBOURG

Bibliothèque Nationale
Address: 37 Boulevard F.-D.-Roosevelt, L-2450 Luxembourg-Ville
Telephone: 26255
Stock: 600,000 volumes, mainly concerning humanities. Special Luxemburgensia collection (approximately 150,000 volumes). 2,300 foreign periodicals and 1,000 Luxembourg periodicals

Bibliothèque de la Ville
Address: 26 Rue E.-Mayrisch, Esch-sur-Alzette
Telephone: 547383/495
Stock: literature in French, German, English and Italian, all disciplines, Luxemburgensia

Centre Universitaire - Bibliothèque
Address: 162A Avenue de la Faiencerie, L-1511 Luxembourg-Ville
Telephone: 21621
Stock: total stock of about 100,000 books and periodicals covering literature, philosophy, history, social sciences, economics, law, linguistics, natural sciences, generalia and dictionaries, etc

MALTA

National Library of Malta
Address: Old Treasury Street, Valletta
Telephone: 224338

University of Malta Library
Address: Msida
Telephone: 314306
Telex: 407
Stock: ca. 300,000 volumes

MONACO

Bibliothèque Louis Notari
Address: 8 rue Louis Notari, Monte Carlo
Telephone: 309509
Stock: ca. 150,000 volumes

NETHERLANDS

Central Bureau of Statistics Library
Address: Prinses Beatrixlaan 428, PO Box 959, NL-2270 AZ Voorburg
Telephone: (070) 3694341
Fax: (070) 3694341
Telex: 32692 CBS NL
Stock: economic and social statistics from all over the world

Erasmus University Library Rotterdam
Address: Burgemeester Oudlaan 50, PO Box 1738, NL-3000 DR Rotterdam
Telephone: (010) 525511
Stock: 600,000 volumes. Strong emphasis on economics, management and law. Also sociology, political sciences, history and philosophy. Separate reading rooms for economics, statistics and periodicals

Gemeente Bibliotheek Rotterdam, afd. Bedrijfsinformatie (City Library Rotterdam, Business Information Department)
Address: Hoogstraat 110, NL-3011 PV Rotterdam
Telephone: (010) 4338911
Fax: (010) 4338338
Stock: provides business information for small and medium sized businesses. Material in Dutch and English, covering the Western world, Japan and China. 1,500 books, 150 journals, Dutch trade journals, national and international newspapers, Dutch official statistics, company and trade directories, microforms (Dutch company reports, American telephone directories)

Koninklijke Bibliotheek (Royal Library - National Library of the Netherlands)
Address: PO Box 90407, 2509 LK The Hague
Telephone: (070) 3140911
Fax: (070) 3140450
Telex: 34402 KBNL
Stock: the Royal Library is a research library which concentrates on the humanities: social sciences, law, history, art, language and literature, theology, philosophy, bibliography and library science. 3 million volumes

Netherlands Foreign Trade Agency (EVD)
Address: 151 Bezuidenhoutseweg, NL-2594 AG The Hague
Telephone: (070) 3798933
Telex: 31099 ECOZA NL
Stock: 150,000 monographs and reports, 1,800 periodicals, 3,800 directories

The Hague Public Library
Address: Bilderdijkstraat 1, NL-2513 CM The Hague
Telephone: (070) 3469235
Stock: general stock including 780,000 volumes of adult books

NORWAY

Bergen University Library
Address: N-5000 Bergen
Telephone: (05) 212500
Telex: 42690 UBB N
Stock: about 1,200,000 volumes on humanities, science, medicine, social sciences and law

Norges Handelshöyskole Biblioteket (Library of the Norwegian School of Economics and Business Administration)
Address: Helleveien 30, N-5035 Bergen Sandviken
Telephone: (05) 959222
Fax: (05) 258100
Stock: covers accounting, auditing, data processing, finance, industrial economics, labour relations, management, statistics, petroleum economics. Material mainly in English and Scandinavian languages. 225,000 books, 1,200 journals, Norwegian and some international statistics, company and trade directories, Norwegian company information

Norges Tekniske Universitetsbibliotek (The Technical University Library of Norway)
Address: N-7034 Trondheim
Telephone: (07) 595110
Fax: (07) 595103
Telex: 55186 NTHHBN
Stock: science and technology, industrial economics, art and architecture. Material mainly in English. 1 million books, 8,000 journals, local, national and international newspapers, patents, standards and microforms

Statistisk Sentralbyrå, Biblioteket (Central Bureau of Statistics Library)
Address: PO Box 8131 Dep, N-0033 Oslo 1
Telephone: (02) 413820
Fax: (02) 864973
Stock: approximately 160,000 volumes. Main subjects: economics, statistics, demography, with a special collection of statistical publications

POLAND

Biblioteka Glowna Politechniki Lodzkiej (Central Library of Lodz Technical University)
Address: 36 Zwinki, 90-924 Lodz
Stock: ca. 225,000 volumes and 98,000 periodicals covering most disciplines

Biblioteka Glowna Politechniki Warszawskiej (Central Library of Warsaw Technical College)
Address: 1 Plac Jednosci Robotniczej, 00-661 Warsaw
Telephone: (22) 211370
Telex: 816467
Stock: ca. 1.3 million books, 238,000 standards

Biblioteka Narodowa (National Library)
Address: 213 Al Niepodleglosci, 00973 Warsaw
Telephone: (22) 259270
Telex: 816761
Stock: ca. 5 million volumes including periodicals; also houses the Bibliographical Institute and the Institute of Books and Public Reading

Biblioteka Sejmowa (Library of the Polish Parliament)
Address: ul. Wiejska 4, 00902 Warsaw
Telephone: (2) 288545
Telex: 812544
Stock: ca. 225,000 volumes including 65,800 periodicals; covers official publications, economic, social, legal and political collections, international publications

Biblioteka Szkoly Glownej Planowania i Statystyki (Library of the Central School of Planning and Statistics)
Address: ul. Rakowiecka 22K, 02521 Warsaw
Telephone: (22) 495098
Stock: ca. 600,000 volumes including 156,500 periodicals

Centralna Biblioteka Statystyczna (Central Statistical Library)
Address: Al. Niepodleglosci 208, 00925 Warsaw
Telephone: (22) 250345
Telex: 816059
Stock: 350,000 volumes; emphasis on scientific, economic and social statistics

PORTUGAL

Biblioteca Nacional
Address: Campo Grande 83, P-1751 Lisbon Codex
Telephone: (01) 767639/764720
Fax: (01) 733607
Telex: 62803 BN P
Stock: general library but good coverage in social sciences and the humanities. Material mainly in Portuguese, covering Portugal. 2 million books, 50,000 journals, Portuguese official statistics, Portuguese company and trade directories

Instituto de Apoio às Pequenas e Médias Empresas e ao Investimento, Euro Info Centre
Address: Rua do Valasco 19C, P-7000 Evora
Telephone: (066) 21875/6
Fax: (066) 29781
Stock: covers EC matters concerning small and medium sized enterprises, international co-operation, grants and loans and technology transfer. EC and Eurostat publications, Portuguese company reports

Instituto Nacional de Estatística Biblioteca
Address: Instituto Nacional de Estatistica Serviço de Documentaçao, Avenida Antonio José de Almeida, P-1078 Lisbon Codex
Telephone: (01) 847 0050
Fax: (01) 848 9480
Telex: 63738 PCDINE P
Stock: holds all publications of the National Statistical Institute

Porto Biblioteca Publica Municipal (Oporto Public Municipal Library)
Address: Passeio de S. Lazaro, P-4099 Oporto Codex
Telephone: (02) 572147/565361/573147
Stock: about 1,300,000 volumes on all subjects, as this library receives the Portuguese copyright intake

ROMANIA

Biblioteca Centrala de Stat (Central State Library)
Address: Str. Ion Ghica 4, Bucharest
Stock: ca. 7.9 million volumes; acts as Copyright Deposit and Centre of Bibliographical Information

Biblioteca Institutului National de Informare si Documentare (Library of the National Institute for Information and Documentation)
Address: Str. Cosmonautilor 27-29, Sector 1, 70141 Bucharest
Telephone: (0) 134010
Telex: 11247
Stock: ca. 650,000 volumes including 88,000 periodicals

Institutul de Economie Mondiala
Address: Bd Republicii 12, 40348 Bucharest
Telephone: (0) 142006
Telex: 11429

SPAIN

Instituto de Estudios Fiscales Biblioteca
Address: Paseo del Prado 6, E-28014 Madrid
Telephone: (91) 222 8519
Stock: 48,426 books, 11,720 pamphlets and 803 periodicals on public finance, economics and law, comparative fiscal law. Collections include foreign tax and trade briefs, guides to European taxation - taxation of companies in Europe, taxation of patents royalties, dividends, interest in Europe etc

Instituto de Información en Ciencias Sociales y Humanidades (ISOC) del CSIC (Institute for Information and Documentation in Social Sciences and Humanities)
Address: Vitrubio 4, E-28006 Madrid
Telephone: (91) 411 0244
Fax: (91) 564 5069
Stock: covers all social sciences and humanities, including business and economics. Holds all Spanish journals in the social sciences and humanities field since 1975. 2,000 journal titles, 600 in the field of economics and business

Ministerio de Hacienda, Archivo Central y Biblioteca
Address: Calle de Alcala 11, E-28014 Madrid
Telephone: (91) 468 2000
Stock: covers economics, finance and law

SWEDEN

Malmö Stadsbibliotek
Address: Regementsgatan 3, S-211 Malmö
Telephone: (040) 77810
Stock: public library but with good coverage of business information and local information. 925,994 volumes, 1,650 journals, trade journals, statistics, Swedish company reports, company and trade directories

Riksdagsbiblioteket (Library of the Swedish Parliament)
Address: Riksdagen, S-10012 Stockholm
Telephone: (08) 786 4000
Fax: (08) 218878
Telex: 10184 PARLBIB S
Stock: about 500,000 volumes and 2,600 periodical titles, of which 1,300 are from abroad. Specialises in political, economic and social sciences, and coverage includes economics, business and industry. Special collections include official publications, publications issued by the UN and its specialised agencies, the OECD, the Council of Europe, the Nordic Council, the EC and other international organisations

Statistika Centralbyrån Biblioteket (Statistics Sweden, Library)
Address: Karlavägen 100, S-11581 Stockholm
Telephone: (08) 783 5066
Fax: (08) 661 5261
Telex: 15261 SWESTAT
Stock: covers official statistics from over 170 countries throughout the world. Also contains non-official statistics for Sweden. Material in all national languages

Stockholms Stadsbibliotek (Stockholm Public Library)
Address: Box 6502, S-11383 Stockholm
Telephone: (08) 236600
Telex: 19478 STOCTEK S
Stock: about 2 million books, 160,000 AV-media, 1,500 newspapers and periodicals covering all subjects

SWITZERLAND

Bundesamt für Statistik, Bibliothek/Office Fédéral de la Statistique, Bibliothèque (Federal Statistical Office Library)
Address: Hallwylstrasse 15, CH-3003 Bern
Telephone: (031) 618628
Fax: (031) 617856
Telex: 32526 SIBBE CH
Stock: covers statistics, economics, social sciences, applied sciences and the environment. 200,000 books, 2,700 journals

Schweizerische Landesbibliothek/Bibliothèque Nationale Suisse
Address: Hallwylstrasse 15, CH-3003 Bern
Telephone: (031) 618911
Telex: 32526 SLBBE CH
Stock: about 1.5 million items of 'Helvetica': books and periodicals written by Swiss authors, both in the original language and in translation, all books dealing with Switzerland, the entire book production of the country. This includes journals and periodicals, including those of institutions and firms, and official publications; there is a periodicals catalogue and a catalogue of official publications

Universität Zürich, Zentrale für Wirtschaftsdokumentation
Address: Wiesenstrasse 9, CH-8008 Zürich
Telephone: (01) 383 5850
Stock: covers economics, energy, labour market, industry, science, technology, finance, banking, insurance, accountancy, regional development, transport and tourism. Material in German, English and French, worldwide in coverage. 15,000 books, 270 journals, 3,000 Swiss company reports, 500 foreign company reports, OECD statistical publications, 130,000 press cuttings

Zentralbibliothek Zürich, Kantons-, Stadt- und Universitätsbibliothek (Zurich Central Library, Canton, City and University Library)
Address: Zähringerplatz 6, CH-8025 Zürich
Telephone: (01) 261 7272
Fax: (01) 262 0373
Stock: all subjects covered in university curriculi. Material mainly in German, English, French and Italian. 2.45 million volumes, ca. 9,000 current periodicals, 150 newspapers (mostly local), general trade directories covering Switzerland and major European countries, statistical yearbooks of main European countries and international organisations. Microfilm collection: The Goldsmiths'-Kress library of economic literature; Saitzew collection: historic literature on economic theory

TURKEY

Bogazici University Library
Address: P.K. 2, 80815 Bebek, Istanbul
Telephone: (91) 1631500, ext. 739
Telex: 26411 BOUN TR
Stock: 200,000 volumes on all subjects; special collection on the Near East

National Library
Address: 06490 Bahcelievler, Ankara
Telephone: (4) 222 4158
Stock: depository library; open to researchers and students

The former **UNION OF SOVIET SOCIALIST REPUBLICS**

Krupskaya N.K., State Public Library of Moldova
Address: Kievskaya ul. 78-a, 277612 Kishinev, Moldova
Telephone: (042) 221475
Stock: ca. 3 million volumes; national and principal depository library of Moldova

State V.I. Lenin Library of the USSR
Address: 3 Pr. Kalinina, 101000 Moscow, Russia
Telephone: (095) 202 4056
Telex: 411167
Stock: ca. 28 million books, periodicals and serials; complete files of newspapers in all the languages of the former Soviet Union and over 150 foreign languages

State Public Scientific and Technical Library
Address: Kuznetsky Most 12, 103031 Moscow, Russia
Telephone: (095) 228 7379
Stock: ca. 10 million books, periodicals, etc; special collections of industrial company catalogues

State ME Saltyko Schedrin Public Library
Address: 18 Sedovayaul, St Petersburg D-59, Russia
Telephone: (812) 152956
Stock: ca. 28 million books

UNITED KINGDOM

British Library Business Information Service
Address: 25 Southampton Buildings, Chancery Lane, London WC2A 1AW
Telephone: (071) 323 7454 (free service), (071) 323 7979 (priced service)
Telex: 266959 SCIREF G
Stock: business material held at the Science Reference and Information Service (formerly the Science Reference Library), where the Business Information Service is based, includes 2,000 trade directories, 2,500 market research reports, product literature and annual reports from 25,000 companies, and 5,000 trade and business journals; British and foreign company information, including Extel, McCarthy and Moody services; supplementary material at the Official Publications and Social Sciences Service (Great Russell Street), which holds all UK and major overseas statistical series, complementing the Export Market Information Centre, formerly the Statistics and Market Intelligence Library (see separate entry for EMIC)

British Library of Political and Economic Science
Address: 10 Portugal Street, London WC2A 2HD
Telephone: (071) 955 7229
Stock: about 3 million separate items. Covers social sciences in widest use of the term. Research collections emphasise economics, politics and sociology. Important collections of statistics, particularly government and inter-governmental, from all over the world. Special collections of bank reports and trade union annual reports

Central Statistical Office Library
Address: Room 1.001, Government Buildings, Cardiff Road, Newport NP9 1XG, Wales
Telephone: (0633) 812973
Fax: (0633) 812599
Telex: 497121
Stock: about 300 serial titles and 1,000 monographs. Complete collection of own *Business Monitor* statistical publications and many other official UK statistical titles. Periodicals and monographs on statistical methodology, automatic data processing and public administration. Collection of UK trade directories

City Business Library (Corporation of London)
Address: 1 Brewers Hall Garden, London Wall, London EC2
Telephone: (071) 638 8215 (Enquiries); (071) 480 7638 (recorded information)
Telex: 9312130747 CB G
Telecom Gold: 74:HAY 3004
Stock: public library covering all aspects of business information, with special emphasis on company data (UK and overseas) and market research materials (principally domestic consumer). Stock includes directories, card services, periodicals, newspapers, quoted company annual reports

City University Business School Library
Address: Level 14, Frobisher Crescent, Barbican, London EC2B 8HB
Telephone: (071) 477 8000
Fax: (071) 588 2756
Telex: 263896
Stock: approximately 25,000 primarily theoretical and academic monographs on business studies subjects, shipping and arts administration. Small collection of basic educational and business reference works. About 400 current journal titles. Stock includes recent acquisitions from the Market Research Society collection

Export Market Information Centre - EMIC
Address: Ashdown House, 123 Victoria Street, London SW1E 6RB
Telephone: (071) 215 5000
Fax: (071) 215 4231
Telex: 8811074/5 DTHQ G
Stock: The Export Market Information Centre is provided by the DTI to give access for British exporters and potential exporters to a wide collection of detailed overseas official statistics, trade directories, development plans and other published information on overseas (i.e. non-UK) markets. Resources available include the British Overseas Trade Information System (BOTIS), the DTI's own database for information on products and markets, overseas agents, distributors and importers, export opportunities, promotional events, and for an index to other published information available for reference in EMIC

Financial Times Business Research Centre
Address: Number One Southwark Bridge, London SE1 9HL
Telephone: (071) 873 3000
Fax: (071) 873 3069
Telex: 8811506
Stock: access to the stock of the Financial Times library covering current affairs, companies, industries and markets, statistics, personalities and international business and commerce; over 60,000 Company Files and 25,000 Personality files and information by subject and country. Access to a variety of external sources

Holborn Library, London Borough of Camden
Address: 198 High Holborn, London WC1
Telephone: (071) 405 6866
Stock: business, employment and legal information. Company information includes: 3,000+ company annual reports (MIRAC), UK Extel cards, CRO microfiche index, trade directories, UK and foreign telephone directories, *Research Index*. Marketing information: *Marketing Surveys Index, Reports Index, Retail Business.* Statistics including *Business Monitor* series. Newspapers and periodicals

Liverpool City Libraries, Commercial and Social Sciences Library
Address: Central Libraries, William Brown Street, Liverpool L3 8EW
Telephone: (051) 225 5434/5435/5436
Fax: (051) 207 1342
Telex: 629500
Stock: contains EC, HMSO, OECD and UN collections, large range of UK and overseas directories, statistical, shipping and law collections. 100,000 books, 500 journals, 300 trade journals, UK company reports, market research reports, UK, European and USA trade directories, local and national newspapers. Special company information service including Extel and McCarthy cards, Prestel and Teletext, Companies House directory on microfiches

London Business School/LBS Information Service
Address: Sussex Place, Regent's Park, London NW1 4SA
Telephone: (071) 262 5050; (071) 724 2300 (LBS Information Service)
Fax: (071) 724 7875
Telex: 27461
Stock: about 25,000 volumes covering all aspects of management and business in the private and public sectors as well as related parts of economics, law, politics, the behavioural sciences, information technology and the sciences generally. Also about 500 periodical titles, 150 of the most important British, European and international published statistical series and 15 daily and weekly newspapers. Collection of company information, including annual reports of all British publicly quoted companies and 500 European companies, Extel cards, McCarthy's press cuttings services and directories and handbooks. Market research reports, government publications, information files on subjects and countries

London Chamber of Commerce and Industry
Address: 69 Cannon Street, London EC4N 5AB
Telephone: (071) 248 4444
Fax: (071) 489 0391
Telex: 888941 LCCI G
Stock: 1,000 trade magazines, 1,500 British and foreign trade directories, extensive collections of UK and foreign government trade regulations, trade statistics worldwide, economic background to most countries of the world, British company information, market research reports and openings for trade worldwide

Manchester Business School, University of Manchester
Address: Booth Street West, Manchester M15 6PB
Telephone: (061) 275 6499
Fax: (061) 273 7732
Telex: 668354
Stock: 30,000 books on all aspects of management and business as well as related aspects of sociology, economics, law, politics and information technology. 800 periodicals. Collection of company information including annual reports of 3,000 British and European companies, Extel cards, McCarthy's Press service and MIRAC. Online access to Textline, Datastar, Dialog, Dun & Bradstreet, Pergamon and other hosts. CD-ROM products include FAME (UK company financial data) and ABI/Inform (international bibliographic database). Market research reports, government publications, and information files

Manchester Commercial Library and Information Service
Address: Central Library, St Peters Square, Manchester M2 5PD
Telephone: (061) 236 9422 ext 283/284, (061) 228 0641/2
Telex: 667149
Stock: comprehensive stock covering all aspects of business information. Approximately 7,500 trade and telephone directories (UK and foreign); company information including card services, Business Ratios, Financial Surveys and in-house database of Manchester companies; large collection of UK, foreign and international statistics; large collection of trade magazines and financial newspapers; fully indexed collection of market reports; maps and travel information; information files on products, industries and services; European Community information; trade names; import/export tariffs. Patents, standards, government publications and wide range of other information are available in the Central Library building

National Institute of Economic and Social Research
Address: 2 Dean Trench Street, Smith Square, London SW1P 3HE
Telephone: (071) 222 7665
Fax: (071) 222 1435
Stock: 30,000 - 40,000 volumes and 500 serials on economics, especially statistics

National Library of Scotland
Address: George IV Bridge, Edinburgh EH1 1EW, Scotland
Telephone: (031) 226 4531
Fax: (031) 220 6662
Telex: 72638 NLSEDI G
Stock: approximately 5 million volumes and pamphlets, and large collections of maps and manuscripts. A copyright deposit library with the right to claim copies of all British and Irish publications. Government publications are acquired and a wide range of foreign books is purchased

National Library of Wales
Address: Aberystwyth, Dyfed, SY23 3BU, Wales
Telephone: (0970) 623816
Fax: (0970) 615709
Telex: 35165
Stock: collections include 2.5 million volumes and bound periodicals and 6,000 current periodicals. The library is entitled to receive copies of most published material originating within the UK and has an extensive stock of technical, scientific and business-related books and journals, including annual editions of trade directories. It is a deposit library for government publications and for the publications of international agencies such as the UN, UNESCO, and the EC. Important publications from other countries are purchased

Newcastle upon Tyne City Libraries, Business and Technical Library
Address: Central Library, PO Box 1DX, Princess Square, Newcastle upon Tyne NE99 1DX
Telephone: (091) 261 0691
Fax: (091) 2611435
Telex: 53373 LINCLE G
Stock: an in-house index to most of the marketing periodicals published in Britain; most UK directories and extensive coverage for Europe, North America, Japan, Australasia, South Africa, Middle East; large economic report files for every country in the world; all Extel and McCarthy card services; large collection of UK marketing periodicals

Northern Ireland Department of Economic Development
Address: Netherleigh, Massey Avenue, Belfast BT4 2JP, Northern Ireland
Telephone: (0232) 63244 ext 2374/2286
Stock: covers commerce, economics, energy, mineral development, industrial development, public administration, training, industrial relations, factory inspection, tourism. Around 500 periodical titles held

Office of Population Censuses and Surveys Library
Address: Room 502, St Catherines House, 10 Kingsway, London WC2B 6JP
Telephone: (071) 242 0262 ext 2235
Fax: (071) 430 1779
Stock: collection of 50,000 books and pamphlets and 400 periodical titles. Main subject areas include demography, vital registration, epidemiology, survey methodology and computing. All published Census data for the UK from 1801 and some unpublished data, eg Small Area Statistics. Other collections include Social Survey reports, foreign censuses and statistical series and international statistics

Sheffield City Libraries and Information Services: Business Library, Science and Technology Library
Address: Central Library, Surrey Street, Sheffield S1 1XZ
Telephone: (0742) 734736-8
Fax: (0742) 735009
Telex: 54243 SHFLIB G
Stock: includes company annual reports, Extel services, CRO indexes and directory, general and specialised trade directories for UK and abroad; collection of detailed local company information; foreign company data; UK and foreign telephone, telex and fax directories; lists of professional and trade services; wide range of business journals

Small Firms and Tourism Division, Department of Employment
Address: Room 112, Steel House, Tothill Street, London SW1H 9NF
Telephone: (071) 273 4941 (Headquarters), Freefone Enterprise for local offices
Stock: information and advice on the establishment of a business and on the running of an existing business

Welsh Office Library
Address: Crown Building, Cathays Park, Cardiff CF1 3NQ, Wales
Telephone: (0222) 823683/
825449
Telex: 498228
Stock: general administration of Wales covering central and local government, education, National Health Service, agriculture, industry, economic planning, transport, highways and physical planning

Westminster Central Reference Library
Address: St Martins Street, London WC2 7HP
Telephone: (071) 798 2034/5
Fax: (071) 798 2040
Stock: covers commercial information and official publications. 100,000 books, 700 journals, market research reports, company and trade directories, statistical collection, national newspapers

The former **YUGOSLAVIA**

Biblioteka Matice srpske (Yugoslav National Library)
Address: Ul. Matice srske 1, 21000 Novi Sad, Serbia
Telephone: (021) 615599
Fax: (021) 28574
Telex: 64367
Stock: ca. 700,000 volumes including 164,000 periodicals; national copyright and deposit library and depository library for FAO and UNESCO publications

Centraina ekonomska Knjiznica (Central Economic Library)
Address: Kardelijeva ploscad 17, Ljubljana, Slovenia
Telephone: (061) 301120
Fax: (061) 301110
Stock: 145,300 volumes and periodicals, ca. 750 current periodicals

Nacionalna i Sveucilisna Biblioteka (National and University Library)
Address: Marolicav trg 21, Zagreb, Croatia
Telephone: (041) 426322
Fax: (041) 426676
Telex: 22206
Stock: ca. 1.4 million volumes, 340 volumes of periodicals, 4,000 microfilms, collections of prints, maps, records and scores; federal deposit and copyright library

Narodna Biblioteka Srbije (National Library of Serbia)
Address: Skerliceva 1, Belgrade, Serbia
Telephone: (011) 451242
Telex: 12208
Stock: over 950,000 volumes, including 190,000 periodicals and 96,850 volumes of newspapers; federal deposit and copyright library

Narodna in Univerzitetna Knjiznica (National and University Library)
Address: Turjaska 1, 61000 Ljubljana, Slovenia
Telephone: (061) 150141
Fax: (061) 150134
Telex: 32285
Stock: ca. 1.6 million volumes; federal copyright and depository library

5. Foreign Trade and Export Departments

ALBANIA

Albkontroll
Address: Bul. Enver Hoxha 45, Durres
Telephone: (52) 2345
Telex: 2181
Notes: Export/import control body with branches throughout Albania

Ministry of Foreign Trade
Address: Ministria e Tregetise te Jashtme, Tirana
Telex: 2152

AUSTRIA

Bundesministerium für Auswärtige Angelegenheiten (Federal Ministry of Foreign Affairs)
Address: Wirtschaftspolitische Sektion, Ballhausplatz 2, A-1014 Vienna
Telephone: (01) 66150
Telex: 13710 AAWN A

Ministry of Trade and Industry, Export/Import Licensing Office (Zentralstelle Aussenhandel u. Zoll)
Address: Landstrasser Hauptstrasse 55-57, A-1030 Vienna
Telephone: (01) 71102-0
Fax: (01) 71102-352
Telex: 131300

Österreichische Exportfonds (Austrian Export Fund)
Address: Gottfried-Keller-Gasse 1, A-1030 Vienna
Telephone: (01) 731213
Telex: 132846

Zoll-und Verbrauchsteuersektion (Customs and Excise Department)
Address: Bundesministerium für Finanzen, Himmelpfortgasse 4 & 8-9, A-1011 Vienna
Telephone: (01) 5333

BELGIUM

Administration des Douanes et Accises (Customs and Excise Department)
Address: Sité Administrative d l'Etat, Tour Finances, Boîte 37, Boulevard du Jardin Botanique, B-1010 Brussels
Telephone: (02) 210 2111

Ministère du Commerce Extérieur (Ministry of Foreign Trade)
Address: 2 Rue des Quatres Bras B-1000 Brussels
Telephone: (02) 516 8311

Ministère des Relations Extérieures (Ministry of External Relations)
Address: 2 Rue des Quatre Bras, B-1000 Brussels
Telephone: (02) 516 8211
Telex: 23979

Office Belge du Commerce Extérieur (Belgian Overseas Trade Office)
Address: World Trade Centre, 162 Boulevard Emile Jacqmain, B-1000 Brussels
Telephone: (02) 219 4450
Telex: 21502
Notes: The Belgian Overseas Trade Office is the official organisation for the promotion of foreign trade under the Ministry of Foreign Trade. The Centre publishes trade opportunities

Office National du Dacroire (Export Credit Guarantee Office)
Address: 40 Square de Meeûs, B-1040 Brussels
Telephone: (02) 511 6580

BULGARIA

Bulgarian Chamber of Commerce and Industry
Address: Bul. Stamboliisky 11a, 1040 Sofia
Telephone: (2) 872631
Fax: (2) 873209
Telex: 22374
Notes: Promotes business contacts between Bulgarian and foreign companies and organisations; also publishes several business information journals

Ministry of Foreign Economic Relations
Address: Sofiska Komuna St. 12, 1000 Sofia
Telephone: (2) 874811
Telex: 22530
Notes: Foreign trade is a state monopoly and is conducted through highly specialised state foreign trade organisations.

CYPRUS

Ministry of Commerce and Industry
Address: 6 Andreas Araouzos St, Nicosia
Telephone: (02) 403441
Fax: (02) 366120
Telex: 2283

The former CZECHOSLOVAKIA

Ceskoslovenska obchodni a prumyslova komora (Czechoslovak Chamber of Commerce and Industry)
Address: Argentinska 38, 170 05 Prague 7, Czech Republic
Telephone: (2) 872 4111
Fax: (2) 879134
Telex: 121862
or:
Address: Gorkeho 9, 81300 Bratislava, Slovak Republic
Telephone: (7) 333272
Fax: (7) 330754
Notes: The membership comprises all the country's foreign trade organisations as well as most of the industrial enterprises and research institutes. Provides a database of all Czech and Slovak enterprises

Ministerstvo Zahranicniho Obchodu (Ministry of Foreign Trade)
Address: Politickych veznuzo, 11249 Prague 1, Czech Republic
Telephone: (2) 2126111
Fax: (2) 2322861
Notes: Publishes a foreign trade bulletin

DENMARK

Direktoratet for Toldvæsenet (Customs and Excise Department)
Address: Amaliegade 44, DK-1256 Copenhagen K
Telephone: 33157300

Industriministeriet (Ministry of Industry)
Address: Slotsholmsgade 12, DK-1216 Copenhagen K
Telephone: 33923350
Telex: 22373
Notes: The Trade Department of the Ministry of Industry also deals with foreign trade

Udenrigsministeriets Handelsafdeling (The Trade Department of the Ministry of Foreign Affairs)
Address: Asiatisk Plads 2, DK-1448 Copenhagen K
Telephone: 31920000
Fax: 31540533
Telex: 31292 ETR DK
Notes: The Department promotes Danish export, collects information on foreign commerce and economies and assists in establishing contacts between Danish and foreign enterprises. Foreign companies interested in making contacts with Danish companies or finding out more about Danish export products should contact the nearest Danish diplomatic or consular office. The Department publishes *The Foreign Office Journal* which carries trade enquiries from foreign companies free of charge, and *Denmark Review/Business News from Denmark*

FINLAND

Finnish Foreign Trade Association
Address: PO Box 908, Arkadiankatu 4-6 B, SF-00101 Helsinki 10
Telephone: (90) 69591
Fax: (90) 6940028
Telex: 121696 TRADE SF
Notes: The FFTA, the central organisation for export promotion, is a semi-official organisation supported by the Confederation of Finnish Industry and 800 affiliated companies. It has 8 regional centres
The FFTA will supply foreign clients with information about:
- Finnish industries and relevant suppliers
- general market conditions
- business opportunities in Finland

The FFTA provides Finnish exporters with:
- market information
- advice on marketing and legal matters
- advice on regulations in foreign trade
- project export services
- sales campaigns and publicity abroad

The FFTA publishes a book, *Finland as a Trading Partner. The Finnish Trade Review* is published 8 times annually and each issue is available in several languages, including English. Commercial Secretaries in the diplomatic corps are under the administration of the Ministry for Foreign Affairs, but the trade-related work is co-ordinated by the Finnish Foreign Trade Association. Finnish and foreign companies can communicate with the Commercial Secretaries either direct or through the FFTA. The Commercial Secretaries supply information on market and sales opportunities and assist companies in marketing

Handels- & Industriministeriet (Ministry of Trade and Industry)
Address: Commercial Department, Aleksanterikatu 10, SF-00171 Helsinki 17
Telephone: (90) 1601
Telex: 124645

Ministeriet för Utrikesärenden (Ministry of Foreign Affairs)
Address: Herikasarmi, Pl 176 SF-00161 Helsinki
Telephone: (90) 1601
Telex: 124636

Tullihallitus (Customs and Excise Department)
Address: Erottaja 2-4, SF 00101 Helsinki
Telephone: (90) 6141

Vientitakuulaitos (Export Guarantee Board)
Address: Eteläranta 6, Box 187, SF-00130 Helsinki
Telephone: (90) 661811
Telex: 121778

FRANCE

Centre Français du Commerce Extérieur
Address: 10 avenue d'léna, F-75783 Paris 16
Telephone: (1) 45053000
Fax: (1) 45053979
Telex: 611934 F
Notes: Centre for the promotion of French foreign trade. Maintains close contacts with industry and commerce. Publicises trade opportunities

Direction Nationale des Statistiques de Commerce Extérieur (Directorate for Foreign Trade Statistics)
Address: 192 rue St-Honoré, F-75056 Paris
Telephone: (1) 42603300
Telex: 230061 DOUSTAT

Ministère du Commerce et de l'Artisanat (Ministry of Commerce and Small Businesses)
Address: Administration Centrale, 80 rue de Lille, F-75007 Paris
Telephone: (1) 45562424
Fax: (1) 47530834

Ministère du Commerce Extérieur (Ministry of Foreign Trade)
Address: 41 quai Branly, F-75007 Paris
Telephone: (1) 45507111
Fax: (1) 45559542
Telex: 205885 F

Ministère des Relations Extérieures (Ministry of Foreign Affairs)
Address: 37 quai d'Orsay, F-75000 Paris
Telephone: (1) 45559540
Fax: (1) 47534753
Telex: 202329 F

Service de Renseignements Douaniers (Customs Information Service)
Address: 182 rue St-Honoré, F-75001 Paris
Telephone: (1) 42603590 (office); (1) 42615602 (overseas trade statistics)

GERMANY

Abteilung III-Zölle, Verbrauchssteuern, Monopole (Customs and Excise Department)
Address: Bundesministerium der Finanzen (Ministry of Finance), Graurheindforstrasse 108, W-5300 Bonn
Telephone: (0228) 682-1
Telex: 886645

Auswärtiges Amt (Ministry of Foreign Affairs)
Address: Adenauerallee 99-103, W-5300 Bonn
Telephone: (0228) 170
Telex: 886591

Bundesstelle für Aussenhandelsinformation (Foreign Trade Information Office)
Address: Agrippastrasse 87/93, Postfach 108007, W-5000 Cologne
Telephone: (0221) 20570
Fax: (0221) 205 7212
Telex: 882735
Notes: Official information office under the German Ministry of Industry dealing with all foreign trade enquiries. Together with the Bundesverband der Deutschen Industrie (Federation of German Industry) the Trade Information Office publish *Nachrichten für den Aussenhandels* (foreign trade information bulletin), *Auslands-Anfragen* (enquiries from abroad)

GIBRALTAR

Gibraltar Chamber of Commerce
Address: 30 Main Street, POB 29, Gibraltar
Telephone: 78376

GREECE

Athens Chamber of Commerce & Industry
Address: 7-9 Academias Street, GR-10671, Athens
Telephone: (01) 362 4280
Telex: 215707 EBEA GR
Notes: The Athens Chamber of Commerce and Industry is a semi-governmental institution under the supervision of the Ministry of Commerce. It deals with all sorts of trade related enquiries and any approaches to other chambers will be referred to the Athens Chamber. It publishes a monthly report and a bi-annual journal, *Trade with Greece*

Customs and Excise Department
Address: 6 Marni Street, Athens
Telephone: (01) 522 3910

Directorate of Foreign Commerce
Address: Ministry of Commerce, Kaningos Square, Athens
Telephone: (01) 361 6241
Telex: 215282/219033

Ministry of Foreign Affairs (Foreign Trade Departments and Export Advisory Bodies)
Address: Zalokosta 2, Athens
Telephone: (01) 361 0581
Telex: 216593

HUNGARY

Magyar Gazdasagi Kamara (Hungarian Chamber of Commerce)
Address: Kossuth Lajostér, PO Box 106, H-1054 Budapest
Telephone: (01) 153 3333
Fax: (01) 153 1285
Telex: 224745
Notes: Promotes foreign trade. Membership includes all Hungarian foreign trade organisations. Publishes *Hungarian Economic Review* and *Investors' Guide to Hungary*

Ministry of Foreign Affairs
Address: Bem Rkp. 47, H-1027 Budapest
Telephone: (01) 156 8000
Telex: 225571

Ministry of Trade and Industry
Address: Martirok u. 85, H-1024 Budapest
Telephone: (01) 132 6570
Fax: (01) 175 0219
Telex: 225376

ICELAND

Customs Department (Head Office)
Address: Tryggvagata 19, Reykjavik
Telephone: (91) 18500
Telex: 2128 CUSTOM IS

Iceland Chamber of Commerce
Address: Hus Verzlunarinnar, IS-103 Reykjavik
Telephone: (91) 83088
Telex: 2316

Ministry of Commerce
Address: Arnarhvali, IS-150 Reykjavik
Telephone: (91) 25000
Telex: 2092

IRELAND

An Roinn Gnothaí Eachtracha (Department of Foreign Affairs)
Address: 80 St. Stephen's Green, Dublin 2
Telephone: (01) 780822
Telex: 25300

An-Roinn Tionscail, Agus Trachtala Turasóireachta (Department of Industry, and Commerce)
Address: Kildare Street, Dublin 2
Telephone: (01) 614444
Telex: 93478
Fax: (01) 762654

Córas Trachtala (CTT) (Irish Export Board)
Address: Merrion Hall, Strand Road, Sandymount, Dublin 4
Telephone: (01) 695011
Telex: 25337 CTT EI
Notes: The CTT is the state organisation for the promotion and development of exports. The organisation has regional offices in Cork, Limerick, Waterford and Sligo as well as 20 overseas offices. The CTT provides a variety of services and incentives to exporters and companies which are planning to enter the export market. A range of services is also available for foreign buyers and importers

Customs and Excise Department
Address: Office of Revenue Commissioners, Dublin Castle, Dublin 2
Telephone: (01) 792777
Fax: (01) 711826
Telex: 93479 REV EI

ITALY

Direzione Generale delle Dogane e Imposte Indirette (Customs and Excise Department)
Address: Viale America, I-00100 Rome
Telephone: (06) 5997/5924931

Istituto Nazionale per il Commercio Estero (ICE) (Institute for Foreign Trade)
Address: Viale Liszt 21, I-00144 Rome
Telephone: (06) 5992
Telex: 610160/610178 ICERM I
Publications: Esportare (fortnightly), *Informazioni per il Commercio Estero* (daily), *Notiziaro ortofrutticolo* (monthly), *Quality* (quarterly), *Pubblicazioni technico informative*
Notes: ICE is the government agency responsible for the promotion of exports. It runs a network of ICE offices overseas

Ministero del Commercio Estero (Ministry of Foreign Trade)
Address: Viale America, I-00144 Rome
Telephone: (06) 5993
Telex: 610471 MINCOMES I

LIECHTENSTEIN

Industrie und Handelskammer (Chamber of Commerce and Industry)
Address: Postfach 232, 9490 Vaduz
Telephone: 22744

LUXEMBOURG

Administration des Douanes (Customs and Excise Department)
Address: 4-6 rue du Saint Esprit, L-1475 Luxembourg-Ville
Telephone: 20951

Ministère des Affaires Etrangères, du Commerce Extérieur et de la Coopération (Ministry of Foreign Affairs, Foreign Trade and Co-operation)
Address: 5 Rue Notre-Dame, L-2240 Luxembourg-Ville
Telephone: 4781
Telex: 3405

MALTA

Department of Trade
Address: Lascaris, Valletta
Telephone: 22441
Fax: 606800
Telex: 1106
Notes: Deals with import, export, trade licenses, etc and promotes foreign trade relations

Ministry of Finance
Address: St. Calcedonius Sq., Floriana
Telephone: 220437
Fax: 229925
Telex: 1512

NETHERLANDS

Central Service for Imports and Exports
Address: Engelse Kamp 2, NL-9722 AX Groningen
Telephone: (050) 239111

Customs and Excise Departments
Information about clearance of goods can be obtained from:

Inspectie der Invoerrechten en Accijnzen
Address: Leeuwendalersweg 21, NL-1055 JE Amsterdam
Telephone: (020) 864441

Inspectie der Invoerrechten en Accijnzen
Address: Westzeekijk 387, NL-3024 EK Rotterdam
Telephone: (010) 4765144

Inspectie der Invoerrechten en Accijnzen
Address: Waldorpstraat 440, NL-2521 CH, The Hague
Telephone: (070) 3889380

Ontvangstkantoor der Invoerrechten en Accijnzen
Address: Stationsgebouw, Stationsweg 1, NL-3151 HR Hoek van Holland
Telephone: (01747) 2370

Directoraat-Generaal voor de Buitenlandse Economische Betrekkingen (Directorate-General for Foreign Economic Affairs)
Address: Bezuidenhoutseweg 30, NL-2594 AV The Hague
Telephone: (070) 3798911

Economische Voorlichtingsdienst, EVD (The Netherlands Foreign Trade Agency)
Address: Bezuidenhoutseweg 151, NL-2594 AG The Hague
Telephone: (070) 3798933
Telex: 31099
Notes: The EVD is the information and export promotion department of the Ministry of Economic Affairs. The EVD collaborates with governmental, semi-governmental and private organisations, such as embassies, the Netherlands Council for Trade Promotion (see below), domestic and bilateral chambers of commerce and the Ministry of Agriculture and Fisheries.
The EVD's function is to support Dutch exports and to supply information on domestic and international economic and commercial developments
The EVD helps trade and industry by finding and exploring new and traditional markets, setting up contracts with foreign companies, promoting Dutch trade and industry in general, supplying information about developments of foreign markets and legislation, and providing an extensive library service. The EVD also produces a *Foreign Trade and Economic Abstracts Database*
Publications include: Export Magazine, *Export Agenda*, as well as sector bulletins and a foreign projects bulletin

Nederlands Centrum voor Handelsbevordering, NCH
(Netherlands Council for Trade Promotion)
Address: Kettingstraat 2, PO Box 10, NL-2501 CA The Hague
Telephone: (070) 3478234
Telex: 32306 NCH NL
Notes: The NCH is a private non-profit-making organisation which aims to assist exports. The NCH collaborates with domestic and foreign governmental and private organisations. It organises and participates in exhibitions abroad, carries out surveys of foreign markets, organises conferences, seminars, etc. and runs an international market intelligence service. The NCH also houses the offices of the following bilateral chambers of commerce: Kamer Griekenland (Greece), Kamer Ierland (Ireland), Kamer Denemarken/IJsland (Denmark/Iceland), Kamer Finland (Finland), Kamer Noorwegen (Norway), Kamer Zweden (Sweden), Kamer Portugal (Portugal)

NORWAY

Departementet for Handel og Skipsfart (Ministry of Commerce and Shipping)
Address: Victoria terrasse 7, N-0030 Oslo 1
Telephone: (02) 314050
Telex: 18670

The Export Council of Norway
Address: Drammensveien 40, N-0255 Oslo 2
Telephone: (02) 437700
Fax: (02) 552628
Telex: 18532
Notes: The Export Council of Norway is part of the Norwegian Foreign Office Overseas Services. It has offices in 34 countries and is represented through embassies and consulates elsewhere. The Council provides a full range of professional services for existing and potential trading partners. This includes promoting contracts between Norwegian exporters and foreign customers and supplying extensive and up-to-date information and advice on the products of the country

Finans- og tolldepartementet (Customs and Excise Department)
Address: Akersgatan 42, N-0030 Oslo 1
Telephone: (02) 119090
Telex: 72095

Utenriksdepartementet (Ministry of Foreign Affairs)
Address: 7 Juni plassen 1, Boks 8114, N-0030 Oslo 1
Telephone: (02) 204170
Telex: 71004

POLAND

Ministry of Foreign Economic Relations
Address: Pl. Trzech Krzyzy 5, 00507 Warsaw
Telephone: (22) 260221
Fax: (22) 274673
Telex: 814501

Polska Izba Handlu Zagranicznego (Polish Chamber of Foreign Trade)
Address: Trebacka 4, PO Box 361, 00950 Warsaw
Telephone: (22) 260221
Telex: 814361

PORTUGAL

Alfandega de Lisboa (Customs and Excise Department)
Address: Terreiro du Trigo, Lisbon
Telephone: (01) 866176

Direccao-Geral do Comercio Externo (General Directorate of Overseas Trade)
Address: Av. da Republica 79, P-1000 Lisbon
Telephone: (01) 730993
Telex: 13418

Instituto do Comércio Externo (ICEP) (Foreign Trade Institute)
Address: Avenida 5 de Outubro 101, P-1000 Lisbon
Telephone: (01) 730103
Telex: 16498 ICEP P
Notes: ICEP's function is to promote Portuguese exports

Instituto do Investimento Estrangeiro (IIE) (Overseas Investment Institute)
Address: Avenida da Liberdade 258, P-1200 Lisbon
Telephone: (01) 570607
Telex: 14712
Notes: The Institute provides support and guidance to foreign investors and foreign exporters of technology

Ministry of Foreign Affairs
Address: Largo do Rilvas, P-1351 Lisbon
Telephone: (01) 601028
Telex: 12276

ROMANIA

Camera de Comert si Industrie a Romaniei (CCIR) (Romanian Chamber of Commerce)
Address: Blvd N Balcescu 22, 79502 Bucharest
Telephone: (0) 154703
Fax: (0) 130091
Telex: 11374
Notes: Advises members on a wide variety of industrial and trade issues and establishes links with foreign companies

Directorate for Foreign Trade Development Strategy
Address: Strada Apolodor 17, Sector 5, Bucharest
Telephone: (0) 120392
Telex: 10564
Notes: Key role in restructuring the basis on which foreign trade is conducted

Ministry of Trade and Tourism Directorate
Address: Strada Apolodor 17, Sector 5, Bucharest
Telephone: (0) 310619
Telex: 10564
Notes: Responsible for drafting customs policy and issuing import/export licences

SPAIN

Consejo Asesor de Exportación (CAE) (Export Advisory Board)
Address: Alcalá 9, Madrid 14
Telephone: (91) 232 6124

Customs and Excise (Head office)
Address: Guzman el Bueno 125, Madrid
Telephone: (91) 254 3200
Telex: 23058

Information Centre of Foreign Trade - CEDIN (Ministry of Economy, Finance and Trade)
Address: Ministerio de Economía Hacienda y Comercio, Paseo de la Castellana 162, E-28046 Madrid
Telephone: (91) 259 0807
*Telex:*44185

Instituto Nacional de Fomento de la Exportación (INFE)
Address: Paseo de la Castellana 14, E-28046 Madrid 1
Telephone: (91) 431 1240
Telex: 47392 IEC E
Notes: INFE is a state institute. Its function is to promote Spanish exports

Ministerio de Asuntos Exteriores (Ministry of Foreign Affairs)
Address: Plaza de la Provincia 1, E-28012 Madrid
Telephone: (91) 265 8605
Telex: 27739/22645

SWEDEN

Generaltullstyrelsen (Department of Customs and Excise)
Address: Box 2267, S-10316 Stockholm
Telephone: (08) 789 7300

Industridepartementet (Ministry of Commerce)
Address: Fredsgatan 8, S-10333 Stockholm
Telephone: (08) 763 1000
Telex: 14180

Sveriges Allmanna Exportforening (General Export Association)
Address: Storgatan 19, Box 5501, S-11485 Stockholm
Telephone: (08) 783 8500

Swedish Trade Council
Address: Storgatan 19, Box 5513, S-11485 Stockholm
Telephone: (08) 783 8500
Fax: (08) 6629093
Telex: 19620 EXPORT S
Contacts: Bo Hampus Israelsson (president)
Notes: The Swedish Trade Council is a semi-official organisation. It is the central organisation for planning, co-ordination, marketing and promotion for Swedish export companies. The STC also assists the less experienced export trader with advice, in collaboration with the 24 Regional Development Funds and the 12 Chambers of Commerce. The STC has 30 Swedish trade offices around the world. The operative part of the STC's international organisation includes the commercial sections of Swedish embassies and consulates. The Council publishes *The Swedish Export Directory Buyer's Guide to Sweden*

Utrikesdepartementet (Ministry of Foreign Affairs)
Address: Handelsavdelingen, Gustav Adolfstorg 1, Box 16121, S-10323 Stockholm
Telephone: (08) 786 6000
Telex: 10590/19350

SWITZERLAND

Federal Department of Finance
Address: Bundeshaus, Bundesgasse 3, CH-3003 Bern
Telephone: (031) 616111

Federal Department of Foreign Affairs
Address: Bundeshaus-West, Bundesgasse, CH-3003 Bern
Telephone: (031) 612111

Internationales Handelszentrum (International Trade Centre)
Address: 54-56 rue de Montbrullant, CH-1202 Geneva; Palais des Nations, CH-1211 Geneva 10
Telephone: (022) 346021
Telex: 289052

Oberzolldirektion (Customs and Excise Department)
Address: Monbijoustrasse 40, CH-3003 Bern
Telephone: (031) 616511

Schweizerische Zentrale für Handelsförderung (Swiss Office for the Development of Trade)
Address: Stampfenbachstrasse 85, CH-8035 Zürich
Telephone: (01) 363 2250
Telex: 53111 OSEC CH

and
Address: Avant-Poste 4, CH-1005 Lausanne
Telephone: (021) 203231
Telex: 25425
Notes: The SODT is a semi-official organisation which collaborates closely with the Swiss government and various economic associations. Its aim is to promote trade relations with foreign countries by bringing together foreign and Swiss companies and agents, advising on buyers, partners for joint ventures and licences, providing addresses of Swiss suppliers, providing information about the Swiss market, organising industrial exhibitions abroad, technical symposia and participation in exhibitions
SODT publishes the following books and journals which are available from all Swiss embassies, consulates and chambers of commerce:
Swiss Export Products and Services (book), *How to Export to Switzerland* (book), *Partner* (book), *Textiles suisses* (journal), *Textiles suisses - Intérieur* (journal), *Swiss economic news* (journal). The SODT has over 2000 members involved in foreign trade

TURKEY

Foreign Trade Association of Turkey
Address: Otim Binasi, A Blok Kat 4, Besiktas, Istanbul
Telephone: (91) 172 3828
Telex: 26689 FTAT TR

IGEME (Export Promotion Research Centre)
Address: Mithatpasa Cad. 60, Kizilay, Ankara
Telephone: (4) 172223
Telex: 4228 IGM TR

Ministry of Industry and Commerce
Address: Sanayi ve Ticaret Bakanligi, Ankara
Telephone: (4) 229 2834
Telex: 44598

Union of Chambers of Commerce, Industry, Maritime Commerce and Commodity Exchanges
Address: Atatürk Bulv. 149, Bakanliklar, Ankara
Telephone: (4) 117 7700
Telex: 42343

The former **UNION OF SOVIET SOCIALIST REPUBLICS**

Chamber of Commerce and Industry
Address: ul. Kuibysheva 6, Moscow 103684, Russia
Telephone: (095) 921 0811
Telex: 411126
Notes: Promotes trade, economic, scientific and technological exchanges between the former Soviet Union and other countries; organises exhibitions, seminars etc and through the Soviet state exhibition organisations. Registers patented inventions, trademarks etc. Presides over arbitration disputes; inspects goods for import and export; provides translation services

Ministry of Foreign Economic Relations of Russia
Address: 5/1 L Tolstogo ul, 119862 Moscow, Russia
Telephone: (095) 246 4483
Telex: 411291/2

Ministry of Foreign Economic Relations of the Ukraine
Address: 6 ul Pushkinskaya, 253034 Kiev, Ukraine
Telephone: (044) 2262112

Vneshekonombank (Bank for Foreign Trade of the USSR)
Address: 37 Plyuschika ul, 119121 Moscow, Russia
Telephone: (095) 246 6973
Telex: 411174
Notes: Apart from normal banking operations, accepts foreign currency from its clients, as well as precious metals, securities and other valuables for custody. Fulfils encashment, letter-of-credit and remittance commissions of its clients and correspondence involved in account-settling and credit operations in export and import trade and services, as well as in account-settling in non-commercial operations; grants and accepts credits; guarantees financial liabilities to Soviet and foreign juristic persons

UNITED KINGDOM

Customs and Excise Department
Address: King Beam House, Mark Lane, London EC3
Telephone: (071) 626 1515

Department of Trade and Industry
Address: 1 Victoria Street, London SW1H 0ET
Telephone: (071) 215 7877
Telex: 8811074

Foreign and Commonwealth Office
Address: Downing Street, London SW1A 2AL
Telephone: (071) 233 3000
Telex: 297711

Overseas Trade Division (OTD)
Address: Department of Trade and Industry, 1 Victoria Street, London SW1H 0ET
Telephone: (071) 215 5000
Fax: (071) 215 5611
Telex: 27366
Notes: The OTD was set up to help British exporters. Its members are drawn from experienced exporters in commerce and industry. The OTD's responsibilities are:
- to advise the government on strategy for overseas trade
- to direct and develop the government export promotion services on behalf of the Secretary of State for Trade and Industry
- to encourage and support industry and commerce in overseas trade with the aid of appropriate governmental and non-governmental organisations at home and overseas
- to contribute to the exchange of views between government and industry and commerce in the field of overseas trade and to search for solutions to problems. (See also the Export Market Information Centre in the section on libraries and information services)

Publications include: Hints to Exporters, Country Profiles, Sector Reports

The former YUGOSLAVIA

Federal Secretariat for Foreign Trade
Address: Kneza Milos a 24, 11000 Belgrade, Serbia
Telephone: (011) 682555
Fax: (011) 682668
Telex: 11143/11728

Institut za Spoljnu Trgovinu (Foreign Trade Institute)
Address: Mose Pijade 8, 11000 Belgrade, Serbia
Telephone: (011) 335391

Privredna Komora Jugoslavije (Federal Chamber of Economy)
Address: Terazije 15, 11000 Belgrade, Serbia
Telephone: (011) 339461
Fax: (011) 326691
Telex: 11638/12423
Notes: Promotes economic and commercial relations with other countries

DATA SECTIONS

Section One

Marketing Geography

MARKETING GEOGRAPHY

This section has been compiled from recent press articles on European countries and current available information. The standard regions are extracted from regional data published by national statistical offices, and the marketing maps from Nielsen and national advertising data sources.

Continued...

Eastern Europe cont'd

Others

Belgium/Luxembourg

Belgium	
Population	10,084,000 (1992)
Urban population	96%
Land area	30,519 sq km
Languages	Dutch (Flemish) and French (Walloon), with German minority
Religion	Mostly Roman Catholic
Currency	Belgian Franc (= 100 centimes)
Head of state	HM King Baudouin (1951)
Head of government	Jean-Luc Dehaene
Ruling party	Christian Democrat parties of French and Dutch speakers lead a grand coalition with their Socialist counterparts
Main urban areas	Brussels (capital, 960,324 in early 1991)
	Antwerp (467,875)
	Charleroi (230,946)
	Ghent (185,201)
	Liège (206,928)
	Bruges (117,100)

Luxembourg	
Population	375,000 (1992)
Urban population	84%
Land area	2,586 sq km
Languages	French (official); Letzeburgesch is the local French dialect, German is also widely spoken as a first language
Religion	Roman Catholic
Currency	Luxembourg Franc (equivalent to the Belgian Franc which is also legal tender)
Head of state	HRH Grand Duke Jean (1964)
Head of government	Jacques Santer
Ruling party	Christian Socialist (in coalition)
Main urban area	Luxembourg-Ville (capital, 88,400)

The Kingdom of Belgium, established in 1830, is officially bilingual, with the northern and western provinces (Flanders, Antwerp, Limburg and northern Brabant) being Dutch-speaking and the southern provinces French-speaking. About 85% of the inhabitants of Brussels speak French. 9% of the population are foreigners. Geographically, the country is divided into two by the river Meuse, with the south-eastern third of the country, the Ardennes, having poorer soils than the lower lands north and west of the river.

With little in the way of natural resources, except coal, the country relies heavily on agriculture. The major crops are potatoes, sugar beet, wheat and barley. Dairy cattle and pigs are the main livestock.

Industrial activity centres on the processing of imported raw materials and the export of finished goods. Antwerp lies at the southern end of the entrepôt area centred on Rotterdam, which supplies raw and processed materials to the industrial areas of Germany via the Rhine. Petrochemicals are therefore a large part of this trade, as well as cement, steel products and processed foodstuffs. Heavy industry, especially in Wallonia, suffered badly in the 1980s, but some recovery has been in evidence since the start of 1990.

Belgium has an economic union with Luxembourg, dating back to 1922, and since 1960 a customs union with the Netherlands. It was a signatory of the 1990 Schengen agreement on the mutual abolition of border controls.

Marketing regions

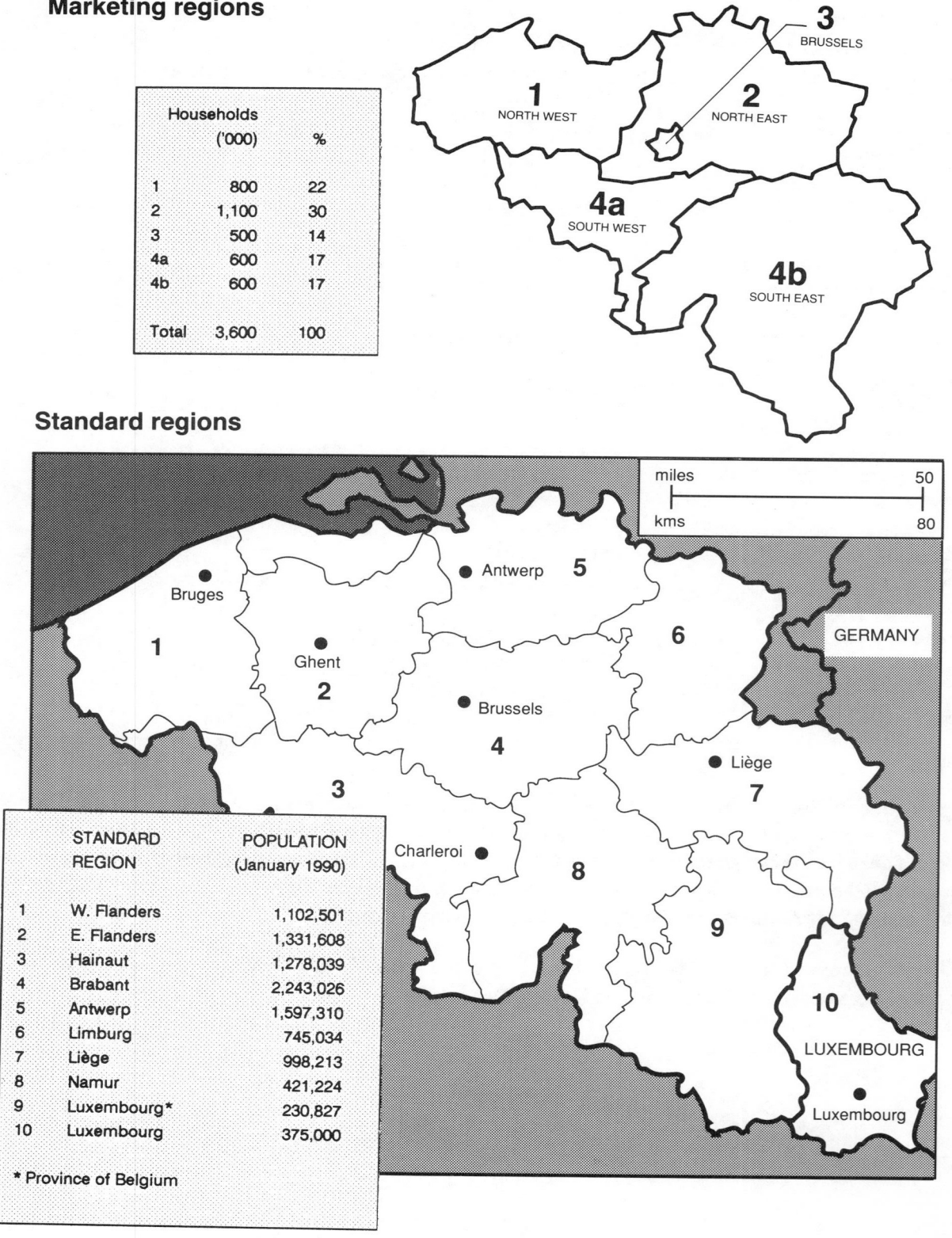

	Households ('000)	%
1	800	22
2	1,100	30
3	500	14
4a	600	17
4b	600	17
Total	3,600	100

Standard regions

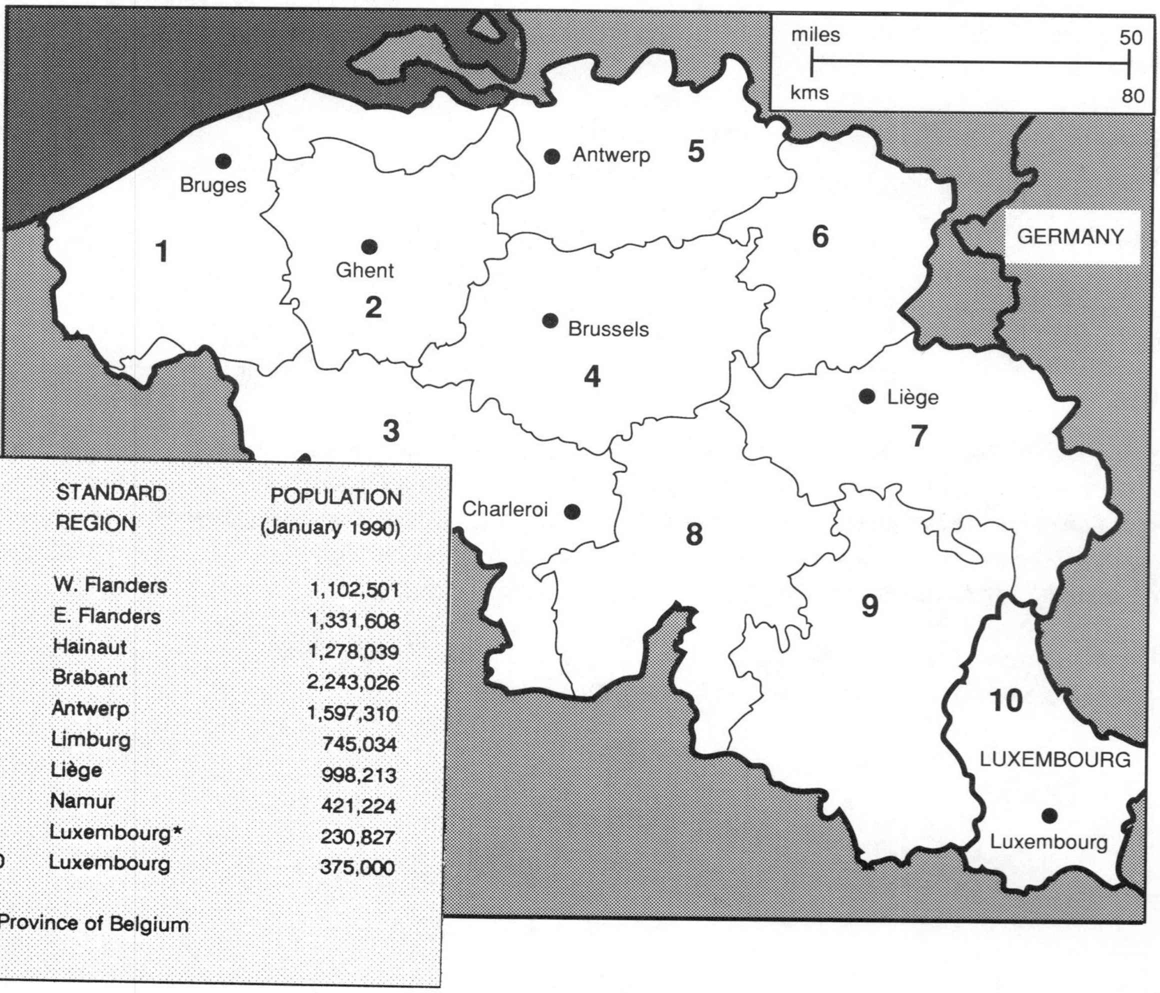

	STANDARD REGION	POPULATION (January 1990)
1	W. Flanders	1,102,501
2	E. Flanders	1,331,608
3	Hainaut	1,278,039
4	Brabant	2,243,026
5	Antwerp	1,597,310
6	Limburg	745,034
7	Liège	998,213
8	Namur	421,224
9	Luxembourg*	230,827
10	Luxembourg	375,000

* Province of Belgium

Denmark

Population	5,155,000 (1992)
Urban population	87%
Land area	43,093 sq km
Language	Danish
Religion	Mostly Protestant
Currency	Kroner (=100 ore)
Head of state	Queen Margrethe II (1972)
Head of government	Poul Schlüter
Ruling party	Conservative (in coalition with Liberals)
Greenland: Head of government	Lars Emil Johansen
Greenland: Ruling party	Siumut leads a coalition with Inuit Ataqatigiit
Main urban areas	Copenhagen (capital, 464,773; 1,336,855 including suburbs, 1991)
	Aarhus (264,136)
	Odense (177,679)
	Aalborg (155,664)
	Esbjerg (81,616)
	Randers (60,970)

The Jutland peninsula, which forms the bulk of the country's land area, has sandy soil, especially in the west, and consequently much of the available arable land is given over to livestock. Pigs and dairy cattle are the main animals, and the export of bacon and dairy products provides a large portion of the country's income.

Although best known as an agricultural country, Denmark's farming produce supports an expanding industrial base which in 1990 produced over 28% of GDP. Barley, for example, supplies a large brewing industry, while pig products are exported all over the world. Other industrial products include agricultural machinery, cement and food products. There is also a significant shipbuilding industry. Biotechnology and financial services are rapidly growing in importance.

Centres of population are concentrated on the numerous islands to the east of Jutland, with Copenhagen facing the Swedish industrial city of Malmö across the Oresund. A system of bridges and causeways links many of the islands, aiding communication and transport, and more are being built. Contracts were awarded in 1991-1992 for a bridge linking Copenhagen with Malmö.

The Kingdom of Denmark also includes the Faroe Islands and Greenland, both of which have some degree of autonomy from the Danish parliament; Greenland withdrew from the European Community in 1985, although it seemed likely to rejoin in the early 1990s. There is also some optimism that Greenland may hold reserves of valuable ores, although extraction is likely to be expensive; at present its 55,558 inhabitants (1990 census figure) rely mainly on fishing.

Marketing regions

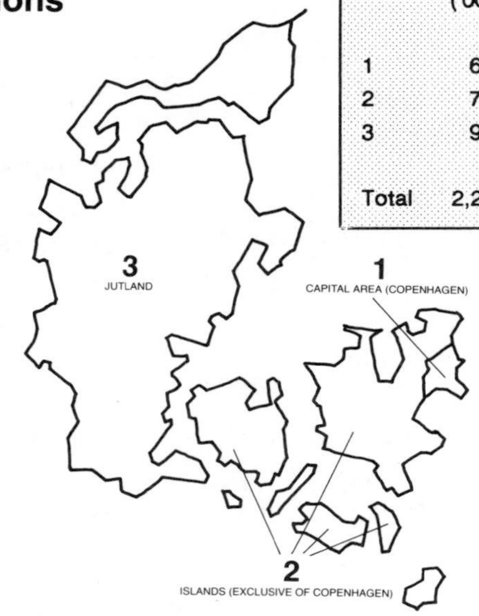

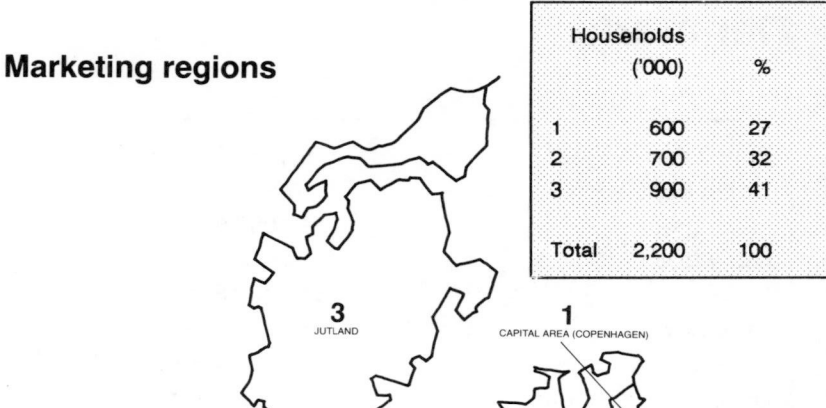

	Households ('000)	%
1	600	27
2	700	32
3	900	41
Total	2,200	100

Standard regions

	STANDARD REGION	POPULATION (1989)
1	N/W Jutland	1,170,000
2	S/SE Jutland	960,000
3	Fyn, Lolland, Bornholm	820,000*
4	Sjaelland	468,000
5	Kobenhavn	1,712,000

* (incl. part of Sjaelland Island)

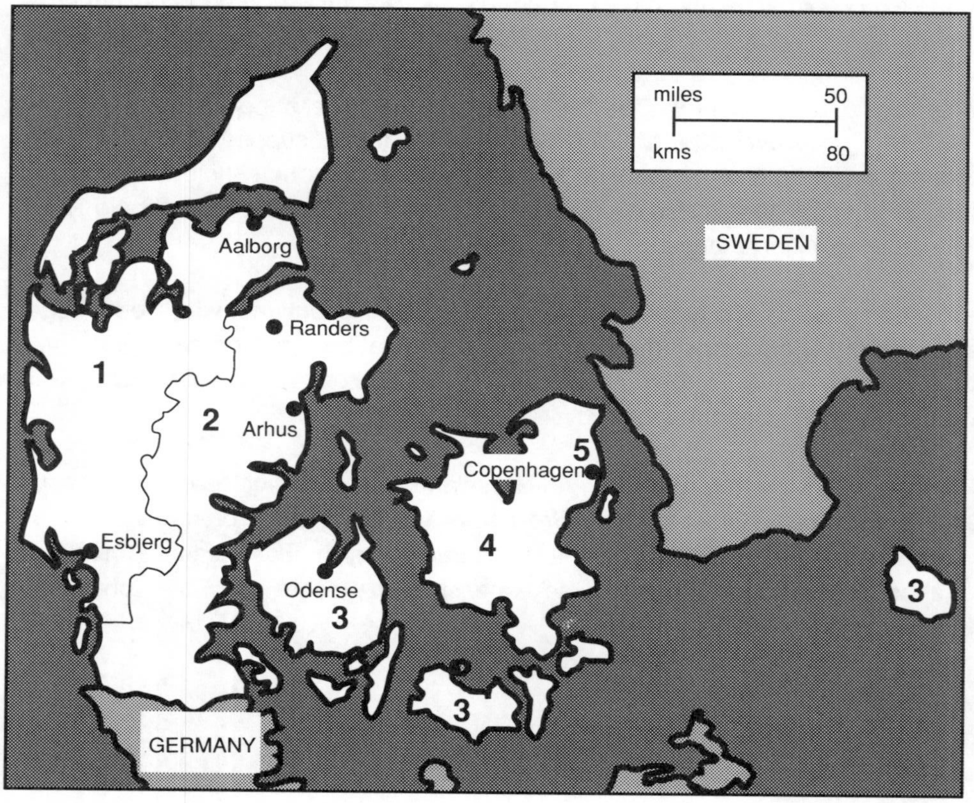

France

Population	56,832,000 (1992)
Urban population	74%
Land area	543,965 sq km
Language	French
Religion	Roman Catholic
Currency	Franc (= 100 centimes)
Head of state	President François Mitterrand (1981)
Head of government	Pierre Bérégovoy
Ruling party	Socialist Party
Main urban areas	Paris (capital, 2,152,423 in 1990 census)
	Marseille (800,500)
	Lyon (415,487)
	Toulouse (358,688)
	Nice (342,439)
	Strasbourg (252,330)
	Nantes (244,995)
	Bordeaux (210,336)

France is the largest country in Western Europe in terms of area, and has a population which is predominantly rural in character and is widely spread. Consumer markets are, therefore, highly regionalised, although the concentration of population in the Ile de France (the area around Paris) makes it by far the most important area in marketing terms.

Compared with the cosmopolitan nature of Paris, the southern cities show a decidedly Mediterranean influence, deriving not least from the numerous immigrants from North Africa. In the south-west, Bordeaux and Toulouse are centres for new high-tech industries, whereas more traditional industries are found in the east (Lyon) and north (Lille). Dependence on heavy industry in the Pas de Calais in the north has created severe economic problems for the area in recent years, but the completion of the Channel Tunnel in 1993 seems likely to bring benefits to the area.

The country supports a variety of climate and soil conditions, producing a number of different crops. Of great importance to the country's economy is the number of vineyards, although other alcoholic beverages such as brandy and cider are also important on a regional basis. Livestock is important to the rural economy, with dairy production particularly important.

France possesses a corresponding diversity of natural resources: natural gas deposits have been exploited in the south-west, and iron ore, coal, uranium and bauxite are also plentiful. France was also one of the first major markets to obtain energy supplies outside the framework provided by the international oil companies: by importing natural gas from the USSR and from its own former colonies, notably Algeria. It has also adopted nuclear energy more enthusiastically than other western nations, deriving some 75% of its electricity from this source.

France is a signatory of the 1990 Schengen agreement on the mutual abolition of border controls.

Marketing regions

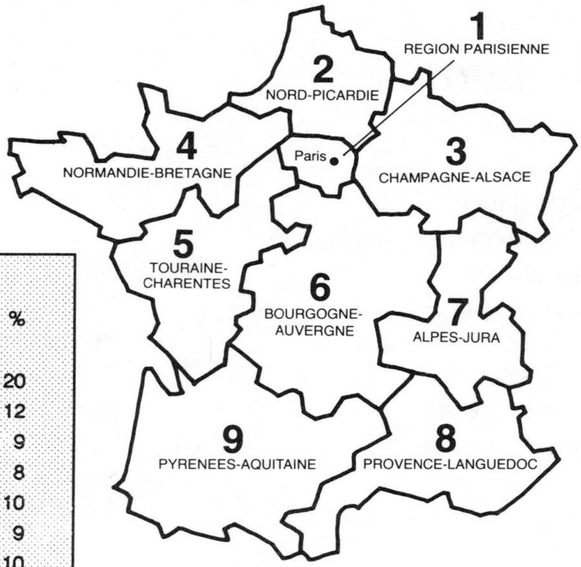

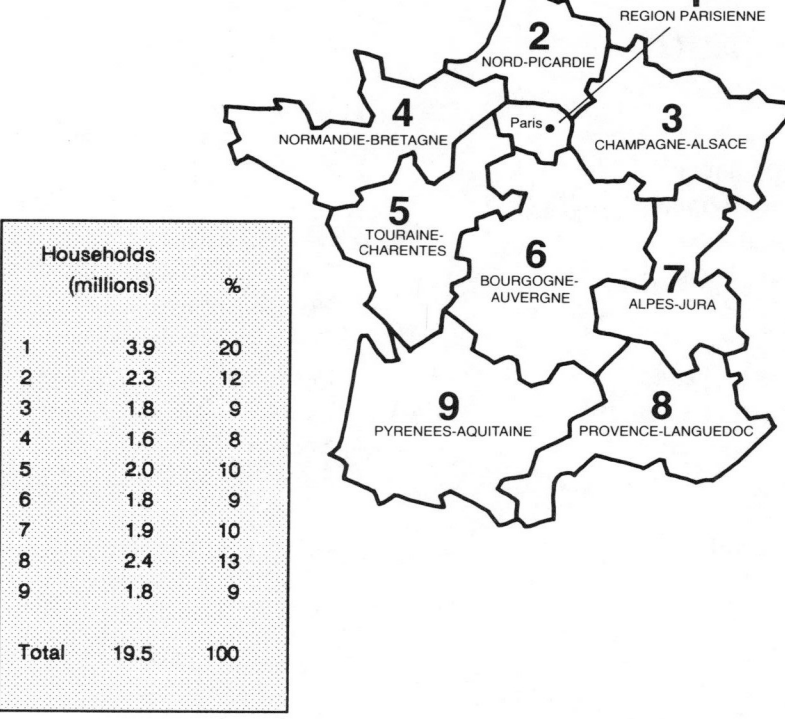

	Households (millions)	%
1	3.9	20
2	2.3	12
3	1.8	9
4	1.6	8
5	2.0	10
6	1.8	9
7	1.9	10
8	2.4	13
9	1.8	9
Total	19.5	100

Standard regions

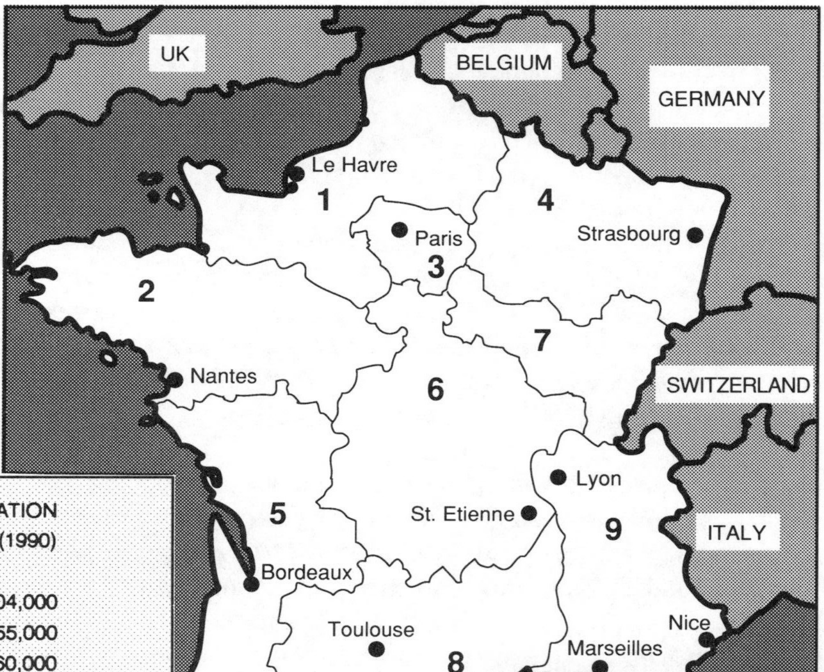

	STANDARD REGIONS	POPULATION (1990)
1	North	8,904,000
2	Brittany, Loire	5,855,000
3	Ile de France	10,660,000
4	Champagne, Alsace, Lorraine	5,278,000
5	Poitou, Aquitaine	4,391,000
6	Centre, Limousin, Auvergne	4,415,000
7	Burgundy, Franche-Compté	2,706,000
8	Pyrénées, Languedoc	4,546,000
9	Rhône, Provence	9,609,000
10	Corsica	250,000

Federal Republic of Germany

Population	78,381,000 (1992)
Urban population	83%
Land area	356,910 sq km
Language	German
Religions	Protestant (50%), Roman Catholic (35%), Jewish (0.5%)
Currency	Deutsche Mark (= 100 Pfennig)
Head of state	President Dr Richard von Weizsäcker (1984)
Head of government	Dr Helmut Kohl
Ruling party	Christian Democrat (in coalition with Bavarian Christian Social Union and Free Democrats)
Main urban areas	Berlin (capital, 3,410,000 in 1990)
	Hamburg (1,626,220)
	Munich (1,206,683)
	Cologne (946,280)
	Bremen (674,000)
	Frankfurt am Main (635,151)
	Essen (624,445)
	Dortmund (594,058)
	Düsseldorf (574,022)
	Stuttgart (570,699)
	Duisburg (532,152)
	Leipzig (530,010)
	Hanover (505,872)
	Dresden (501,417)
	Chemnitz* (301,918)
	Magdeburg (288,355)
	Bonn (287,117)
	Rostock (252,956)
	Halle (236,044)
	* Formerly Karl-Marx-Stadt

The reunification of West Germany, the Federal Republic, with the German Democratic Republic in October 1990 created the most populous as well as the biggest industrial power in Europe; the population increase from 62 to 78 million has meant a period of economic adjustment for the country's EC partners, and the considerable domestic pressures arising from the need to support or to close loss-making industries in the East has been steadily worsening since the start of 1991.

Although per capita incomes in the East of the country are running at about half of those in the West, living standards have been depressed by the very severe redundancy problems which have resulted from the necessary restructuring of the East's chronically overmanned industries. The increased social security burdens on the state have necessitated tax increases in the West of the country, but the authorities are pressing ahead nevertheless with their plans for vast investments, both industrial and infrastructural, as the five Eastern administrative regions (Mecklenburg-Vorpommern, Sachsen, Sachsen-Anhalt, Thüringen and Brandenburg) have been added to the 11 in the West of the country. It was agreed in 1991 that Berlin should take over from Bonn as the capital of a reunited Germany, and should become the seat of the *Bundestag* (Lower House of Parliament) although not of the Upper House, which will remain in Bonn.

By far the greatest industrial heartland in the West of the country is the Ruhrgebiet, a vast conurbation stretching along the Ruhr valley and up the Rhine as far as Cologne. The Rhine provides a transport link for the supply of raw materials and the export of finished goods. The area itself is rich in mineral resources, particularly coal, lignite and iron ore, and there are further important coal reserves further west in the Saarland. The northern cities of Hamburg and Bremen also support metalworking industries, and there are numerous shipyards along the North Sea and Baltic coastlines. In the south of the country, there are lighter manufacturing centres in Bavaria and the upper Rhine valley. Frankfurt, situated in the Main valley east of the Rhine, is the country's financial centre.

In the East, manufacturing is dominated by heavy industries (chemicals, engineering and shipbuilding), but all these are coming under competitive pressure which has heightened the demands on the jobs market. The state is attempting to privatise all the East's enterprises, which were formerly 100% nationalised, but it is having difficulty in finding buyers and is likely to have to continue its wage subsidies to support short-time working for the foreseeable future. The process of privatisation has been further hampered by difficulties in ascertaining the exact ownership of East German property.

Construction industries are now booming in all parts of the country. In 1991 the government established a plan to construct over 1,000 major public buildings in the East, and it set out a group of 17 top-priority transport projects (new motorways, rail links and waterway improvements) costed at some DM62 billion.

Agriculture is only moderately successful for both parts of the reunited country. In the West, productivity is hampered by a comparatively poor soil, and in the East by the often chaotically inadequate infrastructural conditions. Main crops include potatoes, barley, wheat, rye and oats. Apples are grown in large quantities, and the Rhine valley provides a favourable environment for vineyards. Livestock are predominantly cattle (largely dairy) and pigs.

There is a general lack of other energy resources besides brown coal. Some natural gas has been exploited close offshore in the North Sea and on land in the north of the country, but much of the country's oil requirements have to be imported, largely through the Netherlands. For the East, the abrupt cessation of Soviet oil supplies has created special problems.

Both parts of the reunited country share a demographic imbalance arising from the extremely low birth rates of the 1970s and 1980s, combined with the rapid increase in life expectancy which seems likely to produce a significant ageing of the population in the coming decades. Migration, particularly from the East to the West of the country, is creating further problems at present; some 700,000 Eastern Germans are now estimated to have settled in the West, and another 500,000 are commuting on a weekly or monthly basis.

Marketing regions

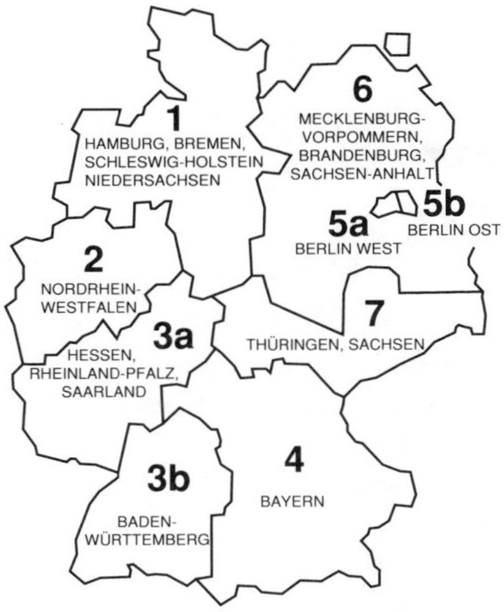

Former West Germany: Households at 1987 census

	('000)	%
1	5,216	19.9
2	7,195	27.4
3a	4,291	16.4
3b	4,529	17.3
4	3,900	14.9
5	1,091	4.2
Total	26,218	100.0

Standard regions

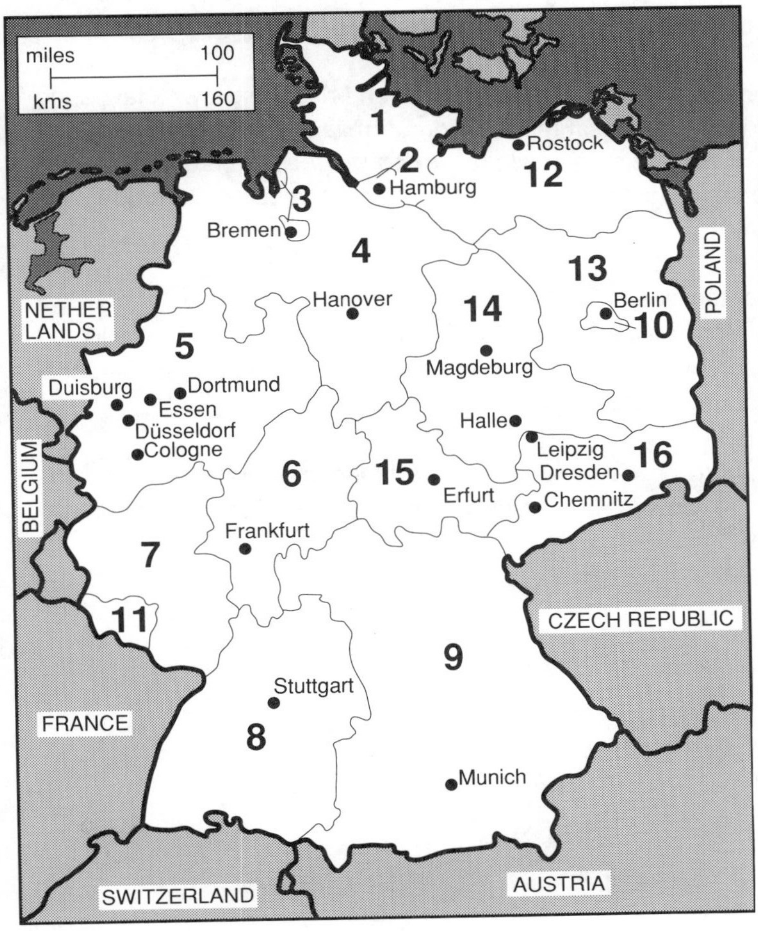

	STANDARD REGION	POPULATION ('000, 1990 estimates)
1	Schleswig-Holstein	2,666
2	Hamburg	1,626
3	Bremen	674
4	Niedersachsen	7,238
5	Nordrhein-Westfalen	17,104
6	Hessen	5,661
7	Rheinland-Pfalz	3,702
8	Baden-Württemberg	9,619
9	Bayern	11,221
10	Berlin	3,410
11	Saarland	1,065
12	Mecklenburg-Vorpommern	1,964
13	Brandenburg	2,641
14	Sachsen-Anhalt	2,965
15	Thüringen	2,684
16	Sachsen	4,901

Greece

Population	10,198,000 (1992)
Urban population	62%
Land area	131, 957 sq km
Language	Greek
Religion	Greek Orthodox
Currency	Drachma (= 100 leptae)
Head of state	President Constantine Karamanlis (May 1990)
Head of government	Constantine Mitsotakis
Ruling party	New Democracy Party
Main urban areas	Athens (capital, 3,449,735 in 1981 census)
	Salonika (Thessaloniki, 759,551)
	Patras (166,280)
	Volos (115,545)
	Larissa (110,167)
	Candia (Iraklion, on Crete) (110,137)

Development in modern Greece has been hampered by the dual disadvantages of poor agricultural and natural resources, and of the country's relatively isolated geographical position: it is the only EC member state which has no borders with other EC members.

The hot climate and parched soils are poor for cereal crops (although wheat and rice are grown), favouring fruits such as olives, peaches, oranges, lemons and grapes. Fresh and dried fruits are an important part of Greece's exports. There is some exploitation of bauxite resources, as well as magnesium ore and oil, and the country has set up petroleum refineries to serve its domestic market - although much of its crude oil is imported.

The country's mountainous topography, and the scattering of island communities, impose a physical restriction on communications and transport. Moreover, a great deal of investment has been necessitated by the development of the electricity system, and by the broadening of the irrigation programmes. Regional aid from the European Community is a major source of development capital at present.

The Greek economy has had to rely on tourism to provide a large part of its income, but there are signs that growth in this sector is beginning to slow down, with tourists from Western European countries venturing further afield.

Marketing regions

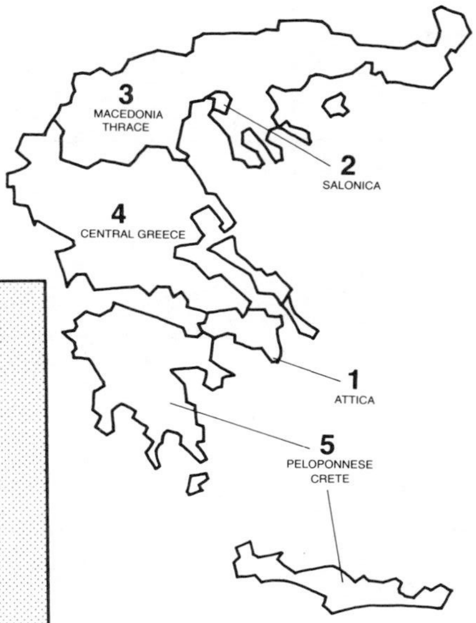

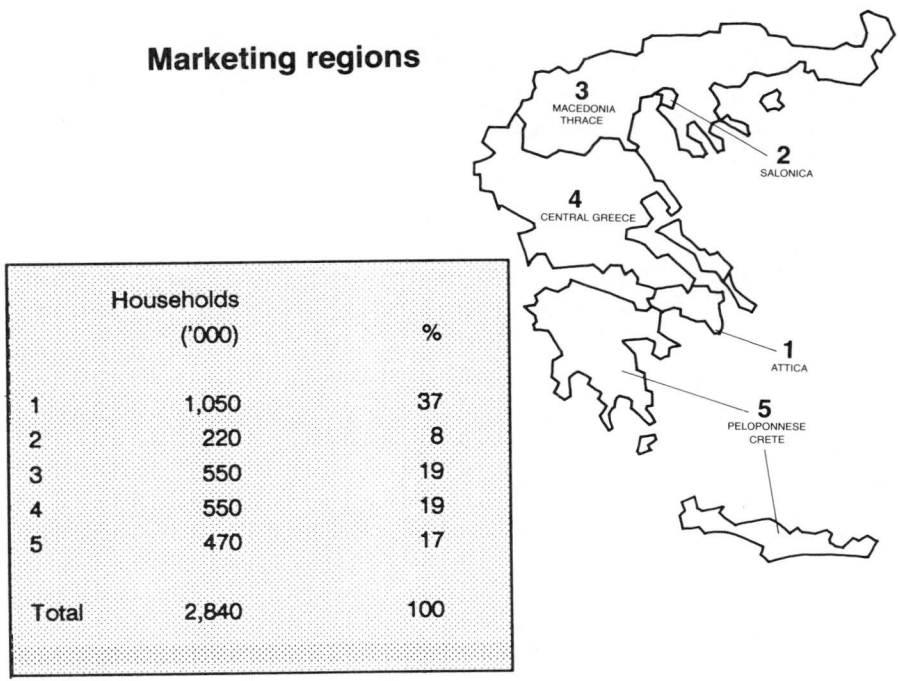

	Households ('000)	%
1	1,050	37
2	220	8
3	550	19
4	550	19
5	470	17
Total	2,840	100

Standard regions

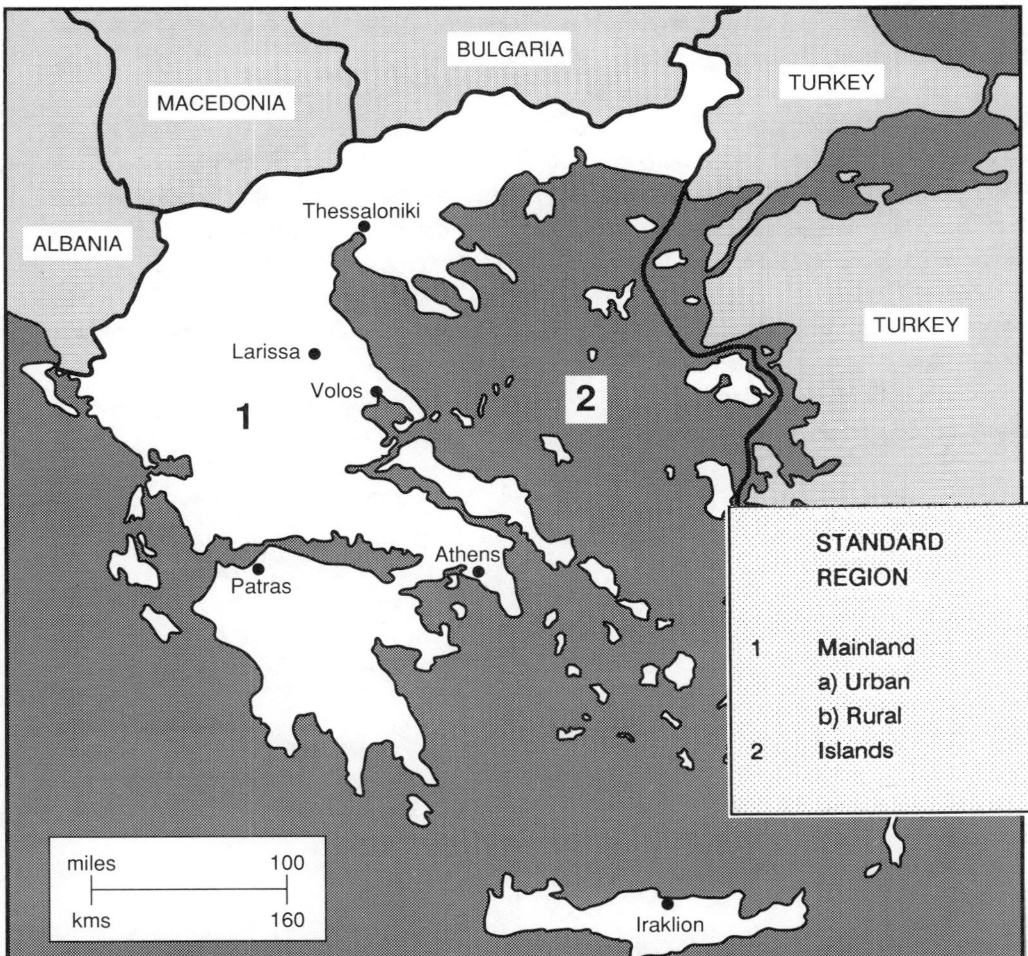

	STANDARD REGION	POPULATION (1983)
1	Mainland	8,724,111
	a) Urban	5,347,880
	b) Rural	3,376,231
2	Islands	1,122,154

Ireland

Population	3,503,000 (1992)
Urban population	60%
Land area	70,283 sq km
Languages	Irish, English
Religions	Catholic (93%), Church of Ireland (3%), Presbyterian (0.4%)
Currency	Punt (= 100 pence)
Head of state	President Mary Robinson (December 1990)
Head of government	Albert Reynolds
Ruling party	Fianna Fail
Main urban areas	Dublin (capital, 1,024,429 in 1991, including county)
	Cork (282,790)
	Galway (129,462)
	Limerick (109,816)

Ireland is a largely low-lying island, exposed to the Atlantic ocean and dominated by a wet climate. The Irish Republic, the southern part of the island, was left when the United Kingdom partitioned Ireland in 1921. The economy is still largely dependent on farming, with potatoes and barley the dominant crops, and with an important dairy and cattle sector.

There is relatively little indigenous manufacturing industry, but considerable growth has been seen in the export-oriented assembly of high-technology and other goods on behalf of Japanese, American and West European companies - all attracted by the generous incentives offered by the government. However, the growth has failed to stem the increase in unemployment which has driven thousands of people into emigration, and the population has been steadily shrinking since the mid-1980s.

The UK remains the country's most important trading partner, although this position has declined somewhat since Ireland's accession to the EC. Food and food products make up the largest part of the country's exports, although the recent development of oil reserves in the Irish Sea has also made a contribution to trade. Manufactured goods and chemicals are the major imports.

Marketing regions

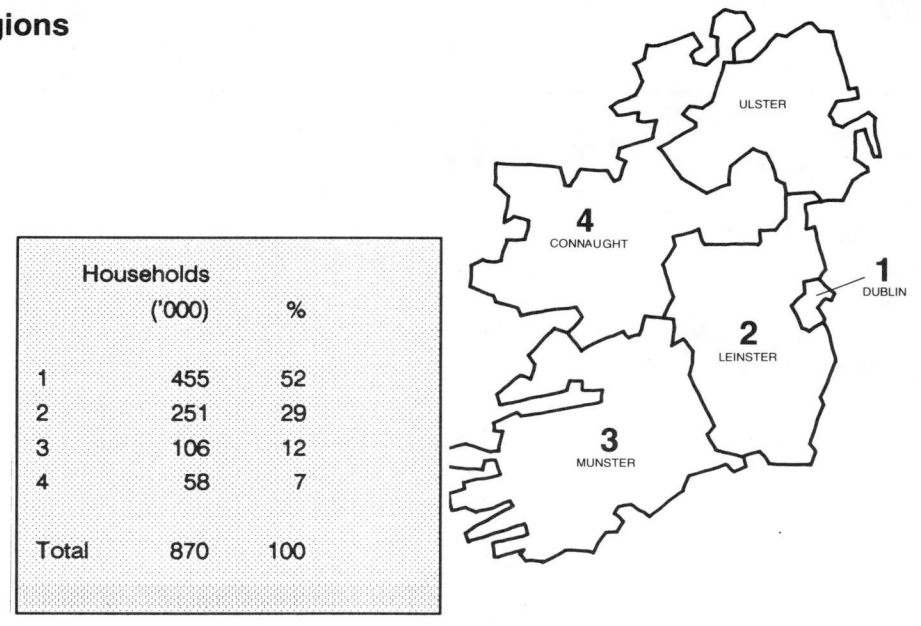

	Households ('000)	%
1	455	52
2	251	29
3	106	12
4	58	7
Total	870	100

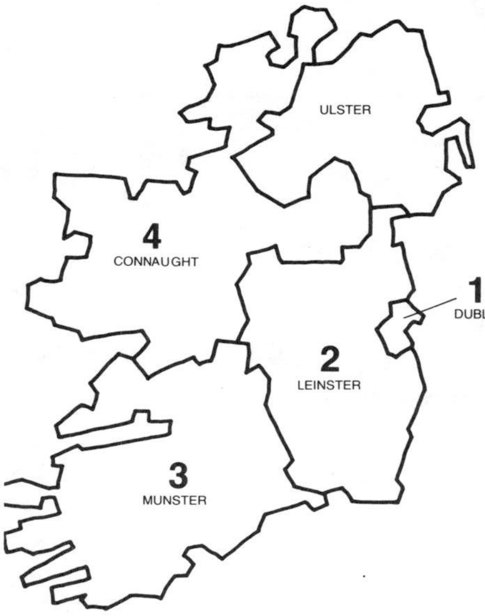

Standard regions

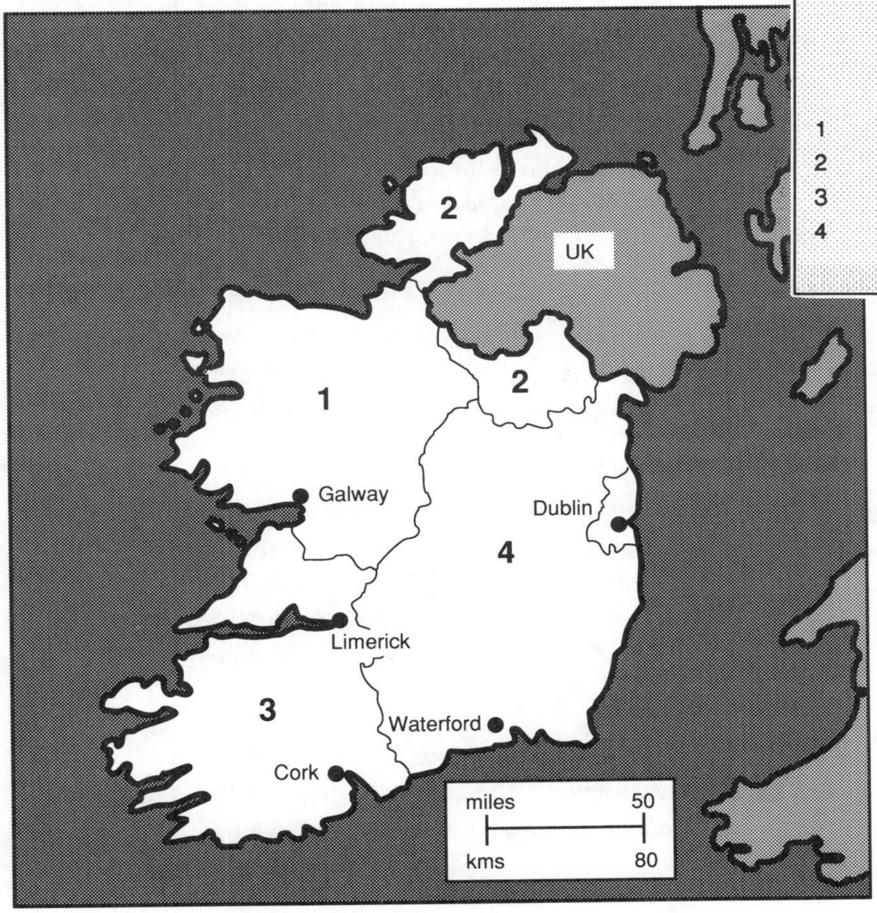

	STANDARD REGION	POPULATION (1991)
1	Connaught	422,909
2	Ulster (part of)	232,012
3	Munster	1,008,443
4	Leinster	1,860,037

Italy

Population	58,024,000 (1992)
Urban population	68%
Land area	301,277 sq km
Language	Italian
Religion	Roman Catholic (90%)
Currency	Lira
Head of state	President Oscar Luigi Scalfaro
Head of government	Giuliano Amato
Ruling party	Christian Democrats (in coalition with Socialist Party)
Main urban areas	Rome (capital, 2,791,354 in January 1991)
	Milan (1,432,184)
	Naples (1,206,013)
	Turin (991,870)
	Palermo (734,238)
	Genoa (701,032)
	Bologna (411,803)
	Florence (408,403)

The size and shape of Italy imply a diversity in all areas of economic life, but broadly speaking the country can be regarded as having two distinct areas: to the north of Rome lie the prosperous industrial areas and fertile arable land: to the south (the Mezzogiorno) the climate is harder with correspondingly poorer agriculture.

Milan is the main industrial centre, with steel, machine tool and automobile industries, and is also the hub of the Lombardy region, which houses much of the country's financial and banking services. West of Milan lies Turin, where 75% of the country's cars are made, and the Piedmont region, where the country's textile industry is concentrated.

In the north-east there has in recent years been some development of light industry, especially in Verona, Trieste and around Venice. Similarly, in Tuscany and Emilia, regions of special agricultural importance, industry has developed: in Florence (leather), in Bologna (food processing), and in numerous smaller towns.

South of Rome, social conditions are different, with higher unemployment and lower standards of living. The government is attempting to encourage industry around Naples and on the Adriatic coast around Bari. There are some industrial plants, notably oil refineries in the east and a steelworks at Taranto. But the soil quality in the south is poor, and agriculture concentrates on fruits (olives, oranges, tomatoes) and nuts. For many southern regions tourism is an important part of the economy, particularly in Sicily and on the Adriatic coast.

The overall Italian economy seems to have recovered from the problems of inflation, balance of payments deficits and industrial unrest which were largely responsible for the poor growth of the 1970s, and there is considerable optimism about the expansion of the country's consumer economy. Yet a major budget crisis erupted in 1992 accompanied by fears about the stability of the lira in the foreign exchange markets, and in September Prime Minister Amato sought emergency powers. Unemployment remains a problem, however, particularly in the south.

Marketing regions

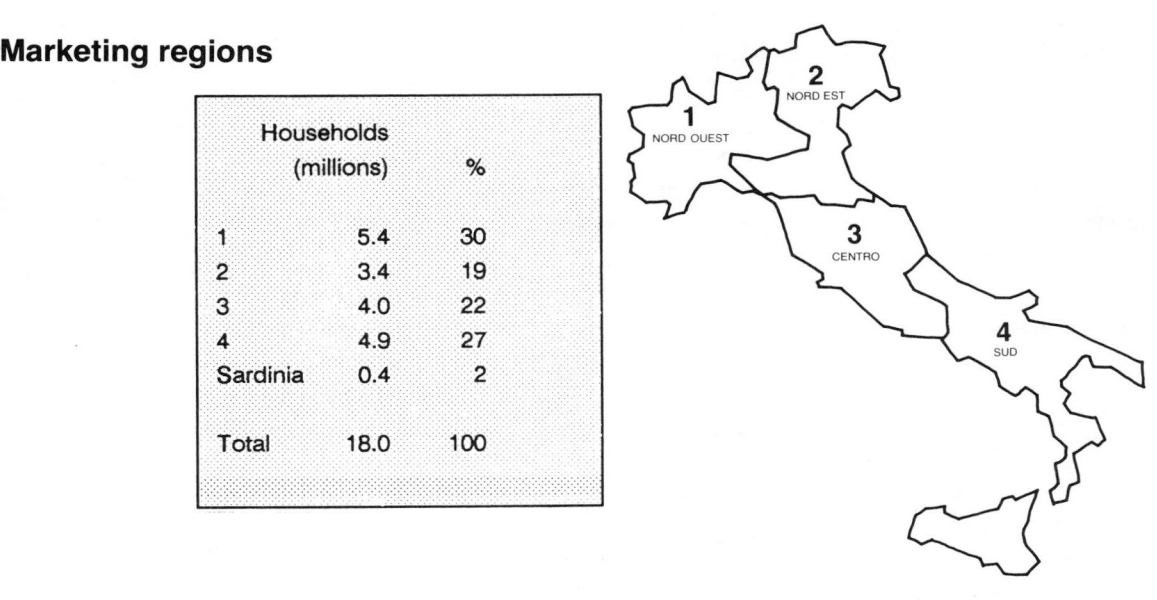

	Households (millions)	%
1	5.4	30
2	3.4	19
3	4.0	22
4	4.9	27
Sardinia	0.4	2
Total	18.0	100

Standard regions

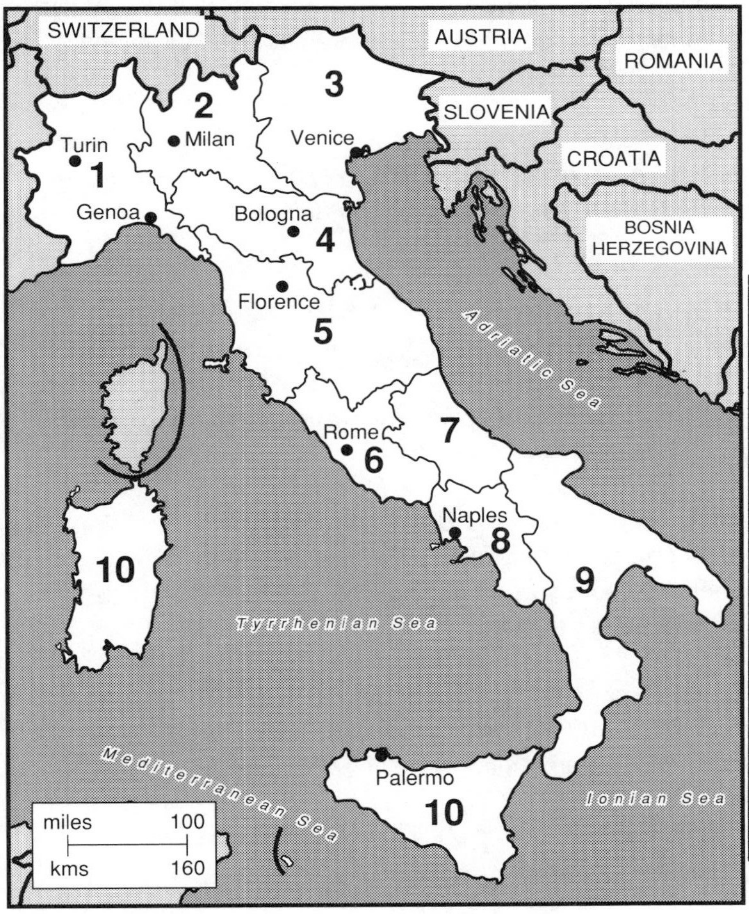

	STANDARD REGION	POPULATION (Jan 1991)
1	Valle d'Aosta, Piedmont, Liguria	6,191,425
2	Lombardia	8,939,429
3	Friuli, Veneto, Trentino	6,490,562
4	Emilia-Romagna	3,928,744
5	Marche, Umbria, Toscana	5,820,864
6	Lazio	5,191,482
7	Abruzzi and Molise	1,601,843
8	Campania	5,853,902
9	Calabria, Basilicata, Puglia	6,859,717
10	Sicilia, Sardinia	6,861,195

Netherlands

Population	15,118,000 (1992)
Urban population	89%
Land area	33,933 sq km
Language	Dutch
Religions	Roman Catholic (38%), Potestant (30%)
Currency	Florin or Guilder (= 100 cents)
Head of state	HM Queen Beatrix (1980)
Head of government	Ruud Lubbers
Ruling party	Christian Democrats and Labour Party (in coalition)
Main urban areas	Amsterdam (capital, 695,162 at January 1990)
	Rotterdam (579,179)
	The Hague (seat of government, 441,506)
	Utrecht (230,358)
	Eindhoven (191,467)
	Groningen (167,872)
	Tilburg (156,421)
	Haarlem (149,269)

With 374 persons per square kilometre, the Netherlands is the most densely populated major European nation. Most of the population live in the southern half of the country, while there has been an increase in the areas reclaimed from the North Sea in recent decades.

Arable land, especially in the reclaimed areas, is very fertile, and the agricultural sector is highly productive, with potatoes, wheat, rye and sugar beet the main crops, and with dairy cattle, poultry and pigs as the main livestock. There is a large horticultural sector exporting flowers and bulbs, and an important fishing industry.

The importance of the Netherlands lies in its position as a trading nation, which for centuries has provided much of the nation's wealth. Its position at the mouth of the rivers Rhine, Maas and Scheldt allows it to act as an entrepôt for materials moving into Western Germany and other central European countries, and industries such as oil and petrochemical refining have grown up to take advantage of this trade, as has a large banking and financial services sector.

There are few metal deposits, but there is some coal mining, and during the 1980s large natural gas reserves were exploited in the north of the country and offshore. Lacking its own iron ore resources, there is little heavy industry: rather, manufacturing activity centres on electrical and mechanical engineering, automobiles, aircraft and defence equipment, and consumer goods.

The Netherlands has three of the largest consumer product companies in Europe: Royal Dutch Shell (oil, plastics and petrochemicals), Unilever (household and personal products) and Philips (domestic appliances and consumer electronics). Shell and Unilever are both co-owned by UK interests.

The country was a signatory of the 1990 Schengen agreement on the abolition of border controls.

Marketing regions

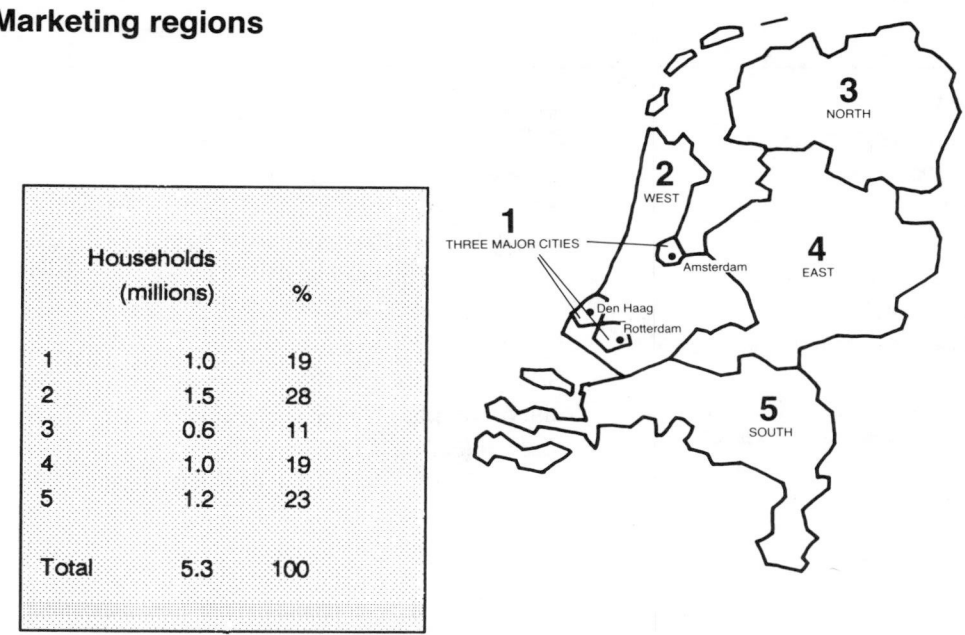

	Households (millions)	%
1	1.0	19
2	1.5	28
3	0.6	11
4	1.0	19
5	1.2	23
Total	5.3	100

Standard regions

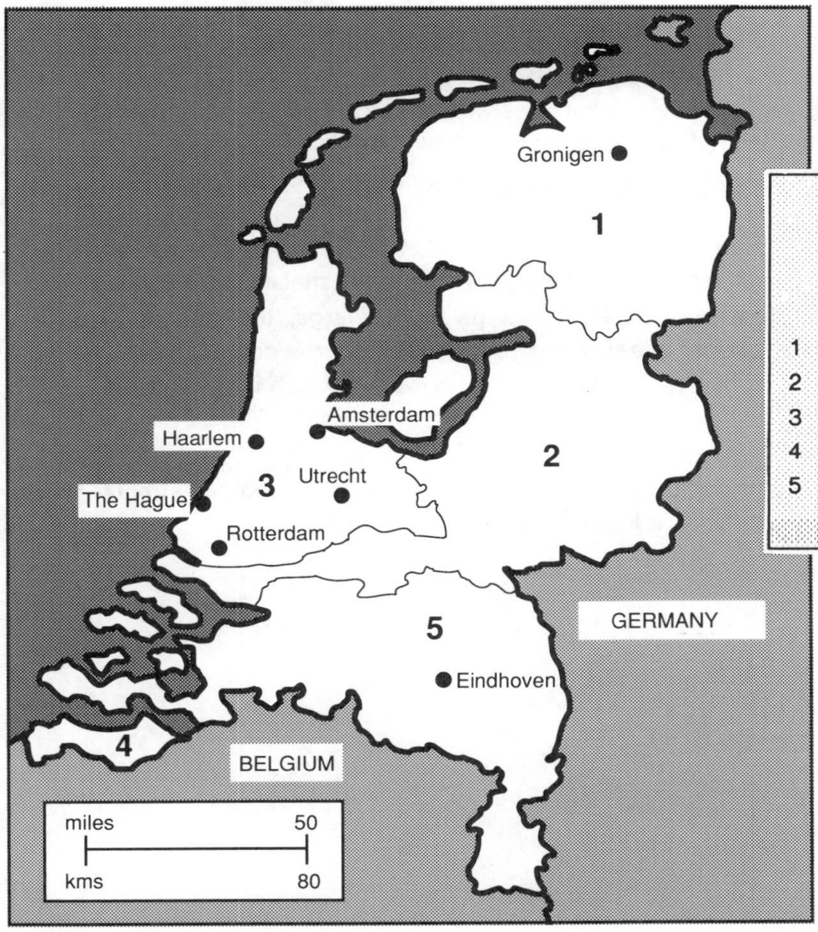

	STANDARD REGION	POPULATION (1991)
1	North	1,591,041
2	East	3,036,140
3	West	6,611,369
4	South West	355,947
5	South	3,293,441

Portugal

Population	10,430,000 (1992)
Urban population	33%
Land area	92,389 sq km
Language	Portuguese
Religion	Mainly Roman Catholic
Currency	Escudo (= 100 centavos)
Head of state	Dr Mario Lopes Soares (1986)
Head of government	Dr Anibal Cavaco Silva
Ruling party	Social Democrat Party
Main urban areas	Lisbon (capital, 830,500 in 1987)
	Oporto (350,368)
	Amadora (95,518 in 1981 census)
	Setubal (77,885)
	Coimbra (74,616)
	Braga (63,033)

Portugal, which acceded to the EC only in 1986, has experienced perhaps the most dramatic economic growth of any member country since then, as foreign investment and EC development aid have continued to flood into the country.

Development assistance is helping a variety of industries, notably textiles, footwear, food processing and wood products. There are also two shipyards, and a modern steelworks. The industrial sector as a whole is as yet still underdeveloped, however, and manufactured goods and raw materials make up a large part of the country's imports. A burgeoning trade deficit has periodically necessitated strict controls on lending to consumers.

Because of the nature of the soil and the hot climate, agricultural products are mainly fruits and potatoes. Cereal crops are largely imported. Its seaboard situation has given it a large, though comparatively unorganised, fishery industry. There are a number of small mineral deposits, but the country lacks coal and oil reserves. It has begun to make use of its hydro-electric potential, however, which is helping the growth of industry.

In recent years tourism has become extremely important, particularly in the Algarve region in the far south, where as much as 90% of the workforce is directly or indirectly involved in the sector.

Marketing regions

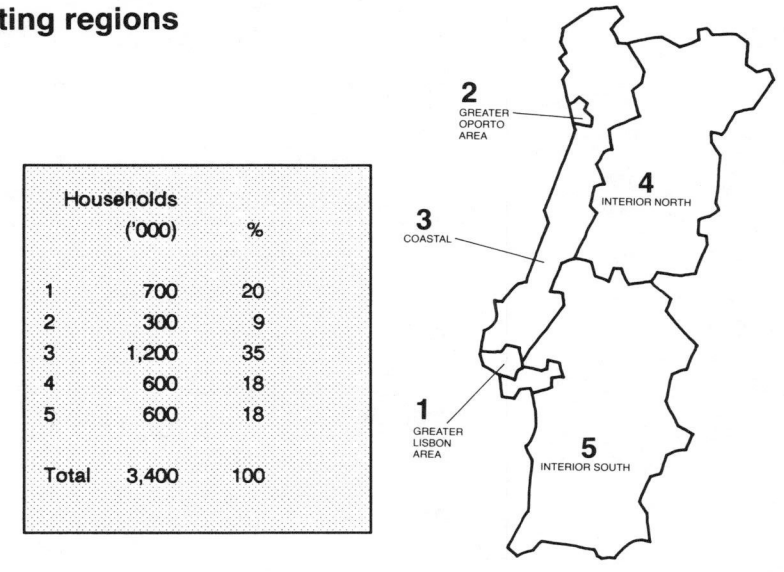

	Households ('000)	%
1	700	20
2	300	9
3	1,200	35
4	600	18
5	600	18
Total	3,400	100

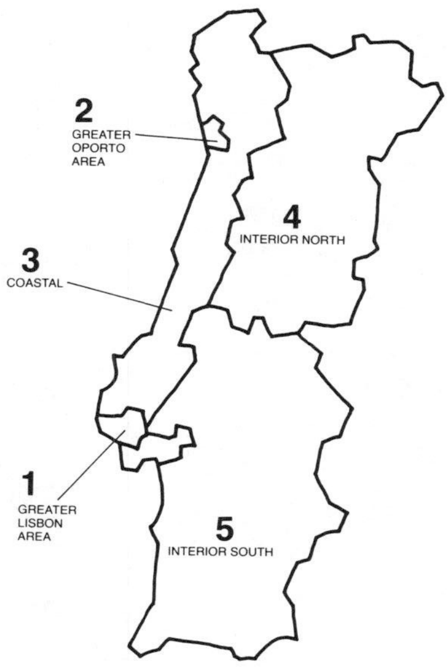

Standard regions

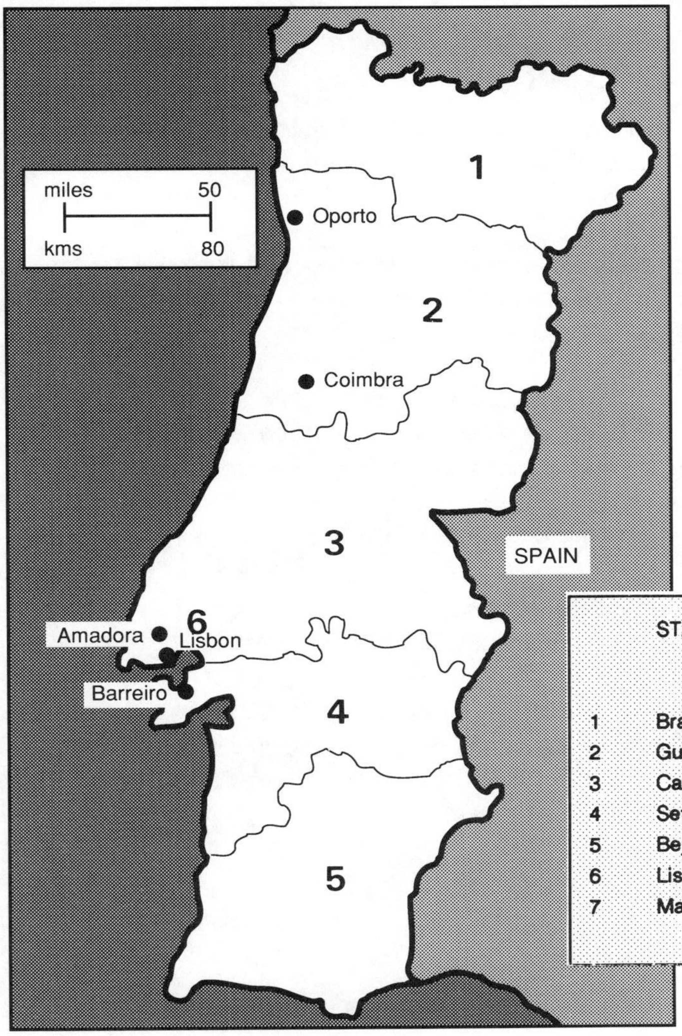

	STANDARD REGION	POPULATION (January 1989)
1	Bragança, Vila Real, Braga, Viana do Castelo	1,490,300
2	Guarda, Viseu, Coimbra, Aveiro, Porto	3,415,400
3	Castelo Branco, Leiria, Santarem, Portalegre	1,253,500
4	Setubal, Evora	971,700
5	Beja, Faro	518,300
6	Lisboa	2,128,700
7	Madeira/Azores	526,800

Spain

Population	38,990,000 (1992)
Urban population	79%
Land area	504,782 sq km
Languages	Spanish (Castilian, Catalan, Galician), Basque
Religion	Mainly Roman Catholic
Currency	Peseta (= 100 centimos)
Head of state	King Juan Carlos I (1975)
Head of government	Felipe Gonzalez Marquez
Ruling party	Socialist Workers' Party (PSOE)
Main urban areas	Madrid (capital, 3,120,732 in January 1990)
	Barcelona (1,777,286)
	Valencia (758,738)
	Seville (678,218)
	Zaragoza (592,686)
	Malaga (560,495)
	Bilbao (383,798)

The interior of Spain is dominated by a relatively fertile plain allowing the cultivation of a variety of fruits (olives, grapes, citrus fruits, tomatoes, peppers, etc), as well as nuts, cereals, hemp and flax. The export of food products is an important contributor to the Spanish economy.

Spain also has numerous mineral deposits, but these are becoming depleted and many of the more accessible reserves have already been mined out. Coal, oil, iron and other metal ores are found throughout the country, and particularly in the north-east.

The main industrial centres are on the east coast (centred on Barcelona) and north coast (around Bilbao); since the accession of Spain to the European Community in 1986 there has been strong interest from foreign investors in Spanish enterprises. Spain acts for Andorra within the European Community.

The consumer boom in Spain since the start of 1987 has been one of the strongest seen anywhere in Europe, with a pronounced shift away from basics and towards luxury goods. However, the growing pressure on the trade balance has occasionally forced the government to restrain consumer spending, especially on luxury goods. Some of these restrictions were being lifted in 1992, however.

Tourism is an important part of the Spanish economy, contributing around 1,500 billion Ptas a year to the balance of payments. French tourists comprise more than 20% of the country's foreign visitors.

Marketing regions

	Households (millions)	%
Metropolitan Barcelona	1.7	12
1	1.6	11
2	2.0	13
3	2.7	18
Metropolitan Madrid	1.8	13
4	1.6	11
5	1.7	12
6	1.4	10
Total	14.4	100

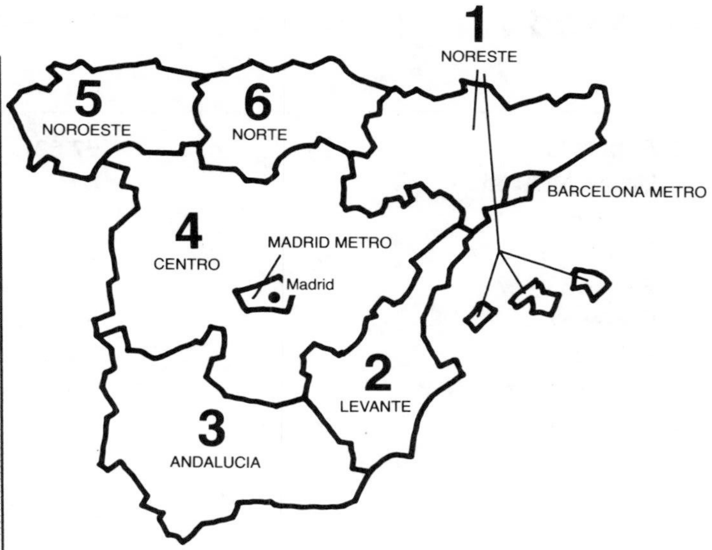

Standard regions

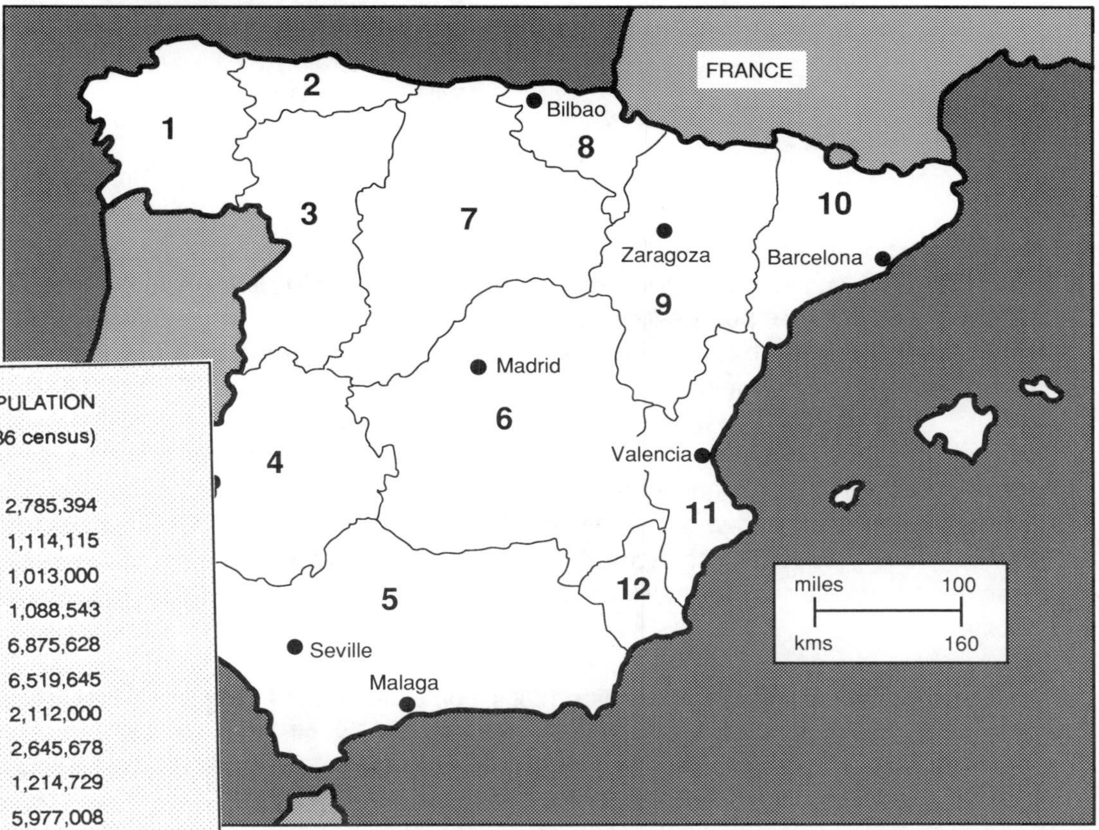

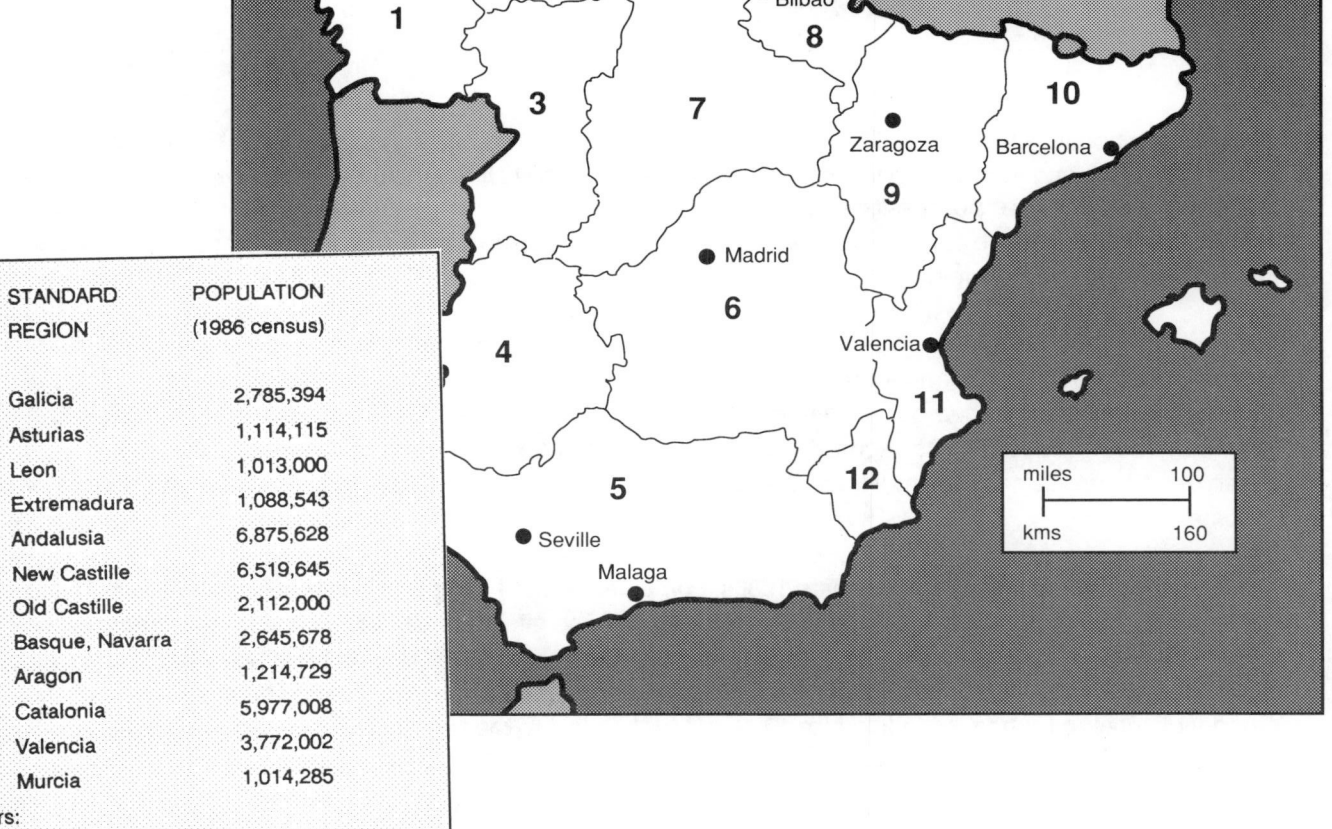

	STANDARD REGION	POPULATION (1986 census)
1	Galicia	2,785,394
2	Asturias	1,114,115
3	Leon	1,013,000
4	Extremadura	1,088,543
5	Andalusia	6,875,628
6	New Castille	6,519,645
7	Old Castille	2,112,000
8	Basque, Navarra	2,645,678
9	Aragon	1,214,729
10	Catalonia	5,977,008
11	Valencia	3,772,002
12	Murcia	1,014,285
Others:		
	Ceuta*	71,403
	Melilla*	55,613
	Baleares	754,777
	Canary Islands	1,614,882

* Became full provinces in 1991

United Kingdom of Great Britain and Northern Ireland

Population	57,521,000 (1992)
Urban population	89%
Land area	244,103 sq km
Language	English
Religion	Protestant
Currency	Pound (= 100 pence)
Head of state	HM Queen Elizabeth II (1952)
Head of government	John Major
Ruling party	Conservative Party
Main urban areas	Greater London (capital, 6,794,000 in 1991)
	Birmingham (993,000)
	Leeds (712,000)
	Glasgow (696,000)
	Sheffield (527,000)
	Bradford (468,000)
	Liverpool (463,000)
	Manchester (447,000)
	Edinburgh (433,000)
	Bristol (374,000)

Britain's position as a wealthy nation was derived initially from the fertile agricultural land, particularly in the east of England, and subsequently from the development of heavy industry in the Midlands and the north of the country. Its imperial possessions in the eighteenth and nineteenth centuries enabled further growth in manufacturing industry by providing raw materials, and its position as a major trading nation helped to make London the world's leading financial centre.

Although many of these factors are now less relevant, the country is managing to replace much of its lost industrial base with new high-tech and light industries. London remains one of the three main financial centres in a vastly expanded global market, and relies on its heavy services income from abroad to offset its equally heavy trade deficits. Agriculture remains extremely efficient, and in the 1970s and 1980s large reserves of hydrocarbons in the North Sea have been exploited to provide another significant source of income.

Over-borrowing by consumers in the late 1980s, combined with a high interest rate policy and a continuing trade deficit, has braked the economy in the early 1990s. The effects have not been felt equally across the country, however: traditional manufacturing areas in the north and the Midlands have been worst affected, while the south in general and Greater London in particular remain more affluent. The completion of the Channel Tunnel to France, scheduled for 1993, will further add to the pressures in the region although it will generate considerable wealth as well.

Marketing regions

	Households (millions)	%
1	4.3	22
2	1.2	6
3	1.5	8
4	2.0	10
5	2.9	15
6	2.7	14
7	2.1	11
8	1.0	5
9	1.8	9
Total	19.5	100

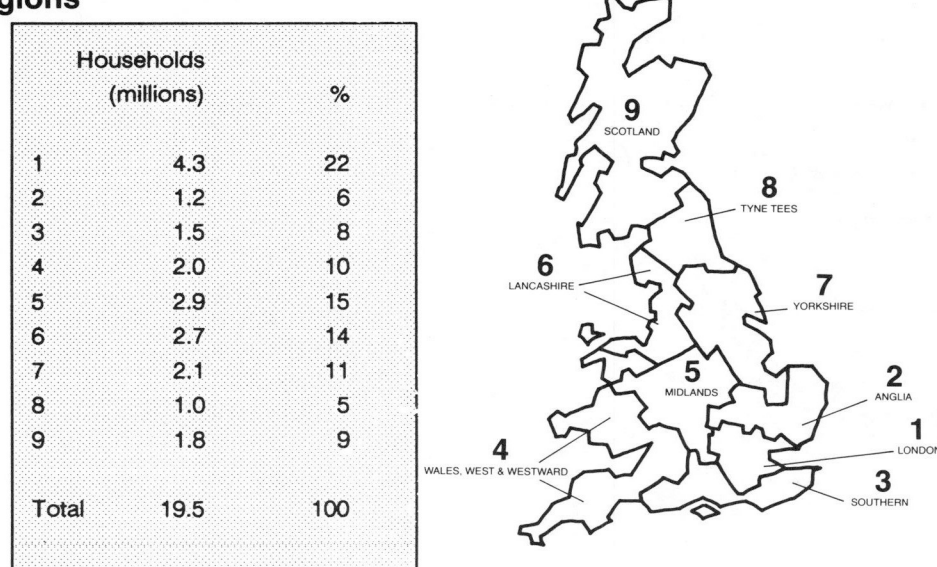

Standard regions

	STANDARD REGION	POPULATION ('000, mid-1990)
1	North	3,075
2	Yorks, Humberside	4,952
3	E. Midlands	4,019
4	E. Anglia	2,059
5	South East	17,458
6	South West	4,666
7	W. Midlands	5,219
8	North West	6,389
9	Wales	2,881
10	Scotland	5,102
11	N. Ireland	1,589

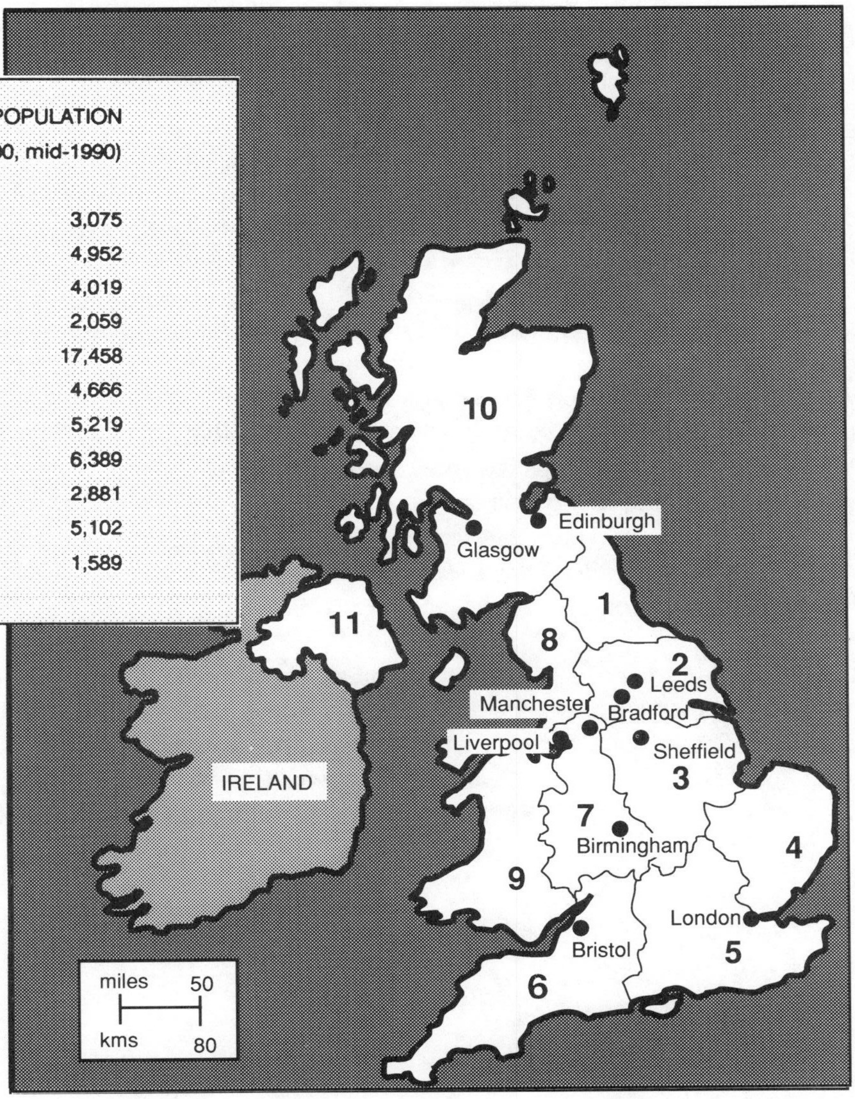

Austria

Population	7,733,000 (1992)
Urban population	58%
Land area	83,857 sq km
Language	German (minorities speak Slovene and Croat)
Religion	Roman Catholic
Currency	Schilling (= 100 Groschen)
Head of state	President Thomas Klestil (1992)
Head of government	Dr Franz Vranitzky
Ruling party	Socialist Party of Austria, in coalition with the People's Party
Main urban areas	Vienna (capital, 1,533,176 in 1991 census)
	Graz (232,155)
	Linz (202,855)
	Salzburg (145,971)
	Innsbruck (114,996)
	Klagenfurt (89,502)

Although Austria is a mountainous country, its climate sustains a variety of crops and fruit, including potatoes, sugar beet, wheat, barley, apples and pears, as well as a large number of vineyards. The main livestock animals are dairy cows, pigs and chickens. With a large proportion of land forested, wood and timber-derived products are also important.

Austria's industrial sector has traditionally been dominated by state-owned enterprises, especially in the important machine tool and engineering sector, but 1987-91 saw moves to privatise these often cumbersome and loss-making concerns. Natural resources include brown coal, magnesium and aluminium ores, and small quantities of oil and natural gas. The terrain lends itself to hydro-electric production; the use of nuclear power was rejected in a referendum in 1987, and the country's only nuclear reactor at Zwentendorf is currently being dismantled.

Tourism is very important to Austria - foreign currency earnings from over 15 million foreign visitors were equivalent to over 28% of total federal income in 1991.

Although Austria shares a common language and heritage with Germany, which represents its overwhelmingly major trade partner, there are some marked differences, due not only to Austria's adherence to Catholicism, but also its links with, and its proximity to, the Slavonic countries of Eastern Europe. Austria has applied to join the European Community, and negotiations are under way with Brussels for an improvement in the road links on which through traffic from Germany and Italy depends.

Marketing regions

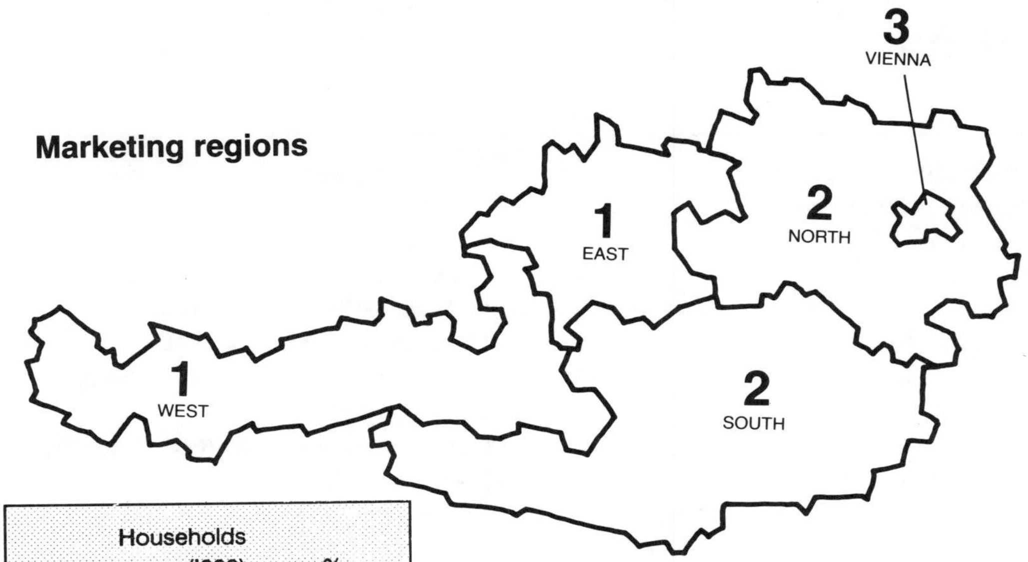

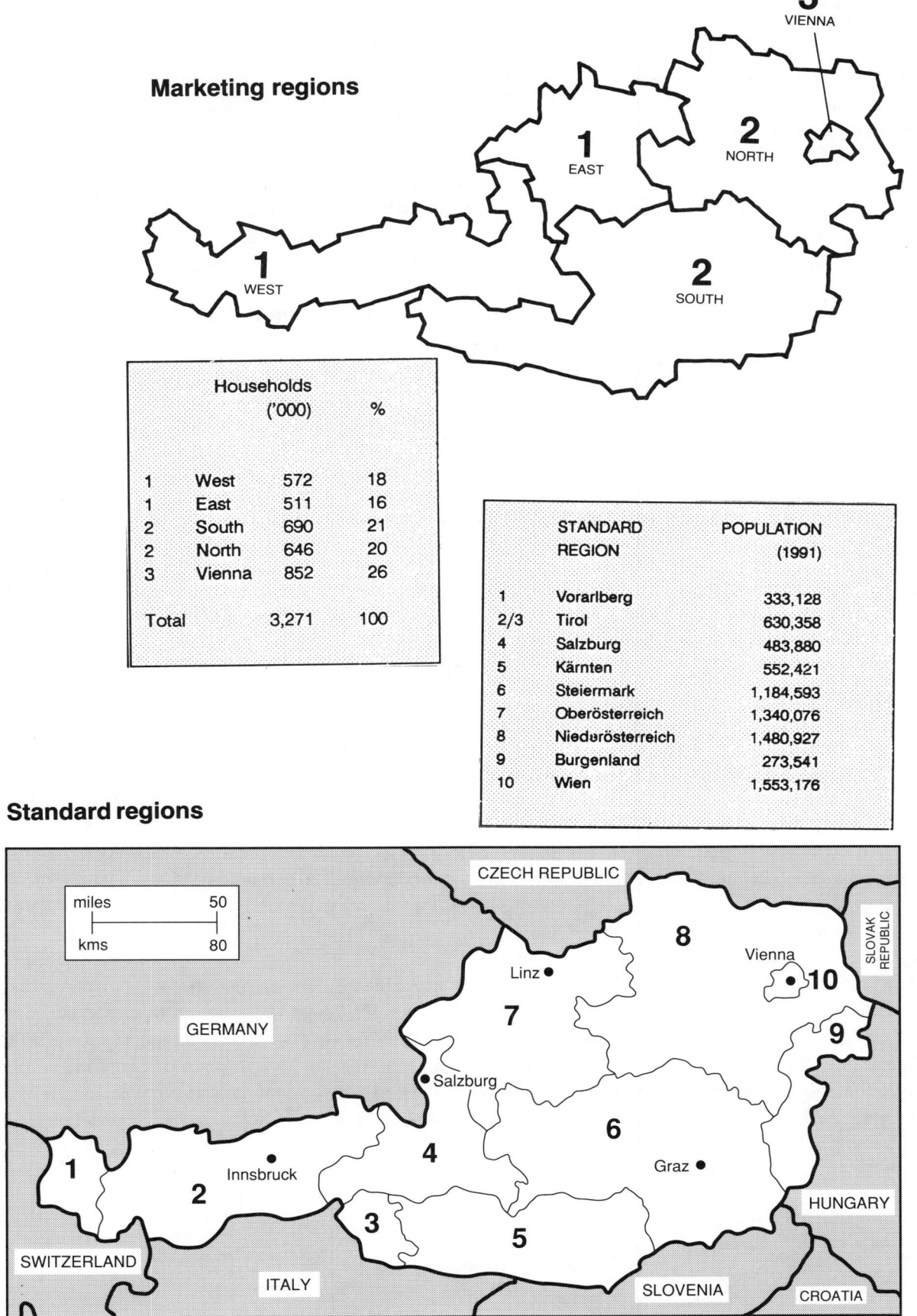

		Households ('000)	%
1	West	572	18
1	East	511	16
2	South	690	21
2	North	646	20
3	Vienna	852	26
Total		3,271	100

	STANDARD REGION	POPULATION (1991)
1	Vorarlberg	333,128
2/3	Tirol	630,358
4	Salzburg	483,880
5	Kärnten	552,421
6	Steiermark	1,184,593
7	Oberösterreich	1,340,076
8	Niederösterreich	1,480,927
9	Burgenland	273,541
10	Wien	1,553,176

Standard regions

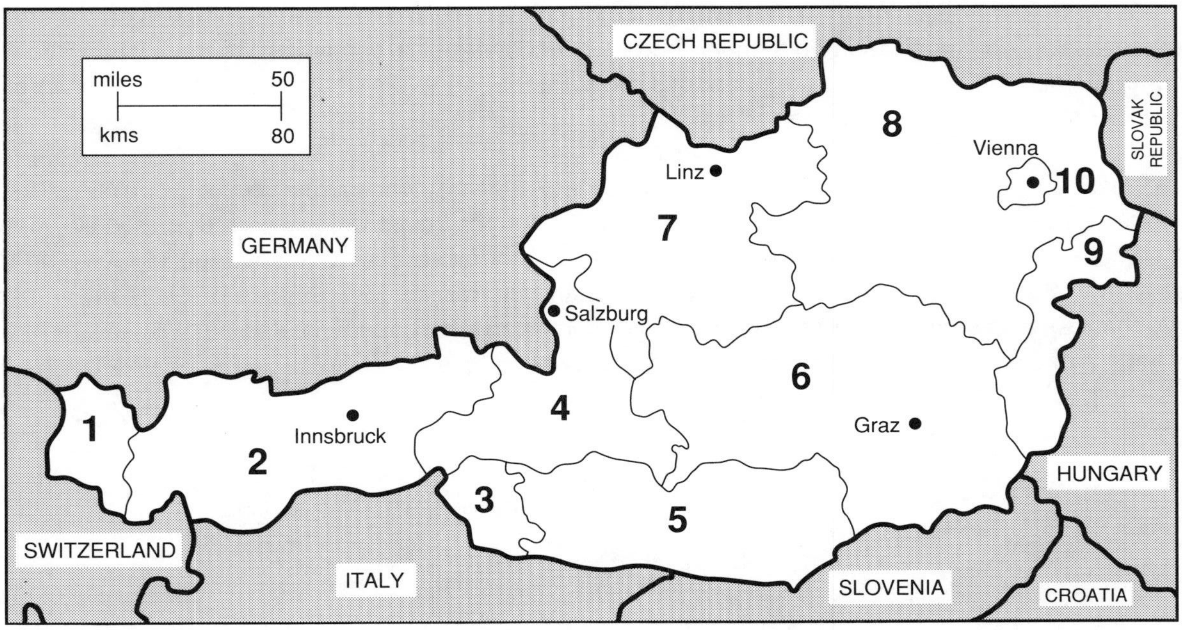

Finland

Population	4,981,000 (1992)
Urban population	60%
Land area	338,145 sq km
Languages	Finnish (93.5%), Swedish (6.3%), Lapp (0.2%)
Religions	Lutheran (90%), Greek Orthodox
Currency	Markkas (= 100 pennia)
Head of state	President Dr Mauno Koivisto (1982)
Head of government	Esko Aho
Ruling party	Centre Party leads a four-party coalition
Main urban areas	Helsinki (capital, 492,400 in mid-1991)
	Espoo (172,629)
	Tampere (172,560)
	Turku (159,180)
	Vantaa (154,933)
	Oulu (101,379)
	Lahti (93,151)

Although most of its economy derives from activities in the southern portion of the country, Finland also possesses huge natural resources in the forests which cover some 65% of the land area in the north and centre. Much of the country's industry centres on processing of wood products, which make up some 41% of exports. Engineering, shipbuilding and chemical sectors have been growing in importance, however, and the country also produces a large quantity of consumer goods, particularly textiles and footwear, and also plastics, electronic equipment, glassware and ceramics.

The country's agricultural sector is limited by the amount of arable land available, and by the poor nature of the soil, which favours livestock rather than crops. At present it accounts for around 6.2% of GDP.

The main centres of population are in the south, notably in Helsinki and in other major cities on the coast. Improvements in communication links have, however, encouraged a spread of the population into the interior of the country, where there are numerous lakes. Further north the population is more thinly spread, being concentrated on the coast.

Finland has been forced since 1991 to impose sharp austerity measures on its population, as a deteriorating trade position, the collapse of trade with the former Soviet Union and a domestic slowdown have combined to force the government's hand. The country faces a serious shortage of labour in the 1990s, due to the low birth rates of previous decades, and the resulting wage/price pressures have been among the major reasons behind its periodic bouts of inflation. The country is also painfully aware of the likely impact of the Single European Market on its trade with EC members, submitted an application for full membership in mid-1992.

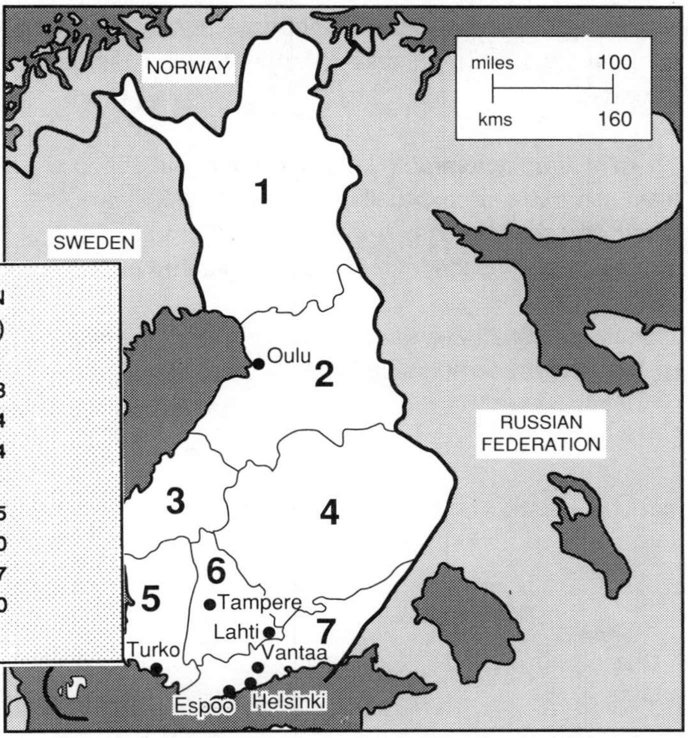

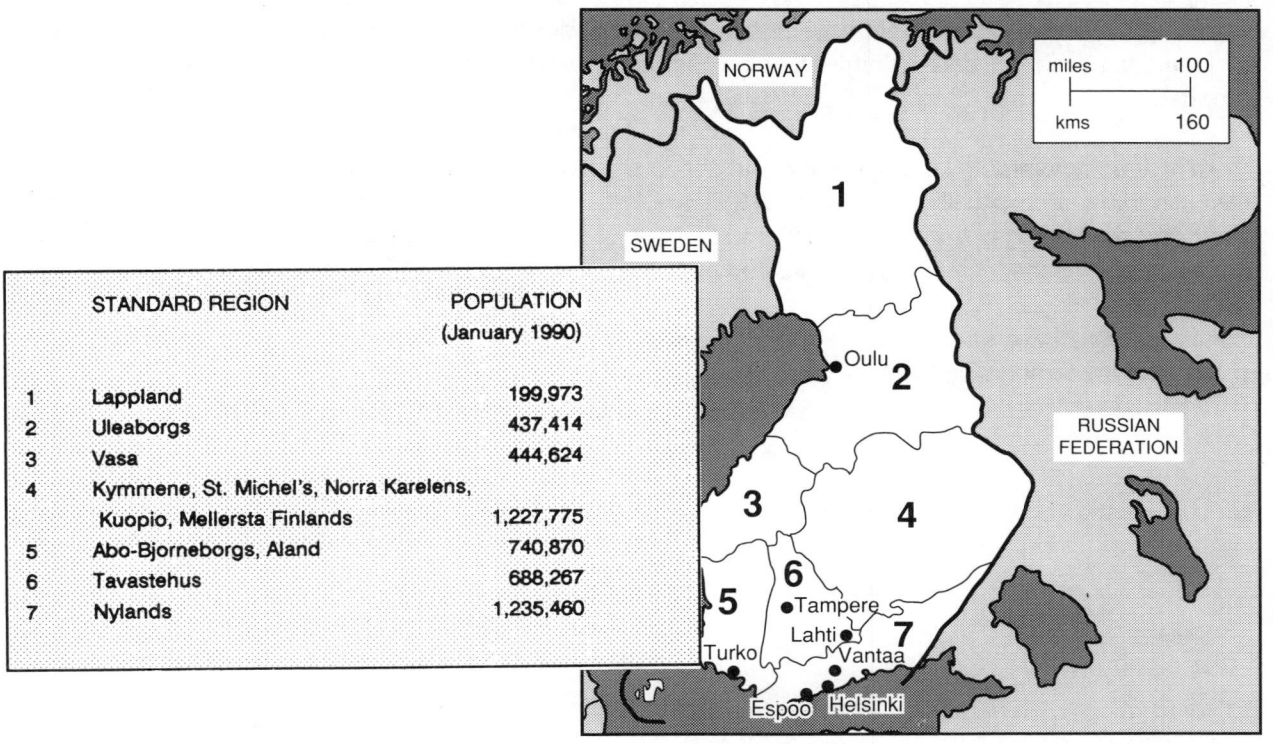

STANDARD REGION		POPULATION (January 1990)
1	Lappland	199,973
2	Uleaborgs	437,414
3	Vasa	444,624
4	Kymmene, St. Michel's, Norra Karelens, Kuopio, Mellersta Finlands	1,227,775
5	Abo-Bjorneborgs, Aland	740,870
6	Tavastehus	688,267
7	Nylands	1,235,460

Iceland

Population	257,000 (1992)
Urban population	90%
Land area	103,000 sq km
Language	Icelandic
Religion	Mainly Evangelical Lutheran Church (93%)
Currency	Krona (= 100 aurar)
Head of state	Vigdis Finnbogadottir (1980)
Head of government	David Oddson
Ruling party	Independence Party heads a coalition with the Social Democrats
Main urban areas	Reykjavik (capital, 97,569 in early 1991) Kopavogur (15,900 in 1990) Hafnarfjordur (14,541) Akureyri (14,091)

Being geographically isolated from the rest of Western Europe, Iceland's economy relies to a large extent on its fishing industry. In recent years the country's natural energy resources have begun to be more widely exploited: in addition to hydro-electric generation the potential for geothermal power is only now beginning to be realised. The abundance of such energy sources has increased the feasibility of building an industry based on energy-intensive manufacturing, although virtually all raw materials need to be imported.

There is almost no arable land in Iceland, but sheep are reared in large numbers on lowland pasture. Apart from fish and lamb, virtually all other foodstuffs are imported. Transport poses a problem for the country: there are no railways, and most main roads (few of which are metalled) are impassable in winter. Consequently, all the main towns are situated on the coast, and transport is effected by sea.

The early 1990s have seen an improvement in relations with the European Community, for which Iceland may apply for membership in future years.

Liechtenstein

Population	28,300 (1992)
Urban population	20%
Land area	160 sq km
Language	German
Religion	Mainly Roman Catholic (87%)
Currency	Swiss Franc (other currencies are widely accepted)
Head of state	Crown Prince Hans Adam (1989)
Head of government	Hans Brunhart
Ruling party	Patriotic Union Party
Main urban area	Vaduz (capital, 4,200)

Liechtenstein operates under a customs union with Switzerland, which also represents the principality in diplomatic matters. It became the 7th member of the European Free Trade Association in May 1991.

The country's economy, once predominantly agricultural in character, has seen a major expansion of light and high-tech industries, and Liechtenstein has acquired a new status as a centre for offshore banking and financial activities. Agriculture is still important, however, and based largely on the rearing of livestock. Tourism has also been developed.

Norway

Population	4,270,000 (1992)
Urban population	75%
Land area	323,878 sq km
Language	Norwegian
Religion	Evangelical Lutheran Church (92%)
Currency	Krone (=100 ore)
Head of state	King Harald V (1991)
Head of government	Gro Harlem Brundtland
Ruling party	Labour
Main urban areas	Oslo (capital, 458,364 in January 1991)
	Bergen (213,356)
	Trondheim (138,126)
	Stavanger (98,136)
	Kristiansand (65,729)
	Drammen (51,969)

Norway's mountainous terrain and craggy coastline make overland transport extremely difficult. Except for the southern areas around Oslo, where the land is somewhat flatter, towns are located on the coast.

Until the 1970s the economy was founded on the fishery industry, which benefited from the warm Gulf Stream feeding the coastal waters. However, the discovery of oil and gas reserves in the Norwegian sector of the North Sea dramatically altered the nature of the economy. In the early 1980s the sector directly employed 18% of the total workforce, and shipbuilders turned to producing drilling equipment, creating a corresponding growth in other service industries. Meanwhile, the exploitation of hydro-electric power also enabled the growth of energy-intensive industries.

Since the mid-1980s, however, the country has been forced by falling oil revenues, increasing government debts and widespread overspending by consumers to impose a series of harsh austerity budgets. Labour shortages are a recurrent feature of the Norwegian economy and these periodically push the wage/price spiral to levels which endanger the external trade balance. An emergency economic programme was introduced in 1991, based on heavy government spending in an effort to stimulate domestic activity, and this was stepped up in 1992.

The country has a number of mineral deposits, although the terrain makes extraction expensive. Aluminium, molybdenum and titanium are exported in significant quantities. Agricultural production is assisted by the Gulf Stream, although the growing season is short. Potatoes and barley are the main crops, and forestry is also important. Sheep and pigs are kept, but the livestock sector is dominated by the fishery industry.

Marketing regions

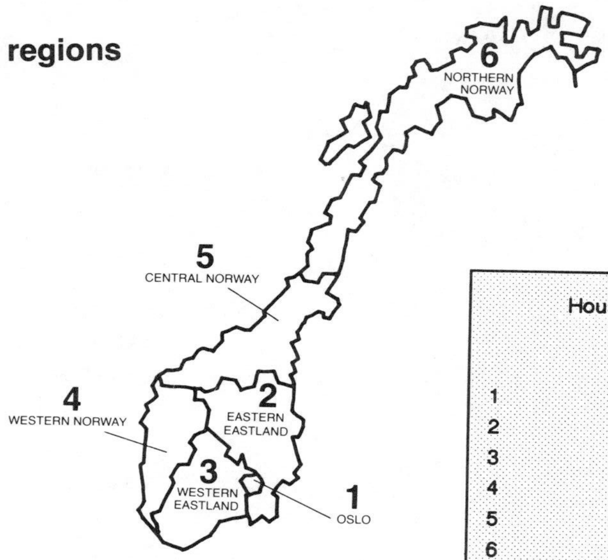

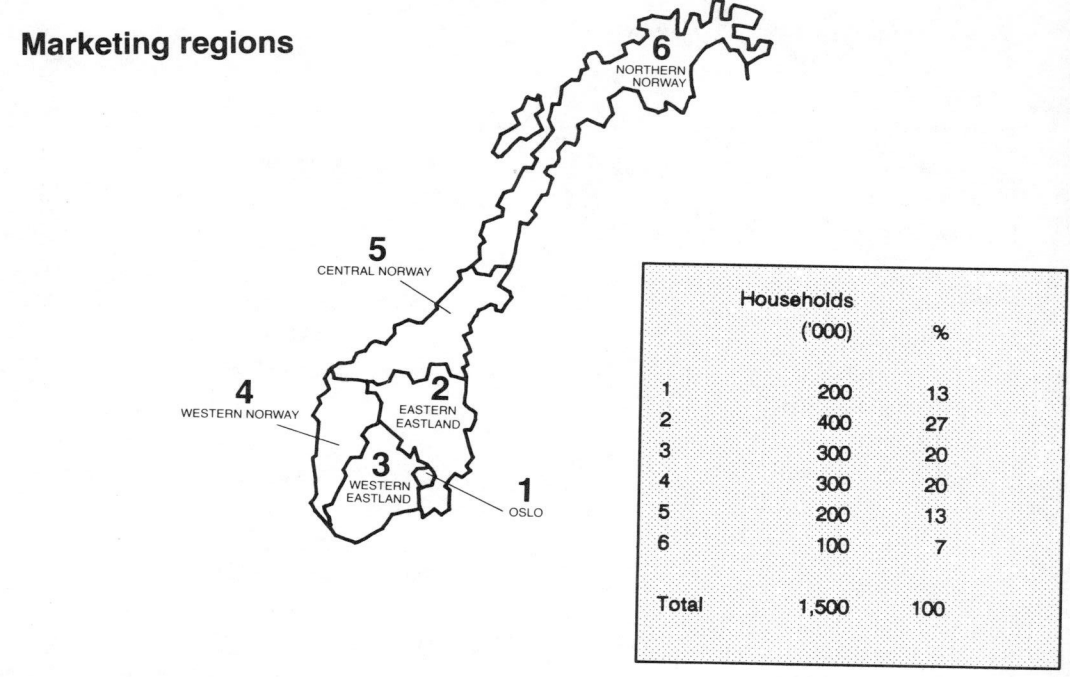

	Households ('000)	%
1	200	13
2	400	27
3	300	20
4	300	20
5	200	13
6	100	7
Total	1,500	100

Standard regions

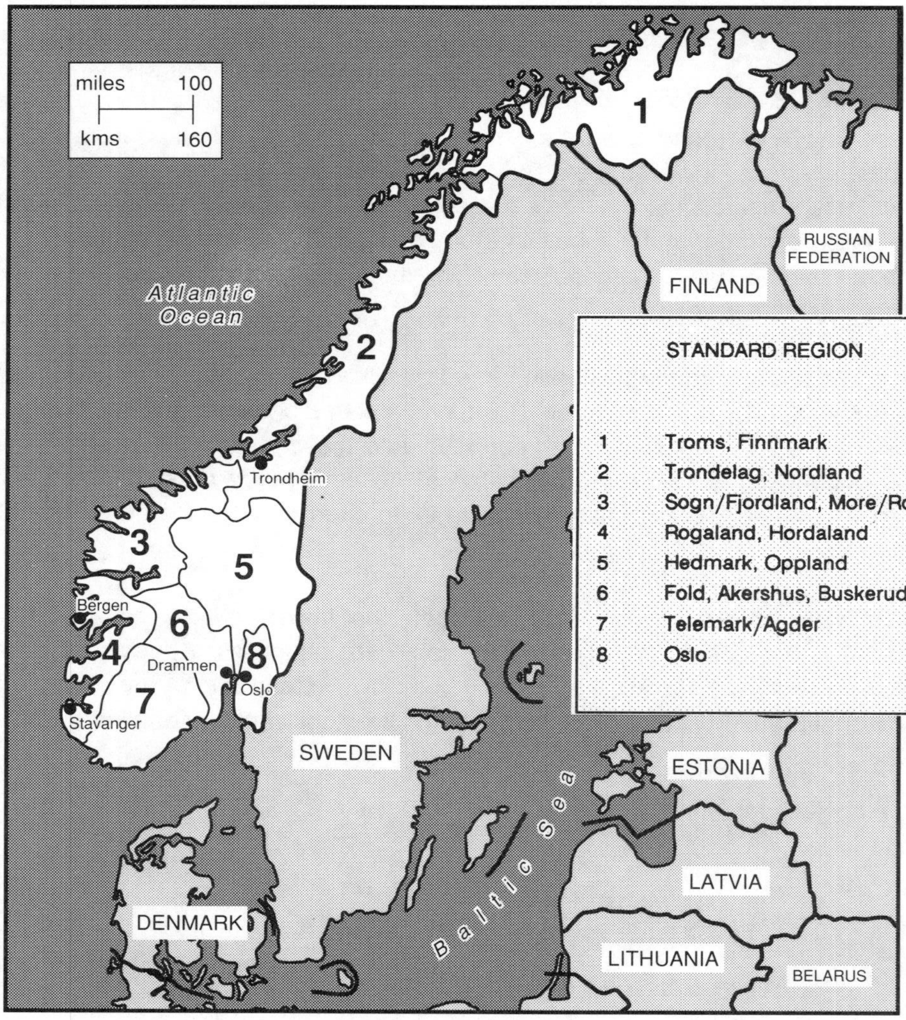

	STANDARD REGION	POPULATION (1991)
1	Troms, Finnmark	221,444
2	Trondelag, Nordland	617,866
3	Sogn/Fjordland, More/Romsdal	344,961
4	Rogaland, Hordaland	748,983
5	Hedmark, Oppland	369,958
6	Fold, Akershus, Buskerud	1,080,071
7	Telemark/Agder	405,407
8	Oslo	461,127

Sweden

Population	8,662,000 (1992)
Urban population	83%
Land area	440,945 sq km
Language	Swedish
Religion	Evangelical Lutheran Church (95%)
Currency	Krona (= 100 ore)
Head of state	King Carl XVI Gustav (1973)
Head of government	Carl Bildt
Ruling party	Moderate Party leads a multi-party coalition
Main urban areas	Stockholm (capital, 1,641,669 in January 1991)
	Gothenburg (433,042)
	Malmö (233,887)
	Uppsala (167,508)
	Linköping (122,268)
	Örebro (120,944)
	Norrköping (120,522)
	Västerås (119,761)

Sweden's profitable industrial sector stems from the country's abundance of natural resources, especially forests, mineral deposits and hydro-electric power.

Forests cover almost half of the country's land area, and have encouraged the growth of large timber, wood pulp and paper industries. Its mineral resources include iron ore, lead, zinc, sulphur, uranium and aluminium. Its manufacturing industries are generally of high quality and specialised, and there is a growing chemical and pharmaceutical sector.

Because of the growth in industrial output, agriculture has declined in importance. A variety of cereals and vegetables are cultivated, and there is a large dairy sector, with pigs also being reared. Hydro-electric resources are particularly important as Sweden has no significant oil or gas deposits, and as its current nuclear power programme is to be discontinued by 2010 as a result of a referendum.

The main population centres are in the low midlands to the east (around Stockholm), and further south on the Kattegat coast, where there are a number of shipyards. Unlike the other Nordic countries, there are sizeable towns throughout the northern regions, as transport is easier.

Sweden faces a recurrent shortage of skilled labour, due mainly to low birth rates in previous decades, and this has periodically worsened the wage/price spiral to the point of necessitating devaluations of the national currency. In 1991 the country presented a formal application to join the European Community, in the course of which the krona was formally linked to the basket of currencies comprising the European Currency Unit.

Marketing regions

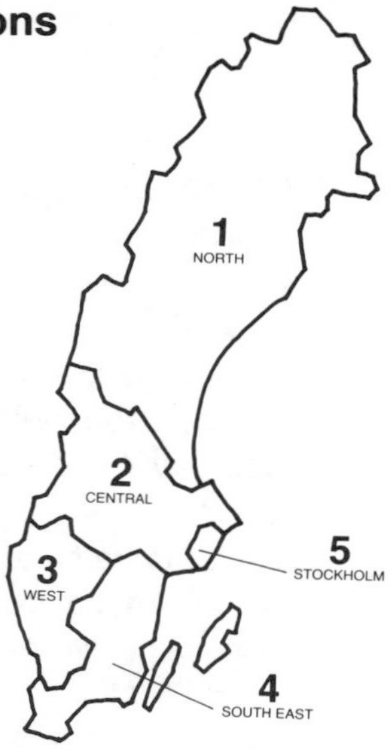

	Households ('000, 1985)	%
1	640	17.4
2	650	17.7
3	750	20.4
4	900	24.5
5	730	19.9
Total	3,670	100.0

Standard regions

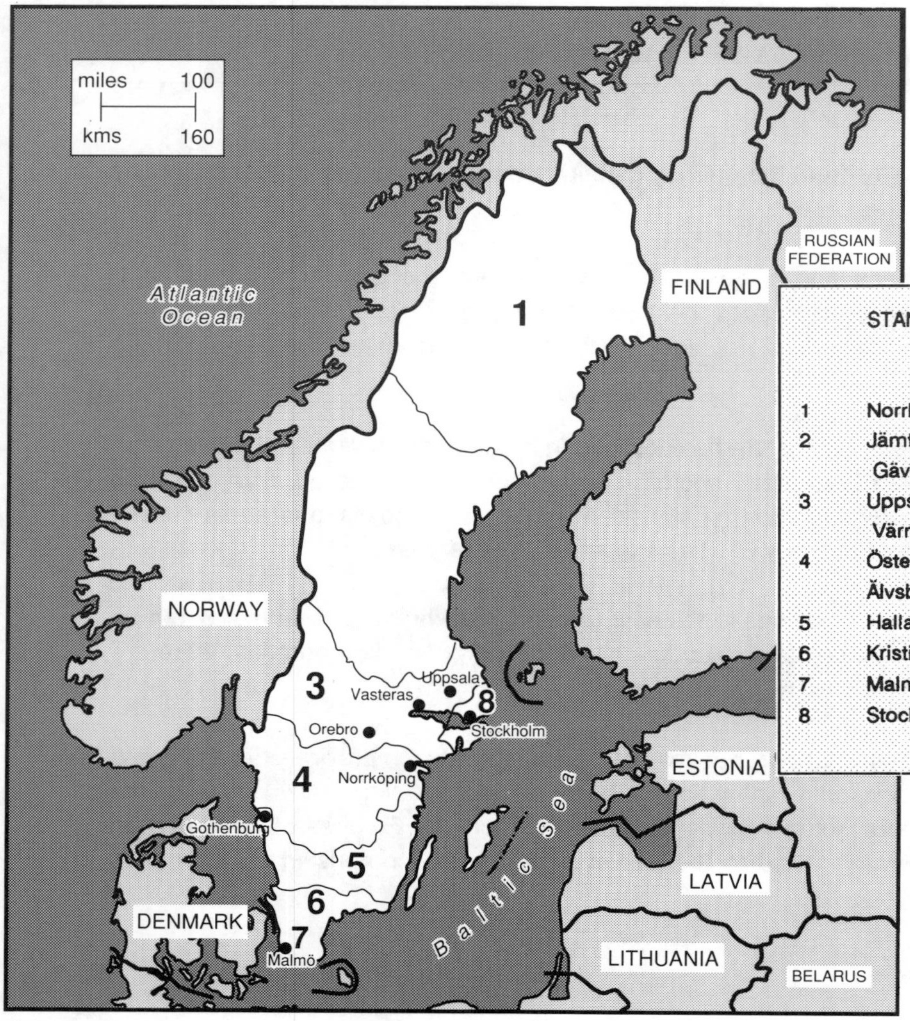

	STANDARD REGION	POPULATION (January 1991)
1	Norrbotten, Västerbotten	517,703
2	Jämtland, Västernorrland, Gävleborg, Kopparberg	975,242
3	Uppsala, Västmanland, Örebro, Värmland, Södermanland	1,338,581
4	Östergötland, Jönköping, Göteborg, Älvsborg, Skaraborg	2,169,467
5	Halland, Kalmar, Kronoborg, Gotland	730,817
6	Kristianstad, Blekinge	439,842
7	Malmöhus	779,309
8	Stockholm	1,641,669

Switzerland

Population	6,740,000 (1992)
Urban population	59%
Land area	41,293 sq km
Languages	German, French, Italian, Romansch
Religions	Roman Catholic (47.6%), Protestant (44.3%)
Currency	Swiss Franc (=100 centimes)
Head of state	René Felber (1992); Adolf Ogi (1993)
Main urban areas	Zurich (342,861 in 1990)
	Geneva (169,587)
	Basel (165,404)
	Berne (capital, 134,343)
	Lausanne (122,600)

Switzerland occupies a unique position within Europe: as a universally recognised neutral confederation of 26 cantons, and as a particularly important financial centre. Banking, insurance and other financial services are vital to the country's economy, and its advantageous tax rates have also attracted international businesses, particularly those associated with commodity trading.

The country itself is largely mountainous, and its heavily subsidised farming sector is contained in the valleys and the flatter country to the north. Despite the high altitude a wide variety of cereals and other crops are grown, and there are a large number of dairy herds. There is also a vigorous wine industry. Industry and population are concentrated in the north of the country, notably in the valley of the river Aare, a tributary of the Rhine which is used a means of transporting raw materials.

The country has few mineral reserves, but a plentiful supply of hydro-electrical power, and sustains a manufacturing industry on the basis of imported raw materials, exporting finished goods, particularly in the electrical and mechanical engineering, clocks and watches, pharmaceuticals, textiles and woodworking fields.

In mid-1992 the country voted to become a full member of the United Nations and the International Monetary Fund; it was also expected to present an application for membership of the European Community before long.

Marketing regions

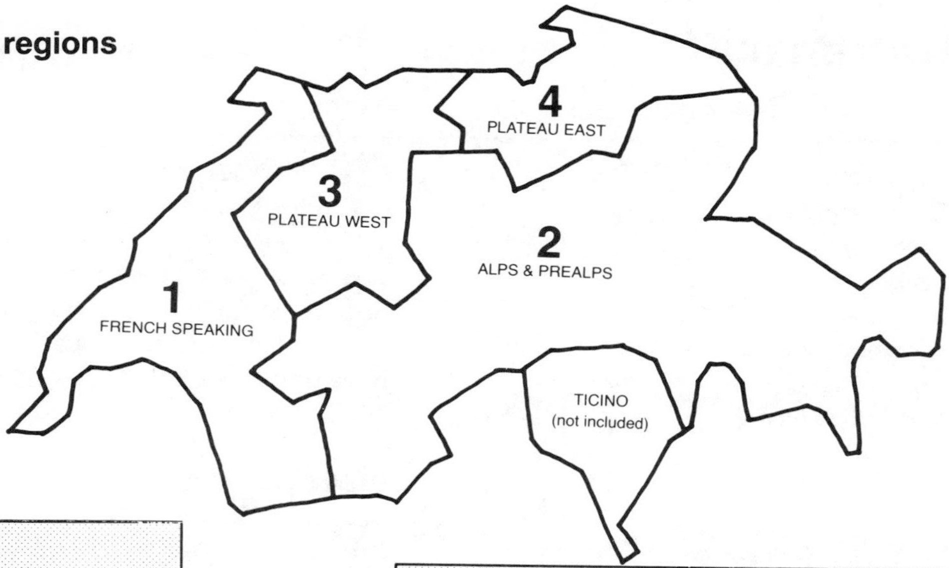

	Households ('000)	%
1	496	18
2	413	15
3	1,295	47
4	551	20
Total	2,755	100

	STANDARD REGION	POPULATION (January 1990)
1	West	2,578,600
2	North	2,555,500
3	Central	245,200
4	South West	254,700
5	East	692,500
6	South East	180,000
7	South	289,800

Standard regions

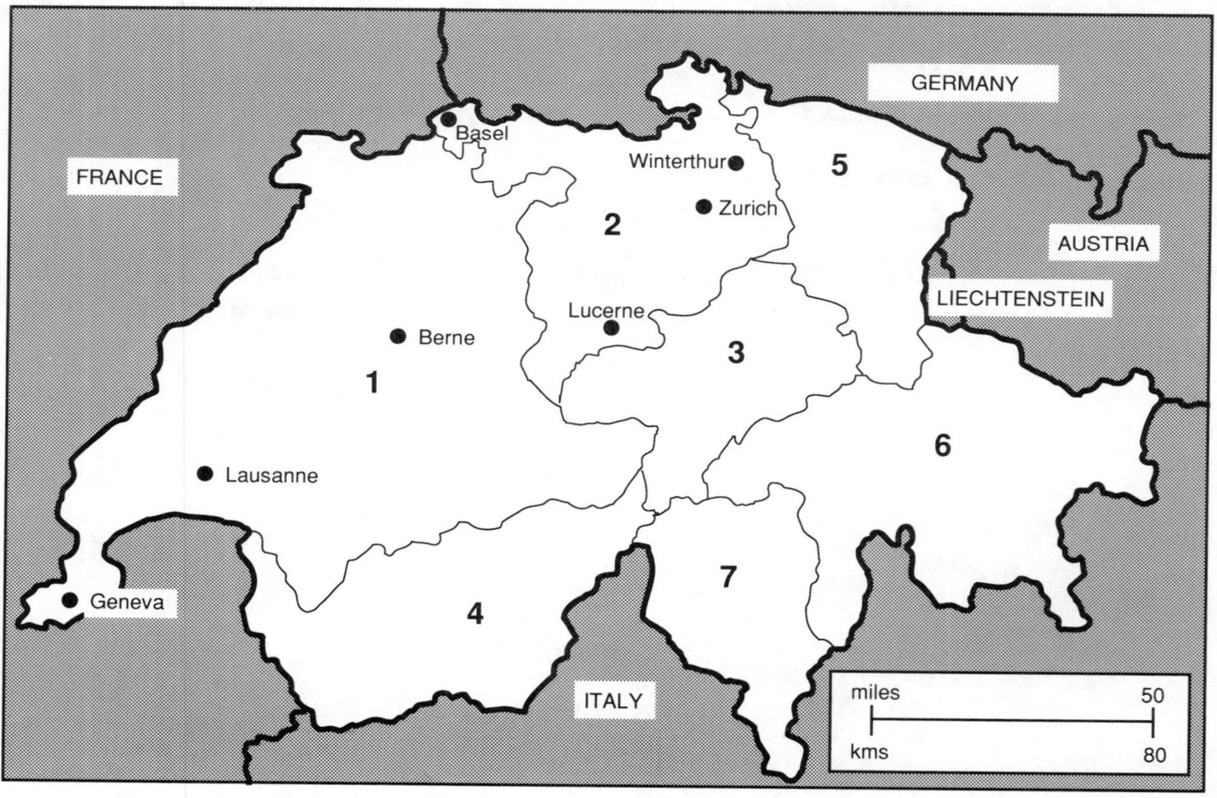

Albania

Population	3,246,000 (1992)
Urban population	36%
Land area	28,748 sq km
Language	Albanian (dialects: Gheg, Tosk)
Currency	Lek (= 100 Quindarkas)
Head of state	President Sali Berisha (1992)
Head of government	Aleksandr Meksi
Ruling party	Democratic Party heads a coalition with Republican Party and Social Democratic Party
Main urban areas	Tirana (capital, 363,100 in 1988)
	Durres (242,500)
	Elbassan (238,600)
	Shkodër (233,000)
	Korcë (213,200)
	Vlorë (174,000)

The Republic of Albania acquired its present title in April 1991, following the collapse of the communist regime which had run the country as the People's Socialist republic of Albania since 1946. A succession of short-lived interim governments followed the dissolution of the former Albanian Party of Labour, but few lasted more than a few months at a time until April 1992, when general elections to the People's Assembly were held.

Until 1991 the country pursued a dogged policy of self-sufficiency, which led it to reject all offers of external aid, including development capital. As a result, the transition to democracy and free enterprise has found the country disastrously under-equipped to face the challenges of the open market.

Unfortunately, Albania's transition to a market economy also coincided with the disastrous political deterioration in neighbouring Yugoslavia, which cut short the country's attempts at trade with Belgrade. Albania has an outstanding territorial dispute with Serbia, the dominant member of the former Yugoslavia, and in mid-1992 the prospect of armed conflict could not be ruled out.

Much of the country's land area is mountainous, with arable land confined to coastal areas and the Koritza Basin. Land reclamation projects have increased the area under cultivation, the main crops being maize, wheat and sugar beet. Sheep and goats are the natural livestock for such an environment, and chickens are also kept in large quantities. Around 50% of the country is forested, and forest products are an important factor in the economy. Other natural resources include chromite or chromium ore (of which Albania has the world's fourth largest resources) and a small amount of petroleum.

At present the country's industry, like its agriculture, is wholly nationalised, but privatisation decrees were approved in April 1991 and these were expected to pass into effect in the next few years. The main products are foodstuffs, textiles, oil products and cement, but more attention is being paid to building up engineering industries.

The 1989 census showed that 3,117,601 (98%) of the 3,181,056 people recorded were ethnic Albanians, 58,758 (1.8%) were Greeks and 4,697 (0.1%) were Macedonians. The census was thought to have been about 40,000 short of the actual total.

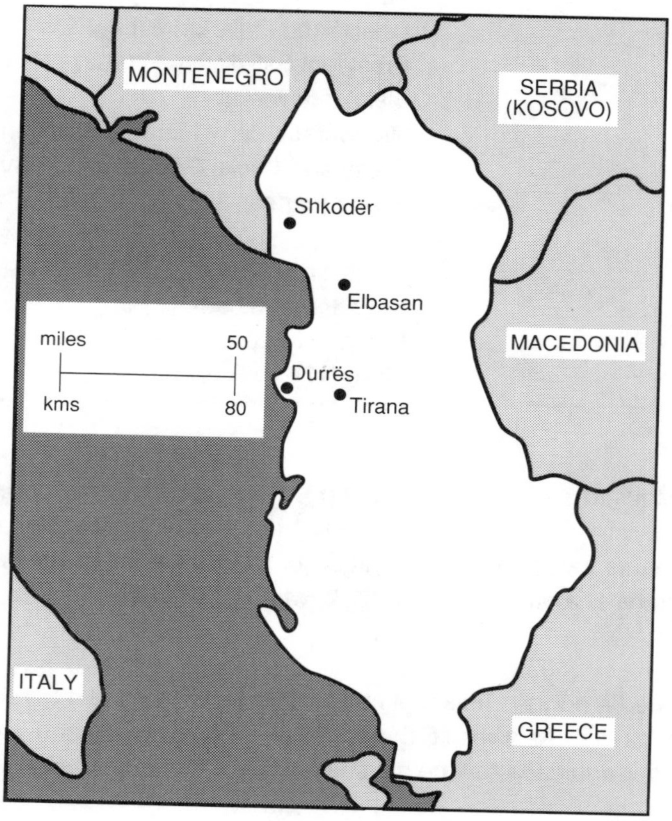

Bulgaria

Population	9,006,000 (1992)
Urban population	68%
Land area	110,994 sq km
Language	Bulgarian
Religion	Bulgarian Orthodox
Currency	Lev (= 100 Stotinki)
Head of state	President Zhelyu Zhelev (August 1990)
Head of government	Filip Dimitrov
Ruling party	Socialist Party (formerly the Bulgarian Communist Party) leads a coalition with the Union of Democratic Forces
Main urban areas:	Sofia (capital, 1,141,142 in January 1991)
	Plovdiv (379,088)
	Varna (314,913)
	Burgas (204,915)
	Ruse (192,365)
	Stara Zagora (164,553)
	Pleven (138,323)
	Dobrich (formerly Tolbukhin) (115,786)

Bulgaria is a largely mountainous country, with most of the centres of population and industry concentrated in the valleys of the Danube (which forms the border with Romania to the north) and the river Maritsa to the south, and on the Black Sea coast in the east. The country has worked hard to establish an industrial base, but it is still significantly dependent on the agricultural sector; it is also more strongly dependent on trade with the former Soviet Union than its Eastern European partners, and the transition to hard-currency trading with that country from 1990 has presented severe difficulties. Agricultural products still provide a major part of the country's exports. The main crops are wheat, maize, barley and tomatoes, and the wine industry is gaining in importance as an export industry. Although there is some growth in foreign investment from the West, the country is hard pressed to keep abreast of its less heavily indebted competitors when it comes to attracting capital.

The removal of the communist head of state Todor Zhivkov in October 1989 marked one of the most decisive stages in the spread of *perestroika* in Eastern Europe, Bulgaria having been among the strongest adherents of old-style Soviet policy. The multi-party elections of mid-1990 showed, however, that opposition groups had made little impression: the communists, now renamed as the Socialist Party, won an easy victory. Since then the country has re-elected its socialist President, Zhelyu Zhelev, and has embarked upon an ambitious privatisation programme.

MAIN URBAN AREA	POPULATION (1991)
Sofia (capital)	1,127,024
Plovdiv	364,162
Varna	306,300
Burgas	200,464
Ruse	190,720
Stara Zagora	158,151
Pleven	136,287
Dobrich (formerly Tolbukhin)	112,582

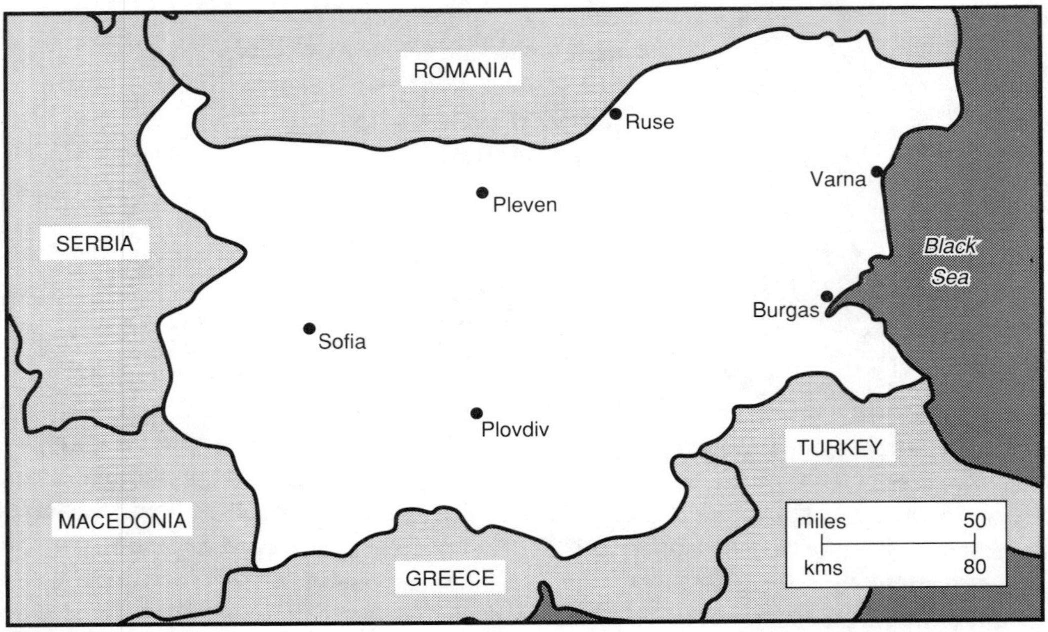

Czech and Slovak Republics (*Former* Czechoslovakia)

Population	15,708,000 (1992)
Urban population	78%
Land area	127,900 sq km
Languages	Czech, Slovak
Religions	Catholic (70%), Protestant (15%)
Currency	Koruna (= 100 Heller)
Head of state	Vaclav Havel (1990)
Head of government	Marian Calfa
Ruling party	Civic Forum/Public Against Violence lead a coalition with Christian Democratic Movement
Main urban areas (early 1991):	Prague (capital, 1,215,076)
	Bratislava (444,482)
	Brno (392,614)
	Ostrava (331,504)
	Kosice (238,343)
	Plzen (224,815)

The Czech and Slovak republics were due to become independent of each other in January 1993, some 74 years after their original amalgamation (in 1918) into the state of Czechoslovakia. The Czech republic, lying to the west, includes some 65% of the population of the combined state and is by far the more industrialised of the two republics: engineering and heavy industries are particular strengths, although recently the motor manufacturing industry has been gaining in prominence. There is also a significant small business and crafts sector.

With its large expanses of fertile arable land, the Slovak republic is notable for the production of potatoes, wheat and barley, and the extensive area under forest produces abundant quantities of wood and wood products. Although there is little in the way of metallic ores, the two republics share large resources of coal and lignite, the basis for their important ferrous metal industries. There are also significant deposits of silver and manganese ores.

Until 1990 the former Czechoslovakian state had no private enterprises at all, having progressively eliminated them in the 1960s and 1970s. However, the Government had no difficulty in attracting investment capital from the West with which to promote an ambitious privatisation scheme; a second round of privatisations took place in May 1992, aimed this time at a wide share ownership among the public.

Although plans were still being drawn up in the autumn of 1992, the Czech and Slovak republics intended to retain a customs union and to share a common currency after their independence.

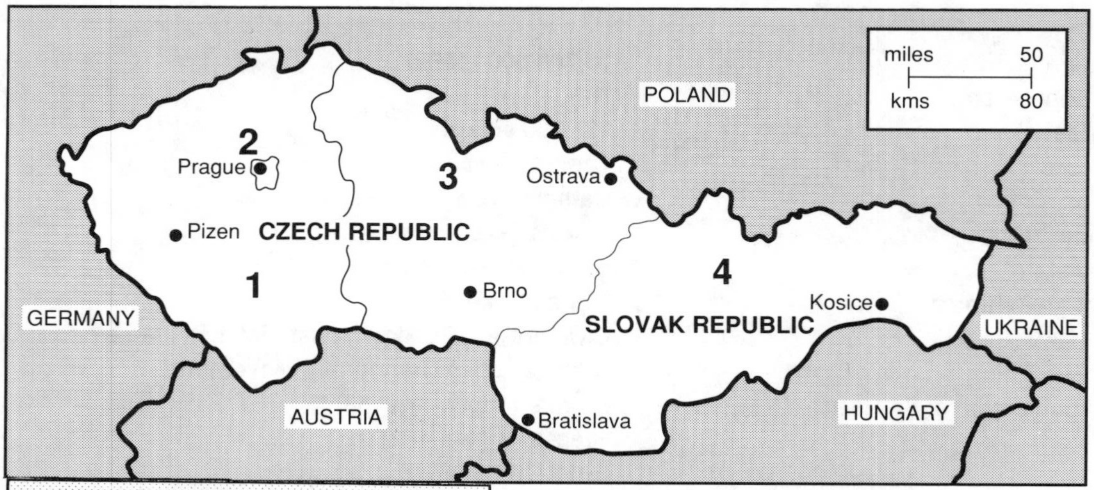

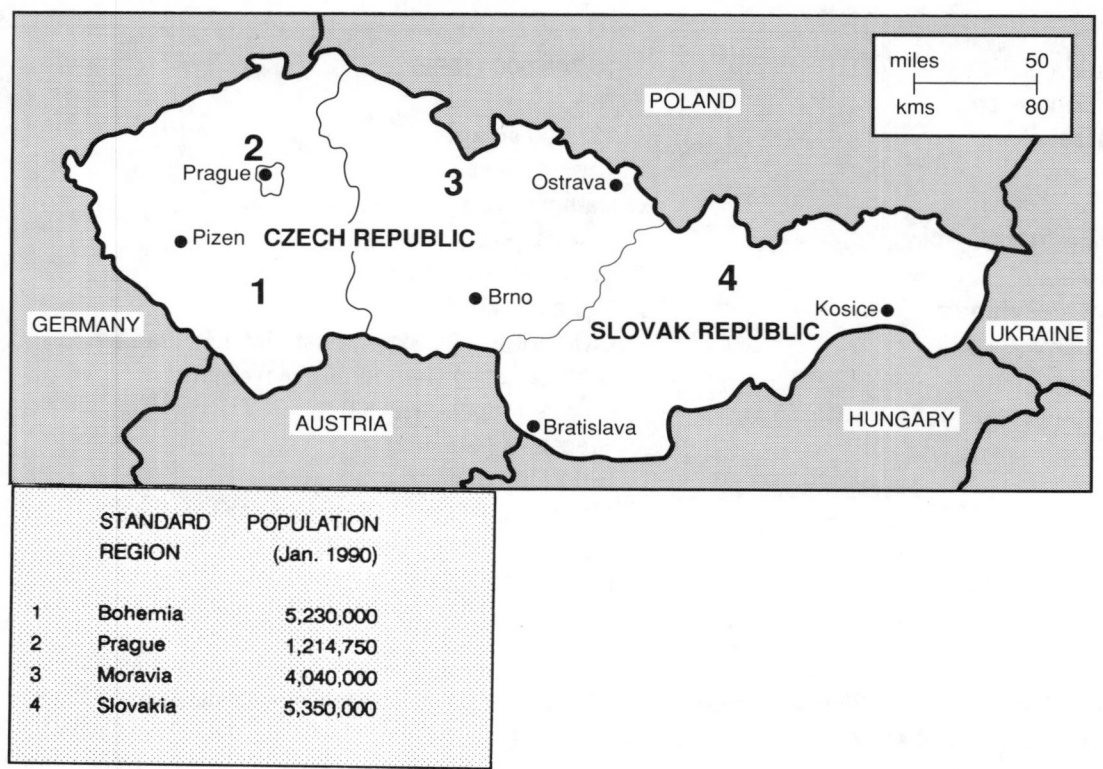

	STANDARD REGION	POPULATION (Jan. 1990)
1	Bohemia	5,230,000
2	Prague	1,214,750
3	Moravia	4,040,000
4	Slovakia	5,350,000

Hungary

Population	10,580,000 (1992)
Urban population	61%
Land area	93,033 sq km
Language	Magyar
Religions	Catholic (65%), Calvinist (30%)
Currency	Forint (= 100 filler)
Head of state	President Arpad Goncz (August 1990)
Head of government	Jozsef Antall (1990)
Ruling party	Democratic Forum heads a coalition with Smallholders' Party and Christian Democrats
Main urban areas	Budapest (capital, 2,018,033 in 1991)
	Debrecen (213,927)
	Miskolc (194,033)
	Szeged (176,135)
	Pécs (170,023)

The opening of Hungary's border with Austria in May 1989 marked the first major practical stage in the liberalisation of Eastern European regimes. The massive outflow of East Germans, Czechoslovakians and Hungarians which followed forced the pace of political change elsewhere in the region - most notably in East Germany, where the Berlin Wall was breached in November in an effort to attract the refugees back to their homeland.

Hungary has long maintained a relatively liberal economy, allowing private enterprise to operate alongside its state-run activities; the country was, then, ideally equipped to attract foreign investment capital from the start, and it has been quick to introduce Western-style banking and stockbroking activities. Moreover, liberal cultural and political traditions paved the way for an easy return to multi-party democracy. The country has yet to cope with its hard-currency debts, however, which have hindered the expansion in national or personal income, and industry is expected to under-perform for some years yet.

Hungary has nevertheless made major strides in its industrial development, with engineering to the fore. Although well equipped with fuel reserves, in the form of brown coal and natural gas, there is little in the way of metallic deposits, however, and much of the country's raw material requirements are met from imports, largely from the USSR, Czechoslovakia and Germany. The main agricultural crops are wheat and maize, and the climate also supports a vigorous wine industry. Pigs and sheep dominate the livestock sector.

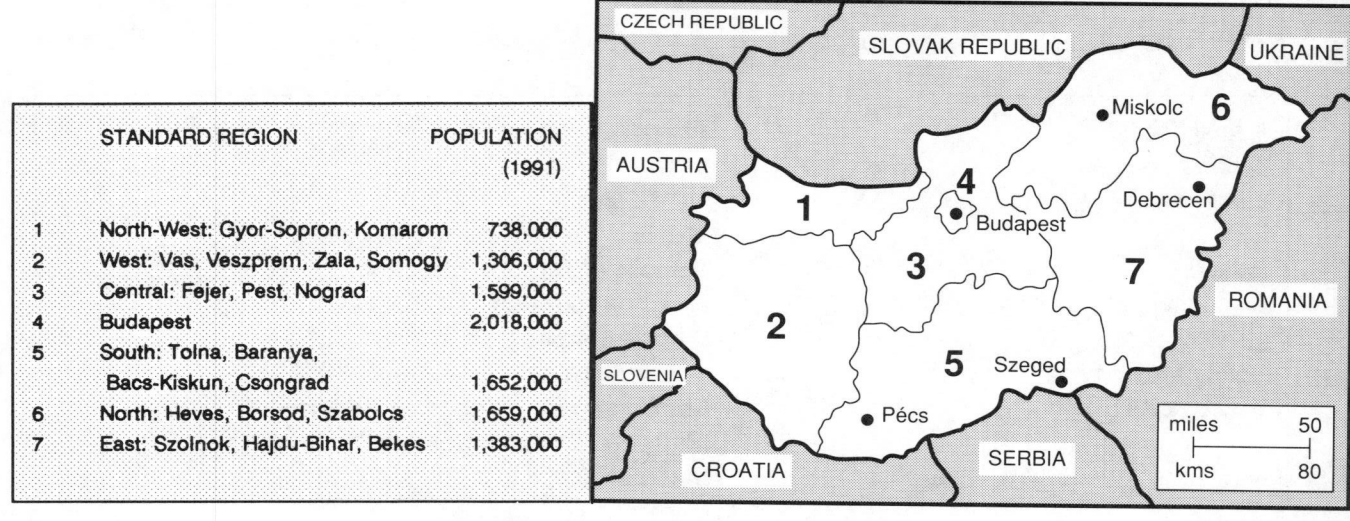

	STANDARD REGION	POPULATION (1991)
1	North-West: Gyor-Sopron, Komarom	738,000
2	West: Vas, Veszprem, Zala, Somogy	1,306,000
3	Central: Fejer, Pest, Nograd	1,599,000
4	Budapest	2,018,000
5	South: Tolna, Baranya, Bacs-Kiskun, Csongrad	1,652,000
6	North: Heves, Borsod, Szabolcs	1,659,000
7	East: Szolnok, Hajdu-Bihar, Bekes	1,383,000

Poland

Population	38,334,000 (1992)
Urban population	62%
Land area	312,683 sq km
Language	Polish
Currency	Zloty (= 100 groszy)
Head of state	President Lech Walesa (December 1990)
Head of government	Hanna Suchocka (July 1992)
Ruling party	Coalition led by Democratic Union
Main urban areas	Warsaw (capital, 1,655,100 in 1990)
	Lodz (851,700)
	Krakow (748,400)
	Wroclaw (642,300)
	Poznan (588,700)
	Gdansk (464,600)
	Szczecin (412,100)
	Bydgoszcz (380,400)
	Katowice (367,000)
	Lublin (349,600)

Poland, one of the most heavily industrialised countries of Eastern Europe, supports a large number of heavy industries, including steelworks, shipbuilding, cement works and chemicals. The nation's economy is based on its plentiful supplies of coal, and on iron ore deposits.

Poland was among the major forerunners of *perestroika* in Eastern Europe, installing non-communist politicians in high offices as long ago as the mid-1980s. By the end of 1989 Poland had already liberalised practically all price mechanisms and had removed state subsidies; by 1992 an ambitious programme of privatisation was under way, but the high unemployment necessitated by the drive toward efficiency was causing severe political tensions, and the government appeared to be entering a period of instability. The resignation of the Finance Minister, Andrzej Olechowski, prompted President Lech Walesa to demand the creation of a French-style executive presidency which would give him wide personal powers.

Although Poland has vast agricultural areas the land is not particularly fertile, and food products often have to be imported. The main crops are beets, rye, wheat and barley, with livestock of all kinds. Coal mining is of major importance to the export economy.

	STANDARD REGION	POPULATION (January 1990)
1	Szczecin, Koszalin, Slupsk, Pila, Zielona Gora, Gorzow	3,515,500
2	Gdansk, Elbiag, Torun, Bydgoszcz, Wloclawek, Plock, Konin	5,571,500
3	Olsztyn, Suwalki, Ciechanow, Ostroleka, Lomza, Bialystok, Siedlce, Biala Podlaska	4,026,500
4	Warsaw	2,419,100
5	Jelenia Gora, Legnica, Leszno, Poznan, Walbrzych, Wroclaw, Kalisz, Opole	6,331,800
6	Sieradz, Lodz, Skiernewice, Piotrkow, Radom, Lublin, Chelm	4,618,800
7	Kielce, Tarnobrzeg, Zamosc, Tarnow, Rzeszow, Przemysl, Nowy Sacz, Krosno	5,117,000
8	Czestochowa, Katowice, Krakow, Bielsko-Biala	6,367,500

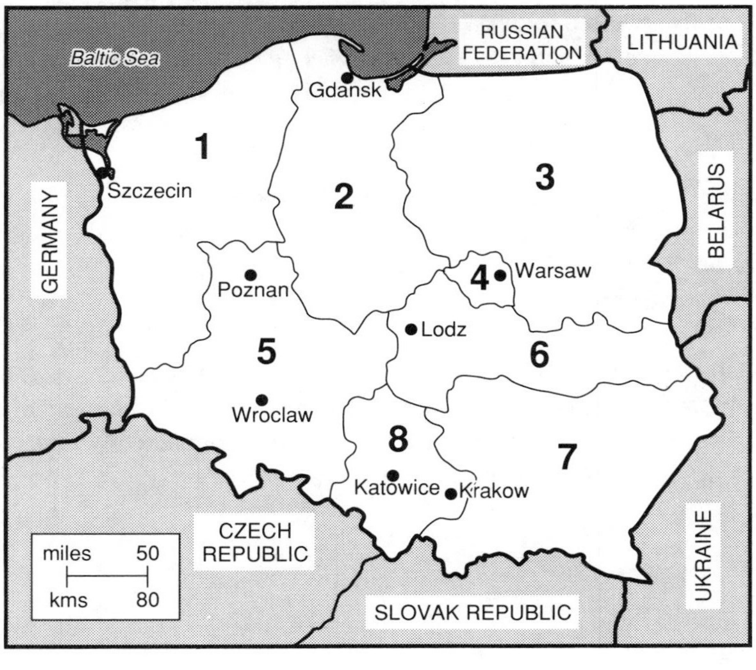

Romania

Population	23,446,000 (1992)
Urban population	53%
Land area	237,500 sq km
Language	Romanian
Religions	Romanian Orthodox, Roman Catholic
Currency	Leu (= 100 Bani)
Head of state	Ion Iliescu (June 1990)
Head of government	Theodor Stolojan
Ruling party	National Salvation Front
Main urban areas	Bucharest (capital, 1,989,823 in 1986)
	Brasov (351,493)
	Constanta (327,676)
	Timisoara (325,272)
	Iasi (313,060)
	Cluj-Napoca (310,017)
	Galati (295,372)

Romania was the last Eastern European member of the former CMEA group to initiate a policy of political change, forcibly removing the Communist president Nicolae Ceausescu in December 1989 and installing in his place an ad hoc alliance of opposition groups. Elections were held in February 1992, resulting in the formation of a governing coalition facing a 14-party coalition of opposition parties. Yet in mid-1992 there was no immediate sign that the government's new policies had slowed the severe shrinkage of the economy to any appreciable extent.

Romania's agricultural areas are among the most fertile in Eastern Europe, and yet productivity has been extremely poor in recent years, with a serious lack of investment undermining the sector. Wallachia (the valley of the Danube) in the south, Moldavia (Siret valley) in the north, and the Transylvanian lowlands to the west support a variety of cereal and beet crops, as well as cattle and sheep rearing, and flax and hemp. The Carpathian and Transylvanian mountains sustain an important forestry sector, and there are vineyards and orchards in the valleys.

Coal, oil, natural gas, iron ore, bauxite and other metal ores are found in quantities, and a number of heavy industries have been developed. A drive by the Ceausescu government to eliminate the country's foreign debts resulted, however, in serious under-investment while simultaneously depriving the population of Romania's food products; major food shortages have resulted.

The deposed Ceausescu government's plans to demolish over 7,000 villages, mainly occupied by ethnic Hungarians, have now been dropped; hostility toward the country's Hungarians continues, however. Meanwhile, there have been isolated calls in the neighbouring republic of Moldova (the former Moldavian Soviet republic) for a a political reunification with Romania.

All Romanian statistics are open to qualification, having been deliberately tampered with since the mid-1980s. While data presented in this volume are given in good faith, this fact should always be borne in mind.

	STANDARD REGION	POPULATION (1987)
1	Satu Mare, Maramures, Bistrita-Nasoud	1,280,763
2	Mures, Sibiu, Brasov	1,819,411
3	Selaj, Cluj, Bihor, Alba, Arad, Timis, Caras-Severin, Hunadoara	3,791,650
4	Mehedint, Gorj, Vilcea, Argesw	1,806,904
5	Dolj, Olt, Teleorman	1,807,917
6	Botosani, Suceava, Neamt, Iasi	2,509,445
7	Harghita, Covasna, Bacau, Vaslui	1,767,899
8	Buzau, Vrancea, Galati, Braila, Ialomita	2,253,806
9	Tulcea, Constanta	995,867
10	Bucharest	2,298,256
11	Prahova, Dimbovita, Giurgiu, Calarasi	2,104,862

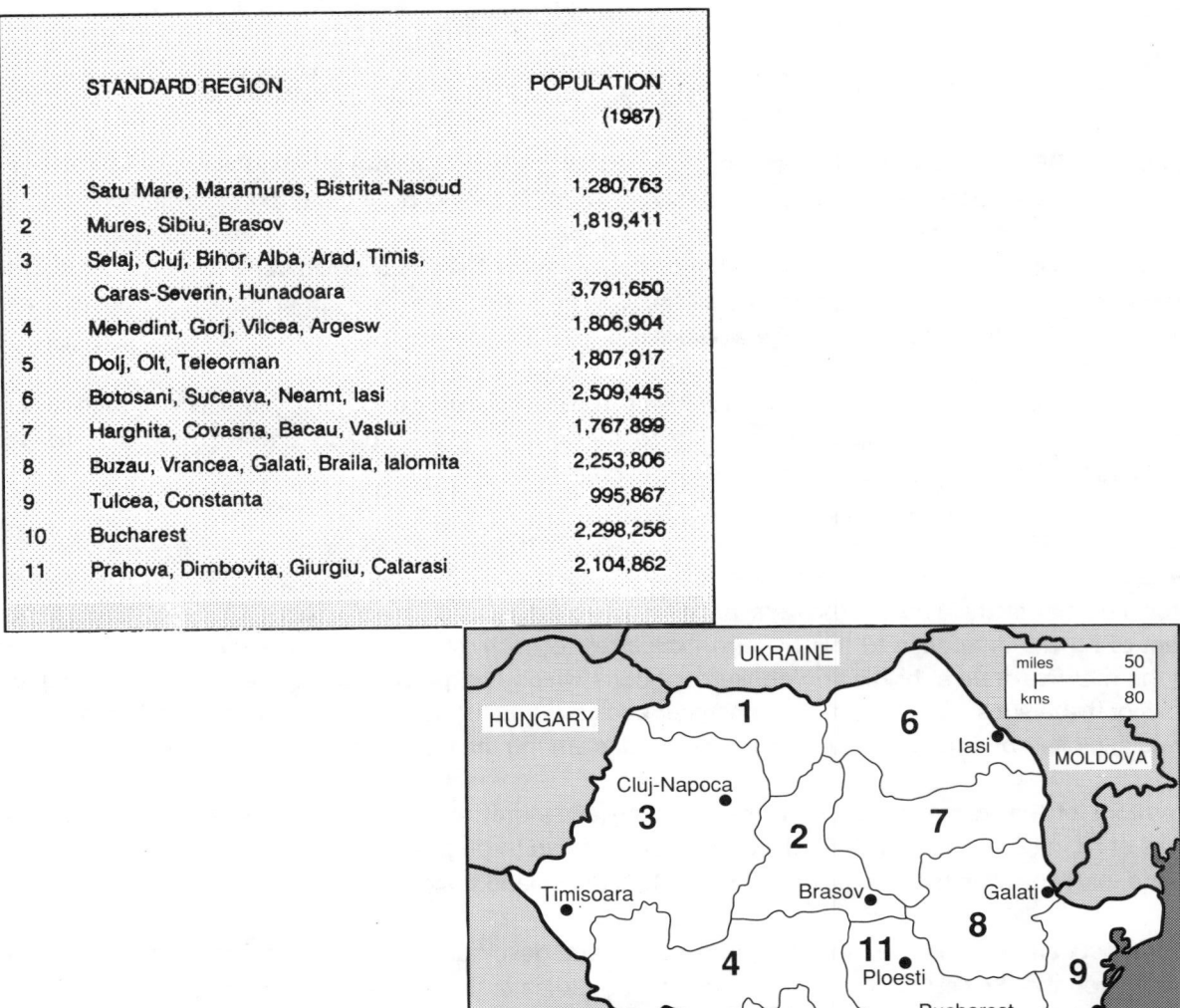

The former Union of Soviet Socialist Republics

Population	285,100,000 (1992)
Urban population	67%
Land area	22,402,200 sq km
Language	Russian (numerous dialects and regional languages)
Currency	Rouble (= 100 kopeks)

The former USSR was officially dissolved on 31 December 1991, and all the institutions of the Soviet state, including the Army and the Presidency, were abolished, to be replaced by the regional institutions formed by the emergent states which formed the old grouping. By mid-1992 the majority of these states had yet to find their feet: all except Georgia and the Baltic states Latvia, Estonia and Lithuania were committed to membership of a new organisation known as the Confederation of Independent States, but it remained uncertain as to how long the new alliance would last.

Because of the historical impossibility of unravelling regional statistics from past years, it was found more appropriate for this book to continue referring to the former USSR, and to present new data for the emergent republics alongside, as and when they become available.

The late years of the Soviet communist leadership were marred by inefficiency, favouritism and corruption, and a lack of industrial willpower engendered by the absence of a profit principle. Gorbachev's market-oriented reforms in the late 1980s were an attempt to address these problems, by re-introducing the concept of private enterprise to this hitherto exclusively collectivist state, and by simultaneously winding down the massive state subsidies on consumer goods which had propped up the economy for decades. The loss of these subsidies prompted a consumer backlash against the necessary price increases, which in turn was exploited by separatist and nationalist factions among the republics.

The territory of the former USSR contains a wealth of natural resources, including the world's largest reserves of oil, natural gas and coal, which are widely spread throughout the county. All kinds of metal ores are found, particularly in the Ural mountains, and 40% of the land is forested.

Overall agricultural efficiency is still poor, and agricultural development has if anything suffered since the dissolution of the Soviet state, which served to co-ordinate the gathering and distribution of crops. Industrial enterprises, struggling to come to terms with their new "co-operative" (ie private) status, have faced even worse problems as the legacy of overcapacity and overmanning has been addressed.

The growing independence of the various republics has been reflected since 1991 by the introduction of their own currencies in many cases, to replace the Soviet rouble. Nearly all nowadays conduct their foreign trade in convertible currencies such as German marks or US dollars; but the admission of Russia to the International Monetary Fund may add new strength to the rouble, which has been badly affected by the inflation which followed price deregulation in the early 1990s.

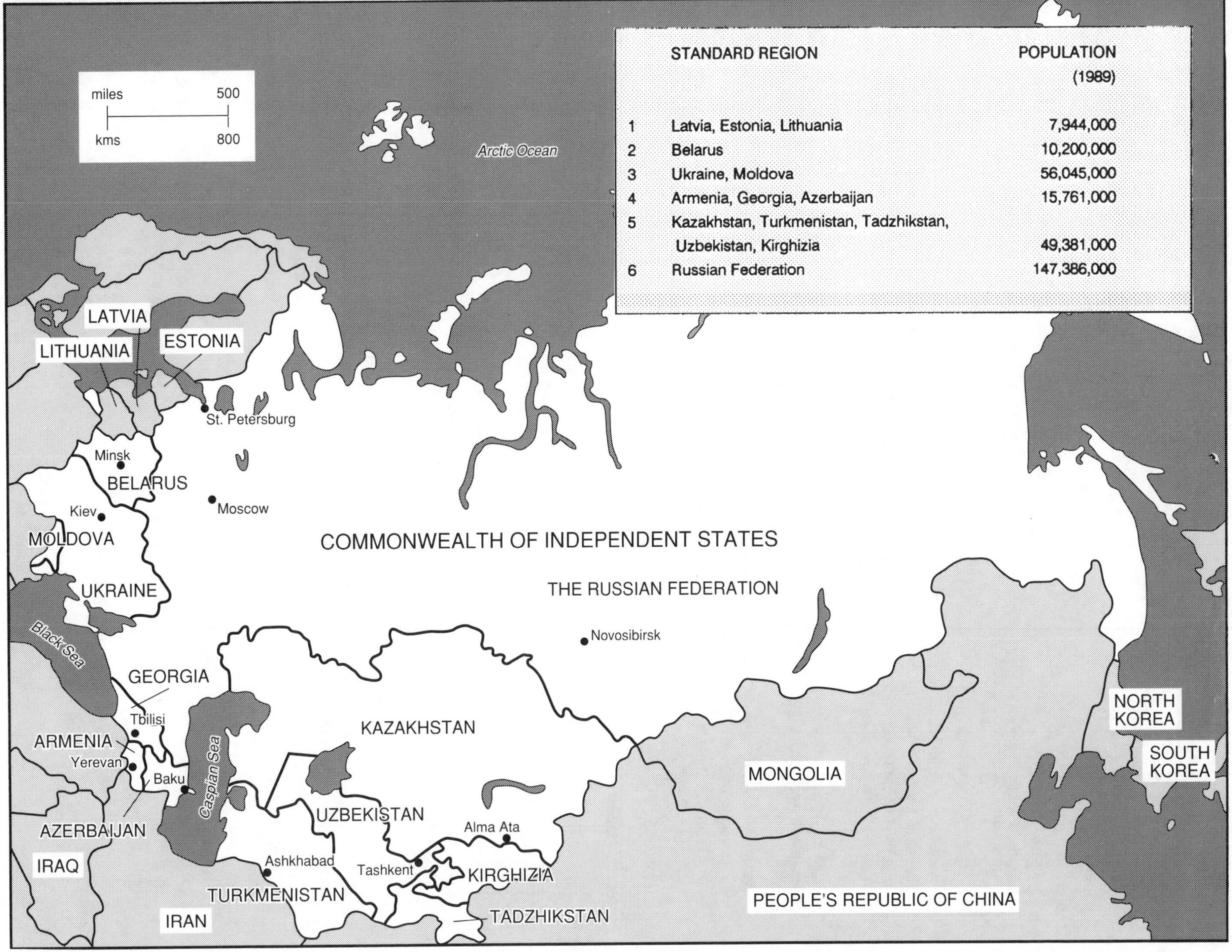

	STANDARD REGION	POPULATION (1989)
1	Latvia, Estonia, Lithuania	7,944,000
2	Belarus	10,200,000
3	Ukraine, Moldova	56,045,000
4	Armenia, Georgia, Azerbaijan	15,761,000
5	Kazakhstan, Turkmenistan, Tadzhikstan, Uzbekistan, Kirghizia	49,381,000
6	Russian Federation	147,386,000

Armenia

Population	3,580,000 (1991)
Population density	110 per sq km
Land area	29,759 sq km
Capital	Yerevan (1,300,000 in 1991)
Net material product per head (1988)	1,757 roubles
President	Levon Ter-Petrosyan
Prime Minister	Gagik Arutunyan

Armenia is a landlocked republic to the east of the Turkish border with its southern tip on the northern border of Iran. Armenia ratified its independence after a referendum on 21 September 1991. It covers an area of almost 30,000 square kilometres and is the smallest of the new republics by area. The main city is Yerevan, in the mountains close to the Turkish border.

Main industrial activities centre on mineral extraction, hydro-electricity, machine tools, rubber, textiles and fertilisers. Agriculture is dominated by cotton, fruit, vines and olives.

As the republic tries to rebuild its economy, it suffers from political isolation; Armenia has often expressed its exasperation with Moscow for the latter's perceived hostility to Armenia's claim with neighbouring Azerbaijan for the control of Nagorno-Karabakh. Its relations are no better with Turkey, which it borders in the south; Turkey has periodically threatened to close the border completely.

Azerbaijan

Population	7,145,600 (1990)
Population density	82 per sq km
Land area	87,000 sq km
Capital	Baku (1,757,000 in 1990)
President	Ayaz Mutalibov
Prime Minister	Feirus Mustafavayev

Azerbaijan, with a population of around 7,130,000, is a predominantly Muslim state located close to the Turkish border in the south of the former USSR. Most inhabitants speak a Turkish or Iranian dialect, reflecting their close links with both countries. Since independence, the country's politics have been dominated by a prolonged and often violent dispute with Armenia as to the control of the Armenian enclave in Nagorno-Karabakh.

Azerbaijan's economy is heavily dominated by the mining sector, with oil, natural gas and numerous metal ores in abundance. However, the whole industrial structure is in poor shape and is badly in need of modernisation. Agriculture is sparse and is subject to periodic droughts, although citrus fruits, cotton and grain are produced.

Belarus

Population	10,259,000 (1990)
Population density	49 per sq km
Land area	207,546 sq km
Capital	Minsk (1,613,000)
Net material product per head (1988)	2,578 roubles
President	Nikolai Demental
Prime Minister	V.F. Kebich

Belarus, formerly known as Byelorussia, occupies 207,546 square kilometres to the east of Poland. Its population is sparse, with Minsk (population 1,613,000) by far the largest settlement. The republic has been independent since 25 August 1991.

The republic's major industries are engineering, machine tools, agricultural equipment, chemicals, motor vehicles and some consumer durables such as watches, televisions and radios. Forestry and agriculture, notably potatoes, grain, peat and cattle, are also important.

Virtually all (90%) of the republic's raw materials are imported from Russia, a fact which underlines the new state's dependence on the future goodwill of its larger neighbour.

Estonia

Population	1,573,000 (1989)
Population density	35 per sq km
Land area	45,099 sq km
Capital	Tallinn (503,000 in 1989)
Net material product per head (1988)	2,590 roubles
President	Arnold Ruutel
Prime Minister	Tiit Vahi

Estonia lies to the south of Gulf of Finland in an area of 45,099 square kilometres, which also includes a number of islands on its west coast. Estonia has now achieved full recognition as a member of the United Nations in its own right.

There are few major industrial sectors, but established activities include electronics, motors, footwear and paper. Fishing and fish-processing are also important along with agricultural activities. There are also a number of sawmills in the area.

Still dependent on Russia and the Ukraine for energy, apart from some local reserves of coal shale, Estonia's economic development is likely to depend on how well it can develop links with Finland and the rest of Scandinavia, and also capitalise on its links with St Petersburg in neighbouring Russia.

Georgia

Population	5,449,000 (1989)
Population density	78 per sq km
Land area	69,670 sq km
Capital	Tbilisi (1,264,000 in 1989)
Net material product per head (1988)	1,891 roubles
Prime Minister (Chair of State Council)	Eduard Shevardnadze

Situated between Armenia and the Russian Federation, with its southern border adjoining Turkey and its western edge overlooking the Black Sea, Georgia occupies an area of 69,670 square kilometres.

The republic declared its independence in April 1991, yet the population of almost 5.5 million considered themselves as a separate country long before this. Unfortunately the republic's own independence process has been marred by ethnic disputes and by bitter infighting, which showed few signs of abating in mid-1992.

Georgia's economy is based around heavy industry and agriculture, notably wine production, tea, fruit, grain and vegetables. Manganese and coal mining, metallurgy, motor vehicles, food-processing and hydro-electric power are the main industrial sectors.

Kazakhstan

Population	16,690,300 (1990)
Population density	6 per sq km
Land area	2,717,300 sq km
Capital	Alma Ata (1,151,300 in 1990)
President	Nursultan Nazarbayev
Prime Minister	U.K. Karamanov

Kazakhstan, one of the largest of the former Soviet republics, is located in the central southern belt which was designated in the 1950s for the production of grain. Its farm production is still regarded as essential to the welfare of Russia, a point which has given it added bargaining power in the aftermath of independence.

In fact Kazakhstan is also well supplied with other activities. Major mineral deposits, including coal, oil and iron ore, are present in quantity, and the republic is particularly important as a producer of industrial goods.

Kirghizia

Population	4,372,000 (1990)
Population density	22 per sq km
Land area	198,500 sq km
Capital	Bishkek (626,900 in 1990)
President	Askar Akayev
Prime Minister	Nasirdin Isanov

Kirghizia, a vast mountainous terrain in the central southern area of the country, is among the poorest regions of the former USSR, but it is widely tipped for economic growth in the 1990s, thanks to the projected exploitation of its oil and gas reserves with foreign assistance. Until now the country's economy has been almost exclusively dominated by agriculture: livestock products, wool, grain and potatoes are produced largely without the aid of irrigation.

Russian expatriates represent rather more than a quarter of the local population and exert most of the political influence together with the native Kirghiz people - a factor which has caused deep resentment among the ethnic Uzbeks who comprise some 12% of the total, but who feel themselves to be disenfranchised. Severe riots have broken out on occasion since the late 1980s, with over 200 killed in one incident.

Latvia

Population	2,681,000 (1989)
Population density	42 per sq km
Land area	63,700 sq km
Capital	Riga (917,000 in 1989)
Net material product per head (1988)	2,630 roubles
President	Anatolis Gorbunovs
Prime Minister	Ivars Godmanis

Latvia is located on the eastern coast of the Baltic Sea, and covers 63,700 square kilometres. One third of the population are ethnic Russians, a fact which has not deterred the population from significant anti-Russian gestures in recent years: Latvia does almost as much trade with Finland as with Russia itself. The republic became a full member of the United Nations in 1991.

Industry is concentrated on electrical equipment and telecommunications, with some paper and woollen goods; forestry, fishing and agriculture are also important. Latvia's history as a trading nation before it was annexed by the Soviet Union in 1940 suggests that it can survive as an independent republic although its sizeable Russian minority might prove a problem in the future.

Lithuania

Population	3,690,000 (1989)
Population density	57 per sq km
Land area	65,190 sq km
Capital	Vilnius (582,000 in 1989)
Net material product per head (1988)	2,427 roubles
President	Vytautas Landsbergis
Prime Minister	Gediminas Vagnorius (acting)

Lithuania, the southernmost of the three Baltic republics, occupies 65,190 square kilometres and is the largest of the three Baltic regions. Its population of 3.7 million is unusually mixed, with 80% comprising Lithuanians, 8.6% Russians and 7.7% Poles. The republic declared independence in March 1990 and was recognised by the USA as independent in September 1991. It is a full member of the United Nations.

Lithuania has strong engineering and shipbuilding sectors, and it is also involved in the production of electrical and electronic goods and car components. Forests cover 1.5 million hectares and agriculture is also a major employer. To the west is Kaliningrad, a large naval base which is now part of Russia. This may be a problem area in the future as the base is cut off from Russia by Lithuania.

Moldova

Population	4,341,000 (1989)
Population density	129 per sq km
Land area	33,669 sq km
Capital	Kishinev (720,000 in 1989)
Net material product per head (1988)	1,789 roubles
President	Mircea Snigur
Prime Minister	Valeriu Muravsky

Sandwiched between the Ukraine in the east and Romania to the west, Moldova covers 33,669 square kilometres. The republic declared its independence from the Soviet system in August 1991, changing its name from Moldavia.

Part of Moldova was part of Romania until 1940, when it was ceded by a weak fascist government to Stalin. Two-thirds of its 4.3 million residents are ethnic Romanians, and with independence the possibility of reunion with Romania has been raised. There are, however, reservations about the idea among the Ukrainians (14% of the total) and the Russians (13%, and largely forcibly settled by Stalin).

Moldova has a fine low-lying soil, growing tobacco, vegetables, grain and wine for export. Sturgeon fishing is an activity in the south. Industrial activities include food-processing, engineering and metallurgy. Domestic appliances, such as washing machines and refrigerators, are produced in the region.

Russian Federation

Population	147,386,000 (1989)
Population density	9 per sq km
Land area	16,834,935 sq km
Main towns	Moscow (capital, 8,967,000 in 1989)
	St Petersburg (5,020,000 in 1989)
Net material product per head 1988	2,623 roubles
President	Boris Yeltsin

Russia remains the dominant force among the former Soviet states, by reason of its sheer size. Its population of 147.7 million, including non-residents, represented more than half the population of the former USSR, and its territory spans eleven time zones from Finland to Alaska, and 2,000 miles from the Arctic Ocean to China. The climate varies from the permafrost of Siberia to the sub-tropical areas of the deep south.

Owing to its vast land mass, Russia has a population density of just nine persons per square kilometre. Major population centres are Moscow, the capital (8,967,000 inhabitants), St Petersburg (formerly Leningrad, with 5,020,000), and Nizhniy Novgorod (formerly Gorky), to the east of Moscow, with 1,438,000 inhabitants.

The republic is rich in natural resources, with vast oil and gas fields, as well as reserves of iron, coal, gold, diamonds, platinum and other minerals. There are also large areas of forest and thousands of square miles of fertile farmland. The republic produces many industrial goods and accounted for 70% of all the Soviet agricultural and industrial output in the late 1980s; yet, like all other republics, it has had to bear the discomfort of closing superfluous and outdated industrial plant, and its extensive urban populations have felt the impact of food price deregulation particularly severely as they do not have their own local resources to fall back on.

Tadzhikstan

Population	5,112,000 (1989)
Population density	36.7 per sq km
Land area	143,000 sq km
Capital	Dushanbe (604,000 in 1989)
Presiden:	Rakhman Nabiyev
Prime Minister	Y. Khaaev

Tadzhikstan, located near the southern border with Afghanistan, remains the least developed region in what was once the USSR. With only a modest land area and a particularly inaccessible location, it has few significant economic activities other than farming, producing mainly livestock products because so little of the land is suitable for arable cultivation. Its mountainous terrain has made it suitable for hydro-electric development, and sales of power make a small contribution to the external economy.

Turkmenistan

Population	3,621,700 (1989)
Population density	7 per sq km
Land area	488,100 sq km
Capital	Ashkhabad (402,000, in 1989)
President	Saparmurad Niyazov
Prime Minister	K. Akhmedov

Located in the far south of the country, Turkmenistan comprises mainly very large tracts of desert where a proportion of the population are nomadic. At present there is little scope for agriculture, but perhaps more for the vast natural gas resources which are piped to the west of the former USSR, and for the developing petroleum industries. This is unlikely to be accomplished without substantial foreign investment, however, and at present there are few indications that Turkmenistan will be able to offer sufficiently bright prospects in return.

Ukraine

Population	51,704,000 (1989)
Population density	116 per sq km
Land area	444,701 sq km
Main towns	Kiev (2,602,000 in 1989)
	Kharkov (1,611,000 in 1989)
	Odessa (1,115,000 in 1989)
	Donetsk (1,110,000 in 1989)
Net material product per head (1988)	1,985 roubles
President	Leonid Kravchuk
Prime Minister	Vitold Fukin

Covering 444,701 square kilometres to the north of the Black Sea, with a western border alongside Poland and Czechoslovakia, the Ukraine is the second largest of the former Soviet republics by area, after Russia. The Ukraine declared its independence in September 1991 and this was ratified in December 1991.

The Ukraine was a central part of the Soviet agricultural and industrial system; its rich agricultural land accounted for 46% of Soviet agricultural output in the 1980s, while 25% of Soviet coal production originated here. Other industries include iron, steel, oil, chemicals, machine tools, food-processing and various consumer goods. Rivalries with Russia run deep, and in mid-1992 the republic was still at odds with Moscow as to the apportionment of defence resources and other state facilities.

Approximately 73% of the population is Ukrainian and 21% Russian. The republic's capital, Kiev, is also its largest city, with a population of 2,602,000, and other major centres are Kharkov, with 1,611,000 residents, and Donetsk and Odessa, with just over a million inhabitants each.

Uzbekistan

Population	20,320,000 (1990)
Population density	45 per sq km
Land area	447,400 sq km
Capital	Tashkent (2,310,000)
President	Islam Karimov
Prime Minister	Shaikh Mirsaidov

Uzbekistan, another of the former republics selected for agricultural production in the 1950s, is now the largest cotton producer among the former Soviet states, and it has substantial mineral resources. Yet, paradoxically, it has no mechanisms for processing these commodities itself - its produce having hitherto been taken to other parts of the USSR for conversion into manufactured goods.

Worse, the quality of the soil is continuing to deteriorate, again for lack of adequate investment. The Aral Sea, which was once one of the world's largest inland seas, has now almost dried up because of the growing need for water with which to compensate for the lack of other growing media. As a result, there seems little likelihood that Uzbekistan's predominantly Turkish population will see an upturn in its living standards in the foreseeable future.

The former Yugoslavia

Population	24,062,000 (1992)
Urban population	56%
Land area	255,804 sq km
Languages	Serbo-Croat, Slovenian, Macedonian, and several other minor Slavonic, Romance and Magyar dialects
Religions	Orthodox, Catholic, Islamic
Currency	Dinar
Head of state	Vacant in July 1992
Head of government	Milan Panic
Capital	Belgrade (1,470,073 at 1981 census)

The political disintegration of Yugoslavia since the end of the 1980s has left the former country in a state of severe tension which erupted into full-scale war during 1992. While the northern states of Slovenia and Croatia have successfully broken away from the old federation, achieving international recognition as sovereign states in their own right, the position remains less clear with regard to Macedonia in the south-east or Bosnia-Herzegovina, whose insistence on self-determination has been rejected by Serbia, the largest and most powerful state in what remains of the Yugoslav Federation. There are further doubts about the status of Kosovo, which is technically an autonomous province to the west of Serbia, but whose predominantly Albanian population has declared itself independent, and about Vojvodina, also an autonomous Serbian region on the Bulgarian border to the east.

The armed conflicts started in 1991, after Serbian minorities attempted to secede from Croatia, leading the Croatian authorities to begin a crackdown. Serbia responded with severe repression of its own minorities, and during the full-scale war which ensued, the Croatian forces were driven back by Serbian forces which were reinforced by the full strength of the former Yugoslavian Army.

In apparent recognition of the federation's break-up, the Yugoslavian Constitution was revised in April 1992, so as to include only Serbia and Montenegro. But as soon as Bosnia-Herzegovina attempted to declare its own independence, it was invaded by Serbian troops which inflicted severe damage on the Bosnian capital of Sarajevo. The republic subsequently became embroiled in the fighting which had hitherto been restricted to Croatia and Serbia, as the two rival republics fought it out on Bosnian soil. UN peacekeeping troops were moved in during June and July in an attempt to secure the airport at Sarajevo.

Having inflicted severe damage on the Croatian port of Dubrovnik, Serbia turned its attentions in 1992 to Bosnia-Herzegovina, attacking and then besieging its capital Sarajevo while conducting what it euphemistically called a policy of "racial cleansing". UN peacekeeping troops were called in during mid-1992, but the possibility of UN military action against Serbia could not be excluded.

The currency was devalued by 80% in January 1992, and by another 20% in March, in an attempt to resume the export effort. But Yugoslavia continued to face strong international pressure including trade sanctions imposed by the United Nations. Under the circumstances, normal economic activity has all but ceased in large areas of the country. In the absence of a developed industrial base, agriculture nowadays dominates the picture. Attention has also been turned towards developments in the mining, energy and transport sectors. Yugoslavia's industry is based on its large reserves of coal and metal ores, particularly iron, bauxite, copper and mercury, located in the central and southern areas.

Although Yugoslavia still existed, in a technical sense, in late 1992 it will be clear that most of its former constituent republics no longer consider themselves members. Slovenia, Bosnia-Herzegovina, Macedonia and Croatia had all declared themselves independent by mid-1992, and the first two had been recognised by most of the developed industrial world. The recognition of Macedonia was proving more problematic, however, because both Greece and Bulgaria were also laying claim to the title, though not the territory, of the republic.

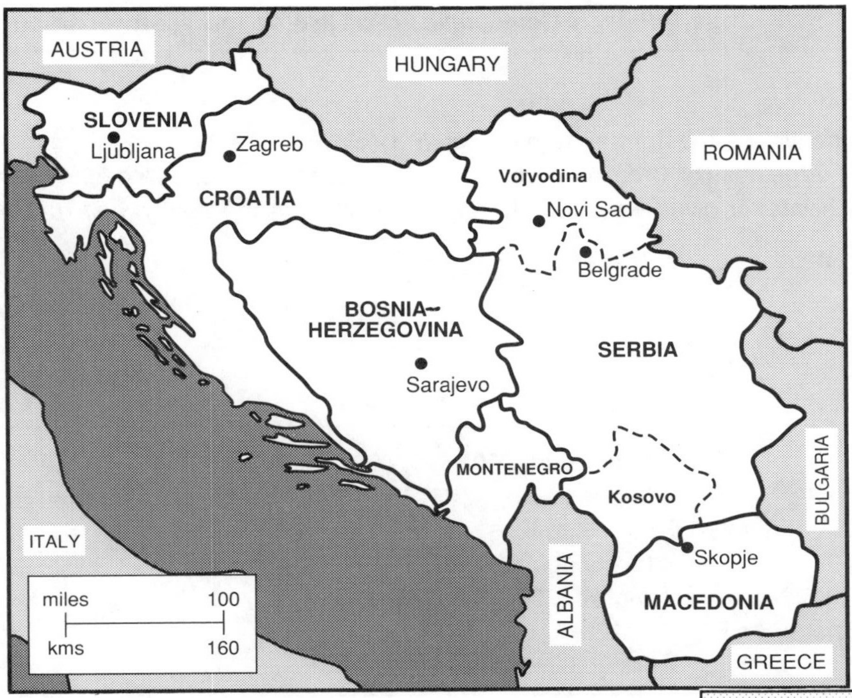

	STANDARD REGION	POPULATION (1990)
1	Slovenia	1,953,000
2	Croatia	4,685,000
3	Bosnia-Herzegovina	4,516,000
4	Serbia	9,880,000
5	Montenegro	644,000
6	Macedonia	2,132,000

Bosnia-Herzegovina

Population	4,516,000 (1990)
Population density	88 per sq km
Land area	51,129 sq km
Households 1981	1,031,000
National income 1989 (million dinars)	24,283
Capital	Sarajevo (448,519 in 1981)
Head of state	President Alija Izetbegovic
Prime Minister	Jure Pelivan
Ruling party	Party of Democratic Action leads a multi-party coalition

Bosnia-Herzegovina lies in the centre of the former territory of Yugoslavia, with its eastern borders alongside Serbia and the western edge against Croatia. It covers 51,129 square kilometres, or 20% of the total land area. The mountainous interior gives way to a stretch of coastline in the south-west running down to the city of Dubrovnik.

Croatia

Population	4,685,000 (1990)
Population density	83 per sq km
Land area	56,538 sq km
Households 1981	1,424,000
Capital	Zagreb (768,700 in 1981)
National income 1989 (million dinars)	51,278
Prime Minister	Franjo Greguric

Croatia lies in the north of the old Yugoslavia, with its western edge straddling the Adriatic coast and sharing an eastern border with Hungary. To the north is Slovenia, with Bosnia and Serbia to the south. The coastal strip and islands soon give way to mountains but, in the east, the hills are replaced by a flat plain. The region covers 56,538 square kilometres and has a population density of 83 persons per square kilometre.

Macedonia

Population	2,132,000 (1990)
Population density	83 per sq km
Land area	25,713 sq km
Households 1981	435,000
Capital	Skopje (506,547 in 1981)
National income 1989 (million dinars)	11,434
Prime Minister	Kiro Gligorov

Macedonia covers 25,713 square kilometres in the far south of the old Yugoslavia and borders three countries: Bulgaria in the east, Albania in the west and Greece to the south. It is characterised by mainly mountainous scenery with a river valley running north to south through its centre. Industries in the area include brewing, flour milling, tobacco, textiles, carpets and cement.

Despite seeking independence, recognition of Macedonia was withheld by the EC in April 1992.

Montenegro

Population	644,000 (1990)
Population density	46 per sq km
Land area	13,812 sq km
Households 1981	143,000
Capital	Podgorica (606,000 in 1981)
National income 1989 (million dinars)	3,789
President	Momir Bulatovic

Montenegro is the smallest of the former Yugoslav regions, with an area of 13,812 square kilometres in the south-west of the old country. Its western border is along the Adriatic and to the south is Albania. A mountainous interior gives way to a thin coastal plain and fertile land around Lake Scutari in the far south. The capital, Titograd, reverted to its former name of Podgorica in March 1992.

Agriculture is central to the local economy, with livestock rearing and grain production the major activities. Tobacco is also produced in the region.

Serbia

Population	9,880,000 (1990)
Population density	112 per sq km
Land area	88,361 sq km
National income 1989 (million dinars)	71,710
Households 1981	2,569,000
Capital	Belgrade (1,470,073 at 1981 census)
Prime Minister	Slobodan Milosevic
Ruling party	Socialist Party of Serbia

Serbia, the largest region in the former Yugoslavia, is the dominant part of what remains of the country, stretching over 88,361 square kilometres and housing 41% of the country's residents. Its northern border is with Hungary and on its eastern side are Romania and Bulgaria. In the centre of the region is Belgrade, the capital and largest town, with a population of 1,480,000. The region is characterised in geographical terms by mountains and deep river valleys. Industrial activities, largely around Belgrade, are machine tools, electrical equipment, pharmaceuticals, textiles, food-processing and light engineering.

Serbia includes the autonomous provinces of Kosovo and Vojvodina, where four million of the region's residents live. Yet Kosovo has gone its own way since 1990. The region held illegal elections in April 1992 to its 130-member Assembly, in which Ibrahim Rugova, the chairman of the Democratic Alliance of Kosovo, was elected as President - a move which has not been recognised by the Serbian authorities in Belgrade.

Slovenia

Population	1,953,000 (1990)
Population density	96 per sq km
Land area	20,251 sq km
National income 1989 (million dinars)	35,297
Households 1981	595,000
Capital	Ljubljana (305,211 in 1981)
Prime Minister	Janez Drnovsek
Ruling party	Liberal Democratic Party

Slovenia, which was recognised as a sovereign state by the European Community in January 1992, lies in the far north of the former Yugoslav Federation, covering an area of 20,251 square kilometres and comprising mountains in the west and gentler flatter land in the east. Three countries border the region - Austria in the north, Italy to the west and Hungary to the east. Ljubljana, in a valley between the mountains, is the republic's capital, with a population of 310,100.

Less than 8% of Slovenia's employees work in agriculture, compared to double figure percentages in other former Yugoslav regions, but agricultural products include maize, wheat, sugar beet and potatoes; forestry is also carried out. Coal, lead, lignite and mercury are mined and industries include cotton fabrics, steel and motor vehicles.

Cyprus

Population	750,000 (1992)
Urban population	51%
Land area	9,251 sq km
Languages	Greek (78%), Turkish (18%), Armenian
Religions	Greek Orthodox (78%), Islamic (18%)
Currency	Cyprus pound (= 100 cents)
Head of state	President Georgios Vassiliou (1988)
Ruling party	Democratic Rally (in coalition)
Main urban areas	Nicosia (capital, 149,100*)
	Limassol (107,200)
	Larnaca (48,300)
	Famagusta (39,500)
	* plus 37,400 in the Turkish sector

Recent Cypriot history has been dominated by the 1974 invasion from Turkey, followed by the partition of the island which left the north sector under the protection of Turkish forces. Turkey has declared this zone a separate state, but it is not internationally recognised as such.

However, there were indications in 1992 that the climate may be easing. Inter-communal talks were resumed during this period, amid declarations by the Turkish and the Greek governments that they intended to negotiate a settlement of the Cyprus issue under UN auspices later in the year.

The economy is dominated by the agricultural sector, which provides much of its exports - mainly citrus and vine fruit and products. There is little potential for further growth in this area, and the government has attempted to promote the island as a natural trading station between the West and the Middle East, a policy which appears to be succeeding, with the installation of a number of international companies' offices. The need to import most raw materials and manufactured goods means that the visible trade balance is regularly in deficit, being offset by income from tourism and British and UN service personnel stationed on the island. Cyprus entered a customs union with the EC in 1988.

Gibraltar

Population	29,800 (1992)
Urban population	100%
Land area	5.5 sq km
Language	English
Religion	Mainly Roman Catholic
Currency	Gibraltar pound (= 100 pence)
Head of state	HM Queen Elizabeth II, represented by the Governor, Sir Derek Reffell
Chief minister	Joe Bossano

Gibraltar's importance to the United Kingdom over nearly three centuries has been as a strategic naval base covering access to the Mediterranean Sea. More recently, its low rates of duty have given it a position as a favoured shopping area and merchant marine base, enhanced by the promotion of tourism.

The reopening in 1986 of the border with Spain has done much to boost the colony's economy. Meanwhile Gibraltar is becoming increasingly important as a centre for financial services related to Mediterranean trade and investment. Yet the issue of sovereignty continues to cause problems between Britain and Spain.

Malta

Population	357,000 (1992)
Urban population	87%
Land area	316 sq km
Languages	Maltese, English
Religion	Roman Catholic
Currency	Maltese Lira (= 100 cents)
Head of state	Vincent Tabone (1989)
Head of government	Dr Edward Fenech Adami
Ruling party	Nationalist Party
Main urban areas	Valletta (capital, 9,100; 120,000 approx including the harbour area) Birkirkara (21,450) Sliema (13,250)

The Maltese economy is remarkably strong for such a small state, and is based on a balance of three areas. The agricultural sector, significant in employment terms, produces a variety of fruit, root crops and legumes, as well as wine and horticultural products. The main industry is shipping and ship repair, but there is also a wide variety of manufacturing industry, producing textiles, clothing, food products, plastics and chemicals. The growth area is now tourism.

Following the election in 1987 of Dr Adami, Malta has made renewed efforts to repair its relations with Western Europe and the United States (hitherto damaged by its close links with the government of Libya), and it has been trying to attract foreign investment as well as strengthening its relations with the European Community, with which it has an Association Agreement.

Monaco

Population	30,000 (1992)
Urban population	100%
Land area	2.0 sq km
Language	French
Currency	French Franc
Head of state	HSH Sovereign Prince Rainier III
Head of government	Jean Ausseil

Monaco's income derives almost exclusively from tourism, and in particular from the Monte Carlo Casino. There is no agriculture, the whole of the principality being built up. Visitors number over 250,000 annually - nearly ten times the population.

Turkey

Population	59,045,000 (1992)
Urban population	61%
Land area	779,452 sq km
Language	Turkish
Religion	Islam (99%)
Currency	Lira (= 100 Kuru)
Head of state	Turgut Özal
Head of government	Süleyman Demirel
Main urban areas	Istanbul (5,482,985 at 1985 census)
	Ankara (capital, 3,306,327)
	Izmir (2,317,829)
	Adana (1,725,940)
	Bursa (1,324,015)
	Eskisehir (597,397)

Agriculture is the most important sector in the Turkish economy, employing 50% of the workforce and contributing 16% of GDP. Wheat is the major crop, grown on the arid tablelands of Anatolia. Other important crops, cultivated in the coastal areas, include barley, grapes, olives and citrus fruits. Around Izmir there are tobacco farms, and also sultana and fig cultivation. Adana is the centre of cotton cultivation. The foothills of Anatolia are widely afforested, although there is concern that depletion of forest resources is proceeding too rapidly.

Turkey has abundant natural resources, many of which are relatively unexploited. Lignite and hard coal are produced in great quantities, as are ores of iron, copper, chrome and boron. Indigenous industries are centred on the exploitation of these resources, and the processing of its agricultural produce.

Turkey has relatively minor energy resources, although there is a great deal of potential for hydro-electric schemes. It has also developed a thriving trade as an entrepôt for the export of oil and gas from Iraq and other Middle Eastern countries via Ceyhan, where there are refineries and petrochemical plants. However, the invasion of Kuwait by Iraq in August 1990, and the onset of economic sanctions which followed in early 1991, were a serious blow for the country's trade prospects. By mid-1991 the plight of Kurdish refugees in the south-east of the country had placed the Turkish authorities in a delicate position because of its own disapproval of Kurdish organisations.

Turkey continues to suffer grave economic problems, the most serious being high inflation and low investment. Unemployment is high, and there is a persistent current account deficit, although this has been reduced in recent years. The government has applied to be considered for membership of the EC, which would presumably assist the country to take advantage of its resources to help stabilise the economy but which has aroused strong protests from Greece. An unstable political scene has also been a problem, and the EC members would obviously like to see evidence that such disturbances are now over before allowing Turkey's accession.

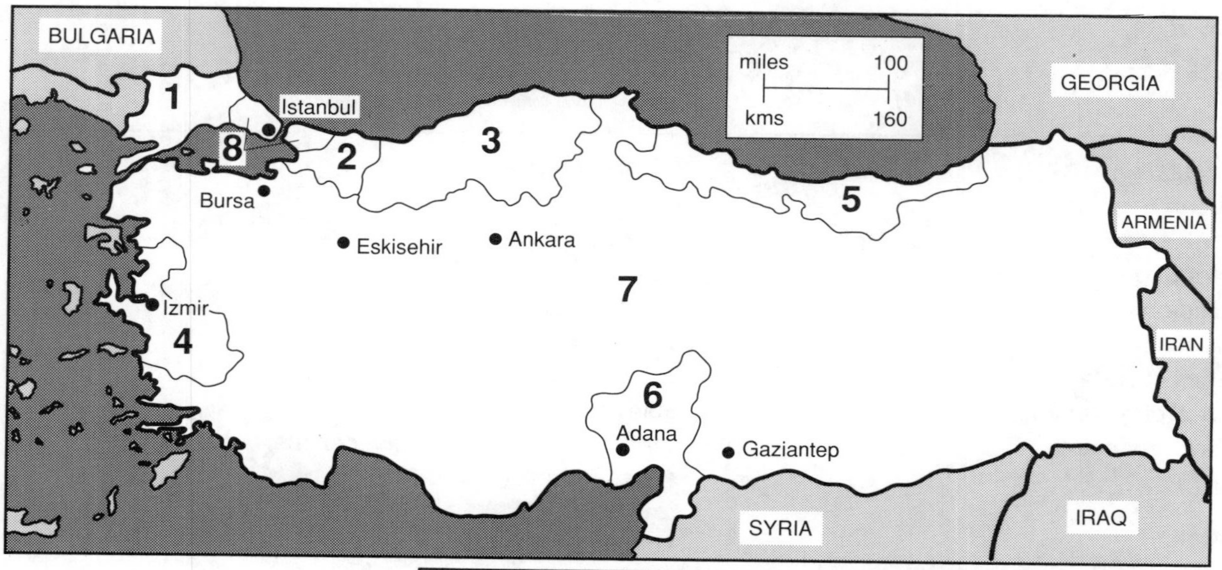

	STANDARD REGION	POPULATION (1985 census)
1	Edirne, Kirklareli, Tekirdag	1,089,457
2	Kocaeli, Sakarya	1,352,745
3	Bolu, Zonguldak	1,549,723
4	Izmir, Aydin	3,061,248
5	Rize, Trabzon, Giresun, Ordu, Samsun	3,535,118
6	Adana, Hatay	2,728,192
7	Central region	31,474,990
8	Istanbul	5,842,990

Section Two

Demographic Trends and Forecasts

Table No: 0201

TOTAL POPULATION

Trends in Total Population 1977-1991: International Estimates

'000

	1977	1978	1979	1980	1981	1982	1983	1984	1985
EC members									
Belgium	9822	9830	9837	9847	9852	9860	9860	9860	9860
Denmark	5088	5104	5117	5123	5122	5118	5114	5112	5114
France	53145	53376	53606	53880	54182	54480	54729	54947	54621
Germany: East	16765	16756	16745	16737	16736	16697	16699	16671	16644
Germany: West	61396	61310	61337	61561	61666	61638	61421	61181	61015
Greece	9268	9360	9449	9643	9729	9790	9847	9896	9935
Ireland	3272	3314	3368	3401	3440	3483	3508	3535	3552
Italy	55929	56127	56292	56416	56502	56639	56836	56983	57128
Luxembourg	361	362	363	364	365	366	366	366	366
Netherlands	13853	13937	14030	14144	14246	14310	14362	14420	14484
Portugal	9736	9796	9841	9884	9855	9930	10010	10190	10160
Spain	36351	36775	37183	37430	37654	37970	38160	38330	38470
United Kingdom	56179	56167	56228	56314	56378	56335	56377	56488	56125
EC total	331165	332214	333396	334744	335727	336616	337289	337879	337474
EFTA members									
Austria	7568	7562	7549	7549	7565	7574	7552	7552	7555
Finland	4739	4753	4765	4780	4800	4827	4856	4882	4908
Iceland	222	224	226	228	231	234	237	239	241
Liechtenstein	24	25	26	26	26	26	26	28	28
Norway	4043	4059	4073	4086	4100	4115	4128	4141	4152
Sweden	8252	8276	8294	8310	8320	8325	8329	8337	8350
Switzerland	6327	6333	6351	6385	6429	6467	6505	6442	6374
EFTA total	31175	31232	31284	31364	31471	31568	31633	31621	31608
Eastern Europe									
Albania	2508	2563	2617	2671	2725	2783	2841	2901	2962
Bulgaria	8804	8814	8826	8862	8891	8917	8940	8961	8950
Czechoslovakia	15030	15137	15237	15311	15320	15369	15414	15458	15500
Hungary	10637	10673	10698	10711	10712	10706	10689	10668	10649
Poland	34698	35010	35257	35578	35902	36227	36571	36914	37203
Romania	21658	21855	22048	22201	22353	22478	22553	22625	23017
USSR	259029	261253	263425	265542	267722	270042	272500	275066	277540
Yugoslavia	21775	21968	22166	22394	22471	22642	22801	22963	23123
East European total	374139	377273	380274	383270	386096	389164	392309	395556	398944
Others									
Cyprus	613	616	620	627	634	641	649	657	665
Gibraltar	30	29	30	30	30	29	29	29	30
Malta	332	340	347	364	364	360	377	380	383
Monaco	25	25	25	26	26	26	27	27	27
Turkey	41768	42640	43530	44438	45366	46690	47860	49070	50310
Total	42768	43650	44552	45485	46420	47746	48942	50163	51415
European total	779247	784369	789506	794863	799714	805094	810173	815219	819441

Table No: 0201 (cont'd)

TOTAL POPULATION

Trends in Total Population 1977-1991: International Estimates

'000

	1986	1987	1988	1989	1990	1991	% growth 1977-1991	% share 1977	% share 1991
EC members									
Belgium	9870	9880	9880	9850	9840	9850	0.29	1.26	1.16
Denmark	5121	5127	5130	5132	5134	5140	1.02	0.65	0.60
France	55392	55632	55858	56160	56640	56640	6.58	6.82	6.66
Germany: East	16624	16641	16650	16630	16700	16700	-0.39	2.15	1.96
Germany: West	61048	61171	61319	61990	63250	63250	3.02	7.88	7.43
Greece	9966	9992	10027	10030	10025	10025	8.17	1.19	1.18
Ireland	3537	3543	3538	3515	3500	3500	6.97	0.42	0.41
Italy	57221	57355	57422	57517	57650	57650	3.08	7.18	6.78
Luxembourg	363	367	370	371	380	380	5.26	0.05	0.04
Netherlands	14563	14661	14760	14830	15060	15060	8.71	1.78	1.77
Portugal	10210	10250	10290	10470	10580	10580	8.67	1.25	1.24
Spain	38660	38720	38881	38890	39480	39480	8.61	4.66	4.64
United Kingdom	56763	56891	57065	57244	57450	57450	2.26	7.21	6.75
EC total	339338	340220	341190	342629	344634	345705	4.39	42.50	40.63
EFTA members									
Austria	7565	7573	7574	7618	7790	7820	3.33	0.97	0.92
Finland	4918	4932	4954	4963	4990	5100	7.62	0.61	0.60
Iceland	243	246	248	251	254	260	17.12	0.03	0.03
Liechtenstein	27	28	28	28	28	28	16.67	0.00	0.00
Norway	4169	4187	4210	4230	4240	4250	5.12	0.52	0.50
Sweden	8370	8399	8440	8490	8560	8600	4.22	1.06	1.01
Switzerland	6504	6538	6558	6650	6710	6750	6.69	0.81	0.79
EFTA total	31796	31903	32012	32230	32572	32808	5.24	4.00	3.86
Eastern Europe									
Albania	3022	3083	3130	3202	3250	3300	31.58	0.32	0.39
Bulgaria	8959	8970	8980	9000	9000	9000	2.23	1.13	1.06
Czechoslovakia	15534	15573	15610	15640	15660	15710	4.52	1.93	1.85
Hungary	10627	10613	10626	10576	10550	10500	-1.29	1.37	1.23
Poland	37456	37664	37860	37850	38180	38200	10.09	4.45	4.49
Romania	23174	22936	22900	23152	23230	23250	7.35	2.78	2.73
USSR	280240	282830	285420	287630	289340	290000	11.96	33.24	34.08
Yugoslavia	23271	23420	23570	23690	23810	23930	9.90	2.79	2.81
East European total	402283	405089	408096	410740	413020	413890	10.62	48.01	48.64
Others									
Cyprus	673	680	700	720	740	750	22.35	0.08	0.09
Gibraltar	30	30	30	31	31	31	3.33	0.00	0.00
Malta	385	344	347	350	353	355	6.93	0.04	0.04
Monaco	27	27	28	28	28	29	16.00	0.00	0.00
Turkey	51430	52560	53710	54890	56100	57300	37.19	5.36	6.73
Total	52545	53641	54815	56019	57252	58465	36.70	5.49	6.87
European total	825962	830853	836113	841618	847478	850868	9.19	100.00	100.00

Sources: UN Demographic Yearbook/UN Population and Statistics Report/IMF

Table No: 0202

TOTAL POPULATION

Trends in Total Population 1977-1992: National Estimates at January 1st

'000

	1977	1980	1983	1984	1985	1986	1987	1988	1989	1990	1991	1992
EC members												
Belgium	9823	9855	9858	9853	9857	9865	9876	9881	9928	9980	10032	10050
Denmark	5080	5122	5116	5112	5111	5116	5125	5129	5130	5135	5146	5160
France	53019	53731	54626	54831	55062	55278	55510	55947	56250	56560	56871	57185
Germany: East	16767	16740	16706	16709	16671	16655	16641	16650	16648	16200	15900	15600
Germany: West	61442	61439	61546	61307	61049	61020	61238	61715	62000	62285	62570	63500
Greece[a]	9308	9643	9847	9896	9919	9950	9978	10004	10058	10105	10152	10200
Ireland[a]	3262	3401	3504	3529	3540	3537	3542	3539	3530	3521	3512	3500
Italy	56123	57000	57342	56933	57080	57202	57291	57399	57505	57576	57746	57835
Luxembourg	361	364	366	366	366	367	370	372	375	375	375	380
Netherlands	13814	14091	14340	14394	14454	14530	14615	14715	14810	14899	15015	15138
Portugal	9403	9714	9969	10050	10129	10185	10230	10304	10310	10350	10390	10500
Spain	36155	37242	38067	38280	38495	38549	38750	38766	38852	38924	38944	39000
United Kingdom	56190	56330	56347	56460	56618	56763	56847	57017	57218	57300	57420	57700
EC total	330747	334672	337634	337720	338351	339017	340013	341438	342614	343210	344073	345748
EFTA members												
Austria[b]	7568	7549	7552	7553	7558	7566	7576	7598	7624	7660	7697	7800
Finland	4731	4771	4842	4870	4894	4911	4932	4950	4954	4974	4998	5020
Iceland	221	227	236	238	241	242	246	249	253	254	256	260
Liechtenstein	24	26	26	27	27	27	28	29	30	30	30	30
Norway	4035	4079	4123	4134	4146	4159	4175	4205	4221	4233	4249	4274
Sweden	8236	8303	8327	8331	8343	8358	8381	8414	8459	8527	8591	8644
Switzerland	6298	6314	6410	6428	6456	6485	6523	6567	6620	6660	6700	6740
EFTA total	31113	31269	31516	31581	31665	31748	31861	32012	32161	32339	32520	32768
Eastern Europe												
Albania[a]	2508	2671	2841	2901	2962	3022	3083	3130	3177	3200	3223	3300
Bulgaria[b]	8804	8862	8940	8961	8960	8950	8960	8950	8987	8993	9000	9000
Czechoslovakia[b]	15030	15311	15414	15458	15500	15534	15573	15600	15627	15654	15681	15700
Hungary	10615	10710	10700	10679	10657	10640	10607	10604	10602	10610	10587	10332
Poland	34528	35414	36399	36745	37063	37341	37663	37850	37889	38050	38195	38330
Romania[b]	21660	22201	22553	22625	22725	22860	22940	23054	23152	23250	23348	23300
USSR[a]	259029	265542	272540	275066	277537	280144	283100	283500	283900	284300	284700	285000
Yugoslavia[a]	21780	22304	22805	22966	23118	23270	23442	23566	23690	23814	23938	23950
E European total	373954	383015	392192	395401	398522	401761	405369	406254	407023	407871	408671	408912
Others												
Cyprus	613	623	645	653	662	669	680	700	720	730	740	750
Gibraltar	30	30	29	29	28	29	30	30	30	30	30	31
Malta	311	323	332	338	340	343	346	349	352	353	355	356
Monaco	25	26	27	27	27	27	27	28	28	28	28	29
Turkey[a]	41768	44438	47864	49070	50664	52150	53250	54176	55102	56028	56954	57500
Total	42747	45440	48897	50117	51721	53218	54333	55283	56232	57169	58107	58666
European total	778561	794396	810239	814819	820259	825744	831576	834987	838030	840589	843372	846094

Sources: National statistical offices: all countries
Notes: See end of section

Table No: 0203

TOTAL POPULATION

Total Population: Latest Official Census Year

'000

	Year	Total	Male	Female	0-14	15-64	65+
EC members							
Belgium	1981	9849	4810	5038	1972	6462	1415
Denmark	1981	5124	2528	2596	968	3151	1005
France	1982	54335					
Germany: East	1981	16706	7849	8857			
Germany: West	1987	61077	29323	31754			
Greece	1981	9740	4780	4960			
Ireland	1986	3541	1770	1771			
Italy	1981	56557	27506	29051	12128	36944	7485
Luxembourg	1981	365	178	187	67	248	50
Netherlands	1971	13060					
Portugal	1981	9833	4738	5095			
Spain	1981	37746	18530	19216	9686	20189	7871
United Kingdom	1981	55089	26803	28286	11455	35465	8169
EFTA members							
Austria	1981	7555	3572	3983	1511	4898	1146
Finland	1985	4911	2378	2533			
Iceland	1970	205	104	101			
Liechtenstein	1981	26	13	13			
Norway	1980	4091	2027	2064	1215	2040	836
Sweden	1985	8360	4128	4232			
Switzerland	1980	6366	3115	3251	1222	4262	882
Eastern Europe							
Albania	1989	3182					
Bulgaria	1985	8948					
Czechoslovakia	1980	15283	7441	7842			
Hungary	1980	10710	5189	5521	2341	6539	1830
Poland	1984	37026	18026	19000			
Romania	1977	21560	10626	10934			
USSR	1989	286717	135499	151218			
Yugoslavia	1981	22425	11084	11341	5488	14804	2133
Others							
Cyprus	1982	643	320	323	161	413	69
Gibraltar	1981	26	13	14	6	18	3
Malta	1985	346	170	176	83	229	34
Monaco	1982	27	13	14			
Turkey	1985	50664	25672	24992			

Sources: UN Population & Vital Statistics Report/national statistical offices

Table No: 0204

VITAL STATISTICS

Number of Live Births 1977-1991

'000

	1977	1980	1983	1984	1985	1986	1987	1988	1989	1990	1991
EC members											
Belgium	121.9	124.4	117.4	115.7	114.0	117.0	118.0	115.5	119.1	120.3	120.0
Denmark	61.9	57.3	50.8	51.8	54.0	55.4	56.4	58.8	61.5	63.5	64.4
France	744.7	800.4	748.8	760.5	769.1	778.9	767.7	771.3	765.5	762.4	758.4
Germany: East	223.2	245.1	233.8	228.1	227.4	222.3	226.0	215.7	198.9	178.5	107.0
Germany: West	582.3	620.7	594.2	584.2	584.8	624.4	642.0	677.3	681.5	727.2	721.3
Greece	143.7	148.1	132.6	126.8	116.7	112.3	105.9	107.7	98.8	100.0	100.0
Ireland	68.9	74.1	67.1	64.2	62.2	61.4	58.9	54.3	51.7	53.0	52.7
Italy	741.1	640.4	600.3	586.0	576.2	580.0	550.6	568.3	567.3	580.7	565.0
Luxembourg	4.1	4.2	4.2	4.2	4.1	4.3	4.2	4.6	4.8	4.6	4.7
Netherlands	173.3	181.3	170.2	174.4	178.2	185.0	186.2	186.6	189.0	191.0	192.0
Portugal	181.1	158.4	144.3	136.9	130.5	128.0	124.2	118.0	113.5	114.0	114.0
Spain	661.1	565.4	477.3	465.7	451.0	434.0	425.0	409.5	411.2	410.0	411.0
United Kingdom	657.0	753.7	721.5	729.6	750.7	755.0	773.7	787.6	777.3	798.6	802.6
EC total	4364.3	4373.4	4062.5	4028.2	4018.8	4057.9	4038.8	4075.2	4040.1	4103.8	4013.1
EFTA members											
Austria	85.6	90.9	90.1	89.2	86.6	86.3	86.3	88.0	87.9	90.5	91.0
Finland	65.7	63.1	66.9	65.1	63.0	60.8	59.8	63.3	63.4	65.6	64.5
Iceland	4.0	4.5	4.4	4.1	3.8	3.9	4.2	4.7	4.7	4.7	4.7
Liechtenstein	0.3	0.4	0.3	0.4	0.4	0.4	0.4	0.4	0.4	0.4	0.4
Norway	50.9	51.0	49.9	50.3	51.4	52.5	54.0	57.5	59.3	60.9	60.7
Sweden	96.1	97.1	91.8	93.9	98.3	102.0	104.7	112.1	116.0	118.3	123.4
Switzerland	72.8	73.7	73.7	74.7	74.7	76.3	76.5	80.3	79.8	80.3	81.0
EFTA total	375.3	380.6	377.1	377.6	378.1	382.1	385.9	406.3	411.6	420.7	425.7
Eastern Europe											
Albania	70.0	70.7	73.8	79.2	77.5	77.5	78.2	80.2	78.9	75.0	75.0
Bulgaria	141.7	128.9	123.0	122.3	117.9	120.4	115.7	117.9	113.4	114.0	114.0
Czechoslovakia	281.3	248.9	229.5	227.8	225.2	220.0	215.9	216.9	208.6	212.9	210.0
Hungary	177.6	148.7	127.3	125.3	129.9	128.5	125.2	124.3	124.4	125.2	126.0
Poland	662.6	692.8	720.8	699.0	677.6	634.7	606.4	584.4	562.5	546.0	546.0
Romania	424.0	398.9	321.5	350.7	358.8	361.0	365.0	367.0	369.5	371.0	370.0
USSR	4693.4	4851.4	5391.9	5386.9	5374.4	5614.7	5605.4	5596.1	5586.7	5577.4	5570.0
Yugoslavia	384.6	382.1	379.3	376.4	367.5	358.3	358.2	355.4	335.9	335.9	310.0
East European total	6835.1	6922.4	7366.9	7367.7	7328.8	7515.1	7470.0	7442.1	7379.9	7357.4	7321.0
Others											
Cyprus	11.3	12.8	14.6	13.5	13.0	13.1	12.7			13.3	
Gibraltar	0.5	0.6	0.5	0.5	0.5	0.5	0.5	0.5	0.5	0.5	
Malta	5.9	5.8	5.7	5.6	5.4	5.4	5.5	5.5	5.6	5.5	
Monaco	0.2	0.5	0.5	0.5	0.5	0.5					
Turkey[a]	650.0	650.0	650.0	650.0	650.0	650.0			1482.1		
Total	667.9	669.7	671.4	670.2	669.5	669.5	18.7	6.0	1488.2	19.3	
European total	12242.7	12346.0	12477.9	12443.7	12395.2	12624.6	11913.5	11929.7	13319.7	11901.3	11759.8

Sources: UN Demographic Yearbook/UN Population & Vital Statistics Report
Note: See end of section

Table No: 0205

VITAL STATISTICS

Number of Deaths 1977-1991

'000

	1977	1980	1983	1984	1985	1986	1987	1988	1989	1990	1991
EC members											
Belgium	112.7	113.7	114.8	109.7	110.8	110.5	106.1	110.6	112.2	120.3	120.4
Denmark	50.5	55.9	57.2	57.1	58.4	58.1	58.0	59.0	59.4	61.0	59.5
France	536.2	547.1	559.7	540.6	552.5	546.9	527.5	524.6	529.3	526.2	425.9
Germany: East	226.2	238.3	222.7	221.2	225.4	223.5	214.7	213.7	205.7	196.0	196.6
Germany: West	704.9	714.1	718.3	696.1	703.4	699.6	687.0	687.5	697.7	709.7	709.0
Greece	83.8	87.3	90.6	88.5	92.1	91.5	95.2	93.0	91.3	93.0	93.1
Ireland	33.6	33.5	33.0	32.2	31.9	33.6	31.2	31.6	31.1	31.8	31.5
Italy	546.7	554.5	564.0	535.0	547.0	542.0	533.4	536.7	531.6	544.4	544.8
Luxembourg	4.1	4.1	4.1	4.1	3.9	4.0	4.0	3.8	3.9	3.9	4.0
Netherlands	110.1	114.3	117.8	119.8	122.4	125.0	121.7	124.2	128.9	130.0	131.0
Portugal	96.2	95.0	96.4	97.2	97.3	97.3	96.3	98.7	98.2	98.5	99.0
Spain	294.3	287.6	296.2	295.4	295.5	306.0	310.0	312.0	313.3	314.0	311.0
United Kingdom	655.1	661.5	659.1	644.9	670.6	660.7	637.2	649.2	657.7	641.8	646.2
EC total	3454.4	3506.9	3533.8	3441.8	3511.2	3498.7	3423.3	3444.6	3460.3	3470.6	3472.0
EFTA members											
Austria	92.4	92.4	93.0	88.5	89.0	86.5	84.9	83.3	82.8	83.0	83.3
Finland	44.1	44.4	45.4	45.1	48.2	47.1	47.1	49.1	49.1	49.1	50.2
Iceland	1.4	1.5	1.7	1.6	1.7	1.7	1.7	1.8	1.9	2.1	2.1
Liechtenstein	0.1	0.2	0.2	0.2	0.2	0.2	0.2	0.2	0.2	0.2	0.2
Norway	39.8	41.3	42.2	42.5	44.2	40.8	45.0	45.4	45.2	46.0	44.8
Sweden	88.2	91.8	90.8	90.5	94.0	93.0	93.2	96.7	92.1	95.2	95.0
Switzerland	55.7	59.1	60.8	58.6	59.6	60.1	59.5	60.6	60.8	61.0	61.4
EFTA total	321.7	330.8	334.0	326.9	336.8	329.3	331.6	337.1	332.1	336.6	337.0
Eastern Europe											
Albania	16.5	17.0	17.4	16.7	17.2	17.0	17.0	17.3	18.2	18.5	18.8
Bulgaria	94.4	98.0	102.2	101.4	107.4	101.8	107.6	108.0	106.2	106.2	106.2
Czechoslovakia	173.4	186.1	186.9	183.9	182.6	184.0	179.1	178.2	181.6	183.7	184.3
Hungary	132.0	145.4	148.6	146.7	147.4	146.4	142.2	140.2	144.7	145.7	146.0
Poland	313.0	350.2	349.4	364.9	381.5	376.3	376.6	378.6	381.2	388.4	404.0
Romania	208.7	231.9	233.9	233.7	246.7	242.0	239.5	239.1	247.3	247.1	247.3
USSR	2494.7	2743.8	2822.6	2964.9	2947.1	2741.2	2802.7	2828.4	2850.3	2867.2	2873.7
Yugoslavia	182.8	197.4	219.3	213.1	211.0	212.0	215.4	211.8	215.5	209.6	210.7
East European total	3615.5	3969.6	4080.4	4225.3	4240.9	4020.7	4080.2	4101.5	4144.9	4166.3	4190.9
Others											
Cyprus	5.5	5.8	5.6	5.3	5.7	5.3	6.1			6.0	
Gibraltar	0.2	0.3	0.3	0.3	0.3	0.3	0.2	0.3	0.2	0.3	
Malta	2.9	3.2	3.1	2.9	2.8	2.8	2.9	2.7	2.6	2.8	
Monaco	0.3	0.5	0.4	0.4	0.4	0.4					
Turkey	122.7	130.1	134.7	136.3	141.3	133.1				423.0	
Total	131.6	139.9	144.1	145.2	150.5	142.0	9.2	3.0	425.8	9.1	
European total	7523.2	7947.2	8092.3	8139.2	8239.5	7990.7	7843.2	7886.2	8363.2	7982.6	7999.9

Sources: UN Demographic Yearbook/UN Population & Vital Statistics Report/national statistical offices

Table No: 0206

VITAL STATISTICS

Birth Rates 1977-1991

Per '000 inhabitants

	1977	1980	1983	1984	1985	1986	1987	1988	1989	1990	1991
EC members											
Belgium	12.4	12.6	11.9	11.7	11.6	11.9	12.0	11.7	12.1	12.2	12.2
Denmark	12.2	11.2	9.9	10.1	10.6	10.8	11.0	11.5	12.0	12.4	12.5
France	14.0	14.9	13.7	13.8	14.1	14.1	13.8	13.8	13.6	13.5	13.4
Germany: East	13.3	14.6	14.0	13.7	13.7	13.4	13.6	12.9	12.0	10.9	6.7
Germany: West	9.5	10.1	9.7	9.6	9.6	10.2	10.5	11.0	11.0	11.3	11.5
Greece	15.5	15.4	13.5	12.8	11.7	11.2	10.6	10.8	9.9	10.0	10.0
Ireland	21.1	21.8	19.1	18.2	17.5	17.4	16.6	15.3	14.7	15.2	15.1
Italy	13.3	11.4	10.6	10.3	10.1	10.1	9.6	9.9	9.9	10.1	9.8
Luxembourg	11.2	11.5	11.4	11.5	11.1	11.9	11.5	12.4	12.9	12.4	12.4
Netherlands	12.5	12.8	11.9	12.1	12.3	12.7	12.7	12.6	12.6	12.7	12.7
Portugal	18.6	16.0	14.4	13.6	12.8	12.5	12.1	11.5	10.8	10.8	10.8
Spain	18.2	15.1	12.5	12.1	11.7	11.2	11.0	10.5	10.6	10.5	10.4
United Kingdom	11.7	13.4	12.8	12.9	13.4	13.3	13.6	13.8	13.6	13.9	14.0
EC average	13.2	13.1	12.0	11.9	11.9	12.0	11.9	11.9	11.8	12.0	11.6
EFTA members											
Austria	11.3	12.0	11.9	11.8	11.5	11.4	11.4	11.6	11.5	11.6	11.6
Finland	13.9	13.2	13.8	13.3	12.8	12.4	12.1	12.8	12.8	13.1	12.6
Iceland	18.0	19.9	18.4	17.2	15.9	16.0	16.9	18.8	18.7	18.5	18.1
Liechtenstein	12.9	15.1	13.4	12.5	12.5	13.0	13.0	14.3	14.3	14.3	14.3
Norway	12.6	12.5	12.1	12.1	12.4	12.6	12.9	13.7	14.0	14.4	14.3
Sweden	11.6	11.7	11.0	11.3	11.8	12.2	12.5	13.3	13.7	13.8	14.3
Switzerland	11.5	11.5	11.3	11.6	11.7	11.7	11.7	12.2	12.0	12.0	12.0
EFTA average	12.0	12.1	11.9	11.9	12.0	12.0	12.1	12.7	12.8	12.9	13.0
Eastern Europe											
Albania	27.9	26.5	26.0	27.3	26.2	25.6	25.4	25.6	24.6	23.1	22.7
Bulgaria	16.1	14.5	13.8	13.6	13.2	13.4	12.9	13.1	12.6	12.7	12.7
Czechoslovakia	18.7	16.3	14.9	14.7	14.5	14.2	13.9	13.9	13.3	13.6	13.4
Hungary	16.7	13.9	11.9	11.7	12.2	12.1	11.8	11.7	11.8	11.9	12.0
Poland	19.1	19.5	19.7	18.9	18.2	16.9	16.1	15.4	14.9	14.3	14.3
Romania	19.6	18.0	14.3	15.5	15.9	15.9	15.9	16.0	16.0	16.0	15.9
USSR	18.1	18.3	19.8	19.6	19.4	20.0	19.8	19.6	19.4	19.3	19.2
Yugoslavia	17.7	17.1	16.6	16.4	15.9	15.4	15.3	15.1	14.2	14.1	13.0
East European average	18.3	18.1	18.8	18.6	18.4	18.7	18.4	18.2	18.0	17.8	17.7
Others											
Cyprus	18.5	20.4	22.5	20.6	19.5	19.5	18.7			18.0	
Gibraltar	16.9	18.3	17.6	17.4	16.6	16.9	17.9	16.7	17.1	16.1	
Malta	17.9	16.0	15.2	14.8	14.2	13.9	15.9	15.9	16.0	15.6	
Monaco	7.5	20.6	19.6	19.6	19.8	19.9					
Turkey	15.6	14.6	13.6	13.2	12.9	12.6					
Average	15.6	14.7	13.7	13.4	13.0	12.7	17.8	16.0	16.1	17.2	
European average	15.7	15.5	15.4	15.3	15.1	15.3	15.3	15.2	15.0	15.0	14.8

Sources: United Nations/national statistical offices

Table No: 0207

VITAL STATISTICS

Death Rates 1977-1991

Per '000 inhabitants

	1977	1980	1983	1984	1985	1986	1987	1988	1989	1990	1991
EC members											
Belgium	11.5	11.5	11.6	11.1	11.2	11.2	10.8	11.2	11.4	12.2	12.2
Denmark	9.9	10.9	11.2	11.2	11.4	11.4	11.3	11.5	11.6	11.9	11.6
France	10.1	10.2	10.2	9.8	10.1	9.9	9.5	9.4	9.4	9.3	9.3
Germany: East	13.5	14.2	13.3	13.3	13.5	13.4	12.9	12.8	12.4	11.8	11.8
Germany: West	11.5	11.6	11.7	11.4	11.5	11.5	11.2	11.2	11.4	11.4	11.3
Greece	9.0	9.1	9.2	8.9	9.6	9.1	9.5	9.3	9.1	9.3	9.3
Ireland	10.3	9.8	9.4	9.1	9.0	9.5	8.8	8.9	8.8	9.1	9.0
Italy	9.8	9.8	9.9	9.4	9.6	9.5	9.3	9.3	9.2	9.4	9.4
Luxembourg	11.3	11.3	11.3	11.1	10.8	10.9	10.9	10.4	10.4	10.5	10.5
Netherlands	7.9	8.1	8.2	8.3	8.5	8.6	8.3	8.4	8.7	8.7	8.7
Portugal	9.9	9.6	9.6	9.6	9.6	9.5	9.4	9.6	9.4	9.4	9.4
Spain	8.1	7.7	7.8	7.7	7.7	7.9	8.0	8.0	8.1	8.1	7.9
United Kingdom	11.7	11.7	11.7	11.4	11.9	11.6	11.2	11.4	11.5	11.2	11.2
EC average	10.4	10.0	10.5	10.2	10.4	10.3	10.1	10.1	10.1	10.1	10.1
EFTA members											
Austria	12.2	12.2	12.3	11.7	11.8	11.4	11.2	11.0	10.9	10.7	10.7
Finland	9.3	9.3	9.3	9.2	9.8	9.6	9.6	9.9	9.9	9.8	9.8
Iceland	6.5	6.7	7.0	6.6	7.1	6.8	6.9	7.3	7.7	8.1	8.1
Liechtenstein	6.2	6.7	5.8	5.7	5.8	6.1	6.4	6.4	6.4	7.1	7.1
Norway	9.9	10.1	10.2	10.3	10.6	9.8	10.7	10.8	10.7	10.8	10.5
Sweden	10.7	11.0	10.9	10.9	11.3	11.1	11.1	11.5	10.8	11.1	11.0
Switzerland	8.8	9.3	9.3	9.1	9.3	9.2	9.1	9.2	9.1	9.1	9.1
EFTA average	10.3	10.6	10.6	10.3	10.7	10.4	10.4	10.5	10.3	10.3	10.3
Eastern Europe											
Albania	6.6	6.4	6.1	5.8	5.8	5.6	5.5	5.5	5.7	5.7	5.7
Bulgaria	10.7	11.1	11.4	11.3	12.0	11.4	12.0	12.0	11.8	11.8	11.8
Czechoslovakia	11.5	12.2	12.1	11.9	11.8	11.8	11.5	11.4	11.6	11.7	11.7
Hungary	12.4	13.6	13.9	13.8	13.8	13.8	13.4	13.2	13.7	13.8	13.9
Poland	9.0	9.8	9.6	9.9	10.3	10.0	10.0	10.0	10.1	10.2	10.6
Romania	9.6	10.4	10.4	10.3	10.7	10.4	10.4	10.4	10.7	10.6	10.6
USSR	9.6	10.3	10.4	10.8	10.6	9.8	9.9	9.9	9.9	9.9	9.9
Yugoslavia	8.4	8.8	9.6	9.3	9.1	9.1	9.2	9.0	9.1	8.8	8.8
East European average	9.7	10.4	10.4	10.7	10.6	10.0	10.1	10.1	10.1	10.1	10.1
Others											
Cyprus	9.0	9.3	8.6	8.0	8.5	7.9	8.9			8.1	
Gibraltar	8.3	9.4	8.7	9.1	9.2	9.7	7.3	10.0	7.1	9.7	
Malta	8.7	8.8	8.3	7.6	7.4	7.3	8.4	7.8	7.4	7.9	
Monaco	10.6	21.1	16.6	16.6	16.3	16.1					
Turkey	2.9	2.9	2.8	2.8	2.8	2.6			7.7		
Average	3.1	3.1	2.9	2.9	2.9	2.7	8.7	8.0	7.7	8.1	
European average	9.7	10.0	10.0	10.1	10.1	9.7	10.1	10.1	9.9	10.1	10.1

Sources: UN/national statistical offices

Table No: 0208

VITAL STATISTICS

Infant Mortality Rate 1977-1991

Per '000 live births

	1977	1980	1983	1984	1985	1986	1987	1988	1989	1990	1991
EC members											
Belgium	13.6	12.1	11.2	10.7	9.4	9.7	9.7	9.7	9.7	7.9	
Denmark	8.7	8.4	7.7	7.7	7.9	8.2	8.3	7.6	8.4	7.5	
France	11.4	10.0	9.1	8.3	8.3	8.0	7.8	7.9	7.5	7.4	7.4
Germany: East	13.1	12.1	10.7	10.0	9.8	9.2	8.5	9.0	7.6	7.6	
Germany: West	15.5	12.6	10.3	9.6	8.9	8.7	8.3	8.3	8.3		
Greece	20.4	17.9	14.6	14.1	14.0	12.3	11.7	12.0	10.4	10.4	
Ireland	15.5	11.1	10.1	9.6	8.8	8.7	7.4	9.2	7.5	8.5	
Italy	18.1	14.6	12.3	11.4	10.5	9.8	9.6	9.6	8.6	8.2	8.2
Luxembourg	10.6	11.5	11.2	11.7	9.0	7.9	9.4	9.5	9.5	7.3	
Netherlands	9.5	8.6	8.4	8.3	8.0	7.7	7.6	7.5	6.8	6.8	
Portugal	30.3	24.3	19.3	16.7	17.8	15.8	14.2	13.6	13.6	13.1	
Spain	16.0	12.3	10.9	9.9	8.5	8.8	8.5	8.1	8.2	7.8	
United Kingdom	14.1	12.1	10.5	9.6	9.3	9.5	9.1	9.0	8.6	8.4	
EC average	15.1	12.6	10.9	10.0	9.5	9.2	8.9	8.9	8.4	8.0	7.8
EFTA members											
Austria	16.8	14.3	11.9	11.4	11.0	10.3	9.8	8.1	8.3	7.9	
Finland	9.1	7.6	6.2	6.5	6.3	5.8	6.3	6.0	5.8	5.8	
Iceland				6.1			3.4	6.2	6.0	6.0	
Liechtenstein											
Norway	9.2	8.1	7.9	8.3	8.5	7.8	8.0	8.4	8.2	7.8	
Sweden	8.0	6.9	7.0	6.4	6.7	5.9	5.7	5.8	6.0	5.6	
Switzerland	9.8	9.1	7.5	7.1	6.9	6.9	6.8	6.8	6.8	6.8	
EFTA average	10.9	9.5	8.4	8.0	8.0	7.5	7.3	6.9	7.0	6.7	
Eastern Europe											
Albania[a]	27.9	50.0	26.0	27.3	44.8	25.6	25.4	25.2	25.0		
Bulgaria	24.0	20.2	16.5	16.1	15.8	14.5	15.0	13.6	14.4	14.4	
Czechoslovakia	19.7	18.4	15.7	15.3	14.0	13.5	13.1	13.2	11.3	11.3	
Hungary	26.2	23.2	19.0	20.4	20.4	18.9	17.4	15.8	16.0	15.9	15.0
Poland	24.6	21.3	19.2	19.2	18.5	17.5	17.5	17.5	16.0	16.0	15.9
Romania	31.2	29.3	23.4	23.4	25.6	25.8	25.9	25.9	26.9	26.9	
USSR[a]		28.0			25.1	25.1	25.1	25.1	25.0	19.6	
Yugoslavia	35.6	31.4	31.6	28.9	28.8	27.3	25.1	24.5	23.7	20.2	
East European average	21.0	27.1	20.4	20.1	24.1	23.1	23.0	22.9	24.4	19.2	15.7
Others											
Cyprus[a]	18.5	12.0	22.6	20.7	16.5	11.5	11.0	11.0	11.0	10.5	
Gibraltar	16.9	18.3	17.6	17.4	17.8	17.5	17.9	16.7	17.7		
Malta	13.8	15.2	14.9	11.7	13.6	10.1	7.9	8.0	8.0	11.3	
Monaco	7.5	20.6	19.6	19.6	19.8	19.9					
Turkey	15.6	14.6	13.6	13.2	13.0	12.5					
Average	15.6	14.6	13.7	13.3	13.1	11.2	10.2	10.2	10.2	10.8	
European average	17.8	19.6	15.6	15.1	16.8	16.7	16.5	16.4	16.0	13.8	

Sources: UN/national statistical offices
Note: See end of section

Table No: 0209

VITAL STATISTICS

Marriage Rate 1977-1990

Per '000 inhabitants

	1977	1980	1983	1984	1985	1986	1987	1988	1989	1990
EC members										
Belgium	7.0	6.7	6.1	6.0	5.8	5.8	5.7	6.0	6.4	6.6
Denmark	6.3	5.2	5.3	5.6	5.8	6.0	6.1	6.3	6.0	6.1
France	6.9	6.2	5.5	5.1	4.9	4.8	4.7	4.9	5.0	5.1
Germany: East	8.8	8.0	7.5	8.0	7.9	8.0	8.2	8.3	7.9	6.5
Germany: West	5.8	5.9	6.0	6.0	6.0	6.1	6.3	6.5	6.4	6.6
Greece	8.2	6.5	7.2	5.5	6.4	5.8	6.6	5.2	6.0	
Ireland	6.1	6.4	5.5	5.2	5.3	5.2	5.1	5.1	5.1	5.0
Italy	6.2	5.7	5.3	5.2	5.2	5.2	5.3	5.5	5.4	5.4
Luxembourg	6.1	5.9	5.4	5.4	5.3	5.1	5.3	5.5	5.8	6.2
Netherlands	6.7	6.4	5.5	5.7	5.7	6.0	6.0	6.0	6.1	6.4
Portugal	9.4	7.4	7.5	6.9	6.7	6.8	6.6	6.9	7.0	
Spain	7.0	5.7	5.1	5.2	5.0	5.3	5.3	5.3	5.6	
United Kingdom	7.2	7.4	6.9	7.0	6.9	6.9	7.0	6.9	6.8	
EC average	6.8	6.3	6.0	5.9	5.8	5.9	5.9	6.0	6.0	5.9
EFTA members										
Austria	6.0	6.1	7.4	6.1	5.9	6.0	5.0	4.7	5.8	5.6
Finland	6.5	6.1	6.0	5.8	5.8	5.3	5.3	5.3	5.1	4.8
Iceland	7.1	5.7	5.9	5.9	5.4					4.5
Liechtenstein	12.2	13.7	13.7	14.0	14.0				11.3	
Norway	5.9	5.4	5.0	5.0	5.0	5.2	5.2	5.2	4.9	
Sweden	4.9	4.5	4.3	4.4	4.5	4.6	5.0	5.2	5.0	4.7
Switzerland	5.2	5.6	5.9	6.0	6.0	6.2	6.5	6.8	6.8	6.9
EFTA average	5.6	5.5	5.7	5.4	5.4	5.5	5.4	5.4	5.6	5.5
Eastern Europe										
Albania	8.0	8.1	9.0	9.1	8.5				8.6	
Bulgaria	8.5	7.9	7.5	7.3	7.2			6.7	7.0	
Czechoslovakia	9.1	7.7	7.8	7.8	7.7	7.6	7.6	7.6	7.5	8.4
Hungary	9.1	7.5	7.1	7.0	6.9	6.5	6.2	6.2	6.3	6.4
Poland	9.4	8.6	8.4	7.7	7.2	7.0	6.5	6.8	6.8	6.7
Romania	9.2	8.2	7.3	7.3	7.1	7.2	7.3	7.5	7.7	8.3
USSR	10.7	10.3	10.4	9.6	9.7					
Yugoslavia	8.2	7.7	7.5	7.3	7.0	6.9	7.0	6.8	6.7	6.3
East European average	10.2	9.6	9.6	9.0	8.9	7.1	6.9	7.0	7.1	7.2
Others										
Cyprus	9.7	8.1	11.2	8.0	10.2	10.3				9.3
Gibraltar	15.3	14.4	14.8	13.9	14.0	14.0	14.1	14.0		
Malta	20.3	17.4	16.3	15.2	14.2	14.0	14.2	14.7		7.4
Monaco	7.0	6.5	7.3	7.3	7.3					
Turkey	3.4	3.7	3.7	3.8	3.8				7.9	
Average	3.6	3.9	3.9	3.9	4.0	11.7	14.2	14.6	7.9	8.7
European average	8.2	7.7	7.6	7.2	7.2	6.1	6.1	6.2	6.4	6.2

Sources: UN/national statistical offices
Note: See end of section

Table No: 0210

VITAL STATISTICS

Divorce Rate 1977-1990

Per '000 inhabitants

	1977	1980	1982	1983	1984	1985	1986	1987	1988	1989	1990
EC members											
Belgium	1.3	1.5	1.6	1.8	1.9	1.9	1.9	1.9	2.0		
Denmark	2.6	2.7	2.9	2.9	2.8	2.8	2.8	2.8	3.0	3.1	2.8
France	1.4	1.5	1.7	1.8	1.9	2.0	2.0	2.2	1.9		
Germany: East	2.6	2.7	3.0	3.0	3.0	3.1				3.3	
Germany: West	1.2	1.6	1.9	2.0	2.1	2.0	2.0	2.1	2.1		
Greece	0.5	0.7	0.6	0.6	0.9	0.8	0.8	0.9			
Ireland											
Italy	0.2	0.2	0.3	0.2	0.3	0.3	0.3	0.5	0.4		
Luxembourg	1.2	1.6	1.7	1.6	1.7	1.8	1.9	2.0	2.1	2.3	
Netherlands	1.6	1.8	2.2	2.3	2.4	2.3	2.4	2.4	2.4	2.2	1.9
Portugal		0.6	0.6	0.8	0.7	0.8	0.8	0.8	0.9		
Spain			0.6	0.5	0.5	0.2	0.2	0.2			
United Kingdom	2.5	2.8	2.8	2.9	2.8	3.1	3.0	3.1	3.1	2.9	
EC average	1.4	1.6	1.6	1.6	1.7	1.7	1.6	1.7	1.9	2.9	2.1
EFTA members											
Austria	1.6	1.8	1.9	1.9	2.0	2.0	2.0	2.0	2.0	2.0	
Finland	2.1	2.0	2.0	2.0	2.0	2.0				2.9	
Iceland	1.8	1.9	1.8	2.1	1.9	2.2					1.8
Liechtenstein										1.0	
Norway	1.5	1.6	1.7	1.9	1.9	1.9				2.2	
Sweden	2.5	2.4	2.5	2.5	2.4	2.3	2.2	2.2	2.1	2.2	2.2
Switzerland	1.7	1.7	1.8	1.8	1.7	1.8					1.9
EFTA average	1.9	1.9	2.0	2.1	2.0	2.0	2.1	2.1	2.1	2.3	2.1
Eastern Europe											
Albania		0.8	0.8	0.8	0.8	0.8				0.8	
Bulgaria	1.5	1.5	1.5	1.6	1.5	1.7					
Czechoslovakia	2.1	2.2	2.2	2.4	2.4	2.5					2.6
Hungary	2.6	2.6	2.7	2.7	2.7	2.7				2.4	
Poland	1.2	1.1	1.3	1.3	1.4	1.3				1.1	1.1
Romania	1.2	1.5	1.5	1.5	1.5						1.4
USSR	3.5	3.5	3.3	3.5	3.4						
Yugoslavia	1.1	1.0	1.0	0.9	0.9	0.9	1.0	1.0	1.0	1.0	0.8
East European average	2.9	2.9	2.8	2.9	2.8	1.6	1.0	1.0	1.0	1.2	1.3
Others											
Cyprus	0.2	0.3	0.3	0.4	0.4	0.5	0.5	0.5	0.6	0.5	0.5
Gibraltar											
Malta											
Monaco		1.9		1.4							
Turkey	0.3	0.4	0.4	0.4						0.4	
Average	0.3	0.4	0.4	0.4	0.4	0.5	0.5	0.5	0.6	0.4	0.5
European average	2.1	2.2	2.1	2.2	2.3	1.7	1.6	1.7	1.8	1.8	1.5

Sources: UN/national statistical offices
Note: See end of section

Table No: 0211

VITAL STATISTICS

Fertility Rate 1977-1989

Children born per female

	1977	1980	1982	1983	1984	1985	1986	1987	1988	1989
EC members										
Belgium	1.8	1.8	1.6	1.6	1.6	1.6	1.5	1.6	1.6	1.6
Denmark	1.7	1.8	1.9	1.4	1.4	1.4	1.5	1.5	1.6	1.6
France	1.9	1.9	1.9	1.8	1.8	1.8	1.8	1.8	1.8	1.8
Germany: East	1.8	1.8	1.9	1.9	1.8	1.8	1.7	1.6	1.6	1.6
Germany: West	1.4	1.5	1.4	1.4	1.4	1.3	1.3	1.4	1.4	1.4
Greece	2.3	2.3	2.3	2.1	2.1	2.0	1.6	1.7	1.5	1.6
Ireland	3.3	3.2	3.0	2.8	2.6	2.5	2.4	2.3	2.2	2.1
Italy	2.1	1.7	1.6	1.5	1.5	1.4	1.5	1.3	1.3	1.4
Luxembourg	1.5	1.5	1.5	1.4	1.4	1.4	1.4	1.4	1.5	1.6
Netherlands	1.6	1.6	1.4	1.5	1.5	1.5	1.6	1.6	1.6	1.6
Portugal	2.5	2.2	2.1	2.0	1.9	1.7	1.6	1.6	1.5	1.5
Spain	2.6	2.2	1.9	1.8	1.7	2.0	1.7	1.5	1.4	1.6
United Kingdom	1.7	1.8	1.8	1.8	1.8	1.8	1.8	1.8	1.8	1.9
EC average	1.9	1.8	1.7	1.7	1.7	1.7	1.6	1.6	1.6	1.6
EFTA members										
Austria	1.6	1.7	1.6	1.6	1.6	1.7	1.5	1.5	1.5	1.5
Finland	1.7	1.7	1.6	1.8	1.7	1.7	1.7	1.6	1.6	1.7
Iceland		2.4	2.2	2.1	2.0	1.9	1.9	2.1	2.3	2.5
Liechtenstein										
Norway	1.8	1.9	1.7	1.7	1.7	1.7	1.7	1.7	1.8	1.8
Sweden	1.7	1.7	1.7	1.7	1.6	1.7	1.8	1.8	2.0	2.0
Switzerland	1.5	1.6	1.9	1.9	1.5	1.5	1.5	1.6	1.5	1.7
EFTA average	1.6	1.7	1.7	1.7	1.6	1.7	1.6	1.6	1.7	1.7
Eastern Europe										
Albania	4.2	3.9	3.6	3.6	3.4	3.4	3.3	3.3	3.3	3.3
Bulgaria	2.2	2.2	2.1	2.0	2.0	2.0	2.0	2.0	2.0	1.9
Czechoslovakia	2.4	2.3	2.2	2.1	2.0	2.1	2.1	2.0	2.0	2.0
Hungary	2.2	2.1	2.0	1.8	1.7	1.7	1.8	1.8	1.8	1.8
Poland	2.3	2.3	2.3	2.4	2.3	2.3	2.3	2.2	2.1	2.1
Romania	2.6	2.5	2.4	2.4	2.2	2.1	2.1	2.1	2.1	2.1
USSR	2.4	2.3	2.4	2.4	2.3	2.3	2.4	2.3	2.2	2.1
Yugoslavia	2.2	2.2	2.0	2.1	2.1	2.1	2.0	2.0	2.0	2.0
E European average	2.4	2.3	2.4	2.4	2.3	2.3	2.3	2.2	2.2	2.1
Others										
Cyprus		2.5	2.5	2.5	2.5	2.4	2.4	2.3	2.3	2.3
Gibraltar										
Malta										
Monaco										
Turkey	4.3	4.4	4.1	4.1	3.9	3.9	3.7	3.8	3.8	3.6
Average	4.3	4.4	4.1	4.1	3.9	3.9	3.7	3.8	3.8	3.8
European average	2.3	2.2	2.2	2.2	2.1	2.1	2.1	2.0	2.0	2.0

Source: World Bank
Note: See end of section

Table No: 0212

VITAL STATISTICS

Life Expectancy: Latest Period Available

Years

	Period	Male	Female
EC members			
Belgium	1986	70.9	77.7
Denmark	1988	72.1	77.7
France	1988	72.3	80.5
Germany: East	1987	71.9	78.3
Germany: West	1986-88	72.1	78.7
Greece	1986	74.1	78.9
Ireland	1985-87	71.0	76.7
Italy	1987	72.9	79.4
Luxembourg	1987	70.6	77.9
Netherlands	1988-89	73.7	80.2
Portugal	1988	70.7	77.6
Spain	1985	72.5	78.8
United Kingdom	1989	72.3	77.9
EC average		72.4	78.9
EFTA members			
Austria	1989	72.1	78.8
Finland	1987	70.7	78.7
Iceland	1989	75.2	79.9
Liechtenstein			
Norway	1989	73.3	79.9
Sweden	1989	74.0	78.0
Switzerland	1988	74.2	80.0
EFTA average		73.0	79.0
Eastern Europe			
Albania			
Bulgaria	1988-89	69.6	75.5
Czechoslovakia	1989	68.6	74.7
Hungary	1988	67.8	75.3
Poland	1989	66.2	74.0
Romania	1988	67.1	75.7
USSR	1987-89	67.1	72.7
Yugoslavia	1988	64.8	73.6
East European average		67.0	73.3
Others			
Cyprus	1980-85	72.5	77.5
Gibraltar	1980-81	71.4	75.5
Monaco			
Malta	1988	72.8	77.6
Turkey	1980-85	60.0	63.3
Yugoslavia	1988	67.7	73.2
Average		62.6	65.9
European average		69.3	75.5

Sources: UN/World Bank

Table No: 0213

VITAL STATISTICS

Population Density 1977-1992

Persons per square kilometre

	1977	1980	1983	1984	1985	1986	1987	1988	1989	1990	1991	1992
EC members												
Belgium	322.2	323.2	323.3	323.2	323.3	323.6	323.9	324.1	325.6	327.3	329.1	329.6
Denmark	118.5	119.5	119.3	119.2	119.2	119.3	119.5	119.6	119.7	119.8	120.1	120.4
France	97.6	98.9	100.6	100.9	101.4	101.8	102.2	103.0	103.5	104.1	104.7	105.3
Germany: East	154.9	154.7	154.3	154.4	154.0	153.9	153.7	153.8	153.8	149.7	146.9	144.1
Germany: West	246.6	246.6	247.0	246.1	245.0	244.9	245.8	247.7	248.8	250.0	251.1	254.9
Greece	70.9	73.5	75.0	75.4	75.6	75.8	76.0	76.2	76.6	77.0	77.3	77.7
Ireland	47.2	49.2	50.7	51.1	51.2	51.2	51.3	51.2	51.1	50.9	50.8	50.6
Italy	186.3	189.2	190.3	189.0	189.5	189.9	190.2	190.5	190.9	191.1	191.7	192.0
Luxembourg	140.0	141.2	141.9	141.9	141.9	142.3	143.5	144.3	145.4	145.4	145.4	147.4
Netherlands	341.2	348.0	354.2	355.5	357.0	358.9	361.0	363.5	365.8	368.0	370.9	373.9
Portugal	106.4	109.9	112.8	113.7	114.6	115.2	115.8	116.6	116.7	117.1	117.6	118.8
Spain	72.9	75.1	76.8	77.2	77.6	77.7	78.1	78.2	78.3	78.5	78.5	78.6
United Kingdom	230.1	230.7	230.7	231.2	231.9	232.4	232.8	233.5	234.3	234.6	235.1	236.3
EC average	179.3	180.3	180.0	180.6	180.7	181.0	181.5	182.3	183.0	183.5	184.1	185.5
EFTA members												
Austria	90.2	90.0	90.0	90.0	90.1	90.2	90.3	90.6	90.9	91.3	91.7	93.0
Finland	14.1	14.2	14.4	14.5	14.6	14.6	14.7	14.8	14.8	14.8	14.9	15.0
Iceland	2.2	2.3	2.3	2.4	2.4	2.4	2.4	2.5	2.5	2.5	2.5	2.6
Liechtenstein	159.2	172.5	172.5	179.1	179.1	179.1	185.7	192.4	199.0	199.0	199.0	199.0
Norway	12.5	12.6	12.8	12.8	12.8	12.9	12.9	13.0	13.1	13.1	13.2	13.2
Sweden	18.4	18.5	18.6	18.6	18.6	18.7	18.7	18.8	18.9	19.1	19.2	19.3
Switzerland	153.4	153.8	156.1	156.6	157.2	158.0	158.9	160.0	161.2	162.2	163.2	164.2
EFTA average	61.8	61.7	62.3	62.4	62.6	62.8	63.1	63.4	63.9	64.3	64.6	65.2
Eastern Europe												
Albania	89.2	95.0	101.0	103.2	105.3	107.5	109.7	111.3	113.0	113.8	114.6	117.4
Bulgaria	79.5	80.0	80.7	80.9	80.9	80.8	80.9	80.8	81.2	81.2	81.3	81.3
Czechoslovakia	118.4	120.6	121.4	121.8	122.1	122.4	122.7	122.9	123.1	123.3	123.5	123.7
Hungary	114.7	115.7	115.6	115.4	115.2	115.0	114.6	114.6	114.6	114.6	114.4	111.6
Poland	112.0	114.9	118.1	119.2	120.2	121.1	122.2	122.8	122.9	123.4	123.9	124.3
Romania	92.0	94.3	95.8	96.1	96.5	97.1	97.4	97.9	98.3	98.8	99.2	99.0
USSR	11.7	12.0	12.3	12.4	12.5	12.7	12.8	12.8	12.8	12.8	12.9	12.9
Yugoslavia	85.9	88.0	89.9	90.6	91.2	91.8	92.5	92.9	93.4	93.9	94.4	94.5
E European average	39.3	40.1	40.7	40.9	41.1	41.3	41.5	41.7	41.8	42.0	42.1	42.1
Others												
Cyprus	66.6	67.7	70.1	70.9	71.9	72.7	73.9	76.1	78.2	79.3	80.4	81.5
Gibraltar	5000.0	5000.0	4833.3	4833.3	4666.7	4833.3	5000.0	5000.0	5000.0	5000.0	5000.0	5166.7
Malta	1075.9	1117.4	1148.5	1169.3	1176.2	1186.6	1197.0	1207.4	1217.7	1221.2	1228.1	1231.6
Monaco	16778.5	17449.6	18120.8	18120.8	18120.8	18120.8	18120.8	18791.9	18791.9	18791.9	18791.9	19463.1
Turkey	54.6	58.1	62.6	64.1	66.2	68.2	69.6	70.8	72.0	73.2	74.5	75.2
Average	75.5	79.0	82.8	84.2	85.5	87.2	88.5	90.2	91.2	92.2	93.1	94.5
European average	101.6	102.2	102.5	102.3	102.3	102.4	102.6	103.2	103.7	104.0	104.4	105.2

Source: Euromonitor

Table No: 0214

URBANISATION

Urban Population 1990, City Population 1985, Growth Rates 1975-1980, 1980-1985

	Urban population '000	% of total population	% in largest city	% in cities over 500,000	No. of cities over 500,000	Average annual growth rates 1975-80	1980-85
EC members							
Belgium	9543	95.6	10.0		3	0.3	0.3
Denmark	4473	87.1	27.8	27.8	1	0.8	0.4
France	41689	73.7	21.6	29.6	6	0.4	0.4
Germany: East[a]	12549	77.5	9.3	17.6	3	0.1	0.2
Germany: West[a]	53606	86.1	4.2	17.1	12	0.2	0.1
Greece	6276	62.1	45.1	55.6	2	2.1	1.3
Ireland	2123	60.3	49.1	49.1	1	1.8	1.8
Italy	39336	68.3	18.7	48.0	6	0.7	0.4
Luxembourg	314	83.7	27.1			1.1	0.8
Netherlands	13239	88.9	7.1	24.3	4	0.5	0.5
Portugal	3455	33.4	60.5	60.5	1	2.1	1.8
Spain	30724	78.9	11.0	23.5	6	1.9	1.4
United Kingdom	50980	88.9	20.2	36.4	5	0.2	0.3
EC total/average	268307	78.3	17.1	32.0		0.7	0.5
EFTA members							
Austria	4426	57.8	39.4	39.4	1	0.5	0.5
Finland	2971	59.7	34.3	34.3	1	1.9	1.9
Iceland	229	90.2	59.8			1.2	1.5
Liechtenstein	6	20.0	71.4			2.4	2.8
Norway	3157	74.5	21.3	21.3	1	1.1	0.9
Sweden	7092	83.2	22.1	30.5	2	0.4	0.2
Switzerland	3958	59.4	19.2	19.2	1	0.2	0.6
EFTA total/average	21839	67.5	27.8	29.7		0.7	0.7
Eastern Europe							
Albania	1143	35.7	26.0			2.8	2.6
Bulgaria	6103	67.9	23.9	23.9	1	2.0	1.7
Czechoslovakia[a]	12135	77.5	11.3	11.3	1	1.7	1.3
Hungary[a]	6464	60.9	34.2	34.2	1	1.7	1.0
Poland[a]	23746	62.4	7.3	19.6	5	1.9	1.9
Romania	12255	52.7	19.7	19.7	1	1.7	1.1
USSR[a]	189895	66.8	4.9	32.8	54		
Yugoslavia	13352	56.1	10.2	16.7	2	2.8	2.5
E European total/average	265093	65.0	8.0	28.8		2.0	1.7
Others							
Cyprus	370	50.7	57.4			2.0	2.5
Gibraltar	30	100.0	100.0			1.4	1.3
Malta	308	87.3	4.7			1.9	1.3
Monaco	28	100.0	100.0			0.8	0.8
Turkey	34274	61.2	9.0	31.3	5	2.8	2.2
Total/average	35010	61.2	9.8				
European total/average	590249	70.2	12.7			1.2	0.9

Sources: UN Prospects of World Urbanisation/UN Demographic Yearbook/national statistical offices
Note: See end of section

Table No: 0215

DEMOGRAPHIC ANALYSIS

Number of Males 1977-1992: National Estimates at January 1st

'000

	1977	1980	1983	1984	1985	1986	1987	1988	1989	1990	1991	1992
EC members												
Belgium	4809	4810	4813	4810	4812	4812	4816	4840	4850	4860	4885	4914
Denmark	2513	2529	2521	2518	2517	2521	2526	2528	2528	2531	2536	2553
France	25950	26247	26662	26751	26852	26948	27053	27162	27290	27417	27542	28097
Germany: East	7813	7847	7868	7867	7870	7881	7913	7952	8143	7924	7777	7662
Germany: West	29263	29317	29428	29306	29180	29190	29285	29419	29574	29729	23196	30441
Greece	4517	4703	4829	4854	4879	4894	4909	4920	4930	4939	4962	5007
Ireland	1640	1705	1755	1776	1771	1768	1770	1768	1755	1743	1738	1739
Italy	27538	27840	27589	27679	27740	27792	27833	27890	27938	27973	28000	27987
Luxembourg	179	178	178	178	178	179	180	181	183	185	185	188
Netherlands	6875	6994	7103	7124	7150	7185	7224	7275	7317	7358	7415	7507
Portugal	4592	4687	4804	4846	4887	4916	4940	4960	4978	4997	5017	5091
Spain	17711	18273	18689	18798	18908	18934	19037	19123	19069	19105	19114	19221
United Kingdom	27269	27412	27428	27476	27537	27615	27692	27750	27813	27853	27911	28165
EC total	160669	162542	163667	163983	164281	164635	165178	165768	166367	166613	160280	168574
EFTA members												
Austria	3548	3551	3577	3578	3582	3589	3601	3610	3633	3658	3676	3741
Finland	2286	2307	2343	2357	2369	2378	2389	2400	2401	2403	2407	2446
Iceland	112	114	119	120	121	122	124	125	127	127	128	131
Liechtenstein												
Norway	2003	2022	2040	2046	2050	2056	2060	2065	2088	2096	2104	2121
Sweden	4093	4116	4117	4116	4121	4127	4145	4155	4190	4212	4245	4287
Switzerland	3069	3073	3121	3130	3145	3160	3202	3230	3229	3228	3247	3280
EFTA total	15111	15183	15317	15347	15388	15432	15521	15585	15668	15724	15807	16007
Eastern Europe												
Albania		1379	1466	1496	1526	1550	1575	1600	1629	1641	1652	1699
Bulgaria	4385	4409	4443	4450	4456	4448	4440	4475	4506	4509	4512	4530
Czechoslovakia	7296	7446	7496	7517	7537	7566	7586	7650	7639	7652	7665	7707
Hungary	5162	5189	5177	5164	5149	5138	5188	5116	5222	5226	5215	5110
Poland	16805	17254	17741	17914	18073	18211	18370	18450	18524	18603	18673	18818
Romania	10677	10953	11129	11165	11214	11261	11340	11395	11343	11391	11439	11463
USSR	120548	123953	127626	128958	130273	131721	133283	135010	135606	135797	135988	136726
Yugoslavia						11438						
E European total	164873	170583	175078	176664	178228	191333	181782	183696	184469	184819	185145	186054
Others												
Cyprus	306	309	321	325	329	333	339	343	354	359	364	370
Gibraltar	16	15	15	15	14	15	15	15	15	15	15	16
Malta	147	154	158	160	161	168	169	170	172	174	175	176
Monaco												
Turkey												
Total	469	478	494	500	504	516	523	528	541	548	554	562
European total	341122	348786	354556	356494	358401	371916	363004	365577	367045	367704	361785	371197

Sources: National statistical offices: all countries
Note: See end of section

Table No: 0216

DEMOGRAPHIC ANALYSIS

Number of Females 1977-1992: National Estimates at January 1st

'000

	1977	1980	1983	1984	1985	1986	1987	1988	1989	1990	1991	1992
EC members												
Belgium	5014	5045	5045	5043	5045	5053	5060	5041	5078	5120	5137	5136
Denmark	2567	2593	2595	2594	2594	2595	2599	2602	2602	2604	2605	2607
France	27069	27484	27964	28080	28210	28330	28457	28588	28727	28886	28987	29088
Germany: East	8954	8893	8831	8842	8801	8774	8728	8698	8505	8276	8106	7938
Germany: West	32179	32122	32118	32001	31869	31830	31953	32296	32426	32556	32640	33059
Greece	4791	4940	5018	5042	5040	5056	5069	5084	5128	5166	5179	5193
Ireland	1622	1696	1749	1753	1769	1769	1772	1771	1775	1778	1770	1761
Italy	28585	29160	29297	29254	29340	29410	29458	29509	29566	29603	29744	29848
Luxembourg	182	186	188	188	188	188	190	191	192	190	190	192
Netherlands	6939	7097	7237	7270	7304	7345	7391	7440	7493	7541	7584	7631
Portugal	4811	5027	5165	5204	5242	5269	5290	5344	5332	5353	5363	5409
Spain	18444	18969	19378	19482	19587	19615	19713	19643	19783	19819	19790	19779
United Kingdom	28921	28918	28919	28984	29081	29148	29155	29267	29405	29447	29450	29535
EC total	170078	172130	173504	173737	174070	174382	174835	175473	176013	176340	176545	177174
EFTA members												
Austria	4020	3998	3975	3975	3976	3977	3975	3988	3991	4002	4013	4059
Finland	2445	2464	2499	2513	2525	2533	2543	2550	2553	2560	2567	2574
Iceland	109	113	117	118	120	120	122	124	127	127	127	129
Liechtenstein												
Norway	2032	2057	2083	2088	2096	2103	2115	2140	2133	2141	2145	2153
Sweden	4143	4187	4210	4215	4222	4231	4236	4259	4269	4315	4339	4357
Switzerland	3229	3241	3289	3298	3311	3325	3321	3337	3391	3432	3446	3460
EFTA total	15978	16060	16173	16207	16250	16289	16312	16398	16463	16577	16637	16731
Eastern Europe												
Albania		1292	1375	1405	1436	1472	1508	1530	1548	1559	1567	1601
Bulgaria	4419	4453	4497	4511	4504	4502	4520	4475	4481	4484	4479	4470
Czechoslovakia	7734	7865	7918	7941	7963	7968	7987	7950	7988	8002	8000	7993
Hungary	5453	5521	5523	5515	5508	5502	5419	5488	5380	5384	5362	5222
Poland	17723	18160	18658	18831	18990	19130	19293	19400	19365	19447	19482	19512
Romania	10983	11248	11424	11460	11511	11599	11600	11659	11809	11859	11885	11837
USSR	138481	141589	144914	146108	147264	148423	149817	148490	148294	148503	148414	148274
Yugoslavia							11832					
E European total	184793	190128	194309	195771	197176	198596	211976	198992	198864	199238	199188	198908
Others												
Cyprus	307	314	324	328	333	336	341	357	366	371	376	380
Gibraltar	14	15	14	14	14	14	15	15	15	15	15	15
Malta	164	169	174	178	179	175	177	179	180	179	180	180
Monaco												
Turkey												
Total	485	498	512	520	526	525	533	551	561	565	570	575
European total	371334	378816	384498	386235	388022	389792	403656	391413	391902	392720	392940	393388

Sources: National statistical offices: all countries
Note: See end of section

Table No: 0217

DEMOGRAPHIC ANALYSIS

Number of Children Aged 0-14 Years 1977-1992: National Estimates at January 1st

'000

	1977	1980	1983	1984	1985	1986	1987	1988	1989	1990	1991	1992
EC members												
Belgium	2118	1971	1917	1897	1874	1844	1874	1803	1805	1777	1786	1789
Denmark	1133	1081	992	969	951	935	901	895	890	881	883	885
France	12388	12002	11924	11832	11744	11652	11539	11425	11339	11456	11519	11583
Germany: East		3102	3133	3127	3114	3100	3209	3228	3240	3153	3095	3036
Germany: West	12664	11363	10177	9738	9341	9126	9045	8941	9129	9170	9212	9349
Greece	2181	2213	2142	2120	2094	2071	2027	1983	1967	1985	1994	2004
Ireland	1004	1034	1054	1050	1046	1041	1025	1009	977	976	973	970
Italy	13223	12699	11778	11497	11178	10877	10548	10219	9924	9990	10020	10035
Luxembourg	70	69	66	64	63	63	63	62	64	65	65	66
Netherlands	3380	3184	3003	2930	2850	2788	2753	2719	2710	2739	2760	2783
Portugal	2710	2601	2458	2435	2410	2369	2323	2269	2217	2237	2245	2269
Spain	9738	9693	9393	9246	9100	8781	8650	8486	8045	8100	8104	8116
United Kingdom	12709	11801	11284	11102	11012	10815	10773	10761	10760	10848	10870	10923
EC total	73318	72813	69321	68007	66777	65462	64729	63798	63065	63377	63527	63809
EFTA members												
Austria	1673	1540	1439	1405	1378	1358	1339	1320	1325	1334	1340	1358
Finland	1017	976	952	950	952	952	952	956	960	966	971	975
Iceland	65	63	63	63	63	63	63	63	63	63	64	65
Liechtenstein												
Norway	945	912	871	854	837	824	808	805	801	814	817	822
Sweden	1695	1641	1556	1534	1521	1512	1502	1505	1508	1522	1533	1543
Switzerland	1358	1248	1188	1166	1149	1134	1046	1122	1128	1141	1148	1154
EFTA total	6753	6380	6069	5972	5900	5843	5710	5771	5786	5840	5873	5917
Eastern Europe												
Albania		1047										
Bulgaria	1955	1960	1972	1960	1946	1865	1905	1905	1916	1917	1919	1919
Czechoslovakia	3561	3703	3757	3774	3781	3773	3766	3751	3779	3786	3792	3797
Hungary		2475	2460	2450	2460	2330	2290	2233	2234	2236	2231	2177
Poland	8237	8550	9047	9243	9400	9558	9657	9642	9700	9741	9779	9813
Romania	5560	5922	5814	5664	5603	5400	5300	5200	5284	5306	5328	5317
USSR		64650			68948	69500	71631	70500	70952	71052	71152	71227
Yugoslavia							5490	5546	5603	5633	5662	5665
E European total	19313	88307	23050	23091	92138	92426	100038	98893	99469	99671	99863	99915
Others												
Cyprus	153	155	162	166	168	171	173	177	182	185	188	190
Gibraltar												
Malta							83	84	85	85	86	86
Monaco												
Turkey					19010				20001	20337	20673	20871
Total	153	155	162	166	19178	171	256	260	20268	20607	20946	21147
European total	99537	167655	98602	97236	183993	163902	170733	168722	188588	189495	190209	190788

Sources: National statistical offices/Statistical Office of the European Community/UN
Note: See end of section

Table No: 0218

DEMOGRAPHIC ANALYSIS

Number of Persons of Working Age (15-64 Years) 1977-1992: National Estimates at January 1st

'000

	1977	1980	1983	1984	1985	1986	1987	1988	1989	1990	1991	1992
EC members												
Belgium	6328	6457	6564	6609	6637	6636	6646	6655	6676	6680	6715	6727
Denmark	3251	3306	3370	3381	3394	3404	3440	3442	3445	3473	3481	3490
France	33362	34050	35505	35901	36262	36394	36577	36761	37094	37096	37300	37506
Germany: East			10688	10758	10776	10799	11220	11640	11670			
Germany: West	39646	40513	42196	42588	42727	42768	42891	43015	43191	43300	43498	44145
Greece	5890	6116	6375	6443	6503	6531	6600	6668	6691	6676	6707	6739
Ireland	1905	1995	2072	2100	2114	2147	2132	2135	2141	2145	2140	2132
Italy	35835	36690	38168	38159	38631	38854	39293	39396	39480	39349	39465	39526
Luxembourg	244	246	250	254	255	257	259	260	257	254	254	257
Netherlands	8920	9292	9649	9756	9874	9972	10064	10156	10226	10238	10318	10402
Portugal	6032	6264	6344	6434	6518	6582	6643	6706	6776	6767	6793	6865
Spain	22616	23520	24261	24536	24810	25111	25345	25561	26135	26114	26127	26165
United Kingdom	35263	36043	36648	36934	37134	37268	37325	37422	37534	37436	37514	37697
EC total	199292	204492	222090	223853	225635	226723	228434	229818	231314	219955	220508	221581
EFTA members												
Austria	4697	4804	5027	5069	5097	5108	5123	5138	5138	5152	5176	5245
Finland	3190	3227	3294	3316	3336	3341	3346	3345	3344	3342	3358	3372
Iceland	136	142	149	151	153	154	157	160	162	162	162	165
Liechtenstein												
Norway	2526	2568	2623	2641	2663	2675	2705	2720	2734	2767	2777	2793
Sweden	5267	5317	5376	5387	5397	5392	5411	5429	5446	5471	5512	5546
Switzerland	4118	4194	4331	4367	4404	4438	4465	4493	4456	4459	4486	4512
EFTA total	19934	20252	20800	20931	21050	21108	21207	21283	21280	21351	21471	21634
Eastern Europe												
Albania		1509										
Bulgaria	5866	5862	5954	6004	6003	6068	5981	5984	5965	5970	5974	5974
Czechoslovakia	9623	9680	9884	9969	10016	10023	10043	10063	10037	10054	10072	10084
Hungary		6452	6394	6382	6380	6368	7002	7002	6955	6960	6945	6778
Poland	22898	23254	23826	24018	24100	24258	24400	24542	24456	24560	24653	24740
Romania	13932	13998	14583	14721	14969	15000	15050	15100	15635	15701	15767	15735
USSR		174233			182714	184800	186900	189000	185423	185684	185945	186141
Yugoslavia							17921	17989	18055	18150	18244	18253
E European total	52319	234988	60641	61094	244182	246517	267297	269680	266537	267092	267616	267774
Others												
Cyprus	398	412	417	421	426	431	436	440	464	470	477	483
Gibraltar												
Malta							227	226	225	226	227	228
Monaco												
Turkey					29432				30385	30896	31406	31707
Total	398	412	417	421	29858	431	662	666	31074	31592	32110	32419
European total	271943	460144	303948	306299	520725	494779	517601	521446	550204	539990	541705	543408

Sources: National statistical offices/Statistical Office of the European Community/UN
Note: See end of section

Table No: 0219

DEMOGRAPHIC ANALYSIS

Number of Persons Aged 65 Years and Over 1977-1992: National Estimates at January 1st

'000

	1977	1980	1983	1984	1985	1986	1987	1988	1989	1990	1991	1992
EC members												
Belgium	1378	1414	1377	1347	1347	1379	1402	1418	1451	1485	1493	1496
Denmark	697	735	755	762	766	777	791	793	796	780	782	784
France	7223	7535	7197	7098	7057	7232	7565	7476	7728	7909	7953	7997
Germany: East			2885	2824	2781	2756	2230	1691	1720	1673	1643	1612
Germany: West	9133	9563	9173	8981	8981	9127	9283	9439	9670	9850	9895	10042
Greece	1157	1259	1304	1309	1323	1348	1352	1375	1405	1420	1427	1433
Ireland	353	364	372	373	377	378	384	394	397	401	400	399
Italy	7065	7611	7396	7273	7271	7490	7689	7887	8113	8273	8297	8310
Luxembourg	48	49	49	48	48	48	49	50	50	52	52	53
Netherlands	1514	1615	1688	1709	1730	1769	1805	1840	1877	1922	1937	1953
Portugal	957	1018	1167	1181	1201	1234	1265	1295	1326	1355	1360	1375
Spain	3801	4029	4413	4498	4584	4653	4756	4868	4981	5092	5094	5102
United Kingdom	7987	8478	8452	8424	8472	8680	8750	8883	8950	9140	9159	9203
EC total	41313	43670	46228	45827	45938	46871	47321	47411	48462	49352	49491	49757
EFTA members												
Austria	1148	1161	1090	1077	1081	1095	1114	1133	1155	1177	1183	1198
Finland	524	568	596	604	606	618	639	645	651	664	667	670
Iceland	21	22	23	24	24	25	26	26	28	29	29	30
Liechtenstein												
Norway	565	598	629	639	646	660	678	681	684	703	706	710
Sweden	1274	1345	1395	1410	1425	1454	1493	1499	1505	1537	1549	1558
Switzerland	823	871	891	895	903	918	933	1000	1014	1039	1045	1051
EFTA total	4355	4565	4624	4649	4685	4770	4883	4984	5036	5149	5178	5218
Eastern Europe												
Albania		118										
Bulgaria	983	1040	1014	997	1011	1017	1054	1090	1111	1111	1112	1112
Czechoslovakia	1846	1928	1773	1715	1703	1715	1712	1786	1823	1826	1829	1831
Hungary		1516	1546	1556	1558	1570	1470	1369	1387	1388	1385	1352
Poland	3393	3610	3526	3484	3500	3525	3545	3519	3586	3601	3615	3628
Romania	2168	2281	2156	2155	2153	2160	2165	2170	2233	2243	2252	2248
USSR		26659			25873	26000	26500	27000	27525	27564	27602	27631
Yugoslavia												
E European total	8390	37152	10015	9907	35798	35987	36445	36934	37664	37733	37796	37802
Others												
Cyprus	63	62	69	70	71	71	71	71	74	75	76	77
Gibraltar												
Malta							34	37	40	40	40	40
Monaco												
Turkey									2750	2796	2842	2870
Total	63	62	69	70	71	71	105	108	2864	2911	2959	2987
European total	54121	85449	60936	60453	86492	87699	88754	89436	94027	95145	95424	95732

Sources: National statistical offices/Statistical Office of the European Community/UN
Note: See end of section

Table No: 0220

DEMOGRAPHIC ANALYSIS

Demographic Breakdown by Age Group: Latest Official Estimates at January 1st

'000

	Year	0-4	5-9	10-14	15-19	20-24	25-29	30-34	35-39	40-44
EC members										
Belgium	1989	585.0	609.7	606.1	687.6	761.5	803.7	770.6	719.9	675.4
Denmark	1989	278.0	276.5	335.0	366.4	413.5	386.3	371.5	372.9	419.6
France	1990	3745.9	3861.8	3677.7	4273.9	4211.4	4267.7	4218.2	4273.9	4108.6
Germany: East	1989	1093.2	1151.6	999.2	1027.0	1287.7	1415.0	1302.6	1227.3	829.2
Germany: West	1988	3083.3	3002.0	2942.9	4040.1	5326.1	5109.1	4401.2	4262.8	3757.4
Greece	1989	564.7	698.5	711.3	719.5	773.6	727.7	682.8	658.9	660.9
Ireland[a]	1989	293.3	345.9	342.2	336.1	269.1	244.1	242.7	233.0	219.9
Italy	1989	2857.1	3143.1	3923.8	4516.3	4854.6	4520.9	4013.3	3817.7	3809.8
Luxembourg	1990	22.7	21.8	20.9	22.4	28.1	32.3	32.1	30.0	27.2
Netherlands	1989	913.1	885.5	911.9	1165.5	1263.2	1278.6	1193.0	1146.5	1145.2
Portugal	1989	636.8	738.3	842.9	864.1	862.3	827.7	727.9	661.4	609.4
Spain	1990	2097.0	2482.8	3098.4	3284.3	3294.1	3200.6	2854.3	2504.5	2424.3
United Kingdom[b]	1989	3807.7	3632.6	3384.6	4078.9	4650.7	4618.7	3971.0	3795.6	4074.5
EFTA members										
Austria	1990	423.9	460.4	439.5	518.7	645.7	674.6	594.9	506.8	504.3
Finland	1989	311.0	325.3	323.6	304.2	363.8	377.8	391.2	417.9	413.4
Iceland	1989	20.8	22.0	20.4	21.2	22.0	22.0	20.5	18.3	15.5
Liechtenstein	1987	1.8	1.8	1.9	2.2	2.5	2.6	2.5	2.4	2.2
Norway	1990	275.5	257.5	268.0	319.1	338.5	321.3	317.9	305.7	315.4
Sweden	1989	516.3	481.2	510.5	560.3	622.6	568.8	574.3	601.9	673.8
Switzerland	1989	344.5	377.9	370.8	431.3	511.1	541.0	517.7	496.5	510.7
Eastern Europe										
Albania	1980	406.1	336.5	304.5	293.8	259.1	195.1	164.3	144.3	126.7
Bulgaria	1989	582.3	600.9	671.7	657.1	596.0	603.7	628.6	651.8	646.5
Czechoslovakia	1989	1071.1	1154.6	1373.0	1246.1	1060.9	1078.1	1154.0	1254.3	1161.2
Hungary	1989	621.0	680.2	872.6	754.8	688.2	650.6	921.3	856.0	728.9
Poland	1988	3218.9	3356.6	3091.9	2652.6	2554.0	2949.0	3351.0	3137.7	2217.5
Romania[b]	1989	1807.1	1736.6	1983.8	1906.2	1831.2	1444.2	1787.1	1697.3	1332.4
USSR	1989	21913.4	24342.3	22581.2	21267.6	20394.1	24355.6	23482.5	20824.2	13828.9
Yugoslavia[c]	1989	1749.8	1829.6	1861.5	1801.6	1815.2	1857.0	1862.4	1849.9	1440.2
Others										
Cyprus	1989	64.1	63.8	52.1	51.2	53.7	60.9	55.2	49.1	47.4
Gibraltar	1981	2.4	2.3	2.1	2.0	2.2	2.3	2.2	2.0	1.9
Malta	1989	26.8	28.0	28.3	25.6	23.7	27.6	28.7	27.6	29.6
Monaco	1982	0.9	1.0	1.3	1.5	1.5	1.7	1.8	2.1	1.8
Turkey[d]	1985	6078.0	6739.0	6193.0	5407.0	4784.0	4041.0	3374.0	2787.0	2208.0

Table No: 0220 (cont'd)

DEMOGRAPHIC ANALYSIS

Demographic Breakdown by Age Group: Latest Official Estimates at January 1st

'000

	Year	45-49	50-54	55-59	60-64	65-69	70-74	75-79	80-84	85-89	90+
EC members											
Belgium	1989	534.1	568.2	594.6	561.0	409.9	361.8	308.7	199.7	95.4	35.3
Denmark	1989	331.1	278.5	252.8	252.0	242.9	202.2	168.0	107.1	53.6	21.9
France	1990	2889.4	2927.3	3047.3	2894.2	2703.5	1331.4	1750.3	1218.8	878.4	
Germany: East	1989	1202.5	1190.3	928.6	811.9	711.8	399.3	540.0	351.6	185.1	
Germany: West	1988	4766.0	4343.1	3543.9	3359.2	2945.3	2010.7	2249.8	1427.3	828.1	
Greece	1989	567.0	676.1	668.3	569.8	390.4	391.2	290.0	180.5	73.1	22.8
Ireland[a]	1989	175.0	153.7	141.6	135.1	129.0	110.7	75.3	42.7	25.4	
Italy	1989	3629.7	3567.6	3461.3	3276.6	2499.3	2007.0	1774.2	997.5	453.0	156.6
Luxembourg	1990	23.8	23.0	22.4	21.0	16.4	11.5	11.5	11.3		
Netherlands	1989	868.2	765.7	726.5	669.5	593.3	479.2	371.1	241.2	167.3	
Portugal	1989	549.0	573.6	562.8	527.2	416.1	359.1	274.1	150.4	74.9	
Spain	1990	2158.0	2022.7	2251.3	2065.6	1764.2	1312.2	1037.1	678.7	428.2	
United Kingdom[b]	1989	3300.0	3093.6	2964.2	2910.4	2957.2	2064.3	1871.0	1226.8	834.7	
EFTA members											
Austria	1990	515.7	449.6	388.7	403.0	395.5	228.0	259.0	177.2	108.0	
Finland	1989	294.7	270.3	260.1	250.1	209.6	168.6	140.9	84.9	35.6	11.5
Iceland	1989	11.8	10.4	10.9	9.7	8.5	6.6	5.0	3.4	1.9	0.9
Liechtenstein	1987	1.7	1.3	1.1	1.1	1.0	0.6	0.6	0.3	0.2	
Norway	1990	241.7	194.3	188.6	198.9	215.5	178.9	140.5	91.0	65.3	18.4
Sweden	1989	540.3	441.2	423.4	439.5	458.7	380.6	319.9	207.4	100.1	37.8
Switzerland	1989	461.0	393.0	365.0	329.0	299.9	226.5	212.8	150.7	107.5	
Eastern Europe											
Albania	1980	109.4	93.6	69.3	53.6	117.5					
Bulgaria	1989	538.7	534.2	582.0	547.3	485.1	239.8	237.6	130.9	58.5	
Czechoslovakia	1989	940.8	754.0	793.0	773.7	720.8	336.5	419.3	239.0	119.2	
Hungary	1989	677.1	607.3	619.7	590.9	534.2	273.3	322.3	174.4	93.2	
Poland	1988	1868.0	2008.8	2033.1	1772.1	1284.0	832.7	836.2	480.2	235.9	
Romania[b]	1989	1265.3	1443.9	1361.1	1206.7	944.6	475.1	536.6	272.5	120.0	
USSR	1989	14919.1	17491.8	14940.2	14854.7	8419.7	6359.9	5939.0	3230.8	1758.7	
Yugoslavia[c]	1989	1338.6	1461.2	1437.4	1194.2	891.5	404.3	493.6	265.0	142.3	
Others											
Cyprus	1989	37.8	34.9	29.1	26.0	22.6	20.0	17.3	11.6		
Gibraltar	1981	1.7	1.6	1.5	1.4	1.1	0.9	0.5	0.3	0.2	
Malta	1989	19.1	18.7	16.9	15.0	14.0	8.6	7.2	4.4	2.3	
Monaco	1982	1.7	1.9	2.0	1.8	1.7	2.9				
Turkey[d]	1985	2009.0	2043.0	1649.0	1130.0	2126.0					

Source: National statistical offices: all countries
Note: See end of section

Table No: 0221

DEMOGRAPHIC ANALYSIS

Demographic Breakdown by Age Group: Latest Official Estimates at January 1st

% total population

	Year	0-4	5-9	10-14	15-19	20-24	25-29	30-34	35-39	40-44
EC members										
Belgium	1989	5.9	6.2	6.1	7.0	7.7	8.1	7.8	7.3	6.8
Denmark	1989	5.4	5.4	6.5	7.1	8.1	7.5	7.2	7.3	8.2
France	1990	6.7	6.9	6.5	7.6	7.5	7.6	7.5	7.6	7.3
Germany: East	1989	6.6	6.9	6.0	6.2	7.7	8.5	7.8	7.4	5.0
Germany: West	1988	5.0	4.9	4.8	6.6	8.7	8.3	7.2	6.9	6.1
Greece	1989	5.6	7.0	7.1	7.2	7.7	7.3	6.8	6.6	6.6
Ireland	1989	8.3	9.8	9.7	9.6	7.7	6.9	6.9	6.6	6.3
Italy	1989	5.0	5.5	6.9	7.9	8.5	7.9	7.0	6.7	6.7
Luxembourg	1990	6.0	5.8	5.5	5.9	7.4	8.5	8.5	7.9	7.2
Netherlands	1989	6.2	6.0	6.2	7.9	8.5	8.6	8.1	7.8	7.7
Portugal	1989	6.2	7.2	8.2	8.4	8.4	8.1	7.1	6.4	5.9
Spain	1990	5.4	6.4	8.0	8.4	8.5	8.2	7.3	6.4	6.2
United Kingdom	1989	6.7	6.3	5.9	7.1	8.1	8.1	6.9	6.6	7.1
EC average		5.8	6.1	6.4	7.4	8.2	8.0	7.2	6.9	6.7
EFTA members										
Austria	1990	5.5	6.0	5.7	6.7	8.4	8.8	7.7	6.6	6.6
Finland	1989	6.3	6.6	6.5	6.1	7.3	7.6	7.9	8.4	8.3
Iceland	1989	8.3	8.7	8.1	8.4	8.7	8.7	8.1	7.3	6.2
Liechtenstein	1987	6.5	6.5	6.8	7.9	9.0	9.4	9.0	8.6	7.9
Norway	1990	6.5	6.1	6.3	7.5	8.0	7.6	7.5	7.2	7.4
Sweden	1989	6.1	5.7	6.0	6.6	7.4	6.7	6.8	7.1	8.0
Switzerland	1989	5.2	5.7	5.6	6.5	7.7	8.1	7.8	7.5	7.7
EFTA average		5.9	6.0	6.0	6.7	7.8	7.8	7.5	7.3	7.5
Eastern Europe										
Albania	1980	15.2	12.6	11.4	11.0	9.7	7.3	6.1	5.4	4.7
Bulgaria	1989	6.5	6.7	7.5	7.3	6.6	6.7	7.0	7.2	7.2
Czechoslovakia	1989	6.8	7.4	8.8	8.0	6.8	6.9	7.4	8.0	7.4
Hungary	1989	5.8	6.4	8.2	7.1	6.5	6.1	8.6	8.0	6.8
Poland	1988	8.5	8.9	8.2	7.0	6.7	7.8	7.7	8.3	5.9
Romania	1989	7.8	7.5	8.6	8.2	7.9	6.2	7.7	7.3	5.8
USSR	1989	7.8	8.7	8.0	7.6	7.3	8.7	8.4	7.4	4.9
Yugoslavia	1989	7.4	7.7	7.9	7.6	7.7	7.8	7.9	7.8	6.1
E European average		7.8	8.4	8.1	7.6	7.2	8.2	8.3	7.5	5.3
Others										
Cyprus	1989	9.2	9.2	7.5	7.3	7.7	8.7	7.9	7.0	6.8
Gibraltar	1981	8.4	8.0	7.3	7.0	7.7	8.0	7.7	7.0	6.6
Malta	1989	7.6	8.0	8.0	7.3	6.7	7.8	8.2	7.8	8.4
Monaco	1982	3.5	3.9	5.1	5.9	5.9	6.6	7.0	8.2	7.0
Turkey	1985	12.0	13.3	12.2	10.7	9.5	8.0	6.7	5.5	4.4
Average		11.9	13.2	12.1	10.6	9.4	8.0	6.7	5.5	4.4
European average		7.1	7.6	7.5	7.7	7.8	8.1	7.7	7.2	5.9

Table No: 0221 (cont'd)

DEMOGRAPHIC ANALYSIS

Demographic Breakdown by Age Group: Latest Official Estimates at January 1st

% total population

	Year	45-49	50-54	55-59	60-64	65-69	70-74	75-79	80-84	85-89	90+	Total
EC members												
Belgium	1989	5.4	5.7	6.0	5.7	4.1	3.7	3.1	2.0	1.0	0.4	100.0
Denmark	1989	6.5	5.4	4.9	4.9	4.7	3.9	3.3	2.1	1.0	0.4	100.0
France	1990	5.1	5.2	5.4	5.1	4.8	2.4	3.1	2.2	1.6		100.0
Germany: East	1989	7.2	7.1	5.6	4.9	4.3	2.4	3.2	2.1	1.1		100.9
Germany: West	1988	7.8	7.1	5.8	5.5	4.8	3.3	3.7	2.3	1.3		100.0
Greece	1989	5.7	6.7	6.7	5.7	3.9	3.9	2.9	1.8	0.7	0.2	100.0
Ireland	1989	5.0	4.4	4.0	3.8	3.7	3.1	2.1	1.2	0.7		100.0
Italy	1989	6.3	6.2	6.0	5.7	4.4	3.5	3.1	1.7	0.8	0.3	100.0
Luxembourg	1990	6.3	6.1	5.9	5.5	4.3	3.0	3.0	3.0			100.0
Netherlands	1989	5.9	5.2	4.9	4.5	4.0	3.2	2.5	1.6	1.1		100.0
Portugal	1989	5.4	5.6	5.5	5.1	4.1	3.5	2.7	1.5	0.7		100.0
Spain	1990	5.5	5.2	5.8	5.3	4.5	3.4	2.7	1.7	1.1		100.0
United Kingdom	1989	5.8	5.4	5.2	5.1	5.2	3.6	3.3	2.1	1.5		100.0
EC average		6.1	5.9	5.6	5.3	4.6	3.2	3.1	2.0	1.2	0.3	100.0
EFTA members												
Austria	1990	6.7	5.8	5.1	5.2	5.1	3.0	3.4	2.3	1.4		100.0
Finland	1989	5.9	5.5	5.2	5.0	4.2	3.4	2.8	1.7	0.7	0.2	100.0
Iceland	1989	4.7	4.1	4.3	3.9	3.4	2.6	2.0	1.4	0.8	0.4	100.0
Liechtenstein	1987	6.1	4.7	4.0	4.0	3.6	2.2	2.2	1.1	0.7		100.0
Norway	1990	5.7	4.6	4.4	4.7	5.1	4.2	3.3	2.1	1.5	0.4	100.0
Sweden	1989	6.4	5.2	5.0	5.2	5.4	4.5	3.8	2.5	1.2	0.4	100.0
Switzerland	1989	6.9	5.9	5.5	4.9	4.5	3.4	3.2	2.3	1.6		100.0
EFTA average		6.4	5.5	5.1	5.1	4.9	3.7	3.3	2.2	1.3	0.4	100.0
Eastern Europe												
Albania	1980	4.1	3.5	2.6	2.0	4.4						
Bulgaria	1989	6.0	5.9	6.5	6.1	5.4	2.7	2.6	1.5	0.7		100.0
Czechoslovakia	1989	6.0	4.8	5.1	4.9	4.6	2.2	2.7	1.5	0.8		100.0
Hungary	1989	6.3	5.7	5.8	5.5	5.0	2.6	3.0	1.6	0.9		100.0
Poland	1988	4.9	5.3	5.4	4.7	3.4	2.2	2.2	1.3	0.6		100.0
Romania	1989	5.5	6.2	5.9	5.2	4.1	2.1	2.3	1.2	0.5		100.0
USSR	1989	5.3	6.2	5.3	5.3	3.0	2.3	2.1	1.2	0.6		100.0
Yugoslavia	1989	5.6	6.2	6.1	5.0	3.8	1.7	2.1	1.1	0.6		100.0
E European average		5.4	6.0	5.4	5.2	3.3	2.2	2.2	1.2	0.6		100.0
Others												
Cyprus	1989	5.4	5.0	4.2	3.7	3.2	2.9	2.5	1.7			100.0
Gibraltar	1981	5.9	5.6	5.2	4.9	3.8	3.1	1.7	1.0	0.7		100.0
Malta	1989	5.4	5.3	4.8	4.3	4.0	2.4	2.0	1.2	0.7		100.0
Monaco	1982	6.6	7.4	7.8	7.0	6.6	11.3					100.0
Turkey	1985	4.0	4.0	3.3	2.2	4.2						
Average		4.0	4.1	3.3	2.3	4.2	5.9	4.7	3.0	1.3		100.0
European average		5.6	5.8	5.3	5.0	4.0	2.7	2.7	1.6	0.9	0.3	100.0

Source: National statistical offices: all countries
Note: See end of section

Table No: 0222

POPULATION FORECASTS

Official Population Projections 1990-2020

'000	Actual 1990	1995	2000	2005	2010	2020	% increase 1990-2020
EC members							
Belgium	9988	9980	10034	10046	10040	9974	-0.14
Denmark	5134	5129	5139	5137	5085	5038	-1.87
France	56462	57188	58196	58889	59430	60229	6.67
Germany: East	16210	16118	16118	16121	16118	15863	-2.14
Germany: West	62661	60701	60318	59511	58407	55889	-10.81
Greece	10035	10124	10193	10247	10249	10139	1.04
Ireland	3492	3900	4086	4462	4462	4808	37.69
Italy	57612	57591	57881	57771	57290	55785	-3.17
Luxembourg	371	368	368	366	363	355	-4.31
Netherlands	14899	15008	15207	15301	15318	15225	2.19
Portugal	10359	10429	10587	10717	10809	10912	5.34
Spain	39324	40060	40812	41420	41831	42366	7.74
United Kingdom	57423	57268	57509	57562	57560	57630	0.36
EC total	343970	343864	346448	347550	346962	344213	0.07
EFTA members							
Austria	7662	7479	7461	7406	7339	7173	-6.38
Finland	4972	5030	5076	5108	5132	5148	3.54
Iceland	254	264	274	283	291	305	20.08
Liechtenstein	28						
Norway	4284	4271	4331	4378	4416	4485	4.69
Sweden	8530	8326	8322	8305	8275	8205	-3.81
Switzerland	6638	6552	6553	6508	6434	6247	-5.89
EFTA total	32368	31922	32017	31988	31887	31563	-2.49
Eastern Europe							
Albania	3274	3521	3795	4061	4316	4792	46.37
Bulgaria	9011	9036	9071	9077	9059	8985	-0.29
Czechoslovakia	15678	15874	16179	16478	16715	17061	8.82
Hungary	10526	10509	10531	10519	10459	10291	-2.23
Poland	37781	39365	40366	41462	42553	44333	17.34
Romania	23230	23816	24346	24731	25013	25521	9.86
USSR	284300	298000	307737	317266	326415	343212	20.72
Yugoslavia	23783	24471	25026	25481	25822	26211	10.21
East European total	407582	424592	437051	449075	460352	480406	17.87
Others							
Cyprus	740	734	765	795	826	882	19.19
Gibraltar	31						
Malta	353	360	366	373	379	388	9.93
Monaco	28						
Turkey	54029	61151	66622	71800	76641	85342	57.96
Total	55181	62245	67753	72968	77846	86612	56.96
European total	839101	862623	883269	901581	917047	942794	12.36

Source: UN World Population Prospects (1988 base)
Note: See end of section

Table No: 0223

POPULATION FORECASTS

Projected Demographic Population by Age and Sex 1995: Official Forecasts

'000

	Total	Male	Female	0-14	15-64	65+
EC members						
Belgium	9729	4747	4982	1766	6404	1559
Denmark	5108	2507	2601	849	3455	804
France[a]	56338	27756	28582	11194	37338	7807
Germany: East[a]	16998	8231	8767	3447	11362	2189
Germany: West[a]	59983	29118	30864	9502	41004	9477
Greece	10168	5053	5115	2347	6434	1387
Ireland[a]	4083	2051	2032	1161	2533	389
Italy	57506	27960	29546	9307	39071	9128
Luxembourg	373	182	191	71	253	49
Netherlands	15028	7413	7615	2653	10325	2050
Portugal	10819	5273	5547	2129	7263	1427
Spain	40022	19706	20316	7647	26745	5630
United Kingdom	58144	28483	29661	11593	37385	9166
EC total	344299	168480	175819	63666	229572	51062
EFTA members						
Austria	7621	3661	3960	1328	5094	1199
Finland	5054	2467	2588	941	3383	731
Iceland	256	129	128	57	170	29
Liechtenstein						
Norway	4273	2109	2163	784	2788	701
Sweden	8498	4188	4309	1502	5472	1524
Switzerland[a]	6382	3115	3266	1036	4347	999
EFTA total	32084	15669	16414	5648	21254	5183
Eastern Europe						
Albania[a]	3759	1903	1856	1235	2322	202
Bulgaria[a]	9392	4656	4737	2006	6069	1318
Czechoslovakia[a]	16155	7896	8259	3461	10746	1949
Hungary[a]	10661	5146	5516	1959	7172	1530
Poland	39600	19324	20276	9410	25786	4404
Romania[a]	24690	12214	12476	5840	16045	2805
USSR	303517	145752	157765	74801	195059	33657
Yugoslavia	24908	12399	12509	5326	16874	2708
East European total	432682	209290	223394	104038	280073	48573
Others						
Cyprus[a]	734	367	366	186	477	71
Gibraltar						
Malta[a]	407	196	211	92	274	41
Monaco						
Turkey[a]	60041	30723	29318	20134	36983	2924
Total	61182	31286	29895	20412	37734	3036
European total	870247	424725	445522	193764	568633	107854

Sources: National statistical offices/UN World Population Prospects
Note: See end of section

Notes to Tables in Section Two:

Table 0202 a Mid-year
b Annual average

Table 0204 a Data for 1977-86 are Euromonitor estimates

Table 0208 Rates are number of deaths of infants under one year per '000 live births
a 1980 = UN estimates for 1975-80
1985 = UN estimates for 1980-85

Table 0209 Rates are the number of legal (recognised) marriages performed and registered per '000 mid-year population

Table 0210 Rates are the number of final divorce decrees granted under civil law per '000 mid-year population

Table 0211 Rate represents the number of children that would be born per woman, if she were to live to the end of her childbearing years and bear children at each age in accordance with prevailing age-specific fertility rates

Table 0214 Data on cities refer to urban agglomerations
a Data on cities refer to cities proper

Table 0215 Data for 1990-1992 include Euromonitor estimates

Table 0216 Data for 1990-1992 include Euromonitor estimates

Table 0217 Most EC data for 1990-1992 and most East European data for 1989-1992 are Euromonitor estimates

Table 0218 Most EC data for 1990-1992 and most East European data for 1989-1992 are Euromonitor estimates

Table 0219 Most EC data for 1990-1992 and most East European data for 1989-1992 are Euromonitor estimates

Table 0220 Last figure for each country includes people of all older age groups
a Annual average
b Mid-year
c Does not include 98,100 people of unknown age
d Does not include 167,400 people of unknown age

Table 0221 Last figure for each country includes people of all older age groups

Table 0222 Allowance has been made for an emigration of 500,000 East Germans to the Western part of the country

Table 0223 a UN estimates (medium variant)

Section Three

Economic Indicators

Table No: 0301

GROSS DOMESTIC PRODUCT

Trends in Total Gross Domestic Product 1977-1991

National currencies (billions)

	1977	1978	1979	1980	1981	1982	1983	1984	1985
EC members									
Belgium[a]	2842	3058	3266	3519	3659	3979	4221	4539	4856
Denmark[a]	279	311	347	374	408	464	513	565	615
France[b]	1918	2183	2481	2808	3165	3626	4007	4362	4700
Germany: East[a,c]	164	176	179	187	196	202	210	222	232
Germany: West[d]	1198	1285	1392	1479	1541	1598	1669	1751	1823
Greece[a]	964	1161	1429	1711	2050	2575	3079	3806	4618
Ireland[a]	6	7	8	9	11	13	15	16	18
Italy[b,e]	190	222	270	390	468	545	633	727	811
Luxembourg[a]	118	129	138	148	162	182	222	222	205
Netherlands[b]	275	297	316	337	353	369	381	400	419
Portugal[a]	626	787	991	1232	1465	1848	2279	2806	3524
Spain[a]	9178	11231	13131	15185	16989	19567	22235	25111	28201
United Kingdom[b]	146	168	197	230	254	276	304	324	356
EFTA members									
Austria[b]	796	842	919	995	1056	1134	1202	1277	1348
Finland[b]	130	144	167	193	218	245	274	310	337
Iceland[a]	4	6	9	15	24	38	66	87	119
Liechtenstein									
Norway	192	213	239	285	328	362	402	453	500
Sweden[b]	370	412	462	525	573	628	710	794	866
Switzerland	146	152	159	170	185	196	204	214	228
Eastern Europe									
Albania									
Bulgaria[a,c]	17	17	19	21	22	23	24	25	26
Czechoslovakia[f]	411	434	456	483	470	491	503	534	677
Hungary[a]	582	630	682	721	780	848	896	979	1034
Poland[a]				2511	2753	5546	6924	8576	10367
Romania[a,c]	513	552	599	620	642	747	786	816	817
USSR[a,g]	413	420	433	454	478	513	536	559	569
Yugoslavia	73	90	117	155	221	293	408	665	1158
Others									
Cyprus[a]	0	1	1	1	1	1	1	1	1
Gibraltar									
Malta	0	0	0	0	0	0	0	0	0
Monaco									
Turkey[a]	860	1273	2182	4328	6414	8578	11532	18212	27552

Table No: 0301 (cont'd)

GROSS DOMESTIC PRODUCT

Trends in Total Gross Domestic Product 1977-1991

National currencies (billions)	1986	1987	1988	1989	1990	1991	% growth 1977-1991	% share 1991	Total $ billion 1991	$ per capita 1991
EC members										
Belgium[a]	5117	5351	5685	6160	6577			2.3	197	19720
Denmark[a]	667	700	732	770	800	832	198.21	1.5	129	25173
France[b]	5337	5337	5722	6136	6485	6701	249.37	13.9	1188	20884
Germany: East[a,c]	238	254	261	240	190			1.4	118	7258
Germany: West[d]	1925	1991	2096	2221	2405	2403	100.58	16.9	1448	23143
Greece[a]	5515	6259	7527	8778	10455			0.8	66	6527
Ireland[a]	19	20	22	24	26			0.5	43	12246
Italy[b,e]	900	984	1092	1193	1307	1396	634.74	13.2	1125	19486
Luxembourg[a]	223	237	248	279	292			0.1	9	23313
Netherlands[b]	428	429	447	476	504	527	19.64	3.3	282	18772
Portugal[a]	4420	5175	6003	7168	8530			0.7	60	5782
Spain[a]	32324	36125	40160	45021	50087			5.7	491	12624
United Kingdom[b]	383	421	467	511	550	571	291.10	11.8	1010	17594
EC total								72.1	6166	17965
EFTA members										
Austria[b]	1416	1474	1565	1664	1778	1903	139.07	1.9	163	21176
Finland[b]	358	392	442	497	524	516	296.92	1.5	128	25529
Iceland[a]	159	208	255	301	341			0.1	6	23007
Liechtenstein										
Norway	514	561	583	623	662	690	259.38	1.2	106	25049
Sweden[b]	946	1021	1110	1224	1340	1410	281.08	2.7	233	27139
Switzerland	243	255	268	290	312	327	123.97	2.7	228	34035
EFTA total								10.1	864	26719
Eastern Europe										
Albania										
Bulgaria[a,c]	27	29	32	35	140			0.4	33	3669
Czechoslovakia[f]	695	711	740	759	819	952	131.63	0.4	32	2059
Hungary[a]	1089	1226	1409	1730	2081			0.4	33	3103
Poland[a]	12953	16940	29629	118319	606726			0.7	64	1678
Romania[a,c]	839	845	857	798	844	47.94		0.4	38	1618
USSR[a,g]	576	586	619	666	670			13.1	1117	3928
Yugoslavia	2259	5031	15371	282268	9997352	0.7		1.0	88	3709
East European total								16.4	1405	3444
Others										
Cyprus[a]	2	2	2	2	2			0.1	4	5995
Gibraltar										
Malta	1	1	1	1	1			0.0	3	8936
Monaco										
Turkey[a]	39288	58299	100826	167457	283187			1.3	109	1938
Total								1.4	116	2031
European total								100.0	8551	10172

Sources: International Monetary Fund (IMF)/Comecon/national statistical offices

Notes: See end of section

Table No: 0302

GROSS NATIONAL PRODUCT

Trends in Total Gross National Product 1977-1991

National currencies (billions)

	1977	1978	1979	1980	1981	1982	1983	1984	1985
EC members									
Belgium[a]	3231	3328	3384	3501	3635	3940	4168	4490	4793
Denmark[a]	276	306	340	365	395	447	494	541	589
France					3181	3625			
Germany: East	164	176	179	187	196	202	210	222	232
Germany: West	1199	1292	1397	1485	1545	1597	1680	1770	1838
Greece[a]	994	1194	1472	1768	2109	2632	3110	3808	4584
Ireland[a]	6	7	8	9	11	12	14	15	16
Italy[a,b]	190	222	271	339	399	467	627	725	805
Luxembourg[a]	121	134	147	164	166	189	207	233	289
Netherlands[a]	275	296	315	336	352	368	382	400	419
Portugal[a]	619	772	969	1199	1439	1745	2160	2628	3328
Spain[a]	9116	11143	13052	15072	16751	19283	21877	24715	27870
United Kingdom	146	169	198	230	255	277	307	329	359
EFTA members									
Austria	789	834	911	986	1047	1125	1193	1268	1341
Finland	128	141	164	189	214	240	269	301	331
Iceland[a]	4	6	8	15	24	37	63	83	114
Liechtenstein									
Norway	156	171	192	234	317	350	389	439	489
Sweden[a]	369	411	461	521	564	614	688	774	845
Switzerland[a]	152	158	165	177	194	205	214	226	241
Eastern Europe									
Albania									
Bulgaria[a,c]	17	17	19	21	22	23	24	25	26
Czechoslovakia[c]	411	434	456	483	470	491	503	541	556
Hungary[c,d]	477	515	556	583	635	696	738	804	842
Poland[a,c]				1992	2160	4753	5924	7182	8586
Romania[a,c]	513	552	599	620	642	747	786	816	817
USSR[d]	413	420	433	454	478	513	536	559	569
Yugoslavia[d,e]								633	1129
Others									
Cyprus[a]	0	1	1	1	1	1	1	1	2
Gibraltar									
Malta[f]	0	0	0	0	0	0	0	1	1
Monaco									
Turkey	873	1291	2200	4435	6554	8722	11551	18375	27797

Table No: 0302 (cont'd)

GROSS NATIONAL PRODUCT

Trends in Total Gross National Product 1977-1991

National currencies (billions)

	1986	1987	1988	1989	1990	1991	% growth 1977-1991	% share 1991	Total $ million 1991	$ per capita 1991
EC members										
Belgium[a]	5070	5302	5634	6127	6521			2.8	195	19553
Denmark[a]	639	672	704	739	767			1.8	124	24134
France		5283	5463			2611	117.76			
Germany: East	238	254	261	2244	2429					
Germany: West	1939	2004	2107	8692	10409			22.3	1573	25261
Greece[a]	5497	6195	7470	21	23			0.9	66	6499
Ireland[a]	17	18	19	1182	1291			0.5	38	10833
Italy[a,b]	893	977	1084	375	397			15.3	1078	18715
Luxembourg[a]	306	305	334	476	509			0.2	12	31697
Netherlands[a]	428	429	447	7055	8476			4.0	280	18761
Portugal[a]	4269	5044	5877	44635	49654	571	291.10	0.8	59	5745
Spain[a]	32028	35820	39749	515	554			6.9	487	12515
United Kingdom	388	425	472					14.4	1010	17631
EC total								69.9	4922	14341
EFTA members										
Austria	1411	1469	1548	1650	1778	1882	138.53	2.3	161	21041
Finland	355	388	421							
Iceland[a]	152	202	246	287	327			0.1	6	22062
Liechtenstein										
Norway	505	552	570	605	646	674	332.05	1.5	104	24561
Sweden[a]	926	1004	1089	1197	1303			3.1	220	25817
Switzerland[a]	255	266	283	305	326			3.3	235	35240
EFTA total								10.3	726	22438
Eastern Europe										
Albania										
Bulgaria[a,c]	27	29	32	35	140		723.53	0.2	17	1853
Czechoslovakia[c]	570	583	606	618	673	822	100.00	0.4	28	1781
Hungary[c,f]	881	1000	1160							
Poland[a,c]	10697	14013	24995	104952	506253			0.8	53	1401
Romania[a,c]	839	845	857	798	844		64.52	0.5	38	1618
USSR[f]	576	585	611	636				15.1	1060	3728
Yugoslavia[e,f]	2206	4927	14856	221862				1.1	77	3239
East European total								18.1	1273	3120
Others										
Cyprus[a]	2	2	2	2	3			0.1	7	8993
Gibraltar										
Malta[d]	1	1	1	1						
Monaco										
Turkey	39370	58565	100582	170412	28754			1.6	110	1965
Total								1.7	117	2041
European total								100.0	7037	8371

Sources: IMF/Comecon/national statistical offices

Notes: See end of section

Table No: 0303

GROSS DOMESTIC PRODUCT

Trends in Total Gross Domestic Product 1977-1991

Current US dollars (billions)

	1977	1978	1979	1980	1981	1982	1983	1984	1985
EC members									
Belgium	79.4	97.1	111.5	120.5	98.6	87.1	82.6	78.5	81.8
Denmark	46.5	56.5	65.5	66.8	57.5	55.9	56.4	54.3	58.0
France	391.4	485.1	577.0	668.6	586.1	549.4	527.2	501.4	522.2
Germany: East[a]	126.2	117.3	99.4	103.9	85.2	84.2	80.8	71.6	89.2
Germany: West	520.9	642.5	773.3	821.7	670.0	665.8	641.9	625.4	628.6
Greece	26.2	31.5	38.6	40.2	37.0	38.5	34.9	33.8	33.4
Ireland	9.5	13.5	15.8	18.7	18.9	19.1	18.4	18.1	20.0
Italy	215.3	261.6	324.9	455.4	411.7	403.0	416.8	413.8	425.2
Luxembourg	3.3	4.1	4.7	5.1	4.4	4.0	4.3	3.8	3.5
Netherlands	110.0	135.0	158.0	168.5	141.2	136.7	131.4	125.0	127.0
Portugal	16.3	17.9	20.3	24.6	23.8	23.2	20.6	19.2	20.7
Spain	120.8	146.4	195.7	211.8	184.1	178.0	155.1	156.2	165.9
United Kingdom	243.3	336.0	394.0	575.0	508.0	460.0	434.3	462.9	445.0
EC total	1909.1	2344.7	2778.8	3280.6	2826.4	2704.9	2604.6	2563.9	2620.5
EFTA members									
Austria	48.2	58.1	68.6	77.1	66.4	66.3	66.8	63.9	65.1
Finland	32.5	35.1	42.8	52.2	50.7	51.0	48.9	51.7	54.4
Iceland	2.0	2.2	2.6	3.1	3.3	3.1	2.7	2.7	2.9
Liechtenstein									
Norway	36.2	41.0	46.9	58.2	57.5	55.7	55.1	55.2	58.1
Sweden	82.2	91.6	107.4	125.0	112.4	99.7	92.2	95.7	100.7
Switzerland	60.8	84.4	93.5	100.0	92.5	98.0	97.1	93.0	91.2
EFTA total	262.0	312.4	361.8	415.6	382.8	373.8	362.8	362.2	372.4
Eastern Europe									
Albania									
Bulgaria[a]	18.3	19.2	20.8	22.8	24.3	22.9	23.5	24.9	25.5
Czechoslovakia[b]	24.7	26.1	27.5	29.1	28.3	29.6	30.3	32.1	39.5
Hungary	14.2	16.6	19.2	22.2	22.7	23.2	21.0	24.5	20.6
Poland	50.0			56.7	53.7	65.4	75.5	75.4	70.4
Romania[a]				34.4	41.6	48.5	44.7	38.3	47.8
USSR[c]	590.0	600.0	618.6	756.7	682.9	732.9	765.7	698.8	711.3
Yugoslavia	36.5	45.0	58.5	77.5	73.7	58.6	45.3	44.3	42.9
East European total	733.7	706.9	744.5	999.4	927.2	981.0	1006.0	938.3	958.0
Others									
Cyprus	0.2	0.2	0.2	0.3	0.4	0.5	0.6	2.2	2.8
Gibraltar									
Malta	0.6	0.7	0.8	1.3	1.1	1.2	1.1	0.9	0.9
Monaco									
Turkey	47.8	52.4	70.2	56.9	57.7	52.8	51.1	49.7	52.8
Total	48.5	53.3	71.2	58.5	59.1	54.4	52.9	52.8	56.6
European total	2953.4	3417.3	3956.3	4754.1	4195.6	4114.1	4026.3	3917.2	4007.4

Table No: 0303 (cont'd)

GROSS DOMESTIC PRODUCT

Trends in Total Gross Domestic Product 1977-1991

Current US dollars (billions)

	1986	1987	1988	1989	1990	1991	% growth 1977-1990	% share 1977	% share 1990
EC members									
Belgium	114.5	143.5	154.5	156.3	196.8		147.9	2.7	2.3
Denmark	82.3	102.9	109.3	105.5	129.3		178.0	1.6	1.5
France	773.5	889.5	953.7	958.8	1191.0	1187.7	204.3	13.1	14.0
Germany: East[a]	119.0	149.4	137.4	126.3	117.6		-6.8	4.2	1.4
Germany: West	875.0	1106.1	1164.4	1168.9	1488.2	1448.0	185.7	17.5	17.5
Greece	39.4	46.2	53.0	54.1	66.0		151.8	0.9	0.8
Ireland	27.1	28.6	31.4	34.3	43.1		353.9	0.3	0.5
Italy	603.7	759.2	839.0	869.5	1090.9	1125.3	406.6	7.2	12.8
Luxembourg	5.0	6.4	6.7	7.1	8.7		165.2	0.1	0.1
Netherlands	171.2	214.5	223.5	226.7	276.8	281.9	151.6	3.7	3.3
Portugal	29.5	36.7	41.7	45.5	59.8		266.1	0.5	0.7
Spain	230.7	292.5	344.7	380.2	491.4		306.9	4.1	5.8
United Kingdom	547.1	701.7	778.3	851.7	982.1	1010.3	303.6	8.2	11.6
EC total	3618.1	4477.2	4837.6	4984.8	6141.7	5053.1	221.7	64.1	72.3
EFTA members									
Austria	92.5	117.0	127.0	126.1	156.4	163.0	224.1	1.6	1.8
Finland	70.2	89.1	105.2	115.6	137.3	127.6	322.4	1.1	1.6
Iceland	3.9	5.4	5.9	5.3	5.9		192.5	0.1	0.1
Liechtenstein									
Norway	69.5	83.7	89.7	90.3	105.8	106.4	191.9	1.2	1.2
Sweden	133.2	162.1	182.0	191.3	226.4	233.2	175.3	2.8	2.7
Switzerland	135.0	170.0	178.7	181.3	224.6	228.0	269.2	2.0	2.6
EFTA total	504.3	627.2	688.5	709.7	856.3	858.2	226.8	8.8	10.1
Eastern Europe									
Albania									
Bulgaria[a]	22.4	22.3	18.8	16.7				0.6	
Czechoslovakia[b]	46.4	51.9	51.5	50.4	45.6	32.3	84.7	0.8	0.5
Hungary	23.8	26.1	26.8	29.3	32.9		131.9	0.5	0.4
Poland	73.9	63.9	68.8	82.2	63.9		27.7	1.7	0.8
Romania[a]	51.8	57.9	59.9	53.6	37.6		46.4	0.9	0.4
USSR[c]	822.9	976.7	1031.7	1110.0	1117.0		89.3	19.8	13.1
Yugoslavia	59.4	68.0	61.0	98.1	88.3		142.0	1.2	1.0
East European total	1100.6	1266.8	1318.6	1440.3	1385.4		82.4	25.5	16.3
Others									
Cyprus	3.0	5.0	4.0	4.0	4.4		2505.0	0.0	0.1
Gibraltar									
Malta	2.5	3.3	3.3	3.3	3.2		425.8	0.0	0.0
Monaco									
Turkey	58.2	68.0	70.9	78.9	108.6		127.2	1.6	1.3
Total	63.7	76.3	78.2	86.3	116.1		139.1	1.6	1.4
European total	5286.8	6447.5	6922.9	7221.1	8499.5		185.3	100.0	100.0

Sources: IMF/Comecon/national statistical offices
Notes: See end of section

Table No: 0304

GROSS DOMESTIC PRODUCT

Trends in Total Gross National Product 1977-1991

Current US dollars (billions)

	1977	1978	1979	1980	1981	1982	1983	1984
EC members								
Belgium	90.3	105.7	115.5	119.9	98.0	86.2	81.6	77.7
Denmark	46.0	55.6	64.2	65.2	55.6	53.9	54.3	52.0
France					589.1	549.2		
Germany: East[a]	126.2	117.3	99.4	103.9	85.2	84.2	80.8	71.6
Germany: West	521.3	646.0	776.1	825.0	671.7	665.4	646.2	632.1
Greece	27.0	32.4	39.8	41.5	38.1	39.4	35.3	33.8
Ireland	9.3	13.1	15.2	18.0	18.1	17.8	16.9	16.3
Italy	215.3	261.6	326.2	395.8	351.0	345.3	412.8	412.6
Luxembourg	3.4	4.3	5.0	5.6	4.5	4.1	4.1	4.0
Netherlands	110.0	134.5	157.5	168.0	140.8	136.3	131.7	125.0
Portugal	16.2	17.6	19.8	23.9	23.4	21.9	19.5	18.0
Spain	119.9	145.3	194.5	210.2	181.5	175.5	152.6	153.7
United Kingdom	243.3	338.0	396.0	575.0	510.0	461.7	438.6	470.0
EC total	1528.2	1871.4	2209.2	2552.1	2766.9	2640.9	2074.2	2066.9
EFTA members								
Austria	47.8	57.5	68.0	76.4	65.8	65.8	66.3	63.4
Finland	32.0	34.4	42.1	51.1	49.8	50.0	48.0	50.2
Iceland	2.0	2.2	2.3	3.1	3.3	3.0	2.5	2.6
Liechtenstein								
Norway	29.4	32.9	37.6	47.8	55.6	53.8	53.3	53.5
Sweden	82.0	91.3	107.2	124.0	110.6	97.5	89.4	93.3
Switzerland	63.3	87.8	97.1	104.1	97.0	102.5	101.9	98.3
EFTA total	256.6	306.1	354.2	406.6	382.2	372.6	361.4	361.2
Eastern Europe								
Albania								
Bulgaria[a]	18.3	19.2	20.8	22.8	24.3	22.9	23.5	24.9
Czechoslovakia	24.7	26.1	27.5	29.1	28.3	29.6	30.3	32.6
Hungary	11.6	13.6	15.6	17.9	18.5	19.0	17.3	20.1
Poland				45.0	42.1	56.0	64.6	63.2
Romania[a]	25.7	30.0	33.3	34.4	42.8	49.8	45.7	38.3
USSR[a]	590.0	600.0	618.6	756.7	682.9	732.9	765.7	698.8
Yugoslavia								42.2
East European total	670.3	688.9	715.7	905.9	838.9	910.2	947.1	920.0
Others								
Cyprus	0.2	0.2	0.2	0.3	0.4	0.5	0.6	1.7
Gibraltar								
Malta	0.6	0.7	0.8	1.4	1.2	1.3	1.2	2.0
Monaco								
Turkey	48.5	53.1	70.7	58.4	58.9	53.6	51.2	50.1
Total	49.3	54.1	71.8	60.0	60.5	55.4	53.1	53.8
European total	2504.4	2920.5	3351.0	3924.6	4048.5	3979.1	3435.7	3401.9

Table No: 0304 (cont'd)

GROSS DOMESTIC PRODUCT

Trends in Total Gross National Product 1977-1991

Current US dollars (billions)

	1985	1986	1987	1988	1989	1990	1991	% growth 1977-1990	% share 1977	% share 1990
EC members										
Belgium	80.7	113.4	142.1	153.1	155.5	195.1		116.2	3.6	2.8
Denmark	55.6	78.9	98.8	105.1	101.2	123.9		169.4	1.8	1.8
France			880.5	910.5						
Germany: East[a]	89.2	119.0	149.4	137.4	126.3	117.6		-6.8	5.0	1.7
Germany: West	633.8	881.4	1113.3	1170.6	1181.1	1503.1	1573.4	188.3	20.8	21.7
Greece	33.2	39.3	45.8	52.6	53.5	65.7		143.1	1.1	0.9
Ireland	17.8	24.3	25.7	27.1	30.0	38.1		308.7	0.4	0.6
Italy	422.0	599.0	753.8	832.8	861.5	1077.5		400.4	8.6	15.6
Luxembourg	4.9	6.8	8.2	9.1	9.5	11.9		251.7	0.1	0.2
Netherlands	127.0	171.2	214.5	223.5	226.7	279.5		154.1	4.4	4.0
Portugal	19.5	28.5	35.8	40.8	44.8	59.5		267.9	0.6	0.9
Spain	163.9	228.6	290.0	341.2	377.0	487.1		306.1	4.8	7.0
United Kingdom	448.8	554.3	708.3	786.7	858.3	989.3	1010.3	306.6	9.7	14.3
EC total	2096.3	2844.7	4466.3	4790.5	4025.4	4948.4		216.1	61.0	69.9
EFTA members										
Austria	64.8	92.2	116.6	125.9	125.0	156.4	161.2	227.0	1.9	2.3
Finland	53.4	69.6	88.2	100.2					1.3	
Iceland	2.7	3.7	5.2	5.7	5.0	5.6		180.5	0.1	0.1
Liechtenstein										
Norway	56.7	68.2	82.4	87.7	87.7	103.2	104.0	250.6	1.2	1.5
Sweden	98.3	130.4	159.4	178.5	187.0	220.1		168.5	3.3	3.2
Switzerland	96.4	141.7	177.3	188.7	190.6	234.7		270.6	2.5	3.4
EFTA total	372.3	505.9	629.1	686.7	595.4	720.0		180.6	10.2	10.4
Eastern Europe										
Albania										
Bulgaria[a]	25.5	22.4	22.3	18.8	16.7				0.7	
Czechoslovakia	32.4	38.0	42.6	42.2	41.1	37.5	27.9	51.8	1.0	0.5
Hungary	16.8	19.2	21.3	22.1					0.5	
Poland	58.3	61.1	52.9	58.1	72.9	53.3				0.8
Romania[a]	47.8	51.8	57.9	59.9	53.6	37.6		46.6	1.0	0.5
USSR[a]	711.3	822.9	975.0	1018.3	1060.0	1117.0		89.3	23.6	16.2
Yugoslavia	41.8	58.1	66.6	59.0	77.1	128.4				
East European total	933.9	1073.4	1238.5	1278.4	1321.4	1245.4			26.8	18.0
Others										
Cyprus	4.0	4.0	5.0	4.0	4.0	6.6		3716.6	0.0	0.1
Gibraltar										
Malta	2.0	2.5	3.3	3.3	3.3				0.0	
Monaco										
Turkey	53.3	58.4	68.3	70.7	80.3	110.1		127.0	1.9	1.6
Total	59.3	64.9	76.7	78.1	87.7	116.7			2.0	1.7
European total	3461.8	4488.9	6410.5	6833.6	5903.4	7030.5			100.0	100.0

Sources: IMF/Comecon/national statistical offices
Notes: See end of section

Table No: 0305

MONEY SUPPLY

Trends in Money Supply 1977-1991

National currencies (billions)

	1977	1980	1983	1984	1985	1986	1987	1988	1989	1990	1991	Total $ billion 1991
EC members												
Belgium	741.0	806.1	929.8	932.5	962.4	1037.3	1086.0	1145.9	1207.7	1217.0		34.2
Denmark[a]	58.9	83.2	114.2	153.8	156.5	168.0	188.5	225.1	226.1	244.5	258.3	47.6
France[b]	508.0	671.0	970.0	1219.0	1312.0	1407.0	1471.0	1532.0	1633.0	1703.0	1576.0	291.6
Germany: East												
Germany: West[b,c]	198.6	243.4	278.2	294.8	314.5	340.2	365.7	408.3	431.6	551.4	561.0	341.2
Greece[b,d]	186.6	303.8	525.6	630.9	743.3	896.0	1057.7	1205.7	1486.4	1848.1	1738.0	
Ireland[e]	1.1	1.7	2.1	2.2	2.3	2.4	2.6	2.8	3.1	3.3	3.4	5.5
Italy[f]	96.9	171.3	244.6	269.6	298.0	331.0	357.2	386.0	433.3	467.5	514.0	388.8
Luxembourg[b]	32.1	38.1	45.8	47.5	44.9	49.2	54.3	58.6	66.7	72.8	79.5	
Netherlands	57.8	65.6	79.7	85.0	90.8	97.2	103.7	111.3	119.0	124.3	129.7	69.0
Portugal[b,g]	286.0	504.6	687.3	799.4	1000.3	1359.4	1537.0	1803.9	1903.4	2453.6	2583.0	
Spain[h]	2836.0	4098.0	5277.0	5746.0	6589.0	7580.0	8899.0	10573.0	12177.0	14674.0	16573.0	143.9
UK[i]	23.5	31.0	42.5	48.1	56.7	69.3	154.1	170.0	195.3	214.9	229.2	383.8
EFTA members												
Austria	127.3	145.1	170.4	176.4	181.9	193.5	213.5	232.2	235.0	247.3	265.8	21.8
Finland[a,b]	9.9	15.0	21.4	24.9	27.7	27.8	30.3	35.9	41.4	44.4	124.1	11.2
Iceland[b,j]	0.3	1.0	3.7	5.3	6.7	9.7	12.9	15.2	19.7	24.8	26.5	0.4
Liechtenstein												
Norway[b]	37.0	45.6	65.9	82.0	98.7	101.8	152.6	187.1	218.3	237.6	241.8	52.0
Sweden[k]	49.6	79.4	86.8	95.7	102.8	112.2	115.4	116.9	119.2	129.2		
Switzerland[l]	56.4	68.3	75.8	75.9	73.9	75.5	85.9	87.8	85.6	84.2	82.9	59.4
Eastern Europe												
Albania												
Bulgaria												
Czechoslovakia				257.6	260.4	261.3	270.7	309.5	317.7	291.2	371.9	16.2
Hungary[b,m]	117.1	160.7	203.1	200.9	239.7	266.5	306.6	302.0	355.0	449.1	442.4	6.1
Poland[b]		910.3	1747.0	2001.0	2449.0	2998.0	3786.0	5748.0	19975.0	101670.0	125266.0	10.4
Romania[b,n]	84.2	114.5	156.3	162.3	165.8	169.5	171.3	199.4	204.5	233.0	445.1	
USSR												
Yugoslavia[b,o]	25.0	45.0	87.0	125.0	182.0	383.0	764.0	2407.0	51030.0	126283.0	170498.0	11.2
Others												
Cyprus[b]	0.1	0.2	0.2	0.3	0.3	0.3	0.3	0.4	0.4	0.4	0.4	0.9
Gibraltar												
Malta	0.2	0.3	0.3	0.3	0.3	0.3	0.4	0.4	0.4	0.4	0.4	1.3
Monaco												
Turkey[b]	210.3	719.8	2090.0	2487.0	3468.0	5432.0	8960.0	11956.0	20302.0	32419.0	40177.0	10.2

Sources: IMF/UN/OECD
Notes: See end of section

Table No: 0306

INFLATION RATES

Annual Rates of Inflation 1979-1991

% growth

	1979	1980	1983	1984	1985	1986	1987	1988	1989	1990	1991
EC members											
Belgium	4.5	6.6	7.7	6.3	4.9	1.3	1.6	1.2	3.1	3.4	3.2
Denmark	9.6	12.3	6.9	6.3	4.7	3.7	4.0	4.6	4.8	2.6	2.4
France	10.8	13.3	9.6	7.4	5.8	2.5	3.3	2.7	3.5	3.4	3.1
Germany: East[a]	0.3	0.4	0.0	0.2	-0.1	0.0	0.0	0.0	2.0	15.0	
Germany: West	4.1	5.4	3.3	2.4	2.2	-0.1	0.2	1.3	2.8	2.7	3.5
Greece	19.0	24.9	20.2	18.4	19.3	23.0	16.4	13.5	13.7	20.4	19.5
Ireland	13.2	18.2	10.5	8.6	5.4	3.8	3.1	2.2	4.0	3.4	3.2
Italy	14.8	21.3	14.6	10.8	9.2	5.9	4.7	5.1	6.3	6.5	6.4
Luxembourg	4.5	6.3	8.7	5.6	4.1	0.3	-0.1	1.5	3.4	3.7	3.1
Netherlands	4.2	6.5	2.8	3.3	2.2	0.2	-0.5	0.7	1.1	2.5	3.9
Portugal	23.6	16.6	25.1	28.9	19.6	11.7	9.4	9.6	12.6	13.4	11.4
Spain	15.7	15.6	12.2	11.3	8.8	8.8	5.3	4.8	6.8	6.7	5.9
United Kingdom	13.4	18.0	4.6	5.0	6.1	3.4	4.1	4.9	7.8	9.5	7.5
EFTA members											
Austria	3.7	6.4	3.3	5.7	3.2	1.7	1.4	1.9	2.6	3.3	3.3
Finland	7.5	11.6	8.4	7.1	5.9	2.9	4.1	5.1	6.6	6.1	4.1
Iceland	45.5	58.5	86.1	30.8	32.0	21.9	17.7	25.8	20.8	15.5	6.8
Liechtenstein	3.6	4.0	3.0	2.9	3.4	0.8	1.4				
Norway	4.8	10.8	8.4	6.3	5.7	7.2	8.7	6.7	4.6	4.1	3.4
Sweden	7.2	13.7	8.9	8.0	7.4	4.2	4.2	5.8	6.4	10.5	9.4
Switzerland	3.6	4.0	3.0	2.9	3.4	0.8	1.4	1.9	3.2	5.4	5.8
Eastern Europe											
Albania											
Bulgaria[b]	4.4	14.0	1.4	0.7	1.7	3.4	0.0	1.3	9.2		
Czechoslovakia	3.8	2.9	0.9	0.8	1.7	0.4	0.1	0.1	1.4	10.0	58.5
Hungary	8.9	9.1	7.3	8.3	7.0	5.3	8.2	16.3	16.9	28.2	
Poland	7.1	9.4	22.1	15.4	14.6	17.7	25.2	60.2	251.1	584.7	70.3
Romania	1.8	1.5	5.2	1.1	-0.4	2.2	1.1	2.8	0.8	4.2	174.4
USSR	1.0	1.1	0.6	-1.0	-2.0	1.9	1.9	2.3	2.3		
Yugoslavia	21.2	30.9	40.2	54.7	72.3	89.8	120.8	194.1	1239.9	587.5	117.4
Others											
Cyprus	9.5	13.5	5.0	6.0	5.0	1.2	2.8	3.4	3.8	4.5	5.1
Gibraltar	16.3	11.9	5.1	6.7	6.0	3.6	5.2	5.2	4.8	5.9	
Malta	7.1	15.8	-0.9	-0.4	-0.2	2.0	0.4	0.9	0.8	3.1	2.6
Monaco											
Turkey	58.7	110.2	32.9	48.4	45.0	34.6	38.8	75.4	69.6	64.4	70.8

Sources: IMF/International Labour Office (ILO)/UN/OECD/Euromonitor

Notes: See end of section

Table No: 0307

PUBLIC CONSUMPTION

Trends in Public Consumption 1977-1991

National currencies (billions)

	1977	1980	1983	1985	1986	1987	1988	1989	1990	1991	Total $ million 1991	$ per capita 1991
EC members												
Belgium[a]	489.0	613.9	57.0	849.0	883.0	891.0	899.0	934.0	983.0		29415	2947
Denmark[a]	66.8	99.7	40.5	155.5	159.4	176.2	188.5	196.5	201.2		32509	6331
France[b]	329.5	509.3	93.5	923.0	972.8	1016.0	1071.1	1122.2	1186.6	1239.1	219617	3862
Germany: East												
Germany: West	235.0	297.8	36.2	365.6	382.7	397.4	412.7	419.0	443.2	467.9	281952	4506
Greece[a]	153.8	280.0	79.4	942.0	1067.2	1229.4	1507.5	1805.3	2221.4		14014	1387
Ireland[a]	1.0	1.9	2.8	3.3	3.5	3.6	3.6	3.7	4.0		6633	1884
Italy[a,c]	30.0	57.0	03.2	135.5	148.4	166.7	186.9	202.5	229.7		191720	3301
Luxembourg[a]	16.3	22.2	27.6	32.3	35.0	38.5	40.5	44.3	47.6		1425	3800
Netherlands[b]	47.9	60.3	66.6	67.7	68.6	70.6	71.2	72.5	75.3	75.6	40434	2693
Portugal[a]	87.8	182.6	48.4	546.9	678.8	787.8	980.2	1182.0	1453.6		10197	985
Spain[a]	921.0	1929.3	90.9	4152.0	4740.0	5452.0	5924.0	6787.0	7579.0		74355	1910
United Kingdom[b]	29.5	49.0	65.9	74.0	79.5	85.3	91.8	99.0	109.7	120.6	213376	3716
EFTA members												
Austria[b]	138.7	178.7	26.9	255.0	270.7	280.4	288.4	302.9	321.2	340.5	29162	3789
Finland[b]	24.0	34.9	53.3	68.2	74.0	81.3	88.7	97.8	110.8	120.5	29797	5962
Iceland[a]	0.4	2.5	11.6	20.1	27.3	36.8	47.5	56.4	63.8		1095	4305
Liechtenstein												
Norway	38.6	53.5	78.2	92.7	101.6	116.0	122.3	130.9	139.3	149.3	23030	5420
Sweden[b]	102.8	151.4	03.5	239.2	257.9	271.2	289.1	317.7	366.0	380.1	62852	7316
Switzerland	19.2	21.7	27.4	30.9	32.3	33.0	35.4	38.5	42.2	45.8	31939	4767
Eastern Europe												
Albania												
Bulgaria												
Czechoslovakia				127.9	135.9	143.8	149.5	155.3	162.8	245.2	8318	530
Hungary[a]	57.8	74.1	90.9	104.6	116.0	126.3	157.4	178.0	222.0		3512	331
Poland[a]		230.8	09.7	1022.9	1178.1	1516.0	2429.0	7067.0	45045.0		4742	125
Romania[a,d]	35.5	42.7	49.5	32.0	30.3	27.8	31.0	32.9	39.6		1765	76
USSR												
Yugoslavia[e,f]	7.3	14.3	35.2	97.0	191.0	415.0	1297.0	13441.0			4674	196
Others												
Cyprus[a]	0.1	0.1	0.2	0.2	0.2	0.2	0.3	0.3	0.3		656	899
Gibraltar												
Malta		0.1	0.1	0.1	0.1	0.1	0.1	0.1			333	944
Monaco												
Turkey	116.0	440.0	54.0	3139.0	4592.0	7254.0	12128.0	26791.0			12627	225

Source: IMF

Notes: See end of section

Table No: 0308

PRIVATE CONSUMPTION

Trends in Private Consumption 1977-1991

National currencies (billions)

	1977	1980	1985	1986	1987	1988	1989	1990	1991	Total $ million 1991	Per capita $ 1991
EC members											
Belgium[a]	1724.5	2171.9	3198.0	3303.0	3464.0	3602.0	3846.0	4084.0		122210	12245
Denmark[a]	158.9	208.8	337.2	366.8	377.9	393.1	406.6	417.1		67394	13124
France[b]	1117.1	1653.3	2858.4	3049.5	3235.6	3433.2	3663.2	3888.5	4040.8	716187	12593
Germany: East											
Germany: West	683.2	840.8	1036.6	1066.9	1108.8	1153.7	1209.6	1299.2	1375.8	829045	13250
Greece[a]	634.9	1104.6	3025.5	3718.9	4346.9	5143.4	6175.7	7563.6		47717	4722
Ireland[a]	3.7	6.2	10.6	11.3	12.0	12.8	13.7	14.2		23549	6688
Italy[b,c]	135.6	239.3	507.8	559.6	614.0	676.2	744.3	812.4	876.1	706191	12229
Luxembourg[a]	61.1	78.1	120.5	126.2	143.7	144.7	154.6	166.5		4985	13293
Netherlands[a]	164.3	205.8	247.7	256.2	263.9	268.9	281.4	298.5		163921	11002
Portugal[a]	450.4	845.5	2386.6	2868.9	3323.8	3895.5	4522.9	5366.6		37647	3637
Spain[a]	6067.3	10080.4	18080.0	20438.0	22864.0	25160.0	28313.0	31259.0		306671	7879
UK[b]	86.3	137.2	217.6	241.3	264.9	298.8	326.5	349.1	363.7	643489	11207
EFTA members											
Austria[a]	456.9	552.5	775.5	804.4	835.5	875.3	927.9	991.9	1037.1	88823	11540
Finland[b]	72.5	104.0	181.7	195.0	214.0	235.0	257.6	273.2	274.9	67977	13601
Iceland[a]	2.3	8.8	74.7	96.9	131.7	158.2	181.0	207.8		3565	14020
Liechtenstein											
Norway	103.9	135.2	245.4	278.9	298.1	308.4	312.0	334.1	345.8	53340	12554
Sweden	198.9	271.8	447.9	492.8	542.5	590.9	638.6	695.6	752.4	124415	14482
Switzerland	92.9	108.3	140.6	144.9	150.2	157.0	166.2	177.6	190.0	132497	19776
Eastern Europe											
Albania											
Bulgaria											
Czechoslovakia	229.8	315.4	297.6	306.1	315.3	330.4	343.0	389.0	377.3	12799	816
Hungary[a]	334.0	441.2	649.3	695.5	778.5	854.5	1050.0	1300.0		20568	1939
Poland[a]		1679.5	6397.0	7916.8	10157.0	16916.0	61216.0	327269.0		34449	905
Romania[a]	269.5	354.2	459.9	466.9	489.1	501.3	508.9	613.3		27340	1176
USSR											
Yugoslavia[d,e]	39.8	81.9	0.6	1.1	2.5	7.5	106.0			36857	1548
Others											
Cyprus[a]	0.3	0.5	0.9	1.0	1.1	1.2	1.3	1.6		3501	4796
Gibraltar											
Malta[e]	0.2	0.3	0.3	0.3	0.4	0.4	0.4			1333	3777
Monaco											
Turkey[e]	573.3	3476.0	19212.0	25916.0	37309.0	61955.0	103649.0			48852	872

Source: IMF
Notes: See end of section

Table No: 0309

GOVERNMENT FINANCE

Government Finance and International Liquidity: Latest Year

National currencies (billions)

	Year	Budget Revenue	Budget Expend-iture	Budget Surplus/ Deficit	Foreign Debt	1991 Gold Reserves (million troy oz)	1991 Foreign Exchange Reserves ($ million)
EC members							
Belgium	1989	2581.9	2942.2	-379.5	1106.5	30.2	11068
Denmark	1990	314.6	320.1	-2.8	119.1	2.0	6807
France[a]	1990	2651.1	2777.7	-140.9	38.4	81.9	28292
Germany: East							
Germany: West	1990	696.9	713.7	-41.9	197.8	95.2	57517
Greece	1990	2888.0	4805.7	-1814.3		3.4	5082
Ireland	1991	9.5	9.7	-0.2		0.4	5320
Italy[b]	1990	406.0	532.4	-145.3		66.7	45495
Luxembourg	1989	135.7	119.2	+9.2	2.0	0.4	
Netherlands	1990	242.1	268.7	-24.7	59.7	43.9	16240
Portugal[c]	1989	2591.1	3006.7	-344.6	72.5	15.9	20261
Spain	1991	11353.4	13022.9	-1946.1	10312.3	15.6	64295
United Kingdom[d]	1989	181.2	176.9	+4.0	18.5	18.9	38730
EFTA members							
Austria	1990	626.2	694.2	-77.7	135.4	20.0	9655
Finland[f]	1990	160.2	158.6	+0.7	22.8	2.0	7108
Iceland[c]	1990	119.4	107.7	+11.8	30.0	0.0	444
Liechtenstein							
Norway	1990	306.8	298.7	+4.4	18.2	1.2	12209
Sweden	1990	595.5	555.4	+42.3	83.6	6.1	17476
Switzerland[e]	1990	30.4	28.8	+1.3	38.4	83.3	29002
Eastern Europe							
Albania							
Bulgaria							
Czechoslovakia	1991	458.4	480.2	=18.6		2.8	3050
Hungary[c]	1990	1105.9	1088.8	+16.7	31.7	0.3	3293
Poland	1988	10966.1	11457.8	-673.0	67.3	0.5	3625
Romania	1991	497.3	537.9	-40.6		2.2	323
USSR							
Yugoslavia	1989	12.0	11.4	+0.6		1.9	2682
Others							
Cyprus	1990	0.7	0.8	-0.1	0.5	0.5	1365
Gibraltar	1990	0.1	0.1	-0.0			
Malta	1989	0.2	0.3	-0.0	0.0	0.1	1212
Monaco							
Turkey[d]	1990	56573.0	68316.0	-11782.0	4384.0	4.2	5098

Sources: IMF/OECD
Notes: See end of section

Table No: 0310

GOVERNMENT EXPENDITURE

Government Expenditure by Object: Latest Year

National currencies (billions)

	Year	A	B	C	D	E	F	G	H	I	Total
EC members											
Belgium	1988	90.6	132.9	344.5	48.8	1183.8	64.4	26.2	278.4	676.1	2845.7
Denmark	1988	22.2	15.5	26.9	3.2	107.8	3.9	5.0	21.1	82.5	288.1
France	1988	149.1	163.5	166.3	374.8	1107.0	34.1	9.3	133.2	320.8	2458.1
Germany: East	1986			12.8	13.0	34.1				186.5	246.4
Germany: West	1988	22.3	53.2	3.8	122.9	305.3	2.2	0.7	51.2	75.8	637.4
Greece	1981	96.2	88.6	79.0	86.7	251.9	20.5	16.1	42.6	80.3	822.3
Ireland	1989	0.8	0.3	1.3	1.3	2.7	0.3	0.0	1.1	2.3	10.1
Italy[a]	1988	37.9	18.4	41.9	57.2	191.9	2.9	4.9	58.0	136.8	549.9
Luxembourg	1989	10.3	2.1	12.1	2.6	61.4	3.4	0.9	19.4	7.0	119.2
Netherlands	1990	16.6	13.5	29.1	31.4	102.7	10.9	1.0	19.8	43.7	268.7
Portugal	1987	139.1	122.9	217.6	177.7	548.1	37.3	18.8	213.7	806.8	2282.0
Spain	1988	400.9	733.5	748.8	1704.0	4932.3	89.6	82.7	1435.9	3193.8	13321.5
United Kingdom	1989	7.2	21.5	5.6	25.8	56.0	5.6	0.8	13.1	41.3	176.9
EFTA members											
Austria	1990	34.4	17.7	63.9	89.2	313.9	20.5	4.6	68..8	81.2	694.2
Finland	1989	11.5	6.7	20.7	15.5	47.6	2.7	2.2	29.8	6.7	143.4
Iceland	1987	3.4		7.6	14.3	10.5	1.5	1.1	12.0	6.8	57.2
Liechtenstein											
Norway	1990	14.7	23.8	28.1	31.2	113.4	3.8	3.6	52.3	27.8	298.7
Sweden	1990	25.9	35.2	48.3	5.1	286.4	24.2	3.7	42.2	84.4	555.4
Switzerland	1984	2.2	4.6	1.4	5.9	22.4	0.3	0.1	5.5	2.7	44.9
Eastern Europe											
Albania											
Bulgaria	1989	1.1	1.9	1.8	1.2	4.9	2.2	0.7	13.9	1.8	29.5
Czechoslovakia	1990	10.9	32.3	8.5	1.9	112.9	9.5		223.2	85.4	484.6
Hungary	1990	147.1	39.3	35.9	86.2	312.2	71.8	20.5	239.9	135.9	1088.8
Poland											
Romania	1990	3.9	29.8	7.9	25.2	91.2		1.8	110.9	19.2	289.9
USSR											
Yugoslavia[b]	1989	1164.0	6113.0			685.0		30.0	2247.0	1209.0	11448.0
Others											
Cyprus[b]	1990	60.3	24.2	79.4	48.3	157.9	31.1	6.4	131.0	220.7	759.3
Gibraltar											
Malta[b]	1989	18.6	6.8	24.6	24.3	93.2	24.3	7.9	62.4	12.3	274.4
Monaco											
Turkey	1990	17215.4	7965.5	13088.4	2437.0	1444.8	1017.8	506.5	12154.5	12486.5	68316.4

Sources: IMF/UN/national statistical offices
Notes: See end of section

Table No: 0311

GROSS DOMESTIC PRODUCT

Origin of Gross Domestic Product: Latest Available Year

National currencies (billions)

	Year	A	B	C	D	E	F	G	H	Total, inc. others
EC members										
Belgium[a]	1989	123.6		1300.9	243.8	321.9	1018.5	448.7	2570.6	6027.9
Denmark[a]	1990	31.4	7.4	132.3	12.7	42.8	92.7	61.2	306.3	686.8
France[a]	1989	214.4	30.2	1304.4	124.2	321.6	943.9	346.5	2827.9	6113.1
Germany: East[a,b,c,d,e]	1989	30.3		170.0		20.1	25.1	15.1	-5.7	254.9
Germany: West[a,b,c]	1989	36.1		695.0		116.0	199.7	129.6	1059.2	2235.6
Greece[a,f]	1989	1337.3	120.9	1346.7	194.1	468.5		598.8	4732.1	8789.4
Ireland[b,c]	1988	2.0		6.3		1.0	2.0	1.2	9.0	21.5
Italy[a,b,g]	1989	41.9		275.7	58.5	63.4	219.7	74.0	454.8	1188.0
Luxembourg[a]	1989	5.9	0.3	78.4	5.4	17.9	44.1	17.4	107.1	276.5
Netherlands[a]	1989	21.1	13.8	95.7	9.0	27.6	61.5	32.0	213.7	474.4
Portugal[a,b]	1989	441.0		2055.9	209.8	452.7	1397.8	413.0	2160.1	7130.3
Spain[b]	1989	2194.4		12111.6		3731.5			26983	45020.9
United Kingdom[a]	1989	6.6				30.3	62.1	30.1	382.8	511.9
EFTA members										
Austria[a]	1989	51.6	5.3	446.5	48.7	114.5	268.6	99.I5	638.5	1673.4
Finland[a]	1990	28.6	1.4	99.8	11.0	44.6	51.6	37.6	186.2	460.8
Iceland[a]	1989	29.0		43.5	10.9	19.7	26.6	16.9	94.7	241.3
Liechtenstein										
Norway[a]	1989	25.3	64.2	90.2	20.7	32.5	60.0	61.3	198.4	552.6
Sweden[a]	1990	36.8	5.2	262.5	35.4	89.8	125.6	84.0	536.0	1175.3
Switzerland	1985	8.2		58.6	5.0	17.3	44.1	14.8	80.0	228.0
Eastern Europe										
Albania										
Bulgaria[a,b,c,d]	1989	3.9		17.6		2.9	2.9	2.8	0.7	30.8
Czechoslovakia[a,b,c,d]	1989	62.2		360.0	65.4	100.1	18.6	2.8	609.1	
Hungary	1988	209.5	55.4	327.2	64.5	96.8	125.9	101.2	429.0	1409.5
Poland[b,c,d]	1989	15089.2		52671.7		10054.9	19502.3	5184.0	2450.0	104952.1
Romania[b,c,d]	1989	110.9		421.9		50.6	48.2	60.0	106.4	798.0
USSR[a,b,c,d]	1989	158.4		282.0		86.4	109.0	37.9		673.7
Yugoslavia[a]	1989	25451.2	5493.9	92947.5	3754.5	14406.3	14900.4	23527.0	54914.2	235395.0
Others										
Cyprus	1989	0.2	0.0	0.3	0.0	0.2	0.5	0.2	0.8	2.2
Gibraltar										
Malta[a,h,i]	1989	22.4	22.3	163.7	54.0		84.8	34.6	288.3	670.1
Monaco										
Turkey[a,j]	1989	25805.0	3253.0	44901.0	7097.0	6625.0	28879.0	16830.0	34380.0	16777.0

Sources: OECD/UN/national statistical offices
Notes: See end of section

Table No: 0312

GROSS DOMESTIC PRODUCT

Origin of Gross Domestic Product: Latest Available Year

% total GDP

	Year	A	B	C	D	E	F	G	H	Total, inc. others
EC members										
Belgium[a]	1989	2.1		21.6	4.0	5.3	16.9	7.4	42.6	100.0
Denmark[a]	1990	4.6	1.1	19.3	1.8	6.2	13.5	8.9	44.6	100.0
France[a]	1989	3.5	0.5	21.3	2.0	5.3	15.4	5.7	46.3	100.0
Germany: East[a,b,c,d,e]	1989	11.9		66.7		7.9	9.8	5.9	-2.2	100.0
Germany: West[a,b,c]	1989	1.6		31.1		5.2	8.9	5.8	47.4	100.0
Greece[a,f]	1989	15.2	1.4	15.3	2.2	5.3		6.8	53.8	100.0
Ireland[b,c]	1988	9.3		29.3		4.7	9.3	5.6	41.9	100.0
Italy[a,b,g]	1989	3.5		23.2	4.9	5.3	18.5	6.2	38.3	100.0
Luxembourg[a]	1989	2.1	0.1	28.4	2.0	6.5	15.9	6.3	38.7	100.0
Netherlands[a]	1989	4.4	2.9	20.2	1.9	5.8	13.0	6.7	45.0	100.0
Portugal[a,b]	1989	6.2		28.8	2.9	6.3	19.6	5.8	30.3	100.0
Spain[b]	1989	4.9		26.9		8.3			59.9	100.0
United Kingdom[a]	1989	1.3				5.9	12.1	5.9	74.8	100.0
EFTA members										
Austria[a]	1989	3.1	0.3	26.7	2.9	6.8	16.1	5.9	38.2	100.0
Finland[a]	1990	6.2	0.3	21.7	2.4	9.7	11.2	8.2	40.4	100.0
Iceland[a]	1989	12.0		18.0	4.5	8.2	11.0	7.0	39.2	100.0
Liechtenstein										
Norway[a]	1989	4.6	11.6	16.3	3.7	5.9	10.9	11.1	35.9	100.0
Sweden[a]	1990	3.1	0.4	22.3	3.0	7.6	10.7	7.1	45.6	100.0
Switzerland	1985	3.6		25.7	2.2	7.6	19.3	6.5	35.1	100.0
Eastern Europe										
Albania										
Bulgaria[a,b,c,d]	1989	12.7		57.1		9.4	9.4	9.1	2.3	100.0
Czechoslovakia[a,b,c,d]	1989	10.2		59.1		10.7	16.4	3.1	0.5	100.0
Hungary	1988	14.9	3.9	23.2	4.6	6.9	8.9	7.2	30.4	100.0
Poland[b,c,d]	1989	14.4		50.2		9.6	18.6	4.9	2.3	100.0
Romania[b,c,d]	1989	13.9		52.9		6.3	6.0	7.5	13.3	100.0
USSR[a,b,c,d]	1989	23.5		41.9		12.8	16.2	5.6		100.0
Yugoslavia[a]	1989	10.8	2.3	39.5	1.6	6.1	6.3	10.0	23.3	100.0
Others										
Cyprus	1989	9.1		13.6		7.3	22.7	7.1	36.4	100.0
Gibraltar										
Malta[a,h,i]	1989	3.3	3.3	24.4	8.1		12.7	5.2	43.0	100.0
Monaco										
Turkey[a,j]	1989	15.4	1.9	26.8	4.2	3.9	17.2	10.0	20.5	100.0

Sources: OECD/UN/national statistical offices
Notes: See end of section

Table No: 0313

GROSS DOMESTIC PRODUCT

Usage of Gross Domestic Product 1990

National currencies (billions)

	A	B	C	D	E	F	Total, inc. others
EC members							
Belgium	983.0	4084.0	32.0	1298.0	4661.0	4482.0	6577.0
Denmark[a]	204.6	436.8	-3.0	142.7	302.7	251.5	832.3
France[a]	1255.3	4063.4	27.6	1402.0	1532.9	1510.0	6771.1
Germany: East							
Germany: West[a]	469.2	1379.1	9.7	570.1	1009.4	821.8	2615.8
Greece	2221.4	7563.6	33.1	2060.7	2279.1	3445.3	10455.0
Ireland	4.0	14.2	0.5	4.8	15.9	13.9	25.7
Italy[b]	229.7	812.1	7.5	264.3	250.9	257.6	1306.8
Luxembourg	47.6	166.5	5.3	73.6	286.8	288.4	291.5
Netherlands	75.4	299.1	-1.1	109.1	287.9	262.1	508.3
Portugal	1453.6	5366.6	205.1	2239.4	3105.4	3840.3	8529.8
Spain	7579.0	31259.0	659.0	12235.0	8616.0	10262.0	50087.0
United Kingdom[a]	121.5	368.1	-4.4	94.9	136.0	140.7	575.4
EFTA members							
Austria[a]	344.8	1054.4	15.2	485.0	786.1	768.7	1916.8
Finland[a]	122.0	275.3	-1.0	116.7	110.3	112.8	510.4
Iceland	63.8	207.8	-1.8	66.2	125.6	120.2	341.3
Liechtenstein							
Norway[a]	149.3	345.8	9.1	125.9	307.0	246.9	690.2
Sweden[a]	382.0	779.4	-25.5	270.3	403.7	378.5	1431.6
Switzerland[a]	45.8	190.0	3.8	84.4	115.7	112.7	327.0
Eastern Europe							
Albania							
Bulgaria							
Czechoslovakia[a]	245.2	377.3	83.2	86.2	359.5	342.3	952.2
Hungary	222.0	1300.0	109.2	370.0	685.1	605.0	2080.9
Poland	45045.0	327269.0	68646.0	115732.0	156211.0	106704.0	606726.0
Romania[c]	39.6	613.3		289.3	165.9	220.5	844.0
USSR							
Yugoslavia[d,e]	13.4	106.0	71.7	34.2	59.5	52.7	282.3
Others							
Cyprus[f]	316.3	1557.8	49.7	611.2	1270.5	1374.4	2477.0
Gibraltar							
Malta[e,f]	119.6	425.5	9.9	188.4	543.5	616.8	670.1
Monaco							
Turkey[b,e]	26.8	103.6	-0.2	38.3	39.2	167.5	

Sources: OECD/UN/national statistical offices
Notes: See end of section

Table No: 0314

GROSS DOMESTIC PRODUCT

Usage of Gross Domestic Product 1990

% total GDP

	A	B	C	D	E	F	Total, inc. others
EC members							
Belgium	14.9	62.1	0.5	19.7	70.9	68.1	100.0
Denmark[a]	24.6	52.5	-0.4	17.1	36.4	30.2	100.0
France[a]	18.5	60.0	0.4	20.7	22.6	22.3	100.0
Germany: East							
Germany: West[a]	17.9	52.7	0.4	21.8	38.6	31.4	100.0
Greece	21.2	72.3	0.3	19.7	21.8	33.0	100.0
Ireland	15.6	55.3	1.9	18.7	61.9	54.1	100.0
Italy	17.6	62.1	0.6	20.2	19.2	19.7	100.0
Luxembourg	16.3	57.1	1.8	25.2	98.4	98.9	100.0
Netherlands	14.8	58.8	-0.2	21.5	56.6	51.6	100.0
Portugal	17.0	62.9	2.4	26.3	36.4	45.0	100.0
Spain	15.1	62.4	1.3	24.4	17.2	20.5	100.0
United Kingdom[a]	21.1	64.0	-0.8	16.5	23.6	24.5	100.0
EFTA members							
Austria[a]	18.0	55.0	0.8	25.3	41.0	40.0	100.0
Finland[a]	23.9	53.9	-0.2	22.9	21.6	22.1	100.0
Iceland	18.7	60.9	-0.5	19.4	36.8	35.2	100.0
Liechtenstein							
Norway[a]	21.6	50.1	1.3	18.2	44.5	35.8	100.0
Sweden[a]	26.7	54.4	-1.8	18.9	28.2	26.4	100.0
Switzerland[a]	14.0	58.1	1.2	25.8	35.4	34.5	100.0
Eastern Europe							
Albania							
Bulgaria							
Czechoslovakia[a]	25.8	39.6	8.7	9.1	37.8	35.9	100.0
Hungary	10.7	62.5	5.2	17.8	32.9	29.1	100.0
Poland	7.4	53.9	11.3	19.1	25.7	17.6	100.0
Romania[b]	4.7	72.7		34.3	19.7	26.1	100.0
USSR							
Yugoslavia[c]	4.7	37.5	25.4	12.1	21.1	18.7	100.0
Others							
Cyprus	12.8	62.9	2.0	24.7	51.3	55.5	100.0
Gibraltar							
Malta[c]	17.8	63.5	1.5	28.1	81.1	92.0	100.0
Monaco							
Turkey[c]	16.0	61.9	-0.1	22.9	22.9	23.4	100.0

Sources: OECD/UN/national statistical offices
Notes: See end of section

Table No: 0315

EXCHANGE RATES

Exchange Rates Against US Dollar 1977-1992

National currency units per US dollar

	1977	1978	1979	1980	1981	1982	1983	1984
EC members								
Belgium	35.8	31.5	29.3	29.2	37.1	45.7	51.1	57.8
Denmark	6.0	5.5	5.3	5.6	7.1	8.3	9.1	10.4
France	4.9	4.5	4.3	4.2	5.4	6.6	7.6	8.7
Germany: East	1.3	1.5	1.8	1.8	2.3	2.4	2.6	3.1
Germany: West	2.3	2.0	1.8	1.8	2.3	2.4	2.6	2.8
Greece	36.8	36.8	37.0	42.6	55.4	66.8	88.1	112.7
Ireland	0.6	0.5	0.5	0.5	0.6	0.7	0.8	0.9
Italy	882.4	848.7	830.9	856.4	1136.8	1352.5	1518.8	1757.0
Luxembourg	35.8	31.5	29.3	29.2	37.1	45.7	51.1	57.8
Netherlands	2.5	2.2	2.0	2.0	2.5	2.7	2.9	3.2
Portugal	38.3	43.9	48.9	50.1	61.6	79.5	110.8	146.4
Spain	76.0	76.7	67.1	71.7	92.3	109.9	143.4	160.8
United Kingdom	0.6	0.5	0.5	0.4	0.5	0.6	0.7	0.7
EFTA members								
Austria	16.5	14.5	13.4	12.9	15.9	17.1	18.0	20.0
Finland	4.0	4.1	3.9	3.7	4.3	4.8	5.6	6.0
Iceland	2.0	2.7	3.5	4.8	7.2	12.4	24.8	31.7
Liechtenstein	2.4	1.8	1.7	1.7	2.0	2.0	2.1	2.3
Norway	5.3	5.2	5.1	4.9	5.7	6.5	7.3	8.2
Sweden	4.5	4.5	4.3	4.2	5.1	6.3	7.7	8.3
Switzerland	2.4	1.8	1.7	1.7	2.0	2.0	2.1	2.3
Eastern Europe								
Albania[a]	0.1	6.7	6.3	6.2	6.1	5.9	6.6	7.3
Bulgaria	0.9	0.9	0.9	0.9	0.9	1.0	1.0	1.0
Czechoslovakia								16.6
Hungary	41.0	37.9	35.6	32.5	34.3	36.6	42.7	40.0
Poland	43.2	41.2	40.2	44.3	51.3	84.8	91.7	113.7
Romania	20.0	18.4	18.0	18.0	15.0	15.0	17.2	21.3
USSR	0.7	0.7	0.7	0.6	0.7	0.7	0.7	0.8
Yugoslavia	0.002	0.002	0.002	0.002	0.003	0.005	0.009	0.015
Others								
Cyprus	2.5	2.7	2.8	2.8	2.4	2.1	1.9	0.6
Gibraltar	0.6	0.5	0.5	0.4	0.5	0.6	0.7	0.7
Malta	0.4	0.4	0.4	0.3	0.4	0.4	0.4	0.5
Monaco	4.9	4.5	4.3	4.2	5.4	6.6	7.6	8.7
Turkey	18.0	24.3	31.1	76.0	111.2	162.6	225.5	366.7

Table No: 0315 (cont'd)

EXCHANGE RATES

Exchange Rates Against US Dollar 1977-1992

National currency units per US dollar

	1985	1986	1987	1988	1989	1990	1991	August 1992	Unit of currency
EC members									
Belgium	59.4	44.7	37.3	36.8	39.4	33.4	34.1	30.2	Belgian Franc
Denmark	10.6	8.1	6.8	6.7	7.3	6.2	6.4	5.7	Danish Kroner
France	9.0	6.9	6.0	6.0	6.4	5.4	5.6	5.0	Franc
Germany: East	2.6	2.0	1.7	1.9	1.9				DDR Mark
Germany: West	2.9	2.2	1.8	1.8	1.9	1.6	1.7	1.5	Deutsche Mark
Greece	138.1	140.0	135.4	141.9	162.4	158.5	182.3	180.1	Drachma
Ireland	0.9	0.7	0.7	0.7	0.7	0.6	0.6	0.6	Pound
Italy	1907.4	1490.8	1296.1	1301.6	1372.1	1198.1	1240.6	1110.0	Lira
Luxembourg	59.4	44.7	37.3	36.8	39.4	33.4	34.1	31.1	Luxembourg Franc
Netherlands	3.3	2.5	2.0	2.0	2.1	1.8	1.9	1.9	Guilder
Portugal	170.4	149.6	140.9	144.0	157.5	142.6	144.5	125.4	Escudo
Spain	170.0	140.1	123.5	116.5	118.4	101.9	103.9	93.6	Peseta
United Kingdom	0.8	0.7	0.6	0.6	0.6	0.6	0.6	0.6	Pound
EFTA members									
Austria	20.7	15.3	12.6	12.3	13.2	11.4	11.7	10.3	Schilling
Finland	6.2	5.1	4.4	4.2	4.3	3.8	4.0	4.0	Markka
Iceland	41.5	41.1	38.7	43.0	57.0	58.3	59.0	54.7	Icelandic Krona
Liechtenstein	2.5	1.8	1.5	1.5	1.6	1.4	1.4	1.4	Swiss Franc
Norway	8.6	7.4	6.7	6.5	6.9	6.3	6.5	5.8	Norwegian Krone
Sweden	8.6	7.1	6.3	6.1	6.4	5.9	6.0	5.3	Swedish Kronor
Switzerland	2.5	1.8	1.5	1.5	1.6	1.4	1.4	1.4	Swiss Franc
Eastern Europe									
Albania[a]	7.7	6.7	6.2	6.0	6.4			50.0	Lek
Bulgaria	1.0	1.2	1.3	1.7	2.1			20.9	Leva
Czechoslovakia	17.1	15.0	13.7	14.4	15.1	18.0	29.5	27.9	Koruny
Hungary	50.1	45.8	47.0	52.5	59.1	63.2	74.7	78.1	Forint
Poland	147.2	175.2	265.1	430.5	1439.2	9500.0	10576.0	13559.7	Zloty
Romania	17.1	16.2	14.6	14.3	14.9	22.4	76.4	314.1	Lei
USSR	0.8	0.7	0.6	0.6	0.6				Rouble
Yugoslavia	0.0	0.0	0.1	0.3	2.9	11.3	19.6	316.8	New Dinar
Others									
Cyprus	0.5	0.5	0.4	0.5	0.5	0.5	0.5	0.4	Cyprus Pound
Gibraltar	0.8	0.7	0.6	0.6	0.6			0.5	Gibraltar Pound
Malta	0.5	0.4	0.3	0.3	0.3	0.3	0.3	0.3	Maltese Lira
Monaco	9.0	6.9	6.0	6.0	6.4	5.4	5.6	5.1	French Franc
Turkey	522.0	674.5	857.2	1422.3	2121.7	2608.6	171.8	6919.6	Turkish Lira

Sources: IMF/UN/national statistical offices
Notes: See end of section

Table No: 0316

EXCHANGE RATES

Exchange Rates Against ECU 1985-1992

National currency units per ECU

	1985	1986	1987	1988	1989	1990	1991	August 1992	Unit of currency
EC members									
Belgium	44.91	43.78	43.04	43.43	43.38	42.43	42.22	41.99	Belgian Franc
Denmark	8.02	7.94	7.88	7.95	8.05	7.86	7.91	7.85	Danish Kroner
France	6.80	6.80	6.93	7.04	7.02	6.92	6.98	6.91	Franc
Germany: East	2.23	2.13	2.07	2.07	2.07	2.05	2.05	2.04	DDR Mark
Germany: West	2.23	2.13	2.07	2.07	2.07	2.05	2.05	2.04	Deutsche Mark
Greece	105.74	137.43	156.22	167.58	178.84	201.41	225.20	251.14	Drachma
Ireland	0.72	0.73	0.78	0.78	0.78	0.77	0.77	0.77	Pound
Italy	1448.00	1461.09	1494.71	1537.33	1510.47	1521.94	1553.30	1542.87	Lira
Luxembourg	44.91	43.78	43.04	43.43	43.38	42.43	42.22	41.99	Luxembourg Franc
Netherlands	2.51	2.40	2.33	2.34	2.34	2.31	2.31	2.30	Guilder
Portugal	130.25	147.09	162.58	170.06	173.41	181.11	175.50	174.10	Escudo
Spain	129.13	137.46	142.19	137.60	130.41	129.32	130.00	130.16	Peseta
United Kingdom	0.59	0.67	0.71	0.66	0.67	0.71	0.70	0.72	Pound
EFTA members									
Austria	20.70	14.98	14.55	14.59	14.57	14.44	14.34	14.35	Schilling
Finland	6.20	4.98	5.07	4.94	4.72	4.86	4.92	5.05	Markka
Iceland	41.50	41.10	38.70	43.00	57.00	58.28	57.40		Icelandic Krona
Liechtenstein	2.50	1.76	1.72	1.73	1.80	1.76	1.85	1.83	Swiss Franc
Norway	8.60	7.28	7.77	7.70	7.60	7.95	8.02	8.03	Norwegian Krone
Sweden	8.60	6.70	7.31	7.24	7.10	7.52	7.49	7.41	Swedish Kronor
Switzerland	2.50	1.76	1.72	1.73	1.80	1.76	1.85	1.83	Swiss Franc
Eastern Europe									
Albania[a]	7.70	6.70	6.20	6.00	6.40	17.95	28.74		Lek
Bulgaria	1.00	1.20	1.30	1.70	2.10	63.21	72.65		Leva
Czechoslovakia	17.14	14.99	13.69	14.36	15.05	9500.00	9500.00		Koruny
Hungary	50.10	45.80	47.00	52.50	59.10	22.43	35.71		Forint
Poland	147.20	175.20	265.10	430.50	1439.20				Zloty
Romania	17.10	16.20	14.60	14.30	14.90	11.32	14.44		Lei
USSR	0.80	0.70	0.60	0.60	0.60				Rouble
Yugoslavia	0.03	0.04	0.07	0.25	2.88				Dinar
Others									
Cyprus	0.50	0.50	0.40	0.50	0.50	0.46	0.45		Cyprus Pound
Gibraltar	0.80	0.70	0.60	0.60	0.60				Gibraltar Pound
Malta	0.50	0.40	0.30	0.30	0.30	0.32	0.32		Maltese Lira
Monaco	6.80	6.80	6.93	7.04	7.02	6.92	6.98		French Franc
Turkey	522.00	674.50	857.20	1422.30	2121.70	2608.60	3134.60		Turkish Lira

Sources: Commission of European Communities/Financial Times
Notes: See end of section

Notes to Tables in Section Three:

Table 0301
- a Dollar and percentage share values based on 1990 results
- b Data for 1991 are estimated
- c Net material product
- d Data for 1991 refer to former West Germany only
- e '000 billion lire
- f 1977-83 data are net material product
- g 1977-86 data are net material product

Table 0302
- a Dollar and percentage share values based on 1990 results
- b '000 billion lire
- c Net material product
- d Dollar and percentage share values based on 1988 results
- e Gross social product
- f Dollar and percentage share values based on 1989 results

Table 0303
- a Net material product
- b 1977-83 data are NMP
- c 1977-86 data are NMP

Table 0304
- a Net material product

Table 0305
- a New series starting 1987 and 1991
- b Data for 1991 are estimated
- c New series starting 1985
- d New series starting 1987
- e New series starting 1982
- f '000 billion lire
- g New series starting 1988
- h New series starting 1982 and 1983
- i New series starting 1981, 1983 and 1987
- j New series starting 1989
- k New series starting 1983
- l New series starting 1984
- m New series starting 1978 and 1986
- n New series starting 1980, 1985, 1988 and 1990
- o Million new dinars

Table 0306
- a 1990 data are calculated from index of retail prices, service charges and fares
- b Calculated from state retail price index

Table 0307
- a Dollar and percentage share values based on 1990 results
- b Data for 1991 are estimated
- c '000 billion lire
- d New series starting 1984
- e Million new dinars
- f Dollar and percentage share values based on 1989 results

Table 0308
- a Dollar and percentage share values based on 1990 results
- b Data for 1991 are estimated
- c '000 billion lire
- d Million new dinars to 1982; billion new dinars from 1983
- e Dollar and percentage share values based on 1989 results

Table 0309 0.0 indicates less than 50,000 troy oz (gold reserves), less than 50 million currency units (other columns)
- a Foreign debt refers to foreign currency debt
- b '000 billion lire
- c Foreign debt in 1987
- d Foreign debt in 1986
- e Foreign debt in 1989
- f Foreign debt in 1988

Table 0310
- A General public services
- B Defence
- C Education
- D Health
- E Social security and welfare
- F Housing and community amenities
- G Other community/social services
- H Economic services
- I Other purposes

- a '000 billion lire
- b Millions

Tables 0311 and 0312
- A Agriculture/forestry/fishing
- B Mining & quarrying
- C Manufacturing
- D Electricity, gas and water
- E Construction
- F Wholesale and retail trade, restaurants and hotels
- G Transport, storage and communications
- H Others

- a GDP total given by government differs significantly from external estimates
- b C includes B
- c C includes D
- d Data refer to net material product
- e Statistical discrepancy results in "others" column
- f H includes F
- g '000 billion lire
- h B includes E
- i Million liri
- j Restaurants and hotels included in "others"

Table 0313
- A Government final consumption expenditure
- B Private final consumption expenditure
- C Increase in stocks
- D Gross fixed capital formation
- E Exports of goods and services
- F Imports of goods and services

- a Data refer to 1990
- b '000 billion
- c Usage of Gross Capital Formation (inc. increase/decrease in stocks)
- d New dinars
- e Data refer to 1989
- f Millions

Table 0314
- A Government final consumption expenditure
- B Private final consumption expenditure
- C Increase in stocks
- D Gross fixed capital formation
- E Exports of goods and services
- F Imports of goods and services

- a Data refer to 1991
- b Usage of Gross Capital Formation (inc. increase/decrease in stocks)
- c Data refer to 1989

Table 0315 Annual average market exchange rates
- a Mid-year exchange data
- b Data for 1991 are estimated

Table 0316 Annual average market exchange rates
- a Mid-year exchange data

Section Four

Finance and Banking

Table No: 0401

INTEREST RATES

Lending Rates 1980-1991

% per annum

	1980	1983	1984	1985	1986	1987	1988	1989	1990	1991
EC members										
Belgium	17.00	13.75	14.00	12.54	10.44	9.33	8.92	11.08	13.00	12.88
Denmark	17.20	14.49	13.38	14.65	12.98	13.62	12.59	13.44		
France[a]	18.73	18.95	18.85	17.77	16.38	15.82	15.65	16.01	16.75	
Germany: East										
Germany: West	12.04	10.05	9.82	9.53	8.75	8.36	8.33	9.94	11.59	12.46
Greece	21.30	20.50	20.50	20.50	20.50	21.81	22.89	23.26	27.62	29.45
Ireland	15.96	14.13	12.92	12.44	12.23	11.15	8.29	9.42	11.29	10.63
Italy	19.03	22.27	20.38	13.36	15.93	13.58	13.57	14.21	14.08	13.89
Luxembourg	9.25	9.38	9.25	8.75	7.75	7.19	6.71	7.25	8.23	8.25
Netherlands	13.50	8.46	8.88	9.25	8.63	8.15	7.77	10.75	11.75	12.40
Portugal[b]	18.50	24.10	27.05	27.29	19.63	18.92	17.53	19.59	21.71	22.87
Spain	16.85	15.00	16.58	13.52	12.19	16.36	12.43	15.84	16.01	14.38
United Kingdom	16.17	9.79	9.65	12.29	10.83	9.63	10.29	13.92	14.75	11.54
EFTA members										
Austria										
Finland[c]	9.77	9.56	10.49	10.41	9.08	8.91	9.72	10.31	11.62	11.81
Iceland	45.00	42.80	22.80	32.60	18.80	26.60	30.30	28.00	16.20	17.50
Liechtenstein										
Norway	12.63	14.35	13.69	13.46	13.62	14.03	14.28	14.39	14.18	18.72
Sweden[c]	15.12	15.07	15.53	16.72	14.18	12.99	13.32	14.36	17.18	14.97
Switzerland		5.49	5.49	5.43	5.46	5.24	5.07	5.85	7.42	7.83
Eastern Europe										
Albania										
Bulgaria										
Czechoslovakia[d]	4.56	4.69	4.68	4.64	4.72	4.73	4.66	5.20	6.16	15.32
Hungary[c]	9.00	13.00	13.00	12.00	11.00	11.50	13.00	17.00	28.00	30.00
Poland[c]	8.00	9.00	9.00	12.00	12.00	12.00	16.70	64.00	101.40	54.60
Romania										
USSR										
Yugoslavia	11.50	38.00	44.50	71.50	82.00	111.25	455.17	4353.75		
Others										
Cyprus	9.00	9.00	9.00	9.00	9.00	9.00	9.00	9.00	9.00	9.00
Gibraltar										
Malta	8.00	8.00	8.00	8.00	8.00	8.00	8.50	8.50	8.50	8.50
Monaco										
Turkey	25.67	35.50	52.33	53.50	52.63	50.00				

Source: International Monetary Fund (IMF)
Notes: See end of section

Table No: 0402

BANK RESERVES

Reserves of Deposit Banks 1980-1991

National currencies (billions)

	1980	1983	1984	1985	1986	1987	1988	1989	1990	1991
EC members										
Belgium	19.5	16.9	21.7	20.0	22.9	21.6	20.9	23.2	23.2	
Denmark[a,b]	1.1	1.3	2.1	25.8	11.2	4.7	8.4	9.1	8.7	19.4
France[c]	47.0	58.0	75.0	112.0	112.0	136.0	123.0	112.0	89.0	80.0
Germany: East										
Germany: West	70.4	69.5	75.6	78.3	80.2	83.6	89.0	96.8	117.7	112.8
Greece[c]	100.8	348.8	600.9	661.4	715.5	984.9	1210.0	1119.7	1384.9	1549.6
Ireland	0.5	0.4	0.5	0.5	0.6	0.6	0.6	0.7	0.8	0.6
Italy	37110.0	456347.0	66988.0	81854.0	89384.0	97168.0	106770.0	117380.0	130970.0	134810.0
Luxembourg		7.2	7.0	6.5	5.5	4.9	5.0			
Netherlands	1.0	1.6	1.9	2.1	2.1	2.1	2.2	2.6	2.9	2.9
Portugal[d]	112.3	297.0	287.0	273.7	256.4	352.4	424.1	1272.1	1354.1	1731.2
Spain	884.0	3601.0	3649.0	3678.0	3789.0	5274.0	5285.0	6003.0	5034.0	5809.0
United Kingdom	2.4	2.4	2.8	2.9	3.6	4.3	5.0	5.8	6.0	5.8
EFTA members										
Austria	43.4	50.6	54.0	55.4	62.0	52.7	48.8	65.3	61.8	59.4
Finland	4.0	6.0	10.4	12.2	11.6	18.6	24.0	29.9	22.4	28.4
Iceland[c]		4.9	7.4	9.1	12.2	13.1	14.4	19.2	14.3	14.8
Liechtenstein		75.2	114.3							
Norway	1.4	2.0	2.2	2.7	3.3	3.9	2.7	2.7	2.8	3.4
Sweden	5.7	4.8	5.3	7.7	13.9	15.4	18.8	19.9	24.9	15.5
Switzerland		18.6	15.8	15.8	17.2	18.7	9.3	8.6	8.3	7.9
Eastern Europe										
Albania										
Bulgaria										
Czechoslovakia										
Hungary[c]	68.0	99.8	76.7	84.6	98.4	148.7	126.8	168.8	300.0	416.0
Poland[c]		1351.1	1363.4	1314.3	1273.1	1151.0	3176.0	18893.0	39089.0	38878.0
Romania[e]	81.3	67.9	43.6	35.9	8.3	0.4	0.4	0.4	8.7	316.1
USSR										
Yugoslavia[c,f]	32.0	116.0	177.0	300.0	541.0	1713.0	6195.0	149223.0	154566.0	309331.0
Others										
Cyprus	0.1	0.2	0.2	0.2	0.3	0.3	0.3	0.3	0.5	0.5
Gibraltar										
Malta[g]	76.5	55.7	58.1	127.2	127.6	113.2	103.6	86.4	58.4	62.8
Monaco										
Turkey[c]	219.5	827.1	1299.1	1833.8	2205.2	2806.0	5635.0	9352.0	11717.0	15548.0

Source: IMF

Notes: See end of section

Table No: 0403

FOREIGN ASSETS

Foreign Assets of Deposit Banks 1980-1991

Current US dollars (millions)

	1980	1983	1984	1985	1986	1987	1988	1989	1990	1991
EC members										
Belgium[a]	60680	66202	71607	92631	117926	149126	150374	164520	192030	175380
Denmark	4833	6654	7975	14158	16033	24150	28780	34660	45550	49070
France[a]	148098	144460	158640	184380	217990	290100	299720	358900	458670	424070
Germany: East										
Germany: West	85171	74756	75232	112932	178478	232608	230045	295247	394780	401960
Greece[a]	1188	1386	1598	1980	1788	1870	2590	2980	3460	3140
Ireland			2650	3220	3840	5900	6260	9860	13540	14370
Italy	31195	31498	35530	45470	54720	60830	65590	84330	96590	99640
Luxembourg	104755	103250	101710	130950	171700	226525	232022	280190	355120	358720
Netherlands	62625	58862	57520	72876	91099	115975	120572	146271	185330	189050
Portugal	1739	1710	1850	2270	2320	2740	4180	4660	5490	6950
Spain[b]		15712	18100	20730	24680	26940	25760	29030	41400	49340
United Kingdom[c]	350946	485210	489710	590070	715560	875220	882660	923590	1068950	1018650
EC total	851230	989700	1022122	1271667	1596134	2011984	2048553	2334238	2860910	2790340
EFTA members										
Austria	21711	25743	26515	36754	48900	58955	54604	58902	65990	66190
Finland	2762	4777	6258	7671	14310	18825	20542	22242	27000	24240
Iceland	35	41	40	58	61	106	99	109		
Liechtenstein										
Norway	627	2540	2997	3644	6880	8680	6510	6680	8080	9420
Sweden[d]	8036	7122	8680	11380	14630	19540	20890	37550	40950	39760
Switzerland[e]	66452	68374	161830	205460	253440	331950	319060	355600	444050	428590
EFTA total	99623	108597	206320	264967	338221	438056	421705	481083	586070	568200
Eastern Europe										
Albania										
Bulgaria										
Czechoslovakia										
Hungary	177	129	182	363	685	636	733			
Poland	1477	1640	1896	2295	2371	2783	2795	2800		
Romania	260	353	317	608	1770	1547	1020	800	680	270
USSR										
Yugoslavia[a]	1811	1896	2283	2676	2173	2037	2089	2950	1690	1070
East European total	3725	4018	4678	5942	6999	7003	6637	6550	2370	1340
Others										
Cyprus	46	67	85	124	178	232	319			
Gibraltar										
Malta	159	125	118	157	199	260	308	425		
Monaco										
Turkey[a]	547	992	2076	1994	2178	2425	3280	3220	4130	4370
Total	752	1184	2279	2276	2555	2917	3907	3645	4130	
European total	955330	1103499	1235399	1544852	1943909	2459960	2480802	2825516		

Source: IMF

Notes: See end of section

Table No: 0404

FOREIGN LIABILITIES

Foreign Liabilities of Deposit Banks 1980-1991

Current US dollars (million)

	1980	1981	1982	1983	1984	1985	1986	1987	1988	1989	1990	1991
EC members												
Belgium[a]	71953	83102	78374	80196	86376	112925	144838	184795	186432	205530	239790	212300
Denmark	4877	5271	5844	7104	8289	14852	16405	23440	27900	35230	44800	47380
France[a]	133554	139433	146101	152020	174370	197180	228290	296360	315900	384690	519670	486630
Germany: East												
Germany: West	72093	66795	64692	57923	58224	75773	101288	131375	131000	159895	226370	230860
Greece[a]	4001	4676	4916	6600	6600	7590	9120	11410	12300	14360	16460	15430
Ireland					5650	6980	9080	11780	11770	14140	19330	19000
Italy	44696	46411	41123	43790	56700	70540	92320	111450	119040	156810	196890	236680
Luxembourg	97263	106184	102158	94730	92880	117540	152480	197857	193060	231280	296030	309580
Netherlands	64353	65181	62732	56217	53052	65677	83456	108672	109884	121329	153430	157360
Portugal[a,b]	808	896	1366	1684	1766	1636	1516	1770	11014	12290	17140	18163
Spain	22856	26175	19349	19417	22990	22620	26630	34640	38660	45960	68370	78740
UK	365601	471122	517063	532027	538220	625740	758930	927460	961770	1028070	1201300	1154800
EC total	882055	1015246	1043718	1051708	1105117	1319053	1624353	2041009	2116280	2409544	2999580	2966923
EFTA members												
Austria	24955	25538	26118	26355	28153	38026	50891	62440	59370	65949	74310	76560
Finland	4566	4909	6293	7205	9441	12812	20531	32917	37756	42581	59910	53450
Iceland[a]	178	209	222	289	300	422	419	630	754	740	673	657
Liechtenstein												
Norway	2738	3439	3979	4336	7500	11300	15630	22470	21110	21070	23570	17410
Sweden	12518	14100	13157	13980	16950	21610	29280	40970	51530	81170	104630	99810
Switzerland[c]	47949	58606	56124	54517	134590	163790	193720	247880	243460	280480	352970	345490
EFTA total	92904	106801	105893	106682	196934	247960	310471	407307	413980	491990	616063	593377
Eastern Europe												
Albania												
Bulgaria												
Czechoslovakia												
Hungary[a]	1752	1555	1312	1237	1284	1415	1851	1750	1917	2165	1642	1594
Poland[a,d]	5676	5279	4209	4391	5166	4764	4666	4183	4046	14263	1768	1163
Romania	8381	9056	8034	7603	6460	6160	6213	5900	1970	510	1720	720
USSR												
Yugoslavia[a]	8261	8986	8113	7866	8291	9615	11363	11757	11003	10300	9640	8230
E European total	24070	24876	21668	21097	21201	21954	24093	23590	18936	27238	14470	11707
Others												
Cyprus[a]	148	174	212	249	286	365	463	600	715	898	1414	1630
Gibraltar												
Malta	19	25	25	30	27	42	49	77	103	120	208	261
Monaco												
Turkey[a]	82	46	343	446	2190	3060	4360	6580	6950	7510	10070	11380
Total	249	245	581	725	2503	3467	4872	7257	7768	8528	11692	13271
European total	999278	1147167	1171860	1180212	1325755	1592433	1963788	2479163	2556964	2937300	3642105	3585278

Source: IMF

Notes: See end of section

Table No: 0405

PRIVATE LENDING

Bank Claims on the Private Sector 1980-1991

National currencies (billions)

	1980	1983	1984	1985	1986	1987	1988	1989	1990	1991
EC members										
Belgium	968.0	1101.3	1181.0	1222.3	1342.4	1493.8	1769.5	2220.8	2335.2	372.0
Denmark[a,b]	94.0	132.9	162.0	190.4	251.9	370.8	371.8	415.8	429.2	6425.0
France[c]				3646.0	4056.0	4599.0	5142.0	5656.0	6314.0	
Germany: East										
Germany: West	1155.2	1399.4	1489.0	1594.6	1665.5	1726.1	1818.5	1952.6	2310.5	2559.1
Greece[c]	516.8	933.5	1078.0	1355.4	1670.9	1712.0	2507.0	2120.8	2406.6	2600.5
Ireland	2.9	4.1	4.5	4.3	4.7	5.0	6.3	7.7	7.8	7.0
Italy	136717.0	203225.0	240607.0	268681.0	296400.0	321429.0	371690.0	455300.0	523400.0	606800.0
Luxembourg	111.8	204.5	218.4	224.9	259.7	280.2	323.6	372.4	446.4	476.4
Netherlands[d]	224.8	250.5	259.5	270.9	290.7	306.4	375.1	399.9	426.2	460.8
Portugal[d]	688.1	1289.0	1500.0	1689.0	1893.0	2024.3	2764.7	2944.8	4008.7	5016.7
Spain	10714.0	15680.0	15832.0	16887.0	18356.0	21063.0	24545.0	28058.0	30746.0	36017.0
United Kingdom[a]	63.7	119.7	146.5	167.4	206.3	376.1	467.6	582.4	644.3	662.1
EFTA members										
Austria	754.2	957.5	788.4	928.8	874.6	914.7	1018.2	1165.2	1330.5	1460.2
Finland[c]	90.3	146.1	170.5	203.2	231.0	271.5	348.1	402.8	449.9	479.2
Iceland[c,e]	4.3	26.0	38.3	50.5	58.2	81.8	111.4	146.2	157.7	168.9
Liechtenstein										
Norway	94.6	143.4	180.1	236.6	303.8	372.6	399.2	433.0	451.6	432.8
Sweden[f]	219.2	289.0	323.5	338.7	397.3	452.8	580.8	704.3	791.2	785.4
Switzerland[g]	195.8	281.6	305.1	335.3	355.2	388.2	431.8	490.0	532.8	552.0
Eastern Europe										
Albania										
Bulgaria										
Czechoslovakia										
Hungary[c]	113.1	167.3	179.6	208.6	240.6	648.7	668.9	792.7	947.5	949.6
Poland[c]	156.0	295.0	364.0	462.0	580.0	742.0	1104.0	1987.0	17193.0	43037.0
Romania[h]		349.8	380.6	439.1	469.8	513.0	546.6	478.9	684.0	1370.3
USSR										
Yugoslavia[i]	140.0	290.0	433.0	645.0	1092.0	2492.0	8507.0	200823.0	301346.0	446427.0
Others										
Cyprus	0.4	0.6	0.7	0.8	0.9	1.0	1.2	1.3	1.6	1.8
Gibraltar										
Malta	0.1	0.2	0.2	0.2	0.2	0.3	0.3	0.4	0.5	0.5
Monaco										
Turkey[c]	660.3	1707.9	3624.8	5725.3	8993.0	13992.0	20013.0	33885.0	59755.0	81273.0

Source: IMF
Notes: See end of section

Table No: 0406

PERSONAL FINANCE

Ownership of Banking Services 1991

% of adults	Bank Account	Cheque Book	Cash Dispenser Card	Use Card Instead of Cash
EC members				
Belgium	81	56	51	18
Denmark	94	43	43	15
France	88	84	53	39
Germany: East				
Germany: West	89	57	38	10
Greece	56	3	2	8
Ireland	63	33	30	14
Italy	57	39	16	6
Luxembourg	87	70	40	31
Netherlands	87	65	61	19
Portugal	68	53	22	7
Spain	69	22	30	13
United Kingdom	81	70	60	41
EFTA members				
Austria	90	49	56	42
Finland	93	13	61	41
Iceland				
Liechtenstein				
Norway	94	55	53	36
Sweden	90	49	56	42
Switzerland	91	18	31	35
Eastern Europe				
Albania				
Bulgaria				
Czechoslovakia				
Hungary				
Poland				
Romania				
USSR				
Yugoslavia				
Others				
Cyprus				
Gibraltar				
Malta				
Monaco				
Turkey				

Source: Reader's Digest Eurodata

Table No: 0407

PERSONAL FINANCE

Eurocard/Mastercard Holders 1987-1991; Accepting Outlets 1989; Eurocheque Holders 1991

'000

	Eurocard/Mastercard holders 1987	1988	1989	1991	Accepting outlets 1989	Eurocheque holders 1991
EC members						
Belgium	107	184	235	309	32	3372
Denmark	99	122	139	159	12	198
France	1423	1840	2753	4167	488	82
Germany: East						
Germany: West	577	835	1827	3241	135	30500
Greece	33	64	99	118	47	0
Ireland	177	204	278	290	13	128
Italy	282	397	477	557	110	1550
Luxembourg	17	29	44	54	3	165
Netherlands	130	186	359	2322	30	4154
Portugal	8	11	19	26	16	178
Spain	256	450	500	406	350	10
United Kingdom	10497	12100	14032	11432	380	1875
EC total	13606	16422	20762	23081	1616	42212
EFTA members						
Austria	60	93	211	309	19	2400
Finland	32	39	50	50	28	82
Iceland	19	26	29	30	5	0
Liechtenstein						
Norway	56	60	70	106	10	57
Sweden	32	39	651	804	44	0
Switzerland	189	248	374	609	32	1960
EFTA total	388	505	1385	1908	138	4499
Eastern Europe						
Albania						
Bulgaria						
Czechoslovakia						
Hungary			0	3	1	14
Poland						
Romania						
USSR			0	182	1	0
Yugoslavia	25	25	27	48	9	22
East European total	25	25	27	233	11	36
Others						
Cyprus		0	0	3	5	3
Gibraltar						
Malta			8	15	1	1
Monaco						
Turkey	8	15	47	107	34	0
Total	8	15	55	125	40	4
European total	14027	16967	22229	25347	1805	46751

Sources: EFMA/Eurocard International/Euromonitor
Notes: See end of section

Table No: 0408

PERSONAL FINANCE

Visa Cardholders and Accepting Outlets 1985-1991

'000

	Visa					Accepting outlets	
	1985	1987	1989	1990	1991	1989	1991
EC members							
Belgium	32	63	497	719	956	30	
Denmark	0	0	161	223	307	11	
France	4629	6352	7291	7769	8189	495	
Germany: East							
Germany: West	119	182	756	1073	1312	121	
Greece	89	87	161	213	267	60	
Ireland	156	224	332	406	430	15	
Italy	1273	1410	2339	3243	3499	177	
Luxembourg	31	51	74	93	107	6	
Netherlands	15	40	113	189	203	25	
Portugal	122	255	481	622	926	16	
Spain	3671	5366	6817	9930	11638	431	
United Kingdom	11243	14212	22569	26090	28282	473	
EC total	21380	28242	41591	50570	56116	1860	
EFTA members							
Austria	45	84	192	244	290	20	
Finland	189	376	645	766	804	27	
Iceland	42	74	83	86	91	8	
Liechtenstein							
Norway	196	404	507	563	605	14	
Sweden	283	503	846	1062	1293	45	
Switzerland	164	249	393	459	536	37	
EFTA total	919	1690	2666	3180	3619	151	
Eastern Europe							
Albania							
Bulgaria							
Czechoslovakia				0	1		
Hungary			1	3	4	1	
Poland					0		
Romania							
USSR			0	0	0	1	
Yugoslavia	2	12	44	76	75	12	
East European total	2	12	45	79	80	14	
Others							
Cyprus	16	27	52	69	89	11	
Gibraltar							
Malta	0	3		6	9	1	
Monaco							
Turkey	1	14	197	419	556	37	
Total	17	41	252	494	654	49	
European total	22318	29985	44554	54323	60469	2074	6200

Source: Visa International
Note: See end of section

Table No: 0409

PERSONAL FINANCE

Ownership of Savings and Investments 1991

% of adults

	Post Office Savings	Stocks and Shares	Government Savings/ Bonds	Employer's Pension Fund	Private Pension Savings Plan
EC members					
Belgium	27	22	9	7	17
Denmark		40	33	13	40
France	37	23	2	8	13
Germany: East					
Germany: West	25	10	10	11	16
Greece	12	2	6	2	1
Ireland	21	9	4	7	4
Italy	15	5	18	3	4
Luxembourg	3	9	2	4	3
Netherlands	30	12	14	29	7
Portugal	5	4	2	7	4
Spain	67	6	5	6	2
United Kingdom	22	22	9	35	21
EFTA members					
Austria	24	7	6	4	9
Finland	1	38	9	3	2
Iceland					
Liechtenstein					
Norway	21	26	6	33	20
Sweden	23	46	34	8	26
Switzerland	26	27	5	60	9
Eastern Europe					
Albania					
Bulgaria					
Czechoslovakia					
Hungary					
Poland					
Romania					
USSR					
Yugoslavia					
Others					
Cyprus					
Gibraltar					
Malta					
Monaco					
Turkey					

Source: Reader's Digest Eurodata

Notes to Tables in Section Four:

Table 0401	a	Data for 1990 are estimated
	b	New series starting 1987 and 1988
	c	Data for 1991 are estimated
	d	Rate for state enterprises
Table 0402	a	New series starting 1987
	b	New series starting 1991
	c	Data for 1991 are estimated
	d	New series starting 1988
	e	New series starting 1985 and 1990
	f	New dinars
	g	Million liri
Table 0403	a	Data for 1991 are estimated
	b	New series starting 1982
	c	New series starting 1985
	d	New series starting 1990
	e	New series starting 1982 and 1984
Table 0404	a	Data for 1991 are estimated
	b	New series starting 1988
	c	New series starting 1984
	d	New series starting 1981
Table 0405	a	New series starting 1987
	b	New series starting 1991
	c	Data for 1991 are estimated
	d	New series starting 1988
	e	New series starting 1989
	f	New series starting 1983
	g	New series starting 1982 and 1984
	h	New series starting 1985 and 1990
	i	New dinars
Table 0407	0 = less than 1,000 1991: year ending September	
Table 0408	0 = less than 1,000	

Lending Rates 1980-1991: Selected Countries

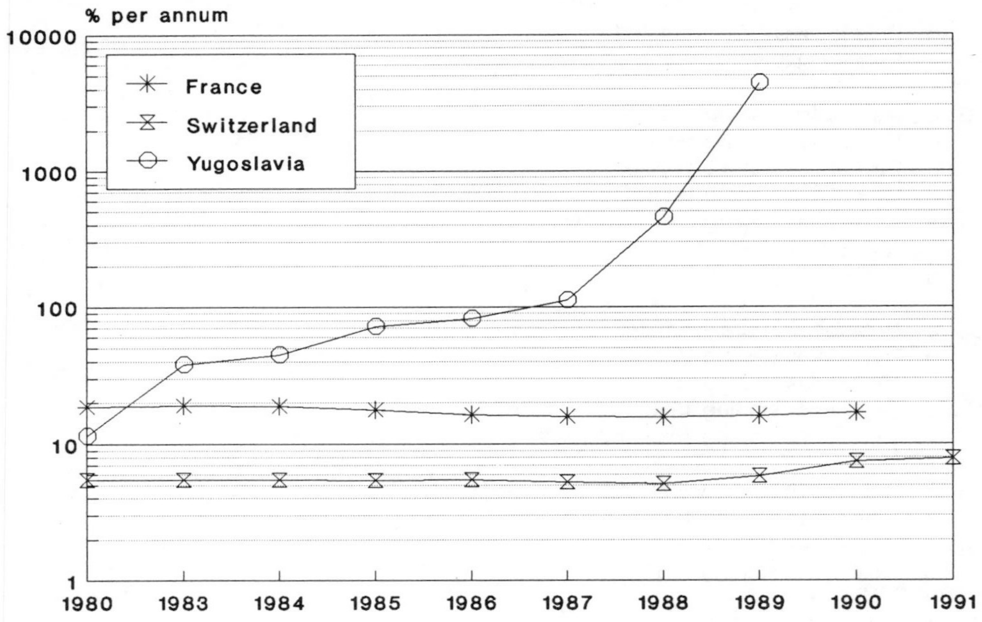

Ownership of Cash Dispenser Cards 1991: Selected Countries

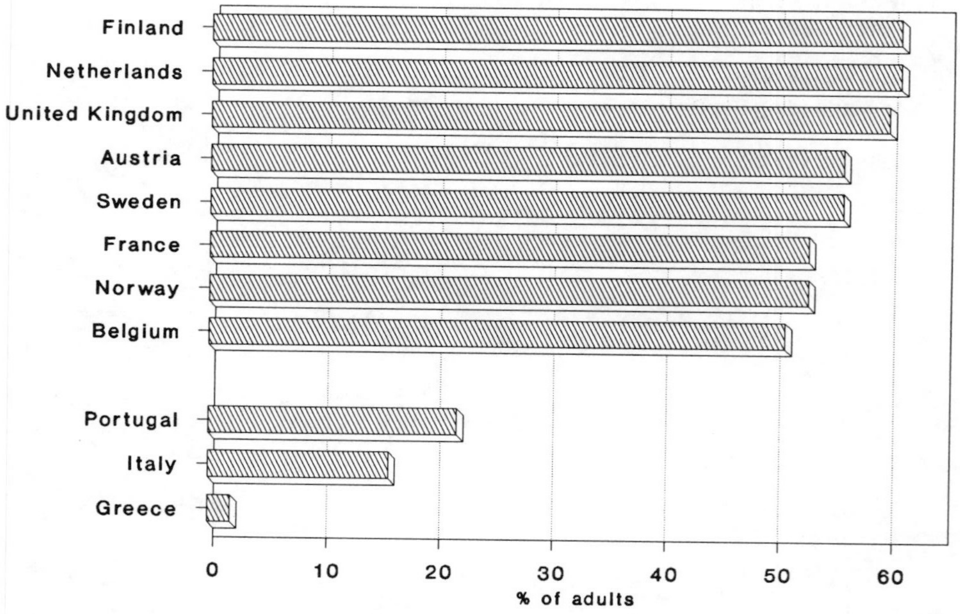

Section Five

External Trade by Destination and Commodity

Table No: 0501

TOTAL IMPORTS

Trends in Total Imports (fob) 1977-1991

National currencies (billions)

	1977	1980	1981	1982	1983	1984	1985	1986	1987
EC members									
Belgium[a]	1404.5	2037.6	2240.3	2573.6	2736.1	3099.7	3218.0	2969.8	3016.6
Denmark	76.4	104.6	119.2	132.8	142.3	164.3	183.1	176.6	166.4
France	331.0	551.0	635.8	705.0	757.5	870.7	931.1	867.4	920.5
Germany: East[b]	49.9	63.0	67.0	69.9	76.2	83.5	86.7	90.5	80.6
Germany: West[c]	227.7	331.4	357.3	365.2	378.5	421.4	451.1	402.9	399.5
Greece[d]	223.1	400.8	437.0	589.3	749.3	959.3	1250.3	1404.8	1569.4
Ireland	2.9	5.2	6.3	6.5	7.0	8.5	9.0	8.8	8.7
Italy[e]	39.6	80.4	99.8	110.2	113.3	139.8	156.3	138.7	151.3
Luxembourg									
Netherlands	106.7	147.0	157.8	161.1	167.6	188.3	204.0	174.9	174.7
Portugal	165.6	422.2	543.6	683.4	817.3	1052.3	1181.1	1307.8	1781.8
Spain	1257.1	2313.4	2808.5	3289.7	3944.1	4366.4	4786.1	4613.6	5688.6
United Kingdom[f]	34.0	46.1	47.6	53.2	61.6	74.8	81.3	82.2	90.7
EC total									
EFTA members									
Austria	227.9	305.7	321.3	320.3	333.1	374.5	411.5	389.8	393.4
Finland	29.3	55.5	58.4	61.7	68.2	71.3	77.9	72.0	82.8
Iceland	1.1	4.4	6.8	10.6	18.7	24.3	34.2	41.7	55.7
Liechtenstein		0.4	0.4	0.4	0.4	0.4	0.4	0.5	
Norway	66.9	81.8	87.8	97.8	95.8	110.3	129.2	146.2	148.2
Sweden	83.9	139.2	143.5	169.2	195.6	213.6	239.1	227.2	251.6
Switzerland	41.9	58.8	58.3	57.3	60.6	68.5	74.0	72.8	74.4
EFTA total									
Eastern Europe									
Albania									
Bulgaria[g]	6.0	8.3	10.0	11.0	12.0	12.8	14.0	14.4	14.0
Czechoslovakia		173.5	150.1	160.3	165.2	187.5	198.3	209.4	213.0
Hungary	262.9	294.6	307.9	319.0	359.2	384.0	402.0	432.1	455.1
Poland	559.9	706.3	623.7	868.9	970.2	1209.7	1594.9	1964.0	2875.6
Romania	140.4	230.7	186.9	146.2	165.7	219.9	178.8	130.6	121.0
USSR[b]	30.1	44.5	52.6	56.4	59.6	65.4	69.1	62.6	60.7
Yugoslavia[h]	8.8	13.8	14.4	12.3	11.1	11.0	11.2	10.8	11.6
East European total									
Others									
Cyprus[d]	0.2	0.4	0.4	0.5	0.6	0.7	0.7	0.6	0.6
Gibraltar							0.1	0.1	0.1
Malta[d]	0.2	0.3	0.3	0.3	0.3	0.3	0.3	0.3	0.4
Monaco									
Turkey[d,g]	100.0	583.0	961.0	1389.0	2018.0	3802.0	5638.0	2562.0	11687.0
Total									
European total									

Table No: 0501 (cont'd)

TOTAL IMPORTS

Trends in Total Imports (fob) 1977-1991

National currencies (billions)

	1988	1989	1990	1991	% growth 1977-91	% share 1991	Total $ billion 1991	$ per capita 1991
EC members								
Belgium[a]	3291.6	3767.1	3881.7	3979.8	183.36	7.0	116.5	11678
Denmark	166.8	186.5	190.0	197.3	158.25	1.9	30.8	6007
France	1030.5	1187.2	1226.7	1251.2	278.01	13.3	221.8	3921
Germany: East[b]	87.1							
Germany: West[c]	428.4	493.2	541.8	634.1	178.48	23.0	382.1	6135
Greece[d]	1555.8	2326.9	2776.8	3436.2	1440.21	1.1	18.9	1866
Ireland	9.7	11.7	11.9	12.3	324.14	1.2	19.9	5643
Italy[e]	168.4	196.4	203.7	211.2	433.33	10.2	170.2	2957
Luxembourg								
Netherlands	186.0	209.4	216.9	222.0	108.06	7.1	118.7	7969
Portugal	2189.1	2722.8	3254.4	3414.9	1962.14	1.4	23.6	2284
Spain	6641.1	7921.1	8394.7	8309.3	560.99	4.8	80.0	2054
United Kingdom[f]	102.0	117.0	120.7	113.8	234.71	12.1	201.3	3514
EC total						83.3	1383.9	4032
EFTA members								
Austria	431.2	491.5	531.3	549.3	141.03	2.8	47.0	6141
Finland	84.8	99.6	98.6	83.9	186.35	1.2	20.7	4171
Iceland	62.7	73.0	88.7	92.3	8290.91	0.1	1.6	6152
Liechtenstein								
Norway	146.9	158.7	162.9	157.4	135.28	1.5	24.3	5736
Sweden	273.0	308.5	314.1	292.6	248.75	2.9	48.4	5674
Switzerland	81.6	94.3	95.7	94.1	124.58	4.0	65.6	9853
EFTA total						12.5	207.6	6421
Eastern Europe								
Albania								
Bulgaria[g]	13.8							
Czechoslovakia	209.6	214.7	238.2	293.7		0.6	10.0	636
Hungary	463.8	515.1	547.5			0.5	8.7	816
Poland	5272.2	14864.0	77520.0	164259.0	29237.20	0.9	15.5	408
Romania	109.1	125.9	204.5			0.5	9.1	392
USSR[b]	65.0							
Yugoslavia[h]	12.1	13.6	17.3	13.5	53.41	0.1	0.9	39
East European total						2.7	44.2	108
Others								
Cyprus[d]	0.8	1.0	1.1	1.1	378.26	0.1	2.4	3266
Gibraltar	0.1	0.2	0.2					
Malta[d]	0.4	0.5	0.6	0.6	200.00	0.1	1.9	5269
Monaco								
Turkey[d,g]	19367.0	31938.0	58755.0	88657.0	885.57	1.3	21.3	379
Total						1.5	25.5	446
European total						100.0	1661.2	1976

Sources: IMF International Financial Statistics/Comecon Foreign Trade Data/national trade statistics
Notes: See end of section

Table No: 0502

TOTAL EXPORTS

Trends in Total Exports (fob) 1977-1991

National currencies (billions)

	1977	1980	1981	1982	1983	1984	1985	1986	1987
EC members									
Belgium[a]	1344.7	1890.4	2062.3	3393.2	2651.3	2992.1	3167.7	3066.6	3100.1
Denmark	60.4	95.7	114.3	128.1	146.7	165.3	179.6	171.8	175.3
France	319.2	490.6	576.7	633.1	723.1	851.0	906.9	864.4	888.9
Germany: East[b]	41.8	57.1	65.9	75.2	84.2	90.4	93.5	91.4	83.6
Germany: West	273.6	350.3	397.0	427.8	432.3	488.2	537.1	526.4	527.4
Greece[c]	101.3	221.1	237.9	286.3	392.7	542.7	629.1	790.0	881.0
Ireland	2.5	4.1	4.8	5.7	6.9	8.9	9.7	9.4	10.7
Italy[d]	40.0	66.7	86.0	99.2	110.6	129.0	149.7	145.3	144.8
Luxembourg									
Netherlands	107.2	147.0	170.8	176.8	184.4	210.7	225.6	197.8	187.5
Portugal	75.7	232.2	254.9	331.7	508.6	760.6	967.4	1082.3	1311.0
Spain	775.3	1493.2	1888.4	2258.0	2838.6	3778.1	4099.2	3799.1	4195.6
United Kingdom	32.0	47.4	50.7	55.6	60.5	70.5	78.3	73.0	79.8
EC total									
EFTA members									
Austria	161.8	226.2	251.8	266.9	277.1	314.5	354.0	342.3	342.4
Finland	30.9	52.8	60.3	63.0	69.9	80.9	84.1	82.7	87.5
Iceland	1.0	4.5	6.5	8.5	18.6	23.6	33.8	45.1	53.1
Liechtenstein		0.9	0.9	0.9	0.9	1.1	1.2	1.2	
Norway	47.3	91.7	104.3	113.2	131.4	154.0	170.7	134.9	144.5
Sweden	85.7	130.7	144.9	168.1	210.5	242.8	260.5	265.1	281.3
Switzerland	42.0	49.6	52.9	52.7	53.8	60.6	66.7	67.0	67.5
EFTA total									
Eastern Europe									
Albania									
Bulgaria	6.0	8.9	9.9	10.9	11.8	13.0	13.7	13.3	13.8
Czechoslovakia		172.1	153.8	165.4	171.6	195.5	204.0	206.7	211.7
Hungary	238.6	281.0	299.5	324.5	374.1	414.0	424.6	420.3	450.1
Poland	430.3	628.6	547.9	951.2	1060.2	1336.1	1691.0	2115.6	3236.5
Romania	140.4	201.8	189.2	173.4	197.8	269.1	208.6	202.6	152.7
USSR[b]	33.3	49.6	57.1	63.2	67.9	74.4	72.5	75.7	68.1
Yugoslavia[e]	5.3	9.0	10.0	10.3	9.9	10.3	10.7	10.4	11.4
East European total									
Others									
Cyprus[c]	0.1	0.2	0.2	0.3	0.2	0.3	0.3	0.2	0.3
Gibraltar									0.0
Malta[c]	0.1	0.2	0.2	0.2	0.2	0.2	0.2	0.2	0.3
Monaco									
Turkey[c]	31.0	221.0	531.0	937.0	1299.0	2608.0	4153.0	5012.0	8844.0
Total									
European total									

Table No: 0502 (cont'd)

TOTAL EXPORTS

Trends in Total Exports (fob) 1977-1991

National currencies (billions)

	1988	1989	1990	1991	% growth 1977-1991	% share 1991	Total $ million 1991	$ per capita 1991
EC members								
Belgium[a]	3382.3	3943.1	3942.9	4001.5	197.58	7.2	117.2	11742
Denmark	185.8	205.3	216.4	229.1	279.30	2.2	35.8	6976
France	997.7	1143.2	1177.2	1221.0	282.52	13.4	216.4	3826
Germany: East[b]								
Germany: West	567.7	641.0	660.7	648.2	136.92	24.1	390.6	6271
Greece[c]	776.4	1231.0	1281.0	1554.6	1434.65	0.5	8.5	844
Ireland	12.3	14.6	14.3	15.0	500.00	1.5	24.2	6882
Italy[d]	166.4	193.0	203.6	209.7	424.25	10.4	169.0	2936
Luxembourg								
Netherlands	203.9	228.5	239.2	248.1	131.44	8.2	132.7	8906
Portugal	1531.7	2015.7	2335.8	2347.1	3000.53	1.0	16.2	1570
Spain	4686.4	5134.5	5630.6	5585.0	620.37	3.3	53.7	1381
United Kingdom	81.7	93.8	103.7	104.8	227.50	11.4	185.4	3236
EC total						83.3	1349.9	3933
EFTA members								
Austria	383.3	429.3	466.1	496.4	206.80	2.6	42.5	5550
Finland	90.9	99.9	101.4	93.1	201.29	1.4	23.0	4628
Iceland	61.7	79.1	92.6	91.6	9060.00	0.1	1.6	6106
Liechtenstein								
Norway	143.9	185.9	211.1	217.0	358.77	2.1	33.5	7908
Sweden	304.2	332.2	340.2	332.7	288.21	3.4	55.0	6452
Switzerland	74.1	84.3	88.3	87.9	109.29	3.8	61.3	9204
EFTA total						13.4	216.9	6706
Eastern Europe								
Albania								
Bulgaria								
Czechoslovakia	220.2	218.2	216.5	321.2		0.7	10.9	696
Hungary	504.1	571.3	603.7			0.6	9.6	900
Poland	6011.8	19476.0	129455.0	157716.0	36552.57	0.9	14.9	392
Romania	148.4	156.5	131.7			0.4	5.9	253
USSR[b]								
Yugoslavia[e]	12.7	13.5	14.3	14.0	164.15	0.1	1.0	41
East European total						2.6	42.2	103
Others								
Cyprus[c]	0.4	0.4	0.5	0.5	400.00	0.1	1.1	1484
Gibraltar	0.0	0.0	0.1					
Malta[c]	0.2	0.3	0.4	0.4	300.00	0.1	1.2	3513
Monaco								
Turkey[c]	16809.0	24819.0	34070.0	37102.0	119583.87	0.5	8.9	159
Total						0.7	11.2	196
European total						100.0	1620.2	1927

Sources: IMF, International Financial Statistics/Comecon, Foreign Trade Data/national trade statistics

Notes: See end of section

Table No: 0503

EXTERNAL TRADE BY DESTINATION AND ORIGIN

Imports by Country of Origin 1990

Current US dollars (millions)

	BLEU	France	Germany	Italy	Netherlands	UK	Total EC	Norway	Sweden	Switzerland	Total EFTA
EC members											
Belgium		18877.0	28702.0	5423.0	21039.0	9904.0	87660.0	1172.0	2681.0	1965.0	7337.0
Denmark	1041.0	1684.0	7068.0	1311.0	1852.0	2405.0	16392.0	1487.0	3651.0	638.0	7211.0
France	20514.0		43969.0	26894.0	11812.0	16905.0	138837.0	3005.0	3572.0	6063.0	16732.0
Germany: East[a]	115.0	221.5		117.2	201.0	154.9	901.8	30.2	93.9	321.7	845.1
Germany: West	24849.0	40692.0		32314.0	34988.0	23124.0	179144.0	4896.0	8253.0	14613.0	46596.0
Greece	740.0	1601.0	4116.0	3048.0	1332.0	1042.0	12733.0	86.0	280.0	356.0	1164.0
Ireland	446.0	943.0	1723.0	528.0	851.0	9078.0	14127.0	175.0	313.0	149.0	888.0
Italy	9252.0	25859.0	38555.0		10420.0	9499.0	104394.0	684.0	2736.0	8292.0	16871.0
Luxembourg											
Netherlands	17551.0	9716.0	32295.0	4716.0		10303.0	801414.0	1746.0	2726.0	1755.0	8726.0
Portugal	1036.8	2852.2	3590.0	2481.8	1436.9	1894.1	17299.0	259.3	357.0	522.4	1696.1
Spain	2728.0	12854.0	14431.0	8891.0	3251.0	6321.0	52198.0	271.0	1578.0	1281.0	4395.0
United Kingdom	10204.0	20771.0	35427.0	11863.0	18700.0		117278.0	7166.0	6388.0	7501.0	26384.0
EFTA members											
Austria	1423.0	2064.0	21538.0	4441.0	1392.0	1266.0	33634.0	163.0	852.0	2222.0	3585.0
Finland	740.0	1155.0	4620.0	1244.0	861.0	2077.0	12431.0	935.0	3504.0	473.0	5297.0
Iceland	30.6	51.1	216.3	51.4	160.0	138.7	813.7	84.1	125.0	20.1	268.0
Liechtenstein											
Norway	633.0	1012.0	3764.0	864.0	1071.0	2415.0	12423.0		4232.0	418.0	5776.0
Sweden	1606.0	2662.0	10463.0	2235.0	2232.0	4354.0	29471.0	4079.0		1036.0	9523.0
Switzerland	2510.0	7721.0	23508.0	7329.0	2869.0	3677.0	49933.0	403.0	1339.0		5029.0
Eastern Europe											
Albania											
Bulgaria[a]	45.4	126.9	893.6	278.8	67.7	86.6	1610.9	5.0	29.6	103.7	291.4
Czechoslovakia[a]	111.4	234.1	2875.8	302.8	172.5	382.2	4264.5	35.8	129.4	586.4	2109.5
Hungary	146.2	177.3	1503.1	349.3	180.6	182.7	2661.7	12.8	128.2	265.3	1321.9
Poland	185.0	287.0	2881.0	535.0	349.0	386.0	4885.0	142.0	211.0	279.0	1098.0
Romania	49.0	179.0	1068.0	112.0	136.0	174.0	1838.0	4.0	20.0	190.0	371.0
USSR[b]	494.0	1645.0	13038.0	2921.0	636.0	1165.0	21092.0	188.0	446.0	805.0	6195.0
Yugoslavia	226.0	1212.0	3491.0	2469.0	380.0	426.0	8680.0	57.0	247.0	412.0	1865.0
Others											
Cyprus	45.5	166.9	235.9	255.7	63.0	325.8	1377.5	10.0	38.3	36.0	120.2
Gibraltar											
Malta	32.7	145.1	231.0	731.7	59.1	294.5	1566.5	33.3	15.8	16.2	96.9
Monaco											
Turkey	617.0	1191.5	3744.4	1662.2	614.0	1117.6	9577.6	101.1	231.9	577.3	1303.1

Table No: 0503 (cont'd)

EXTERNAL TRADE BY DESTINATION AND ORIGIN

Imports by Country of Origin 1990

Current US dollars (millions)

	CMEA	USA	Canada	Brazil	Americas	Total Africa	Japan	China	Asia	Austra-lasia	Total, inc. others
EC members											
Belgium	2030.0	5266.0	665.0	654.0	1272.0	4425.0	2508.0	292.0	3106.0	604.0	119414.0
Denmark	762.0	1964.0	143.0	220.0	800.0	209.0	1307.0	327.0	1288.0	96.0	31573.0
France	5192.0	18956.0	1559.0	1736.0	3348.0	10971.0	9338.0	2213.0	9134.0	1073.0	234460.0
Germany: East[a]	2173.9	102.1	28.4	49.9	105.6	57.3	40.6	158.7	147.1	22.5	9089.0
Germany: West	16018.0	222922.0	2793.0	3183.0	6232.0	7826.0	20466.0	4868.0	18975.0	1714.0	346461.0
Greece	791.0	729.0	66.0	177.0	171.0	366.0	1172.0	118.0	541.0	58.0	19793.0
Ireland	202.0	3000.0	148.0	69.0	126.0	261.0	1153.0	84.0	636.0	36.0	21000.0
Italy	6623.0	9267.0	1452.0	1993.0	2528.0	8821.0	4231.0	1830.0	5424.0	1167.0	181726.0
Luxembourg											
Netherlands	2608.0	9912.0	882.0	1131.0	2053.0	3200.0	4014.0	725.0	5587.0	524.0	125873.0
Portugal	90.3	970.8	189.3	390.7	503.4	1603.4	661.6	70.1	547.5	74.5	25246.0
Spain	1780.0	7269.0	436.0	775.0	2854.0	4185.0	3890.0	745.0	3136.0	463.0	87424.0
United Kingdom	2868.0	25036.0	3984.0	1269.0	2648.0	4869.0	12064.0	1044.0	15188.0	2562.0	223040.0
EFTA members											
Austria	2803.0	1795.0	243.0	162.0	352.0	846.0	2222.0	359.0	1615.0	53.0	49288.0
Finland	3226.0	1839.0	212.0	132.0	372.0	105.0	1726.0	195.0	905.0	87.0	26991.0
Iceland	90.1	235.0	8.9	4.8	7.0	4.6	92.0	6.7	36.9	43.3	1618.4
Liechtenstein											
Norway	601.0	2186.0	590.0	116.0	1177.0	1202.0	1171.0	177.0	913.0	75.0	26834.0
Sweden	1556.0	4615.0	352.0	270.0	686.0	217.0	2781.0	423.0	2260.0	174.0	53382.0
Switzerland	675.0	4260.0	219.0	249.0	1168.0	967.0	3059.0	300.0	2270.0	108.0	69705.0
Eastern Europe											
Albania											
Bulgaria[a]	653.4	92.7	23.5	55.5	73.5	32.2	59.7	62.3	232.6	8.3	4086.2
Czechoslovakia[a]	2241.9	76.2	16.1	107.6	150.6	46.6	63.7	456.1	319.0	96.2	13699.7
Hungary	2401.4	227.9	10.5	140.1	73.5	218.9	180.8	48.9	248.0	8.6	8621.4
Poland	3035.0	305.0	20.0	149.0	41.0	33.0	221.0	128.0	398.0	60.0	10867.0
Romania	3362.0	428.0	19.0	39.0	98.0	49.0	79.0	238.0	87.0	114.0	9358.0
USSR[b]	10792.0	3396.0	1061.0	345.0	886.0	724.0	2819.0	1952.0	4310.0	500.0	64894.0
Yugoslavia	4182.0	854.0	79.0	192.0	303.0	397.0	425.0	166.0	709.0	104.0	19227.0
Others											
Cyprus	84.6	181.4	11.5	13.2	7.6	37.6	294.8	17.6	179.8	3.8	2288.0
Gibraltar											
Malta	44.5	55.5	4.4	9.7	11.7	8.0	98.9	9.1	88.1	6.3	2076.3
Monaco											
Turkey	1182.2	2161.6	234.0	236.7	269.6	746.2	1019.3	133.8	707.0	236.2	20751.7

Sources: OECD Foreign Trade Statistics/IMF Direction of Trade Statistics
Notes: See end of section

Table No: 0504

EXTERNAL TRADE BY DESTINATION AND ORIGIN

Imports by Country of Origin 1990

% total imports	BLEU	France	West Germany	Italy	Nether-lands	UK	Total EC	Norway	Sweden	Switzer-land	Total EFTA
EC members											
Belgium		15.8	24.0	4.5	17.6	8.3	73.4	1.0	2.2	1.6	6.1
Denmark	3.3	5.3	22.4	4.2	5.9	7.6	51.9	4.7	11.6	2.0	22.8
France	8.7		18.8	11.5	5.0	7.2	59.2	1.3	1.5	2.6	7.1
Germany: East[a]	1.3	2.4		1.3	2.2	1.7	9.9	0.3	1.0	3.5	9.3
Germany: West	7.2	1.7		9.3	10.1	6.7	51.7	1.4	2.4	4.2	13.4
Greece	3.7	8.1	20.8	15.4	6.7	5.3	64.3	0.4	1.4	1.8	5.9
Ireland	2.1	4.5	8.2	2.5	4.1	43.2	67.3	0.8	1.5	0.7	4.2
Italy	5.1	14.2	21.2		5.7	5.2	57.4	0.4	1.5	4.6	9.3
Luxembourg											
Netherlands	13.9	7.7	25.7	3.7		8.2	63.7	1.4	2.2	1.4	6.9
Portugal	4.1	11.3	14.2	9.8	5.7	7.5	68.5	1.0	1.4	2.1	6.7
Spain	3.1	14.7	16.5	10.2	3.7	7.2	59.7	0.3	1.8	1.5	5.0
United Kingdom	4.6	9.3	15.9	5.3	8.4		52.6	3.2	2.9	3.4	11.8
EFTA members											
Austria	2.9	4.2	43.7	9.0	2.8	2.6	68.2	0.3	1.7	4.5	7.3
Finland	2.7	4.3	17.1	4.6	3.2	7.7	46.1	3.5	13.0	1.8	19.6
Iceland	1.9	3.2	13.4	3.2	9.9	8.6	50.3	5.2	7.7	1.2	16.6
Liechtenstein											
Norway	2.4	3.8	14.0	3.2	4.0	9.0	46.3		15.8	1.6	21.5
Sweden	3.0	5.0	19.6	4.2	4.2	8.2	55.2	7.6		1.9	17.8
Switzerland	3.6	11.1	33.7	10.5	4.1	5.3	71.6	0.6	1.9		7.2
Eastern Europe											
Albania											
Bulgaria[a]	1.1	3.1	21.9	6.8	1.7	2.1	39.4	0.1	0.7	2.5	7.1
Czechoslovakia[a]	0.8	1.7	21.0	2.2	1.3	2.8	31.1	0.3	0.9	4.3	15.4
Hungary	1.7	2.1	17.4	4.1	2.1	2.1	30.9	0.1	1.5	3.1	15.3
Poland	1.7	2.6	26.5	4.9	3.2	3.6	45.0	1.3	1.9	2.6	10.1
Romania[b]	0.5	1.9	11.4	1.2	1.5	1.9	19.6	0.0	0.2	2.0	4.0
USSR	0.8	2.5	20.1	4.5	1.0	1.8	32.5	0.3	0.7	1.2	9.5
Yugoslavia	1.2	6.3	18.2	12.8	2.0	2.2	45.1	0.3	1.3	2.1	9.7
Others											
Cyprus	2.0	7.3	10.3	11.2	2.8	14.2	60.2	0.4	1.7	1.6	5.3
Gibraltar											
Malta	1.6	7.0	11.1	35.2	2.8	14.2	75.4	1.6	0.8	0.8	4.7
Monaco											
Turkey	3.0	5.7	18.0	8.0	3.0	5.4	46.2	0.5	1.1	2.8	6.3

Table No: 0504 (cont'd)

EXTERNAL TRADE BY DESTINATION AND ORIGIN

Imports by Country of Origin 1990

% total imports	CMEA	USA	Canada	Brazil	Americas	Total Africa	Japan	China	Asia	Austra-lasia	Total, inc. others
EC members											
Belgium	1.7	4.4	0.6	0.5	1.1	3.7	2.1	0.2	2.6	0.5	100.0
Denmark	2.4	6.2	0.5	0.7	2.5	0.7	4.1	1.0	4.1	0.3	100.0
France	2.2	8.1	0.7	0.7	1.4	4.7	4.0	0.9	3.9	0.5	100.0
Germany: East[a]	23.9	1.1	0.3	0.5	1.2	0.6	0.4	1.7	1.6	0.2	100.0
Germany: West	4.6	6.6	0.8	0.9	1.8	2.3	5.9	1.4	5.5	0.5	100.0
Greece	4.0	3.7	0.3	0.9	0.9	1.8	5.9	0.6	2.7	0.3	100.0
Ireland	1.0	14.3	0.7	0.3	0.6	1.2	5.5	0.4	3.0	0.2	100.0
Italy	3.6	5.1	0.8	1.1	1.4	4.9	2.3	1.0	3.0	0.6	100.0
Luxembourg											
Netherlands	2.1	7.9	0.7	0.9	1.6	2.5	3.2	0.6	4.4	0.4	100.0
Portugal	0.4	3.8	0.7	1.5	2.0	6.4	2.6	0.3	2.2	0.3	100.0
Spain	2.0	8.3	0.5	0.9	3.3	4.8	4.4	0.9	3.6	0.5	100.0
United Kingdom	1.3	11.2	1.8	0.6	1.2	2.2	5.4	0.5	6.8	1.1	100.0
EFTA members											
Austria	5.7	3.6	0.5	0.3	0.7	1.7	4.5	0.7	3.3	0.1	100.0
Finland	12.0	6.8	0.8	0.5	1.4	0.4	6.4	0.7	3.4	0.3	100.0
Iceland	5.6	14.5	0.5	0.3	0.4	0.3	5.7	0.4	2.3	2.7	100.0
Liechtenstein											
Norway	2.2	8.1	2.2	0.4	4.4	4.5	4.4	0.7	3.4	0.3	100.0
Sweden	2.9	8.6	0.7	0.5	1.3	0.4	5.2	0.8	4.2	0.3	100.0
Switzerland	1.0	6.1	0.3	0.4	1.7	1.4	4.4	0.4	3.3	0.2	100.0
Eastern Europe											
Albania											
Bulgaria[a]	16.0	2.3	0.6	1.4	1.8	0.8	1.5	1.5	5.7	0.2	100.0
Czechoslovakia[a]	16.4	0.6	0.1	0.8	1.1	0.3	0.5	3.3	2.3	0.7	100.0
Hungary	27.9	2.6	0.1	1.6	0.9	2.5	2.1	0.6	2.9	0.1	100.0
Poland	27.9	2.8	0.2	1.4	0.4	0.3	2.0	1.2	3.7	0.6	100.0
Romania	35.9	4.6	0.2	0.4	1.0	0.5	0.8	2.5	0.9	1.2	100.0
USSR[b]	16.6	2.2	1.6	0.5	1.4	1.1	4.3	3.0	6.6	0.8	100.0
Yugoslavia	21.8	4.4	0.4	0.9	1.6	2.1	2.2	0.9	3.7	0.5	100.0
Others											
Cyprus	3.7	7.9	0.5	0.6	0.3	1.6	12.9	0.8	7.9	0.2	100.0
Gibraltar											
Malta	2.1	2.7	0.2	0.5	0.6	0.4	4.8	0.4	4.2	0.3	100.0
Monaco											
Turkey	5.7	10.4	1.1	1.1	1.3	3.6	4.9	0.6	3.4	1.1	100.0

Sources: OECD Foreign Trade Statistics/IMF Direction of Trade Statistics
Notes: See end of section

Table No: 0505

EXTERNAL TRADE BY DESTINATION AND ORIGIN

Exports by Country of Destination 1990

Current US dollars (millions)

	BLEU	France	West Germany	Italy	Nether-lands	UK	Total EC	Norway	Sweden	Switzer-land	Total EFTA
EC members											
Belgium		23775.0	25116.0	7725.0	15733.0	10229.0	88406.0	586.0	1694.0	2425.0	6836.0
Denmark	735.0	2093.0	6847.0	1735.0	1658.0	3737.0	18129.0	1982.0	4428.0	695.0	8527.0
France	19617.0		36311.0	23827.0	11780.0	19475.0	131500.0	913.0	2485.0	8827.0	15104.0
Germany: East[a]	79.5	230.9		81.3	143.2	176.6	830.9	51.6	123.5	165.6	484.7
Germany: West	29777.0	52159.0		37250.0	33847.0	33957.0	218283.0	3476.0	10430.0	23878.0	65382.0
Greece	163.0	769.0	1784.0	1332.0	277.0	585.0	5127.0	37.0	129.0	109.0	451.0
Ireland	1045.0	2502.0	2785.0	1046.0	1376.0	8044.0	17823.0	193.0	456.0	402.0	1334.0
Italy	5791.0	27830.0	32306.0		5301.0	12026.0	99152.0	741.0	2108.0	7696.0	15795.0
Luxembourg											
Netherlands	19274.0	14672.0	36322.0	8721.0		13364.0	101033.0	1030.0	2359.0	2408.0	8458.0
Portugal	511.8	2525.1	2743.9	662.1	930.9	1987.6	12125.7	223.9	664.3	314.8	1663.9
Spain	1672.0	11561.0	7534.0	5937.0	2625.0	5000.0	38608.0	306.0	533.0	899.0	2403.0
United Kingdom	10066.0	19451.0	23506.0	10035.0	13403.0		98469.0	2289.0	4789.0	4195.0	14553.0
EFTA members											
Austria	894.0	1952.0	1533.0	4026.0	1193.0	1591.0	26733.0	221.0	750.0	2971.0	4286.0
Finland	598.0	1630.0	3371.0	845.0	1135.0	2807.0	12416.0	804.0	3818.0	474.0	5414.0
Iceland	17.5	141.3	200.5	44.0	33.1	396.0	1050.4	22.1	28.0	63.8	133.0
Liechtenstein											
Norway	747.0	2652.0	3790.0	874.0	2709.0	8809.0	21945.0		3889.0	281.0	5298.0
Sweden	2139.0	3046.0	7979.0	2659.0	2992.0	5664.0	30709.0	4808.0		1321.0	10937.0
Switzerland	1467.0	6320.0	14031.0	5670.0	1731.0	4723.0	36941.0	338.0	1046.0		4242.0
Eastern Europe											
Albania											
Bulgaria[a]	20.3	75.6	250.5	132.2	29.8	58.4	716.4	28.3	10.5	13.2	110.1
Czechoslovakia[a]	126.7	315.4	2091.2	369.4	262.2	307.5	3733.0	43.3	112.8	271.7	1248.4
Hungary	110.6	257.2	1629.0	560.6	144.7	193.3	3089.6	20.8	134.1	179.0	1144.7
Poland	234.0	467.0	2644.0	447.0	362.0	594.0	5176.0	63.0	308.0	231.0	1267.0
Romania	60.0	207.0	663.0	533.0	160.0	131.0	1894.0	8.0	34.0	91.0	217.0
USSR[b]	1291.0	3063.0	6680.0	3775.0	1393.0	1453.0	19544.0	347.0	783.0	258.0	4709.0
Yugoslavia	127.0	980.0	1964.0	2519.0	207.0	334.0	6533.0	76.0	135.0	161.0	973.0
Others											
Cyprus	18.2	17.9	51.7	14.3	19.6	219.3	453.0	2.2	5.7	8.4	25.5
Gibraltar											
Malta	26.3	72.9	240.8	387.4	18.3	89.1	843.6	2.6	6.1	4.3	18.0
Monaco											
Turkey	251.1	650.0	2764.1	1001.6	364.1	699.0	6088.3	33.0	81.2	221.8	556.2

Table No: 0505 (cont'd)

EXTERNAL TRADE BY DESTINATION AND ORIGIN

Exports by Country of Destination 1990

Current US dollars (millions)

	CMEA	USA	Canada	Brazil	Americas	Total Africa	Japan	China	Asia	Austra-lasia	Total, inc. others
EC members											
Belgium	1037.0	5081.0	512.0	150.0	732.0	2632.0	1567.0	350.0	4381.0	398.0	117473.0
Denmark	808.0	1753.0	187.0	48.0	583.0	792.0	1167.0	101.0	1105.0	205.0	34840.0
France	2853.0	12740.0	2001.0	735.0	5415.0	13778.0	4055.0	1406.0	8699.0	1000.0	216394.0
Germany:East[a]	2776.1	46.3	9.2	41.2	68.3	107.6	34.4	107.0	202.8	5.8	10167.8
Germany:West	23371.0	29026.0	2917.0	1842.0	5725.0	8219.0	10816.0	2494.0	16775.0	2660.0	409274.0
Greece	343.0	450.0	47.0	3.0	77.0	171.0	78.0	33.0	86.0	71.0	7996.0
Ireland	231.0	1958.0	181.0	27.0	219.0	247.0	436.0	7.0	384.0	168.0	23780.0
Italy	4871.0	12977.0	1507.0	793.0	2625.0	5173.0	3984.0	972.0	6446.0	129.0	169939.0
Luxembourg											
Netherlands	1599.0	5257.0	569.0	270.0	1137.0	2228.0	1120.0	195.0	3577.0	618.0	131465.0
Portugal	96.5	784.5	135.1	47.3	57.4	726.5	165.6	36.9	160.7	45.5	16375.3
Spain	588.0	3239.0	353.0	184.0	1473.0	2088.0	632.0	303.0	1130.0	171.0	55187.0
United Kingdom	2162.0	23280.0	3381.0	589.0	2439.0	5561.0	4709.0	815.0	11977.0	3738.0	185167.0
EFTA members											
Austria	3211.0	1319.0	309.0	51.0	242.0	516.0	657.0	225.0	1033.0	204.0	41392.0
Finland	3657.0	1532.0	290.0	70.0	315.0	337.0	385.0	155.0	855.0	278.0	26570.0
Iceland	44.4	159.0	4.2	3.0	3.6	11.1	86.0	0.3	17.4	1.3	1539.9
Liechtenstein											
Norway	376.0	2187.0	837.0	86.0	459.0	337.0	562.0	108.0	616.0	142.0	33828.0
Sweden	1052.0	5099.0	832.0	265.0	802.0	624.0	1179.0	263.0	2295.0	820.0	56937.0
Switzerland	1637.0	5111.0	511.0	389.0	1119.0	1051.0	3048.0	301.0	4925.0	611.0	63790.0
Eastern Europe											
Albania											
Bulgaria[a]	557.1	47.9	8.1	0.1	27.0	69.8	31.5	85.2	86.1	3.2	2376.2
Czechoslovakia[a]	1378.7	91.3	46.3	26.3	68.7	137.2	88.7	222.6	293.0	35.4	11654.0
Hungary	2696.6	337.5	28.9	21.6	23.8	97.7	110.6	81.8	256.8	19.0	9548.8
Poland	5369.0	358.0	59.0	169.0	33.0	119.0	145.0	295.0	312.0	21.0	14485.0
Romania	2089.0	351.0	28.0	7.0	40.0	91.0	96.0	158.0	146.0	7.0	6027.0
USSR[b]	8630.0	1062.0	140.0	57.0	170.0	685.0	3064.0	1886.0	2871.0	36.0	49649.0
Yugoslavia	3903.0	690.0	62.0	13.0	87.0	481.0	41.0	26.0	240.0	67.0	14356.0
Others											
Cyprus	50.5	15.0	1.7	0.2	8.6	12.3	4.4	0.4	17.9	0.8	952.4
Gibraltar											
Malta	40.8	39.2	1.3		0.5	9.4	6.4		36.2	1.2	1088.2
Monaco											
Turkey	564.1	833.7	62.4	8.4	43.5	377.1	232.0	176.5	608.1	28.1	12367.1

Sources: OECD Foreign Trade Statistics/IMF Direction of Trade Statistics

Notes: See end of section

Table No: 0506

EXTERNAL TRADE BY DESTINATION AND ORIGIN

Exports by Country of Destination 1990

% total exports

	BLEU	France	West Germany	Italy	Nether-lands	UK	Total EC	Norway	Sweden	Switzer-land	Total EFTA
EC members											
Belgium		20.2	21.4	6.6	13.4	8.7	75.3	0.5	1.4	2.1	5.8
Denmark	2.1	6.0	19.7	5.0	4.8	10.7	52.0	5.7	12.8	2.0	24.5
France	9.1		16.8	11.0	5.4	9.0	60.8	0.4	1.1	4.1	7.0
Germany: East[a]	0.8	2.3		0.8	1.4	1.7	8.2	0.5	1.2	1.6	4.8
Germany: West	7.3	12.7		9.1	8.3	8.3	53.3	0.8	2.5	5.8	16.0
Greece	2.0	9.6	22.3	16.7	3.5	7.3	64.1	0.5	1.6	1.4	5.6
Ireland	4.4	10.5	11.7	4.4	5.8	33.8	74.9	0.8	1.9	1.7	5.6
Italy	3.4	16.4	19.0		3.1	7.1	58.3	0.4	1.2	4.5	9.3
Luxembourg											
Netherlands	14.7	11.2	27.6	6.6		10.2	76.9	0.8	1.8	1.8	6.4
Portugal	3.1	15.4	16.8	4.0	5.7	12.1	74.0	1.4	4.1	1.9	10.2
Spain	3.0	20.9	13.7	10.8	4.8	9.1	70.0	0.6	1.0	1.6	4.4
United Kingdom	5.4	10.5	12.7	5.4	7.2		53.2	1.2	2.6	2.3	7.9
EFTA members											
Austria	2.2	4.7	37.0	9.7	2.9	3.8	64.6	0.5	1.8	7.2	10.4
Finland	2.3	6.1	12.7	3.2	4.3	10.6	46.7	3.0	14.4	1.8	20.4
Iceland	1.1	9.2	13.0	2.9	2.1	25.7	68.2	1.4	1.8	4.1	8.6
Liechtenstein											
Norway	2.2	7.8	11.2	2.6	8.0	26.0	64.9		11.5	0.8	15.7
Sweden	3.8	5.3	14.0	4.7	5.3	9.9	53.9	8.4		2.3	19.2
Switzerland	2.3	9.9	22.0	8.9	2.7	7.4	57.9	0.5	1.6		6.6
Eastern Europe											
Albania											
Bulgaria[a]	0.9	3.2	10.5	1.4	1.3	2.5	30.1	1.2	0.4	0.6	4.6
Czechoslovakia[a]	1.1	2.7	17.9	3.2	2.2	2.6	32.0	0.4	1.0	2.3	10.7
Hungary	1.2	2.7	17.1	5.9	1.5	2.0	32.4	0.2	1.4	1.9	12.0
Poland	1.6	3.2	18.3	3.1	2.5	4.1	35.7	0.4	2.1	1.6	8.7
Romania	1.0	3.4	11.0	8.8	2.7	2.2	31.4	0.1	0.6	1.5	3.6
USSR[b]	2.6	6.2	13.5	7.6	2.8	2.9	39.4	0.7	1.6	0.5	9.5
Yugoslavia	0.9	6.8	13.7	17.5	1.4	2.3	45.5	0.5	0.9	1.1	6.8
Others											
Cyprus	1.9	1.9	5.4	1.5	2.1	23.0	47.6	0.2	0.6	0.9	2.7
Gibraltar											
Malta	2.4	6.7	22.1	35.6	1.7	8.2	77.5	0.2	0.6	0.4	1.7
Monaco											
Turkey	2.0	5.3	22.4	8.1	2.9	5.7	49.2	0.3	0.7	1.8	4.5

Table No: 0506 (cont'd)

EXTERNAL TRADE BY DESTINATION

Exports by Country of Destination 1990

% total exports	CMEA	USA	Canada	Brazil	Americas	Total Africa	Japan	China	Asia	Austra-lasia	Total, inc. others
EC members											
Belgium	0.9	4.3	0.4	0.1	0.6	2.2	1.3	0.3	3.7	0.3	100.0
Denmark	2.3	5.0	0.5	0.1	1.7	2.3	3.3	0.3	3.2	0.6	100.0
France	1.3	5.9	0.9	0.3	2.5	6.4	1.9	0.6	6.0	0.5	100.0
Germany:East[a]	27.3	0.5	0.1	0.4	0.7	1.1	0.3	1.1	2.0	0.1	100.0
Germany:West	5.7	7.1	0.7	0.5	1.4	2.0	2.6	0.6	4.1	0.6	100.0
Greece	4.3	5.6	0.6	0.0	1.0	2.1	1.0	0.4	1.1	0.9	100.0
Ireland	1.0	8.2	0.8	0.1	0.9	1.0	1.8	0.0	1.6	0.7	100.0
Italy	2.9	7.6	0.9	0.5	1.5	3.0	2.3	0.6	3.8	0.7	100.0
Luxembourg											
Netherlands	1.2	4.0	0.4	0.2	0.9	1.7	0.9	0.1	2.7	0.5	100.0
Portugal	0.6	4.8	0.8	0.3	0.4	4.4	1.0	0.2	1.0	0.3	100.0
Spain	1.1	5.9	0.6	0.3	2.7	3.8	1.1	0.5	2.0	0.3	100.0
United Kingdom	1.2	12.6	1.8	0.3	1.3	3.0	2.5	0.4	6.5	2.0	100.0
EFTA members											
Austria	7.8	3.2	0.7	0.1	0.6	1.2	1.6	0.5	2.5	0.5	100.0
Finland	13.8	5.8	1.1	0.3	1.2	1.3	1.4	0.6	3.2	1.0	100.0
Iceland	2.9	10.3	0.3	0.2	0.2	0.7	5.6	0.0	1.1	0.1	100.0
Liechtenstein											
Norway	1.1	6.5	2.5	0.3	1.4	1.0	1.7	0.3	1.8	0.4	100.0
Sweden	1.8	9.0	1.5	0.5	1.4	1.1	2.1	0.5	4.0	1.4	100.0
Switzerland	2.6	8.0	0.8	0.6	1.8	1.6	4.8	0.5	7.7	1.0	100.0
Eastern Europe											
Albania											
Bulgaria[a]	23.4	2.0	0.3	0.0	1.1	2.9	1.3	3.6	3.6	0.1	100.0
Czechoslovakia[a]	11.8	0.8	0.4	0.2	0.6	1.2	0.8	1.9	2.5	0.3	100.0
Hungary	28.2	3.5	0.3	0.2	0.2	1.0	1.2	0.9	2.7	0.2	100.0
Poland	37.1	2.5	0.4	1.2	0.2	0.8	1.0	2.0	2.2	0.1	100.0
Romania	34.7	5.8	0.5	0.1	0.7	1.5	1.6	2.6	2.4	0.1	100.0
USSR[b]	17.4	2.1	0.3	0.1	0.3	1.4	6.2	3.8	5.8	0.1	100.0
Yugoslavia	27.2	4.8	0.4	0.1	0.6	3.4	0.3	0.2	1.7	0.5	100.0
Others											
Cyprus	5.3	1.6	0.2	0.0	0.9	1.3	0.5	0.0	1.9	0.1	100.0
Gibraltar											
Malta	3.7	3.6	0.1		0.0	0.9	0.6		3.3	0.1	100.0
Monaco											
Turkey	4.6	6.7	0.5	0.1	0.4	3.0	1.9	1.4	4.9	0.2	100.0

Sources: OECD Foreign Trade Statistics/IMF Direction of Trade Statistics
Notes: See end of section

Table No: 0507

EXTERNAL TRADE BY COMMODITY

Imports by Commodity: SITC Classification 1990

Current US dollars (millions)

	0	1	2	3	4	5	6
EC members							
Belgium[a]	9424.6	1304.3	6856.5	9622.6	406.3	13701.4	28093.0
Denmark	3229.9	376.5	1270.0	2216.2	152.8	3648.8	6173.0
France	19488.2	2294.0	9198.2	22332.0	761.5	24964.8	41275.3
Germany: East[b]	2641.9	570.4	1891.3	4353.1	90.1	2701.9	5583.9
Germany: West	28838.2	3388.7	18290.3	28511.1	946.2	30854.4	60999.2
Greece	2510.7	323.7	982.0	1518.5	81.6	2080.0	4256.7
Ireland	1862.2	256.4	563.0	1332.6	66.7	2581.4	3198.6
Italy	18079.3	1823.5	13758.9	18661.5	1306.6	19860.0	29248.2
Luxembourg							
Netherlands	12170.1	1604.8	6658.3	13243.9	643.7	13253.8	21669.0
Portugal	2287.9	176.1	1484.1	2733.6	63.7	2314.5	4855.6
Spain	7567.9	947.1	5497.0	10441.2	233.2	8668.1	12229.7
United Kingdom	18558.4	3400.0	10200.3	13977.7	672.8	19316.8	39043.1
EFTA members							
Austria	2294.7	188.6	2274.7	3146.6	99.1	4959.3	9464.6
Finland	1125.2	133,3	1422,6	3171.7	26.7	2915.7	4226.7
Iceland	122.6	26.5	84.6	162.8	4.2	134.7	275.5
Liechtenstein							
Norway	1288.1	165.1	2180.7	1203.9	42.7	2227.6	4507.4
Sweden	2781.3	430.1	1845.7	4885.2	103.1	5186.8	9214.8
Switzerland	3411.5	906.2	2054.5	3210.2	69.7	8035.3	15066.9
Eastern Europe							
Albania							
Bulgaria							
Czechoslovakia[c]	1179.5	194.3	1696.7	6498.4	51.8	1567.3	1959.7
Hungary[b]	543.5	65.4	559.3	1036.4		1433.1	1546.7
Poland[c,d]	1005.4	123.4	947.5	1872.5	60.2	1238.0	1443.9
Romania							
USSR							
Yugoslavia	1944.9	152.2	1457.9	3199.4	71.9	2434.7	2957.7
Others							
Cyprus[b]	222.1	50.2	42.0	219.6	17.3	175.6	544.1
Gibraltar							
Malta[b]	155.7	22.7	22.6	95.1	4.7	105.1	333.7
Monaco							
Turkey	1179.9	345.5	1684.6	4622.1	297.5	2850.6	3351.5

Table No: 0507 (cont'd)

EXTERNAL TRADE BY COMMODITY

Imports by Commodity: SITC Classification 1990

Current US dollars (millions)

	7	8	9	Total
EC members				
Belgium[a]	30610.1	12635.1	7071.0	119724.9
Denmark	10038.3	3909.0	540.6	31555.0
France	79577.8	32503.2	129.9	232524.6
Germany: East[b]	9486.7	1681.2	1020.7	30021.1
Germany: West	110917.7	51715.7	6661.5	341122.9
Greece	6124.9	1801.8	21.4	19701.4
Ireland	7444.4	2829.2	581.5	20716.0
Italy	53808.5	13913.8	4240.2	174700.5
Luxembourg				
Netherlands	39012.2	17608.8	258.7	126123.3
Portugal	9362.4	2053.9	0.8	25332.6
Spain	33424.2	8309.3	16.5	87334.2
United Kingdom	84311.3	33012.1	2421.1	224913.4
EFTA members				
Austria	18974.3	8553.3	4.8	49960.1
Finland	10472.6	3603.6	0.1	27098.3
Iceland	580.8	261.1	1.9	1654.6
Liechtenstein				
Norway	11333.9	4242.7	7.6	27199.6
Sweden	21040.1	8678.7	297.5	54463.1
Switzerland	22373.5	15048.9	468.5	70645.3
Eastern Europe				
Albania				
Bulgaria				
Czechoslovakia[c]	8311.7	1140.0	684.6	23283.6
Hungary[b]	2948.1	612.2	74.1	8818.7
Poland[c,d]	3494.5	621.0	37.2	10843.7
Romania				
USSR				
Yugoslavia	5031.4	1580.9	63.0	18894.0
Others				
Cyprus[b]	802.7	181.8	24.9	2280.3
Gibraltar				
Malta[b]	607.9	137.4	91	1494.0
Monaco				
Turkey	7036.5	933.4		22301.6

Sources: OECD/UN
Notes: See end of section

Table No: 0508

EXTERNAL TRADE BY COMMODITY

Imports by Commodity: SITC Classification 1990

% total imports

	0	1	2	3	4	5	6
EC members							
Belgium[a]	7.9	1.1	5.7	8.0	0.3	11.4	23.5
Denmark	10.2	1.2	4.0	7.0	0.5	11.6	19.6
France	8.4	1.0	4.0	9.6	0.3	10.7	17.8
Germany: East[b]	8.8	1.9	6.3	14.5	0.3	9.0	18.6
Germany: West	8.5	1.0	5.4	8.4	0.3	9.0	17.9
Greece	12.7	1.6	5.0	7.7	0.4	10.6	21.6
Ireland	9.0	1.2	2.7	6.4	0.3	12.5	15.4
Italy	10.3	1.0	7.9	10.7	0.7	11.4	16.7
Luxembourg							
Netherlands	9.6	1.3	5.3	10.5	0.5	10.5	17.2
Portugal	9.0	0.7	5.9	10.8	0.3	9.1	19.2
Spain	8.7	1.1	6.3	12.0	0.3	9.9	14.0
United Kingdom	8.3	1.5	4.5	6.2	0.3	8.6	17.4
EFTA members							
Austria	4.6	0.4	4.6	6.3	0.2	9.9	18.9
Finland	4.2	0.5	5.2	11.7	0.1	10.8	15.6
Iceland	7.4	1.6	5.1	9.8	0.3	8.1	16.7
Liechtenstein							
Norway	4.7	0.6	8.0	4.4	0.2	8.2	16.6
Sweden	5.1	0.8	3.4	9.0	0.2	9.5	16.9
Switzerland	4.8	1.3	2.9	4.5	0.1	11.4	21.3
Eastern Europe							
Albania							
Bulgaria							
Czechoslovakia[c]	5.1	0.8	7.3	27.9	0.2	6.7	8.4
Hungary[b]	6.2	0.7	6.3	11.8		16.3	17.5
Poland[c,d]	9.3	1.1	8.7	17.3	0.6	11.4	13.3
Romania							
USSR							
Yugoslavia	10.3	0.8	7.7	16.9	0.4	12.9	15.7
Others							
Cyprus[b]	9.7	2.2	1.8	9.6	0.8	7.7	23.9
Gibraltar							
Malta[b]	10.4	1.5	1.5	6.4	0.3	7.0	22.3
Monaco							
Turkey	5.3	1.5	7.6	20.7	1.3	12.8	15.0

Table No: 0508 (cont'd)

EXTERNAL TRADE BY COMMODITY

Imports by Commodity: SITC Classification 1990

% total imports

	7	8	9	Total
EC members				
Belgium[a]	25.6	10.6	5.9	100.0
Denmark	31.8	12.4	1.7	100.0
France	34.2	14.0	0.1	100.0
Germany: East[b]	31.6	5.6	3.4	100.0
Germany: West	32.5	15.2	2.0	100.0
Greece	31.1	9.1	0.1	100.0
Ireland	35.9	13.7	2.8	100.0
Italy	30.8	8.0	2.4	100.0
Luxembourg				
Netherlands	30.9	14.0	0.2	100.0
Portugal	37.0	8.1	0.0	100.0
Spain	38.3	9.5	0.0	100.0
United Kingdom	37.5	14.7	1.1	100.0
EFTA members				
Austria	38.0	17.1	0.0	100.0
Finland	38.6	13.3	0.0	100.0
Iceland	35.1	15.8	0.1	100.0
Liechtenstein				
Norway	41.7	15.6	0.0	100.0
Sweden	38.6	15.9	0.5	100.0
Switzerland	31.7	21.3	0.7	100.0
Eastern Europe				
Albania				
Bulgaria				
Czechoslovakia[c]	35.7	4.9	2.9	100.0
Hungary[b]	33.4	6.9	0.8	100.0
Poland[c,d]	32.2	5.7	0.3	100.0
Romania				
USSR				
Yugoslavia	26.6	8.4	0.3	100.0
Others				
Cyprus[b]	35.2	8.0	1.1	100.0
Gibraltar				
Malta[b]	40.7	9.2	0.6	100.0
Monaco				
Turkey	31.6	4.2		100.0

Sources: OECD/UN
Notes: See end of section

Table No: 0509

EXTERNAL TRADE BY COMMODITY

Exports by Commodity: SITC Classification 1990

Current US dollars (millions)

	0	1	2	3	4	5	6
EC members							
Belgium[a]	9848.2	786.2	2936.3	4125.1	487.3	16477.2	36731.7
Denmark	8807.0	371.6	1635.3	1171.4	152.6	3062.3	3941.5
France	24264.5	7246.8	7036.4	4913.8	485.4	28339.2	36339.6
Germany: East[b]	1571.1	577.1	929.8	2661.2	32.1	3879.6	5995.8
Germany: West	15587.0	2319.9	7258.8	5083.9	956.9	50597.3	70312.6
Greece	1627.9	443.6	456.8	587.9	302.6	315.2	1887.9
Ireland	4745.0	541.9	820.1	150.4	18.6	3757.3	1911.8
Italy	8515.3	1949.1	1850.2	3352.1	596.0	10920.0	36473.1
Luxembourg							
Netherlands	22581.6	2926.3	7467.2	12891.3	887.5	22478.3	18705.8
Portugal	619.1	470.0	1449.9	575.8	77.9	862.6	3709.9
Spain	6477.7	908.0	1754.0	2854.8	913.7	4584.6	11181.5
United Kingdom	7739.9	4958.1	3870.5	13962.6	157.0	23593.5	28315.7
EFTA members							
Austria	1167.9	186.5	2188.5	422.7	18.9	3547.2	13114.1
Finland	579.6	53.5	2691.6	392.6	22.4	1702.0	11026.4
Iceland	1248.6	2.7	19.7		18.0	1.1	241.4
Liechtenstein							
Norway	2287.0	22.7	1190.2	16259.3	54.9	2257.8	6114.2
Sweden	1032.5	85.0	5063.8	1745.1	108.4	4281.6	14594.0
Switzerland	1408.2	358.7	755.7	46.3	23.8	13776.4	12313.3
Eastern Europe							
Albania							
Bulgaria[c,d]	1959.7	1170.6	730.9	4269.1	15.9	1169.5	1477.8
Czechoslovakia[c]	506.9	92.4	685.0	818.4		1473.0	3774.7
Hungary[b]	1781.6	128.6	397.8	275.4	98.7	1187.2	1635.5
Poland[c,d]	1213.8	62.4	743.1	1373.7	20.4	875.9	2234.1
Romania[c,d]	827.7	74.9	501.5	4740.9	37.1	425.9	2094.3
USSR[c,d]	859.4	106.5	11931.8	72258.5	99.4	5795.5	11278.4
Yugoslavia	908.0	125.5	985.2	352.8	11.7	1397.1	3912.0
Others							
Cyprus[b]	149.7	28.7	7.0	8.9	9.0	35.7	37.0
Gibraltar[e]	0.1	7.0	0.4	55.2		1.5	
Malta[b]	15.9	13.3	7.5	15.4		12.5	85.2
Monaco							
Turkey	2304.2	455.4	749.9	296.3	138.9	747.2	3832.7

Table No: 0509 (cont'd)

EXTERNAL TRADE BY COMMODITY

Exports by Commodity: SITC Classification 1990

Current US dollars (millions)

	7	8	9	Total
EC members				
Belgium[a]	32267.7	9701.4	4641.1	118002.3
Denmark	9289.0	5164.8	187.9	33783.4
France	78378.0	22231.4	255.3	209490.6
Germany: East[b]	11703.1	3847.6	865.7	32063.2
Germany: West	196627.6	44475.2	4626.2	397845.4
Greece	337.5	1878.5	182.7	8020.6
Ireland	7446.9	3384.2	1020.2	23796.4
Italy	62641.8	38638.2	1999.9	166935.7
Luxembourg				
Netherlands	30989.3	12575.3	308.0	131810.7
Portugal	3227.4	5403.3	19.8	16415.7
Spain	21419.5	5215.7	182.6	55492.0
United Kingdom	75448.1	24950.6	2894.8	185890.8
EFTA members				
Austria	15700.6	5525.8	3.9	41876.2
Finland	8251.1	1998.7		26718.1
Iceland	32.9	16.6	9.8	1590.7
Liechtenstein				
Norway	4744.7	1099.9	2.6	34033.3
Sweden	24861.0	5026.6	390.0	57187.9
Switzerland	20527.1	15379.1	408.6	64887.3
Eastern Europe				
Albania				
Bulgaria[c,d]	1721.4	1395.1	244.7	14089.0
Czechoslovakia[c]	12707.6	2671.7	283.6	23016.4
Hungary[b]	2904.7	1011.2	184.3	9605.0
Poland[c,d]	4096.3	960.7	624.5	12204.8
Romania[c,d]	814.7	2972.2	50.1	12542.6
USSR[c,d]	2471.6	644.9	2207.4	107528.4
Yugoslavia	4307.0	2296.1	18.3	14313.7
Others				
Cyprus[b]	22.0	199.9		497.9
Gibraltar[e]	3.4	3.4		70.9
Malta[b]	426.3	280.6	1.2	858.0
Monaco				
Turkey	854.8	3577.8		12957.3

Sources: OECD/UN
Notes: See end of section

Table No: 0510

EXTERNAL TRADE BY COMMODITY

Exports by Commodity: SITC Classification 1990

% total exports	0	1	2	3	4	5	6	7	8	9	Total
EC members											
Belgium[a]	8.3	0.7	2.5	3.5	0.4	14.0	31.1	27.3	8.2	3.9	100.0
Denmark	26.1	1.1	4.8	3.5	0.5	9.1	11.7	27.5	15.3	0.6	100.0
France	11.6	3.5	3.4	2.3	0.2	13.5	17.3	37.4	10.6	0.1	100.0
Germany: East[b]	4.9	1.8	2.9	8.3	0.1	12.1	18.7	36.5	12.0	2.7	100.0
Germany: West	3.9	0.6	1.8	1.3	0.2	12.7	17.7	49.4	11.2	1.2	100.0
Greece	20.3	5.5	5.7	7.3	3.8	3.9	23.5	4.2	23.4	2.3	100.0
Ireland	19.9	2.3	3.4	0.6	0.1	15.8	8.0	31.3	14.2	4.3	100.0
Italy	5.1	1.2	1.1	2.0	0.4	6.5	21.8	37.5	23.1	1.2	100.0
Luxembourg											
Netherlands	17.1	2.2	5.7	9.8	0.7	17.1	14.2	23.5	9.5	0.2	100.0
Portugal	3.8	2.9	8.8	3.5	0.5	5.3	22.6	19.7	32.9	0.1	100.0
Spain	11.7	1.6	3.2	5.1	1.6	8.3	20.1	38.6	9.4	0.3	100.0
United Kingdom	4.2	2.7	2.1	7.5	0.1	12.7	15.2	40.6	13.4	1.6	100.0
EFTA members											
Austria	2.8	0.4	5.2	1.0	0.0	8.5	31.3	37.5	13.2	0.0	100.0
Finland	2.2	0.2	10.1	1.5	0.1	6.4	41.3	30.9	7.5		100.0
Iceland	78.5	0.2	1.2		1.1	0.1	15.2	2.1	1.0	0.6	100.0
Liechtenstein											
Norway	6.7	0.1	3.5	47.8	0.2	6.6	18.0	13.9	3.2	0.0	100.0
Sweden	1.8	0.1	8.9	3.1	0.2	7.5	25.5	43.5	8.8	0.7	100.0
Switzerland	2.2	0.6	1.2	0.1	0.0	21.2	18.9	31.6	23.7	0.6	100.0
Eastern Europe											
Albania											
Bulgaria[c,d]	13.9	8.3	5.2	30.3	0.1	8.3	10.5	12.2	9.9	1.7	100.0
Czechoslovakia[c]	2.2	0.4	3.0	3.6		6.4	16.4	55.2	11.6	1.2	100.0
Hungary[b]	18.5	1.2	4.1	2.9	1.0	12.4	17.0	30.2	10.5	1.9	100.0
Poland[c,d]	9.9	0.5	6.1	11.3	0.2	7.2	18.3	33.6	7.9	5.1	100.0
Romania[c,d]	6.6	0.6	4.0	37.8	0.3	3.4	16.7	6.5	23.7	0.4	100.0
USSR[c,d]	0.8	0.1	11.1	67.2	0.1	5.4	10.5	2.3	0.6	2.1	100.0
Yugoslavia	6.3	0.9	6.9	2.5	0.1	9.8	27.3	30.1	16.0	0.1	100.0
Others											
Cyprus[b]	30.1	5.8	1.4	1.8	1.8	7.2	7.4	4.4	40.1		100.0
Gibraltar[e]	0.2	9.9	0.6	77.8		2.1		4.8	4.8		100.0
Malta[b]	1.9	1.6	0.9	1.8		1.5	9.9	49.7	32.7	0.1	100.0
Monaco											
Turkey	17.8	3.5	5.8	2.3	1.1	5.8	29.6	6.6	27.6		100.0

Sources: OECD/UN
Notes: See end of section

Notes to Tables in Section Five:

Table 0501
- a Belgium-Luxembourg Economic Union (BLEU)
- b Foreign-exchange currency
- c Imports (cif) 1991
- d Data for 1991 are estimated
- e '000 billion lire
- f fob on a b.o.p. basis
- g Imports (cif)
- h Billion US dollars

Table 0502
- a BLEU
- b Foreign-exchange currency
- c Data for 1991 are estimated
- d '000 billion lire
- e Billion US dollars

Table 0503 Due to differing sources, definitions and conversion rates, dollar totals in this table may vary from those in Table 0501

0.0 signifies less than 0.05 million
Americas: all American countries except USA, Canada and Brazil
Australasia: Australia and New Zealand
Asia: excluding Japan and China
CMEA no longer includes former East Germany

- a CMEA data do not include former USSR
- b CMEA data do not include Bulgaria or Czechoslovakia

Table 0504 Americas: all American countries except USA, Canada and Brazil
Australasia: Australia and New Zealand
Asia: excluding Japan and China
CMEA no longer includes former East Germany
Entries of 0.0 = less than 0.05%

- a CMEA data do not include former USSR
- b CMEA data do not include Bulgaria or Czechoslovakia

Table 0505 Due to differing sources, definitions and conversion rates, dollar totals in this table may vary from those in Table 0502

0.0 signifies less than 0.05 million
Americas: all American countries except USA, Canada and Brazil
Australasia: Australia and New Zealand
Asia: excluding Japan and China
CMEA no longer includes former East Germany

- a CMEA data do not include former USSR
- b CMEA data do not include Bulgaria or Czechoslovakia

Table 0506 Americas: all American countries except USA, Canada and Brazil
Australasia: Australia and New Zealand
Asia: excluding Japan and China
CMEA no longer includes former East Germany
Entries of 0.0 = less than 0.05%

- a CMEA data do not include former USSR
- b CMEA data do not include Bulgaria or Czechoslovakia

Table 0507 SITC Classification:
- 0 Food and live animals
- 1 Beverages and tobacco
- 2 Crude materials excluding fuels
- 3 Mineral fuels etc
- 4 Oils and fats
- 5 Chemicals
- 6 Basic manufactures
- 7 Machinery and transport equipment
- 8 Miscellaneous manufactured goods
- 9 Others

- a BLEU
- b Data refer to 1989
- c Data refer to 1987
- d Data are estimates based on trade with industrialised West

Table 0508 SITC Classification:
- 0 Food and live animals
- 1 Beverages and tobacco
- 2 Crude materials excluding fuels
- 3 Mineral fuels etc
- 4 Oils and fats
- 5 Chemicals
- 6 Basic manufactures
- 7 Machinery and transport equipment
- 8 Miscellaneous manufactured goods
- 9 Others

- a BLEU
- b Data refer to 1989
- c Data refer to 1987
- d Data are estimates based on trade with industrialised West

Table 0509 SITC Classification:

0	Food and live animals
1	Beverages and tobacco
2	Crude materials excluding fuels
3	Mineral fuels etc
4	Oils and fats
5	Chemicals
6	Basic manufactures
7	Machinery and transport equipment
8	Miscellaneous manufactured goods
9	Others
a	BLEU
b	Data refer to 1988
c	Data refer to 1986
d	Data are estimates based on trade with industrialised West
e	Data refer to 1987

Table 0510 SITC Classification:

0	Food and live animals
1	Beverages and tobacco
2	Crude materials excluding fuels
3	Mineral fuels etc
4	Oils and fats
5	Chemicals
6	Basic manufactures
7	Machinery and transport equipment
8	Miscellaneous manufactured goods
9	Others
a	BLEU
b	Data refer to 1988
c	Data refer to 1986
d	Data are estimates based on trade with industrialised West
e	Data refer to 1987

Section Six

Labour Force Indicators

Table No: 0601

EMPLOYMENT

General Level of Employment 1977-1990

'000

	1977	1980	1983	1984	1985	1986	1987	1988	1989	1990	% growth 1977-90
EC members											
Belgium[a,b]	3752	3700	3546	3541	3561	3584	3600	3653	3712		
Denmark	2414	2400	2389	2488	2553	2662	2643	2635	2617	2670	10.6
France[a]	21493	21638	21481	21287	21225	21260	21326	21498	21755	22931	6.7
Germany: East[c]	7574	7758	7886	7917	7935	7929	7932	7950	7950		
Germany: West[b]	25041	26528	25809	25869	26062	26431	26626	26835	27209	27946	11.6
Greece[a]		3500	3540	3553	3589	3601	3597	3637	3657		
Ireland	1068	1141	1110	1089	1062	1068	1067	1078	1111		
Italy[a]	20145	20674	20725	20809	20894	20856	20836	21103	21004	21304	5.8
Luxembourg[a]	157	158	158	159	161	165	170	175	182	190	21.0
Netherlands[a,d]	4701	4970	4950	4980	5076	5153	5864	6032	6155	6356	35.2
Portugal[a]	3764	3924	4353	4293	4279	4084	4191	4299	4395	4496	19.4
Spain[a]	12252	11502	10984	10668	10571	10821	11369	11773	12258	12579	2.7
United Kingdom	24538	25004	23624	24235	24539	24568	25083	25922	26693	26889	9.6
EC total	126899	132897	130555	130888	131507	132182	134304	135590	138698	125361	-1.2
EFTA members											
Austria	2737	2789	2735	2745	2760	2780	2785	2810	2862		
Finland[a]	2266	2359	2419	2442	2466	2431	2423	2431	2470	2929	7.0
Iceland[e]	99	106	115	116	121	125	132	128	132	2467	8.9
Liechtenstein											
Norway[a]	1824	1908	1945	1970	2014	2086	2126	2114	2049	2030	11.3
Sweden[a]	4099	4232	4224	4255	4299	4269	4337	4399	4466	4508	10.0
Switzerland	3036	3170	3257	3288	3352	3398	3440	3481	3518	3563	17.4
EFTA total	14061	14564	14695	14816	15012	15089	15243	15363	15497	15497	10.2
Eastern Europe											
Albania											
Bulgaria[c,f]	3870	4025	4114	4098	4095	4077	4084				
Czechoslovakia	7149	7358	7466	7534	7606	6992	7028	7048	7035	6646	-7.0
Hungary	5075	5044	5184	5147	5121	5111	5093	5070	5052		
Poland[c,f]	11910	12000	11583	11608	11674	11769	11756	11632	11472	10448	-12.3
Romania[c,f]	6740	7340	7600	7585	7661	7752	7790	7843	7997		
USSR[c]	120588	125626	128766	129474	130303	130881	130729	128903	127057	124971	3.6
Yugoslavia	5148	5798	6222	6355	6516	6716	6866	6884	6876	6669	29.5
East European total	160480	167191	170935	171801	172976	173298	173346	167380	165489	148734	-7.3
Others											
Cyprus	169	193	207	214	222	224	231	242	249		
Gibraltar		12	11	11	12	13	13				
Malta	114	118	111	111	113	115	122	125	126		
Monaco											
Turkey[b,g]	2191	15031	15412	15611	15790	16092	16450	16908	19373		
Total	2474	15354	15741	15947	16137	16444	16816	17275	19748		
European total	303914	330006	331926	333452	335632	337013	339709	335608	339432	289592	-4.7

Sources: International Labour Office (ILO)/UN
Notes: See end of section

Table No: 0602

UNEMPLOYMENT

Trends in Total Unemployed 1977-1990

'000

	1977	1980	1983	1984	1985	1986	1987	1988	1989	1990	% growth 1977-90
EC members											
Belgium	300.7	368.8	589.5	595.8	558.3	516.8	500.8	459.4	419.3	402.8	34.0
Denmark	163.7	183.8	283.0	276.3	251.8	217.3	221.9	243.9	264.9	269.1	64.4
France	1121.8	1470.5	1960.8	2311.8	2425.9	2516.6	2621.7	2562.9	2532.0	2504.7	123.3
Germany: East											
Germany: West	1030.0	888.9	2258.2	2265.6	2304.0	2228.0	2228.8	2241.6	2037.8	1883.1	82.8
Greece	27.7	37.2	61.6	71.2	89.0	110.5	117.9	115.3			
Ireland	106.4	101.5	192.7	214.2	230.6	236.4	247.3	241.4	231.6	224.7	111.2
Italy	1538.0	1684.0	2264.0	2303.0	2382.0	2611.0	2832.0	2885.0	2865.0	2621.0	70.4
Luxembourg	0.8	1.1	2.5	2.7	2.6	2.3	2.7	2.5	2.3	2.1	162.5
Netherlands[a]	203.5	248.0	800.6	822.4	761.0	710.7	685.5	433.0	390.0	346.0	70.0
Portugal	308.5	330.0	365.7	393.9	397.0	381.6	319.6	262.2	232.8	220.1	-28.7
Spain	539.6	1277.3	2198.9	2475.2	2642.0	2758.7	2924.1	2858.3	2550.3	2350.0	335.5
United Kingdom[b]	1402.7	1664.9	3104.7	3159.8	3271.2	3289.1	2953.4	2370.4	1798.7	1664.5	18.7
EC total	6743.4	8256.0	14082.2	14891.9	15315.4	15579.0	15655.7	14675.9	13324.7	12488.1	85.2
EFTA members											
Austria	51.28	53.2	127.4	130.5	139.5	152.0	164.5	158.6	149.2	165.8	223.8
Finland	140.0	114.0	138.0	133.0	129.0	138.0	130.0	116.0	89.0	88.0	-37.1
Iceland	0.4	0.5	1.2	1.5	1.1	0.8	0.6	0.8	2.1	2.3	475.0
Liechtenstein											
Norway	16.1	22.3	63.5	66.6	51.4	36.2	32.4	49.3	82.9	92.7	475.8
Sweden	34.2	43.6	91.7	91.9	84.9	84.2	78.1	61.1	56.3	66.4	94.2
Switzerland	12.0	6.3	26.3	35.2	30.3	25.7	24.7	22.2	17.5	18.1	50.8
EFTA total	253.9	239.9	448.1	458.7	436.2	436.9	430.3	408.0	397.0	433.3	70.7
Eastern Europe											
Albania											
Bulgaria											
Czechoslovakia											
Hungary											
Poland											
Romania											
USSR											
Yugoslavia	700.4	785.5	910.3	974.8	1039.6	1086.7	1080.6	1131.8	1201.2	1308.5	86.8
East European total	700.4	785.5	910.3	974.8	1039.6	1086.7	1080.6	1131.8	1201.2	1308.5	86.8
Others											
Cyprus	6.1	4.3	7.8	8.0	8.3	9.2	8.7	7.4	6.2	5.1	-16.4
Gibraltar	0.2	0.2	0.4	0.5	0.6	0.5	0.3	0.5	0.6		
Malta	4.6	4.0	10.3	10.4	10.1	9.4	5.8	5.3	4.8		
Monaco											
Turkey	142.7	256.3	549.1	760.9	934.6	1054.6	1124.0	1155.4	1076.2	979.5	586.4
Total	153.6	264.8	567.6	779.8	953.6	1073.7	1138.8	1168.6	1087.8	984.6	541.0
European total	7851.3	9546.2	16008.2	17105.2	17744.8	18176.3	18305.4	17384.3	16010.7	15214.5	93.8

Source: ILO
Notes: See end of section

Table No: 0603

UNEMPLOYMENT

Trends in Total Unemployed 1980-1990

% rate

	1980	1983	1984	1985	1986	1987	1988	1989	1990	% growth 1980-90
EC members										
Belgium	8.9	14.0	14.1	13.3	12.3	11.9	11.1	10.1	9.7	8.99
Denmark	7.0	10.5	10.1	9.1	7.9	7.9	8.7	9.4	9.6	37.14
France	6.3	8.3	9.7	10.2	10.4	10.5	10.0	9.4	9.0	42.86
Germany: East										
Germany: West	3.8	9.1	9.1	9.3	9.0	8.9	8.7	7.9	7.2	89.47
Greece	2.4	3.8	4.2	5.1	6.1	6.4	6.0			
Ireland		14.7	16.4	17.7	18.1	18.8	18.4	17.9	17.2	
Italy	7.6	9.9	10.0	10.3	11.1	11.9	12.0	12.0	11.0	44.74
Luxembourg	0.7	1.6	1.8	1.7	1.5	1.7	1.6	1.4	1.3	85.71
Netherlands[a]	4.6	13.9	14.1	12.9	12.0	11.5	6.5	5.8	4.9	6.52
Portugal	7.8	7.3	8.5	8.5	8.3	7.0	5.7	5.0	4.7	-39.74
Spain	9.8	16.5	18.4	19.5	20.0	20.4	19.5	17.3	16.3	66.33
United Kingdom[b]	6.8	11.7	11.6	11.8	11.8	10.6	8.4	6.3	5.9	-13.24
EFTA members										
Austria	1.9	4.5	4.5	4.8	5.2	5.6	5.3	5.0	5.4	184.21
Finland	4.7	5.5	5.2	5.0	5.4	5.1	4.5	3.5	3.4	-27.66
Iceland	0.4	1.0	1.2	0.9	0.7	0.5	0.7	1.6	1.7	325.00
Liechtenstein										
Norway	1.3	3.1	3.2	2.5	1.8	1.5	2.3	3.8	4.3	230.77
Sweden	1.4	2.8	2.8	2.5	2.5	2.3	1.7	1.6	1.9	35.71
Switzerland	0.2	0.9	1.1	1.0	0.8	0.8	0.7	0.6	0.6	200.00
Eastern Europe										
Albania										
Bulgaria										
Czechoslovakia										
Hungary										
Poland										
Romania										
USSR										
Yugoslavia	11.9	12.8	13.3	13.8	14.1	13.6	14.1	14.9	16.4	37.82
Others										
Cyprus	2.0	3.3	3.3	3.3	3.7	3.4	2.8	2.3	1.8	-10.00
Gibraltar										
Malta		8.5		8.1	6.8	4.4	4.0	3.7		
Monaco										
Turkey		12.1	11.9	11.2			8.3	8.5		

Source: ILO

Notes: See end of section

Table No: 0604

EMPLOYMENT

Level of Paid Employment in Manufacturing 1977-1990

'000

	1977	1980	1983	1984	1985	1986	1987	1988	1989	1990	% growth 1977-90
EC members											
Belgium[a]	952	870	776	767	756	744	725	720	733		
Denmark	378	355	353	371	398	407	397	385	384	384	1.6
France[a]	5449	5235	4882	4747	4608	4506	4398	4331	4351	4395	-19.3
Germany: East[a,b]	3445	3496	3539	3558	3569	3552	3534	3535			
Germany: West[a]	8341	8427	7871	7911	8064	8101	8179	8289	8364		
Greece[a,c,d]	650	675	470	475	471	500	492	489			
Ireland	214	227	203	197	189	185	183	185	189	195	-8.9
Italy[a]	4771	4745	4404	4205	4101	4038	3986	4049	4054	4081	-14.5
Luxembourg[a]	45	41	38	37	37	38	37	36	36	36	-20.0
Netherlands[a]	1056	1028	928	948	955	963	983	965			
Portugal[a]	792	921	960	901	926	927	968		1018	1037	30.9
Spain[a,e]	2839	2620	2272	2191	2116	2163	2251	2299	2394	2461	-13.3
United Kingdom[a]	7316	6936	5474	5363	5320	5190	5129	5162	5146	5100	-30.3
EC total	36248	35576	32170	31671	31510	31314	31252	30445	26669	17689	
EFTA members											
Austria			567	564	565	561	546	534	536	547	
Finland[a,f]	579	608	582	577	578	570	546	527	534	526	-9.2
Iceland	25	25	25	26	26	26	27	24			
Liechtenstein											
Norway[a,g]	393	372	324	326	327	347	340	329	306	301	-23.4
Sweden	634	602	529	533	535	535	548	551	558	540	-14.8
Switzerland	906	924	865	861	872	883	890	883	895	908	0.2
EFTA total	2537	2531	2892	2887	2903	2922	2897	2848	2829	2822	
Eastern Europe											
Albania											
Bulgaria[a,b]	1180	1217	1254	1251	1256	1273					
Czechoslovakia	2323	2370	2399	2411	2420	2435	2434	2428	2407	2221	-4.4
Hungary[a,b]	1444	1384	1269	1261	1278	1269	1243	1209	1145	1047	-27.5
Poland[a,b]	4129	4145	3780	3747	3712	3579	3538	3467	3335	3020	-26.9
Romania[a,b]	3027	3109	3177	3178	3234	3283	3287	3299	3384		
USSR[a,b]	35417	36391	37830	37957	38103	38223	38139	37376	36414	35400	0.0
Yugoslavia[b]	1862	2068	2269	2334	2413	2508	2588	2597	2595		
East European total	49382	50684	51978	52139	52416	52570	51229	50376	49280	41688	
Others											
Cyprus	32	40	43	44	45	46	45	47	48		
Gibraltar[a]	3	3	3	3	3	3	3	3	1		
Malta	42	40	34	34	34	34	36	36	35		
Monaco											
Turkey[a]	1010	1024	1076	1150	1161	1202	1250	1411	1422		
Total	1087	1107	1156	1231	1243	1285	1334	1497	1506		
European total	89254	89898	88196	87928	88072	88091	86712	85166	80284	6299	

Source: ILO

Notes: See end of section

Table No: 0605

HOURS OF WORK

Average Working Week in Non-Agricultural Activities 1977-1990

Hours

	1977	1980	1982	1983	1984	1985	1986	1987	1988	1989	1990	% growth 1977-90
EC members												
Belgium	35.4	33.8	33.6	33.6	33.7	33.3	33.2	33.2	33.6	33.9	33.7	-4.8
Denmark												
France	41.4	40.8	39.5	39.2	39.0	38.9	38.9	39.0	39.0	39.0	39.0	-5.8
Germany: East							35.9	36.0	35.7	35.6		
Germany: West[a]	41.7	41.6	40.7	40.5	40.9	40.7	40.5	40.2	40.2	40.1	39.7	-4.8
Greece												
Ireland												
Italy[b]	7.7	7.8	7.7	7.7	7.8	7.8	7.7					
Luxembourg[a]	39.5	40.2	41.3	41.2	40.1	40.6	41.0	41.2	41.5	40.5		
Netherlands[a]	40.7	40.6	40.4	40.4	40.4	40.3	40.3	40.2	40.1	40.1		
Portugal	38.5	38.4	38.4	38.9	38.2	38.2	38.7	38.7	38.8			
Spain	42.3	40.1	39.5	38.8	37.9	37.5	37.6	36.1	36.5	36.8	36.7	-13.2
United Kingdom			42.1	42.4	42.5	42.8	42.7	43.1	43.5	43.4	42.9	
EFTA members												
Austria												
Finland												
Iceland[a]	49.5	49.3	49.4	48.7	48.9	48.6	48.5	49.2	47.4	46.8		
Liechtenstein												
Norway[c]	36.8	36.3	36.0	35.6	35.9	36.2	36.6	35.9	36.5	36.4	36.0	-2.2
Sweden	35.7	35.4	35.3	35.4	35.8	36.0	36.5	37.1	37.2	37.5	37.7	5.6
Switzerland[a]	44.8	44.3	44.1	43.7	43.5	43.4	43.1	42.8	42.6	42.4	42.2	-5.8
Eastern Europe												
Albania												
Bulgaria												
Czechoslovakia												
Hungary												
Poland[d]		150.0	155.0	158.0	159.0	159.0	159.0	159.0	160.0	155.0	148.0	
Romania												
USSR												
Yugoslavia[a,d]	185.0			182.0		185.0			183.0			
Others												
Cyprus[a]	44.0	42.0	42.0	41.0	41.0	41.0	41.0	41.0	41.0	42.0		
Gibraltar[a]	47.5	43.2	44.7	44.3	45.1	44.5	44.0	42.7	44.9	46.1		
Malta												
Monaco												
Turkey												

Source: ILO

Notes: See end of section

Table No: 0606

HOURS OF WORK

Average Working Week in Manufacturing 1977-1990

Hours

	1977	1980	1982	1983	1984	1985	1986	1987	1988	1989	1990	% growth 1977-90
EC members												
Belgium	35.1	33.4	33.6	33.5	33.7	33.1	33.0	33.0	33.4	33.6	33.4	-4.84
Denmark	32.7	32.6	32.5	33.0	33.0	32.1	32.8	32.1	31.8	32.0	31.8	-2.75
France	41.1	40.6	39.4	38.9	38.7	38.6	38.6	38.7	38.8	38.8	38.8	-5.60
Germany: East							35.2	35.2	35.0	34.9		
Germany: West[a]	41.7	41.6	40.7	40.5	41.0	40.7	40.4	40.1	40.0	39.9	39.5	-5.28
Greece	41.0	40.7	38.6	38.5	38.2	39.3	39.1	39.2	41.1	41.1		
Ireland	42.6	41.1	40.5	40.8	41.1	41.1	41.2	41.1	41.9	41.7	41.4	-2.82
Italy[b]	7.7	7.7	7.7	7.7	7.8	7.8	7.7	7.7	7.8			
Luxembourg[a]	38.9	40.0	41.2	41.0	39.7	40.2	40.5	40.8	41.2	40.3		
Netherlands[a]	40.9	40.8	40.6	40.5	40.3	40.3	40.1	39.9	39.8	39.8		
Portugal	39.8	39.0	38.8	38.6	38.6	38.1	38.9	39.1				
Spain	41.1	38.5	38.0	37.4	36.5	36.3	36.7	35.4	35.8	36.8	36.7	-10.71
United Kingdom			41.0	41.5	41.7	41.8	41.6	42.2	42.4	42.2	41.6	
EFTA members												
Austria[c]	146.9	146.0	145.5	144.3	145.2	144.9	142.1	139.9	141.0	139.6	139.5	-5.04
Finland	32.8	33.2	32.5	32.4	32.3	32.3	33.4	32.1	32.1	31.8		
Iceland												
Liechtenstein												
Norway[d]	38.2	38.3	37.9	37.9	38.0	38.4	38.4	37.2	37.8	37.9	37.3	-2.36
Sweden	37.9	37.6	37.6	37.7	38.1	38.3	38.3	38.4	38.5	38.5	38.5	1.58
Switzerland[a]	44.6	43.8	43.7	43.2	43.0	42.9	42.6	42.4	41.9	41.8	41.6	-6.73
Eastern Europe												
Albania												
Bulgaria												
Czechoslovakia	43.7	43.5	43.1	43.1	43.0	43.1	43.1	43.1	43.0	40.7	40.6	-7.09
Hungary[c]	163.5	160.8	153.9	152.4	147.1	145.2	144.5	147.7	147.3	142.6	143.5	-12.23
Poland[c]	163.0	159.0	149.0	152.0	152.0	153.0	151.0	151.0	154.0	150.0	143.0	-12.27
Romania												
USSR	40.6	40.5	40.4	40.3								
Yugoslavia[a,c]	185.0			181.0		184.0			184.0			
Others												
Cyprus[a]	44.0	41.0	41.0	41.0	41.0	41.0	41.0	41.0	41.0	41.0		
Gibraltar[a]	44.9	45.8	47.7	47.6	50.4	48.7	47.3	43.9	47.1	42.4		
Malta												
Monaco												
Turkey												

Source: ILO
Notes: See end of section

Table No: 0607

ECONOMICALLY ACTIVE POPULATION

Structure of the Economically Active Population: Latest Official Estimates

	Year	Total '000	% Total Population	Males '000	% Total EAP	Females '000	% Total EAP
EC members							
Belgium	1989	4144	41.9	2432	58.7	1712	41.3
Denmark	1990	2912	56.7	1571	53.9	1341	46.1
France	1989	24567	43.9	14077	57.3	10490	42.7
Germany: East[a]	1987	10825	65.0	5608	51.8	5217	48.2
Germany: West	1989	29889	48.3	17994	60.2	11895	39.8
Greece	1987	3884	38.9	2489	64.1	1394	35.9
Ireland	1988	1310	37.0	910	69.5	400	30.5
Italy	1990	24075	42.0	15129	62.8	8946	37.2
Luxembourg	1990	160	42.2	104	65.0	56	35.0
Netherlands	1990	6872	45.3	4179	60.8	2693	39.2
Portugal	1990	4949	47.8	2814	56.9	2135	43.1
Spain	1990	15020	38.8	9742	64.9	52.78	35.1
United Kingdom	1988	28274	49.5	16234	57.4	12040	42.6
EC total		156881		93283	59.5	63597	40.5
EFTA members							
Austria	1989	3455	45.3	2048	59.3	1407	40.7
Finland	1990	2576	51.7	1363	52.9	1213	47.1
Iceland	1986	118	48.4	65	55.1	53	44.9
Liechtenstein	1986	13	47.9	8	61.5	5	38.5
Norway	1990	2142	51.1	1181	55.1	961	44.9
Sweden	1990	4577	53.5	2382	52.0	2195	48.0
Switzerland	1988	3481	52.2	2176	62.5	1305	37.5
EFTA total	13919	16362		9223	56.4	7139	43.6
Eastern Europe							
Albania	1984	1289	44.4	730	56.6	559	43.4
Bulgaria[a]	1987	5004	55.7	2650	53.0	2355	47.0
Czechoslovakia	1986	7705	49.7	4091	53.1	3614	46.9
Hungary	1990	4795	46.2	2595	54.1	2201	45.9
Poland[a]	1988	18452	48.7	10070	54.6	8382	45.4
Romania	1985	7660	33.7	4260	55.6	3400	44.4
USSR	1989	143324	50.2	74120	51.7	69204	48.3
Yugoslavia	1985	6493	28.1	4039	62.2	2454	37.8
East European total		194722		102555	52.7	92169	47.3
Others							
Cyprus	1989	274	48.1	171	62.6	102	37.4
Gibraltar	1989	15	47.2	10	66.1	5	33.9
Malta	1989	131	37.2	98	74.8	33	25.2
Monaco							
Turkey	1989	21175	38.5	14253	67.3	6922	32.7
Total		21595		14532	67.3	7062	32.7
European total		389560		219593	56.4	169967	43.6

Sources: National statistical offices/Statistical Office of the European Community/ILO/Euromonitor
Notes: See end of section

Table No: 0608

ECONOMICALLY ACTIVE POPULATION

Economically Active Population by Industry: Latest Year

% total economically active population

	Year	A	B	C	D	E	F	G	H	I	J	Total
EC members												
Belgium[a]	1989	2.4	0.3	18.8	0.7	5.4	15.1	6.1	7.6	33.0	10.5	100.0
Denmark	1990	5.4	0.1	19.9	0.7	6.9	14.7	6.8	8.8	35.0	1.8	100.0
France[a]	1989	5.7	0.4	18.9	0.8	6.5	15.2	5.7	8.5	27.8	10.5	100.0
Germany: East[b,c]	1986	10.8	40.8			6.7	10.3	7.3	24.1			100.0
Germany: West[a]	1989	3.4	0.7	28.8	0.8	6.0	14.8	5.4	7.2	26.0	6.8	100.0
Greece[a]	1988	24.6	0.6	18.8	0.9	6.2	15.6	6.4	4.1	17.6	5.1	100.0
Ireland[a]	1988	12.7	0.5	15.8	1.1	5.5	14.7	4.9	6.4	21.5	17.1	100.0
Italy[a]	1990	7.9	1.0	19.8		7.7	18.8	4.8	3.7	24.9	12.5	100.0
Luxembourg[a]	1990	3.7		19.1	0.9	8.5	19.8	6.5	12.2	27.2	2.0	100.0
Netherlands[a]	1990	4.2	0.2	17.2	0.6	6.0	16.1	5.6	9.4	32.4	8.3	100.0
Portugal[a]	1990	17.1	0.7	23.5	0.9	7.8	14.7	4.3	4.2	22.2	4.6	100.0
Spain[a]	1990	11.2	0.6	20.5	0.7	9.5	18.9	5.1	4.8	21.4	7.2	100.0
United Kingdom[a]	1990	2.0	0.8	19.0	1.0	6.3	19.1	5.4	11.1	28.7	5.5	100.0
EFTA members												
Austria[a]	1989	7.8	0.4	27.1	1.2	8.4	18.3	6.3	6.1	23.5	1.0	100.0
Finland[a,b]	1990	8.3	0.2	20.9	1.1	8.6	15.6	7.1	8.0	29.7	0.6	100.0
Iceland[a]	1987	10.5		21.5	0.9	9.3	15.7	6.5	7.4	27.8	0.4	100.0
Liechtenstein												
Norway[a]	1990	6.1	1.0	15.0	1.1	7.0	17.3	7.7	7.1	34.9	2.7	100.0
Sweden[a]	1990	3.3	0.3	20.8	0.8	6.8	14.1	7.0	8.4	36.9	1.6	100.0
Switzerland	1990	5.5		25.4		9.5	20.6	6.1	10.6	22.2		100.0
Eastern Europe												
Albania												
Bulgaria[d]	1985	17.0	37.0			7.8	8.3	6.8	21.6		1.5	100.0
Czechoslovakia												
Hungary[b,c,d]	1990	19.6	29.9			6.9	10.8		8.6	24.2		100.0
Poland	1988	27.8	2.8	24.6	1.0	7.9	8.1	6.7	1.7	19.3		100.0
Romania												
USSR	1989	19.3		45.9			7.4			25.9	1.6	100.0
Yugoslavia	1981	30.6	25.2			7.9	9.4	5.1	2.3	18.1	1.5	100.0
Others												
Cyprus[a]	1989	13.6	0.2	18.2	0.5	8.4	20.5	5.1	5.2	18.0	10.2	100.0
Gibraltar[a]	1989			7.0	1.6	13.1	21.5	4.4	10.1	31.7	10.5	100.0
Malta[a]	1989	2.5	0.6	27.1	1.4	4.5	9.6	7.0	3.5	40.3	3.7	100.0
Monaco												
Turkey[a]	1989	45.9	0.7	13.0	0.1	4.7	9.8	3.8	2.0	11.5	8.5	100.0

Sources: UN/ILO/national statistical offices
Notes: See end of section

Table No: 0609

ECONOMICALLY ACTIVE POPULATION

Economically Active Population by Age Group: Latest Year

'000

	Year	Under 15	15-19	20-24	25-29	30-34	35-39	40-44
EC members								
Belgium	1981		209.5	580.1	624.0	579.5	436.5	400.7
Denmark	1990		250.9	333.2	357.7	346.4	343.0	381.5
France	1989		520.2	2749.8	3625.5	3544.8	3587.0	3441.3
Germany: East	1981	0.2	366.8	1186.5	1237.4	1038.8	908.5	1280.0
Germany: West	1989		1515.0	3954.0	4086.0	3620.0	3395.0	3057.0
Greece	1987	8.9	150.0	345.6	467.8	481.3	497.0	448.8
Ireland	1988		96.0	216.2	198.3	169.5	147.0	129.5
Italy[a]	1990		1166.0	2881.0	3267.0	3130.0	2989.0	3024.0
Luxembourg	1990		6.0	20.7	26.0	24.1	22.2	20.1
Netherlands	1990		465.0	972.0	1059.0	973.0	941.0	881.0
Portugal	1990	42.8	423.0	544.1	536.4	567.5	561.4	561.6
Spain	1990		874.7	2155.3	2179.9	1945.4	1703.1	1595.3
United Kingdom[b]	1988		2584.0	3734.0	6747.0		6659.0	
EC total		51.9	8627.1	19672.5	24412.0	16420.3	22189.7	15220.8
EFTA members								
Austria	1989		266.1	482.5	516.1	456.2	403.5	391.4
Finland	1990		118.0	259.0	327.0	345.0	373.0	411.0
Iceland								
Liechtenstein								
Norway	1990		113.0	245.0	261.0	275.0	269.0	283.0
Sweden	1989		224.0	501.0	544.0	538.0	553.0	632.0
Switzerland								
EFTA total			721.1	1487.5	1648.1	1614.2	1598.5	1717.4
Eastern Europe								
Albania								
Bulgaria								
Czechoslovakia								
Hungary								
Poland[c]	1988		526.9	1773.0	2342.0	2898.8	2819.6	2090.2
Romania								
USSR[d]	1988		6158.5	16095.0	22448.4	22255.4	19957.5	13247.5
Yugoslavia[e]	1981		403.1	1224.2	1450.0	1266.3	917.3	1050.4
East European total			7088.5	19092.2	26240.0	26420.5	23694.4	16388.1
Others								
Cyprus	1989		18.2	31.8	38.3	37.3	32.2	30.5
Gibraltar								
Malta								
Monaco								
Turkey	1989	1036.8	3193.8	2481.9	2786.1	2431.6	2359.6	1804.1
Total		1036.8	3212.0	2513.7	2824.4	2468.9	2391.8	1834.6
European total		1088.7	19648.7	42765.9	55124.9	46923.9	49874.4	35160.9

Table No: 0609 (cont'd)

ECONOMICALLY ACTIVE POPULATION

Economically Active Population by Age Group: Latest Year

'000

	Year	45-49	50-54	55-59	60-64	65+	Total
EC members							
Belgium	1981	391.7	357.8	262.0	74.5	27.0	3943.3
Denmark	1990	322.2	244.1	183.7	93.5	56.1	2912.3
France	1989	2340.1	2196.6	1761.2	599.3	201.0	24566.7
Germany: East	1981	1021.0	875.5	663.3	328.6	173.7	9080.2
Germany: West	1989	3649.0	3425.0	2161.0	768.0	261.0	29889.0
Greece	1987	425.2	411.3	334.8	190.4	122.4	3883.6
Ireland	1988	103.2	87.9	72.5	51.3	38.3	1309.8
Italy[a]	1990	2472.0	2248.0	1572.0	773.0	403.0	24075.0
Luxembourg	1990	16.1	13.0	7.9	2.8	0.9	159.8
Netherlands	1990	665.0	485.0	329.0	101.0		6872.0
Portugal	1990	484.8	436.8	370.7	230.5	189.3	4948.6
Spain	1990	1358.7	1207.8	1178.3	678.8	142.6	14019.9
United Kingdom[b]	1989	5054.0		1986.0	1078.0	432.0	28274.0
EC total		18303.0	11988.8	10882.4	4969.7	2047.3	154934.2
EFTA members							
Austria	1989	427.6	282.5	177.7	36.4	15.2	3455.0
Finland	1990	274.0	236.0	155.0	60.0	18.0	2576.0
Iceland							
Liechtenstein							
Norway	1990	229.0	164.0	130.0	108.0	65.0	2142.0
Sweden	1989	564.0	424.0	349.0	249.0		4577.0
Switzerland							
EFTA total		1494.6	1106.5	811.7	453.4	98.2	12750.0
Eastern Europe							
Albania							
Bulgaria							
Czechoslovakia							
Hungary							
Poland[c]	1988	1564.3	1526.6	1228.5	766.1	898.2	18452.2
Romania							
USSR[d]	1988	14017.3	15096.3	8138.7	3819.2	2038.4	143324.0
Yugoslavia[e]	1981	1042.3	821.5	475.9	214.6	463.6	9358.7
East European total		16623.9	17444.4	8743.1	4799.9	3400.2	171134.9
Others							
Cyprus	1989	24.9	21.2	16.3	12.1	11.0	273.5
Gibraltar							
Malta							
Monaco							
Turkey	1989	1383.3	1198.7	1180.8	746.3	572.3	21175.4
Total		1407.9	1219.9	1197.1	758.4	583.3	21448.9
European total		37829.4	31759.6	22734.3	10981.4	6129.0	360268.0

Sources: UN/ILO/national statistical offices
Notes: See end of section

Table No: 0610

ECONOMICALLY ACTIVE POPULATION

Economically Active Population by Age Group: Latest Year

% total economically active population

	Year	Under 15	15-19	20-24	25-29	30-34	35-39	40-44
EC members								
Belgium	1981		5.3	14.7	15.8	14.7	11.1	10.2
Denmark	1990		8.6	11.4	12.3	11.9	11.8	13.1
France	1989		2.1	11.2	14.8	14.4	14.6	14.0
Germany: East	1981	0.0	4.0	13.1	13.6	11.4	10.0	14.1
Germany: West	1989		5.1	13.2	13.7	12.1	11.4	10.2
Greece	1987	0.2	3.9	8.9	12.0	12.4	12.8	11.6
Ireland	1988		7.3	16.5	15.1	12.9	11.2	9.9
Italy[a]	1990		4.8	12.0	13.6	13.0	12.4	12.6
Luxembourg	1990		3.8	13.0	16.3	15.1	13.9	12.6
Netherlands	1990		6.8	14.1	15.4	14.2	13.7	12.8
Portugal	1990	0.9	8.5	11.0	10.8	11.5	11.3	11.3
Spain	1990		5.8	14.3	14.5	13.0	11.3	10.6
United Kingdom[b]	1988		9.1	13.2	23.9		23.6	
EC total		0.0	5.6	12.7	15.8	10.6	14.3	9.8
EFTA members								
Austria	1989	7.7	14.0	14.9	13.2	11.7	11.3	
Finland	1990		4.6	10.1	12.7	13.4	14.5	16.0
Iceland								
Liechtenstein								
Norway	1990	5.3	11.4	12.2	12.8	12.6	13.2	
Sweden	1989	4.9	10.9	11.9	11.8	12.1	13.8	
Switzerland								
EFTA total		5.7	11.7	12.9	12.7	12.5	13.5	
Eastern Europe								
Albania								
Bulgaria								
Czechoslovakia								
Hungary								
Poland[c]	1988		2.9	9.6	12.7	15.7	15.3	11.3
Romania								
USSR[d]	1988		4.3	11.2	15.7	17.7	13.9	9.2
Yugoslavia	1981		4.3	13.1	15.5	13.5	9.8	11.2
East European total			4.1	11.2	15.3	15.4	13.8	9.6
Others								
Cyprus	1989	4.9	15.1	11.7	13.2	11.5	11.1	8.5
Gibraltar								
Malta								
Monaco								
Turkey	1989	4.9	15.1	11.7	13.2	11.5	11.1	8.5
Total		4.8	15.0	11.7	13.2	11.5	11.2	8.6
European total		0.3	5.5	11.9	15.3	13.0	13.8	9.8

Table No: 0610 (cont'd)

ECONOMICALLY ACTIVE POPULATION

Economically Active Population by Age Group: Latest Year

% total economically active population

	Year	45-49	50-54	55-59	60-64	65+	Total
EC members							
Belgium	1981	9.9	9.1	6.6	1.9	0.7	100.0
Denmark	1990	11.1	8.4	6.3	3.2	1.9	100.0
France	1989	9.5	8.9	7.2	2.4	0.8	100.0
Germany: East	1981	11.2	9.6	7.3	3.6	1.9	100.0
Germany: West	1989	12.2	11.5	7.2	2.6	0.9	100.0
Greece	1987	10.9	10.6	8.6	4.9	3.2	100.0
Ireland	1988	7.9	6.7	5.5	3.9	2.9	100.0
Italy[a]	1990	10.3	9.3	6.5	3.2	1.7	100.0
Luxembourg	1990	10.1	8.1	4.9	1.8	0.6	100.0
Netherlands	1990	9.7	7.1	4.8	1.5		100.0
Portugal	1990	9.8	8.8	7.5	4.7	3.8	100.0
Spain	1990	9.0	8.0	7.8	4.5	0.9	100.0
United Kingdom[b]	1988	17.9		7.0	3.8	1.5	100.0
EC total		11.8	7.7	7.0	3.2	1.3	100.0
EFTA members							
Austria	1989	12.4	8.2	5.1	1.1	0.4	100.0
Finland	1990	10.6	9.2	6.0	2.3	0.7	100.0
Iceland							
Liechtenstein							
Norway	1990	10.7	7.7	6.1	5.0	3.0	100.0
Sweden	1989	12.3	9.3	7.6	5.4		100.0
Switzerland							
EFTA total		11.7	8.7	6.4	3.6	0.8	100.0
Eastern Europe							
Albania							
Bulgaria							
Czechoslovakia							
Hungary							
Poland[c]	1988	8.5	8.3	6.7	4.2	4.9	100.0
Romania							
USSR[d]	1988	9.8	10.5	5.7	2.7	1.4	100.0
Yugoslavia	1981	11.1	8.8	5.1	2.3	5.0	100.0
East European total		9.7	10.2	5.8	2.8	2.0	100.0
Others							
Cyprus	1989	9.0	7.8	6.0	4.4	4.0	100.0
Gibraltar							
Malta							
Monaco							
Turkey	1989	6.5	5.7	5.6	3.5	2.7	100.0
Total		6.6	5.7	5.6	3.5	2.7	100.0
European total		10.5	8.8	6.3	3.0	1.7	100.0

Sources: UN/ILO/national statistical offices
Notes: See end of section

Table No: 0611

ECONOMICALLY ACTIVE POPULATION

Economically Active Population by Status: Latest Year

'000

	Year	AB	C	D	E	F	G	HIJ	K	Total
EC members										
Belgium	1981	623.2	75.2	701.2	309.2	327.1	117.8	1331.9	33.5	3519.1
Denmark	1990	667.2	112.0	522.2	219.9	308.2	131.3	875.1	76.5	2912.4
France	1982	3359.1	58.3	4062.5	1866.7	2544.1	1803.4	7346.8	166.0	21206.9
Germany: East	1981	1080.4	561.5	1864.5	379.9	696.8	512.4	2555.1	1429.6	9080.2
Germany: West	1989	4490.2	1033.2	5607.6	2537.9	3092.8	1065.4	9049.6	3012.2	29888.9
Greece	1988	461.9	72.1	382.0	388.0	352.4	977.1	1097.7	229.6	3960.8
Ireland	1988	187.3	33.6	167.0	118.6	117.6	168.0	283.6	234.4	1310.1
Italy	1981	2600.8	3609.7	2164.6	2501.1	2610.1	2097.3	4662.9		20246.5
Luxembourg	1990	20.2	1.6	40.5	13.0	22.0	7.0	52.6	2.8	159.7
Netherlands	1990	1509.0	274.0	1122.0	692.0	778.0	314.0	1535.0	649.0	6872.0
Portugal	1990	418.5	99.6	632.3	446.5	565.7	839.4	1571.8	374.6	4948.4
Spain	1990	1444.0	238.1	1763.3	1500.2	1975.7	1672.0	5262.8	1164.0	15019.9
United Kingdom	1981	4137.8	2311.7	3945.3	1404.1	3062.7	353.3	8004.7	220.8	23440.4
EFTA members										
Austria	1989	492.3	212.1	542.9	310.6	376.7	268.4	1207.3	44.7	3455.0
Finland	1990	612.0	112.0	362.0	248.0	273.0	218.0	704.0	48.0	2576.0
Iceland										
Liechtenstein										
Norway	1990	478.0	130.0	216.0	218.0	273.0	128.0	548.0	153.0	2142.0
Sweden	1990	1454.0	735.0		423.0	424.0	150.0	1309.0	82.0	4577.0
Switzerland										
Eastern Europe										
Albania										
Bulgaria	1985	1218.1	138.0	47.6	283.3	188.7	594.0	2216.0	0.5	4686.2
Czechoslovakia										
Hungary										
Poland	1988	3856.2	110.8	1063.2		982.0	4367.4	7569.3	503.3	18452.2
Romania										
USSR										
Yugoslavia	1981	922.1	153.7	890.7	476.9	529.4	2518.0	2947.9	341.0	8779.7
Others										
Cyprus	1989	25.4	4.8	34.2	25.5	30.5	36.1	82.5	24.1	263.1
Gibraltar	1989	1.7	0.8	3.1	1.2	2.6		4.5	0.6	14.5
Malta										
Monaco										
Turkey	1989	1023.9	294.4	807.4	1407.6	1374.4	9700.1	4681.6	1886.0	21175.4

Sources: UN/ILO/national statistical offices
Notes: See end of section

Table No: 0612

ECONOMICALLY ACTIVE POPULATION

Economically Active Population by Status: Latest Year

% total economically active population

	Year	AB	C	D	E	F	G	HIJ	K	Total
EC members										
Belgium	1981	17.7	2.1	19.9	8.8	9.3	3.3	37.8	1.0	100.0
Denmark	1990	22.9	3.8	17.9	7.6	10.6	4.5	30.0	2.6	100.0
France	1982	15.8	0.3	19.2	8.8	12.0	8.5	34.6	0.8	100.0
Germany: East	1981	11.9	6.2	20.5	4.2	7.7	5.6	28.1	15.7	100.0
Germany: West	1989	15.0	3.5	18.8	8.5	10.3	3.6	30.3	10.1	100.0
Greece	1988	11.7	1.8	9.6	9.8	8.9	24.7	27.7	5.8	100.0
Ireland	1988	14.3	2.6	12.7	9.1	9.0	12.8	21.6	17.9	100.0
Italy	1981	12.8	17.8	10.7	12.4	12.9	10.4	23.0		100.0
Luxembourg	1990	12.6	1.0	25.4	8.1	13.8	4.4	32.9	1.8	100.0
Netherlands	1990	22.0	4.0	16.3	10.1	11.3	4.6	22.3	9.4	100.0
Portugal	1990	8.5	2.0	12.8	9.0	11.4	17.0	31.8	7.6	100.0
Spain	1990	9.6	1.6	11.7	10.0	13.2	11.1	35.0	7.7	100.0
United Kingdom	1981	17.7	9.9	16.8	6.0	13.1	1.5	34.1	0.9	100.0
EFTA members										
Austria	1989	14.2	6.1	15.7	9.0	10.9	7.8	34.9	1.3	100.0
Finland	1990	23.8	4.3	14.1	9.6	10.6	8.5	27.3	1.9	100.0
Iceland										
Liechtenstein										
Norway	1990	22.3	6.1	10.1	10.2	12.7	6.0	25.6	7.1	100.0
Sweden	1990	31.8	16.1		9.2	9.3	3.3	28.6	1.8	100.0
Switzerland										
Eastern Europe										
Albania										
Bulgaria	1985	26.0	2.9	1.0	6.0	4.0	12.7	47.3	0.0	100.0
Czechoslovakia										
Hungary										
Poland	1988	20.9	0.6	5.8		5.3	23.7	41.0	2.7	100.0
Romania										
USSR										
Yugoslavia	1981	10.5	1.8	10.1	5.4	6.0	28.7	33.6	3.9	100.0
Others										
Cyprus	1989	9.7	1.8	13.0	9.7	11.6	13.7	31.4	9.2	100.0
Gibraltar	1989	11.7	5.5	21.4	8.3	17.9		31.0	4.1	100.0
Malta										
Monaco										
Turkey	1989	4.8	1.4	3.8	6.6	6.5	45.8	22.1	8.9	100.0

Sources: UN/ILO/national statistical offices
Notes: See end of section

Notes to Tables in Section Six:

Table 0601
- a Including armed forces
- b New series starting 1980
- c Employees only
- d New series starting 1987
- e Number of 'work years'
- f Social sector only
- g New series starting 1988

Table 0602
- a New series starting 1988
- b Compilation date changed in 1986; subsequent data not strictly comparable

Table 0603
- a New series starting 1988
- b Compilation date changed in 1986; subsequent data not strictly comparable

Table 0604
- a Employees only
- b Social sector only
- c Employment in establishments with more than 10 workers
- d New series starting 1981
- e New series starting 1987
- f Includes mining, quarrying, electricity, gas, water
- g New series starting 1988

Table 0605
- a Hours paid for
- b Hours per day; estimates for 1985 and 1986
- c New series starting 1988
- d Hours per month

Table 0606 Data refer to hours actually worked
- a Hours paid for
- b Hours per day
- c Hours per month
- d New series starting 1988

Table 0607 EAP = economically active population
- a Population of working age only

Table 0608
- A Agriculture/forestry/fishing
- B Mining and quarrying
- C Manufacturing
- D Electricity, gas and water
- E Construction
- F Wholesale/retail trade, restaurants and hotels
- G Transport, storage and communications
- H Finance, insurance, real estate and business services
- I Community, social and personal services
- J Not adequately defined
- a Column J includes unemployed
- b Division B includes divisions C and D
- c Division H includes divisions I and J
- d National figures differ significantly from external estimates

Table 0609
- a Total includes 150,000 persons of unknown age
- b Blank denotes column figure included in previous column
- c Total includes 17,974 persons of unknown age
- d Total includes 51,714 persons of unknown age
- e Total includes 29,500 persons of unknown age

Table 0610 0.0 = less than 0.05%
- a Total includes 150,000 persons of unknown age
- b Blank denotes column figure included in previous column
- c Total includes 17,974 persons of unknown age
- d Total includes 51,714 persons of unknown age
- e Total includes 29,500 persons of unknown age

Table 0611/12
- AB Professional, technical and related workers
- C Administrative and managerial workers
- D Clerical and related workers
- E Sales workers
- F Service workers
- G Agricultural, animal husbandry and forestry workers, fishermen and hunters
- HIJ Production/related workers, transport equipment operators and labourers
- K Workers not classifiable by occupation, armed forces and unemployed

Section Seven

Industrial Resources and Output

Table No: 0701

INDUSTRIAL OUTPUT

Indices of General Industrial Production 1977-1990

1980 = 100

	1977	1978	1979	1980	1981	1982	1983	1984	1985	1986	1987	1988	1989	1990
EC members														
Belgium	95	97	101	100	97	98	99	102	104	105	107	113	118	123
Denmark	94	97	100	100	100	102	106	116	121	129	125	127	130	131
France	93	96	100	100	98	97	98	99	98	101	104	108	112	114
Germany: East	87	91	95	100	105	108	112	117	122	127	131	135	133	
Germany: West	92	95	100	100	98	95	96	99	104	107	107	111	117	123
Greece	87	93	99	100	101	102	101	104	107	107	106	111	113	110
Ireland	88	95	101	100	105	104	111	125	128	132	146	162	184	184
Italy	87	88	95	100	98	95	92	95	97	99	103	108	114	114
Luxembourg	96	100	103	100	94	90	99	113	121	124	125	130	143	142
Netherlands	97	98	101	100	98	94	97	102	106	106	107	107	112	116
Portugal	83	88	95	100	100	105	107	106	118	123	128	136	142	161
Spain	96	98	99	100	99	98	101	101	103	107	112	115	120	120
United Kingdom	100	103	107	100	96	98	102	103	108	110	114	119	119	118
EFTA members														
Austria	88	91	97	100	99	98	99	104	109	110	111	116	123	132
Finland	80	84	92	100	103	104	107	112	116	118	123	128	132	130
Iceland														
Liechtenstein														
Norway	81	89	96	100	99	99	108	118	121	126	135	142	165	171
Sweden	96	94	100	100	98	97	101	107	110	110	113	116	118	114
Switzerland	93	93	95	100	99	96	95	97	103	108	108	115	119	122
Eastern Europe														
Albania														
Bulgaria	85	91	96	100	105	110	115	120	124	129	134	143	149	
Czechoslovakia	89	93	97	100	102	104	107	111	115	118	122	124	125	120
Hungary	95	99	102	100	103	105	106	109	110	112	116	115	111	102
Poland	96	99	101	100	86	85	90	95	99	103	106	111	110	81
Romania				100							147			
USSR	90	94	97	100	103	106	111	115	119	125	129	136	136	135
Yugoslavia	82	89	96	100	102	104	105	111	114	119	120	122	120	
Others														
Cyprus														
Gibraltar														
Malta														
Monaco														
Turkey				100			128	142	149	166	184	187	194	212

Sources: UN/OECD/Comecon

Table No: 0702

INDUSTRIAL OUTPUT

Indices of Mining Production 1977-1990

1980 = 100

	1977	1980	1981	1982	1983	1984	1985	1986	1987	1988	1989	1990
EC members												
Belgium	115	100	94	95	89	90	84	75	65	56	46	32
Denmark	102	100	80	84	89	100	110	138	122	124	132	116
France	101	100	96	89	92	91	88	85	84	82	75	72
Germany: East												
Germany: West	96	100	99	96	92	92	93	91	87	85	84	84
Greece	97	100	101	148	161	178	183	184	181	189	180	174
Ireland	79	100	91	88	92	108	73	80	84	70	85	84
Italy	97	100	104	98	97	99	100	101	108	117	128	130
Luxembourg	183	100	77	46	37	32	29	27	72	30	39	43
Netherlands	108	100	91	78	84	86	93	87	88	78	86	86
Portugal	75	100	88	87	81	97	109	100	84	96	237	422
Spain	73	100	114	120	129	131	130	124	107	102	110	104
United Kingdom	62	100	107	117	124	118	129	133	130	120	102	100
EFTA members												
Austria	90	100	104	109	107	113	110	108	112	84	83	104
Finland	85	100	103	115	115	119	123	127	125	147	142	141
Iceland												
Liechtenstein												
Norway	42	100	96	97	114	131	138	147	164	181	230	243
Sweden	93	100	86	74	87	98	103	102	103	91	100	101
Switzerland												
Eastern Europe												
Albania												
Bulgaria												
Czechoslovakia	95	100	99	99	101	102	101	101	102	107	100	91
Hungary	101	100	97	100	97	97	99	99	99	95	88	78
Poland	101	100	85	97	99	102	104	104	106	105	106	78
Romania												
USSR	96	100	101	102	104	105	107	111	113	116	115	111
Yugoslavia	91	100	102	105	107	109	115	116	117	116	113	
Others												
Cyprus	103	100	85	79	75	65	71	64	68	66	55	55
Gibraltar												
Malta												
Monaco												
Turkey					107	113	119	153	161	152	171	182

Sources: UN/OECD/Comecon

Table No: 0703

INDUSTRIAL OUTPUT

Indices of Manufacturing Production 1977-1990

1980 = 100

	1977	1980	1981	1982	1983	1984	1985	1986	1987	1988	1989	1990
EC members												
Belgium	94	100	98	98	100	102	104	106	109	114	120	126
Denmark	93	100	100	102	106	117	122	131	127	129	133	133
France	95	100	98	97	97	97	98	98	100	105	108	110
Germany: East												
Germany: West	92	100	98	95	96	99	104	107	107	112	118	124
Greece	87	100	101	99	97	98	101	100	98	103	106	103
Ireland	88	100	106	105	114	125	131	134	150	169	190	196
Italy	87	100	98	95	92	95	96	99	103	108	113	112
Luxembourg	95	100	93	90	99	114	122	125	125	126	144	142
Netherlands	94	100	100	99	101	106	109	112	112	128	123	129
Portugal	82	100	101	105	106	105	117	122	128	136	138	150
Spain	98	100	98	96	99	99	101	105	111	114	119	119
United Kingdom	109	100	92	95	97	101	104	105	111	119	124	123
EFTA members												
Austria	88	100	98	97	99	104	109	110	109	115	124	133
Finland	79	100	103	104	107	112	116	118	123	128	133	130
Iceland												
Liechtenstein												
Norway	101	100	99	99	98	104	106	108	110	109	109	110
Sweden	96	100	98	97	102	107	110	110	113	117	118	114
Switzerland	93	100	107	108	94	97	103	107	107	115	120	123
Eastern Europe												
Albania												
Bulgaria												
Czechoslovakia	89	100	102	104	107	111	116	119	122	124	125	121
Hungary	95	100	103	106	107	110	110	112	117	117	111	101
Poland	96	100	86	84	89	94	97	102	105	111	69	80
Romania												
USSR	88	100	104	107	112	116	120	126	131	136	139	139
Yugoslavia	81	100	101	103	105	112	114	117	119	117	120	
Others												
Cyprus												
Gibraltar												
Malta												
Monaco												
Turkey					131	146	152	168	187	188	191	210

Sources: UN/OECD/Comecon

Table No: 0704

INDUSTRIAL OUTPUT

Indices of Construction Output 1977-1990

1980 = 100

	1977	1980	1982	1983	1984	1985	1986	1987	1988	1989	1990
EC members											
Belgium	126	100	80	64	57	54	54	54	60	63	77
Denmark		100	72	71	80	85	97				
France	103	100	95	89	84	83	87	92	98	104	107
Germany: East	97	100	97	99	104	104					
Germany: West	95	100	88	90	91	84	89	89	92	97	102
Greece											
Ireland											
Italy											
Luxembourg	91	100	95	91	81	74	80	86	92	100	103
Netherlands	106	100	87	85	87	87	88	90	98	101	108
Portugal											
Spain											
United Kingdom	100	100	92	98	83	100	104	112	123	130	132
EFTA members											
Austria											
Finland											
Iceland											
Liechtenstein											
Norway											
Sweden											
Switzerland											
Eastern Europe											
Albania											
Bulgaria[a]	81	100	107	111	111	107					
Czechoslovakia	89	100	100	100	102	104					
Hungary	91	100	98	99	100	93					
Poland	104	100	84	88	92	90					
Romania	73	100	102	104	109	108					
USSR	97	100	104	109	112	115					
Yugoslavia											
Others											
Cyprus											
Gibraltar											
Malta											
Monaco											
Turkey											

Sources: UN/OECD/Comecon
Note: See end of section

Table No: 0705

MINERAL PRODUCTION

Production of Selected Minerals 1991

'000 metric tonnes unless otherwise stated

	Iron ore	Bauxite	Copper ore	Lead ore	Tin	Zinc	Silver (tonnes)	Gold (tonnes)
EC members								
Belgium								
Denmark								
France	8724	5	0.3	1.7		27.1	21.0	4.1
Germany: East[a]			3.6		1.8		20.0	
Germany: West	84			7.6		54.0		
Greece		2182		31.9		30.0	62.4	
Ireland				39.9		187.5	10.5	
Italy		9		14.0		36.3	178.4	
Luxembourg								
Netherlands								
Portugal	13		164.8		3.1			0.4
Spain	3030		10.0	49.9		261.0	270.0	7.2
United Kingdom	55		0.2	1.0	1.1	0.8		
EFTA members								
Austria	2300			1.1		14.8		
Finland[b]	35		11.7	1.3		55.5	30.3	2.2
Iceland								
Liechtenstein								
Norway	2081		17.4	3.5		18.9		
Sweden	37900		80.5	86.5		155.0	211.2	4.0
Switzerland								
Eastern Europe								
Albania[b,c]	1200		15.4					
Bulgaria[a]	1079		32.9	45.2		34.7	54.0	
Czechoslovakia[a]	1831		3.6	3.0	0.3	7.4	15.0	
Hungary[d]		2037						0.6
Poland[a]	7		329.3	45.4		154.8	832.0	
Romania[e]	580	218	9.5	15.3		11.5	10.0	2.0
USSR[f]	2360000	5350	900.10	490.0	13.0	870.0	1380.0	220.0
Yugoslavia	4132	2626	113.0	75.8		57.3	92.2	8.2
Others								
Cyprus			0.2					
Gibraltar								
Malta								
Monaco								
Turkey[g]	5000	520	45.6	13.2		35.0		

Source: World Bureau of Metal Statistics
Notes: See end of section

Table No: 0706

METAL PRODUCTION

Production of Selected Metals 1991

'000 metric tonnes

	Pig iron (1990)	Crude steel (1990)	Aluminium	Smelter copper	Refined copper	Refined lead	Refined tin	Slab zinc
EC members								
Belgium	9437	11414		87.6	287.0	99.3	0.2	297.6
Denmark		610						
France	14415	19015	286.1	6.6	55.7	283.3		299.6
Germany: East[a]	2159	5560	67.0	39.9	56.7	45.5	3.0	12.7
Germany: West	30098	38433	690.3	253.2	522.5	372.9	0.4	344.7
Greece		1050	152.4				0.3	
Ireland		326				15.0		
Italy	11882	25510	224.6		82.5	207.6		254.1
Luxembourg	2645	3560						
Netherlands	4960	5412	253.6			32.6	6.3	201.3
Portugal	339	746				6.8	0.1	5.5
Spain	5482	12935	355.2	149.1	189.9	112.6	1.3	273.4
United Kingdom	12319	17841	293.5		70.1	300.6	5.2	100.7
EFTA members								
Austria	3452	4291	80.4	44.8	52.8	22.7		16.3
Finland	2283	2860		90.1	64.5			170.4
Iceland			89.2					
Liechtenstein								
Norway	54	385	883.9	38.4	38.4			124.6
Sweden	2736	4454	96.9	108.0	96.6	88.0		
Switzerland	70	1105	57.2			6.0		
Eastern Europe								
Albania[b]				12.0	9.0			
Bulgaria[b]	1143	2401		30.3	24.1	66.6		73.5
Czechoslovakia[b]	9667	14873	69.6	8.2	24.6	23.7	0.1	
Hungary[c]	1708	2866	63.3		6.0			
Poland[d]	8423	13633	45.8	341.6	440.2	46.8		125.4
Romania[a]	6355	9754	163.1	24.7	29.0	26.9		11.5
USSR[a]	110167	154414	2300.0	990.0	1260.0	730.0	14.0	920.0
Yugoslavia	2313	3608	308.9	132.8	131.5	100.7		96.2
Others								
Cyprus								
Gibraltar								
Malta								
Monaco								
Turkey	4827	9322	55.8	28.4	90.0	9.0	20.1	

Source: World Bureau of Metal Statistics
Notes: See end of section

Table No: 0707

PRODUCTION OF SOAP AND DETERGENTS 1989

Production of Selected Soaps and Detergents 1989

Tonnes	A	B	C	D	E	F	G	H	I	J	K	L	M
EC members													
Belgium[a]	2532	478	10015	125	135950	14994		1700	11865	47932	67098	62106	11000
Denmark	1798	412	9732	51	60070	530		927	1275	14696	19915	20005	65
France	66420	9000	46500	26458	599196	57122	1063	4534	200728	133978	108990	162230	16103
Germany: East													
Germany: West	74565	4478	79538	2465	746042	69901	1000	2972	76400	183362	252751	97994	31524
Greece	2360	1600	8800	2850	74400	2250			2100	25600	15500	70000	3640
Ireland													
Italy													
Luxembourg													
Netherlands	8419			680	140710	1923		566	21431	38955	40978	18882	27575
Portugal	10706	708	9407	46310	67741	2206		2679	6437	49547	5094	24952	7718
Spain	11500	3400	39000	10000	542017	11845			43806	288360	262025	115658	20766
United Kingdom	117000	4300	44500	3200	499000			32000	154800	183000	199300	292300	56000
EFTA members													
Austria	796	187	3236	402	86765	8486		649	10678	10033	17224	4993	6581
Finland	770	368	2555	27	36020	7261				8953	7226	12804	6
Iceland													
Liechtenstein													
Norway	3126			249	15422	2956				6106	5705	7950	1986
Sweden	2511		10000		70422				69250				
Switzerland	4097			310	68506	14334	13536	6832	11881		19542	7680	5980
Eastern Europe													
Albania													
Bulgaria													
Czechoslovakia													
Hungary													
Poland													
Romania													
USSR													
Yugoslavia													
Others													
Cyprus													
Gibraltar													
Malta													
Monaco													
Turkey	86500			77000	182677	248			294	40823	5580	6759	16020

Source: Association Internationale de la Savonnerie et de la Détergence
Notes: See end of section

Table No: 0708

TEXTILE PRODUCTION

Production of Selected Textiles 1990

'000 metric tonnes

	Cotton yarn	Woven cotton fabric	Wool Yarn	Woven wool fabric	Rayon and acetate	Rayon & acetate fabrics
EC members						
Belgium[a]	29.9	39.5	88.5	2.8	7.6	179.4
Denmark	1.7		3.0			
France[a,b]	107.7	107.8	59.9	33.1	2.4	18.4
Germany: East[a,b,c,d]	54.3	19.6	37.5	92.4	120.0	49.6
Germany: West	185.4	169.8	40.0	34.7	176.8	53.4
Greece	136.3	60.0			7.2	
Ireland	14.1		9.1			
Italy[a]	230.6	179.9	507.1	178.6	35.5	
Luxembourg						
Netherlands[d]	5.0	10.5	3.9	1.5		
Portugal[a]	160.6	85.6	32.8	10.6		1.4
Spain	104.6	83.7	74.9			
United Kingdom[e,f]	30.0	27.0	131.3	35.7	19.8	15.4
EFTA members						
Austria	16.7	7.4	8.4	2.3		3.7
Finland[d]	3.8	6.5		0.2		
Iceland						
Liechtenstein						
Norway	2.6	1.8	2.4	0.5		
Sweden[a]	4.9	7.6	0.2	1.3		7.7
Switzerland	50.1	20.0	9.9	5.2		
Eastern Europe						
Albania						
Bulgaria[d,f,g]	77.6	39.4	28.5	3.4		35.8
Czechoslovakia[d,e]	143.8	79.0	57.3	87.2	16.1	
Hungary[c,d,e]	42.8	28.5	14.0	7.5	4.1	14.8
Poland[d,e,f]	126.7	56.6	50.0	85.4	13.9	52.9
Romania	157.4	89.5	58.1			
USSR[c,d,g]	1704.0	1065.0	421.2	495.4		978.0
Yugoslavia[b,c,d,e]	98.1	49.6	37.6	83.2		51.2
Others						
Cyprus						
Gibraltar						
Malta						
Monaco						
Turkey	330.8	327.2				

Sources: OECD/UN/International Wool Study Group/International Cotton Advisory Committee
Notes: See end of section

Notes to Tables in Section Seven:

Table 0704	a	Output of construction materials industry
Table 0705	a	Data refer to 1990
	b	Data for iron ore refer to 1988
	c	Data for copper refer to 1990
	d	Data for gold refer to 1990
	e	Data for copper, lead, silver and gold refer to 1990
	f	Data for bauxite, copper, lead and silver refer to 1990
	g	Data for silver refer to 1988
Table 0706	a	Data refer to 1990 except for aluminium
	b	All data refer to 1990
	c	Data for refined copper refer to 1990
	d	Data for smelter copper refer to 1990
Table 0707	A	Toilet soap
	B	Shaving products
	C	Shampoos
	D	Household soap
	E	Fabric washing powders
	F	Dishwashing powders (automatic)
	G	Dishwashing powders (hand)
	H	Powdered surface cleaners
	I	Fabric washing liquids
	J	Dishwashing liquids
	K	Liquid fabric conditioners
	L	Liquid surface cleaners
	M	Liquid scourers
	a	Includes Luxembourg
Table 0708	a	Data for rayon/acetate refer to 1989
	b	Data for rayon/acetate fabrics refer to 1989
	c	Data for rayon/acetate fabrics are in million square metres
	d	Data for woven wool fabric refer to 1989
	e	Data for woven wool fabric are in '000 square metres
	f	Data for rayon/acetate fabrics are in million metres
	g	Data for woven wool fabric are in '000 metres

Section Eight

Energy Resources and Output

Table No: 0801

ENERGY CONSUMPTION

Primary Energy Consumption: Selected Materials, 1991

Million tonnes of oil equivalent	Solid Fuels	Crude Oil	Natural Gas	Hydro-Electricity	Nuclear Electricity	Total Primary Energy
EC members						
Belgium[a]	10.9	25.9	8.6	0.0	10.4	55.8
Denmark	6.5	9.1	2.0			17.6
France	20.3	94.4	27.6	4.2	65.0	211.5
Germany: East[b]	56.4	14.7	6.6	0.0	1.4	79.1
Germany: West[b]	112.4	133.4	56.8	1.3	38.0	341.9
Greece	8.2	15.5	0.2	0.2		24.1
Ireland	4.3	4.6	1.4	0.1		10.4
Italy	14.2	91.7	41.4	3.5		150.8
Luxembourg						
Netherlands	9.2	35.4	33.5		1.0	79.1
Portugal	0.8	11.4	0.0	0.3		12.5
Spain	18.7	46.1	5.5	2.2	13.0	85.5
United Kingdom	63.4	82.9	54.2	0.3	15.5	216.3
EC total	325.3	565.1	237.8	12.1	144.3	1284.6
EFTA members						
Austria	3.8	11.2	5.7	2.8		23.5
Finland	3.6	10.6	2.4	1.1	4.8	22.5
Iceland	0.1	0.6	0.0	0.4		1.1
Liechtenstein						
Norway	0.5	8.9	0.0	8.3		17.7
Sweden	2.0	14.6	0.7	5.3	18.6	41.2
Switzerland	0.3	13.0	1.5	2.8	5.6	23.2
EFTA total	10.3	58.9	10.3	20.7	29.0	129.2
Eastern Europe						
Albania[c]	1.0	1.2	0.4			2.9
Bulgaria[c]	15.8	8.5	5.7			30.8
Czechoslovakia	31.7	13.2	10.2	0.4	5.9	61.4
Hungary	5.8	7.4	90.2	0.0	3.4	25.8
Poland	79.7	13.5	8.1	0.1		101.4
Romania[c]	22.5	16.3	32.1			72.7
USSR	253.4	420.1	560.0	20.2	54.7	1308.4
Yugoslavia[c]	19.4	14.5	5.7			42.3
East European total	429.3	494.7	631.4	20.7	64.0	1645.7
Others						
Cyprus[c]	0.1	1.2				1.8
Gibraltar						
Malta[c]	0.2	0.3				0.5
Monaco						
Turkey	22.5	22.0	3.8	1.4		49.7
Total	22.8	23.5	3.8	1.4		52.0
European total	787.7	1142.2	883.3	54.9	237.3	3111.5

Sources: UN Energy Statistics Yearbook/OECD/BP Statistical Review of World Energy/national accounts
Notes: See end of section

Table No: 0802

ENERGY PRODUCTION

Primary Energy Production: Hydrocarbons, 1991

Million tonnes of oil equivalent

	Solid Fuels	Crude Oil	Natural Gas
EC members			
Belgium	0.8		
Denmark		7.4	
France	8.4		3.2
Germany: East			
Germany: West[a]	102.2		16.3
Greece	7.3		
Ireland			
Italy	0.2		15.6
Luxembourg[b]			
Netherlands			62.2
Portugal			
Spain	15.6		
United Kingdom	56.6	91.6	48.8
EC total	190.3	99.0	146.1
EFTA members			
Austria	0.8		
Finland			
Iceland			
Liechtenstein			
Norway		93.4	24.6
Sweden			
Switzerland			
EFTA total	0.8	93.4	24.6
Eastern Europe			
Albania			
Bulgaria	5.0		
Czechoslovakia	35.3		
Hungary	4.7		
Poland	90.6		
Romania	6.0		
USSR	263.8	515.2	652.3
Yugoslavia	20.4		
East European total	425.8	515.2	652.3
Others			
Cyprus			
Gibraltar			
Malta			
Monaco			
Turkey	20.2		
Total	20.2		
European total	637.1	707.6	823.0

Source: BP
Notes: See end of section

Table No: 0803

ENERGY PRODUCTION

Refinery Capacities, Latest Year

Million tonnes of oil per year

	Year	
EC members		
Belgium[a]	1991	35.0
Denmark	1989	9.3
France[b]	1991	84.4
Germany: East	1989	26.7
Germany: West[c]	1991	109.7
Greece	1989	19.2
Ireland	1989	2.8
Italy	1991	114.4
Luxembourg		
Netherlands	1991	69.2
Portugal	1989	15.6
Spain	1991	70.5
United Kingdom	1991	90.6
EFTA members		
Austria	1989	10.2
Finland	1989	12.0
Iceland		
Liechtenstein		
Norway	1989	14.7
Sweden	1989	22.0
Switzerland[d]	1989	6.6
Eastern Europe		
Albania	1989	3.7
Bulgaria	1989	15.0
Czechoslovakia	1989	22.7
Hungary	1989	11.0
Poland	1989	19.5
Romania	1989	30.9
USSR	1991	610.6
Yugoslavia	1989	16.5
Others		
Cyprus	1989	0.8
Gibraltar		
Malta		
Monaco		
Turkey	1989	28.5

Sources: OECD/UN Energy Statistics Yearbook/BP
Notes: See end of section

Table No: 0804

ENERGY CONSUMPTION

Consumption of Refined Products 1991

'000 tonnes

	Motor Gasoline	Diesel/ Gasoil	Aviation Fuels	Liquefied Gases
EC members				
Belgium	2726	8951	965	550
Denmark	1701	4379	641	90
France[a]	17904	36729	3660	2878
Germany: East[b]	4269	5131	12	207
Germany: West	31752	60415	4839	2853
Greece	2533	5022	1011	288
Ireland	905	1760	227	136
Italy	15702	26158	2170	3288
Luxembourg	479	930	133	20
Netherlands	3449	5927	1652	2753
Portugal	1485	2642	584	827
Spain	8402	14091	2423	2637
United Kingdom	24046	19323	6176	2654
EC total	115353	191458	24493	19181
EFTA members				
Austria	2815	3873	366	177
Finland	1985	3867	431	133
Iceland	133	245	71	
Liechtenstein				
Norway	1736	2904	455	1073
Sweden	4474	4898	545	772
Switzerland[c]	3867	6739	1064	180
EFTA total	15010	22526	2932	2335
Eastern Europe				
Albania[b]	210	320	70	
Bulgaria[b]	1533	1584	220	90
Czechoslovakia[b]	2100	3716	465	130
Hungary[b]	1353	3079	238	314
Poland[b]	4162	6059	270	280
Romania[b]	1688	4009	656	193
USSR[b]	59900	91700	33340	9470
Yugoslavia[b]	2130	4260	0	398
East European total	73076	114727	35259	10875
Others				
Cyprus[b]	155	274	10	47
Gibraltar[b]	12			
Malta[b]	45	45	5	15
Monaco				
Turkey	3102	7048	483	1710
Total	3314	7367	498	1772
European total	206753	336078	63182	34163

Sources: OECD/UN
Notes: See end of section

Table No: 0805

MOTOR GASOLINE

Consumption of Motor Gasoline 1978-1991

'000 tonnes

	1978	1980	1983	1984	1985	1986	1987	1988	1989	1990	1991
EC members											
Belgium	3148	2940	2605	2603	2576	2785	2890	2936	2879	2726	2726
Denmark	1756	1523	1456	1507	1544	1550	1594	1582	1526	1605	1701
France[a]	17210	16321	18051	18090	16525	16591	16914	17107	16619	18264	17904
Germany: East	2852	3109	2673	3438	3575	3644	4016	4075	4269		
Germany: West	23035	22897	25462	25725	24236	25265	26051	26798	29849	31621	31752
Greece	1360	1377	1569	1672	2055	2102	2222	2288	2363	2445	2533
Ireland	943	1032	969	907	874	867	833	848	881	885	905
Italy	11213	13948	11283	10978	12104	12180	12309	12477	12946	14087	15702
Luxembourg	247	286	297	293	308	308	327	330	379	410	479
Netherlands	4325	3849	3614	4183	3635	4266	4125	3372	3423	3453	3449
Portugal	794	752	821	802	855	939	1081	1193	1272	1370	1485
Spain	5476	5758	5536	5579	6015	6264	6778	7197	7728	8108	8402
United Kingdom	17436	18553	18658	19615	20409	21501	22210	23277	23952	24338	24046
EC total	89795	92345	92994	95392	94711	98262	101350	103480	108086	109312	111084
EFTA members											
Austria	2322	2523	2544	2709	2425	2471	2517	2552	2610	2572	2815
Finland	1392	1370	1550	1574	1527	1648	1740	1819	1950	1985	1985
Iceland	91	89	91	98	98	120	118	124	108	91	133
Liechtenstein											
Norway	1402	1446	1495	1494	1687	1793	1762	1779	1783	1786	1736
Sweden	3660	3516	3578	3718	3961	4189	4303	4455	4588	4378	4474
Switzerland[b]	2608	2751	3010	3086	3066	3204	3343	3471	3529	3728	3867
EFTA total	11475	11695	12268	12679	12764	13425	13783	14200	14568	14540	15010
Eastern Europe											
Albania	140	160	225	200	200	200	210	215	210		
Bulgaria[c]	1720	1850	1800	1800	1800	1210	1218	1383	1533		
Czechoslovakia	1710	1639	1763	1902	1900	1900	2010	2100	2100		
Hungary[c]	1376	1401	1211	1219	1467	1617	1626	1653	1353		
Poland	3553	3988	3019	2956	2909	3519	3510	3698	4162		
Romania[c]	2303	1847	1729	1656	1405	1680	2717	1800	1688		
USSR[c]	62090	65900	69000	71000	70800	58000	58600	60100	59900		
Yugoslavia	2028	2176	2192	3300	2978	2190	1954	2100	2130		
East European total	74920	78961	80939	84033	83459	70316	71845	73049	73076		
Others											
Cyprus	100	100	111	118	124	130	140	148	155		
Gibraltar	3	4	4	4	5	4	8	12	12		
Malta	41	39	45	41	20	46	40	45	45		
Monaco											
Turkey	2214	1862	1784	1770	1940	2171	2408	2675	2729	3204	3102
Total	2358	2005	1944	1933	2089	2351	2596	2880	2941	3204	3102
European total	178548	185006	188145	194037	193023	184354	189574	193609	198671	127056	

Sources: UN Energy Statistics Yearbook/OECD Quarterly Oil Statistics and Energy Balances
Notes: See end of section

Table No: 0806

ELECTRICAL ENERGY

Electrical Energy: Supply, Production 1989

GWh	Public Supply	Self-Producer Supply	Net Total Production	% Conventional Thermal	% Nuclear	% Hydro Electric/ Geo-Thermal/ Wind Power	Per Capita Consumption (kWh per annum)
EC members							
Belgium	64706	2776	63909	37.4	61.2	1.4	5762
Denmark	21962	795	21215	97.8	0.1	2.1	5574
France	381207	27455	387391	12.5	74.5	13.0	5605
Germany: East	111336	7641	107109	88.0	10.6	1.4	5898
Germany: West	378243	62651	411491	61.1	34.3	4.6	6349
Greece	33683	773	31616	93.3		6.7	2906
Ireland	13606	227	13018	92.5		7.5	3243
Italy	184478	26272	199704	80.0		20.0	3674
Luxembourg	862	513	1326	39.3		60.7	10945
Netherlands	61996	11054	70652	94.6	5.4		4897
Portugal	24512	1296	24608	75.7		24.3	2143
Spain	142925	3665	139166	47.5	38.6	13.9	3173
United Kingdom[a]	288543	19687	288031	78.3	19.3	2.4	4826
EC total	1708059	164805	1759236	57.8	33.7	8.4	64995
EFTA members							
Austria	43288	6879	48624	28.0		72.0	5528
Finland	45365	8334	51073	39.6	35.3	25.1	11513
Iceland	4699	5	4480	0.1		99.9	16384
Liechtenstein							
Norway[b]	91523	18497	117968	0.4		99.6	21962
Sweden[c]	130767	7884	139763	4.1	44.9	51.0	14936
Switzerland	50403	4344	53110	2.0	40.6	57.4	6842
EFTA total	366045	45943	415018	9.9	24.7	65.4	77165
Eastern Europe							
Albania							
Bulgaria	39978	4353	39664	59.4	33.9	6.7	4144
Czechoslovakia	79143	10057	83033	67.3	27.6	5.1	5016
Hungary	28647	941	26988	51.1	48.3	0.6	3209
Poland	136900	8572	135289	97.2		2.8	3192
Romania	72530	3321	70553	82.3		17.7	3173
USSR	1644000	73000	1598204	73.7	12.4	13.9	4956
Yugoslavia[a]			78452	62.2	5.0	32.8	2959
East European total	2001198	100244	2032183	74.3	12.4	13.3	26649
Others							
Cyprus	1831	15	1757	100.0			2390
Gibraltar							
Malta	1095		1006	100.0			2294
Monaco							
Turkey[b]	44872	3177	48855	63.8		36.2	753
Total	47798	3192	51618	65.7		34.3	5437
European total	4123100	314184	4258055	61.1	22.2	16.6	174246

Source: UN ECE Annual Bulletin of Electrical Energy Statistics for Europe
Notes: See end of section

Table No: 0807

ELECTRICAL ENERGY

Electricity: Supplies to Households 1977-1988

'000 GWh

	1977	1980	1981	1982	1983	1984	1985	1986	1987	1988
EC members										
Belgium	14.8	13.8	14.1	14.4	14.9	15.3	16.2	16.6	17.6	16.8
Denmark	6.9	7.4	7.4	7.4	7.4	7.8	8.4	8.7	9.2	8.9
France		60.2	64.3	67.1	74.0	79.9	83.7	89.6	94.7	
Germany: East	10.1	12.0	12.2	12.6	13.2	14.5	15.3	16.2	17.5	17.4
Germany: West		84.5	86.8	88.0	90.2	94.1	97.1	97.6	100.7	97.7
Greece[a]	4.2	9.2	9.7	10.1	6.8	7.2	7.7	7.8	8.5	8.8
Ireland[b]	3.0	3.6	3.6	3.6	3.7	3.8	4.0	4.1	4.2	4.2
Italy	31.9	37.8	38.9	41.1	41.0	43.4	44.5	45.7	48.1	49.3
Luxembourg[b]	0.6	1.0	1.1	1.1	1.2	1.2	1.3	1.3	0.6	
Netherlands	13.6	15.6	15.4	15.7	15.3	15.9	16.6	16.2	16.6	15.5
Portugal	2.6	3.3	3.5	3.5	4.2	4.3	4.5	4.7	4.9	5.1
Spain	14.4	19.6	20.4	20.3	21.8	23.5	23.3	24.9	26.6	27.5
United Kingdom	85.9	86.1	84.4	82.8	83.0	83.9	88.2	91.7	93.3	
EC total	188.0	354.1	361.8	367.7	376.7	394.8	410.8	425.1	442.5	251.2
EFTA members										
Austria	7.7	8.8	8.9	9.1	9.4	9.7	10.2	10.4	10.8	
Finland	6.4	8.2	8.7	9.1	9.4	10.4	12.2	12.5	13.8	14.2
Iceland[b]	0.5	0.6	0.7	0.7	0.8	0.8	0.7	0.8		
Liechtenstein										
Norway	21.3	23.6	25.1	25.1	25.8	28.2	28.9	30.2	30.2	29.9
Sweden	20.0	22.8	23.9	26.2	27.6	30.2	34.6	35.1		
Switzerland	8.2	9.7	9.8	9.6	10.1	10.9	11.8	12.1	12.5	12.7
EFTA total	64.1	73.7	77.1	79.8	83.1	90.2	98.4	101.1	67.3	56.8
Eastern Europe										
Albania										
Bulgaria	5.5	6.8								
Czechoslovakia	7.4	8.6	8.8	9.0	9.7	10.3	11.0	11.5	11.9	12.2
Hungary	4.0	5.0	5.4	5.9	6.4	7.0	7.4	7.5	8.1	8.2
Poland	8.5	10.7	12.2	12.6	11.9	14.1	16.2	16.9	18.5	19.3
Romania	4.8	4.9	5.1	5.1	5.0	4.8		5.0	4.8	
USSR[c]					199.7	208.0	219.0	231.0	240.0	
Yugoslavia	12.1	15.6	16.1	17.2		17.2	17.8	18.6	20.3	21.1
East European total	42.3	51.6	47.6	49.8	232.7	261.4	271.4	290.5	303.6	60.8
Others										
Cyprus	0.2	0.2	0.2	0.2	0.2	0.2	0.3	0.3	0.3	0.4
Gibraltar										
Malta										
Monaco										
Turkey	2.6	3.0	3.2	3.5	4.1	4.6	5.0	5.2	5.9	7.2
Total	2.8	3.2	3.4	3.7	4.3	4.8	5.3	5.5	6.2	7.6
European total	297.2	482.6	489.9	501.0	696.8	751.2	785.9	822.2	819.6	376.4

Source: UN ECE Annual Bulletin of Electrical Energy Statistics for Europe
Notes: See end of section

Table No: 0808

SOLID FUEL

Solid Fuels: Production, Final Consumption 1990

'000 tonnes

	Production	Final Consumption
EC members		
Belgium	1.38	4.88
Denmark	1.02	0.79
France	12.19	13.89
Germany: East[a]	304900.00	319781.86
Germany: West	77.79	18.67
Greece	7.67	1.75
Ireland	1.43	1.68
Italy	1.27	5.76
Luxembourg	0.02	0.96
Netherlands	0.20	2.28
Portugal	1.27	1.65
Spain	12.36	4.62
United Kingdom	52.70	12.59
EFTA members		
Austria	2.95	4.22
Finland	5.44	5.33
Iceland		0.06
Liechtenstein		
Norway	1.16	1.69
Sweden	5.60	5.93
Switzerland	0.83	0.80
Eastern Europe		
Albania[a]	2722.32	2649.72
Bulgaria[a]	31760.40	40934.62
Czechoslovakia[a]	125226.72	119328.36
Hungary[a]	19963.68	23793.08
Poland[a]	249546.00	222595.03
Romania[a]	56261.28	62577.06
USSR[a]	740471.04	716387.58
Yugoslavia[a]	74410.08	75263.07
Others		
Cyprus		
Gibraltar		
Malta		
Monaco		
Turkey	19.09	15.71

Sources: Energy Information Administration 1988/OECD Energy Balances Yearbook
Notes: See end of section

Table No: 0809

SOLID FUELS

Solid Fuels: Household Consumption 1977-1990

Million tonnes

	1977	1980	1981	1982	1983	1984	1985	1986	1987	1988	1989	1990
EC members												
Belgium[a]	1.7	1.5	1.4	1.5	1.4	1.4	1.7	1.6	0.2	0.1	0.8	0.8
Denmark	0.1	0.0	0.0	0.1	0.1	0.1	0.1	0.1	0.5	0.0	0.0	0.0
France	5.8	5.0	4.4	4.1	4.2	4.1	4.2	4.0	3.3	2.9	2.7	2.6
Germany: East	14.3	17.0	17.0	17.1	15.4	16.0	18.2	18.3	19.1	17.1		
Germany: West	8.0	7.7					5.0	4.5	3.9	2.9	2.6	2.4
Greece	0.1	0.1	0.1	0.1	0.1	0.1	0.1	0.1	0.1	0.1	0.0	0.0
Ireland[b]	0.7	1.0					1.2	1.3	1.2	1.1	1.1	0.8
Italy		0.6			0.2	0.3	0.3	0.2	0.2	0.5	0.1	0.1
Luxembourg	0.0	0.0	0.1	0.1	0.1	0.0	0.0	0.0	0.0	0.0	0.0	0.0
Netherlands	0.1	0.1	0.1	0.1	0.1	0.1	0.1	0.1	0.1	0.1	0.0	0.0
Portugal		0.0	0.0	0.0	0.0						0.0	0.0
Spain	0.5	0.4	0.6	0.8	0.6	0.7	0.7	0.6	0.4	0.5	0.5	0.5
United Kingdom	14.8	11.7	10.9	10.8	10.1	8.0	10.7	10.5	9.2	8.6	7.4	6.2
EFTA members												
Austria[b]	1.4	1.8	1.4	1.5	1.3	1.9	1.6	1.5	1.5	1.4	1.2	1.2
Finland	0.1	0.1	0.1	0.1	0.1	0.1	0.0	0.0	0.0		0.0	0.0
Iceland												
Liechtenstein												
Norway	0.1	0.0	0.1	0.0	0.0	0.0	0.0	0.0	0.0	0.0	0.0	0.0
Sweden								0.0			0.1	
Switzerland	0.2	0.1	0.1	0.1	0.1	0.1	0.1	0.1	0.1	0.1	0.0	0.0
Eastern Europe												
Albania												
Bulgaria	1.0	1.4	1.4	1.4	1.4	1.2			2.4		2.6	2.1
Czechoslovakia	10.3	11.0	10.4								11.8	
Hungary	4.5	5.1	5.1	4.4	5.2	5.4	6.5	5.8	5.9	5.8	5.2	4.5
Poland[b]	34.4								35.6	27.7	35.0	17.9
Romania											2.1	2.3
USSR												
Yugoslavia[b]	6.1							7.3	6.8		0.0	1.8
Others												
Cyprus												
Gibraltar												
Malta												
Monaco												
Turkey	3.1	5.5			6.2	6.0	7.4	10.4	11.4	11.4	11.9	10.7

Source: UN ECE Annual Bulletin of Coal Statistics for Europe 1992
Notes: See end of section

Table No: 0810

GAS

Gas: Production, Gross Consumption 1989

Terajoules	Production	Gross Consumption	Gas Used in Electricity Production
EC members			
Belgium	134135	469262	81378
Denmark	125815	82319	4929
France	441858	1373709	44030
Germany: East	268565	501145	126048
Germany: West	1081254	2565674	239810
Greece	37663	32263	3148
Ireland[a]	71635	76186	32034
Italy[a]	885768	1802025	316716
Luxembourg	16155	34258	6345
Netherlands	2599890	1691669	371290
Portugal[a]	33146	52487	574
Spain[a]	226002	362296	18494
United Kingdom	1980448	2365357	46781
EC total	7902334	11408650	1291577
EFTA members			
Austria[a]	121334	266577	50274
Finland	30682	113260	16487
Iceland			
Liechtenstein			
Norway	1226144	185263	
Sweden	28187	70865	10726
Switzerland[b]	10743	76243	1872
EFTA total	1417090	712208	79359
Eastern Europe			
Albania			
Bulgaria	28942	260591	
Czechoslovakia[a]	246553	597978	
Hungary	239565	433043	86135
Poland	356587	610340	7093
Romania	1308813	1554644	287454
USSR[a]	28703332	25049254	
Yugoslavia	165679	323811	18077
East European total	31049471	28829661	398759
Others			
Cyprus	2106	3074	
Gibraltar			
Malta		663	
Monaco			
Turkey[a]	110767	178134	51231
Total	112873	181871	51231
European total	40481768	41132390	1820926

Source: UN Annual Bulletin of Gas Statistics for Europe 1991
Note: See end of section

Table No: 0811

GAS

Gas Supplies to Households 1977-1989

'000 terajoules

	1977	1980	1981	1982	1983	1984	1985	1986	1987	1988	1989
EC members											
Belgium	105.7	132.4	129.9	122.1	122.9	123.4	133.8	117.1	117.6	108.8	108.6
Denmark		5.5		6.0	5.8		17.0	30.5	34.2	33.9	33.3
France	291.4	430.8	443.6	440.0	463.1	490.8	517.8	494.8	482.6	456.3	450.1
Germany: East	32.2	38.8	39.1	40.5	40.4	43.9	46.4	46.2	49.6	45.5	45.6
Germany: West	341.1	472.7	498.8	489.2	530.4	593.2	638.4	582.4	642.4	574.3	582.6
Greece	5.9	7.3	6.4	5.3	5.7	5.1	5.1	4.5	4.5	4.4	4.4
Ireland					5.9	5.6	5.7	6.2	6.4	5.6	
Italy	398.1	461.5	471.4	500.8	506.6	543.1	594.1	574.5	607.2	636.0	
Luxembourg	4.1	5.6	6.1	6.2	6.5	6.8	7.5	6.4	7.7	7.0	7.2
Netherlands	463.2	536.9	496.8	454.2	445.1	427.3	474.0	402.3	391.6	334.4	331.4
Portugal	4.2	3.9	6.1	5.4	8.1	12.0	17.5	17.4	18.0	19.2	
Spain	93.2	107.8	101.1	102.3	96.1	106.2	109.8	101.1	103.6	108.0	
United Kingdom	701.6	901.8	936.0	931.3	945.8	957.9	1038.1	1017.2	1031.2	1007.6	974.7
EFTA members											
Austria	40.7	53.2	48.8	43.0	42.7	46.5	55.8	49.8	50.3	51.8	
Finland	1.8	1.5	1.6	1.4	1.4	1.6	1.5	1.2	1.6	1.7	1.4
Iceland											
Liechtenstein											
Norway		0.5	0.5	0.2	0.2	0.1	0.1	0.1	0.1	0.1	0.1
Sweden		2.4		2.5	2.0	1.9	3.0	3.6		5.1	5.7
Switzerland		16.1	18.1	16.1	17.6	19.2	21.9	19.2	21.1	22.3	24.4
Eastern Europe											
Albania											
Bulgaria							3.3	4.0			
Czechoslovakia	42.3	54.2		53.0		59.0	63.8	65.5	71.4	70.5	
Hungary	31.0	38.5	38.8	42.4	42.4	48.5	54.8	60.3	69.5	69.5	74.5
Poland		75.6	79.2	91.5	84.6	85.6	105.9	112.0	124.9	131.6	135.2
Romania											60.2
USSR	644.3	1674.0								1316.9	
Yugoslavia[a]	16.7	16.3	17.3	18.0	16.7	17.7				34.7	33.4
Others											
Cyprus	1.5	1.7	1.7	1.9	2.0	2.0	2.1	2.0	2.1	2.3	2.2
Gibraltar											
Malta	1.0	0.5		0.6	0.7	0.7			0.7	0.7	0.7
Monaco											
Turkey	31.1	27.7		40.7	45.7	46.7	48.4	51.6	53.6	60.5	

Source: UN ECE Annual Bulletin of Gas Statistics for Europe 1991
Note: See end of section

Table No: 0812

NUCLEAR ENERGY

Nuclear Energy Capacity 1988/2005

	Nuclear Stations (number at end-1988)	Installed capacity (MW, net): 1988	2005 forecast
EC members			
Belgium	7	5500	3800
Denmark			
France	55	52863	66900
Germany: East	5	1702	6100
Germany: West	23	22707	20200
Greece			
Ireland			
Italy[a]	3	1300	4800
Luxembourg			
Netherlands	2	516	0
Portugal			
Spain	10	7544	12200
United Kingdom	41	14064	13300
EFTA members			
Austria			
Finland	4	2310	2300
Iceland			
Liechtenstein			
Norway			
Sweden	12	9683	6500
Switzerland	5	2931	1900
Eastern Europe			
Albania			
Bulgaria	5	2585	6500
Czechoslovakia	8	3144	12100
Hungary	4	1640	5500
Poland			
Romania			
USSR	56	34477	109000
Yugoslavia	1	632	600
Others			
Cyprus			
Gibraltar			
Malta			
Monaco			
Turkey			

Source: Comité Professional du Pétrole
Note: See end of section

Table No: 0813

NUCLEAR ENERGY

Nuclear Energy Consumption 1983-1991

Million tonnes of oil equivalent (MTOE)

	1983	1984	1985	1986	1987	1988	1989	1990	1991
EC members									
Belgium[a]	5.3	6.4	7.9	9.1	9.7	9.6	9.5	10.4	10.4
Denmark									
France	30.1	38.5	45.1	51.9	53.8	54.7	59.9	62.0	65.0
Germany: East									
Germany: West	16.0	22.3	29.9	27.5	30.0	33.4	34.3	39.4	38.0
Greece									
Ireland									
Italy	2.1	1.7	1.8	2.2					
Luxembourg									
Netherlands	0.9	0.9	1.0	1.2	0.8	0.9	0.9	0.9	1.0
Portugal									
Spain	2.5	5.2	6.3	8.4	9.1	11.3	12.5	14.1	13.0
United Kingdom	10.7	11.5	13.0	12.6	11.7	13.5	15.4	14.2	15.5
EFTA members									
Austria									
Finland	4.2	4.4	4.5	4.5	4.6	4.6	4.5	4.5	4.8
Iceland									
Liechtenstein									
Norway									
Sweden	10.7	12.7	14.5	16.8	16.2	16.6	15.7	16.8	18.6
Switzerland	3.8	4.5	3.5	3.5	5.6	5.5	5.6	5.8	5.6
Eastern Europe									
Albania									
Bulgaria									
Czechoslovakia	1.6	1.9	3.1	4.7	5.8	6.1	6.4	6.4	5.9
Hungary	0.6	0.9	1.6	1.9	2.8	3.4	3.5	3.5	3.4
Poland									
Romania									
USSR	28.7	37.1	43.6	41.9	48.7	56.2	55.4	55.2	54.7
Yugoslavia									
Others									
Cyprus									
Gibraltar									
Malta									
Monaco									
Turkey				1.7					

Source: BP
Notes: See end of section

Notes to Tables in Section Eight:

Table 0801 MTOE: the energy content of the fuel in question in terms of oil
Hydro-electricity production includes other sources (wind generation, geothermal, etc)
- a Includes Luxembourg
- b East German data refer to 1990; West German refer to unified country in 1991
- c Data refers to 1989; total includes electricity consumption

Table 0802
- a Unified Germany
- b Includes Luxembourg

Table 0803
- a Includes Luxembourg
- b Includes Monaco
- c Unified Germany
- d Includes Liechtenstein

Table 0804
- a Includes Monaco
- b Data refer to 1989
- c Includes Liechtenstein

Table 0805 Data for some Eastern European countries are estimates based on assumed refinery output and trade with Western Europe
- a Includes Monaco
- b Includes Liechtenstein
- c New series starting 1986

Table 0806
- a Data refer to 1988
- b Gross supply data refer to 1988
- c Gross supply data refer to 1986

Table 0807
- a Change in methodology between 1979 and 1982
- b Includes power supplied to agriculture, forestry and fishing industries
- c Includes commercial, agricultural etc, and public use

Table 0808
- a '000 tonnes 1989; gross consumption

Table 0809 Entries of 0.0 signify consumption of less than 50,000 tonnes
- a New series starting 1987
- b Includes commercial, retailing, catering, agricultural and public sectors

Table 0810 Production includes natural gas, gaswork output, LPG, other petroleum gases and coke-oven/blast furnace gases
- a Data refer to 1988
- b Data for gas used in electricity production refer to 1988

Table 0811
- a Includes other consumers

Table 0812
- a Data on installed capacity refer to 1986/2000

Table 0813 MTOE: the amount of oil required to fuel an oil fired plant in order to generate the same amount of electricity
- a Includes Luxembourg

Total Primary Energy Consumption 1991: Selected countries

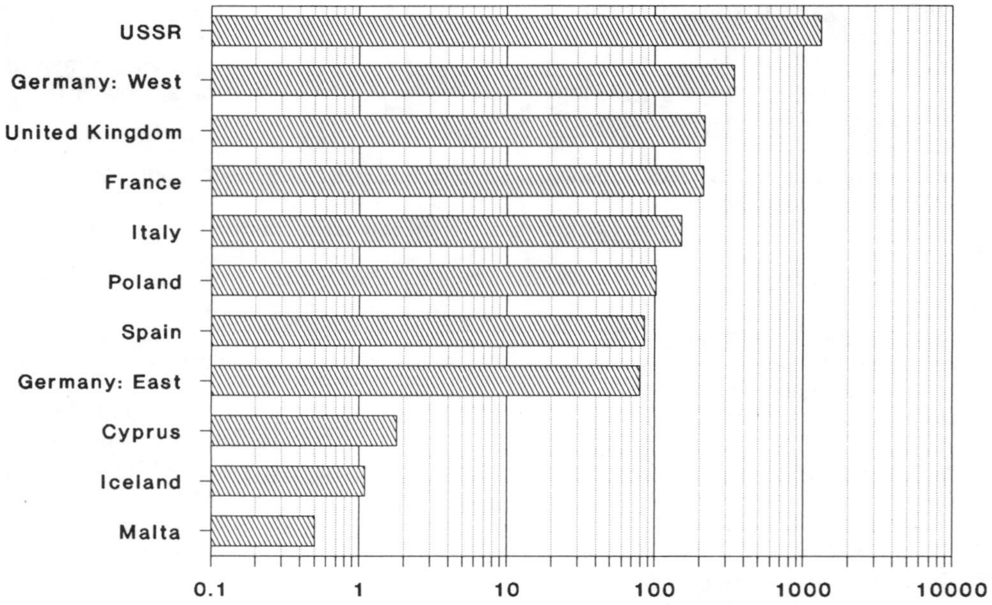

Net Total Electrical Energy Production 1989: Selected countries

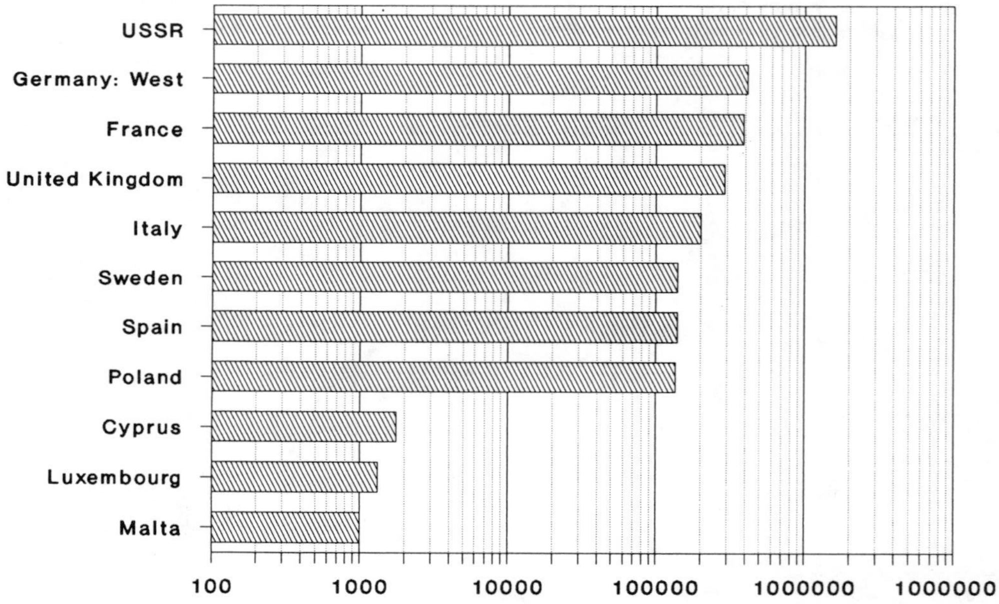

Section Nine

Defence

Table No: 0901

DEFENCE SPENDING AND PERSONNEL

Defence Expenditure and Personnel 1991

Current US dollars (millions)/persons

	Defence Spending	% of GDP	Regular Forces	Reserve Forces	Army Personnel	Naval Personnel	Air Force Personnel	Conscripts as % of Regular Forces
EC members								
Belgium	3250	1.6	85450	234000	62700	4550	18200	39
Denmark	2850	2.2	29400	72300	17900	5000	6500	35
France[a]	37340	3.1	453100	419000	280300	65300	92900	50
Germany: East								
Germany: West[a]	34360	2.4	476300	1009400	335000	37600	103700	42
Greece	4520	6.8	158500	406000	113000	19500	26000	79
Ireland	553	1.3	12900	16100	11200	900	800	0
Italy	21310	1.9	361400	584000	234700	49000	78200	59
Luxembourg[b]	100	1.1	800	0	800	0	0	0
Netherlands	8290	2.9	101400	152400	64100	16600	16000	44
Portugal[b]	1540	2.6	61800	190000	33100	15300	13400	53
Spain	8970	1.8	257400	2400000	182000	39800	35600	61
United Kingdom	43559	4.3	300100	347200	149600	61800	88700	0
EFTA members								
Austria	1680	1.0	44000	242000	38000	0	6000	50
Finland	2420	1.9	31800	700000	27300	2000	2500	75
Iceland[c]								
Liechtenstein								
Norway	3760	3.5	32700	285000	15900	7300	9500	69
Sweden	6240	2.7	63000	709000	43500	12000	7500	74
Switzerland[d,e]	4100	1.8	3500	625000	565000	0	60000	90
Eastern Europe								
Albania	129	3.4	48000	155000	35000	2000	11000	46
Bulgaria	1980	6.0	107000	472500	75000	10000	22000	65
Czechoslovakia[f]	2800	8.8	154000	495000	87300	0	44800	56
Hungary	1230	3.7	86500	210000	66400	0	20100	53
Poland	2110	3.3	305000	507000	199500	19500	86000	62
Romania[d]	1440	3.8	200800	626000	161800	19200	19800	63
USSR	133700	12.0	3400000	5239000	1400000	450000	475000	58
Yugoslavia[d]	3520	4.0	169000	510000	129000	11000	29000	56
Others								
Cyprus[g]	155	3.9	10000	108000	10000			100
Gibraltar								
Malta	25	0.8	1650	0				0
Monaco								
Turkey	4400	4.0	579200	1107000	470000	52000	57200	86

Source: International Institute for Strategic Studies
Notes: See end of section

Table No: 0902

DEFENCE EQUIPMENT

Defence Equipment 1991

Numbers

	Combat Aircraft	Tanks	Submarines	Aircraft Carriers	Other Combat Vessels
EC members					
Belgium	144	334	0	0	3
Denmark	106	499	4	0	49
France	845	1349	17	2	72
Germany: East			0	0	47
Germany: West	638	7000	24	0	59
Greece	375	1879	10	0	54
Ireland	13	14	0	0	7
Italy	449	1220	9	1	50
Luxembourg	0	0	0	0	0
Netherlands	181	913	5	0	15
Portugal	83	146	3	0	35
Spain	247	838	8	1	82
United Kingdom	530	1314	24	2	82
EFTA members					
Austria	54	159	0	0	0
Finland	118	120	0	0	22
Iceland					
Liechtenstein					
Norway	85	211	11	0	40
Sweden	470	785	12	0	42
Switzerland	289	870	0	0	0
Eastern Europe					
Albania	95	190	2	0	37
Bulgaria	266	2149	3	0	24
Czechoslovakia	297	3200	0	0	0
Hungary	111	1482	0	0	0
Poland	506	2850	3	0	22
Romania	465	2875	1	0	110
USSR	4095	54400	317	5	600
Yugoslavia	489	1850	5	0	69
Others					
Cyprus	1	40	0	0	0
Gibraltar					
Malta	0	0	0	0	0
Monaco					
Turkey	530	3783	15	0	67

Source: International Institute for Strategic Studies

Notes to Tables in Section Nine:

Table 0901	a	Regular forces includes inter-service staff
	b	Defence budget data refer to 1990
	c	Iceland has no armed forces
	d	Data refer to 1990
	e	Army and air force consist of reserve forces
	f	Regular forces includes Civil Defence
	g	Army consists of National Guard. Data refer to 1989

Section Ten

Environmental Data

Table No: 1001

AIR POLLUTION

Total Emissions of Air Pollutants: Latest Year

'000 tonnes

	Year	SOx	NOx	CO	HC	Particulate Matter
EC members						
Belgium	1990	420	300			
Denmark[a]	1989	193	249		146	
France[b]	1990	1207	1742	6198	1877	278
Germany: East						
Germany: West	1989	1001	2707	8872	2536	268
Greece						
Ireland	1987	174	115	457	108	107
Italy	1988	2006	1705	5923	827	452
Luxembourg[c]	1985	10	22	240	20	3
Netherlands	1990	217	530	1054	381	73
Portugal[d]	1988	205	122	267	156	93
Spain[e]	1985	2156	826	1822	843	
United Kingdom	1989	3699	2690	6522	2066	512
EFTA members						
Austria[f]	1988	121	179	1161	466	39
Finland[a]	1989	242	276		181	
Iceland						
Liechtenstein						
Norway	1990	59	212	557	226	20
Sweden[g]	1990	168	371	1754	440	170
Switzerland	1990	63	184	431	297	20
Eastern Europe						
Albania						
Bulgaria						
Czechoslovakia						
Hungary						
Poland						
Romania						
USSR						
Yugoslavia[j]	1989	1550	430			
Others						
Cyprus						
Gibraltar						
Malta						
Monaco						
Turkey						

Source: OECD
Notes: See end of section

Table No: 1002

AIR POLLUTION

Concentration in Acid Precipitation: Latest Year

	Year	pH Value	SO4 (mg/l)	NO3 (mg/l)
EC members				
Belgium	1989	5.03	2.94	2.57
Denmark	1988	4.48	0.90	0.53
France	1989	6.10	2.75	1.61
Germany: East				
Germany: West	1989	4.46	2.68	2.54
Greece				
Ireland	1988	5.39	4.98	0.44
Italy	1988	4.23	4.02	3.85
Luxembourg	1989	4.68	3.41	2.67
Netherlands	1989	4.63	4.65	2.47
Portugal	1989	5.60	0.73	0.08
Spain	1989	6.22	3.81	2.83
United Kingdom	1989	4.79	1.38	1.02
EFTA members				
Austria	1988	5.30	4.26	2.75
Finland	1989	4.45	2.20	2.17
Iceland	1988	5.32	1.20	0.44
Liechtenstein				
Norway	1990	4.40	0.72	0.47
Sweden	1989	4.08	3.96	3.50
Switzerland	1990	5.11	2.28	1.99
Eastern Europe				
Albania				
Bulgaria				
Czechoslovakia				
Hungary				
Poland				
Romania				
USSR				
Yugoslavia	1989	5.03	5.95	4.48
Others				
Cyprus				
Gibraltar				
Malta				
Monaco				
Turkey				

Source: OECD
Notes: See end of section

Table No: 1003

WASTE

Amounts of Waste Generated 1989

'000 tonnes and kg per inhabitant

	Municipal Waste:		Industrial Waste:			
	Total	Per inhabitant	Total	Per inhabitant	Of which: hazardous	Per inhabitant
EC members						
Belgium	3470	349	26700	2685	915	92
Denmark[a]	2400	469	2400	469	112	22
France	17000	303	50000	891	3000	53
Germany: East						
Germany: West[b]	19483	318	61424	1003	14210	232
Greece	3147	314	4304	429	423	42
Ireland[a,c]	1100	311	1580	447	20	6
Italy	17300	301	39978	696	3640	63
Luxembourg	170	466	1300	3564	742	2034
Netherlands	6900	465	6687	451	1500	101
Portugal[a,b]	2350	231	662	65	165	16
Spain[a,b]	12546	322	5108	131	1708	44
United Kingdom	18000	357	50000	992	2200	44
EFTA members						
Austria	2700	355	13258	1743	400	53
Finland[b]	2500	504	10500	2117	230	46
Iceland						
Liechtenstein						
Norway	2000	473	2186	517	200	47
Sweden[a]	2650	317	4000	478	500	60
Switzerland	2850	424				
Eastern Europe						
Albania						
Bulgaria						
Czechoslovakia						
Hungary						
Poland						
Romania						
USSR						
Yugoslavia						
Others						
Cyprus						
Gibraltar						
Malta						
Monaco						
Turkey						

Source: OECD
Notes: See end of section

Table No: 1004

WASTE

Levels of Recycling of Packaging Waste 1980-1990

% total consumption

	Paper and Cardboard			Glass				Aluminium
	1980	1985	1989	1980	1985	1989	1990	1989
EC members								
Belgium	14.7			42.0	39.0		59.0	
Denmark	25.6	31.3	29.7	53.9	55.0		40.0	
France	37.0	41.3	45.7	26.0	26.1	28.5	41.0	
Germany: East								
Germany: West	33.9	43.6	43.0	35.5	39.4	42.3	54.0	3.0
Greece							16.0	21.0
Ireland	15.0			7.0	8.0		19.0	2.0
Italy				25.0	38.0		48.0	8.0
Luxembourg								
Netherlands	45.5	50.3	58.4	53.0	62.0	55.2	66.0	
Portugal	38.0			10.0	14.0		23.0	
Spain	38.1	44.1		13.1	22.0		27.0	
United Kingdom	29.0	27.0	27.0	12.0	14.0	18.0	21.0	
EFTA members								
Austria				38.0	44.0		60.0	3.0
Finland	30.0	36.8		21.0	25.0		46.0	
Iceland								
Liechtenstein								
Norway	21.9	21.1	23.2			10.0	34.0	
Sweden	34.0	40.0			20.0	22.0	35.0	82.0
Switzerland[a]	38.0			36.0	46.0	47.0	61.0	31.0
Eastern Europe								
Albania								
Bulgaria								
Czechoslovakia								
Hungary								
Poland								
Romania								
USSR								
Yugoslavia								
Others								
Cyprus								
Gibraltar								
Malta								
Monaco								
Turkey								

Source: OECD
Notes: See end of section

Table No: 1005

WATER TREATMENT

Population Served by Waste Water Treatment Plants 1970-Late 1980s

% total population

	1970	1975	1980	1985	Late 1980s	Primary treatment only Late 1980s	Population not served (millions)
EC members							
Belgium							
Denmark	54	71	80	91	98	8	0.1
France	19	31	43	50	52		26.8
Germany: East							
Germany: West	62	75	82	88	90	2	6.3
Greece							
Ireland							
Italy	14	22	30		60		23.1
Luxembourg	26		81	83	91	5	
Netherlands		45	72	85	89	7	1.6
Portugal	3	6	9	9	11		
Spain		14	18	29	48	6	20.3
United Kingdom[a]			82	83	84	6	9.1
EFTA members							
Austria	17	27	33	65	72	5	2.1
Finland	27	50	65	72	75		1.2
Iceland							
Liechtenstein							
Norway	21	27	34	43	43	6	2.4
Sweden	63	81	82	94	95	1	0.4
Switzerland	35	55	70	83	90		0.7
Eastern Europe							
Albania							
Bulgaria							
Czechoslovakia							
Hungary							
Poland							
Romania							
USSR							
Yugoslavia							
Others							
Cyprus							
Gibraltar							
Malta							
Monaco							
Turkey							

Source: OECD
Note: See end of section

Table No: 1006

PROTECTED AREAS

Protected Areas 1970-1990

'000 square kilometres

	1970	1980	1985	1989	1990	% of land area 1990
EC members						
Belgium	0.0	0.0	0.1	0.8	0.8	2.4
Denmark	0.1	0.1	1.3	2.8	4.2	9.8
France	4.7	12.8	16.5	45.0	47.8	2.3
Germany: East						
Germany: West	1.3	2.9	5.3	27.6	29.6	11.9
Greece					1.0	0.8
Ireland	0.1	0.1	0.2	0.2	0.3	0.4
Italy	3.0	4.1	5.2	12.7	13.0	4.3
Luxembourg						
Netherlands	0.9	1.1	1.6	1.5	3.6	8.7
Portugal	0.7	2.5	3.8	6.2	4.5	4.9
Spain	9.2	16.8	17.0	25.6	35.1	7.0
United Kingdom	13.0	13.2	15.5	25.7	46.4	18.9
EFTA members						
Austria	2.6	2.6	3.0	15.9	15.9	19.0
Finland	4.8	4.8	8.0	8.1	8.1	2.4
Iceland					9.2	8.9
Liechtenstein						
Norway	2.1	37.9	47.2	47.6	47.6	14.7
Sweden	5.0	10.6	15.9	17.1	17.6	3.9
Switzerland	0.2	0.2	1.2	1.2	1.1	2.7
Eastern Europe						
Albania						
Bulgaria						
Czechoslovakia						
Hungary						
Poland						
Romania						
USSR						
Yugoslavia					7.9	3.1
Others						
Cyprus						
Gibraltar						
Malta						
Monaco						
Turkey	0.5	2.3	2.9	2.5	2.7	0.3

Source: OECD
Note: See end of section

Table No: 1007

THREATENED SPECIES

Threatened Species Late 1980s

% of local species

	Mammals	Birds	Fish	Reptiles	Amphibians	Vascular Plants
EC members						
Belgium[a]	21.5	29.0		75.0	100.0	24.0
Denmark	28.6	17.4	7.8		21.4	13.7
France[b]	52.2	39.8	18.6	38.9	62.1	8.4
Germany: East						
Germany: West[c,d]	46.8	32.1	70.0	75.0	57.9	28.2
Greece						
Ireland	16.1	23.7			33.3	
Italy	13.4	14.3	13.9	52.2	46.4	10.0
Luxembourg						
Netherlands[d]	48.3	33.1	22.4	85.7	66.7	
Portugal[b]	51.2	39.6	28.2	37.1	23.5	
Spain[b]	14.8	14.5	18.2	14.1	4.2	2.5
United Kingdom[e]	31.2	15.0	3.4	45.5	33.3	9.6
EFTA members						
Austria[c]	29.4	28.4	36.2	46.2	10.5	15.9
Finland	11.3	6.0	12.1	20.0	20.0	5.6
Iceland						
Liechtenstein						
Norway	7.4	10.2	1.2	20.0	40.0	4.5
Sweden	15.4	6.8	4.6		38.5	8.2
Switzerland	46.3	50.9		80.0	78.9	25.8
Eastern Europe						
Albania						
Bulgaria						
Czechoslovakia						
Hungary						
Poland						
Romania						
USSR						
Yugoslavia						
Others						
Cyprus						
Gibraltar						
Malta						
Monaco						
Turkey	30.5	16.9	18.7	50.5	72.2	

Source: OECD
Notes: See end of section

Notes to Tables in Section Ten:

Table 1001 SOx = Oxides of sulphur (SO_2 equivalent weight)
NOx = Oxides of nitrogen (NO_2 equivalent weight)
CO = Carbon monoxide
HC = Hydrocarbons (excluding methane)

- a Data for HC refer to 1985, SOx 1988
- b Data for HC refer to 1985, CO 1987
- c Data for SOx refer to 1990
- d Data for CO and particulate matter refer to 1983
- e Data for CO and HC refer to 1983
- f Data for NOx refer to 1990
- g Data for HC refer to 1988

Table 1002 Based on data collected from specific monitoring stations
pH = Average degree of acidity in rainwater
SO_4 = Sulphates
NO_3 = Nitrates

Table 1003
- a Data for municipal waste refer to 1985
- b Data for industrial waste refer to 1987
- c Data for industrial waste refer to 1984

Table 1004 This table shows recovery rates for paper and glass and excludes recycling within industrial establishments. Recovery rates refer to the materials utilised in the production process relative to total consumption

- a Data for glass recycling exclude returnable empties

Table 1005 a England and Wales only

Table 1006 0.0 indicates less than 500 sq km

Table 1007
- a Brussels region only
- b Data for known fish species refer only to freshwater fish
- c Including extinct and/or vanished species
- d The number of bird species known includes occasional visitors
- e Fish species concerns only those found within the 200 mile limit

Per Capita Generation of Hazardous Industrial Waste 1989: Selected countries

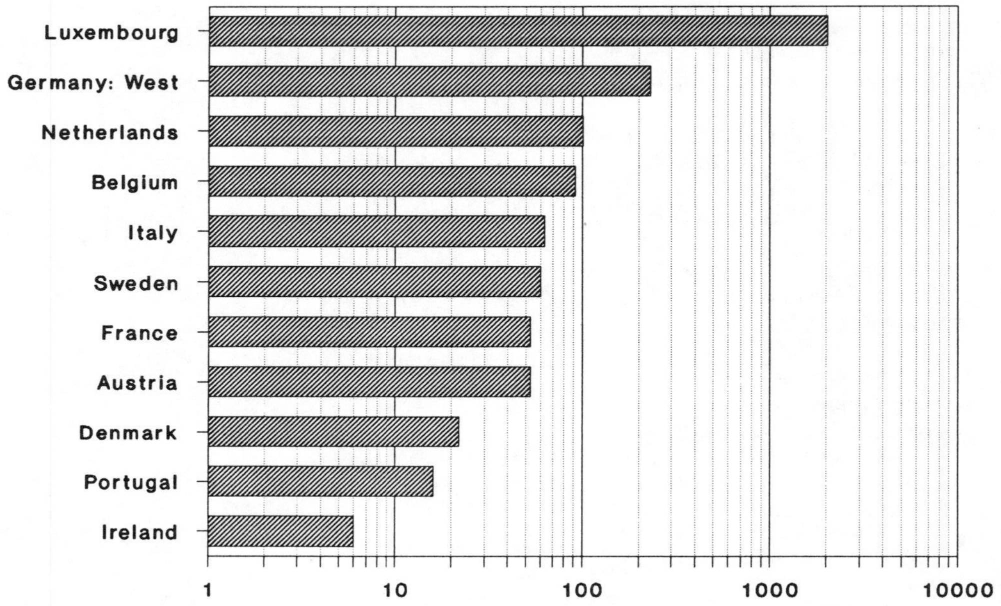

Levels of Recycling of Waste Glass 1990: Selected countries

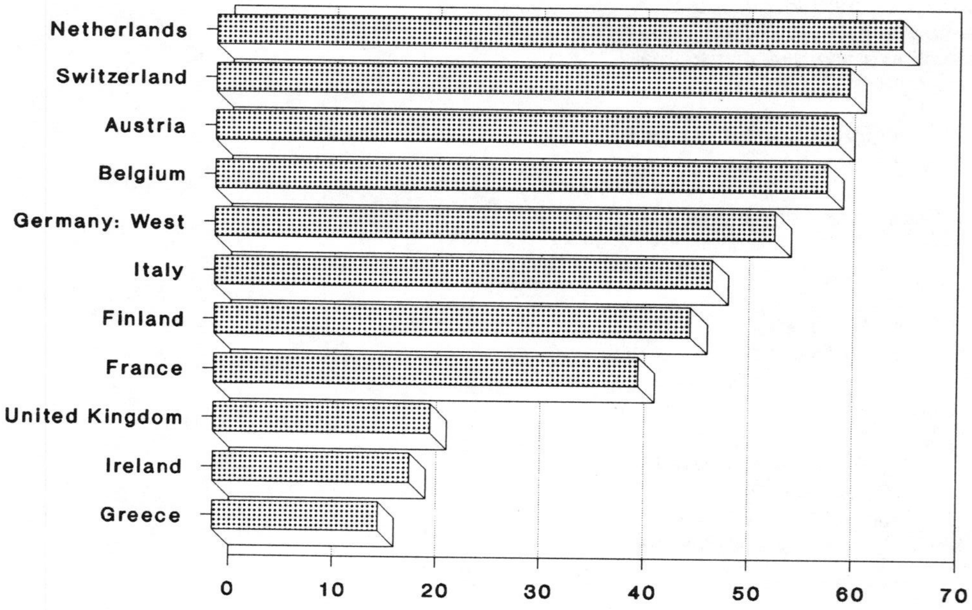

Section Eleven

Consumer Expenditure Patterns

Table No: 1101

TOTAL EXPENDITURE

Total Consumer Expenditure 1977-1991

National currencies (millions)

	1977	1980	1981	1982	1983	1984	1985	1986
EC members								
Belgium	1764125	2212366	2396200	2622204	2762708	2961397	3199155	3300349
Denmark	158900	208814	228566	255639	279963	307889	337215	363131
France	1111354	1645072	1897908	2190339	2424143	2639171	2858393	3049520
Germany: East	103891	115154	126806	153118	164284	173120	178557	183897
Germany: West	669560	834030	879200	910280	947320	1003570	1038340	1068610
Greece	643102	1094389	1362300	1694750	2023350	2623899	2998500	3693000
Ireland	3660	6158	7490	8001	8814	9652	10490	11168
Italy[a]	133433	233737	280127	329417	378379	428050	497350	559550
Luxembourg	60877	79242	86969	96544	109600	117575	125834	131348
Netherlands	165470	205780	213230	221830	229860	234730	247720	247720
Portugal	450400	820725	1019300	1399273	1584000	1986600	2387700	2868900
Spain	6990726	10080400	11457900	13143300	14808100	16313200	18079989	20437730
United Kingdom	86679	137234	152544	167362	182877	195711	217023	239535
EC total								
EFTA members								
Austria	456860	550900	594800	640200	694840	733180	775050	803170
Finland	71268	99320	112035	134200	149600	160503	175330	188430
Iceland	2345	8842	14393	23088	39674	54551	75830	97970
Liechtenstein	332	402	431	443	452	518	540	580
Norway	103915	135242	155205	175310	192979	210921	245439	278909
Sweden	197806	270049	298681	333897	362697	397911	437795	447931
Switzerland	92480	108040	115685	122060	127340	133610	140555	144925
EFTA total								
Eastern Europe								
Albania[b]	8200	12000	15300	17100	19400	22900	25200	28200
Bulgaria[b]	11000	14000	15800	16500	17100	18300	19100	19900
Czechoslovakia	230812	257325	262627	271232	279736	287339	300000	315500
Hungary	327600	441200	477700	515100	551200	600500	649300	695500
Poland	1230200	1658000	2041000	3476700	4486900	5427600	6397000	7916800
Romania[b]	250000	354200	381300	442500	439800	456100	490700	510000
USSR[b]	290000	340000	360000	380000	400000	430000	450000	480000
Yugoslavia[b]	510000	818800	1143300	1510600	2087700	3207200	5659400	11324630
East European total								
Others								
Cyprus[b]	305	508	566	669	739	815	895	950
Gibraltar[b]	38	40	46	48	50	53	55	57
Malta[c]	170	254	279	306	307	318	333	343
Monaco[c]	571	852	982	1127	1243	1341	1410	1484
Turkey	1300000	2993900	4494500	6067600	8449000	14369000	19035000	26400000
Total								
European total								

Table No: 1101 (cont'd)

TOTAL EXPENDITURE

Total Consumer Expenditure 1977-1991

National currencies (millions)

	1987	1988	1989	1990	1991	% growth 1977-1991	% share 1991	Total $ million 1991	$ per capita 1991
EC members									
Belgium	3347040	3587783	3874719	3945355	4084400	131.53	2.33	119609	11923
Denmark	377878	393084	409713	424079	436782	174.88	1.33	68290	13269
France	3231100	3422341	3650029	3885010	4063400	265.63	14.01	720193	12733
Germany: East	195100	206303	214555	245450	262632	152.79	3.08	158260	9953
Germany: West	1108020	1153690	1209570	1299230	1379100	105.97	16.16	831033	13282
Greece	4319400	5104500	6060700	7272840	8727408	1257.08	0.93	47882	4717
Ireland	11782	12376	13728	14231	14744	302.75	0.46	23819	6782
Italy[a]	614020	676182	744248	812064	901515	575.63	14.13	726677	12561
Luxembourg	143700	144700	154600	165506	170471	180.03	0.10	4992	13312
Netherlands	263930	268930	281440	298300	304266	83.88	3.16	162735	10838
Portugal	3323800	3895500	4522900	5366600	6088190	1251.73	0.82	42139	4056
Spain	22864067	25160268	28313302	31259000	33134540	373.98	6.20	318877	8188
United Kingdom	264880	298796	327386	348528	368091	324.66	12.67	651258	11342
EC total							75.37	3875763	11301
EFTA members									
Austria	835090	880100	928300	991900	1054445	130.80	1.76	90309	11733
Finland	210909	231314	248742	263897	275258	286.23	1.32	68066	13690
Iceland	129715	156203	184534	213218	238500	10070.58	0.08	4043	15816
Liechtenstein	582	584	588	632	670	102.11	0.01	500	16677
Norway	297641	307499	311994	334049	345786	232.76	1.04	53338	12540
Sweden	542541	589270	638550	695631	779439	294.04	2.51	128886	14997
Switzerland	150210	156970	166150	177605	189975	105.42	2.58	132479	19773
EFTA total							9.29	477621	14772
Eastern Europe									
Albania[b]	30500	32800	33000	19800		141.46	0.06	3094	967
Bulgaria[b]	20497	21094	23030	10893		-0.97	0.10	5187	577
Czechoslovakia	323300	330360	343010	388990	377270	63.45	0.25	12797	816
Hungary	778100	886800	1050400	1300000	1462500	346.43	0.38	19569	1848
Poland	10157000	16789600	61216000	327269000	594647004	48237.43	1.09	56226	1472
Romania[b]	489100	501400	508900	613300		145.32	0.53	27340	1176
USSR[b]	510000	540000	560000	336000		15.86	10.89	560000	1970
Yugoslavia[b]	25059430	7526952010718388202429289600				476231.29	0.42	21464	901
East European total							13.72	705678	1709
Others									
Cyprus[b]	1015	1210	1347	1558		411.09	0.07	3409	4670
Gibraltar[b]	59	61	63	71		88.53	0.00	131	4358
Malta[c]	351	388	426	461	484	184.67	0.03	1500	4226
Monaco[c]	1578	1672	1806	1922	2010	252.06	0.01	356	12725
Turkey	37035000	61719000	105314000	180000000	324000000	24823.08	1.51	77664	1364
Total							1.62	83060	1453
European total							100.00	5142123	6043

Sources: National accounts/Euromonitor
Notes: See end of section

Table No: 1102

TOTAL EXPENDITURE

Consumer Expenditure by Object 1991

Current US dollars (millions)

	Food	Alcoholic Drinks	Non-Alcoholic Drinks	Tobacco	Clothing	Footwear	Housing	Household Fuels
EC members								
Belgium	20287	3448	1241	1755	7666	1481	14560	5006
Denmark	10198	1976	375	1809	3306	473	14588	4043
France	107951	13279	3644	7444	38952	7631	88505	49484
Germany: East[a]	34817	15035	2532	3165	12028	3323	4971	3766
Germany: West	133129	21185	8426	9630	52963	14685	179110	63796
Greece	13492	649	265	812	5429	560	6764	1879
Ireland	5018	2803	342	1008	1328	319	1263	1309
Italy	132655	8035	2700	10158	55539	16558	74817	26553
Luxembourg[a]	702	72	29	238	288	29	608	378
Netherlands	24950	1873	619	2937	8493	2649	18935	10565
Portugal[b]	14672	637	76	542	2065	638	3867	
Spain	56201	4130	17968	5093	22103	12141	38041	9799
United Kingdom	71978	41672	6391	17505	30761	6403	77369	19837
EC total	626050	114794	44609	62095	240919	66891	523399	196415
EFTA members								
Austria	15950	1883	589	1677	6942	1912	13976	5892
Finland[a]	11577	2122	321	1080	2623	522	9815	2312
Iceland[a,b,c]	1147	96	18	89	324		430	
Liechtenstein[a]	58	30	5	10	31	5	94	25
Norway	9793	1802	613	1202	3313	715	6612	3659
Sweden[a]	18576	3586	593	2370	7321	1365	26039	5861
Switzerland[a]	25185	6079	1080	2141	5006	1177	18525	5550
EFTA total	82286	15599	3220	8569	25560	5697	75490	23299
Eastern Europe								
Albania[a,d]	1187	154	56	69	231	45	148	122
Bulgaria[a,d]	1452	601	53	135	383	135	136	135
Czechoslovakia[a]	3669	1154	240	708	754	183	479	478
Hungary[a]	3262	1206	245	490	675	289	1164	487
Poland[e]	24310	1051		925	4645	1322	2904	3092
Romania[a,d]	9309	1925	640	629	2160	574	711	258
USSR[a,d]	202342	68271	6241	13454	87633	20177	23545	22073
Yugoslavia[a,d]	8349	1146	398	534	1216	696	944	1395
East European total	253881	75507	7873	16943	97696	23421	30032	28041
Others								
Cyprus[a,d]	673	48	44	43	505	38	213	69
Gibraltar[a,b,d]	41	1	1	1	13	3	18	
Malta[a,f]	451	77	64	59	140	38	74	41
Monaco[a,f]	63	8	2	5	26	6	45	25
Turkey[a,d]	25574	837	1878	6545	3265	1260	6191	3953
Total	26801	972	1988	6653	3947	1344	6541	4089
European total	989018	206873	57689	94260	368122	97352	635462	251844

Table No: 1102 (cont'd)

TOTAL EXPENDITURE

Consumer Expenditure by Object 1991

Current US dollars (millions)

	Household Goods & Services	Health	Transport	Communi-cations	Leisure	Others	Total
EC members							
Belgium	15715	13823	14220	1211	11862	7334	119609
Denmark	4302	1266	10080	983	7113	7778	68290
France	58004	68211	108248	15378	53193	100271	720193
Germany: East[a]	20257	6647	23739		15351	12627	158260
Germany: West	59703	38518	117962	14444	88111	29370	831033
Greece	3757	3022	4149	548	2812	3744	47882
Ireland	1739	364	2682	321	2408	2914	23819
Italy	66108	45328	78909	7481	63207	138628	726677
Luxembourg[a]	433	341	878		191	807	4992
Netherlands	14115	21341	16319	2200	15717	22024	162735
Portugal[b]	2639	1275	4667	1287	1195	9773	42139
Spain	24897	13773	55664	3758	24515	30794	318877
United Kingdom	34493	7708	82740	9846	53836	190718	651258
EC total	306162	221618	520258	57456	339510	556783	3875763
EFTA members							
Austria	7315	4795	12674	1685	5328	9690	90309
Finland[a]	4550	3010	11507		6247	12381	68066
Iceland[a,b,c]	438	254	337		358	553	4043
Liechtenstein[a]	25	63	61		70	23	500
Norway	3699	2204	5822	841	4759	8305	53338
Sweden[a]	8189	1998	21706		11840	19440	128886
Switzerland[a]	6532	15975	15682		13717	15831	132479
EFTA total	30747	28298	67789	2526	42319	66222	477621
Eastern Europe							
Albania[a,d]	304	112	213		160	292	3094
Bulgaria[a,d]	732	158	428		360	479	5187
Czechoslovakia[a]	1834	1401	1003		567	1727	12797
Hungary[a]	1052	887	1337		2096	6381	19569
Poland[e]	1912	2412	932	3283	6198	3239	56226
Romania[a,d]	752	875	1009		1750	6749	27340
USSR[a,d]	22361	15146	19774		46216	12765	560000
Yugoslavia[a,d]	936	872	1567		901	2510	21464
East European total	29883	21863	26264	3283	58249	34142	705678
Others							
Cyprus[a,d]	379	81	581		183	553	3409
Gibraltar[a,b,d]	12	11	13		12	7	131
Malta[a,f]	176	65	293		121	-99	1500
Monaco[a,f]	49	54	38		26	11	356
Turkey[a,d]	7331	7627	4173		1105	7925	77664
Total	7947	7838	5098		1447	8396	83061
European total	374739	279618	619408	63266	441526	665543	5142123

Sources: National accounts/Euromonitor
Notes: See end of section

Table No: 1103

TOTAL EXPENDITURE

Consumer Expenditure by Object 1991

% total expenditure

	Food	Alcoholic Drinks	Non-Alcoholic Drinks	Tobacco	Clothing	Footwear	Housing	Household Fuels
EC members								
Belgium	17.0	2.9	1.0	1.5	6.4	1.2	12.2	4.2
Denmark	14.9	2.9	0.5	2.6	4.8	0.7	21.4	5.9
France	15.0	1.8	0.5	1.0	5.4	1.1	12.3	6.9
Germany: East[a]	22.0	9.5	1.6	2.0	7.6	2.1	3.1	2.4
Germany: West	16.0	2.5	1.0	1.2	6.4	1.8	21.6	7.7
Greece	28.2	1.4	0.6	1.7	11.3	1.2	14.1	3.9
Ireland	21.1	11.8	1.4	4.2	5.6	1.3	5.3	5.5
Italy	18.3	1.1	0.4	1.4	7.6	2.3	10.3	3.7
Luxembourg[a]	14.1	1.4	0.6	4.8	5.8	0.6	12.2	7.6
Netherlands	15.3	1.2	0.4	1.8	5.2	1.6	11.6	6.5
Portugal[b]	34.8	1.5	0.2	1.3	4.9	1.5	9.2	
Spain	17.6	1.3	5.6	1.6	6.9	3.8	11.9	3.1
United Kingdom	11.1	6.4	1.0	2.7	4.7	1.0	11.9	3.0
EC total	16.2	3.0	1.2	1.6	6.2	1.7	13.5	5.1
EFTA members								
Austria	17.7	2.1	0.7	1.9	7.7	2.1	15.5	6.5
Finland[a]	17.0	3.1	0.5	1.6	3.9	0.8	14.4	3.4
Iceland[a,b,c]	28.4	2.4	0.4	2.2	8.0		10.6	
Liechtenstein[a]	11.7	6.0	1.1	1.9	6.1	1.0	18.9	5.1
Norway	18.4	3.4	1.1	2.3	6.2	1.3	12.4	6.9
Sweden[a]	14.5	2.8	0.5	1.8	5.7	1.1	20.2	4.5
Switzerland[a]	19.0	4.6	0.8	1.6	3.8	0.9	14.0	4.2
EFTA total	17.2	3.3	0.7	1.8	5.4	1.2	15.8	4.9
Eastern Europe								
Albania[a,d]	38.4	5.0	1.8	2.2	7.5	1.4	4.8	4.0
Bulgaria[a,d]	28.0	11.6	1.0	2.6	7.4	2.6	2.6	2.6
Czechoslovakia[a]	28.7	9.0	1.9	5.5	5.9	1.4	3.7	3.7
Hungary[a]	16.7	6.2	1.3	2.5	3.4	1.5	5.9	2.5
Poland[e]	43.2	1.9		1.6	8.3	2.4	5.2	5.5
Romania[a,d]	34.1	7.0	2.3	2.3	7.9	2.1	2.6	0.9
USSR[a,d]	36.1	12.2	1.1	2.4	15.6	3.6	4.2	3.9
Yugoslavia[a,d]	38.9	5.3	1.9	2.5	5.7	3.2	4.4	6.5
East European total	36.0	10.7	1.1	2.4	13.8	3.3	4.3	4.0
Others								
Cyprus[a,d]	19.7	1.4	1.3	1.3	14.8	1.1	6.2	2.0
Gibraltar[a,b,d]	30.9	1.1	0.5	1.0	9.7	2.0	13.4	
Malta[a,f]	30.0	5.2	4.2	3.9	9.3	2.6	4.9	2.8
Monaco[a,f]	17.7	2.3	0.5	1.3	7.2	1.6	12.5	6.9
Turkey[a,d]	32.9	1.1	2.4	8.4	4.2	1.6	8.0	5.1
Total	32.3	1.2	2.4	8.0	4.8	1.6	7.9	4.9
European total	19.2	4.0	1.1	1.8	7.2	1.9	12.4	4.9

Table No: 1103 (cont'd)

TOTAL EXPENDITURE

Consumer Expenditure by Object 1991

% total expenditure

	Households Goods & Services	Health	Transport	Communi-cations	Leisure	Others	Total
EC members							
Belgium	13.1	11.6	11.9	1.0	9.9	6.1	100.0
Denmark	6.3	1.9	14.8	1.4	10.4	11.4	100.0
France	8.1	9.5	15.0	2.1	7.4	13.9	100.0
Germany: East[a]	12.8	4.2	15.0		9.7	8.0	100.0
Germany: West	7.2	4.6	14.2	1.7	10.6	3.5	100.0
Greece	7.8	6.3	8.7	1.1	5.9	7.8	100.0
Ireland	7.3	1.5	11.3	1.3	10.1	12.2	100.0
Italy	9.1	6.2	10.9	1.0	8.7	19.1	100.0
Luxembourg[a]	8.7	6.8	17.6		3.8	16.2	100.0
Netherlands	8.7	13.1	10.0	1.4	9.7	13.5	100.0
Portugal[b]	6.3	3.0	11.1	3.1	2.8	23.2	100.0
Spain	7.8	4.3	17.5	1.2	7.7	9.7	100.0
United Kingdom	5.3	1.2	12.7	1.5	8.3	29.3	100.0
EC total	7.9	5.7	13.4	1.5	8.8	14.4	100.0
EFTA members							
Austria	8.1	5.3	14.0	1.9	5.9	10.7	100.0
Finland[a]	6.7	4.4	16.9		9.2	18.2	100.0
Iceland[a,b,c]	10.8	6.3	8.3		8.9	13.7	100.0
Liechtenstein[a]	5.0	12.6	12.3		14.0	4.5	100.0
Norway	6.9	4.1	10.9	1.6	8.9	15.6	100.0
Sweden[a]	6.4	1.6	16.8		9.2	15.1	100.0
Switzerland[a]	4.9	12.1	11.8		10.4	11.9	100.0
EFTA total	6.4	5.9	14.2		8.9	13.9	100.0
Eastern Europe							
Albania[a,d]	9.8	3.6	6.9		5.2	9.5	100.0
Bulgaria[a,d]	14.1	3.0	8.3		6.9	9.2	100.0
Czechoslovakia[a]	14.3	11.0	7.8		4.4	13.5	100.0
Hungary[a]	5.4	4.5	6.8		10.7	32.6	100.0
Poland[e]	3.4	4.3	1.7	5.8	11.0	5.8	100.0
Romania[a,d]	2.8	3.2	3.7		6.4	24.7	100.0
USSR[a,d]	4.0	2.7	3.5		8.3	2.3	100.0
Yugoslavia[a,d]	4.4	4.1	7.3		4.2	11.7	100.0
East European total	4.2	3.1	3.7		8.3	4.8	100.0
Others							
Cyprus[a,d]	11.1	2.4	17.1		5.4	16.2	100.0
Gibraltar[a,b,d]	9.0	8.2	9.6		9.0	5.0	100.0
Malta[a,f]	11.7	4.4	19.5		8.1	-6.6	100.0
Monaco[a,f]	13.9	15.3	10.6		7.3	3.0	100.0
Turkey[a,d]	9.4	9.8	5.4		1.4	10.2	100.0
Total	9.6	9.4	6.1		1.7	10.1	100.0
European total	7.3	5.4	12.0		8.6	12.9	100.0

Sources: National accounts/Euromonitor
Notes: See end of section

Table No: 1104

EXPENDITURE ON FOOD

Consumer Expenditure on Food 1977-1991

National currencies (millions)	1977	1980	1981	1982	1983	1984	1985	1986
EC members								
Belgium	349354	403876	415188	471420	519822	560649	590649	607503
Denmark	28760	35894	40265	44526	47182	52049	53872	54500
France	230513	291393	332360	377700	416615	457389	484970	506727
Germany: East	38052	41127	42024	42792	43305	44586	45483	46636
Germany: West	138820	163088	173552	182464	186632	191216	193984	197920
Greece	219713	405359	528343	621245	755050	886235	1109000	1360000
Ireland	986	1548	1819	2024	2217	2383	2409	2495
Italy[a]	35216	56787	66260	77437	87949	105274	110065	116770
Luxembourg	12064	13103	14202	15681	16832	18014	18697	19121
Netherlands	26990	30630	32390	33910	33630	35310	36110	37045
Portugal	165180	250400	300000	437865	541800	753000	980000	1200000
Spain	1930800	2620600	2936800	3404900	3788100	4219900	4139676	4651180
United Kingdom	16047	22876	24207	25649	26379	27591	28642	30064
EC total								
EFTA members								
Austria	88130	110740	118460	123620	131700	137170	140680	145554
Finland	16286	22131	27108	27370	29406	31829	33776	35370
Iceland	801	2522	3972	6237	11805	15097	23208	26519
Liechtenstein	58	64	67	66	58	67	68	71
Norway	21480	27285	31381	35744	38758	41858	46706	51597
Sweden	41996	49699	57205	60719	66643	74112	79506	85386
Switzerland	18880	21750	23290	24470	25530	26985	28250	29360
EFTA total								
Eastern Europe								
Albania[b]	1312	2259	3074	3538	4018	5770	6259	6578
Bulgaria[b]	1949	2409	2772	3123	3147	3256	3570	3776
Czechoslovakia	59374	77843	81985	82503	83884	87163	90960	97346
Hungary	80111	107456	113979	120251	129951	141742	169589	184808
Poland	353900	516900	661400	1314800	1489200	1548400	1916000	2394307
Romania[b]	57120	67080	75300	80100	90660	96670	98880	99100
USSR[b]	92100	85770	98910	107730	117630	128700	133650	137160
Yugoslavia[b]	240108	315238	449317	602125	842178	1402509	2163060	4274940
East European total								
Others								
Cyprus	76	121	130	145	161	180	187	189
Gibraltar[b]	12	14	14	15	16	16	17	18
Malta	49	75	84	92	94	101	98	100
Monaco	119	145	175	198	226	247	263	272
Turkey	572000	1197560	1887690	2305688	3295110	5747600	7652070	10560000
Total								
European total								

Table No: 1104 (cont'd)

EXPENDITURE ON FOOD

Consumer Expenditure on Food 1977-1991

National currencies (millions)

	1987	1988	1989	1990	1991	% growth 1977-1991	% share 1991	Total $ million 1991	$ per capita 1991
EC members									
Belgium	609965	611996	644418	684694	692749	98.29	2.05	20287	2022
Denmark	55859	57690	59626	63089	65227	126.80	1.03	10198	1982
France	521311	545555	548702	582330	609069	164.22	10.91	107951	1909
Germany: East	49555	52484	54497	53999	57779	51.84	3.52	34817	2190
Germany: West	201202	179905	191712	208133	220928	59.15	13.46	133129	2128
Greece	1399156	1438312	1707744	2049292	2459151	1019.26	1.36	13492	1329
Ireland	2580	2642	2780	2948	3106	215.10	0.51	5018	1429
Italy[a]	121561	127366	135994	144488	164572	367.32	13.41	132655	2293
Luxembourg	19545	19969	22587	23269	23967	98.67	0.07	702	1872
Netherlands	37423	39550	41718	44752	46648	72.84	2.52	24950	1662
Portugal	1293550	1467047	1640543	1868600	2119851	1183.36	1.48	14672	1412
Spain	4930516	4131577	4434419	5509301	5839859	202.46	5.68	56201	1443
United Kingdom	31672	33593	36045	38427	40682	153.52	7.28	71978	1254
EC total							63.30	626050	1825
EFTA members									
Austria	149987	152669	163612	175184	186230	111.31	1.61	15950	2072
Finland	37575	40436	43094	44747	46818	187.47	1.17	11577	2328
Iceland	35127	43735	52343	60479	67650	8345.75	0.12	1147	4486
Liechtenstein	70	69	68	74	78	35.47	0.01	58	1946
Norway	55681	57110	59356	61332	63487	195.56	0.99	9793	2302
Sweden	90451	91903	99415	105687	112339	167.50	1.88	18576	2162
Switzerland	29945	31035	31935	34105	36116	91.29	2.55	25185	3759
EFTA total							8.32	82286	2545
Eastern Europe									
Albania[b]	7320	8099	7914	7598		479.19	0.12	1187	371
Bulgaria[b]	3894	4013	4298	3049		56.48	0.15	1452	161
Czechoslovakia	102696	103050	104500	111531	108170	82.18	0.37	3669	234
Hungary	212609	210405	217533	216687	243773	204.29	0.33	3262	308
Poland	2890382	5032000	15347007	163180251	257104986	72549.05	2.46	24310	637
Romania[b]	109200	120285	115520	208829		265.60	0.94	9309	400
USSR[b]	142800	148157	155648	121405		31.82	20.46	202342	712
Yugoslavia[b]	9299300	28467370	415050140	944993654		393470.25	0.84	8349	351
East European total							25.67	253881	657
Others									
Cyprus	198	231	262	308		303.17	0.07	673	922
Gibraltar[b]	18	19	20	22		88.46	0.00	41	1352
Malta	103	102	116	138	145	196.60	0.05	451	1269
Monaco	287	302	320	340	356	198.98	0.01	63	2252
Turkey	14640000	20112000	34424989	59272089	106689761	18552.06	2.59	25574	449
Total							2.71	26801	469
European total							100.00	989018	1177

Sources: National accounts/Euromonitor
Notes: See end of section

Table No: 1105

EXPENDITURE ON ALCOHOLIC DRINKS

Consumer Expenditure on Alcoholic Drinks 1977-1991

National currencies (millions)

	1977	1980	1981	1982	1983	1984	1985	1986
EC members								
Belgium	62692	77032	81222	89331	95364	96062	100239	100157
Denmark	6478	7953	8819	9785	11112	11489	12037	12562
France	30181	39430	44305	49751	54129	56026	58920	63253
Germany: East	13196	14990	15631	16015	16399	17040	17681	18065
Germany: West	16500	20978	22323	23470	24010	24240	24830	25312
Greece	17850	26673	32337	41008	45923	48850	50050	52500
Ireland	423	695	844	1010	1041	1155	1234	1338
Italy[a]	2548	4097	4700	5322	6097	6687	6624	7199
Luxembourg	1058	1423	1620	1750	1784	1787	1885	1963
Netherlands	3930	4060	4250	4620	4578	4580	4650	4760
Portugal	12056	20167	26461	31110	33350	35500	43700	51680
Spain	85890	131200	143900	159400	174100	235000	270919	303895
United Kingdom	6545	9955	11152	12003	13370	14430	15783	16403
EC total								
EFTA members								
Austria	14300	15440	16191	17360	18470	18130	18610	19237
Finland	2916	4330	4860	5563	6229	6683	7020	7885
Iceland	79	265	400	694	1130	1682	2201	2697
Liechtenstein	20	24	25	27	28	32	34	34
Norway	3848	4826	5309	5393	6144	6629	7522	8200
Sweden	8456	9977	11007	12189	13182	14068	14982	15836
Switzerland	4789	5307	5727	6167	6398	6673	7007	7382
EFTA total								
Eastern Europe								
Albania[b]	413	667	820	888	1127	1192	1276	1409
Bulgaria[b]	1610	1924	1864	1924	1961	2009	2033	2130
Czechoslovakia	26408	28306	29515	30205	30723	30895	31586	32104
Hungary	30439	39554	41059	46662	49003	51178	62885	65979
Poland	151000	184700	189800	396700	558900	616300	762300	995600
Romania[b,c]	23340	26340	28140	28680	29700	30600	32400	34800
USSR[b]	34100	35100	41490	43200	45540	51030	54180	57150
Yugoslavia[b]	27795	49619	71571	96074	129855	213920	355950	706440
East European total								
Others								
Cyprus[b]	8	11	12	12	14	14	15	15
Gibraltar[b]	1	1	1	1	1	1	1	1
Malta	10	22	23	17	16	15	15	16
Monaco	16	21	23	26	29	30	32	34
Turkey[b]	13000	35927	53934	72811	101388	172428	228420	316800
Total								
European total								

Table No: 1105 (cont'd)

EXPENDITURE ON ALCOHOLIC DRINKS

Consumer Expenditure on Alcoholic Drinks 1977-1991

National currencies (millions)

	1987	1988	1989	1990	1991	% growth 1977-1991	% share 1991	Total $ million 1991	$ per capita 1991
EEC members									
Belgium	104679	106008	110450	114323	117747	87.82	1.67	3448	344
Denmark	12600	12652	12706	12223	12638	95.09	0.96	1976	384
France	66530	67788	68179	72357	74923	148.25	6.42	13279	235
Germany: East	19315	20583	21455	23318	24950	89.07	7.27	15035	946
Germany: West	25421	27892	30921	33121	35157	113.07	10.24	21185	339
Greece	60864	58587	82196	98636	118363	563.10	0.31	649	64
Ireland	1371	1468	1613	1725	1735	310.36	1.35	2803	798
Italy[a]	7545	7760	8132	8752	9969	291.23	3.88	8035	139
Luxembourg	2041	2119	2319	2363	2458	132.33	0.03	72	192
Netherlands	4811	3808	3057	3294	3502	-10.89	0.91	1873	125
Portugal	58210	66017	68829	81913	91998	663.09	0.31	637	61
Spain	333373	274774	322616	404825	429114	399.61	2.00	4130	106
United Kingdom	17451	18754	19817	21738	23553	259.86	20.14	41672	726
EC total							55.49	114794	335
EFTA members									
Austria	19778	19333	19518	20684	21988	53.76	0.91	1883	245
Finland	8377	8574	8763	8876	8581	194.27	1.03	2122	427
Iceland	3903	4172	4209	5056	5655	7095.45	0.05	96	375
Liechtenstein	35	35	35	38	40	102.86	0.01	30	998
Norway	9582	10626	10214	11402	11685	203.66	0.87	1802	424
Sweden	17573	17684	19130	20720	21689	156.49	1.73	3586	417
Switzerland	7400	7391	7729	8232	8717	82.03	2.94	6079	907
EFTA total							7.54	15599	482
Eastern Europe									
Albania[b]	1525	1641	1639	983		138.36	0.07	154	48
Bulgaria[b]	2193	2256	2670	1263		-21.55	0.29	601	67
Czechoslovakia	33376	33450	33100	35428	34017	28.82	0.56	1154	74
Hungary	76507	75500	78877	81738	90116	196.05	0.58	1206	114
Poland	1139600	1883000	6865543	6219718	11111632	7258.70	0.51	1051	28
Romania[b,c]	34320	33834	32570	43176		84.99	0.93	1925	83
USSR[b]	61200	65310	68271	40963		20.13	33.00	68271	240
Yugoslavia[b]	1555520	3909870	57232970	129716760		466590.99	0.55	1146	48
East European total							36.50	75507	185
Others									
Cyprus[b]	15	17	19	22		186.18	0.02	48	66
Gibraltar[b]	1	1	1	1		54.67	0.00	1	49
Malta	17	17	20	24	25	158.63	0.04	77	218
Monaco	36	39	41	44	46	195.63	0.00	8	292
Turkey[b]	439200	771360	1278682	2183855		16698.89	0.40	837	15
Total							0.47	972	17
European total							100.0	206873	246

Sources: National accounts/Euromonitor
Notes: See end of section

Table No: 1106

EXPENDITURE ON NON-ALCOHOLIC DRINKS

Consumer Expenditure on Non-Alcoholic Drinks 1977-1991

National currencies (millions)

	1977	1980	1981	1982	1983	1984	1985	1986
EC members								
Belgium	16760	20561	21814	24619	27626	29361	29361	32973
Denmark	1046	1262	1313	1453	1628	1751	1932	2100
France	3000	7338	8583	10317	11760	12784	13847	14794
Germany: East	1922	2306	2306	2434	2434	2562	2691	2947
Germany: West	7319	9314	9690	10274	10505	10857	11196	11497
Greece	7098	10836	12351	16335	19345	22938	22210	23800
Ireland	44	79	109	110	129	131	151	154
Italy[a]	360	606	723	863	1002	1246	1523	1813
Luxembourg	281	355	426	511	560	567	685	771
Netherlands	900	1090	1140	1310	1360	1360	1480	1580
Portugal	1094	1724	2143	2921	2700	3000	4000	5000
Spain	150000	446000	501000	563000	628000	750000	90283	997370
United Kingdom	1161	1602	1568	1595	1896	2107	2339	2586
EC total								
EFTA members								
Austria	3100	4100	4303	4615	5210	5110	5240	5405
Finland	379	640	675	688	771	864	917	1012
Iceland	13	40	55	90	170	250	330	499
Liechtenstein	3	4	5	5	5	6	6	6
Norway	1045	1327	1377	1726	1824	2008	2309	2841
Sweden	1024	1410	1460	1530	1633	1752	2009	2183
Switzerland	799	956	1031	1110	1152	1202	1262	1314
EFTA total								
Eastern Europe								
Albania[b]	83	154	179	203	236	260	296	403
Bulgaria[b]	133	157	194	194	194	194	182	194
Czechoslovakia	4315	5351	5178	3797	5351	5523	5868	6214
Hungary	5937	9868	10202	11624	12209	12794	16056	17143
Poland[c]								
Romania[b]	5160	5940	7020	7080	7860	8280	8940	9180
USSR[b]	2800	2790	3420	3330	3420	3600	3780	3960
Yugoslavia[b]	7089	14411	17950	24019	32359	53560	112200	223780
East European total								
Others								
Cyprus[b]	6	8	9	9	9	11	11	12
Gibraltar[b]	0	0	0	0	0	0	0	0
Malta	4	5	7	10	10	11	13	14
Monaco	2	4	5	5	6	7	8	8
Turkey[b]	12675	68860	121352	182028	253470	445439	571050	726000
Total								
European total								

Table No: 1106 (cont'd)

EXPENDITURE ON NON-ALCOHOLIC DRINKS

Consumer Expenditure on Non-Alcoholic Drinks 1977-1991

National currencies (millions)

	1987	1988	1989	1990	1991	% growth 1977-1991	% share 1991	Total $ million 1991	$ per capita 1991
EC members									
Belgium	34419	36643	38967	41140	42372	152.82	2.15	1241	124
Denmark	2108	2351	2411	2319	2398	129.27	0.65	375	73
France	16070	18233	18338	19462	20559	585.31	6.32	3644	64
Germany: East	3024	3093	3218	3927	4202	118.65	4.39	2532	159
Germany: West	11544	11854	12732	13173	13983	91.05	14.61	8426	135
Greece	26045	23942	33590	40308	48369	581.45	0.46	265	26
Ireland	176	194	204	212	212	378.12	0.59	342	97
Italy[a]	2090	2383	2662	3131	3350	830.60	4.68	2700	47
Luxembourg	810	830	911	945	983	249.84	0.05	29	77
Netherlands	1600	1264	1011	1090	1158	28.69	1.07	619	41
Portugal	6468	7335	8203	9644	11050	910.05	0.13	76	7
Spain	1147970	1205500	1389900	1761341	1867022	12346.81	31.15	17968	461
United Kingdom	2800	3000	3200	3406	3612	211.11	11.08	6391	111
EC total							77.33	44609	130
EFTA members									
Austria	5769	6051	6108	6473	6881	121.98	1.02	589	77
Finland	1075	1150	1233	1241	1298	242.51	0.56	321	65
Iceland	585	703	787	928	1038	7734.90	0.03	18	69
Liechtenstein	6	6	6	7	7	113.81	0.01	5	176
Norway	3194	3438	3405	3801	3974	280.26	1.06	613	144
Sweden	2378	2869	3103	3376	3589	250.45	1.03	593	69
Switzerland	1320	1308	1378	1463	1549	93.84	1.87	1080	161
EFTA total							5.58	3220	100
Eastern Europe									
Albania[b]	488	588	598	359		335.18	0.10	56	18
Bulgaria[b]	205	217	234	111		-16.87	0.09	53	6
Czechoslovakia	6419	6625	6500	7225	7077	64.01	0.42	240	15
Hungary	19892	17700	20757	15961	18315	208.48	0.42	245	23
Poland[c]									
Romania[b]	9360	9540	9160	14351		178.12	1.11	640	28
USSR[b]	4233	4509	4801	3745		33.72	10.82	6241	22
Yugoslavia[b]	499770	1412510	19895690	45092967		635997.72	0.69	398	17
East European total							13.65	7873	19
Others									
Cyprus[b]	13	15	17	20		264.44	0.08	44	60
Gibraltar[b]	0	0	0	0		240.65	0.00	1	20
Malta	15	15	16	20	21	446.85	0.11	64	180
Monaco	9	9	10	10	11	593.94	0.00	2	68
Turkey[b]	988200	1704004	2947699	4898272		38545.86	3.25	1878	34
Total							3.45	1988	35
European total							100.00	57689	69

Sources: National accounts/Euromonitor
Notes: See end of section

Table No: 1107

EXPENDITURE ON TOBACCO

Consumer Expenditure on Tobacco 1977-1991

National currencies (millions)

	1977	1980	1981	1982	1983	1984	1985	1986
EC members								
Belgium	32057	35400	37616	45147	49159	53441	54422	55635
Denmark	5832	7130	7554	8425	9292	10174	10653	11560
France	12384	18029	20950	25030	28125	31034	32410	33998
Germany: East	2998	3459	3536	3690	3767	3920	4074	4228
Germany: West	14310	16309	16500	16600	16200	15500	14850	14300
Greece	17090	27433	34817	46766	58889	61500	68700	71100
Ireland	151	239	297	368	422	455	499	519
Italy[a]	2484	4013	4996	6595	7776	8334	8989	9350
Luxembourg	1800	4500	6000	6250	7000	7414	8028	7757
Netherlands	3280	3830	3970	4020	4230	4510	4460	4470
Portugal	7825	17488	22551	31768	28500	31000	38000	44000
Spain	62700	122300	165600	183600	206900	230500	301640	340798
United Kingdom	3628	4821	5515	5881	6209	6622	7006	7471
EC total								
EFTA members								
Austria	11750	13620	14090	14420	15540	15500	16210	17000
Finland	1532	2296	2240	2739	3189	3562	3462	3854
Iceland	85	270	346	563	990	1456	1967	2646
Liechtenstein	8	8	9	10	10	11	12	12
Norway	2191	2764	3190	3557	4017	4436	5064	5906
Sweden	4475	5585	6114	6731	7420	8250	8667	9200
Switzerland	1952	1887	2036	2192	2274	2372	2490	2610
EFTA total								
Eastern Europe								
Albania[b]	165	349	448	483	545	596	615	604
Bulgaria[b]	242	327	375	412	448	472	484	545
Czechoslovakia	14153	17605	17778	17605	17778	17605	18296	18468
Hungary	5854	8697	9115	10537	11038	11540	13380	14216
Poland	33100	41300	60900	77200	98400	100400	120000	157500
Romania[b]	6480	8100	8640	9060	10500	10800	11160	11460
USSR[b]	7600	7740	8640	9090	9630	10440	10980	11520
Yugoslavia[b]	4488	22600	30800	40900	60000	87100	158960	288470
East European total								
Others								
Cyprus[b]	8	14	14	13	14	14	13	14
Gibraltar[b]	0	0	0	1	1	1	1	1
Malta	8	14	14	14	13	13	13	13
Monaco	6	10	11	13	15	17	18	18
Turkey[b]	18052	89817	139330	188096	261919	494329	988978	1574492
Total								
European total								

Table No: 1107 (cont'd)

EXPENDITURE ON TOBACCO

Consumer Expenditure on Tobacco 1977-1991

National currencies (millions)

	1987	1988	1989	1990	1991	% growth 1977-1991	% share 1991	Total $ million 1991	$ per capita 1991
EC members									
Belgium	54629	55709	56789	58192	59936	86.97	1.86	1755	175
Denmark	11600	11644	11789	11193	11573	98.44	1.92	1809	352
France	35997	37998	38217	40559	41997	239.12	7.90	7444	132
Germany: East	4448	4665	4892	4909	5253	75.20	3.36	3165	199
Germany: West	14450	13946	14551	15055	15980	11.67	10.22	9630	154
Greece	78818	73234	102746	123295	147954	765.73	0.86	812	80
Ireland	522	534	550	588	624	313.04	1.07	1008	287
Italy[a]	9821	10555	11352	11778	12602	407.35	10.78	10158	176
Luxembourg	7486	7633	7780	7959	8116	350.90	0.25	238	634
Netherlands	4542	4725	5034	5305	5491	67.40	3.12	2937	196
Portugal	51095	57948	58601	68970	78244	899.92	0.57	542	52
Spain	376923	401100	410000	504288	529200	744.02	5.40	5093	131
United Kingdom	7653	7945	8196	8784	9894	172.71	18.57	17505	305
EC total							65.88	62095	181
EFTA members									
Austria	17200	17964	17377	18415	19576	66.61	1.78	1677	218
Finland	4094	4378	4696	4547	4369	185.19	1.15	1080	217
Iceland	2987	3644	4163	4714	5273	6103.29	0.09	89	350
Liechtenstein	12	11	12	12	13	57.89	0.01	10	317
Norway	6456	6445	6882	7683	7793	255.70	1.28	1202	283
Sweden	10000	12067	13053	13613	14335	220.34	2.51	2370	276
Switzerland	2615	2655	2730	2899	3070	57.25	2.27	2141	319
EFTA total							9.09	8569	265
Eastern Europe									
Albania[b]	671	741	740	444		169.20	0.07	69	22
Bulgaria[b]	553	562	600	284		17.24	0.14	135	15
Czechoslovakia	20111	20150	20100	21513	20865	47.42	0.75	708	45
Hungary	16509	16023	24500	33528	36587	525.04	0.52	490	46
Poland	185918	290054	1057555	4752144	9783827	29458.39	0.98	925	24
Romania[b]	11700	11941	11705	14106		117.68	0.67	629	27
USSR[b]	12240	12960	13454	8072		6.22	14.27	13454	47
Yugoslavia[b]	619640	1729450	26649650	60400609		1345724.62	0.57	534	22
East European total							17.98	16943	42
Others									
Cyprus[b]	14	15	17	20		153.67	0.05	43	59
Gibraltar[b]	1	1	1	1		68.09	0.00	1	43
Malta	13	13	15	18	19	147.06	0.06	59	166
Monaco	20	21	23	25	26	300.89	0.00	5	163
Turkey[b]	2681785	5786623	9893298	17073076		94477.52	6.94	6545	117
Total							7.06	6653	116
European total							100.00	94260	112

Sources: National accounts/Euromonitor
Notes: See end of section

Table No: 1108

EXPENDITURE ON CLOTHING

Consumer Expenditure on Clothing 1977-1991

National currencies (millions)	1977	1980	1981	1982	1983	1984	1985	1986
EC members								
Belgium	95903	124316	131942	150088	153049	157713	167515	178501
Denmark	8605	10183	9533	12208	13562	14986	16904	18236
France	101059	112016	129561	143144	157436	169638	183385	199677
Germany: East	15118	17040	16912	16271	16271	16912	17681	18065
Germany: West	55200	61853	63498	63022	64974	66789	69726	73379
Greece	64518	100245	117550	139049	145001	200500	286000	365000
Ireland	225	370	390	406	472	538	627	653
Italy[a]	9202	16119	18468	20940	22537	25605	37616	40601
Luxembourg	4384	5278	5750	6060	6624	6703	7303	7869
Netherlands	9140	12240	12600	12440	12446	11380	12230	12562
Portugal	31649	75752	94424	102000	116480	130000	159000	168000
Spain	400800	639300	725600	800400	895600	946700	1066300	1194991
United Kingdom	5520	8103	8506	8856	9860	10735	12298	13663
EC total								
EFTA members								
Austria	41309	50050	53115	57120	61370	64900	66840	73184
Finland	3062	4517	5436	5845	6510	7134	8158	8015
Iceland[b]	278	972	1549	2432	4002	6211	8503	9089
Liechtenstein	21	24	25	25	27	31	32	34
Norway	7088	9001	9773	11671	11914	13179	15866	17946
Sweden	13488	16530	17843	19375	21141	23515	26664	28682
Switzerland	3850	4743	5030	5100	5293	5408	5679	5980
EFTA total								
Eastern Europe								
Albania[c]	825	1242	1588	1948	2273	3002	3371	3422
Bulgaria[c]	992	1307	1356	1416	1404	1440	1464	1489
Czechoslovakia	17778	18296	19331	20539	21057	22438	23301	23819
Hungary	23164	28850	31275	32028	35206	37213	44571	46294
Poland	128000	156000	185600	209800	284700	357200	494517	696914
Romania[c]	31140	34200	36300	37320	37680	38400	39600	41340
USSR[c]	45000	45000	47790	52920	62100	66600	71370	75600
Yugoslavia[c]	23001	40039	52020	90032	100001	144324	319420	654490
East European total								
Others								
Cyprus[c]	25	46	56	67	75	104	126	141
Gibraltar[c]	4	4	4	4	5	5	5	5
Malta	16	24	24	21	21	23	28	30
Monaco	52	59	68	75	85	92	100	107
Turkey[c]	66300	149695	256187	364056	515389	790295	970785	1185360
Total								
European total								

Table No: 1108 (cont'd)

EXPENDITURE ON CLOTHING

Consumer Expenditure on Clothing 1977-1991

National currencies (millions)

	1987	1988	1989	1990	1991	% growth 1977-1991	% share 1991	Total $ million 1991	$ per capita 1991
EC members									
Belgium	182022	220995	245550	254160	261773	172.96	2.08	7666	764
Denmark	19100	19307	19235	19980	21144	145.71	0.90	3306	642
France	216302	191300	200230	212244	219770	117.47	10.58	38952	689
Germany: East	19510	21001	21885	18654	19960	32.03	3.27	12028	756
Germany: West	76136	74960	76030	82801	87892	59.22	14.39	52963	846
Greece	471874	578747	687161	824593	989512	1433.70	1.47	5429	535
Ireland	684	690	765	793	822	265.22	0.36	1328	378
Italy[a]	42344	54558	59743	64395	68902	648.77	15.09	55539	960
Luxembourg	8158	8447	8736	9450	9831	124.25	0.08	288	768
Netherlands	13499	14008	14072	14976	15879	73.74	2.31	8493	566
Portugal	189182	214556	223749	265614	298315	842.57	0.56	2065	199
Spain	1409677	1577429	1744002	2166740	2296744	473.04	6.00	22103	568
United Kingdom	14599	15736	16533	17157	17386	214.96	8.36	30761	536
EC total							65.45	240919	702
EFTA members									
Austria	74169	72932	75093	79375	81050	96.20	1.89	6942	902
Finland	8366	10584	11371	11591	10607	246.42	0.71	2623	528
Iceland[b]	11709	13158	14636	17080	19106	6772.54	0.09	324	1267
Liechtenstein	34	35	36	39	41	98.72	0.01	31	1026
Norway	18062	18354	18219	20750	21479	203.04	0.90	3313	779
Sweden	31012	35802	37872	39516	44277	228.27	1.99	7321	852
Switzerland	6050	6195	6440	6711	7178	86.45	1.36	5006	747
EFTA total							6.94	25560	791
Eastern Europe									
Albania[c]	3752	4090	4103	1477		79.04	0.06	231	72
Bulgaria[c]	1537	1586	1698	803		-19.06	0.10	383	43
Czechoslovakia	23500	23200	21200	23382	22224	25.01	0.20	754	48
Hungary	54441	52222	51289	43940	50421	117.67	0.18	675	64
Poland	794344	1357000	4947712	30469631	49128786	38281.86	1.26	4645	122
Romania[c]	41600	41846	40203	48451		55.59	0.59	2160	93
USSR[c]	79050	82371	87633	52580		16.84	23.81	87633	308
Yugoslavia[c]	1496200	4257870	60715540	137609897		598177.89	0.33	1216	51
East European total							26.54	97696	240
Others									
Cyprus[c]	151	181	204	231		809.00	0.14	505	691
Gibraltar[c]	5	6	6	7		90.15	0.00	13	427
Malta	32	33	36	43	45	179.89	0.04	140	394
Monaco	114	120	130	138	144	176.30	0.01	26	915
Turkey[c]	1647000	2899042	5024453	8515822		12744.38	0.89	3265	58
Total							1.07	3947	69
European total							100.0	368122	438

Sources: National accounts/Euromonitor
Notes: See end of section

Table No: 1109

EXPENDITURE ON FOOTWEAR

Consumer Expenditure on Footwear 1977-1991

National currencies (millions)

	1977	1980	1981	1982	1983	1984	1985	1986
EC members								
Belgium	19976	26270	28550	31319	32034	35279	38343	38989
Denmark	1581	2053	2010	2138	2157	2223	2335	2547
France	16010	23532	26204	29842	32041	33681	36060	39501
Germany: East	3075	3459	3587	3587	3715	3844	4100	4228
Germany: West	9930	14862	15257	15143	15612	16048	16754	17380
Greece	7288	11324	13278	16009	16396	21433	27800	35555
Ireland	26	90	115	108	111	114	126	143
Italy[a]	2100	4486	4875	6780	8020	9500	11131	12122
Luxembourg	496	596	649	684	748	757	824	847
Netherlands	3240	3740	3560	3690	3790	3960	4140	4210
Portugal	9827	18938	23606	33501	29100	34000	40100	53230
Spain	126274	200500	217900	240400	258400	333000	470805	535598
United Kingdom	1110	1761	1853	2068	2314	2525	2766	2999
EC total								
EFTA members								
Austria	11261	14100	13400	15290	16310	17250	17770	19450
Finland	645	799	861	1025	971	1062	1277	1355
Iceland[b]								
Liechtenstein	4	5	5	5	5	6	6	6
Norway	1507	2031	2207	2279	2438	2635	2972	3406
Sweden	2010	2871	3099	3348	3657	4038	4915	5475
Switzerland	1005	1041	1104	1119	1161	1187	1246	1520
EFTA total								
Eastern Europe								
Albania[c]	124	236	243	265	309	362	410	430
Bulgaria[c]	278	315	327	351	375	399	424	508
Czechoslovakia	2762	3279	3452	3538	3711	3797	3797	3884
Hungary	4348	5017	5519	5603	6188	6774	8028	8272
Poland	21700	31300	33500	49000	89600	101600	138553	182355
Romania[c]	5160	5940	6060	5520	6960	7860	8580	9660
USSR[c]	11200	11160	12780	12690	14130	15120	15480	16290
Yugoslavia[c]	10700	19800	26400	35600	51800	95994	160200	348550
East European total								
Others								
Cyprus[c]	6	8	7	7	8	8	9	10
Gibraltar[c]	1	1	1	1	1	1	1	1
Malta[c]	2	5	5	5	5	4	5	6
Monaco[c]	8	12	14	16	17	18	20	21
Turkey[c]	16900	65866	98879	133487	185878	344856	437805	580800
Total								
European total								

Table No: 1109 (cont'd)

EXPENDITURE ON FOOTWEAR

Consumer Expenditure on Footwear 1977-1991

National currencies (millions)

	1987	1988	1989	1990	1991	% growth 1977-1991	% share 1991	Total $ million 1991	$ per capita 1991
EC members									
Belgium	39362	39155	47448	49112	50583	153.22	1.52	1481	148
Denmark	2600	2760	2750	2856	3023	91.18	0.49	473	92
France	43389	45801	39226	41580	43054	168.92	7.84	7631	135
Germany: East	4487	4747	4935	5154	5515	79.36	3.41	3323	209
Germany: West	17914	19873	21099	22959	24370	145.42	15.08	14685	235
Greece	47630	59704	70888	85066	102079	1300.65	0.58	560	55
Ireland	155	163	208	225	198	675.28	0.33	319	91
Italy[a]	13383	16317	17812	19198	20542	878.20	17.01	16558	286
Luxembourg	879	911	938	945	974	96.33	0.03	29	76
Netherlands	4380	4488	4578	4828	4953	52.86	2.72	2649	176
Portugal	58210	66017	70894	82106	92215	838.38	0.66	638	61
Spain	596121	866448	957943	1190144	1261553	899.06	12.47	12141	312
United Kingdom	3088	3192	3357	3545	3619	226.04	6.58	6403	112
EC total							68.71	66891	195
EFTA members									
Austria	20026	20006	19872	21005	22330	98.29	1.96	1912	248
Finland	1448	1977	2082	2304	2109	226.97	0.54	522	105
Iceland[b]									
Liechtenstein	6	6	6	7	7	66.26	0.01	5	172
Norway	3897	4089	3930	4477	4634	207.50	0.73	715	168
Sweden	5841	6834	6728	7370	8258	310.82	1.40	1365	159
Switzerland	1565	1575	1530	1594	1688	67.97	1.21	1177	176
EFTA total							5.85	5697	176
Eastern Europe									
Albania[c]	458	484	478	287		131.73	0.05	45	14
Bulgaria[c]	533	558	597	283		1.49	0.14	135	15
Czechoslovakia	4279	4711	4920	5258	5406	95.76	0.19	183	12
Hungary	9422	9635	15963	19211	21612	397.02	0.30	289	27
Poland	226955	345300	1000000	6988448	13976895	64309.66	1.36	1322	35
Romania[c]	10400	11193	10686	12879		149.60	0.59	574	25
USSR[c]	17850	19492	20177	12106		8.09	20.73	20177	71
Yugoslavia[c]	803330	2443570	34735550	78727052		735666.84	0.71	696	29
East European total							24.06	23421	57
Others									
Cyprus[c]	11	13	15	17		175.55	0.04	38	51
Gibraltar[c]	1	1	1	1		70.37	0.00	3	88
Malta[c]	8	9	10	12	12	652.68	0.04	38	108
Monaco[c]	24	26	28	30	31	276.74	0.01	6	198
Turkey[c]	732000	1168727	1942733	3286322		19346.05	1.29	1260	22
Total							1.38	1344	24
European total							100.00	97352	116

Sources: National accounts/Euromonitor
Notes: See end of section

Table No: 1110

EXPENDITURE ON HOUSING

Consumer Expenditure on Housing 1977-1991

National currencies (millions)

	1977	1978	1979	1980	1981	1982	1983	1984	1985	1986
EC members										
Belgium	167755	187187	205350	228050	258752	285313	313481	341095	365970	387100
Denmark	27858	31781	35478	39359	43447	48761	54234	59061	63281	67495
France	112550	127277	147114	172780	203612	232297	263750	292864	322202	338986
Germany: East	1000	1153	1409	1537	2050	2050	2178	2434	2691	3075
Germany: West	81590	85990	97170	104430	111420	119270	135000	150090	159340	166240
Greece	61469	76010	93203	114624	140414	173505	192990	242237	347132	390611
Ireland	210	204	275	327	387	462	505	560	625	669
Italy[a]	14600	17018	19050	24018	28381	33426	40213	49557	54857	61242
Luxembourg	7805	8318	8857	9549	10405	11452	12960	14385	15600	16569
Netherlands	15010	16590	19970	22100	24500	26900	30740	32150	32150	32834
Portugal[b]	31807	49614	68985	94690	118030	167503	210000	230000	250000	300000
Spain	756875	900681	1101100	1469900	1649200	1890000	2094100	2295200	2313945	2439620
United Kingdom	9978	11358	13353	16048	19445	22236	23525	25012	26922	30147
EC total										
EFTA members										
Austria	48000	60000	73760	87340	97466	112987	125215	139920	144257	151000
Finland	10979	12150	13392	14992	17740	20142	22799	22294	23324	24500
Iceland[b]	406	612	856	1391	2224	3493	7654	9469	12754	13984
Liechtenstein	51	54	57	59	63	72	80	93	98	100
Norway	10071	11379	12320	13864	16036	18484	21138	23623	25766	29270
Sweden	35948	41577	46292	51394	66857	74332	81073	88050	92510	101048
Switzerland	12505	12705	12970	13360	14175	15750	16885	17580	18425	19440
EFTA total										
Eastern Europe										
Albania[c]	330	437	442	493	525	857	982	1107	1253	1350
Bulgaria[c]	278	290	290	303	327	351	375	399	412	436
Czechoslovakia	7249	7077	7249	7594	8630	8630	9148	9148	9148	9493
Hungary	11540	12293	13296	14216	15721	16223	18397	20070	22746	25171
Poland	36600	40100	48100	66700	76900	101700	300500	561007	731628	902333
Romania[c]	7980	8220	8400	8640	8880	9060	9240	9660	9840	10080
USSR[c]	9200	9600	9900	9180	10710	11070	13410	13950	14670	15390
Yugoslavia[c]	8313	8586	13090	18587	22752	30061	41754	73445	154590	304010
East European total										
Others										
Cyprus[c]	18	28	28	33	36	50	53	56	60	62
Gibraltar[b,c]	5	5	6	6	7	7	7	7	8	8
Malta	8	9	14	17	17	15	15	14	15	16
Monaco	58	66	75	92	107	122	143	158	175	185
Turkey[c]	42403	142296	275153	209573	328099	473273	684369	1178258	1617975	2138400
Total										
European total										

Table No: 1110 (cont'd)

EXPENDITURE ON HOUSING

Consumer Expenditure on Housing 1977-1991

National currencies (millions)

	1987	1988	1989	1990	1991	% growth 1977-1991	% share 1991	Total $ million 1991	$ per capita 1991
EC members									
Belgium	412713	435750	461757	482727	497187	196.38	2.29	14560	1451
Denmark	73011	79123	85291	90591	93305	23493	2.30	14588	2835
France	368003	415555	445948	472705	499354	343.67	13.93	88505	1565
Germany: East	3122	3159	3218	6200	8250	725.00	0.78	4971	313
Germany: West	188800	232202	253191	280019	297234	264.30	28.19	179110	2863
Greece	555853	721095	856174	1027408	1232890	1905.71	1.06	6764	666
Ireland	698	744	707	754	782	272.33	0.20	1263	359
Italy[a]	66616	73227	79084	87564	92817	535.74	11.77	74817	1293
Luxembourg	17538	18507	19572	20169	20774	166.16	0.10	608	1622
Netherlands	33012	32835	34355	34171	35403	135.86	2.98	18935	1261
Portugal[b]	336323	381432	426541	482858	558739	1656.65	0.61	3867	372
Spain	2566038	2727577	3001573	3729140	3952889	422.26	5.99	38041	977
United Kingdom	32777	36508	40295	39328	43729	338.25	12.18	77369	1347
EC total							82.37	523399	1526
EFTA members									
Austria	155050	136400	143969	153502	163181	239.96	2.20	13976	1816
Finland	28554	30917	33824	38053	39691	261.52	1.54	9815	1974
Iceland[b]	19515	17406	19625	22676	25365	6147.46	0.07	430	1682
Liechtenstein	104	109	108	119	126	147.09	0.01	94	3146
Norway	31555	33477	37345	40597	42863	325.61	1.04	6612	1554
Sweden	110091	111672	121018	139147	157470	338.05	4.10	26039	3030
Switzerland	20375	21335	22510	24835	26565	112.43	2.92	18525	2765
EFTA total							11.88	75490	2335
Eastern Europe									
Albania[c]	1464	1579	1578	947		186.99	0.02	148	46
Bulgaria[c]	447	458	466	287		2.93	0.02	136	15
Czechoslovakia	9756	10018	11000	11657	14133	94.95	0.08	479	31
Hungary	29797	36414	40040	64421	86968	653.62	0.18	1164	110
Poland	1279100	1996600	7279737	18540063	30713075	83815.51	0.46	2904	76
Romania[c]	10400	10726	10178	15946		99.82	0.11	711	31
USSR[c]	16473	17571	18112	14127		53.56	3.71	23545	83
Yugoslavia[c]	1102615	3311859	47160908	106888742		1285702.27	0.15	944	40
East European total							4.73	30032	74
Others									
Cyprus[c]	66	79	86	97		435.66	0.03	213	292
Gibraltar[b,c]	8	8	8	10		89.76	0.00	18	587
Malta	17	17	19	23	24	192.94	0.01	74	208
Monaco	197	210	226	241	252	332.41	0.01	45	1594
Turkey[c]	3001200	5336034	9334749	16150833		37989.03	0.97	6191	111
Total							1.03	6541	114
European total							100.00	635462	756

Sources: National accounts/Euromonitor
Notes: See end of section

Table No: 1111

EXPENDITURE ON FUEL

Consumer Expenditure on Fuel 1977-1991

National currencies (millions)

	1977	1980	1981	1982	1983	1984	1985	1986
EC members								
Belgium	91497	138347	161400	179304	184544	202797	229089	190381
Denmark	8366	16473	18878	20459	19243	19655	21508	23294
France	52562	93994	108964	125469	144501	159389	177287	186522
Germany: East	769	1153	1537	1666	1666	1666	1666	1409
Germany: West	29050	40300	45550	52910	54490	59740	64340	55900
Greece	15900	28976	41554	51789	66146	83025	94789	101838
Ireland	197	350	442	503	528	562	628	644
Italy[a]	2987	9286	11733	14176	17425	20227	23732	22214
Luxembourg	3554	6711	8048	8578	9108	9979	10803	9771
Netherlands	6500	10530	11500	12770	13305	13840	15670	16004
Portugal[b]								
Spain	185500	246600	344000	400100	459700	467500	480902	540144
United Kingdom	4219	6355	7728	8696	9399	9575	10657	10061
EC total								
EFTA members								
Austria	18850	39895	41300	47020	51730	54250	56799	59200
Finland	2362	3210	3722	4078	6059	6698	7567	6657
Iceland[b]								
Liechtenstein	14	15	16	17	17	18	19	20
Norway	4205	7406	8846	10285	11570	13086	15927	18093
Sweden	8518	15484	10576	12247	13762	22142	24285	23446
Switzerland	3400	8050	8095	8105	8235	8890	9380	7625
EFTA total								
Eastern Europe								
Albania[c]	206	287	512	701	764	873	1048	1120
Bulgaria[c]	133	182	230	242	206	218	278	363
Czechoslovakia	2934	3797	4315	4660	4660	5868	6559	6386
Hungary	8362	10704	13547	13965	15805	17895	18230	17895
Poland	12500	21700	21300	75900	72700	89900	105200	135000
Romania[c]	3060	4200	5160	6180	6480	7500	4680	4680
USSR[c]	7600	9450	11700	13680	16380	16560	17370	18405
Yugoslavia[c]	22287	43069	63567	82177	112318	147210	367861	736101
East European total								
Others								
Cyprus[c]	4	9	10	12	14	16	18	19
Gibraltar								
Malta[c]	5	6	7	7	7	8	8	9
Monaco[c]	27	50	58	66	79	87	97	105
Turkey[c]	52000	164665	269670	333718	506940	862140	1027890	1399200
Total								
European total								

Table No: 1111 (cont'd)

EXPENDITURE ON FUEL

Consumer Expenditure on Fuel 1977-1991

National currencies (millions)

	1987	1988	1989	1990	1991	% growth 1977-1991	% share 1991	Total $ million 1991	$ per capita 1991
EC members									
Belgium	173997	157715	163622	165972	170944	86.83	1.99	5006	499
Denmark	25034	23576	25018	25106	25858	209.08	1.61	4043	786
France	197018	222211	249333	264293	279193	431.17	19.65	49484	875
Germany: East	1561	1723	1716	5154	6250	713.04	1.50	3766	237
Germany: West	58250	62409	66572	99738	105869	264.44	25.33	63796	1020
Greece	151071	200304	237826	285391	342469	2053.90	0.75	1879	185
Ireland	639	604	734	782	811	311.86	0.52	1309	373
Italy[a]	23618	24112	28068	31077	32942	1002.85	10.54	26553	459
Luxembourg	10000	10229	11542	12774	12894	262.79	0.15	378	1007
Netherlands	16004	16005	16257	18005	19753	203.89	4.20	10565	704
Portugal[b]									
Spain	629808	707000	765500	960564	1018198	448.89	3.89	9799	252
United Kingdom	10250	10400	10888	11050	11212	165.75	7.88	19837	345
EC total							77.99	196415	573
EFTA members									
Austria	60984	57222	60257	64716	68797	264.97	2.34	5892	766
Finland	6620	7148	7842	8965	9351	295.90	0.92	2312	465
Iceland[b]									
Liechtenstein	20	21	21	32	34	144.68	0.01	25	847
Norway	18555	21419	21508	23380	23718	464.04	1.45	3659	860
Sweden	24809	25854	28495	31632	35443	316.10	2.33	5861	682
Switzerland	7225	6770	7300	7670	7958	134.06	2.20	5550	828
EFTA total							9.25	23299	721
Eastern Europe									
Albania[c]	1220	1321	1304	782		279.22	0.05	122	38
Bulgaria[c]	410	462	600	284		113.17	0.05	135	15
Czechoslovakia	7702	8000	11000	12117	14103	380.63	0.19	478	31
Hungary	20939	20050	21587	29389	36368	334.91	0.19	487	46
Poland	176200	360400	1314042	10910978	32705935	261547.48	1.23	3092	81
Romania[c]	4836	4995	4580	5796		89.40	0.10	258	11
USSR[c]	19584	20766	21022	13244		74.26	8.76	22073	78
Yugoslavia[c]	1628863	4892519	69669523	157903824		708401.92	0.55	1395	59
East European total							11.13	28041	69
Others									
Cyprus[c]	20	24	28	32		614.82	0.03	69	95
Gibraltar									
Malta[c]	9	9	11	13	13	167.66	0.02	41	117
Monaco[c]	110	116	125	133	139	407.91	0.01	25	882
Turkey[c]	1939800	3406840	5972369	10312599		19731.92	1.57	3953	71
Total							1.62	4089	72
European total							100.00	251844	300

Sources: National accounts/Euromonitor
Notes: See end of section

Table No: 1112

EXPENDITURE ON HOUSEHOLD GOODS AND SERVICES

Consumer Expenditure on Household Goods and Services 1977-1991

National currencies (millions)

	1977	1980	1981	1982	1983	1984	1985	1986
EC members								
Belgium	260754	310803	318564	335029	341451	364200	385500	422400
Denmark	13316	15333	16049	17563	19112	20808	23097	24520
France	108898	156976	176713	202667	216449	226027	239196	254969
Germany: East	9609	10506	13709	14478	17553	18834	20756	21909
Germany: West	76760	96640	97560	97700	82090	91200	92170	95610
Greece	54231	89740	111604	135334	172267	216884	275470	334810
Ireland	270	449	470	498	589	610	721	799
Italy[a]	11560	24766	29338	32132	34730	38193	42868	48088
Luxembourg	6212	7000	8191	8741	9412	10581	11565	12203
Netherlands	17000	18590	17570	17190	15223	17511	17920	18990
Portugal	46685	84510	95000	121000	152000	162000	177000	200560
Spain	555684	810500	888200	989500	1123900	1209300	1209568	1475693
United Kingdom	6340	9956	10553	11217	12172	12999	14067	14085
EC total								
EFTA members								
Austria	43130	43230	46100	48760	51790	54250	55680	58678
Finland	4594	9931	10880	12488	13304	12312	12310	13260
Iceland	180	610	781	1261	2000	5579	7455	9674
Liechtenstein	20	28	29	29	29	30	32	34
Norway	9672	11878	13215	14099	15086	16507	19060	21633
Sweden	15381	19051	19987	21779	23521	27570	33490	37346
Switzerland	4940	6315	6550	6625	6735	6925	7125	7435
EFTA total								
Eastern Europe								
Albania[b]	797	1335	1627	1964	2509	2300	2506	2858
Bulgaria[b]	1331	1912	2663	3195	2856	3038	3147	3268
Czechoslovakia	23474	34002	40388	45221	48328	50572	51607	54369
Hungary	23164	29603	33031	34286	37296	35122	44571	50091
Poland	129600	179100	199400	283200	357100	365500	477100	530000
Romania[b]	20760	22200	22020	22200	24180	25080	25800	28200
USSR[b]	28000	29160	34560	35100	36000	34290	35910	38250
Yugoslavia[b]	43809	77622	102783	135048	178498	304043	503687	903911
East European total								
Others								
Cyprus[b]	36	61	69	82	90	96	104	112
Gibraltar[b]	4	4	4	4	5	5	5	5
Malta	24	38	36	36	35	36	34	35
Monaco	65	93	108	125	147	162	180	200
Turkey[b]	130000	299390	539340	679571	887145	1580590	1922535	2587200
Total								
European total								

Table No: 1112 (cont'd)

EXPENDITURE ON HOUSEHOLD GOODS AND SERVICES

Consumer Expenditure on Household Goods and Services 1977-1991

National currencies (millions)

	1987	1988	1989	1990	1991	% growth 1977-1991	% share 1991	Total $ million 1991	$ per capita 1991
EC members									
Belgium	443200	461814	513654	521031	536638	105.80	4.19	15715	1566
Denmark	24790	26601	26133	26592	27517	106.65	1.15	4302	836
France	267567	283165	298165	316055	327262	200.52	15.48	58004	1026
Germany: East	23412	24936	25961	31418	33617	249.85	5.41	20257	1274
Germany: West	101480	96228	104769	93340	99078	29.07	15.93	59703	954
Greece	367675	400540	475571	570685	684822	1162.79	1.00	3757	370
Ireland	840	867	955	1019	1076	298.51	0.46	1739	495
Italy[a]	55851	62212	69818	77008	82014	609.46	17.64	66108	1143
Luxembourg	12670	13138	13605	14414	14772	137.80	0.12	433	1154
Netherlands	20490	21500	22700	26022	26391	55.24	3.77	14115	940
Portugal	219904	249398	278892	332744	381259	716.66	0.70	2639	254
Spain	1624165	1774305	1965241	2490438	2587076	365.56	6.64	24897	639
United Kingdom	16250	17500	18750	18459	19496	207.50	9.20	34493	601
EC total							81.70	306162	893
EFTA members									
Austria	60984	66008	73336	80344	85410	98.03	1.95	7315	950
Finland	14800	16474	17624	17639	18398	300.49	1.21	4550	915
Iceland	14049	18424	20183	23087	25825	14247.15	0.12	438	1713
Liechtenstein	34	35	35	31	33	62.79	0.01	25	826
Norway	22773	22745	22561	23401	23981	147.94	0.99	3699	870
Sweden	37346	40667	45085	48083	49523	221.97	2.19	8189	953
Switzerland	7630	7970	8320	8670	9367	89.61	1.74	6532	975
EFTA total							8.20	30747	951
Eastern Europe									
Albania[b]	3050	3236	3239	1943		143.99	0.08	304	95
Bulgaria[b]	3372	3476	3250	1537		15.47	0.20	732	81
Czechoslovakia	54300	54800	55232	60607	54079	130.38	0.49	1834	117
Hungary	56374	56636	56459	69875	78609	239.36	0.28	1052	99
Poland	650713	1100000	4010673	12209106	20225346	15505.98	0.51	1912	50
Romania[b]	28600	28995	27990	16866		-18.76	0.20	752	32
USSR[b]	40800	43369	44723	13417		-52.08	5.97	22361	79
Yugoslavia[b]	1975924	3280684	46716977	105882587		241591.40	0.25	936	39
East European total							7.97	29883	73
Others									
Cyprus[b]	118	138	151	173		380.03	0.10	379	519
Gibraltar[b]	5	5	6	6		81.00	0.00	12	395
Malta	38	40	45	54	57	134.57	0.05	176	495
Monaco	218	236	250	266	279	329.61	0.01	49	1763
Turkey[b]	3660000	6559184	11121704	19124437		14611.11	1.96	7331	131
Total							2.12	7947	139
European total							100.00	374739	446

Sources: National accounts/Euromonitor
Notes: See end of section

Table No: 1113

EXPENDITURE ON HEALTH

Consumer Expenditure on Health Goods and Medical Services 1977-1991

National currencies (millions)

	1977	1980	1981	1982	1983	1984	1985	1986
EC members								
Belgium	183474	229713	252048	278363	304962	324787	347233	368164
Denmark	2805	3760	4176	4632	5100	5572	6001	5669
France	82352	127284	148094	169808	195354	222606	246474	270716
Germany: East	3459	3331	4100	5509	6022	6662	6662	7431
Germany: West	29268	36020	38700	40340	42550	47460	49310	51000
Greece	21096	43216	50269	58883	78012	97919	111793	120410
Ireland	69	122	116	128	147	159	165	170
Italy[a]	5906	10685	13802	17830	20681	23110	27900	31037
Luxembourg	4361	5863	6362	7043	7287	7941	8390	9070
Netherlands	17430	24830	26580	28410	29220	29790	30640	31610
Portugal	17856	37057	45556	63536	68200	81000	85000	88000
Spain	293207	394400	447700	528900	591500	662400	681002	749474
United Kingdom	732	1261	1489	1752	2064	2284	2604	2916
EC total								
EFTA members								
Austria	17730	24870	26890	28840	33300	37200	39680	40891
Finland	1844	2404	4176	4063	4832	5499	6087	6713
Iceland	90	545	861	1372	2000	2947	3891	6093
Liechtenstein	41	52	55	59	63	71	75	73
Norway	4400	5676	6387	7407	8180	8586	9298	10301
Sweden	2953	3973	4432	5034	5786	6539	7244	7878
Switzerland	9140	10660	11475	12410	13255	13960	14840	15810
EFTA total								
Eastern Europe								
Albania[b]	248	411	538	779	745	809	934	1006
Bulgaria[b]	352	469	526	596	548	581	671	800
Czechoslovakia[b]	10287	11927	13394	14550	16725	18589	19055	20885
Hungary	18648	24920	27429	29436	32111	28516	40139	40725
Poland	93500	134300	158900	190000	215050	241000	357100	478100
Romania[b]	9240	10500	10980	11520	13920	16080	16800	19020
USSR[b]	10100	9630	10890	11160	11790	12060	12420	12690
Yugoslavia[b]	10710	30787	41273	51058	71399	121553	235997	431488
East European total								
Others								
Cyprus[b]	5	10	12	16	19	20	21	22
Gibraltar[b]	2	4	4	4	4	4	4	5
Malta	8	11	10	12	13	13	13	15
Monaco	54	91	106	123	144	159	177	193
Turkey[b]	8219	91564	119664	164442	263563	937749	2541496	5448807
Total								
European total								

Table No: 1113 (cont'd)

EXPENDITURE ON HEALTH

Consumer Expenditure on Health Goods and Medical Services 1977-1991

National currencies (millions)

	1987	1988	1989	1990	1991	% growth 1977-1991	% share 1991	Total $ million 1991	$ per capita 1991
EC members									
Belgium	387438	409833	438381	458290	472017	157.27	4.94	13823	1378
Denmark	6933	7454	7664	7860	8095	188.61	0.45	1266	246
France	285316	313027	340325	360745	384855	367.33	24.39	68211	1206
Germany: East	7804	8169	8582	10309	11031	218.87	2.38	6647	418
Germany: West	53160	52298	56386	60219	63921	118.40	13.78	38518	616
Greece	221293	322177	382528	459034	550841	2511.12	1.08	3022	298
Ireland	173	182	202	217	226	228.81	0.13	364	104
Italy[a]	36362	41878	46207	51168	56234	852.14	16.21	45328	784
Luxembourg	9750	10430	11110	11307	11647	167.06	0.12	341	909
Netherlands	32320	33240	34460	37310	39901	128.92	7.63	21341	1421
Portugal	113186	128367	143548	162423	184263	931.94	0.46	1275	123
Spain	824184	933909	1086729	1350147	1431156	388.10	4.93	13773	354
United Kingdom	3375	3600	3825	4044	4357	495.18	2.76	7708	134
EC total							79.26	221618	646
EFTA members									
Austria	43424	46557	49200	52670	55991	215.80	1.71	4795	623
Finland	7526	8667	9477	10616	12172	560.10	1.08	3010	605
Iceland	8326	10181	11575	13374	14960	16521.82	0.09	254	992
Liechtenstein	73	72	74	79	84	104.62	0.02	63	2097
Norway	11203	12105	11922	13664	14285	224.66	0.79	2204	518
Sweden	8571	9638	10393	10785	12082	309.14	0.71	1998	232
Switzerland	16780	17710	18865	20445	22908	150.64	5.71	15975	2384
EFTA total							10.12	28298	875
Eastern Europe						189.87	0.04	112	35
Albania[b]	1098	1191	1196	717		-6.06	0.06	158	18
Bulgaria[b]	820	840	700	331		144.53	0.50	1401	90
Czechoslovakia[b]	20090	20500	22500	25155	66322	255.65	0.32	887	84
Hungary	48320	49238	50647	59548	25507834	27181.11	0.86	2412	63
Poland	593200	1275900	4652016	11041747		112.40	0.31	875	38
Romania[b]	20176	21394	20356	19626		-10.02	5.42	15146	53
USSR[b]	13515	14344	15146	9088		921126.14	0.31	872	37
Yugoslavia[b]	889044	3057001	4351729	98663320			7.82	21863	54
East European total									
Others									
Cyprus[b]	24	29	31	37		642.53	0.03	81	111
Gibraltar[b]	5	5	5	6		154.18	0.00	11	360
Malta	15	15	17	20	21	158.95	0.02	65	184
Monaco	221	252	276	293	307	464.06	0.02	54	1943
Turkey[b]	5490000	7007464	11692849	19895385		241954.19	2.73	7627	136
Total							2.80	7838	137
European total							100.00	279618	333

Sources: National accounts/Euromonitor
Notes: See end of section

Table No: 1114

EXPENDITURE ON TRANSPORT

Consumer Expenditure on Transport 1977-1991

National currencies (millions)

	1977	1980	1981	1982	1983	1984	1985	1986
EC members								
Belgium	194686	256125	275821	302172	328447	351596	372493	364571
Denmark	22872	27515	30103	34376	40598	46059	48666	51233
France	175555	232904	256195	281814	309995	340995	376666	421222
Germany: East[a]	2370	2819	3075	3203	3459	3587	3715	3972
Germany: West	90088	114808	120263	123851	131862	135513	139776	145035
Greece	75759	126099	160818	207700	240560	301840	340265	379451
Ireland	482	782	945	1011	1057	1169	1253	1221
Italy[a,b]	12948	25538	31761	37511	47966	54958	59035	63629
Luxembourg[a]	8740	13359	15454	17878	18916	20028	21282	22065
Netherlands	15870	16700	18670	20990	22718	24130	22900	23388
Portugal	55981	115802	153549	219482	243300	299200	368800	372542
Spain	734400	1320900	1505100	1701400	2016600	2256700	2497620	2837455
United Kingdom	11455	20300	22765	24538	27577	28966	31866	34826
EC total								
EFTA members								
Austria	66560	83450	91378	95030	103656	108577	113680	120500
Finland[a]	11114	17628	20384	23715	25501	28806	30918	32134
Iceland[a]	480	1095	1446	2414	4100	6919	6725	8390
Liechtenstein[a]	42	54	59	60	60	66	68	72
Norway	14328	18389	20799	23619	25711	36356	37037	42758
Sweden[a]	20485	39325	44413	51616	55792	61039	68835	77379
Switzerland[a]	10540	12755	13925	14240	14400	14770	15310	15800
EFTA total								
Eastern Europe								
Albania[a,c]	413	698	768	935	1091	1384	1822	2000
Bulgaria[a,c]	944	1380	1501	1501	1501	1513	1586	1755
Czechoslovakia	11737	15534	19849	21748	21748	21230	21575	24509
Hungary[a]	20906	28014	30857	33031	36794	40139	55275	66899
Poland	87800	131100	166600	240900	370800	399900	420000	590600
Romania[a,c]	10380	14400	14520	15000	15780	17100	18120	20220
USSR[a,c]	9900	10170	10800	11250	12060	12690	13230	13770
Yugoslavia[a,c]	47685	100303	138797	177042	243843	355037	629891	993528
East European total								
Others								
Cyprus[c]	68	106	111	119	132	137	146	155
Gibraltar[c]	4	5	5	5	5	5	6	6
Malta	28	51	51	51	51	51	58	60
Monaco	61	83	95	113	127	130	145	154
Turkey[c]	156000	353280	539340	740247	1013880	1436900	1713150	2112000
Total								
European total								

Table No: 1114 (cont'd)

EXPENDITURE ON TRANSPORT

Consumer Expenditure on Transport 1977-1991

National currencies (millions)

	1987	1988	1989	1990	1991	% growth 1977-1991	% share 1991	Total $ million 1991	$ per capita 1991
EC members									
Belgium	393077	423619	460090	471460	485582	149.42	2.30	14220	1417
Denmark	54333	58682	60053	62597	64472	181.88	1.63	10080	1959
France	471288	498297	540079	572484	610746	247.89	17.48	108248	1914
Germany: East[a]	4097	4212	7200	36818	39395	1562.07	3.83	23739	1493
Germany: West	152300	179207	165520	184421	195759	117.30	19.04	117962	1885
Greece	410874	454511	525149	630179	756215	898.18	0.67	4149	409
Ireland	1241	1371	1743	1889	1660	244.78	0.43	2682	764
Italy[a,b]	70634	76171	84437	90642	97894	656.05	12.74	78909	1364
Luxembourg[a]	23272	24479	26065	27733	29994	243.18	0.14	878	2342
Netherlands	24825	21774	26370	27678	30511	92.25	2.63	16319	1087
Portugal	420404	476790	496166	594425	674351	1104.61	0.75	4667	449
Spain	3410371	3858710	4392025	5456632	5784030	687.59	8.99	55664	1429
United Kingdom	37000	39000	45672	44279	46765	308.25	13.36	82740	1441
EC total							83.99	520258	1517
EFTA members									
Austria	123615	125555	127822	139205	147983	122.33	2.05	12674	1647
Finland[a]	36198	41965	47003	47484	46534	318.70	1.86	11507	2314
Iceland[a]	11059	13256	15090	17785	19893	4044.45	0.05	337	1319
Liechtenstein[a]	72	71	70	78	82	98.00	0.01	61	2047
Norway	40006	35379	35162	36460	37741	163.41	0.94	5822	1369
Sweden[a]	90534	106880	111221	117153	131267	540.80	3.50	21706	2526
Switzerland[a]	16355	17155	18800	20070	22488	113.36	2.53	15682	2341
EFTA total							10.94	67789	2097
Eastern Europe									
Albania[a,c]	2135	2266	2273	1364		230.68	0.03	213	67
Bulgaria[a,c]	1845	1937	1900	899		-4.80	0.07	428	48
Czechoslovakia	24674	25890	30000	32100	29576	152.00	0.16	1003	64
Hungary[a]	72480	73355	74725	90632	99922	377.96	0.22	1337	126
Poland	823500	1404400	5120536	7200000	9860565	11130.71	0.15	932	24
Romania[a,c]	20800	21389	20865	22631		118.02	0.16	1009	43
USSR[a,c]	14790	15831	16479	11865		19.84	3.19	19774	70
Yugoslavia[a,c]	1829338	5494675	78244234	177338141		371795.02	0.25	1567	66
East European total							4.24	26264	64
Others									
Cyprus[c]	167	201	227	266		288.73	0.09	581	
Gibraltar[c]	6	6	6	7		72.05	0.00	13	422
Malta	65	67	76	90	95	237.69	0.05	293	825
Monaco	166	178	191	203	212	247.64	0.01	38	1345
Turkey[c]	2562000	3937150	6529871	10885159		6877.67	0.67	4173	74
Total							0.82	5098	89
European total							100.00	619408	737

Sources: National accounts/Euromonitor
Notes: See end of section

Table No: 1115

EXPENDITURE ON COMMUNICATIONS

Consumer Expenditure on Communications 1977-1991

National currencies (millions)	1977	1980	1981	1982	1983	1984	1985	1986
EC members								
Belgium	14499	19568	20913	23177	25143	27271	29158	30544
Denmark	1962	2714	3353	3830	4099	4200	4310	4677
France	9726	18391	21576	25409	28526	36666	51500	55256
Germany: East[a]								
Germany: West	10363	13172	13798	14209	15128	15547	16036	16645
Greece	9364	16124	20563	28880	31030	39055	48932	48900
Ireland	21	42	63	66	86	108	137	154
Italy[b]	967	1947	2564	3196	3355	3550	5123	6398
Luxembourg[a]								
Netherlands	1980	2450	2610	2750	2892	3080	3190	3260
Portugal	19168	39028	54030	70000	80000	88000	99000	105000
Spain	48600	88100	106700	123300	141600	160500	163685	176024
United Kingdom	1244	2247	2793	3101	3182	3527	3940	4256
EC total								
EFTA members								
Austria	9000	13670	14281	16909	16203	16427	18145	16169
Finland[a]								
Iceland[a]								
Liechtenstein[a]								
Norway	1307	1831	2287	2883	3477	3908	4300	4378
Sweden[a]								
Switzerland[a]								
EFTA total								
Eastern Europe								
Albania[a]								
Bulgaria[a]								
Czechoslovakia[a]								
Hungary[a]								
Poland	5000	8600	9100	11800	16600	19900	29000	39300
Romania[a]								
USSR[a]								
Yugoslavia[a]								
East European total								
Others								
Cyprus[a]								
Gibraltar[a]								
Malta[a]								
Monaco[a]								
Turkey[a]								
Total								
European total								

Table No: 1115 (cont'd)

EXPENDITURE ON COMMUNICATIONS

Consumer Expenditure on Communications 1977-1991

National currencies (millions)

	1987	1988	1989	1990	1991	% growth 1977-1991	% share 1991	Total $ million 1991	$ per capita 1991
EC members									
Belgium	32333	35366	38400	40143	41346	185.16	1.91	1211	121
Denmark	5091	5612	5855	6103	6286	220.37	1.55	983	191
France	73311	77513	78258	82953	86762	792.07	24.31	15378	272
Germany: East[a]									
Germany: West	17914	21268	22191	22582	23970	131.31	22.83	14444	231
Greece	53642	59996	69321	83185	99822	966.02	0.87	548	54
Ireland	173	187	180	192	199	841.77	0.51	321	91
Italy[b]	7038	7471	8005	8594	9281	859.77	11.82	7481	129
Luxembourg[a]									
Netherlands	3486	3596	3850	3880	4113	107.71	3.48	2200	146
Portugal	97016	110029	139843	163884	185920	869.95	2.03	1287	124
Spain	214221	269638	293586	368397	390501	703.50	5.94	3758	96
United Kingdom	4575	4700	4886	5166	5565	347.36	15.56	9846	171
EC total							90.82	57456	168
EFTA members									
Austria	16482	15434	16993	18507	19674	118.60	2.66	1685	219
Finland[a]									
Iceland[a]									
Liechtenstein[a]									
Norway	5110	5442	4954	5266	5451	317.08	1.33	841	198
Sweden[a]									
Switzerland[a]									
EFTA total							3.99	2526	
Eastern Europe									
Albania[a]									
Bulgaria[a]									
Czechoslovakia[a]									
Hungary[a]									
Poland	41832	50300	183397	3574844	34725731	694414.61	5.19	3283	86
Romania[a]									
USSR[a]									
Yugoslavia[a]									
East European total							5.19	3283	
Others									
Cyprus[a]									
Gibraltar[a]									
Malta[a]									
Monaco[a]									
Turkey[a]									
Total									
European total							100.00	63266	

Sources: National accounts/Euromonitor
Notes: See end of section

Table No: 1116

EXPENDITURE ON LEISURE AND EDUCATION

Consumer Expenditure on Leisure and Education 1977-1991

National currencies (millions)

	1977	1980	1981	1982	1983	1984	1985	1986
EC members								
Belgium	155756	194417	214000	237200	257400	279300	298700	312900
Denmark	15321	18992	21407	23936	26383	29608	32440	35353
France	80960	119956	137310	160177	173581	188423	201960	220494
Germany: East	4228	6022	8072	8840	9225	11018	11146	11531
Germany: West	70000	84090	87523	89900	92300	95810	98980	103950
Greece	29189	52917	59906	67830	89271	112051	127928	160430
Ireland	351	619	780	750	830	904	1008	1088
Italy[a]	9010	15343	19000	22495	30212	35499	41433	47591
Luxembourg	2410	2707	2930	3457	3833	4193	4336	4729
Netherlands	14490	20050	20300	20500	20830	21950	22590	23510
Portugal[b]	21773	39671	49546	50000	60000	75000	82000	90000
Spain	562000	708400	813600	943800	1076100	1194800	1266177	1475477
United Kingdom	8073	12727	14031	15412	16651	18013	19593	24262
EC total								
EFTA members								
Austria	30120	34940	37780	38460	41430	37390	39560	40962
Finland	5314	8158	9925	10750	12576	16841	16908	18789
Iceland						4214	6184	8021
Liechtenstein[b]	35	44	47	50	52	58	70	79
Norway	9048	11626	13403	14488	15882	17572	20196	23861
Sweden[b]	19978	26469	29626	32201	34871	38430	41058	46076
Switzerland	8395	9925	10700	11315	11870	12345	13325	14020
EFTA total								
Eastern Europe								
Albania[b]	413	657	832	1013	1164	1171	1367	1500
Bulgaria[b]	944	1162	1283	1331	1452	1513	1634	1694
Czechoslovakia	10183	12082	12945	13118	13635	13808	14326	14671
Hungary	32530	45491	51679	56195	59875	65226	79861	83624
Poland	45000	55662	60422	99200	110000	135493	134273	200250
Romania[b]	23340	26040	26940	26460	26460	27720	28260	29700
USSR[b]	19700	19170	22680	22860	25470	34110	35910	39600
Yugoslavia[b]	17901	33407	45275	59367	82464	127738	170025	475634
East European total								
Others								
Cyprus[b]	16	37	46	52	52	50	53	54
Gibraltar[b]	4	4	4	4	5	5	5	5
Malta	14	22	23	23	21	23	21	25
Monaco	42	61	69	78	90	97	102	109
Turkey[b]	37794	149695	179780	242704	236988	259560	331320	420000
Total								
European total								

Table No: 1116 (cont'd)

EXPENDITURE ON LEISURE AND EDUCATION

Consumer Expenditure on Leisure and Education 1977-1991

National currencies (millions)

	1987	1988	1989	1990	1991	% growth 1977-1991	% share 1991	Total $ million 1991	$ per capita 1991
EC members									
Belgium	333200	361980	379974	393297	405078	160.07	2.69	11862	1182
Denmark	36048	37545	40383	44174	45497	196.96	1.61	7113	1382
France	236089	252986	270700	286942	300118	270.70	12.05	53193	940
Germany: East	12291	12997	13323	23809	25475	502.54	3.48	15351	965
Germany: West	108866	119588	128778	137752	146220	108.89	19.96	88111	1408
Greece	230109	299787	355945	427134	512561	1656.01	0.64	2812	277
Ireland	1226	1374	1336	1424	1491	325.27	0.55	2408	686
Italy[a]	51599	59289	67530	75909	78414	770.30	14.32	63207	1093
Luxembourg	5122	5515	5908	6325	6515	170.31	0.04	191	509
Netherlands	24640	25740	27180	29100	29385	102.80	3.56	15717	1047
Portugal[b]	113186	128367	143548	170325		682.28	0.27	1195	115
Spain	1607772	1750461	1934498	2427445	2547361	353.27	5.55	24515	629
United Kingdom	25000	26500	28000	29102	30428	276.91	12.19	53836	938
EC total							76.89	339510	990
EFTA members									
Austria	43424	53686	55698	58522	62212	106.55	1.21	5328	692
Finland	20659	22392	25236	27603	25262	375.38	1.41	6247	1256
Iceland	10798	13575	16352	18894	21134		0.08	358	1402
Liechtenstein[b]	80	80	82	88	94	170.04	0.02	70	2329
Norway	25896	27701	28262	30107	30853	240.99	1.08	4759	1119
Sweden[b]	50622	54716	59969	63918	71604	258.42	2.68	11840	1378
Switzerland	14695	15430	16530	17555	19670	134.31	3.11	13717	2047
EFTA total							9.58	42319	1309
Eastern Europe									
Albania[b]	1617	1738	1711	1026		148.83	0.04	160	50
Bulgaria[b]	1742	1793	1600	757		-19.83	0.08	360	40
Czechoslovakia	14977	15403	15715	17237	16717	64.16	0.13	567	36
Hungary	96640	100050	112500	139233	156637	381.52	0.47	2096	198
Poland	226400	1450000	5286797	32775819	65551638	145570.31	1.40	6198	162
Romania[b]	30160	30740	32570	39251		68.17	0.40	1750	75
USSR[b]	42330	44820	46216	27729		40.76	10.47	46216	163
Yugoslavia[b]	1052496	3161320	45017230	102030163		569869.07	0.20	901	38
East European total							13.19	58249	143
Others									
Cyprus[b]	54	64	73	83		415.15	0.04	183	250
Gibraltar[b]	5	6	6	6		70.60	0.00	12	396
Malta	27	27	31	37	39	182.00	0.03	121	341
Monaco	116	123	132	141	147	247.20	0.01	26	930
Turkey[b]	555000	974738	1688184	2883516		7529.59	0.25	1105	20
Total							0.33	1447	25
European total							100.00	441526	525

Sources: National accounts/Euromonitor
Notes: See end of section

Table No: 1117

EXPENDITURE ON HOTELS AND RESTAURANTS

Consumer Expenditure on Hotels and Restaurants 1977-1989

National currencies (millions)	1977	1978	1979	1980	1981	1982	1983	1984	1985
EC members									
Belgium			85963	95759	70190	74330	79380	82070	90060
Denmark	7719	8327	9336	9738	10788	12486	13509	14923	16210
France	77554	87126	100294	117956	136379	156880	177288	192472	207273
Germany: East									
Germany: West									
Greece	34810	40932	51634	61481	78437	89201	113414	142355	165525
Ireland									
Italy[a]	9058	10461	12959	15899	19647	24263	27773	31502	36000
Luxembourg									
Netherlands	4230	4620	5080	9660	10050	10560	10880	11610	11980
Portugal	37689	49232	66142	77288	92917	123409	140000	154400	151000
Spain	746086	891573	1062200	1178800	1422900	1755800	2052500	2300500	2670700
United Kingdom	4955	5605	6765	7970	8239	8837	10278	11215	12339
EC total									
EFTA members									
Austria	49550	53190	57970	63630	70190	74330	79380	82070	90060
Finland	4107	4782	5600	6495	7458	8477			
Iceland									
Liechtenstein									
Norway	3958	4240	4560	5150	6042	6960	8009	9148	10865
Sweden	6521	6830	7406	8253	8591	12683	18770	20272	22907
Switzerland									
Eastern Europe									
Albania									
Bulgaria									
Czechoslovakia									
Hungary									
Poland				30500	30700	44600			
Romania									
USSR									
Yugoslavia									
Others									
Cyprus						70	89	112	
Gibraltar									
Malta									
Monaco									
Turkey									

Table No: 1117 (cont'd)

EXPENDITURE ON HOTELS AND RESTAURANTS

Consumer Expenditure on Hotels and Restaurants 1977-1989

National currencies (millions)

	1986	1987	1988	1989	% growth 1977-1989	% share 1989	Total $ million 1989	$ per capita 1989
EC members								
Belgium	94441	93772	101871	109971		1.61	2791	279
Denmark	18992	19188	20149	20521	165.86	1.62	2811	547
France	229801	233015	245966	271227	249.73	24.44	42379	750
Germany: East								
Germany: West								
Greece	249342	247075	291984	304819	775.67	1.08	1876	187
Ireland								
Italy[a]	50568	51772	61900	72028	695.19	30.28	52494	911
Luxembourg								
Netherlands	12676	12623	13198	13773	225.62	3.78	6558	440
Portugal	194032	187564	212721	237878	531.16	0.87	1510	145
Spain	3275860	3509850	3851965	4194080	462.14	20.43	35422	900
United Kingdom	14625	14750	15635	16520	233.40	15.88	27533	479
EC total						100.00	173378	504
EFTA members								
Austria								
Finland								
Iceland								
Liechtenstein								
Norway								
Sweden								
Switzerland								
Eastern Europe								
Albania								
Bulgaria								
Czechoslovakia								
Hungary								
Poland								
Romania								
USSR								
Yugoslavia								
Others								
Cyprus								
Gibraltar								
Malta								
Monaco								
Turkey								

Sources: National accounts/World Tourism Organisation (WTO)/OECD
Note: See end of section

Notes to Tables in Section Eleven:

Table 1101
- a Billion lire
- b Dollar and percentage share values based on 1988 results
- c Dollar and percentage share values are partly based on 1990 results

Table 1102 Entries of 0 signify less than $0.5 million
- a Communications included in transport
- b Household fuels included in housing
- c Footwear included in clothing
- d Data refer to 1990
- e Non-alcoholic drinks included in alcoholic drinks
- f Data for footwear and household fuels refer to 1990

Table 1103
- a Communications included in transport
- b Household fuels included in housing
- c Footwear including in clothing
- d Data refer to 1990
- e Non-alcoholic drinks included in alcoholic drinks
- f Data for footwear and household fuels refer to 1990

Table 1104
- a Billion lire
- b Dollar and percentage share values based on 1990 results

Table 1105
- a Billion lire
- b Dollar and percentage share values based on 1990 results
- c Includes non-alcoholic drinks

Table 1106
- a Billion lire
- b Dollar and percentage share values based on 1990 results
- c Included in alcoholic drinks

Table 1107
- a Billion lire
- b Dollar and percentage share values based on 1990 results

Table 1108
- a Billion lire
- b Includes footwear
- c Dollar and percentage share values based on 1990 results

Table 1109
- a Billion lire
- b Included in clothing
- c Dollar and percentage share values based on 1990 results

Table 1110
- a Billion lire
- b Includes household fuels
- c Dollar and percentage share values based on 1990 results

Table 1111
- a Billion lire
- b Included in housing
- c Dollar and percentage share values based on 1990 results

Table 1112
- a Billion lire
- b Dollar and percentage share values based on 1990 results

Table 1113
- a Billion lire
- b Dollar and percentage share values based on 1990 results

Table 1114
- a Includes communications
- b Billion lire
- c Dollar and percentage share values based on 1990 results

Table 1115
- a Included in transport
- b Billion lire

Table 1116
- a Billion lire
- b Dollar and percentage share values based on 1990 results

Table 1117
- a Billion lire

Section Twelve

Retailing and Retail Distribution

Table No: 1201

RETAIL SALES

Trends in Retail Sales 1977-1990

National currencies (billions)	1977	1978	1979	1980	1981	1982	1983	1984	1985
EC members									
Belgium	850	920	1005	1055	1110	1252	1318	1388	1472
Denmark	72	73	76	82	90	104	119	131	131
France	560	625	795	810	890	977	1073	1160	1244
Germany: East[a]	89	92	96	100	102	104	104	109	113
Germany: West	310	330	343	355	368	385	403	418	432
Greece	415	490	580	690	835	975	1250	1500	1850
Ireland	2	2	3	3	4	4	4	5	5
Italy[b]	93	85	103	123	136	164	189	192	281
Luxembourg	34	36	38	42	48	52	55	58	61
Netherlands	85	88	89	93	95	98	99	101	105
Portugal	344	425	495	577	693	869	975	1125	1450
Spain[c]	4300	4500	4900	5291	6189	7147	8295	8806	10100
United Kingdom	39	42	51	60	64	70	76	82	90
EC total									
EFTA members									
Austria	175	170	200	220	235	250	263	266	255
Finland	40	43	50	57	63	69	74	77	83
Iceland[a]						9	16	22	30
Liechtenstein									
Norway	40	47	54	58	64	71	76	83	96
Sweden	96	103	109	126	154	162	177	193	200
Switzerland	44	44	44	48	50	51	53	56	60
EFTA total									
Eastern Europe									
Albania[a]		6							
Bulgaria	10	10	10	12	13	13	14	14	15
Czechoslovakia[a]	227	241	250	255	261	269	277	285	296
Hungary[a]	256	281	313	342	381	411	441	480	520
Poland	1049	1131	1235	1334	1511	2690	2979	4370	5150
Romania[a]	138	155	165	219	230	257	265	278	277
USSR	231	241	247	255	304	304	314	324	333
Yugoslavia						612	804	1236	2104
East European total									
Others									
Cyprus	0	1	1	1	1	1	1	1	1
Gibraltar									
Malta	0	0	0	0	0	0	0	0	
Monaco									
Turkey[a]	240	302	661	1044	1490	1490	2256	4500	7500
Total									
European total									

Table No: 1201 (cont'd)

RETAIL SALES

Trends in Retail Sales 1977-1990

National currencies (billions)

	1986	1987	1988	1989	1990	% growth 1977-1990	% share 1990	Total $ billion 1990	$ per capita 1990
EC members									
Belgium	1467	1505	1539	1646	1725	102.94	2.0	51.6	5172
Denmark	140	142	146	150	153	112.50	0.9	24.7	4814
France	1338	1401	1469	1566	1657	195.89	11.6	304.3	5380
Germany: East[a]	118	122	127	129			2.6	67.9	4078
Germany: West	440	466	483	507	560	80.65	13.2	346.5	5564
Greece	2335	2720	3165	3710	4550	996.39	1.1	28.7	2841
Ireland	6	7	7	7	8	263.64	0.5	13.3	3768
Italy[b]	302	329	358	392	427	359.14	13.6	356.4	6190
Luxembourg	63	65	67	69	73	114.71	0.1	2.2	5828
Netherlands	105	109	111	116	124	45.88	2.6	68.1	4570
Portugal	1638	1917	2185	2120	2226	547.09	0.6	15.6	1509
Spain[c]	8642	9981	11285	12660	14045	226.63	5.2	137.8	3540
United Kingdom	96	103	113	121	129	229.92	8.8	230.4	4020
EC total							62.7	1647.5	4809
EFTA members									
Austria	275	286	298	311	334	90.86	1.1	29.4	3835
Finland	89	96	104	112	115	187.50	1.1	30.1	6046
Iceland[a]	38	45	55	62				1.1	4299
Liechtenstein									
Norway	108	116	119	122	129	222.50	0.8	20.6	4868
Sweden	222	239	257	282	302	214.58	1.9	51.0	5984
Switzerland	61	65	67	69	72	63.64	2.0	51.8	7783
EFTA total							7.0	184.0	5721
Eastern Europe									
Albania[a]	18								
Bulgaria	15	16	17	17			0.3	8.1	901
Czechoslovakia[a]	304	314	329	341	381	67.84	0.8	21.2	1356
Hungary[a]	564	640	697	681	804	215.06	0.5	12.7	1199
Poland	6203	8047	13545	4625			1.2	32.0	844
Romania[a]	280	290	291	296	357	158.70	0.6	15.9	685
USSR	341	351	376	405			25.7	675.0	2378
Yugoslavia	4496	9887	26784	300000	1807652		0.6	16.0	671
East European total							29.7	780.9	1919
Others									
Cyprus	1	1	1						
Gibraltar									
Malta									
Monaco		2							
Turkey[a]	9800	12000	20000	35000			0.6	16.5	299
Total							0.6	16.5	299
European total							100.0	2628.9	3137

Source: Euromonitor
Notes: See end of section

Table No: 1202

RETAIL SALES

Index of Retail Sales Volume 1985-1991

1985 = 100

	1985	1986	1987	1988	1989	1990	1991
EC members							
Belgium	100	104	103	105	109	117	
Denmark	100	103	101	100	100	100	102
France	100	102	105	108	110	110	114
Germany: East	100						
Germany: West	100	104	107	111	114	123	129
Greece	100	97	102	118	118	116	109
Ireland	100	96	98	100	105	107	98
Italy	100	103	107	111	119		
Luxembourg	100	102	103	105	107		
Netherlands	100	103	109	110	115	120	120
Portugal	100	101	104	109	115		
Spain	100	109	113	123	134	146	142
United Kingdom	100	105	111	119	120	120	139
EFTA members							
Austria	100	100	102	105	109	114	119
Finland	100	102	108	113	118	112	104
Iceland	100	101	102	99	96		
Liechtenstein							
Norway	100	106	100	91	89	91	
Sweden	100	106	110	110	111	108	106
Switzerland	100	103	103	103	104	104	102
Eastern Europe							
Albania							
Bulgaria	100	104	108	111	102		
Czechoslovakia	100	105	105	105			
Hungary	100	104	110	104	109		
Poland	100				118		
Romania	100	99	100				
USSR	100	104	106	112			
Yugoslavia	100	100	100	100	100		
Others							
Cyprus							
Gibraltar							
Malta							
Monaco							
Turkey							

Source: Euromonitor

Table No: 1203

TOTAL RETAIL TRADE

Numbers of Retail Outlets, Employees: Latest Year

'000

	Year	Total Outlets	Food Outlets	Non-food Outlets	Employment
EC members					
Belgium[a]	1990	113.0	34.2	78.8	173.6
Denmark[b]	1987	42.0	14.3	27.7	200.0
France[a]	1989	518.7	167.4	351.3	1214.2
Germany: East[c]	1991	17.8	6.9	10.9	874.8
Germany: West[d]	1988	348.5	85.2	263.4	2713.0
Greece	1985	148.9	63.6	121.3	301.3
Ireland	1988	31.7	18.2	13.5	89.7
Italy[e]	1989	871.4	312.0	559.4	
Luxembourg[f]	1988	3.3	1.0	2.3	16.5
Netherlands	1991	163.4	45.4	118.0	
Portugal[a]	1989	109.6	58.8	50.8	231.5
Spain[g]	1989	906.8	102.0	804.9	
United Kingdom[d]	1989	334.6	157.8	187.7	2245.0
EFTA members					
Austria	1988	38.3	9.0	29.3	243.6
Finland[d,g]	1990	36.6	12.4	24.2	152.2
Iceland[g]	1987	1.9	0.8	1.1	9.4
Liechtenstein	1986	0.3			0.9
Norway	1989	33.8	11.6	22.2	128.2
Sweden[a]	1990	45.0	18.0	27.0	262.5
Switzerland	1989	45.0	18.0	27.0	340.6
Eastern Europe					
Albania	1978	12.6			
Bulgaria	1990	41.7	28.3	13.4	281.0
Czechoslovakia	1989	62.6	23.0	39.7	271.8
Hungary[h]	1990	77.3	25.1	52.2	341.4
Poland	1989	249.5			
Romania[i]	1990	52.9	17.7	35.2	281.2
USSR	1989	744.7			6581.0
Yugoslavia	1989	98.2			413.0
Others					
Cyprus[j]	1990				36.8
Gibraltar	1986				1.1
Malta	1987	2.5			11.0
Monaco					
Turkey	1985	369.1	170.5	198.6	170.5

Source: Euromonitor

Notes: See end of section

Table No: 1204

TOTAL RETAIL TRADE

Retail Trade by Form of Organisation 1990

% total retail sales

	Co-op	DVS	Mult	Affi	Inde	Total
EC members						
Belgium		8	14	10	68	100
Denmark[a]	20		19	34	27	100
France	1	7	22	31	40	100
Germany: East[b]	31	23	16	19	11	
Germany: West	31	20	21	15	14	100
Greece			15	10	75	
Ireland[c]	1	6	38	7	48	100
Italy	10	2	8	13	67	100
Luxembourg		6	10	20	64	100
Netherlands[d]	11	2	35	19	33	100
Portugal	9	7	25		59	100
Spain	2		27	13	58	100
United Kingdom	5	16	51	5	23	100
EFTA members						
Austria[e]		27	37	30	26	100
Finland	20	3	17	32	28	100
Iceland						
Liechtenstein						
Norway[f]	13		32	23	32	100
Sweden	16		16	45	23	100
Switzerland	27	10	25	10	28	100
Eastern Europe						
Albania						
Bulgaria						
Czechoslovakia						
Hungary						
Poland						
Romania						
USSR						
Yugoslavia						
Others						
Cyprus						
Gibraltar						
Malta						
Monaco						
Turkey						

Source: Euromonitor
Notes: See end of section

Table No: 1205

TOTAL RETAIL TRADE

Retail Sales by Form of Outlet 1989/1990

% total retail sales

	Mail order	Dept Store	Variety Store	Hyper-market	Super-market	Other self-service	Other	Total
EC members								
Belgium[a,b]	1		7		17	75		100
Denmark[c]	5		10	6	20	8	51	100
France[b]	2	2	2	20	12		61	100
Germany: East								
Germany: West[b,d]	4	5		5	15	10	61	100
Greece								
Ireland								
Italy[b,e]			11				89	100
Luxembourg								
Netherlands[f,g]	2		5	4	17	26	46	100
Portugal								
Spain								
United Kingdom								
EFTA members								
Austria[b]	3	2		5	9	5	76	100
Finland[d]	4	10		4	14	19	49	100
Iceland								
Liechtenstein								
Norway[g]		21		2	16	27	34	100
Sweden	3	8		4	29	7	49	100
Switzerland[d]	3	7		10	15	23	42	100
Eastern Europe								
Albania								
Bulgaria								
Czechoslovakia								
Hungary								
Poland								
Romania								
USSR								
Yugoslavia								
Others								
Cyprus								
Gibraltar								
Malta								
Monaco								
Turkey								

Source: Euromonitor
Notes: See end of section

Table No: 1206

FOOD RETAILING

Numbers of Food Outlets by Type: Latest Year

Number of outlets

	Year	General	Fruit/ Veg	Dairy	Meat	Fish	Bakery	Confect- ionery	Drinks	Tobacco
EC members										
Belgium	1987	14209	2359	2367	8647	1431	2198	1190	1686	664
Denmark	1987	6497	1319		1622	474	457	504		1992
France	1989	57021	17033	4880	49138	7717		21370	5383	4887
Germany: East										
Germany: West	1985	59592							7895	10469
Greece	1978	37734	5193	2097	11558	1227	815	3125	1590	
Ireland	1988	6575	327	772	1690	111	337	2882	1405	
Italy	1986	197709	43545		66542	9965	56685		13765	
Luxembourg	1988	652								
Netherlands	1991	8349	5857	3604	6614	2116	5407	1557	3361	3312
Portugal	1987	35622			4908	1801			395	
Spain										
United Kingdom	1988	35319	14623	11264	18215	2802	5895		8736	47774
EFTA members										
Austria	1988	9013								3400
Finland	1982	5647		528					210	
Iceland										
Liechtenstein										
Norway	1989	7323	6525		216	285	565		108	
Sweden	1990								333	2000
Switzerland	1985				3083	4103				
Eastern Europe										
Albania										
Bulgaria	1988	7569	3134	202	1208		2803			
Czechoslovakia	1989	22995								
Hungary	1989	22537								
Poland										
Romania	1990		3267		1185		2512			
USSR	1988	66942	13479		3179		11421			
Yugoslavia	1986									1591
Others										
Cyprus	1983	1912			576					
Gibraltar										
Malta										
Monaco										
Turkey										

Source: Euromonitor

Table No: 1207

NON-FOOD RETAILING

Number of Non-Food Specialists by Type: Latest Year

Number of outlets

	Year	Chemists/ Drugstores	Perfum-eries	Opticians	Photo-graphic	Book-shops	Stationers	News-agents	Fashion
EC members									
Belgium	1987	5796	1901	1230	965	2249	1149	2825	8997
Denmark[a,b]	1987	380	910		505	899		690	3014
France[c,d,e]	1989	22159			7640	28674			92955
Germany: East									
Germany: West[d,f,g]	1988	31554			3460	5161	20476		69695
Greece[h]	1984	6594						14041	20276
Ireland	1988	1269							
Italy[j]	1986			16571		28332		19354	150978
Luxembourg[f]	1988	143				170			307
Netherlands[b,d]	1991	2827	1566	1634	1835	3345	971		17676
Portugal[g,l]	1987	11070							4004
Spain									
United Kingdom[e]	1988	13294			861	7862			43841
EFTA members									
Austria[c,d,k]	1988	2660			510	1450		3400	5650
Finland[f,g,l]	1988	1486							5740
Iceland									
Liechtenstein									
Norway[b,d,k]	1989	407	780		409	690			3529
Sweden[b]	1986	857			703	1173		2583	7374
Switzerland	1985	2642			1157		4381		
Eastern Europe									
Albania									
Bulgaria[m]	1988					1816			3495
Czechoslovakia[f]	1989	1679				1110			6781
Hungary[f,n]	1989	1475				4435			11486
Poland									
Romania[f]	1990	1448	358			2249			8490
USSR	1988	30017				8738			5277
Yugoslavia[d]	1986	109	303		143	686	821		7899
Others									
Cyprus	1980	285				168			1411
Gibraltar									
Malta									
Monaco									
Turkey[g]	1985	11612							66876

Table No: 1207 (cont'd)

NON-FOOD RETAILING

Number of Non-Food Specialists by Type: Latest Year

Number of outlets

	Year	Foot-wear	House-wares/ Hardware	Furnish-ings	Furni-ture	Appliances	TV/Audio	Records	DIY
EC members									
Belgium	1987	2828	3275	1670	2533	2473	1730	733	
Denmark[a,b]	1987	882	1512		3952		2305		
France[c,d,e]	1989	15776	9456	7872	12014	17701			
Germany: East									
Germany: West[d,f,g]	1988				39589	26620		2701	
Greece[h]	1984	9783	11708	3321	15298				
Ireland	1988	671	2072			1242			
Italy[i]	1986	38823	54493		33931	36401			
Luxembourg[f]	1988	95			328				
Netherlands[b,d]	1991	3866	7488	2129	2462	12669			9102
Portugal[g,j]	1976	1908	4091	180	2385	2561			1793
Spain									
United Kingdom[e]	1988	12066	11485	5074	14743	16304			8180
EFTA members									
Austria[c,d,k]	1988	1450	1200	1370		1730			
Finland[f,g,l]	1988	677	4037	1518	1267	1369			3414
Iceland									
Liechtenstein									
Norway[b,d,k]	1989	765	686		816	1316		600	2693
Sweden[b]	1986	1484	6242		2337	1404	2221		1500
Switzerland	1985	1514	2204		1247	698			
Eastern Europe									
Albania									
Bulgaria[m]	1988	463			388	383			
Czechoslovakia[f]	1989				515				
Hungary[f,n]	1989		2263						3546
Poland									
Romania[f]	1990		4061		757	2120			7737
USSR	1988	2568			2397				
Yugoslavia[d]	1986					344			
Others									
Cyprus	1980	292	336			379			
Gibraltar									
Malta									
Monaco									
Turkey[g]	1988				3884				

Table No: 1207 (cont'd)

NON-FOOD RETAILING

Number of Non-Food Specialists by Type: Latest Year

Number of outlets

	Year	Clocks/ Jewellery	Pets	Toys/ Sports	Florists	Total (inc. others)
EC members						
Belgium	1987	1930	916	2089	3887	49176
Denmark[a,b]	1987	1411		526	1126	27932
France[c,d,e]	1989	10404			20122	247963
Germany: East						
Germany: West[d,f,g]	1988	9598	4298	8309	14158	263395
Greece[h]	1984			2946		83967
Ireland	1977	360		410		
Italy[i]	1984	18931		12709	18913	
Luxembourg[f]	1988					
Netherlands[b,d]	1991	2480	1993	3384	8433	83860
Portugal[g,j]	1976	1321			462	
Spain						
United Kingdom[e]	1988	7985		9804	7854	133007
EFTA members						
Austria	1988	1340				
Finland[c,d,k]	1988					
Iceland[f,g,l]						
Liechtenstein						
Norway[b,d,k]	1989	1230		1224	1370	
Sweden[b]	1986	2400		5957	2106	
Switzerland	1985	1566	272	1400	1232	18313
Eastern Europe						
Albania						
Bulgaria[m]	1988					6545
Czechoslovakia[f]	1989	610				
Hungary[f,n]	1989					7279
Poland						
Romania[f]	1990					
USSR	1988			2210		
Yugoslavia[d]	1986					
Others						
Cyprus	1980					
Gibraltar						
Malta						
Monaco						
Turkey[g]	1985					82372

Source: Euromonitor
Notes: See end of section

Table No: 1208

HYPERMARKETS AND SUPERSTORES

Food Distribution by Form of Organisation: Latest Year

% total food sales

	Year	Co-op	Multi	Affi	Inde	Other	Total
EC members							
Belgium[a]	1990		22		67	11	100
Denmark	1990	37	21			42	100
France[b]	1990	1	23	45		31	100
Germany: East							
Germany: West	1989	14	23	40		23	100
Greece							
Ireland							
Italy	1990	15	10	24	51		100
Luxembourg							
Netherlands	1990	1	64		35		100
Portugal[a]	1987	1	10		86	3	100
Spain	1987		15	1	80	4	100
United Kingdom	1987	12	58			30	100
EFTA members							
Austria[b]	1987	15	44	36		5	100
Finland[b]	1987	31	3	63		3	100
Iceland							
Liechtenstein							
Norway	1990	22	27	30		22	100
Sweden[b]	1987	21	8	44		27	100
Switzerland	1990	34		14	34	18	100
Eastern Europe							
Albania							
Bulgaria							
Czechoslovakia							
Hungary							
Poland							
Romania							
USSR							
Yugoslavia							
Others							
Cyprus							
Gibraltar							
Malta							
Monaco							
Turkey							

Source: Euromonitor
Notes: See end of section

Table No: 1209

HYPERMARKETS AND SUPERSTORES

Numbers of Hypermarkets and Superstores 1980-1990

Number of stores

	1980	1981	1982	1983	1984	1985	1986	1987	1988	1989	1990
EC members											
Belgium[a]	79	80	81	82	86	86	88	88	88	98	110
Denmark[b]	29	30	36	38	38	42	42	44	44	49	50
France	421	447	482	515	553	585	629	679	725	780	790
Germany: East											
Germany: West[c]	813	840	860	880	910	1522	1561	1572	1583	1625	1656
Greece			1	2	2	4	6				
Ireland[d]							35				
Italy							45	49	64	75	80
Luxembourg	3	3	3	4	4	5	5				
Netherlands	37	39	37	35	34	35	35	35	35	36	38
Portugal[d]										20	
Spain	34	38	48	58	62	80	89	100	108	121	130
United Kingdom	201	232	260	287	316	393	433	457	500	578	590
EFTA members											
Austria	51	53	54	53	56	58	67	69	71	77	80
Finland	27	28	28	30	32	33	35	40	44	50	57
Iceland											
Liechtenstein											
Norway	67	70	72	73	75	78	80				
Sweden	65	68	70	73	73	72	89	99	108	121	
Switzerland	81	82	82	82	83	90	94	94	94	106	
Eastern Europe											
Albania											
Bulgaria											
Czechoslovakia											
Hungary											
Poland											
Romania											
USSR											
Yugoslavia											
Others											
Cyprus											
Gibraltar											
Malta											
Monaco											
Turkey											

Sources: Retail trade associations/national statistical offices/Euromonitor
Notes: See end of section

Table No: 1210

HYPERMARKETS AND SUPERSTORES

Hypermarkets and Superstores: Market Shares, Selling Space, Turnover: 1988/1989/1990

%/000 m^2/million units of national currency

	% market share, total retail sales 1988	% market share food sales 1990	Sales area '000m^2 1989	Turnover (million units of national currency 1989)
EC members				
Belgium	15		619	86828
Denmark[a,b]	6		260	9180
France[b,c]	19	25	4583	291431
Germany: East				
Germany: West[c]	7	12	7500	27210
Greece	0			
Ireland	5			
Italy[d]		1	314	25000
Luxembourg	11			
Netherlands	3	5	152	
Portugal			131	
Spain[c]	9	18	709	240000
United Kingdom	9	60	2225	12391
EFTA members				
Austria[a,c]	5	13	415	
Finland[a,b]	7	7	184	6700
Iceland				
Liechtenstein				
Norway	1	4	42	1274
Sweden	5	8	879	57650
Switzerland	8	17	535	6042
Eastern Europe				
Albania				
Bulgaria				
Czechoslovakia				
Hungary				
Poland				
Romania				
USSR				
Yugoslavia				
Others				
Cyprus				
Gibraltar				
Malta				
Monaco				
Turkey				

Sources: Retail trade associations/national statistical offices/Euromonitor
Notes: See end of section

Table No: 1211

LARGE MIXED RETAILERS

Retail Sales Through Department and Variety Stores 1981-1990

National currencies (billions)

	1981	1982	1983	1984	1985	1986	1987	1988	1989	1990	Total $ million 1989
EC members											
Belgium	41.0	44.0	45.0	46.0	47.0	49.0	50.1	51.0	51.7		1312.2
Denmark	11.0	12.0	13.3	14.5	16.1	18.2	20.3	21.0	21.0		2876.7
France	45.5	49.0	52.0	54.0	55.0	55.5	56.0	56.5	61.8		9656.3
Germany: East											
Germany: West	29.0	28.1	28.4	27.5	27.8	27.6	28.1	28.7	30.1	32.3	19987.6
Greece											
Ireland	0.2	0.3	0.3	0.3	0.3	0.3	0.3	0.4		0.2	331.7
Italy[a]	1.5	2.0	2.4	2.5	3.2	3.6	3.9	4.0	5.5		4008.5
Luxembourg											
Netherlands	4.6	4.7	4.8	4.9	5.2	5.4	5.7	5.9	6.0	6.1	3349.8
Portugal											
Spain	270.0	300.0	335.0	380.0	425.0	450.0	490.0	530.0			
United Kingdom	9.9	11.2	12.4	13.5	14.7	15.6	16.7	16.8			
EFTA members											
Austria	14.0	14.0	14.0	13.6	13.4	13.0	12.5	12.5	14.0		1060.6
Finland	10.1	10.9	12.2	12.8	13.7	14.6	15.0	16.0	17.5	18.0	4707.1
Iceland											
Liechtenstein											
Norway[b]	4.5	4.8	5.3	5.8	6.3	8.1	7.0	7.9	7.2		1043.5
Sweden[b]	14.5	15.0	15.5	15.8	16.1	16.5	17.4	17.8	18.4	21.3	3598.6
Switzerland	4.9	5.0	5.2	5.5	5.7	5.8	6.0	6.5	6.9		4312.5
Eastern Europe											
Albania											
Bulgaria											
Czechoslovakia									35.9		2385.4
Hungary											
Poland											
Romania											
USSR											
Yugoslavia											
Others											
Cyprus											
Gibraltar											
Malta											
Monaco											
Turkey											

Source: Euromonitor
Notes: See end of section

Table No: 1212

LARGE MIXED RETAILERS

Department and Variety Stores: Numbers 1988, Market Shares 1980-1990

	Department Stores 1988	Variety Stores 1988	% market share 1980	% market share 1987	% market share 1988	% market share 1989	% market share 1990
EC members							
Belgium[a]	631		3.7	3.3	3.3		
Denmark	13	100	13.4	13.2	13.0		
France[b]	185	600	5.0	4.0	3.9	4.0	
Germany: East	29	232					
Germany: West	480	275	7.9	6.0	5.9	5.9	5.8
Greece[b]	22	20	0.3	0.5	0.6	0.8	1.0
Ireland	12	74	6.8	6.2	2.8		3.2
Italy[c]	830		0.8	1.4	1.4	1.3	1.3
Luxembourg							
Netherlands[d]	148	225	4.8	5.2	5.3	5.0	4.9
Portugal	30		0.8	1.2			1.0
Spain[c]	140		4.7	4.2			
United Kingdom	639	1300	15.0	16.2	16.4		
EFTA members							
Austria[b]	200	2850	6.8	8.0	8.0	7.0	7.0
Finland[e]	214		14.0	12.0	11.5	12.1	13.0
Iceland							
Liechtenstein							
Norway	120		6.9	6.4	6.2	5.9	
Sweden[e]	162		9.5	7.5	7.6		7.9
Switzerland	200	75	8.3	9.0	9.0	7.0	7.0
Eastern Europe							
Albania							
Bulgaria							
Czechoslovakia[b]	160	1027			12.5		
Hungary		196					
Poland							
Romania							
USSR							
Yugoslavia							
Others							
Cyprus							
Gibraltar							
Malta							
Monaco							
Turkey[c]	748						

Source: Euromonitor
Notes: See end of section

Table No: 1213

CO-OPERATIVES

Co-operatives: Numbers, Members, Market Shares: Latest Year

	Year	Number Major Co-ops	Member Outlets	Market Share Total %	Market Share Grocery %
EC members					
Belgium	1989	1		0	0
Denmark[a]	1989	747	1511	18	37
France	1990	5	1147	1	1
Germany: East	1990		26000	31	
Germany: West[b]	1988		1300	4	2
Greece					
Ireland	1988		28	0	3
Italy	1990	431	1281	2	15
Luxembourg	1987	1		0	
Netherlands	1990	20	7685	3	1
Portugal					
Spain	1990	8	83	2	3
United Kingdom	1988	83	4270	4	17
EFTA members					
Austria	1989	1	1025	8	15
Finland	1990	3	2365	19	31
Iceland					
Liechtenstein					
Norway[c]	1990	464	1350	13	22
Sweden[d]	1990	132	1635	15	20
Switzerland	1990	2	2000	27	34
Eastern Europe					
Albania					
Bulgaria	1988		27051	30	
Czechoslovakia	1989	25129	24		
Hungary	1988		15091	30	
Poland	1988		33183	30	
Romania	1989	140000	23		
USSR	1989	327000	28		
Yugoslavia					
Others					
Cyprus					
Gibraltar					
Malta					
Monaco					
Turkey					

Source: Euromonitor
Notes: See end of section

Table No: 1214

MAIL ORDER

Sales Through Mail Order Groups 1981-1991

National currencies (billions)

	1981	1982	1983	1984	1985	1986	1987	1988	1989	1990	1991
EC members											
Belgium	15.0	15.5	16.2	18.6	19.7	20.6	21.8	22.9	23.4	24.6	26.5
Denmark	1.5	1.7	1.9	2.1	2.3	2.6	2.9	2.8	4.2	4.2	4.2
France	20.1	23.3	25.5	28.4	30.5	34.1	36.5	37.6	39.2	40.9	42.8
Germany: East											
Germany: West	23.5	22.2	21.7	22.4	22.5	24.0	26.4	25.3	25.1	29.4	36.6
Greece[a]				0.1	0.2	0.2	0.2	0.2			
Ireland											
Italy[a]	0.7	0.8	0.9	1.0	1.2	1.3	1.5	1.7	1.7	1.6	1.7
Luxembourg											
Netherlands	1.3	1.3	1.4	1.6	1.7	1.7	1.8	1.9	1.8	1.9	2.2
Portugal							0.5				
Spain							20.0		41.5	51.3	70.1
United Kingdom	2.2	2.4	2.6	2.7	3.0	3.3	3.5	3.8	3.5	3.8	3.8
EFTA members											
Austria	6.4	6.8	7.4	7.6	8.0	8.5	8.8	9.0	12.8	13.9	14.6
Finland	0.4	0.5	0.7	0.7	0.8	0.9	1.2	1.7	2.0	2.3	2.1
Iceland											
Liechtenstein											
Norway	1.1	1.2	1.5	1.9	2.4	2.8	3.2	3.1		3.1	
Sweden	1.7	2.3	3.3	3.9	4.5	5.9	6.9	6.7	6.2	8.2	6.8
Switzerland	1.0	1.1	1.2	1.3	1.4	1.5	1.6	1.6	1.7	1.8	1.8
Eastern Europe											
Albania											
Bulgaria											
Czechoslovakia											
Hungary											
Poland											
Romania											
USSR											
Yugoslavia											
Others											
Cyprus											
Gibraltar											
Malta											
Monaco											
Turkey											

Sources: Euromonitor/mail order trade associations
Notes: See end of section

Table No: 1215

MAIL ORDER

Mail Order Market Shares 1987-1990

% total retail sales

	Total Sales			Non-Food Sales		
	1987	1988	1990	1987	1988	1990
EC members						
Belgium	1.4	1.5	1.4	2.3	2.4	2.7
Denmark	2.0	1.9	2.8	4.0	4.0	4.8
France	2.7	2.6	2.5	5.4	5.3	5.1
Germany: East						
Germany: West	5.7	5.2	4.3	8.0	8.1	
Greece						
Ireland	0.3			0.7		
Italy	0.4	0.5	0.3	0.8	0.9	1.4
Luxembourg	1.2			2.0		
Netherlands	1.7	1.7	1.6	3.5	3.5	2.7
Portugal						
Spain	0.1	0.1	0.5	0.2	0.2	
United Kingdom	3.4	3.3	2.8	5.5	5.3	4.6
EFTA members						
Austria	3.1	3.0	3.9	5.5	5.3	
Finland	1.2	1.7	1.5	2.2	3.0	2.3
Iceland						
Liechtenstein						
Norway	2.9	2.9	2.0	5.6	5.7	2.6
Sweden	2.9	3.1	2.8	5.5	5.7	4.8
Switzerland	2.5	2.6	2.6	4.5	4.7	5.0
Eastern Europe						
Albania						
Bulgaria						
Czechoslovakia						
Hungary						
Poland						
Romania						
USSR						
Yugoslavia						
Others						
Cyprus						
Gibraltar						
Malta						
Monaco						
Turkey						

Sources: Euromonitor/mail order trade associations

Table No: 1216

RETAIL TECHNOLOGY

Scanning Stores 1991

	Number of Scanning Stores	of which: Self-service Grocery	Department Stores	General Stores
EC members				
Belgium	1651	1146		505
Denmark	1500			
France	7750	4400	180	3170
Germany: East				
Germany: West	7238			
Greece	1		1	
Ireland	127	124	2	1
Italy	3950	3790	160	
Luxembourg	20			
Netherlands	1520	1160	60	300
Portugal	621	50	7	564
Spain	7653	4653		3000
United Kingdom	7869			
EFTA members				
Austria	1672			
Finland	2240	1917	203	120
Iceland	60	36		24
Liechtenstein				
Norway	1480	960	55	465
Sweden	3171	2114	57	1000
Switzerland	638	198	5	435
Eastern Europe				
Albania				
Bulgaria				
Czechoslovakia	10	5	1	4
Hungary	165	40	5	120
Poland	17	11	1	5
Romania				
USSR	2			
Yugoslavia	86	37	46	3
Others				
Cyprus	7	5	2	
Gibraltar				
Malta				
Monaco				
Turkey				

Sources: European Article Numbering Association/national numbering associations/Euromonitor estimates

Table No: 1217

RETAIL TECHNOLOGY

Number of Scanning Stores 1980-1991

Number of stores	1980	1981	1982	1983	1984	1985	1986	1987	1988	1989	1990	1991
EC members												
Belgium	6	35	47	67	125	201	278	344	648	863	1157	1651
Denmark							97	193	530	1061	1300	1500
France			35	162	480	1023	1626	1945	3471	4648	6650	7750
Germany: East									2	3		
Germany: West	19	43	76	175	429	719	966	1246	2252	3600	4849	7238
Greece												1
Ireland							7		30		101	127
Italy[a]							450	618	1250	3434	3690	3950
Luxembourg									18		20	
Netherlands		5	34	90	131	163	300	488	740	800	1100	1520
Portugal									83	220	269	621
Spain							123	281	912	1603	5039	7653
United Kingdom		10	41	83	185	520	793	843	2792	3999	6043	7869
EFTA members												
Austria							150	275	354	552	1200	1672
Finland							73	186	838	1310	1940	2240
Iceland									14	20	32	60
Liechtenstein												
Norway							225	449	998	1136	1284	1480
Sweden							425	650	1050	1725	2180	3171
Switzerland							45	75	344	575	638	638
Eastern Europe												
Albania												
Bulgaria										0		
Czechoslovakia							1	1	1	1	3	10
Hungary							1		10	18	83	165
Poland												17
Romania											1	
USSR									2	2	2	2
Yugoslavia							44		49	62	73	86
Others												
Cyprus							3		5	5	7	7
Gibraltar												
Malta												
Monaco												
Turkey											1	

Sources: International Article Numbering Association/national numbering associations

Note: See end of section

Table No: 1218

DIRECT SELLING

Sales Through Direct Selling Companies, Direct Salespersons 1991

As stated: sales value in million units of national currency

	Number of Companies	Sales Staff ('000)	Sales Value	Sales Value ($ million)
EC members				
Belgium	13	8.6	3600	111
Denmark	2	1.5	86	14
France	73	260.0	5600	1055
Germany: East				
Germany: West	19	175.0	3000	1950
Greece	7	21.6	5405	30
Ireland	7	3.0	7	13
Italy[a]	27	167.9	1317	1109
Luxembourg				
Netherlands[b]	9	10.9	185	105
Portugal[b]	11	50.0	16000	114
Spain	15	92.3	80623	808
United Kingdom[b]	33	495.3	471	862
EFTA members				
Austria	7	4.0	15	139
Finland	8	6.4	230	53
Iceland				
Liechtenstein				
Norway	8	4.1	355	57
Sweden	42	23.0	237	41
Switzerland[b]	29	5.9	223	161
Eastern Europe				
Albania				
Bulgaria				
Czechoslovakia				
Hungary				
Poland				
Romania				
USSR				
Yugoslavia				
Others				
Cyprus				
Gibraltar				
Malta				
Monaco				
Turkey				

Source: Federation of European Direct Selling Associations
Notes: See end of section

Table No: 1219

SERVICE STATIONS

Outlets, Fuel Sales 1989/90

	Outlets ('000) 1988	% Major Group Owned 1988	Self-service Outlets ('000) 1990	Average Fuel Sales/Outlet 1989
EC members				
Belgium[a]	6.3	65		750
Denmark	3.0		3.0	480
France	25.7	68	10.1	659
Germany: East				
Germany: West	18.1	60	16.9	1414
Greece	5.8			389
Ireland	3.2			269
Italy	31.0	70		386
Luxembourg				
Netherlands	7.4	50		459
Portugal				
Spain	5.0			1546
United Kingdom	19.5	35	11.0	1211
EFTA members				
Austria	4.0		1.2	645
Finland	1.9		1.7	1027
Iceland				
Liechtenstein				
Norway	2.4		2.6	734
Sweden	4.1		2.0	1052
Switzerland	3.9		3.4	880
Eastern Europe				
Albania				
Bulgaria				
Czechoslovakia				
Hungary	1.2			
Poland				
Romania				
USSR				
Yugoslavia				
Others				
Cyprus				
Gibraltar				
Malta				
Monaco				
Turkey				

Sources: National petrol federations/Comité Professional du Pétrole/national statistical offices
Note: See end of section

Table No: 1220

OWN BRANDS

Retailers' Own Brand Shares 1981-1990

% total food sales

	1981	1985	1987	1988	1990
EC members					
Belgium	16	16	17	17	18
Denmark					
France	19	19	19	20	20
Germany: East					
Germany: West[a]	5	10	14	14	16
Greece					
Ireland					
Italy[b]	5	7	8	8	8
Luxembourg					
Netherlands	13	21	23	25	27
Portugal					
Spain					12
United Kingdom	17	25	30	32	36
EFTA members					
Austria	13	17	20		
Finland					
Iceland					
Liechtenstein					
Norway	11	14	16		
Sweden	21	24	28	29	
Switzerland					
Eastern Europe					
Albania					
Bulgaria					
Czechoslovakia					
Hungary					
Poland					
Romania					
USSR					
Yugoslavia					
Others					
Cyprus					
Gibraltar					
Malta					
Monaco					
Turkey					

Source: Euromonitor
Notes: See end of section

Table No: 1221

FRANCHISING

Franchisors, Franchisees: Latest Year

	Year	No. of Franchisors	No. of Franchisees	Sales Value (ECU million)
EC members				
Belgium	1989	82	3102	2400
Denmark	1988	80	2500	
France	1989	740	32500	16000
Germany: East				
Germany: West	1988	180	9000	4800
Greece	1983	25	1800	
Ireland				
Italy	1990	218	12900	
Luxembourg				
Netherlands	1989	271	8432	5600
Portugal	1983	37	680	220
Spain	1989	117	14500	
United Kingdom	1989	295	16600	3500
EFTA members				
Austria	1983	53	1583	
Finland				
Iceland				
Liechtenstein				
Norway	1988	120	850	500
Sweden	1988	44	752	400
Switzerland	1988	200		
Eastern Europe				
Albania				
Bulgaria				
Czechoslovakia				
Hungary				
Poland				
Romania				
USSR				
Yugoslavia				
Others				
Cyprus				
Gibraltar				
Malta				
Monaco				
Turkey				

Source: European Franchise Federation
Notes: See end of section

Notes to Tables in Section Twelve:

Table 1201 Retail sales exclude vehicle and petrol sectors
0 = less than 500 million
- a Dollar values based on 1989 results
- b '000 billion lire
- c Data for years prior to 1986 are estimated

Table 1203
- a Employment refers to 1988
- b Employment refers to 1985
- c Employment refers to 1989
- d Employment refers to 1990
- e Fixed outlets only
- f Businesses, not outlets, employment figures refer to 1981
- g Including vehicle and fuel outlets
- h Employment refers to 1987
- i Outlets exclude kiosks
- j Employment excludes wholesale trade

Table 1204
- DVS Department and variety stores, mail order
- Multi Multiples, including hypermarkets
- Affi Voluntary associations and buying groups
- Inde Non-affiliated independents

- a Affiliated includes department and variety stores
- b Independents in the former East Germany were stores in private ownership
- c Data refer to 1989
- d Multiples include department and variety stores. Co-ops include voluntary associations
- e Affiliated includes co-ops
- f Independents include department and variety stores

Table 1205
- a Variety stores include department stores and hypermarkets
- b Data refer to 1989
- c Variety stores include department stores and discounters
- d Other self-service includes discounters and other food stores
- e Variety stores include all large stores and all large self-service stores
- f Variety stores include department stores
- g Other self-service includes discounters and superstores

Table 1207
- a Clocks/jewellery includes opticians; TV/radio includes records; housewares/hardware includes appliances
- b Bookshops include stationers; opticians included with clocks/jewellery
- c Photo includes opticians
- d Appliances includes TV/audio
- e Bookshops includes stationers/newsagents
- f Fashion includes footwear; books includes stationers/newsagents
- g Chemists includes perfumeries; furniture includes furnishings
- h Chemists/drugstores includes perfumeries; newsagents include books; cigarettes; footwear includes leather; appliances includes TV/audio; toys/sports include guns
- i Fashion includes furnishings; opticians includes photographic
- j Fashion includes footwear
- k Furniture includes furnishings
- l Chemists/drugstores includes cosmetics
- m Fashion includes textiles; appliances includes TV/audio
- n State and co-operative outlets only; chemists/drugstores are pharmacists only; housewares/hardware includes technical goods and glassware

Table 1208
- a Affiliated included with independents
- b Independents included with affiliated
- Co-op Co-operatives
- Multi Food multiples
- Affi Voluntary associations and buying groups
- Inde Non-affiliated independents
- Other Department and variety stores, specialists

Table 1209
- a Data for 1990 are estimated
- b Data are estimated, except 1980

c Data for 1981-1984 are estimated
d Data are estimated

Table 1210 a Market share (total retail sales) refers to 1988
b Turnover refers to 1990
c Sales area refers to 1990
d Billion units of national currency

Table 1211 a Dollar value based on 1990 results
b '000 billion lire
c Excludes merchants' department stores

Table 1212 a Data for department stores refer to 1987; change of market shares classification between 1980 and 1988
b Data for department/variety stores refer to 1989
c First column is department and variety stores combined
d Data for department/variety stores refer to 1991
e Data for department/variety stores refer to 1990

Table 1213 Market shares of 0 refer to levels of less than 0.5 per cent
a 747 regional co-ops, all members of one federation
b Outlets refer to Co-op AG only
c 464 regional co-ops, all members of one federation
d 132 regional coops, all members of one federation

Table 1214 a '000 billion
b Data refer to 1990

Table 1217 a Data for 1988 are estimated

Table 1218 a Sales value in billions of lire
b Data refer to 1990

Table 1219 a Data for average fuel sales refers to 1987

Table 1220 a Excludes Aldi
b Data refer to 1989

Table 1221 NB figures exclude vehicles, petrol, soft drinks bottling and hotels

Retail Sales Per Capita 1990: Selected countries

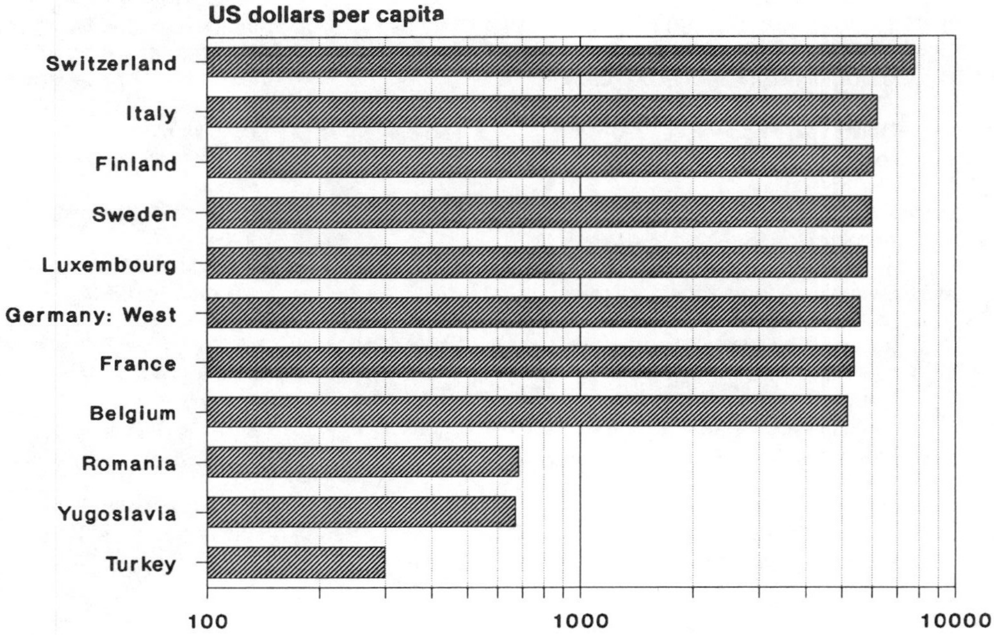

Index of Retail Sales Volume 1985-1991: Selected countries

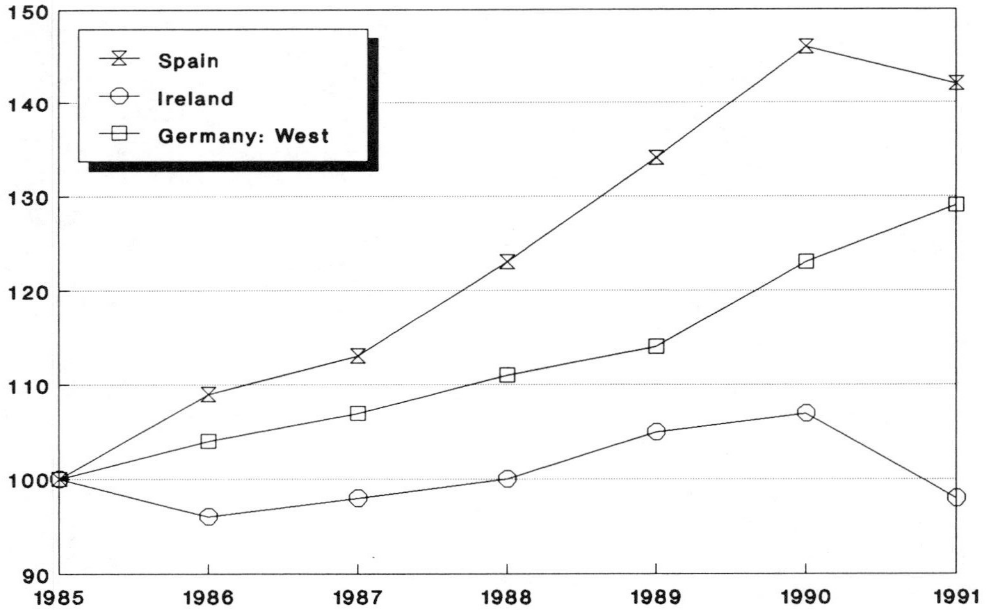

Section Thirteen

Advertising Patterns and Media Access

Table No: 1301

ADVERTISING EXPENDITURE

Trends in Advertising Expenditure 1982-1990

National currencies (millions)	1982	1983	1984	1985	1986	1987	1988	1989	1990
EC members									
Belgium	18057	21113	23449	25534	27730	32209	35296	39171	42866
Denmark	3350	3626	4000	4350	4715	4690	5340	5430	5600
France	17955	21655	23945	26945	30865	35775	41320	46390	50765
Germany: East									
Germany: West	11957	12598	13828	14425	15105	15790	16756	17534	17925
Greece	9210	10845	13846	16651	23603	30581	42681	58654	83627
Ireland	72	72	82	98	116	141	154	175	190
Italy[a]	2096	2729	3306	3981	4742	5805	6594	7341	8543
Luxembourg									
Netherlands	2892	2938	3146	3310	3532	3795	4120	4211	4815
Portugal	5922	7376	9283	12580	18275	29771	42654	54614	68541
Spain	140400	164400	197100	240000	317000	413000	520100	654625	782852
United Kingdom	3115	3564	4039	4418	5088	5781	6779	7311	7360
EFTA members									
Austria	5020	5752	6419	7003	7529	8230	9221	10303	11211
Finland	2931	3551	4158	4649	5063	5511	6322	7209	7250
Iceland									
Liechtenstein									
Norway	2835	2970	3520	3978	4690	5125	5032	5024	5150
Sweden	4063	4628	5858	6431	6855	7863	9877	10251	11828
Switzerland	1831	1957	2063	2294	2478	2737	2887	3095	3275
Eastern Europe									
Albania									
Bulgaria									
Czechoslovakia									
Hungary									
Poland									
Romania									
USSR									
Yugoslavia									
Others									
Cyprus									
Gibraltar									
Malta									
Monaco									
Turkey	26500	28836	44594	76285	89725	151054	315084	490900	999950

Source: National advertising associations
Note: See end of section

Table No: 1302

ADVERTISING EXPENDITURE

Advertising Expenditure by Medium 1990

Current US dollars (millions)

	TV	News-papers	Magazines	Radio	Cinema	Outdoor	Total
EC members							
Belgium	219.0	342.6	236.5	7.4	13.1	114.4	933.0
Denmark[a]	88.5	1217.9	318.7	15.3	8.0	19.3	1667.8
France	2260.6	2605.1	2506.4	600.3	73.4	1062.1	9107.9
Germany: East							
Germany: West	1433.7	5511.8	3316.2	459.4	111.9	370.0	11203.0
Greece	219.0	160.9	174.9	35.3	na	29.6	619.7
Ireland	82.7	269.4	23.0	26.2	na	21.5	422.8
Italy	2851.8	1840.1	1588.5	90.0	na	238.4	6608.8
Luxembourg							
Netherlands	234.6	1315.6	726.2	58.5	7.0	270.5	2612.3
Portugal	239.8	162.5	140.1	43.1	na	61.2	646.8
Spain[a]	1646.9	3423.0	1149.3	608.1	42.2	278.7	7148.2
United Kingdom	3459.4	5010.3	2188.9	253.2	55.2	388.9	11356.0
EFTA members							
Austria	257.6	751.2	261.3	115.9	5.2	63.3	1454.5
Finland[a]	153.5	812.3	120.7	45.4	0.8	29.8	1162.4
Iceland							
Liechtenstein							
Norway	19.6	594.6	121.3	7.8	9.4	17.2	769.8
Sweden[a]	23.3	1280.4	242.8	na	10.9	61.4	1618.8
Switzerland	154.0	1400.1	385.7	39.9	21.7	291.2	2292.7
Eastern Europe							
Albania							
Bulgaria							
Czechoslovakia							
Hungary							
Poland							
Romania							
USSR							
Yugoslavia							
Others							
Cyprus							
Gibraltar							
Malta							
Monaco							
Turkey							

Sources: National advertising associations/International Journal of Advertising 1992
Note: See end of section

Table No: 1303

PRESS

Number of National Newspapers 1991

Number	Nationals	Sundays	Total
EC members			
Belgium[a]	16		16
Denmark	9	6	15
France	12	5	17
Germany: East	15		15
Germany: West	5	3	8
Greece	2		2
Ireland	4	5	9
Italy	24	20	44
Luxembourg			
Netherlands	8		8
Portugal	12		12
Spain	15	5	20
United Kingdom	13	10	23
EFTA members			
Austria	6	4	10
Finland	11	2	13
Iceland			
Liechtenstein			2
Norway	8		8
Sweden	6	4	10
Switzerland	11		11
Eastern Europe			
Albania[b]			2
Bulgaria	2		2
Czechoslovakia	8		8
Hungary	8		8
Poland	9		9
Romania	4		4
USSR	11		11
Yugoslavia	8		8
Others			
Cyprus			10
Gibraltar			1
Malta			4
Monaco			2
Turkey	14		14

Sources: Press/media associations/UNESCO
Notes: See end of section

Table No: 1304

PRESS

National Newspapers: Circulation 1991

'000

	Daily	Sunday	Total
EC members			
Belgium[a,b]	1908		1908
Denmark	1024	1124	2148
France	4334	2068	6402
Germany: East[a]	4435		4435
Germany: West	5850	2900	8750
Greece[a]	1520		1520
Ireland	453	949	1402
Italy	5905	5522	11427
Luxembourg			
Netherlands[a]	2016		2016
Portugal[a]	1050		1050
Spain	2388	1109	3497
United Kingdom	14024	16603	30627
EFTA members			
Austria	1997	1757	3754
Finland	1374	663	2037
Iceland			
Liechtenstein			
Norway[a]	1360		1360
Sweden	1700	1498	3198
Switzerland[a]	1730		1730
Eastern Europe			
Albania[c]			135
Bulgaria[a]	1599		1599
Czechoslovakia[a]	4573		4573
Hungary[a]	1340		1340
Poland[a]	1720		1720
Romania			
USSR[a]	10500		10500
Yugoslavia[a]	875		875
Others			
Cyprus			
Gibraltar			
Malta			
Monaco			
Turkey[a]	3400		3400

Sources: Press/media associations
Notes: See end of section

Table No: 1305

PRESS

Mainstream Consumer Publications 1990

	Consumer Publications (Number)	Combined Circulation ('000)	Total Audited Publications (Number)
EC members			
Belgium	41	4900	130
Denmark	19	4730	34
France	86	40000	827
Germany: East	33	20647	
Germany: West	69	65000	2500
Greece	28	1750	300
Ireland	11	414	60
Italy	60	20000	250
Luxembourg			
Netherlands	52	15000	96
Portugal	17	1600	200
Spain	47	10000	900
United Kingdom	65	23257	1600
EFTA members			
Austria	32	9000	200
Finland	25	3740	60
Iceland			
Liechtenstein			
Norway	32	3673	44
Sweden	38	8350	150
Switzerland	35	7560	2500
Eastern Europe			
Albania			
Bulgaria	7	499	
Czechoslovakia	16	4506	
Hungary	12	3663	
Poland	20	na	
Romania			
USSR	10	82390	
Yugoslavia	16	1944	
Others			
Cyprus			
Gibraltar			
Malta			
Monaco			
Turkey	22	556	

Sources: Press/media organisations/Euromonitor
Note: See end of section

Table No: 1306

TV AND RADIO

Number of TV and Radio Stations 1991

Number

	Radio Stations: National Commercial	National Non-Commercial	Local Commercial	National TV Stations: Commercial	Non-Commercial
EC members					
Belgium	5	3	c680	4	3
Denmark		3	200	2	1
France	4	5	1249	6	
Germany: East		6		2	
Germany: West[a]		1	137	4	2
Greece	3	1	c500	8	
Ireland	3		23	2	
Italy	5		c1000	14	
Luxembourg					
Netherlands	12	2	c200	4	
Portugal	3	1	c300	2	
Spain[b]	4		800+	13	
United Kingdom		5	107	3	2
EFTA members					
Austria	3	1	11	2	
Finland	1		57	6	
Iceland					
Liechtenstein					
Norway		2	425	3	1
Sweden		3	0	0	2
Switzerland	7	9	32	4	1
Eastern Europe					
Albania					
Bulgaria					2
Czechoslovakia	1	6		2	
Hungary	2	3		2	
Poland		1		2	
Romania					
USSR		14			2
Yugoslavia			200		
Others					
Cyprus					
Gibraltar					
Malta					
Monaco					
Turkey	1			6	

Source: Industry sources
Notes: See end of section

Table No: 1307

CINEMA

Cinema Screens, Attendances: Latest Year

	Year	Screens (number)	Attendances (millions)	Box Office Revenue national currencies (millions)
EC members				
Belgium	1990	382	16	200.0
Denmark	1990	350	10	310.0
France	1990	4753	122	3900.0
Germany: East	1988	808	69	263.0
Germany: West	1990	3206	102	800.0
Greece	1990	600	17	9000.0
Ireland	1990	150	8	19.3
Italy[a]	1990	3500	93	580.0
Luxembourg	1989	14	1	78.4
Netherlands	1990	430	15	180.0
Portugal	1990	270	12	4950.0
Spain	1990	2160	131	28000.0
United Kingdom	1990	1580	89	227.0
EC total		18203	685	
EFTA members				
Austria	1990	378	11	744.0
Finland	1990	340	6	184.0
Iceland	1982	na	2	
Liechtenstein				
Norway	1990	300	14	375.0
Sweden	1990	550	19	55.0
Switzerland	1990	325	16	145.0
EFTA total		1893	67	
Eastern Europe				
Albania[b]	1983	103		
Bulgaria	1989	550	79	106.0
Czechoslovakia	1989	2778	70	1000.0
Hungary[c]	1990	1963	37	2950.0
Poland[d]	1990	1600	86	100000.0
Romania	1988	630	212	
USSR	1989	4854	3640	
Yugoslavia[b]	1989	1221	65	
East European total		13699	4189	
Others				
Cyprus				
Gibraltar	1981		170	
Malta[b]	1987	16	1	
Monaco[b]	1981	3	1	
Turkey	1988	250	38	
Total		269	210	
European total		34064	5151	

Sources: Cinema associations and film companies, various countries/UNESCO
Notes: See end of section

Table No: 1308

OUTDOOR ADVERTISING

Number of Sites 1987-1990

Number	1987	1989	1990
EC members			
Belgium	95000	105000	176100
Denmark	17670	17672	17375
France	525000	550000	575000
Germany: East			
Germany: West	257527	260175	308647
Greece	23300	24450	9500
Ireland	6668	7000	7964
Italy	88124	108100	108100
Luxembourg			
Netherlands	69250	75000	75000
Portugal	6150	6200	14270
Spain		45000	45000
United Kingdom	120319	122363	112328
EFTA members			
Austria	110000	120000	130000
Finland	60851	65000	99700
Iceland			
Liechtenstein			
Norway	19225	19140	15356
Sweden	25000	25400	25500
Switzerland	149000	150000	150000
Eastern Europe			
Albania			
Bulgaria			
Czechoslovakia			
Hungary			
Poland			
Romania			
USSR			
Yugoslavia			
Others			
Cyprus			
Gibraltar			
Malta			
Monaco			
Turkey	4590	4590	2889

Source: Local industry

Table No: 1309

DIRECT MARKETING

Volume of Addressed Direct Mail 1983-1989

Million items	1983	1984	1985	1986	1987	1989
EC members						
Belgium	409	449	474	506	533	750
Denmark	140	150	165	190	225	240
France	1603	1737	1973	2000	2376	2850
Germany: East						
Germany: West	3004	3113	3078	3261	3357	3750
Greece						
Ireland	7	9	13	19	20	40
Italy						
Luxembourg						
Netherlands	451	512	541	558	588	850
Portugal	58	58	61	66	85	105
Spain						
United Kingdom	1084	1261	1303	1401	1626	2117
EC total	6756	7289	7608	8001	8810	10702
EFTA members						
Austria						
Finland	171	199	213	220	240	
Iceland	121	135	177	204	215	
Liechtenstein						
Norway	404	434	457	481	511	
Sweden	534	542	565	582	615	
Switzerland						
EFTA total	1230	1310	1412	1487	1581	
Eastern Europe						
Albania						
Bulgaria						
Czechoslovakia						
Hungary						
Poland						
Romania						
USSR						
Yugoslavia						
East European total						
Others						
Cyprus						
Gibraltar						
Malta						
Monaco						
Turkey						
Total						
European total	7986	8599	9020	9488	10391	10702

Source: Services Postaux Européens

Table No: 1310

MEDIA ACCESS

Home Ownership of Media Equipment 1990

% homes equipped with

	Radio	TV	VCR	Viewdata	Satellite Dish
EC members					
Belgium	90	98	34	neg	3
Denmark	98	96	40	na	5
France	98	97	41	5	3
Germany: East[a]	99	20			
Germany: West	84	98	41	9	4
Greece	92	94	44		0
Ireland	95	94	38	21	5
Italy	92	99	25	1	3
Luxembourg		98	53		3
Netherlands	97	97	54	20	2
Portugal	60	92	27	neg	1
Spain	95	98	40	neg	6
United Kingdom	90	97	62	18	4
EFTA members					
Austria	95	97	41	7	6
Finland	96	96	50	22	2
Iceland					
Liechtenstein[b]	18	9			
Norway	98	98	52	na	5
Sweden	93	96	45	13	5
Switzerland	99	93	45	na	3
Eastern Europe					
Albania[c]	500	260			
Bulgaria[a]	95	106			
Czechoslovakia	75	52			
Hungary[a]	40	117			
Poland[a]	79	106			
Romania[d]	45	3645			
USSR	96	98			
Yugoslavia	85	61			
Others					
Cyprus[b]		56			
Gibraltar[b]					
Malta[d]					
Monaco[b]					
Turkey	75	96	10		

Sources: Industry sources/Euromonitor
Notes: See end of section

Table No: 1311

MEDIA ACCESS

Cable and Direct to Home Satellite Television 1990

	Television Households ('000)	Cable Households ('000)	Cable Households (% of TVHH)	Satellite Households (000s)	Satellite Households (% of TVHH)	Cable and Satellite TV Advertising (% of TV advertising)
EC members						
Belgium	3500	3300	94.3	5	0.1	0.8
Denmark	2200	800	36.4	30	1.4	6.8
France	20102	500	2.5	40	0.2	
Germany: East				10	0.2	
Germany: West	24500	8500	34.7	800	3.3	39.7
Greece	3110	neg	0.0	1	0.0	
Ireland	983	350	35.6	20	2.0	5.1
Italy	17084	neg	0.0	30	0.2	
Luxembourg[a]	140	90	64.3	neg	0.0	
Netherlands	5800	4500	77.6	80	1.4	2.1
Portugal	3111	neg	0.0	15	0.5	
Spain	14330	1500	10.5	50	0.4	
United Kingdom	21375	350	1.6	1500	7.0	0.7
EFTA members						
Austria	2775	600	21.6	40	1.4	3.6
Finland	1820	680	37.4	7	0.4	2.8
Iceland[a]	79	0	0.0	neg	0.0	
Liechtenstein						
Norway	1637	500	30.5	65	4.0	100.0
Sweden	3659	1500	41.0	100	2.7	
Switzerland	2595	1650	63.6	10	0.4	10.1
Eastern Europe						
Albania						
Bulgaria	2285	0	0.0	1	0.0	
Czechoslovakia	4450	neg	0.0	30	0.7	
Hungary	2900	500	17.2	50	1.7	
Poland	10000	0	0.0	100	1.0	
Romania	4100	0	0.0	4	neg	
USSR	93500	neg	0.0	neg	0.0	
Yugoslavia	4550	250	5.5	70	1.4	
Others						
Cyprus						
Gibraltar						
Malta						
Monaco						
Turkey	12000	2	0.0	38	0.3	

Sources: Screen Digest/Euromonitor
Note: See end of section

Notes to Tables in Section Thirteen:

Table 1301 a Billion lire

Table 1302 a Data refer to 1989

Table 1303 Non-EC/EFTA data refer to 1984
a Includes Luxembourg
b Data refer to 1988

Table 1304 a No Sunday newspapers
b Includes Luxembourg
c Data refer to 1988

Table 1305 "Mainstream" includes TV guides, business, men's and women's, motoring, home and general interest

Table 1306 a Regional commercial radio stations are state-owned, also numerous private stations
b There are six important regional commercial TV stations

Table 1307 a Billion lire
b Number of cinemas, not screens
c Revenue data refer to 1989
d Attendance and revenue data refer to 1989

Table 1310 a TV, per 100 households
b '000 receivers in use, 1986
c '000 receivers in use 1988
d '000 licences issued

Table 1311 a Data refer to 1989

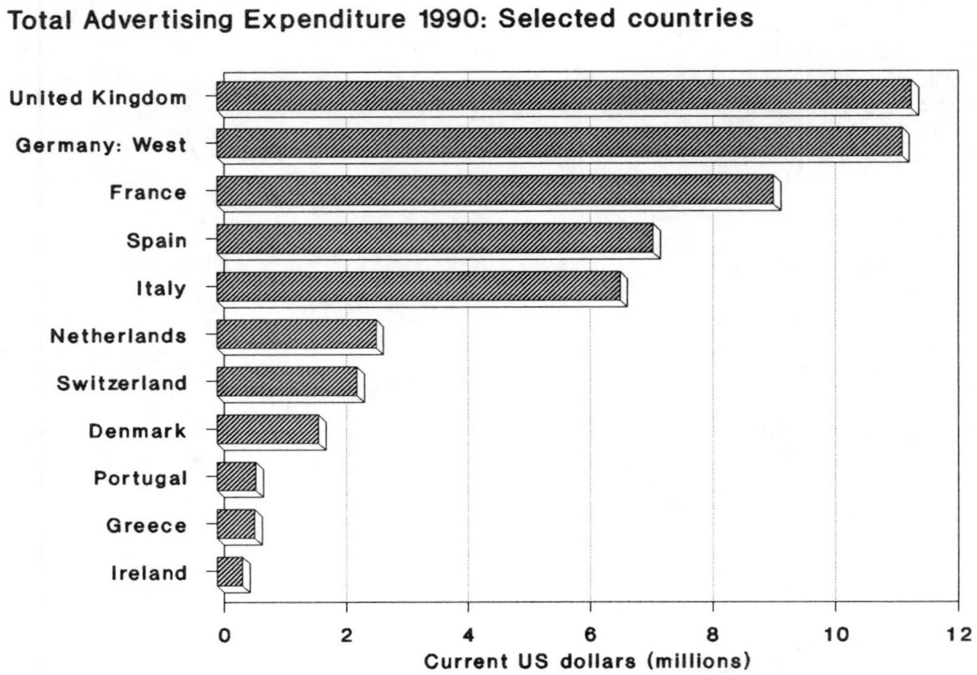
Total Advertising Expenditure 1990: Selected countries
United Kingdom
Germany: West
France
Spain
Italy
Netherlands
Switzerland
Denmark
Portugal
Greece
Ireland
0
2
4
6
8
10
12
Current US dollars (millions)

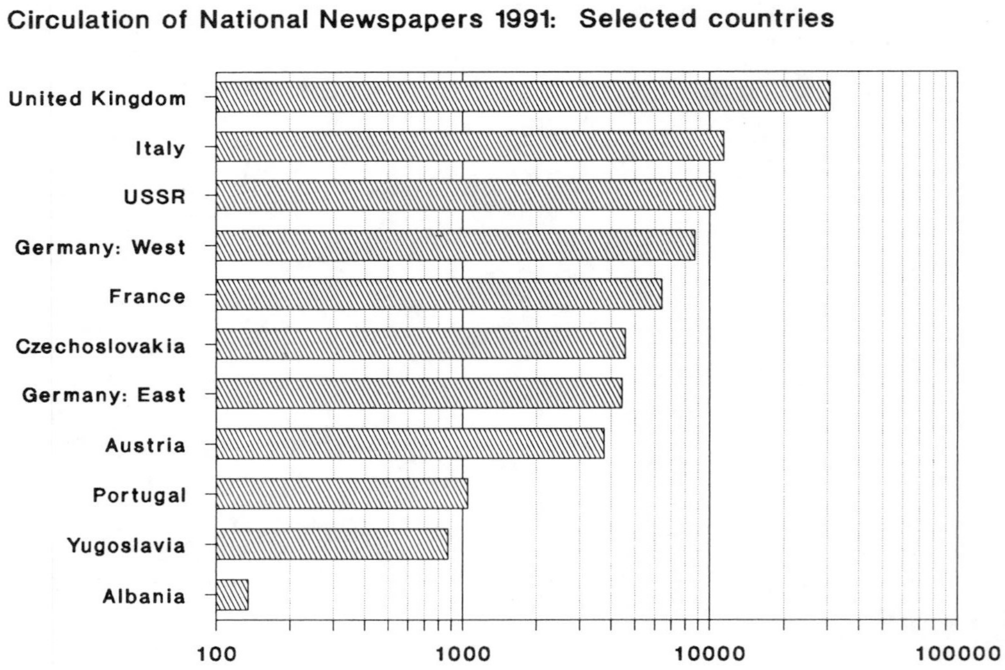
Circulation of National Newspapers 1991: Selected countries
United Kingdom
Italy
USSR
Germany: West
France
Czechoslovakia
Germany: East
Austria
Portugal
Yugoslavia
Albania
100
1000
10000
100000

Section Fourteen

Consumer Market Sizes

Table No: 1401

MEAT AND FISH CONSUMPTION

Per Capita Consumption of Meat and Fish 1991

Kg per inhabitant

	Total Meat	Beef and Veal	Pork	Mutton, Lamb, Goat	Poultry	Fresh Fish	Dried Fish	Shell Fish
EC members								
Belgium[a]	81.9	20.5	43.0	1.9	16.5	4.9	0.7	4.8
Denmark	73.2	21.4	38.9	1.0	11.9	1.5	1.4	0.5
France	96.1	29.9	38.1	5.6	22.5	6.2	0.4	4.0
Germany: East	72.6	20.1	43.0	0.5	9.0	7.4		
Germany: West	66.5	13.8	39.6	1.0	12.1	7.0	0.5	0.2
Greece	63.7	17.7	17.7	11.8	16.5	3.6	1.3	2.4
Ireland	78.9	17.1	31.3	8.5	22.0	12.6	0.3	
Italy	74.7	26.5	27.1	1.8	19.3	6.0	0.9	3.4
Luxembourg								
Netherlands	87.9	19.8	48.9	1.0	18.2	3.9	0.0	4.2
Portugal	69.7	16.2	27.9	3.7	21.8	14.4	9.1	2.0
Spain	88.8	11.5	47.6	6.3	23.3	13.5	1.0	6.5
United Kingdom	69.0	17.9	24.4	7.4	19.3	0.9	0.3	2.3
EC average	77.6	20.1	35.2	4.1	18.3	6.4	0.9	3.0
EFTA members								
Austria	92.4	22.5	54.3	0.5	15.1	1.9	0.1	0.1
Finland	63.3	21.9	35.2	0.2	6.0	5.4	1.2	
Iceland								
Liechtenstein								
Norway	49.5	18.2	20.3	5.9	5.2	12.9	1.9	9.2
Sweden	56.5	17.5	32.2	0.5	6.3	6.1	0.0	1.7
Switzerland	79.8	25.1	41.3	1.5	11.9	3.4	0.3	0.8
EFTA average	70.1	21.1	38.3	1.4	9.4	5.3	0.5	2.2
Eastern Europe								
Albania	17.9	6.3	2.1	6.1	3.5	2.8		
Bulgaria	74.5	18.6	55.9			8.0		
Czechoslovakia	83.9	24.8	59.1			5.1		
Hungary	97.5	10.9	86.5			2.3		
Poland	68.8	18.6	50.2			6.8		
Romania	52.5	11.7	40.8					
USSR	51.0	28.2	22.8			16.2		
Yugoslavia	40.2	10.2	17.8	2.0	10.2	2.6		
E European average	54.8	24.4	29.6	2.5	9.4	13.3		
Others								
Cyprus								
Gibraltar								
Malta								
Monaco								
Turkey								
Average								
European average	65.4	22.4	32.4	3.7	17.0	9.9	0.8	3.0

Source: Euromonitor
Note: See end of section

Table No: 1402

FRESH PRODUCE CONSUMPTION

Per Capita Consumption of Fresh Produce 1991

Kg per inhabitant

	Cereals Total	Rice	Vegetables	Potatoes	Fruit	Citrus Fruit	Non-Citrus Fruit	Dried Fruit
EC members								
Belgium	100.0	5.4	99.6	96.2	75.6	20.8	54.9	1.3
Denmark	93.2	2.4	85.5	62.3	66.5	16.7	49.8	2.1
France	103.1	4.1	124.8	72.7	73.7	21.4	52.3	1.3
Germany: East	130.0		103.5	98.2	74.8	74.8		
Germany: West	101.5	3.0	79.1	75.0	119.1	34.8	84.3	1.5
Greece	146.2	6.4	202.8	85.2	43.9	39.7	4.2	2.9
Ireland	147.3	2.6	99.3	139.6	49.4	17.0	32.4	2.6
Italy	162.2	5.4	174.7	37.8	102.7	33.9	68.8	0.6
Luxembourg								
Netherlands	75.3	5.4	100.8	85.8	144.1	80.7	63.4	3.1
Portugal	125.6	15.7	125.0	91.0	35.8	12.3	23.5	0.9
Spain	98.4	91.9	123.8	98.3	87.1	36.3	50.8	0.4
United Kingdom	120.2	3.8	81.9	105.1	64.0	26.9	37.1	2.8
EC average	117.2	15.1	116.1	79.5	87.6	33.8	56.5	1.5
EFTA members								
Austria	93.3	4.0	72.5	60.1	94.7	18.9	75.8	1.6
Finland	92.5	4.9	35.7	63.8	61.6	17.6	44.0	1.9
Iceland								
Liechtenstein								
Norway	85.5	1.9	41.4	62.4	59.6	15.1	44.5	1.7
Sweden	81.7	3.9	98.9	60.9	66.8	13.9	52.9	1.7
Switzerland	79.2	5.9	82.1	48.8	80.1	19.3	60.7	1.4
EFTA average	86.2	4.2	71.6	58.9	74.5	16.9	57.5	1.6
Eastern Europe								
Albania				43.1				
Bulgaria	216.0		141.7	27.6	111.4	1.2	110.2	
Czechoslovakia	171.0		78.1	81.1	67.0			
Hungary	215.0		148.5	49.2				
Poland	197.4		119.1	142.0				
Romania	125.7		197.5	59.0				
USSR	166.6		102.1	100.0	41.0			
Yugoslavia	152.0		80.5	44.1	49.1	3.7	45.4	0.2
Average	168.8		109.0	94.3	44.7	3.0	63.1	0.2
Others								
Cyprus								
Gibraltar								
Malta								
Monaco								
Turkey	195.6	4.9	191.5	65.8	93.8	13.7	80.2	3.9
Average	195.6	4.9	191.5	65.8	93.8	13.7	80.2	3.9
European average	146.4	12.9	116.3	85.0	68.7	28.0	60.0	1.8

Sources: OECD/Euromonitor

Table No: 1403

DAIRY PRODUCTS CONSUMPTION

Per Capita Consumption of Dairy Products and Eggs 1991

Kg per capita except milk (litres) and eggs (units)

	Eggs	Butter	Cheese	Cream	Yoghurt	Milk
EC members						
Belgium[a]	206.7	8.4	12.9	4.2	7.4	86.7
Denmark	179.4	6.8	11.7	7.6	8.4	101.4
France	229.9	7.7	23.0	1.5	16.2	55.8
Germany: East		12.0	15.0			61.5
Germany: West[b]	216.6	6.8	19.0	5.7	6.2	68.4
Greece	244.1	1.0	19.0	0.3	7.7	72.0
Ireland	170.8	3.6	5.9	0.8	3.4	140.9
Italy	170.5	1.1	15.8	0.7	3.2	47.9
Luxembourg				2.9	8.3	
Netherlands	166.8	1.8	13.7	2.9	22.0	61.6
Portugal	152.4	1.0	4.5	1.3	6.7	68.0
Spain	225.7	0.1	5.0	1.3	9.3	98.3
United Kingdom	156.1	1.8	4.4	0.9	4.4	115.7
EC average	196.4	4.1	13.8	2.2	7.9	75.4
EFTA members						
Austria	247.3	5.7	8.2	5.4	10.0	76.7
Finland[c]	165.3	6.0	12.0	6.4	11.6	162.4
Iceland				2.5		
Liechtenstein						
Norway	181.0	2.7	13.9	5.6	5.7	156.5
Sweden	107.5	1.9	13.4	7.2	9.4	108.6
Switzerland	188.3	4.5	13.1	6.6	16.7	93.8
EFTA average	176.6	4.1	11.9	6.3	10.9	105.9
Eastern Europe						
Albania						
Bulgaria	176.0	16.3		0.1		
Czechoslovakia		8.5	7.1	1.1		1266.5
Hungary[d]	380.0	2.6		1.6		1000.0
Poland[e]		3.0		0.9		
Romania[f]	233.6					
USSR	243.6	6.5		1.4		
Yugoslavia	174.0	17.1	4.5			
East European average	240.6	7.0	5.5	1.3		1159.8
Others						
Cyprus						
Gibraltar						
Malta						
Monaco						
Turkey[f]		2.2				
Average		2.2				
European average	201.4	5.3	12.9	2.0	8.1	148.7

Sources: OECD/US Department of Agriculture/Euromonitor
Notes: See end of section

Table No: 1404

BAKERY PRODUCTS CONSUMPTION

Per Capita Consumption of Bakery Products 1991

Kg per inhabitant

	Bread	Breakfast Cereals	Pasta	Flour	Biscuits
EC members					
Belgium	86.4	1.2	1.8		5.3
Denmark	30.1	3.9	2.4	78.2	2.0
France	65.1	0.9	6.6		6.6
Germany: East	99.0	2.0			
Germany: West	61.8	0.8	5.4	65.7	3.2
Greece	80.0	1.1	6.0		8.1
Ireland	79.7	8.6	0.7		13.8
Italy	69.8	0.2	25.5		8.9
Luxembourg	48.6				
Netherlands	60.1	1.3	1.5	34.4	4.7
Portugal	86.0	1.7	5.6		6.3
Spain	56.9	0.4	4.0		3.8
United Kingdom	35.1	5.8	3.5	4.4	10.8
EC average	62.1	1.8	8.3	37.8	6.7
EFTA members					
Austria	51.1	1.9	3.5	69.5	5.3
Finland	32.4	5.0	2.2	76.3	3.7
Iceland					
Liechtenstein					
Norway	51.5	1.3	0.2		1.8
Sweden	32.9	2.3	3.3	23.4	4.1
Switzerland	22.8	4.2	9.3	6.1	6.4
EFTA average	37.5	2.9	4.0	41.6	4.5
Eastern Europe					
Albania					
Bulgaria	140.0			50.0	
Czechoslovakia	118.0				
Hungary	118.0	3.0		108.0	
Poland	122.0	5.7			
Romania	132.0				
USSR	130.0	7.0			
Yugoslavia	109.1	12.0			
East European average	127.6	7.1		81.2	
Others					
Cyprus					
Gibraltar					
Malta					
Monaco					
Turkey		2.0			
Average		2.0			
European average	95.2	4.2	7.9	42.9	6.5

Source: Euromonitor from various sources

Table No: 1405

CONSUMPTION OF CONVENIENCE AND MISCELLANEOUS FOODS

Per Capita Consumption of Convenience and Miscellaneous Foods 1991

Kg per inhabitant, except soup (litres)

	Frozen Foods	Canned Foods	Soups	Sugar	Jams and preserves
EC members					
Belgium[a]	17.8	34.2		43.5	3.6
Denmark	48.0	10.8	2.4	46.7	2.3
France	23.3	44.0	5.3	38.0	2.1
Germany: East				40.8	
Germany: West	29.1	34.4	13.1	34.9	3.3
Greece		28.2		33.9	1.1
Ireland		22.8	18.8	52.4	2.6
Italy	4.6	13.5	7.0	30.7	0.5
Luxembourg					
Netherlands	17.0	14.7	27.3	53.4	1.1
Portugal		6.8		35.4	1.0
Spain	14.8	14.8	3.4	29.4	1.0
United Kingdom	14.3	22.0		43.3	1.5
EC average	18.1	25.4	9.0	37.2	1.8
EFTA members					
Austria	12.3	11.3		50.0	1.4
Finland	14.4	21.3	1.0	47.4	1.0
Iceland					
Liechtenstein					
Norway	20.6	12.5		38.2	2.4
Sweden	14.7	16.1	2.5	45.8	5.1
Switzerland	23.1	14.9	4.3	42.4	1.2
EFTA average	16.6	15.0	2.7	45.4	2.4
Eastern Europe					
Albania					
Bulgaria				35.7	
Czechoslovakia				37.3	
Hungary				34.0	
Poland				46.1	
Romania				26.0	
USSR				46.6	
Yugoslavia				38.9	
East European average				44.0	
Others					
Cyprus[b]				33.0	
Gibraltar					
Malta[b]				45.0	
Monaco					
Turkey				30.0	
Average				30.1	
European average	18.0	24.5	8.5	40.3	1.8

Source: Euromonitor from various sources
Notes: See end of section

Table No: 1406

CONSUMPTION OF SNACK FOODS AND HOT BEVERAGES

Per Capita Consumption of Snack Foods and Hot Beverages 1991

Kg per inhabitant

	Confectionery: Chocolate	Confectionery: Sugar	Ice Cream	Savoury Snacks	Tea	Coffee
EC members						
Belgium[a]	7.1	5.4	9.9	3.3	0.1	6.8
Denmark	5.0	4.7	8.9	1.8	0.3	6.8
France	5.4	3.1	6.4	2.0	0.1	4.4
Germany: East						
Germany: West	6.0	8.7	8.2	3.6	0.3	7.8
Greece	2.4	2.7	4.2		0.0	3.1
Ireland	6.3	5.7	8.3		3.1	1.7
Italy	1.3	3.1	5.6	1.1	0.2	2.9
Luxembourg						
Netherlands	5.3	4.8	7.5	5.3	0.7	8.4
Portugal	0.5	2.4	1.9	1.4	0.0	2.6
Spain	2.4	2.7	4.7	1.1	0.0	1.5
United Kingdom	8.6	5.3	7.8	4.0	2.2	2.3
EC average	4.8	4.7	6.6	2.6	0.6	4.2
EFTA members						
Austria	7.8	2.6	4.5		0.2	10.6
Finland	3.3	4.1	8.3	1.0	0.2	12.8
Iceland						
Liechtenstein						
Norway	7.9	4.6	12.1	4.4	0.2	9.9
Sweden	6.0	4.6	13.9	2.6	0.2	7.3
Switzerland	10.6	3.1	7.8	1.5	0.2	8.2
EFTA average	7.2	3.7	9.3	2.3	0.2	9.5
Eastern Europe						
Albania						
Bulgaria					0.1	
Czechoslovakia					0.2	
Hungary					0.2	2.7
Poland					0.9	2.7
Romania					0.1	
USSR					0.5	
Yugoslavia					0.2	
East European average					0.5	2.7
Others						
Cyprus						
Gibraltar						
Malta						
Monaco						
Turkey					2.6	
Average					2.6	
European average	5.0	4.6	6.9	2.6	0.6	4.5

Sources: Euromonitor/International Tea Committee
Notes: See end of section

Table No: 1407

DRINKS CONSUMPTION

Per Capita Consumption of Drinks 1991

Litres per inhabitant

	Carbonated Drinks	Mineral Water	Fruit Juices	Beer	Wine	Spirits
EC members						
Belgium[a]	76.7	74.3	16.0	125.1	23.3	3.1
Denmark	50.5	10.9	19.4	116.6	21.7	3.3
France	30.8	87.9	9.9	40.0	69.5	4.4
Germany: East				137.4	11.2	5.0
Germany: West	91.0	62.2	41.5	148.3	25.6	7.5
Greece	38.0	21.3	4.4	23.8	24.7	14.6
Ireland	68.3	4.8	8.7	91.0	3.9	4.1
Italy	46.8	119.3	4.1	23.0	70.7	3.2
Luxembourg						
Netherlands	72.8	14.5	24.1	90.8	15.4	6.1
Portugal	31.5	28.5	3.4	46.0	55.4	2.6
Spain	64.8	55.0	15.0	73.0	37.3	8.8
United Kingdom	114.9	7.7	17.4	109.8	12.5	3.7
EC average	68.2	60.7	17.5	83.1	38.9	5.4
EFTA members						
Austria	52.7	65.3	39.2	123.6	6.0	3.8
Finland	48.2	8.3	19.3	57.4	8.6	6.0
Iceland						
Liechtenstein						
Norway	90.1	4.9	12.5	52.7	6.5	2.2
Sweden	38.0	6.6	12.1	58.5	11.6	4.2
Switzerland	74.6	61.9	14.9	72.6	47.0	32.5
EFTA average	57.6	32.2	20.4	76.1	16.5	10.0
Eastern Europe						
Albania						
Bulgaria				62.0	26.0	3.6
Czechoslovakia				131.8	11.9	3.3
Hungary				97.1	21.1	4.2
Poland				29.0	7.8	4.6
Romania						
USSR				17.0	15.3	3.2
Yugoslavia				48.3	27.5	5.3
East European average				28.0	15.6	3.5
Others						
Cyprus						
Gibraltar						
Malta				48.9	27.9	4.3
Monaco						
Turkey				6.4	0.2	1.1
Average				6.6	0.4	1.1
European average	67.3	58.1	17.7	51.5	24.3	4.4

Source: Euromonitor
Note: See end of section

Table No: 1408

TOBACCO CONSUMPTION

Consumption of Tobacco Products 1991

Total consumption (millions)/units per inhabitant

	Cigarettes (millions)	Cigars/Cigarillos per capita	Cigarettes per capita
EC members			
Belgium	16885	66.5	1714.2
Denmark	6837	58.3	1330.2
France	95608	25.7	1688.0
Germany: East	29220		1749.7
Germany: West	136304	15.6	2155.0
Greece	29276	0.5	2920.3
Ireland	6129	5.1	1751.1
Italy	93843	2.9	1627.8
Luxembourg			
Netherlands	18424	36.5	1223.4
Portugal	14320	2.4	1353.5
Spain	85624	18.3	2168.8
United Kingdom	99153	30.3	1725.9
EC total/average	631623	20.2	1829.1
EFTA members			
Austria	14517	4.2	1856.4
Finland	7143	13.1	1400.6
Iceland			
Liechtenstein			
Norway	3001	3.5	706.1
Sweden	10546	10.3	1226.3
Switzerland	13154	40.0	1948.8
EFTA total/average	48362	14.6	1487.1
Eastern Europe			
Albania			
Bulgaria	9151		1016.8
Czechoslovakia	25804		1642.5
Hungary	26646		2537.7
Poland	99769		2611.7
Romania	35402		1522.7
USSR	382418		1318.7
Yugoslavia	40441		1690.0
East European total/average	619630		1509.1
Others			
Cyprus			
Gibraltar			
Malta	1062		2990.3
Monaco			
Turkey	72976		1273.6
Total/average	74038		1284.2
European total/average	1373653	17.0	1623.5

Source: Euromonitor/World Tobacco

Table No: 1409

CONSUMPTION OF HOUSEHOLD CLEANING PRODUCTS

Per Capita Consumption of Household Cleaning Products 1991

Kg per inhabitant

	Textile Washing Powders	Textile Washing Liquids	Fabric Conditioners	Dishwashing Liquids	Automatic Dishwashing Powders	Toilet Soaps	Surface Cleaners
EC members							
Belgium[a]	10.0	1.1	5.3	5.3	1.6	0.8	3.5
Denmark	9.0	1.9	4.5	1.4	1.9	1.0	10.1
France	10.6	3.4	3.0	1.7	0.9	0.6	2.9
Germany: East							
Germany: West	9.4	1.7	4.3	2.6	1.1	0.6	3.1
Greece	5.6	4.0	0.7	3.1	0.2	0.8	2.5
Ireland	4.8	1.4	1.1	2.6	0.6	0.6	2.0
Italy	8.5	1.4	2.3	4.7	0.4	0.7	4.6
Luxembourg							
Netherlands	10.1	1.7	2.8	2.9	0.4	0.7	2.2
Portugal	5.3	1.0	0.3	5.2	0.2	0.7	2.9
Spain	13.4	1.2	5.6	6.7	0.3	0.3	3.2
United Kingdom	7.0	3.5	2.7	2.4	1.2	1.2	6.9
EC average	9.2	2.2	3.3	3.4	0.8	0.7	4.0
EFTA members							
Austria	7.8	0.2	2.3	1.4	1.0	0.7	1.7
Finland	5.0	1.0	1.4	1.8	0.8	0.4	2.8
Iceland							
Liechtenstein							
Norway	4.7	1.7	2.4	1.9	0.9	1.2	7.8
Sweden	11.4			8.2	0.7	0.6	8.2
Switzerland	9.2	1.7	2.4	1.7	2.3	0.9	4.8
EFTA average	8.2	1.0	2.2	3.4	1.2	0.7	5.0
Eastern Europe							
Albania							
Bulgaria				6.8	2.7	0.4	
Czechoslovakia				8.5	0.8	0.2	
Hungary				9.3	2.0	0.4	
Poland				0.8	0.2	0.1	
Romania							
USSR			0.1	0.1	0.0		
Yugoslavia				2.1	0.5	0.2	
East European average				1.0	0.2	0.1	
Others							
Cyprus							
Gibraltar							
Malta							
Monaco							
Turkey						1.1	
Average						1.1	
European average	9.1	2.1	3.2	2.2	0.5	0.4	4.1

Sources: Euromonitor/Association Internationale de la Savonnerie et la Détergence
Note: See end of section

Table No: 1410

MARKET SIZES: PAPER PRODUCTS

Retail Sales of Disposable Paper Products 1991

Current US dollars (millions)

	Toilet Tissues	Facial Tissues	Sanitary Products	Disposable Nappies	Kitchen Towels	Moist Wipes
EC members						
Belgium	120.5	7.1	40.5	19.9		
Denmark	46.9	4.3	21.0	20.8	31.3	
France	531.7	195.0	336.8	709.0	252.6	23.9
Germany: East						
Germany: West	528.3	277.5	422.9	503.5		
Greece	66.6	9.5	51.8	10.7		
Ireland	56.5	7.9	23.4	24.8		4.2
Italy	321.8	73.3	281.1	366.4		
Luxembourg	3.4		1.6	0.4		
Netherlands	154.0	36.7	238.7	79.3	44.9	14.4
Portugal	76.1	8.7	14.4	20.4	9.7	21.6
Spain	347.1	41.0	223.3	461.3	64.1	26.0
United Kingdom	1017.3	244.0	316.7	790.9	221.2	70.8
EC total	3270.3	905.1	1972.3	3007.4		
EFTA members						
Austria	75.3	31.1	127.4	29.4		
Finland	55.1	6.3	16.8	44.5		
Iceland						
Liechtenstein						
Norway	66.7	4.2	6.3	34.4		
Sweden	155.1	9.9	82.7	157.1	76.4	5.0
Switzerland	77.4	30.7	118.6	53.7	22.3	
EFTA total	429.6	82.1	351.8	319.1		
Eastern Europe						
Albania						
Bulgaria						
Czechoslovakia						
Hungary						
Poland						
Romania						
USSR						
Yugoslavia						
East European total						
Others						
Cyprus						
Gibraltar						
Malta						
Monaco						
Turkey						
Total						
European total						

Source: Euromonitor

Table No: 1411

MARKET SIZES: COSMETICS AND TOILETRIES

Retail Sales of Cosmetics and Toiletries 1991

Current US dollars (millions)

	Women's Fragrances	Shaving Products	Colour Cosmetics	Skincare	Suncare	Haircare
EC members						
Belgium	73.7	36.0	83.1	126.6	10.7	170.0
Denmark	34.0	11.0	37.0	63.8	5.8	73.8
France	1081.2	309.0	957.0	1639.0	119.6	1595.2
Germany: East		21.1	65.0	121.9	56.9	146.2
Germany: West	866.0	629.0	591.7	1092.9	135.3	1200.0
Greece	42.2	9.0	18.0	52.7	12.9	100.0
Ireland	22.9	21.0	36.1	23.8	7.3	47.9
Italy	653.0	605.0	732.9	930.8	139.9	1085.0
Luxembourg						
Netherlands	122.5	46.0	122.5	225.0	29.3	332.1
Portugal	46.5	13.0	22.1	19.0	4.2	45.5
Spain	333.9	119.0	239.0	356.1	123.1	425.6
United Kingdom	690.0	410.0	796.2	509.2	155.7	1146.0
EC total	3965.9	2229.1	3700.8	5160.8	800.6	6367.4
EFTA members						
Austria	64.9	65.0	91.5	195.4	31.6	260.0
Finland	35.6	9.0	45.6	86.6	6.2	115.2
Iceland						
Liechtenstein						
Norway	30.9	6.0	75.6	112.6	4.1	117.2
Sweden	41.3	36.0	90.0	104.2	18.0	177.7
Switzerland	76.1	54.0	84.0	163.9	38.4	156.9
EFTA total	248.8	170.0	387.6	662.7	98.3	827.0
Eastern Europe						
Albania						
Bulgaria		1.8	3.6	9.0	0.4	22.5
Czechoslovakia		5.0	11.0	22.7	0.8	43.8
Hungary		5.2	8.4	21.9	0.6	36.6
Poland		11.4	22.8	45.7	1.5	102.7
Romania		4.6	7.0	16.2	0.7	55.7
USSR		57.1	85.7	199.9	8.6	685.4
Yugoslavia		11.4	18.6	48.9	1.4	69.8
East European total		96.5	157.1	364.3	14.0	1016.5
Others						
Cyprus						
Gibraltar						
Malta						
Monaco						
Turkey						
Total						
European total						

Source: Euromonitor

Table No: 1411 (cont'd)

COSMETICS AND TOILETRIES

Retail Sales of Cosmetics and Toiletries 1991

Current US dollars (millions)

	Bath and Shower Products	Deodorants	Oral Hygiene	Baby Care
EC members				
Belgium	36.0	68.6	52.9	14.8
Denmark	17.8	29.6	56.2	6.3
France	381.1	265.9	443.1	75.3
Germany: East	91.0	58.5	113.7	
Germany: West	365.2	477.3	670.0	181.3
Greece	7.7	12.1	28.2	2.0
Ireland	12.9	15.8	29.9	7.1
Italy	328.9	316.8	447.0	52.9
Luxembourg				
Netherlands	100.5	95.7	139.0	24.7
Portugal	10.8	12.3	12.9	5.6
Spain	158.7	172.8	229.1	77.6
United Kingdom	197.0	362.7	573.3	286.6
EC total	1707.7	1888.0	2795.2	734.1
EFTA members				
Austria	64.0	65.3	76.0	13.2
Finland	24.4	23.7	19.2	2.1
Iceland				
Liechtenstein				
Norway	20.8	44.7	33.2	4.7
Sweden	31.0	66.0	61.2	8.3
Switzerland	75.3	65.0	99.7	18.1
EFTA total	215.5	264.7	289.3	46.4
Eastern Europe				
Albania				
Bulgaria	7.1	4.5	13.5	
Czechoslovakia	15.7	15.7	31.3	
Hungary	12.5	12.5	26.1	
Poland	30.4	22.8	54.7	
Romania	16.2	11.6	32.5	
USSR	199.9	142.8	399.8	
Yugoslavia	27.9	27.9	58.2	
East European total	309.7	237.8	616.1	
Others				
Cyprus				
Gibraltar				
Malta				
Monaco				
Turkey				
Total				
European total				

Source: Euromonitor

Table No: 1412

MARKET SIZES: OTC HEALTHCARE

Retail Sales of OTC Healthcare Products 1991

Current US dollars (millions)

	Analgesics	Cough/Cold Remedies	Digestive Remedies	Medicated Skincare	Vitamins/ Tonics	Total
EC members						
Belgium	64.8	27.6	33.6	20.8	42.3	189.1
Denmark	50.0	81.3	12.5	7.8	15.6	167.2
France	77.1	354.5	110.8	554.8	170.2	1267.4
Germany: East						
Germany: West	388.7	527.3	298.0	352.3	454.6	2020.9
Greece	8.0	11.8	5.3	6.6	5.1	36.7
Ireland	16.2	15.8	8.3	10.0	25.1	75.4
Italy	142.1	245.0	192.1	88.0	38.3	705.4
Luxembourg	3.8	1.7	1.9	1.2	2.5	11.3
Netherlands	45.3	24.3	22.9	22.7	34.1	149.4
Portugal	7.5	11.9	4.1	7.4	7.3	38.2
Spain	37.0	106.1	41.7	43.7	73.7	302.2
United Kingdom	279.6	359.3	178.7	200.0	156.3	1173.9
EC total	1120.1	1766.6	909.9	1315.3	1025.1	6137.1
EFTA members						
Austria	25.2	34.5	22.9	16.6	66.8	166.1
Finland	21.0	13.9	17.2	13.1	6.3	71.5
Iceland						
Liechtenstein						
Norway	14.2	11.4	6.3	6.0	10.9	48.7
Sweden	62.5	35.4	26.3	22.0	6.7	152.9
Switzerland	37.0	41.8	33.5	24.4	108.1	244.8
EFTA total	159.9	137.0	106.2	82.1	198.8	684.0
Eastern Europe						
Albania						
Bulgaria						
Czechoslovakia						
Hungary						
Poland						
Romania						
USSR						
Yugoslavia						
East European total						
Others						
Cyprus						
Gibraltar						
Malta						
Monaco						
Turkey						
Total						
European total						

Source: Euromonitor

Table No: 1413

MARKET SIZES: CLOTHING AND FOOTWEAR

Retail Sales of Clothing and Footwear 1990/91

Current US dollars (millions) except footwear (million pairs)

	Men's Outerwear	Women's Outerwear	Underwear, Nightwear	Knitwear	Socks, Stockings and Tights	Clothing Accessories	Footwear
EC members							
Belgium	1381.5	2333.9	883.4	638.0	346.8	293.6	39.1
Denmark	600.8	997.9	339.1	268.8	106.7	118.8	23.7
France	6807.2	8241.8	4120.9	4652.6	1905.4	2368.7	330.0
Germany: East				1271.3	424.5		78.1
Germany: West	12481.0	19065.4	5798.1	5923.1	3087.8	2272.0	312.9
Greece	468.4	811.9	43.9	349.3	105.7	90.9	23.2
Ireland	189.2	269.3	72.7	114.7	61.4	41.2	14.0
Italy	9169.1	11262.1	5263.5	5041.3	1740.9	1607.7	303.5
Luxembourg	43.8	85.9	31.8	36.8	14.3	10.7	
Netherlands	1710.6	2925.7	760.2	1670.6	187.2	460.8	65.0
Portugal	421.9	763.1	296.0	314.7	100.9	81.6	23.6
Spain	2445.2	4738.4	1651.7	1863.7	537.8	418.3	150.8
United Kingdom	6645.0	11858.4	4287.1	3516.6	813.9	1449.3	256.0
EC total	42363.6	63353.9	23548.3	25661.6	9433.5	9213.6	1619.9
EFTA members							
Austria	1701.4	2592.3	1090.8	921.5	303.3	276.5	38.7
Finland	597.2	967.9	344.0	441.5	99.6	173.3	20.5
Iceland							
Liechtenstein							
Norway	683.2	1037.2	157.7	283.5	121.6	188.5	16.6
Sweden	1611.3	2336.4	214.9	627.9	228.1	103.2	30.3
Switzerland	945.6	1603.9	645.1	557.9	198.7	179.9	39.0
EFTA total	5538.6	8537.7	2452.5	2832.2	951.3	921.4	145.1
Eastern Europe							
Albania							
Bulgaria				198.2	81.5		21.6
Czechoslovakia				801.1	256.7		88.1
Hungary			99.1	185.8	51.8		21.2
Poland				651.3	217.2		72.7
Romania				509.8	98.4		54.4
USSR				18616.2	4111.4		799.7
Yugoslavia							40.1
East European total				20962.5	4816.9		1097.8
Others							
Cyprus							3.0
Gibraltar							
Malta							2.1
Monaco							
Turkey							
Total							
European total							

Sources: Euromonitor/Shoe & Allied Trades Research Association

Table No: 1414

MARKET SIZES: HOME FURNISHINGS AND HOUSEWARES

Retail Sales of Home Furnishings and Housewares 1991

Current US dollars (millions)

	Furniture	Floor Coverings	Household Textiles	Glassware	China and Porcelain	Ceramic Housewares	Cutlery
EC members							
Belgium	2250.3	973.2	1201.9	169.9	62.7	51.3	59.9
Denmark	1570.9	308.8	451.6	29.2	37.9	17.5	14.4
France	10634.5	772.5	4076.6	744.4	576.0	182.7	646.9
Germany: East							
Germany: West	16089.2	2950.4	3141.1	1512.3	811.2	620.5	312.5
Greece	519.8			23.6	23.5	34.9	35.9
Ireland	244.5	120.9	142.4	72.7	9.8	19.6	6.9
Italy	12021.8	1475.7	4821.3	957.1	382.1	241.1	236.3
Luxembourg							2.4
Netherlands	2893.6	976.1	1868.9	184.3	82.2	36.4	68.4
Portugal	529.0			234.1	44.9	66.1	28.3
Spain	5505.2	678.8	2207.7	631.4	153.6	153.6	162.2
United Kingdom	6309.1	1557.3	4057.5	513.3	265.4	474.3	109.7
EC total	58567.8	9813.7	21968.9	5072.2	2449.3	1897.9	1683.8
EFTA members							
Austria	2189.7	697.5	1238.2	40.1	50.2	33.4	45.9
Finland	494.6	202.8	383.7	89.3	20.8	72.4	53.2
Iceland							
Liechtenstein							
Norway	956.4	202.6	562.0	124.9	30.9	26.3	42.0
Sweden	2397.5	355.5	979.0	150.9	90.7	36.7	30.7
Switzerland	1917.7	575.3	976.3	113.0	25.1	21.0	20.9
EFTA total	7955.9	2033.6	4139.3	518.2	217.6	189.8	192.6
Eastern Europe							
Albania	381.7						
Bulgaria	660.2						
Czechoslovakia	355.5						
Hungary	231.6						
Poland	891.7						
Romania	10600.0						
USSR	444.6						
Yugoslavia							
East European total	13565.3						
Others							
Cyprus							
Gibraltar							
Malta							
Monaco							
Turkey							
Total							
European total							

Source: Euromonitor

Table No: 1415

MARKET SIZES: WHITE GOODS

Retail Sales of White Goods 1991

'000

	Refriger-ators	Fridge-Freezers	Freezers	Cookers	Microwave Ovens	Washing Machines	Tumble Dryers	Dish-washers
EC members								
Belgium	229.9	142.5	166.0	226.5	227.3	294.9	120.3	65.1
Denmark	157.7	149.8	76.0	155.3	62.5	125.5	42.7	52.0
France	1506.9	560.0	782.1	2290.0	1150.0	1964.6	480.0	780.0
Germany: East								
Germany: West[a]	3300.0	161.0	1100.0	2600.0	2200.0	2390.0	600.0	1100.0
Greece	356.7	355.2	387.1	311.1	27.2	62.9	20.7	12.5
Ireland	41.7	20.3	59.2	102.6	39.5	121.2	26.4	26.0
Italy	836.0	660.0	388.3	1000.7	600.0	1470.0	27.6	440.0
Luxembourg	10.5	10.7	12.7	19.6	20.4	13.5	11.7	9.2
Netherlands	450.0	126.1	170.0	364.6	375.0	486.6	260.0	75.0
Portugal	501.5	517.4	94.0		49.6	234.5	13.1	24.2
Spain	682.0	2234.5	231.0	796.8	521.0	1130.0	85.9	255.0
United Kingdom	956.0	820.0	452.0	1943.0	950.0	1780.0	420.0	325.0
EC total	9028.8	5757.5	3918.4	9810.1	6222.5	10073.7	2108.5	3163.9
EFTA members								
Austria	227.0	236.0	126.4	185.5	146.9	203.0	29.7	112.1
Finland	100.0	16.5	76.0	129.0	155.0	130.0	15.5	69.0
Iceland								
Liechtenstein								
Norway	60.7	59.5	68.3	99.5	115.0	118.0	34.3	56.6
Sweden	205.0	155.0	215.0	470.0	320.0	220.0	75.0	145.0
Switzerland	295.0	300.0	90.0	131.2	110.0	216.0	38.0	115.0
EFTA total	887.7	767.0	575.7	1015.2	846.9	887.0	192.5	497.7
Eastern Europe								
Albania								
Bulgaria[a,b,c]	192.6			154.3		95.1		
Czechoslovakia[a,b,c]	628.1	519.0				216.6		
Hungary[a,c]	606.1					135.8	112.9	
Poland[a,b,c]	813.4					396.0		
Romania[c]	221.0					266.3		
USSR[a,b,c]	4794.0					6130.2		
Yugoslavia		572.0		248.0		283.5		
East European total	7255.2					7523.5		
Others								
Cyprus								
Gibraltar								
Malta								
Monaco								
Turkey								
Total								
European total								

Sources: Euromonitor/Comecon
Notes: See end of section

Table No: 1416

MARKET SIZES: CONSUMER ELECTRONICS5

Retail Sales of Consumer Electronics 1991

'000

	Colour TVs	Video Recorders	Video Cameras	Home Computers	Audio Separates	CD Players
EC members						
Belgium	398.8	347.4	5.3	137.4	230.1	65.3
Denmark	335.0	240.0	45.0	49.0	480.0	41.0
France	3400.0	2000.0	700.0	1273.5	2402.7	1185.7
Germany: East						
Germany: West	5700.0	3200.0	1000.0	2060.0	6276.4	1799.3
Greece	196.5	192.8	2.1	31.6	76.3	10.4
Ireland	137.4	69.2	1.1	37.7	92.3	9.6
Italy	2791.1	1481.6	314.3	985.3	1614.5	417.4
Luxembourg	88.9				83.2	6.5
Netherlands	691.8	575.0	225.0	203.3	925.0	136.0
Portugal	284.0	165.1		22.3	296.8	17.7
Spain	2550.0	1447.0	260.0	422.4	713.1	64.1
United Kingdom	3975.4	2051.3	455.0	1374.4	2963,5	465.1
EC total	20549.0	11769.4	3007.7	6597.0	16153.9	4218.1
EFTA members						
Austria	345.1	294.2		97.5	412.2	45.0
Finland	285.0	190.0	28.0	39.7	198.9	41.4
Iceland						
Liechtenstein						
Norway	165.0	95.0	45.0	41.8	453.0	10.4
Sweden	520.0	316.0	110.0	96.3	508.8	97.4
Switzerland	380.0	280.0	44.0	110.3	600.0	229.4
EFTA total	1695.1	1175.2	227.0	385.6	2172.9	423.7
Eastern Europe						
Albania						
Bulgaria	209.0	30.0				
Czechoslovakia	654.0	101.0				
Hungary	327.0	183.0				
Poland	768.5	15.0				
Romania	586.6	5.0				
USSR	11006.2	908.0				
Yugoslavia	716.3	1.0				
E European total	14267.6	1243.0				
Others						
Cyprus						
Gibraltar						
Malta						
Monaco						
Turkey						
Total						
European total						

Table No: 1416 (cont'd)

MARKET SIZES: CONSUMER ELECTRONICS5

Retail Sales of Consumer Electronics 1991

'000

	Personal Stereos	Portable Cassettes	Radio Recorders	Portable Radios	In-Car Entertainment
EC members					
Belgium	266.8	93.2	294.0	122.9	507.2
Denmark	95.1	123.0	271.0	96.4	246.0
France	2747.6	594.5	2138.4	850.0	3600.0
Germany: East					
Germany: West	4494.4	904.6	4056.2	1510.1	5994.4
Greece	307.2	158.9	97.3	334.3	94.4
Ireland	141.3	103.5	124.3	30.1	182.7
Italy	1700.6	381.5	1029.9	877.5	1649.6
Luxembourg					
Netherlands	874.9	269.1	415.6	297.0	700.0
Portugal	194.7	215.1	179.8	311.5	173.1
Spain	882.0	438.5	1345.9	1640.5	946.4
United Kingdom	4032.0	258.9	2261.8	1853.3	3670.8
EC total	15736.6	3540.7	12214.1	7923.7	17764.6
EFTA members					
Austria	262.9	51.0	349.6	121.1	346.8
Finland	203.0	123.1	265.1	58.5	136.0
Iceland					
Liechtenstein					
Norway	81.2	64.0	183.3	82.8	375.0
Sweden	363.4	130.9	532.7	189.4	760.0
Switzerland	385.6	83.1	284.9	503.8	330.0
EFTA total	1296.1	452.1	1615.6	955.6	1947.8
Eastern Europe					
Albania					
Bulgaria					
Czechoslovakia					
Hungary					
Poland					
Romania					
USSR					
Yugoslavia					
E European total					
Others					
Cyprus					
Gibraltar					
Malta					
Monaco					
Turkey					
Total					
European total					

Sources: Euromonitor/Comecon

Table No: 1417

MARKET SIZES: PERSONAL AND LEISURE GOODS

Retail Sales of Personal and Leisure Goods 1991

	Compact Discs (millions)	Singles EPs (millions)	LP Records (millions)	Blank Video Cassettes (millions)	Gardening Products ($ million)	Bicycles ('000)	Books ($ million)
EC members							
Belgium[a]	9.0	8.0	1.0	15.8	731.3	450.7	350.0
Denmark	3.2	0.9	4.0	9.6		428.8	355.0
France	55.0	28.0	7.0	56.9	5228.6	2440.5	2410.5
Germany: East	1.0	2.0	11.0				
Germany: West	76.0	28.0	45.0	91.5		3631.9	7540.0
Greece	1.0	0.9	4.8	4.2		160.6	119.0
Ireland	0.3	0.9	1.0	7.3		111.9	106.6
Italy	15.0	2.0	14.0	43.4	116.8	1893.8	2952.6
Luxembourg	0.8						7.6
Netherlands	35.0	6.0	3.0	23.5	1069.5	1356.8	343.3
Portugal	0.5	1.0	8.0	2.1		196.5	215.0
Spain	7.0	1.9	18.0	37.6		1216.7	2261.6
United Kingdom	51.0	58.0	25.0	49.5	4954.0	2384.5	3500.0
EC total	254.9	137.6	141.8	341.5	12100.2	14272.7	20161.1
EFTA members							
Austria	5.0	2.0	4.0	13.3	415.7	416.1	350.0
Finland	3.0	0.9	5.0	6.4		722.0	304.2
Iceland							
Liechtenstein							
Norway	3.1	0.9	1.9	8.6	127.3	296.5	524.5
Sweden	8.0	4.5	9.0	18.5	348.7	534.0	644.8
Switzerland	13.0	1.9	1.0	13.9	322.8	225.0	523.0
EFTA total	32.1	10.2	20.9	60.7	1214.5	2193.5	2346.5
Eastern Europe							
Albania							
Bulgaria[b]		1.0	4.0			142.0	
Czechoslovakia[b]	1.0	1.0	8.0			565.0	
Hungary[b]	2.0	1.0	2.0				
Poland[b]	1.0	1.0	9.0				
Romania[b]	1.0	1.0	6.0				
USSR[b]	1.0	31.0	150.0			375.0	3000.0
Yugoslavia[b]		1.0	5.0				
East European total	6.0	37.0	184.0				
Others							
Cyprus							
Gibraltar							
Malta							
Monaco							
Turkey							
Total							
European total							

Table No: 1417 (cont'd)

MARKET SIZES: PERSONAL AND LEISURE GOODS

Retail Sales of Personal and Leisure Goods 1990/91

	Watches ($ million)	Jewellery ($ million)	Toys/Games ($ million)	Cameras ('000)	Films (millions)	Pre-recorded Cassettes (millions)	Blank Audio Cassettes (millions)
EC members							
Belgium[a]	137.0	418.0	287.4	386.3	21.6	3.1	29.9
Denmark	88.7	157.9	146.9	94.9	14.3	2.0	11.2
France	1063.5	2038.3	3101.7	1880.4	85.4	40.2	51.3
Germany: East						7.2	
Germany: West	318.8	1756.0	3313.3	3828.0	126.5	63.8	126.5
Greece	27.4	1371.6	137.2	73.5	10.5	3.2	7.4
Ireland	28.1	361.0	70.7	171.6	6.2	2.1	3.1
Italy	522.8	3231.8	1494.5	1066.0	74.8	24.6	56.4
Luxembourg	5.1						
Netherlands	201.1	967.3	594.7	790.5	29.6	3.1	42.8
Portugal	198.6	75.2	86.3	52.0	5.2	2.1	6.2
Spain	474.6	1290.5	1042.5	614.3	29.4	28.4	41.0
United Kingdom	738.2	2566.4	1620.9	3822.0	88.2	81.3	105.8
EC total	3803.9	14234.0	11896.1	12779.3	491.8	261.0	481.6
EFTA members							
Austria	133.5	475.0	162.6	115.5	13.1	2.0	18.1
Finland	41.7	179.0	185.5	140.7	18.4	4.9	13.6
Iceland							
Liechtenstein							
Norway	67.3	169.7	216.0	96.0	12.9	4.0	14.9
Sweden	32.7	347.2	578.7	178.2	26.7	5.0	19.8
Switzerland	69.7	383.5	296.4	236.9	23.7	7.2	12.4
EFTA total	345.0	1554.4	1439.2	767.2	94.8	23.0	78.7
Eastern Europe							
Albania							
Bulgaria[b]						2.7	
Czechoslovakia[b]						3.1	
Hungary[b]	393.8					1.0	
Poland[b]						21.4	
Romania[b]						4.0	
USSR[b]						39.9	
Yugoslavia[b]						3.0	
East European total						75.1	
Others							
Cyprus							
Gibraltar							
Malta							
Monaco							
Turkey							
Total							
European total							

Source: Euromonitor
Notes: See end of section

Table No: 1418

MARKET SIZES: SMALL ELECTRICAL APPLIANCES

Retail Sales of Small Electrical Appliances 1990

'000

	Electric Blankets	Drinks Makers	Food Processors	Hair Dryers	Irons	Shavers	Space Heaters	Vacuum Cleaners	Toasters
EC members									
Belgium	55	470	1049	559	634	410	255	699	240
Denmark	22	373	314	225	157	176	319	186	78
France	300	4000	800	2289	3700	2750	3700	2900	1200
Germany: East								356	
Germany: West	1321	5632	2358	4151	5650	2900	1981	5500	1679
Greece	15	39	20	168	257	66	307	139	5
Ireland	113	10	176	186	137	98	75	100	164
Italy	262	291	1534	1553	3210	970	951	1527	223
Luxembourg	19	20	49	29	27	25	12	32	
Netherlands	85	1133	669	878	825	785	409	399	454
Portugal	14	96	200	240	322	111	149	192	
Spain		490	1105	2657	1742	488	1429	170	
United Kingdom	1533	2222	1589	2867	3299	2800	2333	3000	2167
EC total	3738	14775	9863	15804	19961	11579	11919	15201	6210
EFTA members									
Austria	139	464	443	557	495	196	247	299	103
Finland	70	421	79	141	187	227	264	180	8
Iceland									
Liechtenstein									
Norway	92	323	47	255	153	127	62	125	
Sweden	108	606	75	359	410	290	725	355	103
Switzerland	223	335	358	578	375		98	350	132
EFTA total	632	2150	1002	1890	1620	840	1397	1309	346
Eastern Europe									
Albania									
Bulgaria								91	
Czechoslovakia									
Hungary								185	
Poland								761	
Romania[a]								133	
USSR[b]								3418	
Yugoslavia									
East European total									
Others									
Cyprus									
Gibraltar									
Malta									
Monaco									
Turkey									
Total									
European total									

Sources: Euromonitor/Comecon
Notes: See end of section

Notes to Tables in Section Fourteen:

Table 1401 a Includes Luxembourg

Table 1403
a Includes Luxembourg, except cream and yoghurt
b Data for eggs refers to unified Germany
c Data for yoghurts refer to 1989
d Data refer to 1988, except for cream
e Data refer to 1987, except for cream
f Data refer to 1987

Table 1405
a Includes Luxembourg
b Data refer to 1988

Table 1406 Entries of 0.0 denote consumption levels below 50 grammes per capita
a Includes Luxembourg, except for ice cream

Table 1407 a Includes Luxembourg

Table 1409 a Includes Luxembourg

Table 1415
a Refrigerators includes fridge/freezers and freezers
b Washing machines include dryers
c Washing machines: 1991. Most other data: 1990

Table 1417 Compact discs exclude CD singles
a Includes Luxembourg, except for CDs and books
b Most data refer to 1990

Table 1418
a Data refer to 1980
b Data refer to 1985

Per Capita Consumption of Wine 1991: Selected countries

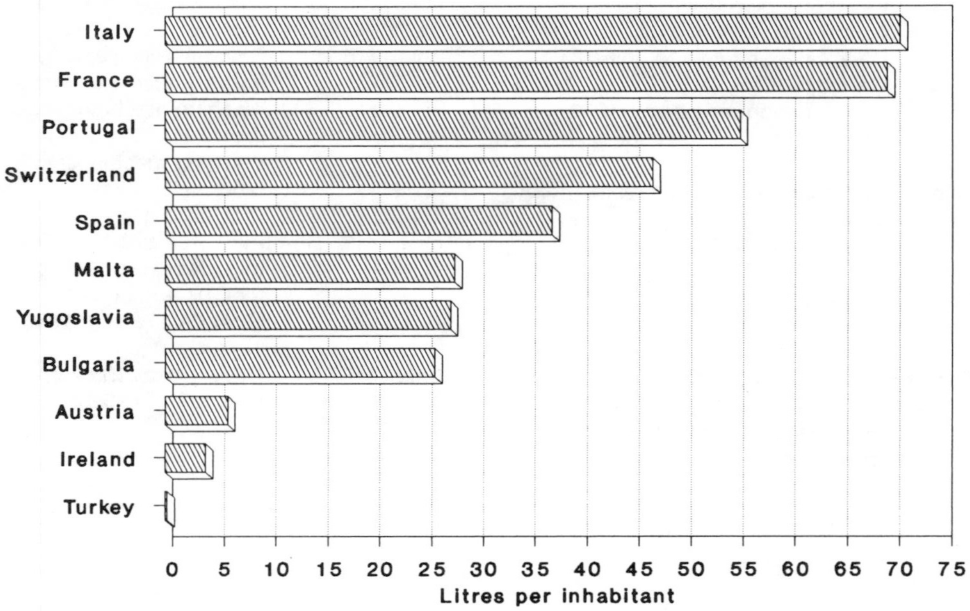

Per Capita Consumption of Fabric Conditioners 1991: Selected countries

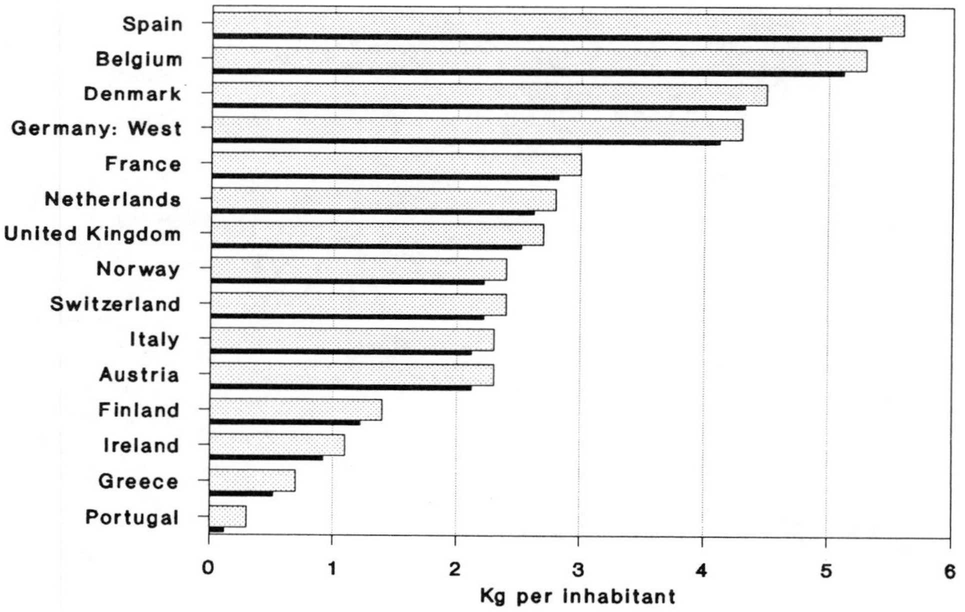

Section Fifteen

Consumer Prices and Costs

Table No: 1501

CONSUMER PRICES

Trends in Consumer Prices 1980-1991

1985 = 100	1980	1983	1984	1985	1986	1987	1988	1989	1990	1991
EC members										
Belgium	71.2	89.7	95.4	100.0	101.3	102.9	104.1	107.3	111.0	114.6
Denmark	68.3	89.8	95.5	100.0	103.6	107.8	112.7	118.1	121.2	124.1
France	63.3	88.0	94.6	100.0	102.6	106.0	108.8	112.6	116.4	120.0
Germany: East	99.9	100.1	100.1	100.0	100.0	100.0	100.1			
Germany: West	82.6	95.5	97.9	100.0	99.9	100.1	101.4	104.2	107.0	110.7
Greece	39.1	70.9	83.8	100.0	123.1	143.3	162.5	184.8	222.5	265.9
Ireland	56.1	87.3	94.9	100.0	103.8	107.1	109.4	113.8	117.6	121.4
Italy	51.8	82.6	91.6	100.0	105.9	110.9	116.5	123.8	131.7	140.1
Luxembourg	70.8	90.0	96.1	100.0	100.3	101.0	101.7	105.1	109.0	112.4
Netherlands	81.5	94.7	97.8	100.0	100.1	99.3	100.3	101.2	103.7	107.7
Portugal	32.5	64.8	83.6	100.0	111.8	122.3	133.9	150.8	170.9	190.3
Spain	56.2	82.6	91.9	100.0	108.8	114.6	120.0	128.2	136.8	144.9
United Kingdom	70.7	89.8	94.4	100.0	103.5	107.7	113.0	121.8	133.4	141.1
EFTA members										
Austria	78.8	91.6	96.8	100.0	101.7	103.2	105.1	107.8	111.3	115.0
Finland	66.4	88.3	94.4	100.0	103.5	107.2	112.5	120.0	127.4	132.6
Iceland	13.9	58.5	75.5	100.0	121.4	146.3	180.5	218.0	251.8	268.9
Liechtenstein	81.0	93.9	96.7	100.0	100.7	101.4				
Norway	64.9	89.0	94.6	100.0	107.1	116.4	124.3	130.0	135.4	140.0
Sweden	65.0	86.2	93.1	100.0	104.2	108.6	114.9	122.3	135.1	147.8
Switzerland	81.0	93.9	96.7	100.0	100.7	102.1	104.1	107.4	113.2	119.8
Eastern Europe										
Albania										
Bulgaria	95.6	97.7	98.4	100.0	103.5	103.5	104.2			
Czechoslovakia	91.0	97.5	98.4	100.0	100.9	101.0	100.7	102.1	112.3	178.0
Hungary	71.9	86.3	93.5	100.0	105.2	113.9	132.5	155.0	198.7	
Poland	25.4	75.5	86.9	100.0	117.7	147.4	236.1	828.9	5684.3	9680.2
Romania	79.0	99.3	100.4	100.0	99.9	100.3	103.0	105.0	110.0	274.4
USSR	95.6	100.6	99.6	100.0	101.8	102.3	103.9	105.8	111.3	
Yugoslavia	14.5	37.5	58.1	100.0	190.9	419.0	1232.0	16511.0	112780.0	245183.0
Others										
Cyprus	72.7	89.8	95.3	100.0	101.4	104.2	107.3	111.7	116.7	122.6
Gibraltar	77.0	88.5	94.3	100.0	103.6	108.5	112.5	117.4	124.4	
Malta	84.7	99.1	99.5	100.0	100.4	100.9	103.4	104.3	107.4	110.2
Monaco										
Turkey	19.6	46.5	69.0	100.0	134.6	259.8	327.8	535.2	857.9	1414.0

Sources: International Monetary Fund (IMF)/International Labour Office (ILO)/national statistical offices
Notes: See end of section

Table No: 1502

FOOD PRICES

Trends in Food Prices 1980-1991

1980 = 100

	1980	1983	1984	1985	1986	1987	1988	1989	1990	1991
EC members										
Belgium[a]	100.0	126.0	135.9	140.6	143.3	142.7	142.7	147.2	152.6	108.9
Denmark[b]	100.0	130.0	142.0	148.0	151.0	152.0	158.0	164.0	164.8	165.0
France	100.0	140.3	151.4	158.9	164.4	167.3	169.9	177.2	184.4	188.6
Germany: East	100.0	100.1	100.1	100.1	100.1	100.1	100.1	100.1		
Germany: West	100.0	114.3	116.0	116.9	117.6	117.0	117.3	120.0	123.5	127.0
Greece	100.0	185.8	219.8	262.7	315.9	355.7	395.4	467.4	566.9	666.3
Ireland[c]	100.0	140.6	154.3	160.2	167.2	171.8	176.6	184.9	461.7	468.1
Italy[d]	100.0	152.0	165.9	180.3	190.2	198.3	206.1	219.1	232.6	243.6
Luxembourg[e]	100.0	129.4	138.1	103.7	106.7	105.2	106.4	109.8	114.1	103.4
Netherlands	100.0	112.3	116.9	117.8	116.7	115.1	115.4	116.4	119.0	122.7
Portugal[g]	100.0	185.5	242.6	285.5	311.6	338.9	371.4	424.8	482.7	529.0
Spain[h]	100.0	144.6	162.8	178.3	197.2	207.2	214.8	231.4	246.4	253.6
United Kingdom	100.0	120.7	127.4	131.4	135.7	139.9	144.7	152.9	165.2	177.9
EFTA members										
Austria	100.0	113.4	119.8	122.5	125.4	126.3	127.3	129.0	132.7	138.1
Finland	100.0	135.9	146.0	157.3	163.0	166.4	170.1	176.2	183.2	187.4
Iceland[h]	100.0	437.6	572.7	788.5	968.0	1119.0	1524.0	1816.0	2047.0	2095.3
Liechtenstein										
Norway	100.0	144.7	154.2	164.2	178.9	194.1	205.2	210.7	217.6	221.3
Sweden	100.0	144.2	161.0	172.9	185.3	191.1	201.6	213.2	228.6	239.1
Switzerland	100.0	120.6	125.1	128.9	130.6	132.1	135.3	137.6	145.1	151.7
Eastern Europe										
Albania										
Bulgaria	100.0	103.9	105.4	107.8	112.4	115.2				
Czechoslovakia[h]	100.0	110.0	110.8	113.7	114.1	114.3	114.0	114.1	126.8	184.2
Hungary[g]	100.0	113.9	127.7	135.7	138.7	151.4	175.0	206.0	278.5	336.9
Poland	100.0	353.0	400.7	448.4	517.0	638.0	985.7	3945.8	4984.8	7727.0
Romania[i]	100.0	141.4	142.9	142.9	142.2	144.0	143.5	143.0	149.2	195.1
USSR	100.0	106.5	106.6	108.5	114.2	119.3	121.4	122.3	125.2	
Yugoslavia[b]	100.0	288.0	423.0	721.0	1370.0	2889.0	8700.0	118400.0	748200.0	1263166.7
Others										
Cyprus	100.0	125.7	136.3	142.6	146.7	151.4	157.6	164.8	172.6	184.3
Gibraltar[j]	100.0	113.2	118.6	124.0	128.4	134.0	138.6	144.8	154.1	164.2
Malta[k,l]	100.0	119.0	117.5	116.4	119.1	121.3	120.7	119.4	121.1	
Monaco										
Turkey[m]	100.0	235.2	198.0	278.5	363.3	507.8	183.2	310.1	509.6	851.0

Sources: ILO/UN
Notes: See end of section

Table No: 1503

FOOD COSTS

Costs of Selected Food and Drink 1990

National currencies

	Rump Steak 1 kg	Milk 1 litre	Chicken 1 kg	Butter 250 g	Pota-toes 1 kg	Apples 1 kg	Sugar 1 kg
EC members							
Belgium	388.0	26.7	141.0	52.3	15.8	66.8	40.2
Denmark	100.0	6.0	30.0	10.0	5.0	15.0	20.0
France	138.5	4.4	42.9	10.9	6.8	14.8	6.6
Germany: East[a]		0.7	8.4	2.4	0.2	1.3	1.6
Germany: West	43.0	1.3	5.4	2.1	0.9	3.6	2.0
Greece	1200.0	158.0	542.0	248.5	110.0	182.0	155.0
Ireland	8.4	0.6	2.7	0.8	0.5	1.0	0.8
Italy	19000.0	1490.0	4750.0	2375.0	1000.0	4000.0	1600.0
Luxembourg[a]		28.5	144.0	49.0	8.6	49.0	49.0
Netherlands	36.0	1.1	8.0	0.4	0.5	5.5	2.0
Portugal	1700.0	105.0	420.0	250.0	40.0	180.0	150.0
Spain	1400.0	100.0	400.0	300.0	50.0	300.0	120.0
United Kingdom	8.8	0.5	2.3	0.7	0.3	1.3	0.6
EFTA members							
Austria	187.0	10.4	43.0	20.8	8.5	25.9	15.3
Finland	130.0	4.0	30.0	10.0	5.0	10.0	8.5
Iceland[a]		55.4	536.7	94.5	115.6	116.0	35.0
Liechtenstein							
Norway	130.0	7.0	50.0	7.5	4.0	15.0	12.0
Sweden	107.0	5.5	46.0	10.5	3.0	10.0	7.5
Switzerland	46.0	1.9	7.0	4.3	1.3	3.0	1.7
Eastern Europe							
Albania							
Bulgaria[b]		0.4	3.2	1.4	0.6	0.8	1.2
Czechoslovakia[c]		5.2	30.0	16.1	1.6	6.0	14.1
Hungary[d]		18.2	129.0	46.8	8.9	12.3	41.4
Poland[a]		36.5	340.0	222.3	46.3	176.1	165.0
Romania		4.5			3.0	11.9	14.0
USSR[e]			2.5	0.9	0.2	5.0	0.9
Yugoslavia[a,f]		1.4	7.5	3.5	0.7	1.0	2.7
Others							
Cyprus							
Gibraltar							
Malta							
Monaco							
Turkey[a]		939.0	2836.0	2063.0	207.0	501.0	524.0

Table No: 1503 (cont'd)

FOOD COSTS

Costs of Selected Food and Drink 1990

National currencies

	Instant Coffee 250 g	Tea 100 g	Table Wine 1 litre	Lager 1/3 l	Scotch Whisky Bottle	20 Cigar-ettes
EC members						
Belgium	495.0	46.0	82.1	123.0	494.0	84.0
Denmark	112.5	5.0	30.0	20.0	280.0	27.0
France	40.0	38.0	10.8	15.0	80.0	11.0
Germany: East[a]		2.4	11.2	0.5		0.2
Germany: West	17.3	4.2	4.0	1.6	25.0	4.2
Greece	1177.5	300.0	390.0	350.0	2000.0	200.0
Ireland	4.4	0.5	6.0	1.0	11.0	2.0
Italy	17500.0	2000.0	6000.0	2500.0	18000.0	2300.0
Luxembourg[a]	368.8	110.0	47.0	13.2		56.0
Netherlands	14.3	1.9	5.0	2.0	30.0	3.9
Portugal	320.0	292.0	170.0	325.0	3450.0	215.0
Spain	1000.0	140.0	250.0	70.0	1250.0	88.0
United Kingdom	3.6	0.4	2.4	0.9	9.8	1.7
EFTA members						
Austria	125.0	1.6	41.0	25.0	168.0	30.0
Finland	57.5	14.0	40.0	23.0	180.0	15.0
Iceland[a]	511.6	164.0	1040.0			
Liechtenstein						
Norway	50.0	6.0	44.0	22.7	340.0	31.6
Sweden	62.5	24.8	50.0	45.0	250.0	25.0
Switzerland	10.0	3.8	4.0	3.0	50.0	3.0
Eastern Europe						
Albania						
Bulgaria[b]	30.0	1.7	1.2	1.2		1.3
Czechoslovakia[c]	140.0	19.0	34.0	2.6		0.7
Hungary[d]	490.0	14.4	48.0	8.0		51.0
Poland[a]		220.0	1175.0	93.3		4500.0
Romania						7.0
USSR[e]		0.8	4.1	0.6		1.6
Yugoslavia[a,f]		1.5	2.8	0.7		1.5
Others						
Cyprus						
Gibraltar						
Malta						
Monaco						
Turkey[b]	2250.0	350.0	2800.0	377.0		3100.0

Sources: Confederation of British Industry/ILO/Euromonitor
Notes: See end of section

Table No: 1504

COSTS OF CONSUMER GOODS

Costs of Miscellaneous Consumer Goods 1990

National currencies

	Colour TV (51cm)	Fridge-Freezer	Gas Cooker	Vacuum Cleaner	Men's Suit	Women's Dress	Men's Shoes	Women's Shoes
EC members								
Belgium	36762	18476	18150	6752	10702	7575	3215	2779
Denmark	5000	4250	5000	1350	3500	1700	750	800
France	3900	3160	2200	1260	2500	1500	700	600
Germany: East								
Germany: West	1100	1100	600	250	500	500	175	160
Greece	48000	105000	70000	100000	50000	55000	13000	12000
Ireland	450	300	600	130	175	200	50	60
Italy	800000	900000	700000	300000	825000	500000	200000	150000
Luxembourg								
Netherlands	1100	900	900	300	600	225	190	120
Portugal	138900	151500	58900	23750	42500	37500	13000	10000
Spain	80000	90000	30000		30000	25000	8000	8000
United Kingdom	360	420	450	122	200	155	80	55
EFTA members								
Austria	13100	5470	8000	3280	3260	2910	900	930
Finland	2000	4000	3000	1000	1800	1300	350	300
Iceland								
Liechtenstein								
Norway[a]	5000	4400	4500	1000	2500	2700	700	800
Sweden	6000	7000	5500	1700	3500	2900	900	700
Switzerland	925	800	1350	500	750	250	140	130
Eastern Europe								
Albania								
Bulgaria[b]		513			140			
Czechoslovakia[c]	13363				2500	900	490	450
Hungary[b,d,e]	27790				7000	4000	5500	4500
Poland[d]		6440			250000	250000	60000	80000
Romania[b]		6776			2726			854
USSR[d]	716	325		46	150	70	40	40
Yugoslavia[b]	2008	560		290			78	43
Others								
Cyprus								
Gibraltar								
Malta								
Monaco								
Turkey								

Source: Confederation of British Industry/Euromonitor
Notes: See end of section

Table No: 1505

COSTS OF SERVICES

Costs of Miscellaneous Services 1990

National currencies

	Telephone Rental (a)	Local Call unit fee	Telex Rent (b)	Inland Letter	Electricity (c)	Gas (c)	Water (c)	Heating Oil (d)	Car Hire (e)
EC members									
Belgium	476.0	6.0	3063.0	14.0	3000.0	80.0	575.0	700.0	13000.0
Denmark	96.3	0.3	793.0	3.5	500.0	365.0	180.0	398.0	2835.0
France	40.0	0.7	1200.0	2.3	500.0	125.0	200.0	300.0	3577.0
Germany: East									
Germany: West[f]	27.4	0.2	3104.0	1.0	105.0	150.0	85.0	38.5	550.0
Greece		5.3		50.0	7500.0	1100.0	1250.0	3583.0	99000.0
Ireland[g]	10.0	0.1	75.0	0.3	50.0	70.0	15.0	25.0	227.0
Italy	19400.0	140.0	500000.0	750.0	90000.0	70000.0	35000.0	90000.0	1047200.0
Luxembourg[h]	250.0	5.0			2500.0	2000.0	500.0	800.0	15000.0
Netherlands	21.2	0.2	360.0	0.8	110.0	225.0	100.0	120.0	750.0
Portugal	1365.0	8.5	18750.0	32.0	12500.0	7000.0	6000.0	4800.0	92100.0
Spain	1000.0	4.0	19800.0	25.0	35000.0	5500.0	4250.0	3500.0	68000.0
United Kingdom	6.6	0.0	265.6	0.2	60.0	70.0	20.0	35.0	172.5
EFTA members									
Austria	180.0	4.0	1200.0	5.0	2000.0	1500.0	200.0	450.0	4165.0
Finland	57.0	0.5	2184.0	2.0	80.0	30.0	150.0	115.0	3000.0
Iceland									
Liechtenstein									
Norway	120.0	1.0	500.0	3.2	1250.0	2700.0	700.0	170.0	6240.0
Sweden	62.3	0.3	410.0	2.5	350.0	2900.0	225.0	381.0	950.0
Switzerland[i]	17.5	0.1		0.8	150.0	75.0	80.0	30.0	616.0
Eastern Europe									
Albania									
Bulgaria									
Czechoslovakia[h]	50.0	1.0			60.0	45.0	490.0	175.0	8500.0
Hungary[h]		2.0			600.0	1750.0	140.0	920.0	23000.0
Poland[h]	4960.0	90.0			90000.0	100000.0	30000.0	190000.0	6000000.0
Romania									
USSR[h]	2.7	0.0			6.0	4.0	5.0	40.0	215.0
Yugoslavia[h,j]	31.4	0.2			1013.0	132.4	200.0	260.0	5000.0
Others									
Cyprus									
Gibraltar									
Malta									
Monaco									
Turkey		150.0			50000.0	20000.0	50000.0	67000.0	1500000.0

Source: Confederation of British Industry/Euromonitor

Notes: See end of section

Notes to Tables in Section Fifteen:

Table 1501 Data for 1991 are derived from a series rebased to October 1990

Table 1502
- a Data for 1991 are derived from a series rebased to 1988
- b Data for 1990 refer to the year to end September
- c Series linked to former series
- d Data for 1990 refer to the year to end May
- e Data for 1985-1990 are derived from a series rebased to 1984
- f Data for 1991 are derived from a series rebased to 1990
- g Data for 1991 refer to the year to end November
- h Data for 1991 refer to the year to end October
- i Data for 1982-1991 are not comparable with previous series. Data for 1991 are derived from a series rebased to December 1990 and refer to the year to end September
- j Data for 1991 refer to the year to end August
- k Data for 1984-1990 are derived from a series rebased to 1983
- l Data for 1991 refer to the year to end June
- m Data for 1988-1991 are derived from a series rebased to 1987

Table 1503
- a Data refer to 1989; lager figure refers to beer
- b Data refer to 1989 except for milk, chicken, potatoes, apples, lager and cigarettes; lager figure refers to beer
- c Data refer to 1989 except for milk, butter, sugar; lager figure refers to beer
- d Data refer to 1989 except for milk, chicken, butter and sugar; lager figure refers to beer
- e Data refer to 1989 except for chicken, apples and cigarettes; lager figure refers to beer
- f New dinars at 1990 rates after currency reform (1 new dinar = 1,000 dinars)

Table 1504 All prices of consumer durables are inclusive of tax
- a Refers to electric cookers, not gas
- b Fridge-freezers figure refers to fridges only
- c Data refer to 1989 except for colour TVs
- d Data refer to 1989
- e Colour TV figure refers to 56cm set

Table 1505 0.0 = less than 0.05
- a Per month
- b Quarterly
- c Average cost for family of four, 1989
- d Cost for 100 litres, 1989
- e Per week
- f Data for car hire refer to 1989
- g Telex maintenance charge
- h Data refer to 1989
- i Telex no longer used
- j New dinars at 1990 rates after currency reform (1 new dinar = 1,000 old dinars)

Section Sixteen

Housing and Household Facilities

Table No: 1601

HOUSING STOCK

Total Housing Stock 1977-1991

'000

	1977	1980	1983	1984	1985	1986	1987	1988	1989	1990	1991
EC members											
Belgium	3686	3811	3959	3979	3997	4020	4060	4085	4124	4165	4198
Denmark	2033	2118	2188	2208	2228	2260	2282	2307	2328	2353	2375
France	17310	21573	24264	24528	24758	24988	25219	25464	25709	25961	26080
Germany: East	6423	6540	6695	6763	6831	6911	6964	7002	7003	7017	6887
Germany: West	24369	25406	26399	26782	27081	27317	27529	27670	27928	28120	28254
Greece	2210	2425	2716	2890	2930	3000	3133	3208	3313	3412	3428
Ireland	841	901	951	969	985	991	999	1005	1021	1036	1051
Italy	18719	20995	23150	23190	24051	24903	25110	25219	25397	25561	25683
Luxembourg	131	138	143	144	144	145	145	146	146	147	147
Netherlands	4577	4850	5178	5289	5384	5483	5589	5669	5802	5908	5969
Portugal	3301	3319	3356	3386	3403	3459	3505	3534	3566	3596	3630
Spain	12714	14580	15205	15253	15300	15317	15475	15631	15786	15966	15974
United Kingdom	20378	21031	21520	21711	21891	22655	22829	22987	22619	22839	22972
EC total	116692	127687	135724	137092	138983	141449	142839	143927	144743	146083	146649
EFTA members											
Austria	2694	3042	3115	3128	3140	3151	3249	3275	3280	3285	3381
Finland	1687	1838	1923	1945	1975	2000	2044	2098	2152	2166	2205
Iceland	67	73	78	79	81	82	85	86	87	89	89
Liechtenstein	10	10	11	11	11	12	12	12	12	12	12
Norway	1480	1524	1635	1670	1694	1720	1748	1778	1803	1769	1788
Sweden	3505	3599	3705	3797	3863	3897	3930	3958	4001	4042	4092
Switzerland	2590	2701	2793	2833	2878	2970	3012	3055	3098	3140	3159
EFTA total	12033	12787	13260	13463	13642	13832	14080	14263	14433	14503	14726
Eastern Europe											
Albania	608	660	700	714	730	745	745	745	745	750	756
Bulgaria	2643	2839	3035	3100	3162	3205	3266	3326	3363	3383	3385
Czechoslovakia[a]	5154	5441	5526	5600	5867	5747	5807	5869	5922	5955	6007
Hungary	3699	3542	3629	3677	3735	3779	3810	3848	3850	3853	3845
Poland	9090	9326	10310	10253	10666	10834	11003	10789	10924	11024	11066
Romania	7010	7220	7420	7550	7600	7700	7700	7723	7770	7806	7839
USSR	66995	72460	77902	79050	79900	80050	82300	83861	85841	87259	87382
Yugoslavia	5932	6322	6539	6620	6700	6848	6995	7173	7350	7453	7556
East European total	101131	107810	115061	116563	118360	118907	121626	123333	125765	127484	127835
Others											
Cyprus	121	151	172	174	180	187	200	205	211	216	219
Gibraltar	7	7	8	8	8	8	8	8	8	8	8
Malta	100	104	112	112	113	114	116	116	116	116	117
Monaco	11	11	12	12	12	12	12	12	12	12	12
Turkey	10980	11441	11685	11740	11821	11950	12150	12234	12343	12436	12641
Total	11220	11715	11988	12046	12134	12270	12486	12574	12690	12788	12997
European total	241076	259999	276034	279165	283119	286459	291031	294097	297630	300858	302207

Sources: National statistical offices/UN/Statistical Office of the European Community
Notes: See end of section

Table No: 1602

HOUSING STOCK

New Dwellings Completed 1977-1991

Units

	1977	1980	1984	1985	1986	1987	1988	1989	1990	1991
EC members										
Belgium	71382	46839	24400	28919	24444	29340	35429	43220	41604	44022
Denmark	36276	30345	26863	22613	28489	26912	25500	26880	27237	20035
France	450900	502600	343500	349800	356200	380600	414800	322222	336250	336250
Germany: East	106826	120209	121657	99000	101000	91000	93500	83400	57000	
Germany: West	409012	363094	366816	252248	251940	217343	208344	238617	256738	178565
Greece	158269	136044	72852	88477	109643	108432	107034	117327	13144	
Ireland	24548	27785	24944	23948	22680	18292	15654	18068	19539	19652
Italy	227475	222000	192386	173605	166750	184450	200800	197500	182450	180000
Luxembourg	1583	2469	1363	1348	1417	1475	1746			
Netherlands	111047	113756	103355	98131	108900	115700	123500	111233	97384	82888
Portugal	37220	38231	41250	35983	36061	38333	36000	35500	40054	44813
Spain	126101	130485	176333	178190	193410	202600	239493	233063		
United Kingdom	313500	251814	203172	212172	178299	188131	199905	175793	156995	176700
EC total	2074139	1985671	1698891	1564434	1579233	1602608	1701705	1602823	1228395	
EFTA members										
Austria	43500	73300	37600	37300	38838	38494	39226	37946	36553	36200
Finland	56966	49648	50337	50306	41910	43635	46537	58244	65397	52000
Iceland	2300	2200	1601	1601	1515	1543	1842	1665	1754	
Liechtenstein										
Norway	38597	38092	30866	26114	25784	28381	30406	27979	27120	25500
Sweden	54800	51438	34988	32932	28791	30884	40575	50402	58426	66900
Switzerland	32297	40070	45449	44228	42570	40230	40965	40705	39984	
EFTA total	228460	254748	200841	192481	179408	183167	199551	216941	229234	
Eastern Europe										
Albania										
Bulgaria	73157	73300	67800	63600	64870	63640	62926	40154	26200	
Czechoslovakia	137693	128876	91863	104524	78700	79600	82900	88500	69300	68727
Hungary	86333	89100	70432	72507	69428	57200	50566	51487	42800	
Poland	267000	217100	195900	217900	185700	191400	189600	150200	134200	
Romania	161500	197800	131900	105600	108100	110400	103300	60400	48600	
USSR	1060000	2004000	2035000	2100000	2100000	2265000	2230000	2120000	189100	
Yugoslavia										
E European total	1785683	2710176	2592895	2664131	2606798	2767240	2719292	2510741	510200	
Others										
Cyprus		9200	6300	7500	6586	6727	6915	6850		
Gibraltar										
Malta										
Monaco										
Turkey		139200	115600	118200	168600	191000	119332	121450		
Total		148400	121900	125700	175186	197727	126247	128300		
European total		5098995	4614527	4546746	4540625	4750742	4746795	4458805		

Sources: National statistical offices/UN/OECD

Table No: 1603

HOUSING STOCK

Dwellings by Number of Rooms: Latest Year

% dwellings

	Year	1 room	2 rooms	3 rooms	4 rooms	5 or more rooms	Total
EC members							
Belgium	1985	1.0	18.0	21.4	24.0	35.6	100.0
Denmark	1991	6.3	17.7	23.1	26.2	26.7	100.0
France[a]	1983	9.1	11.9	16.6	26.5	35.9	100.0
Germany: East	1981	8.0	33.0	37.0	15.1	6.9	100.0
Germany: West	1989	2.3	5.8	21.0	29.2	42.0	100.0
Greece	1985	9.3	15.3	26.4	28.2	20.8	100.0
Ireland[b]	1981	2.4	4.9	11.7	23.1	57.9	100.0
Italy	1981	1.7	10.2	21.4	32.0	34.6	100.0
Luxembourg[b]	1981	2.3	3.1	9.9	19.8	64.9	100.0
Netherlands[a]	1985	5.9	8.9	20.7	56.3	8.2	100.0
Portugal	1986	15.0	25.0	30.0	26.0	4.0	100.0
Spain	1986	11.5	20.0	26.0	19.0	23.5	100.0
United Kingdom	1986	9.1	12.0	23.5	30.3	25.1	100.0
EC average		8.4	15.0	23.7	26.7	26.2	100.0
EFTA members							
Austria	1990	6.0	15.0	29.0	28.0	22.0	100.0
Finland	1989	27.8	23.1	21.6	17.3	10.2	100.0
Iceland[c]	1986	10.0	20.4	34.2	25.9	9.5	100.0
Liechtenstein	1980	8.2	9.0	12.7	20.9	49.3	100.0
Norway	1990	14.2	10.4	18.2	23.2	33.9	100.0
Sweden	1990	11.5	22.0	24.1	19.0	23.0	100.0
Switzerland[d]	1980	8.5	12.8	21.9	32.8	24.0	100.0
EFTA average		9.6	13.5	21.5	28.4	27.0	100.0
Eastern Europe							
Albania	1986	29.0	30.0	32.0	4.5	4.5	100.0
Bulgaria	1985	4.0	21.0	35.0	27.2	12.8	100.0
Czechoslovakia	1986	25.0	41.2	28.9	3.2	1.7	100.0
Hungary	1991	16.1	44.6	20.0	12.8	6.5	100.0
Poland	1988	1.3	6.3	25.7	46.0	20.7	100.0
Romania	1970	12.0	35.0	34.8	13.9	4.3	100.0
USSR	1986	15.0	39.0	30.0	12.0	4.0	100.0
Yugoslavia	1984	23.9	40.5	24.2	7.7	3.7	100.0
East European average		18.1	37.2	28.3	11.6	4.7	100.0
Others							
Cyprus[a]	1986	0.5	3.0	6.5	15.0	75.0	100.0
Gibraltar	1981	8.2	19.0	37.6	24.6	10.6	100.0
Malta	1986	10.0	20.0	30.0	24.0	16.	Malta
Monaco	1986	8.0	12.2	20.6	26.8	32.4	100.0
Turkey[a]	1987	0.7	9.9	37.5	32.8	19.1	100.0
Average		4.3	11.1	29.2	29.8	25.6	100.0
European average		12.9	25.5	26.2	19.6	15.7	100.0

Sources: National statistical offices/UN/Statistical Office of the European Community/Euromonitor
Notes: See end of section

Table No: 1604

HOUSING STOCK

Housing Amenities: Latest Available Year

% households with specific amenities

	Year	Water supply	Bath or shower	Central heating	Own toilet
EC members					
Belgium	1985	99.5	99.3	92.8	90.5
Denmark	1991	96.9	89.1	94.8	96.6
France	1984	99.6	84.7	69.7	97.2
Germany: East	1985	99.2	74.0	50.0	68.0
Germany: West	1987	98.0	84.0	51.0	87.0
Greece	1981	80.0	69.0	30.0	78.0
Ireland	1981	90.0	82.0	39.0	89.8
Italy	1984	92.3	87.6	39.7	96.0
Luxembourg	1981	99.9	86.1	73.9	97.2
Netherlands	1985	100.0	96.0	72.3	100.0
Portugal	1983	58.2	46.8	10.0	63.4
Spain	1981	90.5	70.0	21.0	91.0
United Kingdom	1989	99.0	97.0	77.5	97.0
EC average		95.3	84.5	54.4	91.5
EFTA members					
Austria	1991	99.0	99.0	88.0	99.0
Finland	1989	94.7	86.5	88.0	92.1
Iceland[a]	1986	99.6	99.6	75.1	95.0
Liechtenstein	1980	99.0	92.1	88.4	86.4
Norway	1990	98.2	96.0	91.0	96.9
Sweden	1990	99.0	99.0	96.0	98.0
Switzerland	1986	99.5	97.0	78.0	100.0
EFTA average		98.4	96.3	88.4	97.6
Eastern Europe					
Albania	1986	72.0	67.0	40.0	60.0
Bulgaria	1986	80.2	75.0	20.0	65.0
Czechoslovakia	1980	89.5	75.0	35.0	77.2
Hungary	1991	83.6	77.6	35.0	74.7
Poland	1988	56.5	43.0	33.4	38.9
Romania	1986	82.4	68.2	20.0	70.0
USSR[b]	1987	92.6	85.0	77.9	90.7
Yugoslavia	1984	45.2	53.5	15.9	70.0
East European average		85.2	77.4	61.7	81.7
Others					
Cyprus[a]	1986	100.0	100.0	8.7	100.0
Gibraltar	1981	96.6	87.8	24.0	87.6
Malta	1986	90.0	80.0	15.0	90.0
Monaco	1986	100.0	99.2	82.0	100.0
Turkey[a]	1987	99.0	85.0	13.4	90.0
Average		98.9	85.2	13.4	90.2
European average		91.4	82.1	57.4	87.6

Sources: National statistical offices/UN/Statistical Office of the European Community/Euromonitor
Notes: See end of section

Table No: 1605

HOUSEHOLD COMPOSITION

Number of Households 1977-1991

'000

	1977	1978	1979	1980	1981	1982	1983	1984
EC members								
Belgium	3305	3313	3325	3336	3348	3380	3307	3590
Denmark	2013	2040	2075	2062	2080	2094	2114	2136
France	18274	18515	18910	19136	19343	19590	20100	20222
Germany: East	6409	6423	6471	6485	6510	6510	6510	6525
Germany: West	24165	24221	24280	24229	24544	24835	25131	25345
Greece	2678	2702	2738	2755	2974	3061	3151	3290
Ireland	800	813	832	850	850	852	856	857
Italy	17190	17351	17413	17509	17520	17614	17767	17823
Luxembourg	123	124	126	127	128	128	129	129
Netherlands	4680	4768	4841	5006	5111	5215	5318	5420
Portugal	2750	2804	2866	2900	3075	3105	3150	3203
Spain	12522	12823	12889	13016	13202	13450	13603	13881
United Kingdom	19580	19646	19819	19995	19943	19990	20270	20560
EC total	114489	115543	116585	117406	118628	119824	121406	122981
EFTA members								
Austria	2649	2652	2655	2860	2764	2766	2752	2771
Finland	1695	1720	1754	1728	1745	1820	1839	1850
Iceland	93	94	95	96	97	98	99	100
Liechtenstein	9	9	9	9	10	10	10	10
Norway	1378	1387	1398	1410	1524	1536	1557	1570
Sweden	3443	3486	3536	3595	3610	3615	3610	3690
Switzerland	2280	2353	2417	2459	2500	2575	2646	2666
EFTA total	11547	11701	11864	12157	12250	12420	12513	12657
Eastern Europe								
Albania	675	687	698	720	740	775	800	840
Bulgaria	2603	2643	2655	2680	2695	2708	2800	2873
Czechoslovakia	5061	5127	5187	5274	5308	5319	5380	5411
Hungary	3692	3749	3768	3719	3740	3786	3798	3831
Poland	10718	10948	11065	11175	11230	11290	11330	11660
Romania	6855	6960	7050	7115	7160	7196	7250	7310
USSR	63274	63950	64733	65600	65580	65800	66010	66300
Yugoslavia	6187	6310	6578	6780	6945	7100	7189	7234
East European total	99065	100374	101734	103063	103398	103974	104557	105459
Others								
Cyprus	187	188	190	192	194	197	201	204
Gibraltar	7	7	7	7	7	7	7	7
Malta	96	98	98	101	102	102	103	105
Monaco	10	10	10	11	11	11	12	12
Turkey	7510	7725	8522	8603	8670	8900	8950	8995
Total	7810	8028	8827	8914	8984	9217	9273	9323
European total	232911	235646	239010	241540	243260	245435	247748	250420

Table No: 1605 (cont'd)

HOUSEHOLD COMPOSITION

Number of Households 1977-1991

'000

	1985	1986	1987	1988	1989	1990	1991
EC members							
Belgium	3615	3620	3628	3650	3671	3694	3706
Denmark	2160	2182	2205	2224	2226	2229	2230
France	20413	20623	21100	21305	21428	21559	21614
Germany: East	6540	6572	6586	6621	6627	6455	6323
Germany: West	26553	26785	26939	27200	27850	28715	28247
Greece	3387	3444	3455	3538	3560	3580	3589
Ireland	859	863	870	875	874	873	869
Italy	17891	17967	18003	18081	18133	18174	18224
Luxembourg	130	131	132	132	134	134	134
Netherlands	5613	5735	5820	5935	6026	6127	6162
Portugal	3289	3300	3330	3360	3365	3381	3387
Spain	14015	14329	14389	14534	14580	14622	14600
United Kingdom	20879	21005	21025	21050	21145	21196	21198
EC total	125344	126556	127481	128506	129619	130199	130284
EFTA members							
Austria	2810	2863	2870	2875	2882	2937	2945
Finland	1888	1943	1948	1979	1983	1989	1989
Iceland	101	102	103	104	106	107	107
Liechtenstein	10	11	11	11	11	11	11
Norway	1592	1620	1624	1651	1660	1668	1671
Sweden	3670	3680	3688	3714	3738	3772	3794
Switzerland	2687	2701	2707	2745	2770	2790	2801
EFTA total	12758	12920	12950	13080	13150	13274	13318
Eastern Europe							
Albania	900	912	914	914	929	937	942
Bulgaria	2912	2949	2955	3010	3025	3030	3026
Czechoslovakia	5450	5470	5481	5540	5555	5570	5568
Hungary	3852	3877	3885	3924	3927	3934	3918
Poland	11923	12213	12238	12000	12024	12087	12108
Romania	7372	7423	7438	7509	7548	7588	7605
USSR	66750	67000	67134	68408	68573	68738	68697
Yugoslavia	7256	7289	7304	7332	7378	7424	7448
East European total	106415	107133	107350	108635	108959	109308	109311
Others							
Cyprus	212	216	217	222	229	232	235
Gibraltar	7	7	7	7	7	7	7
Malta	107	109	110	110	111	111	111
Monaco	12	12	12	12	12	12	12
Turkey	9043	9090	9108	9171	9337	9503	9641
Total	9381	9434	9454	9522	9696	9865	10006
European total	253898	256043	257235	259743	261424	262646	262919

Source: Euromonitor/national statistical offices

Table No: 1606

HOUSEHOLD COMPOSITION

Household Size by Number of Persons: Latest Year

% households

	Year	1 person	2 persons	3 persons	4 persons	5+ persons	Un-specified	Total
EC members								
Belgium	1981	23.2	29.7	20.0	15.7	11.4		100.00
Denmark	1991	34.0	33.0	15.0	13.1	4.9		100.00
France	1984	24.2	29.2	18.5	16.8	11.3		100.00
Germany: East	1983	27.1	29.2	20.9	15.0	7.8		100.00
Germany: West	1990	35.0	30.5	17.1	12.5	4.9		100.00
Greece[a]	1989	18.5	26.0	19.5	22.5	13.5		100.00
Ireland	1986	18.2	20.3	14.8	16.1	30.6		100.00
Italy	1982	12.9	22.0	22.4	21.2	17.6	3.9	100.00
Luxembourg	1988	21.8	29.0	21.0	16.5	11.7		100.00
Netherlands	1990	29.3	28.9	15.6	18.5	6.0	1.7	100.00
Portugal[a]	1988	15.0	23.0	27.0	20.0	15.0		100.00
Spain[a]	1986	12.0	24.0	27.0	18.5	18.5		100.00
United Kingdom	1987	25.0	32.0	17.1	13.1	6.0	6.8	100.00
EFTA members								
Austria	1991	27.9	27.7	18.0	15.9	10.5		100.00
Finland	1989	31.1	29.1	16.7	15.3	7.9		100.00
Iceland[a]	1986	14.0	31.3	22.7	16.9	15.1		100.00
Liechtenstein	1980	23.9	23.9	16.8	18.9	16.5		100.00
Norway	1990	35.4	25.9	15.2	15.1	8.3	0.1	100.00
Sweden	1990	40.6	31.1	12.3	11.8	4.2		100.00
Switzerland	1983	13.4	15.9	20.2	33.1	17.4		100.00
Eastern Europe								
Albania[a]	1986	8.0	30.0	26.0	26.0	10.0		100.00
Bulgaria	1975	17.0	20.7	21.6	21.1	19.6		100.00
Czechoslovakia	1970	17.9	23.5	20.8	20.9	16.9		100.00
Hungary	1970	13.1	25.4	23.1	20.5	17.9		100.00
Poland	1984	14.6	20.8	21.0	22.6	21.0		100.00
Romania	1970	14.2	23.4	23.3	19.9	19.2		100.00
USSR[b]	1970		25.4	26.2	24.1	24.3		100.00
Yugoslavia	1971	12.9	16.3	19.0	21.3	30.5		100.00
Others								
Cyprus[a]	1986	12.0	30.3	23.3	20.7	13.7		100.00
Gibraltar	1981	12.5	24.2	18.2	21.3	23.8		100.00
Malta[a]	1986	10.0	24.6	26.2	20.9	18.3		100.00
Monaco[a]	1986	24.0	31.2	26.7	15.0	3.1		100.00
Turkey	1980	6.5	11.3	12.7	16.2	53.3		100.00

Sources: Statistical Office of the European Community/UN
Notes: See end of section

Table No: 1607

HOUSEHOLD COMPOSITION

Average Household Size 1977-1991

Persons per average household unit

	1977	1980	1981	1982	1983	1984	1985	1986	1987	1988	1989	1990	1991
EC members													
Belgium	2.82	2.81	2.80	2.77	2.83	2.61	2.59	2.59	2.59	2.57	2.57	2.57	2.57
Denmark	2.40	2.36	2.34	2.36	2.30	2.27	2.25	2.23	2.21	2.19	2.19	2.19	2.19
France	2.76	2.67	2.65	2.63	2.58	2.58	2.56	2.55	2.50	2.49	2.48	2.48	2.49
Germany: East	2.49	2.45	2.44	2.44	2.44	2.43	2.42	2.41	2.40	2.39	2.39	2.38	2.39
Germany: West	2.42	2.41	2.39	2.36	2.33	2.30	2.18	2.16	2.16	2.16	2.11	2.10	2.10
Greece	3.30	3.33	3.11	3.04	2.97	2.86	2.78	2.74	2.74	2.69	2.68	2.68	2.69
Ireland	3.87	3.80	3.85	3.88	3.89	3.91	3.92	3.89	3.87	3.84	3.84	3.83	3.84
Italy	3.10	3.09	3.06	3.05	3.07	3.03	3.03	3.02	3.02	3.02	3.01	3.01	3.02
Luxembourg	2.79	2.72	2.71	2.72	2.70	2.70	2.67	2.66	2.67	2.67	2.66	2.66	2.66
Netherlands	2.80	2.67	2.64	2.60	2.56	2.52	2.45	2.41	2.39	2.36	2.33	2.31	2.31
Portugal	3.25	3.18	3.03	3.03	3.01	2.98	2.93	2.93	2.92	2.91	2.91	2.91	2.91
Spain	2.74	2.72	2.70	2.67	2.66	2.62	2.61	2.56	2.56	2.53	2.53	2.53	2.53
United Kingdom	2.73	2.68	2.68	2.68	2.64	2.61	2.58	2.57	2.57	2.57	2.57	2.57	2.57
EC average	2.77	2.73	2.71	2.69	2.67	2.61	2.56	2.54	2.53	2.52	2.53	2.50	2.51
EFTA members													
Austria	2.71	2.51	2.60	2.60	2.61	2.59	2.56	2.51	2.51	2.51	2.51	2.48	2.48
Finland	2.65	2.62	2.61	2.51	2.50	2.50	2.46	2.40	2.41	2.38	2.37	2.37	2.38
Iceland	2.26	2.25	2.24	2.26	2.26	2.26	2.27	2.25	2.28	2.28	2.27	2.26	2.26
Liechtenstein	2.68	2.66	2.50	2.55	2.49	2.54	2.49	2.42	2.42	2.50	2.59	2.59	2.60
Norway	2.78	2.75	2.55	2.54	2.52	2.50	2.47	2.44	2.44	2.42	2.42	2.41	2.42
Sweden	2.27	2.19	2.19	2.19	2.19	2.14	2.16	2.16	2.16	2.15	2.15	2.15	2.15
Switzerland	2.62	2.44	2.41	2.35	2.30	2.29	2.28	2.28	2.29	2.27	2.27	2.27	2.27
EFTA average	2.57	2.46	2.44	2.42	2.40	2.37	2.36	2.33	2.34	2.32	2.32	2.31	2.32
Eastern Europe													
Albania	3.53	3.52	3.50	3.41	3.37	3.28	3.13	3.15	3.20	3.25	3.25	3.24	3.25
Bulgaria	3.21	3.14	3.13	3.13	3.03	2.96	2.92	2.88	2.88	2.83	2.82	2.82	2.83
Czechoslovakia	2.82	2.76	2.74	2.74	2.72	2.71	2.70	2.70	2.70	2.68	2.67	2.67	2.68
Hungary	2.73	2.74	2.72	2.69	2.68	2.65	2.63	2.61	2.59	2.57	2.56	2.56	2.57
Poland	3.06	3.01	3.02	3.03	3.05	2.99	2.95	2.90	2.92	3.00	2.99	2.99	3.00
Romania	3.00	2.96	2.97	2.97	2.96	2.94	2.93	2.93	2.93	2.92	2.91	2.91	2.92
USSR	3.89	3.85	3.88	3.90	3.92	3.94	3.95	3.97	4.01	3.94	3.93	3.93	3.94
Yugoslavia	3.34	3.13	3.07	3.03	3.01	3.02	3.03	3.03	3.05	3.05	3.05	3.05	3.05
E European average	3.64	3.58	3.60	3.61	3.63	3.56	3.56	3.56	3.59	3.55	3.55	3.54	3.55
Others													
Cyprus	3.11	3.08	3.09	3.07	3.05	3.04	2.97	2.94	2.98	3.00	2.99	2.99	3.00
Gibraltar	4.07	4.07	4.07	3.94	3.94	3.94	3.80	3.94	3.94	3.94	4.07	4.07	4.08
Malta	3.08	3.04	3.04	3.05	3.06	3.06	3.02	2.99	3.00	3.03	3.01	3.02	3.03
Monaco	2.38	2.25	2.25	2.33	2.23	2.14	2.14	2.14	2.06	2.13	2.22	2.22	2.22
Turkey	5.28	4.91	4.99	4.98	5.08	5.18	5.32	5.45	5.55	5.61	5.61	5.60	5.61
Average	5.23	4.87	4.95	4.94	5.04	5.11	5.24	5.36	5.46	5.52	5.51	5.51	5.52
European average	3.31	3.25	3.26	3.26	3.27	3.09	3.07	3.06	3.07	3.05	3.05	3.04	3.05

Source: Euromonitor

Table No: 1608

HOUSEHOLD OWNERSHIP

Ownership of Consumer Electronics 1990

% households

	Radio	Cassette recorder	Record player	Music centre	CD player	Personal stereo	Home computer
EC members							
Belgium	90	75	30		26	25	15
Denmark	98	82	60	30	20	30	14
France	98	76	65	39	23	37	14
Germany: East	99	64	50				
Germany: West	84	74	72	54	24	31	16
Greece	92	72	46		5	17	6
Ireland		73	61		14	34	12
Italy	92	64	60	16	9	22	12
Luxembourg		69			30	30	12
Netherlands	97	80	81		43	33	20
Portugal	60	36	40		9	13	7
Spain	95	67	49	27	11	21	8
United Kingdom	90	82	29	32	20	37	22
EC average	91	72	55	34	19	29	15
EFTA members							
Austria	95	82	27	30	24	30	11
Finland	96	85	62	34	19	37	16
Iceland							
Liechtenstein							
Norway	98	87	64		21	43	16
Sweden	93	88	64	48	17	45	12
Switzerland	99	82	65	42	39	29	14
EFTA average	96	85	55	39	24	37	13
Eastern Europe							
Albania							
Bulgaria	95	46					
Czechoslovakia	75	52					
Hungary	40	53	36	21			
Poland	79		33	32			
Romania	45		20				
USSR	96	39					
Yugoslavia	85	59	40				
East European average	88	42	32	29			
Others							
Cyprus							
Gibraltar							
Malta							
Monaco							
Turkey	75						
Average	75						
European average	89	58	50	34	19	30	14

Table No: 1608 (cont'd)

HOUSEHOLD OWNERSHIP

Ownership of Consumer Electronics 1990

% households

	Colour/ mono TV	Video recorder	Video camera	Cable TV	Satellite TV	Tele-phone	Cordless phone	Mobile phone
EC members								
Belgium	97	42	6	88	3	79	7	1
Denmark	98	39	5	34	5	87	5	3
France	94	35	6	9	3	89	5	
Germany: East	43							
Germany: West	97	42	6	29	4	89	2	3
Greece	94	37	1	0	0	75	2	0
Ireland	98	38	2	40	5	53	5	3
Italy	98	25	4	0	3	89	4	3
Luxembourg	98	39	9	89	3	75	4	1
Netherlands	98	48	7	87	2	96	5	6
Portugal	92	22	4	4	1	52	2	
Spain	98	40	4	22	6	66	4	1
United Kingdom	98	58	4	3	4	85	6	4
EC average	94	40	5	23	4	84	4	3
EFTA members								
Austria	96	37		6	6	85	2	1
Finland	94	46		2	2	79	5	4
Iceland								
Liechtenstein								
Norway	97	41		5	5	89	5	8
Sweden	97	48		5	5	97	5	6
Switzerland	93	41		3	3	97	4	5
EFTA average	95	43		4	4	90	4	5
Eastern Europe								
Albania								
Bulgaria	93							
Czechoslovakia	95							
Hungary	21							
Poland	70							
Romania	77							
USSR	45							
Yugoslavia	61							
East European average	53							
Others								
Cyprus	56							
Gibraltar								
Malta								
Monaco								
Turkey								
Average	56							
European average	73	40	5	21	4	84	4	3

Sources: Euromonitor/Reader's Digest Eurodata
Notes: See end of section

Table No: 1609

HOUSEHOLD OWNERSHIP

Ownership of Major Appliances 1990

% households

	Micro-wave Oven	Tumble Dryer	Separate Spin Dryer	Washing Machine	Vacuum Cleaner	Hair Dryer
EC members						
Belgium	21	39	28	88	92	66
Denmark	14	22	5	76	96	
France	25	12	66	88	89	79
Germany: East				94	65	
Germany: West	36	17	16	88	96	78
Greece	2			74	52	39
Ireland	20	19	8	81	87	
Italy	6	10	12	96	56	83
Luxembourg	16	35	13	93	88	45
Netherlands	19	23	30	91	98	63
Portugal	4	2	7	66	62	45
Spain	9	5	10	87	29	46
United Kingdom	48	32	7	78	98	85
EC average	24	17	22	87	77	73
EFTA members						
Austria	31	6	13	86	92	86
Finland	53	3	6	76	93	95
Iceland						
Liechtenstein						
Norway	34	29	23	87	90	75
Sweden	37	18	6	72	97	83
Switzerland	15	27	12	78	93	93
EFTA average	33	16	11	79	93	87
Eastern Europe						
Albania						
Bulgaria				96	32	
Czechoslovakia				86	55	
Hungary			80	90	85	
Poland				40	40	
Romania					35	
USSR						
Yugoslavia						
Average			80	65	46	
Others						
Cyprus						
Gibraltar						
Malta						
Monaco						
Turkey						
Average						
European average	25	17	23	83	72	74

Table No: 1609 (cont'd)

HOUSEHOLD OWNERSHIP

Ownership of Major Appliances 1990

% households

	Dish-washer	Separate fridge	Deep Freezer	Fridge freezer	Food Processor	Toaster	Drinks Maker
EC members							
Belgium	26	54	86	53	91	56	79
Denmark	26	52	92	56	83	76	80
France	33	54	77	50	83	59	78
Germany: East		99	40				
Germany: West	34	66	73	43	92	53	88
Greece	11	70	27	24	24		
Ireland	15	54	58	43	41	53	51
Italy	18	21	89	83	48	37	81
Luxembourg	50	55	91	54	90		
Netherlands	12	62	82	60	84	66	65
Portugal	14	27	91	87	37	34	
Spain	11	43	55	51	50	85	22
United Kingdom	11	48	39	53	80	57	59
EC average	21	51	67	56	71	56	69
EFTA members							
Austria	35	62	61	42	82	41	75
Finland	31	52	52	49	72	69	45
Iceland	45						
Liechtenstein							
Norway	37	72	80	34	74	80	
Sweden	31	57	70	50	77	80	65
Switzerland	32	11	68	86	91	81	57
EFTA average	33	50	66	53	80	69	62
Eastern Europe							
Albania							
Bulgaria		96	13				
Czechoslovakia		92					
Hungary		90	30				
Poland		91					
Romania		30					
USSR							
Yugoslavia							
Average		77	22				
Others							
Cyprus							
Gibraltar							
Malta							
Monaco							
Turkey							
Average							
European average	22	56	65	56	71	57	68

Sources: Euromonitor/Reader's Digest Eurodata

Notes to Tables in Section Sixteen:

Table 1601	a	State sector only
Table 1603		Averages are based on 1989 dwelling stock
	a	New dwellings only
	b	Based on households
	c	Including holiday homes
	d	Occupied dwellings only
Table 1604		Averages calculated on the basis of the 1989 housing stock
	a	New dwellings only
	b	Urban households only
Table 1606	a	Estimate based on current trends
	b	Households of 2 or more members only
Table 1608		Values of 0 (EC countries only) signify that the service was not available

Section Seventeen

Health and Living Standards

Table No: 1701

MEDICAL SERVICES

Provision of Medical Services: Latest Year

Numbers

	Year	In-Patient Beds	Practising Doctors	Practising Dentists	Nurses	Active Pharmacists
EC members						
Belgium	1988	51001	33027	6448	9599	11629
Denmark[a]	1988	31300	13679	5100	89500	1476
France	1987	573635	143323	34946	233313	49606
Germany: East	1988	165950	41639	12932	116600	4310
Germany: West	1988	672384	171487	38826	267423	33903
Greece	1986	52864	30491	9131	24364	6261
Ireland[b]	1988	13632	5180	1131	25261	
Italy[c,d]	1988	424417	89620	3697	232091	1430
Luxembourg	1987		666	175	112	274
Netherlands	1989	175357	35852	7882	1095	2153
Portugal	1988	48805	26869	684		5010
Spain	1987	202969	138506	7304	148723	32307
United Kingdom[e]	1989	372823	83600	17830	397641	17589
EC total		2785137	813939	146086	1545722	165948
EFTA members						
Austria[f,g]	1990	78648	24895	1099	52624	1954
Finland[h]	1988	59731	11212	4221	81104	580
Iceland	1987	2798	675	215	3153	160
Liechtenstein	1986		26	9		2
Norway[i,j]	1988	24493	9443	3702	72448	3041
Sweden[k,l]	1988	55331	26577	9514	161264	1246
Switzerland	1987	54470	10491	3147	51101	1417
EFTA total		275471	83319	21907	421694	8400
Eastern Europe						
Albania	1977	11087	4957		6968	532
Bulgaria	1984	84300	24718	5623	57500	4235
Czechoslovakia	1985	158300	55871		106968	7261
Hungary	1988	109832	36188	3988	67985	4501
Poland	1988	263300	77496	17679	191800	16004
Romania	1985	203200	40050	7300		6558
USSR[m]	1987	3720000	1234316			91000
Yugoslavia[n]	1988	142957	55140		91253	6321
East European total		4692976	1528736	34590	522474	136412
Others						
Cyprus	1987	3360	998	374	2279	92
Gibraltar						
Malta	1982		413	57	3187	396
Monaco	1982		59	32	214	56
Turkey	1988	113010	42502	9639	38923	14567
Total		116370	43972	10102	44603	15111
European total		7869954	2469966	212685	2534493	325871

Sources: OECD, Measuring Health Care 1960-1983/World Health Organisation (WHO)/Comecon/national statistical offices
Notes: See end of section

Table No: 1702

ILLNESS

Incidence of Major Illnesses

Death rate per 100,000 population

	A	B	C	D	E	F	G	H
EC members								
Belgium[a]	16.8	554.1	927.7	112.2	82.5	90.7	42.1	45.0
Denmark[b]	10.2	602.2	1033.1	155.8	78.1	162.6	28.3	52.3
France[b]	23.7	493.0	649.0	120.3	101.2	118.9	36.8	41.4
Germany: East	7.8	418.7	1412.2	134.8	108.1	64.8	23.4	52.4
Germany: West	16.3	549.8	1099.5	133.2	104.8	40.1	24.9	33.5
Greece[b]	13.1	380.5	954.4	92.9	50.6	85.3	37.5	8.2
Ireland	9.8	404.4	845.3	230.4	50.5	33.1	25.9	15.0
Italy	7.9	499.6	822.7	121.0	104.1	79.3	31.5	15.5
Luxembourg	10.1	508.0	1001.3	133.0	111.0	44.2	37.3	39.8
Netherlands[b]	8.9	480.8	698.8	118.0	59.4	43.0	17.9	20.7
Portugal	16.5	340.5	809.2	126.9	87.5	50.3	55.3	14.7
Spain[c]	17.1	419.8	680.9	140.2	94.9	72.6	34.8	14.6
United Kingdom	10.2	566.4	1059.4	273.8	73.3	28.9	19.6	15.4
EC average	14.2	498.8	901.1	152.1	92.2	67.6	29.7	26.1
EFTA members								
Austria	9.2	499.2	1140.3	104.2	110.7	61.4	39.3	50.8
Finland[b]	14.9	390.1	998.5	139.9	69.5	115.6	25.7	57.8
Iceland	8.0	351.3	623.4	160.8	28.6	49.7	17.4	17.4
Liechtenstein								
Norway[b]	14.7	474.3	1012.6	209.2	64.4	92.9	17.3	33.8
Sweden[b]	16.6	480.4	1195.0	184.9	103.3	71.7	19.3	37.9
Switzerland	21.0	500.4	811.7	118.7	52.8	124.8	28.6	46.0
EFTA average	15.2	472.8	1043.3	148.0	83.7	89.5	26.6	45.0
Eastern Europe								
Albania								
Bulgaria	12.9	341.3	1455.4	150.5	75.1	60.4	26.2	32.7
Czechoslovakia	7.0	488.8	1270.7	138.9	98.7	90.0	22.6	35.9
Hungary	22.2	578.9	1431.0	109.9	170.6	110.9	44.0	84.5
Poland	16.6	378.4	1050.9	88.2	63.5	69.5	39.9	56.3
Romania								
USSR	41.4	323.9	1117.6	160.1	57.6	103.9	37.4	40.3
Yugoslavia	25.4	310.8	927.2	81.6	73.6	48.5	31.0	32.6
East European average	33.0	320.6	1049.5	136.1	60.3	89.4	34.2	39.5
Others								
Cyprus								
Gibraltar								
Malta	10.3	316.3	749.9	118.9	48.1	46.8	9.2	13.2
Monaco								
Turkey								
Average								
European average								

Sources: WHO/Euromonitor
Notes: See end of section

Table No: 1703

ILLNESS

Reported AIDS Cases by Date of Report 1986-1990

Numbers

	1986	1987	1988	1989	1990	Total
EC members						
Belgium	258	115	137	147	107	764
Denmark	142	100	124	171	168	705
France	1926	2004	2680	2828	280	9718
Germany: East						
Germany: West[a]	1083	1036	1250	1406	725	5500
Greece	35	53	82	107	98	375
Ireland	17	20	37	50	37	161
Italy	688	994	1728	2335	1831	7576
Luxembourg	6	3	4	11	6	30
Netherlands	255	237	319	382	294	1487
Portugal	57	58	95	150	162	522
Spain	637	900	1825	2162	1523	7047
United Kingdom	802	631	790	833	828	3884
EC total	5906	6151	9071	10582	6059	37769
EFTA members						
Austria	54	82	103	139	96	474
Finland	17	8	17	15	14	71
Iceland	4		6	3	1	14
Liechtenstein						
Norway	35	35	30	45	40	185
Sweden	102	78	85	125	97	487
Switzerland	189	164	348	455	392	1548
EFTA total	401	367	589	782	640	2779
Eastern Europe						
Albania						
Bulgaria	0	2	0	5	0	7
Czechoslovakia	6	2	4	7	5	24
Hungary	1	7	9	15	16	48
Poland	1	2	2	24	18	47
Romania	6	4	14	198	833	1055
USSR	1	3	3	21	12	40
Yugoslavia	8	18	39	44	49	158
East European total	23	38	71	314	933	1379
Others						
Cyprus						
Gibraltar						
Malta	5	2	7	0	1	15
Monaco	0	0	0	2	2	4
Turkey						
Total	5	2	7	2	3	19
European total	6335	6558	9738	11680	7635	41946

Source: WHO
Note: See end of section

Table No: 1704

HEALTH EXPENDITURE

Health Expenditure 1980-1990

As stated

	Total health expenditure as % of GDP 1980	1985	1990	Per capita health expenditure (US$) 1990	Drugs as % of health expenditure 1990
EC members					
Belgium	6.7	7.4	7.4	1087	17.3
Denmark	6.8	6.3	6.2	963	11.6
France	7.6	8.5	8.9	1379	17.1
Germany: East					
Germany: West[a]	8.4	8.7	8.1	1287	15.4
Greece[b]	4.3	4.9	5.3	406	31.0
Ireland[c]	9.0	8.3	7.1	697	8.3
Italy	6.8	7.0	7.6	1113	16.6
Luxembourg	6.8	6.8	7.2	1300	
Netherlands	8.0	8.0	8.1	1182	8.2
Portugal	5.9	7.0	6.7	529	30.7
Spain[d]	5.6	5.7	6.6	730	14.3
United Kingdom[d]	5.6	5.8	6.1	909	11.6
EFTA members					
Austria[b]	7.9	7.6	8.4	1192	10.8
Finland	6.5	7.2	7.4	1156	9.2
Iceland	6.5	7.4	8.5	1372	
Liechtenstein					
Norway	6.6	6.4	7.2	1281	8.0
Sweden	9.4	8.8	8.7	1421	8.8
Switzerland	7.3	7.6	7.4	1389	12.5
Eastern Europe					
Albania					
Bulgaria					
Czechoslovakia					
Hungary					
Poland					
Romania					
USSR					
Yugoslavia					
Others					
Cyprus					
Gibraltar					
Malta					
Monaco					
Turkey	4.0	2.8	4.0	197	

Source: Association of Danish Pharmaceutical Industry/OECD
Notes: See end of section

Notes to Tables in Section Seventeen:

Table 1701 Nurses includes professionals, midwives and (except in Denmark, Finland, Iceland, Norway and Sweden) auxiliaries

- a Nurses figure refers to 1983
- b Personnel figure refers to 1987
- c Dentists figure refers to 1987
- d Pharmacists practising in hospitals only
- e Data for beds, nurses and pharmacists refer to 1988
- f Data for beds and pharmacists refer to 1988
- g Doctors includes dental physicians practising in hospitals
- h Data for beds and pharmacists refer to 1987
- i Data for doctors, dentists and pharmacists refer to 1986
- j Nurses figure refers to 1985
- k Doctors figure refers to 1989
- l Pharmacists figure refers to 1987
- m Pharmacists figure refers to 1986
- n Doctors include dentists

Table 1702

- A Infectious and parasitic diseases
- B Malignant neo-plasms
- C Diseases of the circulatory system
- D Diseases of the respiratory system
- E Diseases of the digestive system
- F Injury (other than traffic accidents) and poisoning
- G Motor traffic accidents
- H Suicide and self-inflicted injury

- a Data refer to 1986
- b Data refer to 1988
- c Data refer to 1987

Table 1703 a Data refer to unified Germany

Table 1704

- a Data refer to unified Germany
- b Data refer to 1989
- c Data refer to public health expenditure only
- d Data refer to 1988

Section Eighteen

Literacy and Education

Table No: 1801

BASIC EDUCATION INDICATORS

Adult Literacy Rates, School Leaving Age: Latest Year

	Year	Adult Literacy Rate (%)	School Leaving Age
EC members			
Belgium	1983	98	18
Denmark	1981	99	15
France	1984	99	16
Germany: East	1985	99	16
Germany: West	1985	99	18
Greece	1990	93	15
Ireland	1984	99	15
Italy	1990	97	13
Luxembourg	1982	100	15
Netherlands	1984	98	16
Portugal	1990	85	14
Spain	1990	95	15
United Kingdom	1984	99	16
EFTA members			
Austria	1983	98	15
Finland	1982	99	16
Iceland	1984	100	15
Liechtenstein	1985	100	14
Norway	1984	100	15
Sweden	1982	99	15
Switzerland	1984	100	15
Eastern Europe			
Albania	1983	75	13
Bulgaria	1983	95	16
Czechoslovakia	1981	99	16
Hungary	1983	98	16
Poland	1983	98	14
Romania	1983	98	14
USSR	1989	98	17
Yugoslavia	1990	93	15
Others			
Cyprus	1987	94	15
Gibraltar	1985	98	15
Malta	1985	86	16
Monaco	1983	99	16
Turkey	1985	70	14

Sources: UNESCO/national statistical offices

Table No: 1802

PRE-PRIMARY EDUCATION

Pre-Primary Schools, Pupils, Staff: Latest Year

	Year	Pre-Primary Schools	Pupils ('000)	Staff ('000)
EC members				
Belgium[a]	1987	4060	371.5	19.8
Denmark[b]	1988		51.8	3.7
France	1989	18676	2536.0	74.5
Germany: East	1989	13452	747.1	73.4
Germany: West	1988	29089	1646.0	84.8
Greece	1987	5389	155.2	7.9
Ireland	1988		135.9	4.6
Italy	1989	28038	1566.4	109.6
Luxembourg	1989		8.0	0.5
Netherlands	1984	7951	399.4	22.5
Portugal[a]	1989	2822	128.9	6.4
Spain	1987	15948	1054.2	37.0
United Kingdom	1988	1312	716.0	27.0
EFTA members				
Austria	1989	3876	192.9	9.0
Finland	1989		49.8	
Iceland	1989		4.4	
Liechtenstein	1987		0.8	
Norway	1989	4310	128.2	33.1
Sweden[c]	1989	12850	307.8	
Switzerland	1989		136.8	
Eastern Europe				
Albania	1989	3330	125.3	5.4
Bulgaria	1989	4562	317.6	28.3
Czechoslovakia	1989	11380	636.6	50.5
Hungary	1989	4748	392.3	33.8
Poland	1989	26212	1316.7	90.0
Romania	1989	12108	835.9	31.3
USSR	1989	143000	12718.0	1579.0
Yugoslavia	1989	4157	435.9	46.4
Others				
Cyprus	1989	540	22.0	0.9
Gibraltar[d]	1984	2	0.2	
Malta	1988	57	11.3	0.5
Monaco[e]	1990	9	0.9	
Turkey	1989	3601	112.1	7.2

Source: UNESCO/national statistical offices
Notes: See end of section

Table No: 1803

PRIMARY EDUCATION

Primary Schools, Pupils, Staff: Latest Year

	Year	Primary Schools	Pupils ('000)	Staff ('000)
EC members				
Belgium	1987	4263	728.7	71.1
Denmark[a]	1989	255	355.3	30.0
France	1989	44972	4163.2	265.6
Germany: East	1988	5703	956.2	57.5
Germany: West[b]	1989	13595	2473.7	136.2
Greece	1987	8178	868.3	39.1
Ireland	1988	3310	423.7	15.4
Italy	1989	25163	3140.1	258.0
Luxembourg[c]	1987		23.4	1.8
Netherlands[d]	1988	8426	1428.6	82.6
Portugal[e]	1989	12692	1003.6	75.5
Spain	1987	18532	3246.7	131.4
United Kingdom	1988	24482	4415.0	225.0
EFTA members				
Austria[f]	1989	3717	367.0	33.8
Finland	1989	4235	389.1	25.1
Iceland[g]	1989	183	25.5	1.4
Liechtenstein	1987		1.7	0.1
Norway	1989	3442	310.6	50.9
Sweden[h]	1989	4640	578.5	92.9
Switzerland	1989		394.1	
Eastern Europe				
Albania	1989	1700	550.7	28.4
Bulgaria	1989	2884	991.6	61.2
Czechoslovakia	1989	6206	1961.7	98.0
Hungary	1989	3527	1183.6	90.6
Poland[i]	1989	17537	5141.4	325.8
Romania	1989	13357	2891.8	139.0
USSR	1989	128000	25040.0	3004.0
Yugoslavia	1989	11841	1406.6	62.1
Others				
Cyprus	1989	378	60.8	2.8
Gibraltar	1984	13	2.8	0.2
Malta	1988	112	36.7	1.8
Monaco	1990	7	1.8	0.1
Turkey	1989	51170	6848.1	224.7

Sources: UNESCO/national statistical offices
Notes: See end of section

Table No: 1804

SECONDARY EDUCATION

Secondary Schools, Pupils, Staff: Latest Year

	Year	Secondary Schools	Total Pupils ('000)	Staff ('000)	Pupils in Training Colleges ('000)	Pupils at Tech. Colleges ('000)
EC members						
Belgium	1987	2314	805.6	114.6		372.4
Denmark	1988	164	483.5			155.8
France	1989	11181	5398.6	434.0		1200.4
Germany: East	1988	1429	1418.3	158.3		360.5
Germany: West	1988	5416	6219.2	443.7		2259.0
Greece	1987	3134	840.0	54.2		131.5
Ireland[a]	1988	815	341.8	18.9		23.1
Italy	1989	17615	5245.1	571.6	189.0	1939.1
Luxembourg[b]	1987		22.5	1.7	0.1	14.8
Netherlands[c,d]	1988	3316	1289.4	98.0	0.1	571.0
Portugal[e]	1989	1511	544.9	40.3		16.1
Spain	1987	4861	4798.3	229.1		1290.3
United Kingdom	1988	5020	4365.9			429.8
EFTA members						
Austria	1989	2069	601.1	71.1	10.2	160.9
Finland[f]	1989	1082	410.6	37.4	0.2	110.4
Iceland[a,g]	1989	115	29.1	2.4	0.3	7.0
Liechtenstein	1987	10	3.9	0.2		
Norway	1989	937	375.1		0.9	117.1
Sweden[b,f]	1989	534	598.0	51.5	0.1	212.6
Switzerland	1989		371.1		7.7	27.2
Eastern Europe						
Albania	1989	397	202.9	9.4	2.1	137.7
Bulgaria	1989	526	397.4	27.6		239.5
Czechoslovakia	1989	2269	857.0	86.9	8.5	395.9
Hungary[a]	1989	587	487.2	22.8	4.9	366.0
Poland[h]	1989	10544	1829.7	161.9	26.2	1389.4
Romania[i]	1989	1728	1652.4	44.4	5.5	1422.0
USSR	1989	48600	21124.0		209.0	2959.0
Yugoslavia	1989	1490	2361.7	139.5	22.1	785.8
Others						
Cyprus	1989	92	43.2	3.6		3.1
Gibraltar	1986		1.7	0.1		0.1
Malta	1988	87	30.2	2.5		6.9
Monaco	1990		2.9			0.7
Turkey	1989	7809	3621.0	155.7	9.4	830.7

Sources: UNESCO/national statistical offices
Notes: See end of section

Table No: 1805

HIGHER EDUCATION

Higher Education: Establishments, Staff, Students: Latest Year

	Year	Establish-ments	Teaching Staff ('000)	Students ('000)	University Teachers ('000)	University Students ('000)	% Students at University
EC members							
Belgium	1987	190	19.5	254.3	5.3	103.5	40.7
Denmark	1988	50		126.7		100.5	74.3
France	1989			1587.2	46.3	1124.1	70.8
Germany: East[a]	1988	54	42.7	438.9	30.9	156.3	35.6
Germany: West	1988	238	198.2	1686.9	151.0	1464.6	86.8
Greece	1987	107	12.8	189.2	7.4	117.2	61.9
Ireland	1988	25	5.1	81.1	2.5	43.6	53.8
Italy	1989	796	54.5	1358.3	53.8	1348.5	99.3
Luxembourg[b]	1986		0.4	0.7			
Netherlands	1988	451		415.8		171.2	41.2
Portugal	1989	126	13.2	156.7	10.6	113.7	72.6
Spain	1987	254	52.2	1036.4	51.5	978.3	94.4
United Kingdom	1988	719	84.7	1113.3	34.2	383.6	34.5
EFTA members							
Austria	1989	44	13.0	199.8	11.8	186.6	93.4
Finland	1989	571		155.3	7.7	108.1	69.6
Iceland	1989	3		5.4			
Liechtenstein							
Norway	1988	198	9.6	114.9	4.3	47.9	41.7
Sweden	1989			184.8			
Switzerland[a,c]	1989	12		132.8	7.0	83.3	62.7
Eastern Europe							
Albania	1990	8	1.8	22.1	1.8	22.1	100.0
Bulgaria	1989	30	20.8	157.9	19.2	138.0	87.4
Czechoslovakia	1989	36	25.4	186.1	25.4	186.1	100.0
Hungary	1989	54	16.3	100.9	12.1	65.5	64.9
Poland[a]	1989	92		505.7	65.9	408.1	80.7
Romania	1989	44	11.7	164.5	11.7	164.5	100.0
USSR[d]	1989	5301	404.0	5273.0			
Yugoslavia	1989	340	26.5	342.6	23.5	295.3	86.2
Others							
Cyprus	1989	16	0.5	5.9			
Gibraltar							
Malta	1988	1	0.1	1.7	0.1	1.7	100.0
Monaco							
Turkey	1989	310	32.1	685.5	30.6	394.5	57.5

Sources: UNESCO/national statistical offices
Notes: See end of section

Table No: 1806

QUALIFICATIONS

School Leavers and Qualifications 1991

% of adults

	School Leaving Age 15 or less	16	17	18 or more	Degree or Professional Qualification	Trade or Craft Qualification
EC members						
Belgium	29	8	8	54	36	24
Denmark	17	3	2	71	19	49
France	33	10	9	41	55	2
Germany: East						
Germany: West	9	6	13	59	19	44
Greece	49	3	2	46	24	1
Ireland	36	16	13	34	13	11
Italy	58	4	4	34	29	10
Luxembourg	36	10	11	43	31	17
Netherlands	20	12	11	53	33	25
Portugal	53	6	4	29	21	7
Spain	63	6	4	28	20	6
United Kingdom	43	26	6	24	22	20
EFTA members						
Austria	37	6	10	44	44	13
Finland	27	10	4	57	25	31
Iceland						
Liechtenstein						
Norway	17	6	6	68	51	18
Sweden	22	6	5	63	58	5
Switzerland	30	37	6	27	25	55
Eastern Europe						
Albania						
Bulgaria						
Czechoslovakia						
Hungary						
Poland						
Romania						
USSR						
Yugoslavia						
Others						
Cyprus						
Gibraltar						
Malta						
Monaco						
Turkey						

Source: Reader's Digest Eurodata
Note: See end of section

Notes to Tables in Section Eighteen:

Table 1802	a	Figure for staff refers to 1985
	b	Figure for staff refers to 1986
	c	Figure for schools refers to 1983
	d	Pupils = 150, staff = 5
	e	Figure for schools refers to 1982
Table 1803	a	Figure for schools refers to 1988
	b	Data for schools and staff refer to 1988
	c	Figure for staff refers to 1986
	d	Data for schools and staff refer to 1987
	e	Data for schools and staff refer to 1986
	f	Figure for staff refers to 1983
	g	Data for schools and staff refer to 1975
	h	Figure for schools refers to 1984
	i	Figure for staff refers to 1988
Table 1804	a	Figure for staff refers to 1975
	b	Figure for pupils at training colleges refers to 1985
	c	Figure for pupils at training colleges refers to 1986
	d	Figure for staff refers to 1987
	e	Figure for staff refers to 1984
	f	Figure for staff refers to 1983
	g	Data for pupils at training colleges and at tech. colleges refer to 1987
	h	Figure for staff refers to 1988
	i	Figure for pupils at tech. colleges refer to 1987
Table 1805	a	Establishments refers to universities only
	b	Figure for staff refers to 1985
	c	Figure for staff refers to 1987
	d	Data include evening and correspondence courses
Table 1806		School leavers do not always sum to 100% owing to lack of data in some countries

Section Nineteen

Agricultural Resources

Table No: 1901

AGRICULTURAL OUTPUT

Indices of Agricultural Output 1977-1990

1979-1981 = 100

	1977	1980	1982	1983	1984	1985	1986	1987	1988	1989	1990
EC members											
Belgium[a]	91.0	96.9	101.2	96.7	105.9	106.6	115.9	110.0	115.9	117.0	119.1
Denmark	97.3	99.3	110.6	101.0	125.7	122.5	119.6	115.3	121.5	128.0	139.0
France	86.1	101.7	104.7	100.1	109.3	106.9	106.8	109.2	106.0	102.7	103.3
Germany: East	91.3	98.5	95.7	97.5	107.7	114.0	116.5	118.8	114.1	115.4	115.2
Germany: West	95.3	101.0	108.3	105.8	112.3	108.1	115.9	110.4	114.2	113.5	112.9
Greece	89.4	104.0	107.4	102.2	105.4	112.3	107.0	104.0	110.6	111.3	103.2
Ireland	98.1	109.4	98.8	102.8	112.2	112.6	114.9	115.8	110.3	107.6	117.4
Italy	92.1	102.2	99.3	108.2	99.7	101.2	100.9	104.2	100.5	102.6	96.3
Luxembourg											
Netherlands	88.9	96.2	109.2	107.2	110.2	108.5	119.3	115.7	115.6	125.3	126.0
Portugal	91.7	97.7	104.2	92.5	103.0	106.4	105.1	115.2	93.4	118.7	127.1
Spain	86.6	106.6	105.2	97.4	114.6	110.3	108.0	121.2	115.3	115.7	119.4
United Kingdom	92.2	102.5	103.9	105.1	115.1	110.4	109.9	108.6	106.1	109.8	110.5
EFTA members											
Austria	93.8	103.6	111.5	105.6	109.9	107.7	109.1	107.4	113.3	106.3	105.5
Finland	97.0	103.8	106.0	117.1	116.4	113.1	112.1	98.6	102.5	114.2	118.3
Iceland	95.6	100.2	103.8	103.3	103.1	107.2	101.1	98.2	91.1	89.9	89.2
Liechtenstein											
Norway	93.5	100.3	108.4	103.3	110.7	107.4	103.2	107.1	103.8	105.8	103.5
Sweden	97.1	99.3	105.8	104.3	115.5	108.6	105.9	92.5	91.3	99.4	106.8
Switzerland	95.4	100.2	104.1	104.2	108.0	107.9	109.8	106.1	106.3	113.5	108.7
Eastern Europe											
Albania	92.3	99.2	103.3	113.3	111.0	107.6	109.1	113.8	110.3	113.9	112.7
Bulgaria	89.1	95.4	109.9	98.6	107.7	94.1	104.0	98.9	97.5	99.3	90.6
Czechoslovakia	100.7	102.4	109.6	114.7	119.9	117.7	118.2	120.8	124.5	126.7	125.3
Hungary	95.6	102.7	113.1	107.0	112.8	106.8	108.1	108.5	114.8	110.2	104.7
Poland	98.1	95.7	99.0	103.4	106.8	109.5	117.6	110.7	113.8	115.7	113.5
Romania	96.8	99.9	104.6	101.7	117.5	106.5	117.5	106.2	104.8	99.7	95.7
USSR	101.5	99.9	104.3	109.2	109.6	110.3	117.2	117.2	117.1	120.4	119.0
Yugoslavia	100.1	99.5	109.3	104.6	108.8	100.3	112.3	105.9	100.3	103.3	94.0
Others											
Cyprus[b]	97.9	104.0	101.3	82.4	99.3	96.5	90.2	95.2	111.0	111.9	114.3
Gibraltar											
Malta	99.1	106.6	114.9	114.9	106.0	113.5	118.2	112.7	104.5	113.9	114.4
Monaco											
Turkey	94.3	99.8	106.2	105.2	105.6	108.6	113.8	115.1	122.2	113.5	122.3

Source: FAO Production Yearbook
Notes: See end of section

Table No: 1902

AGRICULTURAL OUTPUT

Indices of Food Output 1977-1990

1979-1981 = 100

	1977	1980	1982	1983	1984	1985	1986	1987	1988	1989	1990
EC members											
Belgium[a]	91.0	96.96	105.19	96.68	105.84	106.49	115.82	110.07	115.87	116.93	119.02
Denmark	97.3	99.36	100.66	102.98	125.73	122.48	114.10	115.33	121.68	128.01	139.04
France	86.0	101.18	104.74	100.42	109.37	106.98	106.49	109.31	100.07	102.87	103.43
Germany: East	91.3	98.42	95.70	95.38	101.23	117.78	116.08	118.35	113.51	114.75	114.57
Germany: West	95.3	100.98	108.33	105.83	112.35	108.14	115.93	110.45	114.20	113.37	112.89
Greece	88.6	104.67	108.05	102.69	105.18	110.50	103.31	100.82	106.90	107.37	99.02
Ireland	98.1	109.40	98.88	102.89	112.28	112.59	114.84	115.70	110.00	107.40	116.95
Italy	92.2	102.30	99.14	108.01	99.42	100.80	106.76	103.91	99.92	101.95	95.43
Luxembourg											
Netherlands	88.9	96.40	109.16	106.96	109.82	108.10	119.02	115.37	113.26	123.05	125.58
Portugal	91.3	104.68	103.23	105.06	105.55	115.38	103.80	113.80	93.51	119.02	127.41
Spain	86.8	106.68	106.27	97.99	114.86	111.33	107.65	121.23	114.82	115.81	119.25
United Kingdom	92.2	102.51	103.93	105.09	115.18	110.30	109.85	108.53	105.94	109.54	110.28
EFTA members											
Austria	93.7	103.61	111.50	105.60	109.90	107.72	109.08	107.41	113.34	106.32	105.54
Finland	97.0	103.75	105.97	117.05	116.40	113.05	112.69	98.50	102.50	114.17	118.32
Iceland	97.0	100.95	102.95	103.49	103.42	107.66	101.27	98.32	91.05	89.78	89.06
Liechtenstein											
Norway	93.5	100.31	108.40	103.15	110.70	107.38	102.96	107.07	103.82	105.81	103.48
Sweden	97.1	99.30	105.84	104.38	115.48	108.57	105.98	92.46	91.28	99.43	95.10
Switzerland	95.4	100.20	109.16	104.21	107.90	107.89	109.87	106.11	106.32	113.52	108.77
Eastern Europe											
Albania	93.6	99.38	105.83	114.73	111.72	107.76	109.19	113.82	108.72	114.12	112.56
Bulgaria	98.2	96.11	110.63	100.69	107.98	94.36	106.32	99.80	100.12	106.02	96.83
Czechoslovakia	100.8	102.39	109.56	114.62	119.84	117.62	118.82	120.40	124.67	120.69	125.30
Hungary	95.4	102.98	113.09	106.99	113.40	105.97	108.39	108.77	115.49	110.89	105.21
Poland	98.0	95.84	99.29	103.66	109.17	102.39	117.15	110.91	114.59	117.12	115.09
Romania	96.5	99.74	104.73	101.81	117.51	106.55	117.58	105.99	104.64	99.58	95.10
USSR	101.3	100.74	104.51	109.97	109.52	111.66	119.29	119.62	118.16	123.04	122.50
Yugoslavia	99.9	99.70	109.80	104.74	108.67	99.78	111.66	105.66	100.73	103.85	94.23
Others											
Cyprus[b]	98.1	104.03	101.46	82.32	99.28	96.46	90.08	94.99	111.15	111.88	114.44
Gibraltar											
Malta	99.1	106.63	114.94	114.99	105.98	113.61	118.30	102.73	104.32	114.02	114.52
Monaco											
Turkey	93.1	99.53	106.63	105.03	105.58	109.16	114.87	115.84	122.30	113.89	122.61

Source: FAO Production Yearbook
Notes: See end of section

Table No: 1903

LAND USE

Land Use and Irrigation 1990

'000 hectares

	Total Area	Land Area	Arable Land	Permanent Crops	Permanent Pasture	Forest and Woodland	Other Land	Irrigated Land	% of Land Area
EC members									
Belgium[a]	3310	3282	806	16	682	699	1079	1	0.03
Denmark	4307	4237	2550	5	219	493	970	430	10.15
France	55150	55010	17899	1220	11598	14782	9511	1160	2.11
Germany: East	10833	10519	4676	237	1258	2983	1365	150	1.43
Germany: West	24858	24428	7273	205	4407	7401	5142	330	1.35
Greece	13199	13085	2875	1049	5255	2620	1286	1190	9.09
Ireland	7028	6889	950	3	4690	341	905		
Italy	30127	29406	9043	2990	4877	6733	5759	3100	10.54
Luxembourg									
Netherlands	3733	3392	905	29	1070	300	1088	550	16.21
Portugal	9239	9195	2906	865	761	2968	1695	634	6.90
Spain	50478	49944	15570	4775	10210	15650	3739	3360	6.73
United Kingdom	24488	24160	6685	51	11197	2364	3863	157	0.65
EFTA members									
Austria	8385	8273	1459	74	2015	3200	1525	4	0.05
Finland	33813	30461	2453		123	23222	4663	62	0.20
Iceland	10300	10025	8		2274	120	7623		
Liechtenstein	16	16	4		6	3	3		
Norway	32390	30683	878		111	8330	21364	95	0.31
Sweden	44996	41162	2853		558	28020	9731	112	0.27
Switzerland	4129	3977	391	21	1609	1052	904	25	0.63
Eastern Europe									
Albania	2875	2740	582	128	403	1046	584	423	15.44
Bulgaria	11091	11055	3848	298	2022	3868	1019	1253	11.33
Czechoslovakia	12787	12537	4976	133	1641	4615	1173	310	2.47
Hungary	9303	9234	5052	235	1197	1688	1062	175	1.90
Poland	31268	30445	14414	345	4048	8746	2892	100	0.33
Romania	23750	23034	9902	448	4410	6372	1902	3458	15.01
USSR	2240220	2227200	226700	4536	371100	946000	679410	21064	0.95
Yugoslavia	25580	25540	7039	727	6352	9334	2088	168	0.66
Others									
Cyprus	925	924	104	52	5	123	640		
Gibraltar	1	1					1		
Malta	32	32	12	1			19	1	3.13
Monaco									
Turkey	77945	76963	24868	3017	8600	20199	20219	2220	2.88

Source: FAO Production Yearbook
Note: See end of section

Table No: 1904

LIVESTOCK

Circulation of Livestock 1990

'000 head

	Horses	Cattle	Pigs	Sheep	Goats
EC members					
Belgium[a]	21	3069	6350	195	9
Denmark	35	2190	9300	100	
France	265	21200	12200	11900	1220
Germany: East	107	5724	12013	2603	19
Germany: West	375	14563	22165	1533	58
Greece	60	715	1160	10353	5904
Ireland	53	5899	995	5782	9
Italy	250	8746	9254	11569	1246
Luxembourg					
Netherlands	65	4731	13634	1702	35
Portugal	26	1393	2490	5380	746
Spain	241	50331	16910	27400	3200
United Kingdom	169	11933	7183	29521	40
EC total	1667	130494	113654	108038	12486
EFTA members					
Austria	48	2562	3773	289	36
Finland	44	1363	1348	61	4
Iceland	57	74	12	700	
Liechtenstein		9	10	3	
Norway	19	953	708	2211	89
Sweden	58	1698	2175	395	
Switzerland	49	1848	1157	370	70
EFTA total	275	8507	9183	4029	199
Eastern Europe					
Albania	102	700	183	1630	1150
Bulgaria	119	1575	4352	8130	433
Czechoslovakia	42	5129	7498	1051	50
Hungary	75	1598	3668	2069	15
Poland	941	10049	19464	4158	10
Romania	663	6291	11671	15435	1100
USSR	5920	118400	78900	137000	6500
Yugoslavia	314	4705	7231	7596	
East European total	8176	148447	132967	177069	9258
Others					
Cyprus	1	49	281	325	208
Gibraltar					
Malta	1	21	101	6	5
Monaco					
Turkey	620	11600	10	31500	13100
Total	622	11670	392	31831	13313
European total	10740	299118	256196	320967	35256

Source: FAO Production Yearbook
Note: See end of section

Table No: 1905

FOOD PRODUCTION

Production of Dairy Products 1990

'000 metric tonnes

	Cow Milk Fresh	Cow Milk Dried	Evaporated Milk	Cheese	Butter and Ghee	Hen Eggs	Honey
EC members							
Belgium[a]	3810	50	25	69	82	180	1
Denmark	4730	185	8	302	94	82	
France	26000	232	221	1400	539	876	23
Germany: East	9100		100	208	286	345	9
Germany: West	23725	145	433	1124	391	732	23
Greece	670			206	6	137	13
Ireland	5605	33	16	78	151	33	
Italy	10376	2	18	702	79	697	10
Luxembourg							
Netherlands	1180	157	449	596	175	615	0
Portugal	1544	5	2	53	12	88	3
Spain	6100	12	81	167	46	620	21
United Kingdom	15284	100	138	312	138	603	3
EC total	108124	921	1491	5217	1999	5008	106
EFTA members							
Austria	3360	12	16	113	41	96	5
Finland	2730	22		93	62	77	1
Iceland	110	0		4	1	3	
Liechtenstein	19						
Norway	1912	1	10	84	19	52	1
Sweden	3523	6	11	116	74	117	3
Switzerland	3772	10	3	129	37	37	2
EFTA total	15426	51	40	539	234	382	12
Eastern Europe							
Albania	316			14	13	14	0
Bulgaria	2112			199	21	143	10
Czechoslovakia	6931		138	212	158	283	10
Hungary	2897	8	4	99	38	236	20
Poland	16170	41	21	446	335	414	14
Romania	4400			97	42	380	17
USSR	106275	360	610	2111	1820	4540	270
Yugoslavia	4500	14		135	18	241	4
East European total	143601	423	773	3313	2445	6251	345
Others							
Cyprus	100			7		7	0
Gibraltar							
Malta	24					6	
Monaco							
Turkey	3000	0	148	143	119	380	40
Total	3124	0	148	150	119	393	40
European total	270275	1395	2452	9219	4797	12034	503

Source: FAO Production Yearbook
Note: See end of section

Table No: 1906

FOOD PRODUCTION

Production of Meat 1990

'000 metric tonnes

	Beef and Veal	Mutton and Lamb	Pig Meat	Horse Meat	Goat Meat	Poultry	Total (incl. others)
EC members							
Belgium[a]	326	7	825	4		185	1371
Denmark	202	1	1200	1		129	1536
France	1878	148	1870	17	9	1384	5716
Germany: East	430	21	1390	2		160	2017
Germany: West	1792	37	3356	4		428	5652
Greece	80	99	150	3	41	153	521
Ireland	491	84	145			67	788
Italy	1176	76	1280	56	4	1104	3907
Luxembourg							
Netherlands	505	14	1641	2	1	458	2621
Portugal	114	26	239	1	4	144	538
Spain	455	225	1730	5	18	825	3352
United Kingdom	1003	370	955	11		1101	3326
EC total	8452	1108	14781	106	77	6138	31345
EFTA members							
Austria	216	4	410			78	715
Finland	118	1	178	1		33	342
Iceland	3	10	2	1		2	21
Liechtenstein							
Norway	82	24	85	1		20	225
Sweden	146	5	313	2		44	535
Switzerland	164	4	270	1	1	33	477
EFTA total	729	48	1258	6	1	210	2315
Eastern Europe							
Albania	28	19	9		9	14	80
Bulgaria	118	74	415		5	182	798
Czechoslovakia	402	9	909			244	1602
Hungary	112	5	1040			490	672
Poland	702	28	1780	4		332	2864
Romania	230	65	920	7	7	390	1635
USSR	8700	950	6600		25	3280	19860
Yugoslavia	302	69	825			350	1555
East European total	10594	1219	12498	11	46	5282	29066
Others							
Cyprus	4	5	29		4	21	64
Gibraltar							
Malta	2		8			4	15
Monaco							
Turkey	265	315		4	75	302	963
Total	271	320	37	4	79	327	1042
European total	20046	2695	28574	127	203	11957	63768

Source: FAO Production Yearbook
Notes: See end of section

Table No: 1907

FOOD PRODUCTION

Production of Cereals 1990

'000 metric tonnes

	Wheat	Barley	Maize	Oats	Rye	Rice	Total (incl. others)
EC members							
Belgium[a]	1527	625	60	60	12		1043
Denmark	4101	5030		109	565		9815
France	33363	10067	8996	875	248	109	54838
Germany: East	4734	4878	1	580	1945		12334
Germany: West	11053	9195	1545	1535	2056		25889
Greece	1580	400	1700	47	30	100	3860
Ireland	603	1337		136	1		2077
Italy	8109	1703	5864	307	21	1282	17411
Luxembourg							
Netherlands	1076	219	5	16	36		1352
Portugal	268	62	643	62	77	153	1315
Spain	4760	9415	3051	524	274	569	18786
United Kingdom	13900	7900		535	32		2242
EC total	85074	50831	21865	4786	5297	2213	171162
EFTA members							
Austria	1370	1437	1400	262	375		4945
Finland	627	1720		1662	244		4283
Iceland							
Liechtenstein							
Norway	207	590		404	4		1180
Sweden	2173	2052		1614	340		5491
Switzerland	572	347	231	55	19		1411
EFTA total	4949	6146	1631	3997	982		17310
Eastern Europe							
Albania	615	42	302	30	10	9	1043
Bulgaria	5095	1345	1241	107	48	23	7888
Czechoslovakia	6707	4071	468	360	736		12492
Hungary	6159	1359	4500	149	226	35	12500
Poland	9026	4217	290	2186	6044		28014
Romania	7320	2680	6810	168	59	57	17189
USSR	108000	57000	16000	16828	21000	2473	228854
Yugoslavia	6359	650	6270	279	72	440	15664
East European total	149281	71364	35881	20107	28195	3037	323644
Others							
Cyprus	8	90		1			98
Gibraltar							
Malta	5	4					9
Monaco							
Turkey	20000	7200	2000	2166	250	235	29983
Total	20013	7294	2000	2167	250	235	30090
European total	259317	135635	61377	31057	34724	5485	542206

Source: FAO Production Yearbook
Note: See end of section

Table No: 1908

FOOD PRODUCTION

Production of Selected Crops 1990

'000 metric tonnes

	Sugar Beet	Hops	Rapeseed	Potatoes	Tomatoes	Apples	Grapes
EC members							
Belgium[a]	6200	0	8	1750	235	223	27
Denmark	3300		819	1614	18	30	
France	29925	0	2011	6000	770	2400	7340
Germany: East	6100	3	437	8900	78	700	
Germany: West	23778	32	1720	7716	19	1958	1240
Greece	2500			1100	2124	296	1600
Ireland	1550		15	687	12	9	
Italy	13800		34	2479	5186	1970	8450
Luxembourg							
Netherlands	8623		26	7036	650	333	1
Portugal	27	0		999	1005	143	1500
Spain	7223	2	30	5399	2928	642	6481
United Kingdom	8000	4	1231	6504	153	249	
EC total	111026	41	6331	50184	13178	8953	26639
EFTA members							
Austria	2760	0	97	850	19	338	400
Finland	995		117	881	30	15	
Iceland				10	1		
Liechtenstein				12			
Norway			8	440	10	50	
Sweden	2550		401	1233	16	150	
Switzerland	965		43	760	20	320	174
EFTA total	7270	0	666	4186	96	873	574
Eastern Europe							
Albania	250			88	160	17	75
Bulgaria	576	0		427	792	355	708
Czechoslovakia	5609	10	380	2534	123	350	221
Hungary	4674	0	97	1200	406	950	700
Poland	16700	2	1206	36313	414	740	
Romania	3278	0	11	2852	2350	545	955
USSR	81200	10	430	63700	6700	5800	5000
Yugoslavia	5920	4	52	2200	440	500	1000
East European total	118207	26	2176	109314	11385	9257	8659
Others							
Cyprus				185	28	10	215
Gibraltar							
Malta				17	19	1	3
Monaco							
Turkey	13986		2	4000	5850	1800	3420
Total	13986	0	2	4202	5897	1811	3638
European total	250489	67	9175	167886	30556	20894	39510

Source: FAO Production Yearbook
Notes: See end of section

Table No: 1909

FORESTRY PRODUCTS

Production of Forestry/Paper Products 1990

As stated

	A	B	C	D	E	F	G	H
EC members								
Belgium[a,b]	4682	572	1184	507	1195	734	118	101
Denmark[b]	2107	427	861	123	326	130	18	
France[c]	44718	10442	10655	1905	7006	2773	321	379
Germany: East[c]	11251	710	2521	179	1351	194		126
Germany: West	73456	3656	12203	3489	11873	4788	829	1118
Greece[b]	2037	1346	355	147	282	62	85	10
Ireland[d]	1527	50	393	15	34			
Italy	8038	3703	1950	2099	5582	2242	261	233
Luxembourg								
Netherlands	1411	151	455	669	2770	819	167	300
Portugal	10443	598	1790	50	740	154	51	
Spain[c,d]	17758	2590	2826	437	3446	832	232	173
United Kingdom[c,d]	6455	255	2191	1928	4980	1487	453	696
EC total	183883	24500	37384	11548	39585	14215	2535	3136
EFTA members								
Austria	17280	2680	7332	373	2872	1377	98	333
Finland	41647	2984	7503	81	8781	4590	167	1430
Iceland								
Liechtenstein								
Norway[c]	11794	919	2413	67	1819	339	40	910
Sweden	55854	4424	11830	192	8426	1655	283	2273
Switzerland[c]	6778	877	1985	339	1295	370	150	280
EFTA total	133353	11884	31063	1052	23193	8331	738	5226
Eastern Europe								
Albania[b]	2330	1608	200		21			2
Bulgaria	4099	1518	985	90	322	52		
Czechoslovakia[c]	17854	1782	4702	47	1307	152	55	75
Hungary[c,d]	6604	2944	1257	273	443	142	20	
Poland[e]	19622	2774	4630	84	1065	242	120	25
Romania[b]	17321	3846	2851	71	819	139	23	108
USSR[b]	364600	80700	92000	150	10657	1365		1719
Yugoslavia[c]	13577	4045	4496	215	1302	307		36
East European total	446007	99217	111121	930	15936	2399	218	1965
Others								
Cyprus[b]	68	20	22					
Gibraltar								
Malta								
Monaco								
Turkey[b]	15524	9796	4923	100	436	75	3	151
Total	15592	9816	4945	100	436	75	3	151
European total	778835	145417	184513	13630	79150	25020	3494	10478

Source: FAO Yearbook of Forestry Products/Timber Bulletin Forest Products Statistics
Notes: See end of section

Table No: 1910

FISHERY PRODUCTS

Production of Fishery Products 1990

'000 metric tonnes

	A	B	C	D	E	F
EC members						
Belgium[a]	39.9	10.9	4.2	12.6		1.0
Denmark	1927.5	190.1	31.2	81.9	85.7	332.9
France	875.8	122.4	14.0	67.0	3.7	19.2
Germany: East	174.2	26.0	29.8	53.9		
Germany: West	233.9	206.0	15.2	133.2	7.4	25.3
Greece	128.9	5.8	10.2	1.4		
Ireland	245.0	84.3	5.7	1.8	3.8	7.0
Italy	550.9	60.9	6.6	111.9		4.0
Luxembourg						
Netherlands	421.6	190.0	29.3	18.0		
Portugal	331.8	44.2	1.6	50.0	1.7	6.9
Spain	1370.0	349.2	25.2	111.8	8.5	82.2
United Kingdom	792.8	203.1	34.2	16.5	7.1	49.0
EC total	7092.3	1492.9	207.2	660.0	117.9	527.5
EFTA members						
Austria	5.0		0.6			
Finland	110.8	11.7	4.8	1.4		4.0
Iceland	1504.7	176.3	87.7	2.4	53.7	143.6
Liechtenstein						
Norway	1899.9	324.3	87.0	57.1	77.2	199.6
Sweden	257.8	12.2	5.5	37.9	4.0	20.0
Switzerland	4.4	0.9	1.0	0.2		
EFTA total	3782.6	525.4	186.6	99.0	134.9	367.2
Eastern Europe						
Albania	11.9	0.3		0.8		
Bulgaria	102.0	69.2	4.5	13.2		7.3
Czechoslovakia	21.2		7.0	21.5		
Hungary	38.2	4.3		1.3		
Poland	654.8	162.9	52.4	60.1	0.5	61.8
Romania	267.6	93.0	37.5	11.0	0.2	9.2
USSR	11310.0	3405.9	760.3	1460.1	118.8	751.7
Yugoslavia	71.6	3.3	0.1	34.7	0.4	2.0
East European total	12477.3	3738.9	861.8	1602.7	119.9	832.0
Others						
Cyprus	2.6					
Gibraltar						
Malta	6.9					
Monaco	2.0					
Turkey	457.1	24.0	3.5	1.1	3.9	45.0
Total	468.6	24.0	3.5	1.1	3.9	45.0
European total	23820.8	5781.2	1259.1	2362.8	376.6	1771.7

Source: FAO Yearbook of Fishery Statistics
Note: See end of section

Notes to Tables in Section Nineteen:

Table 1901 Break in series 1988
- a Includes Luxembourg
- b Data are year ending mid-1981 = 100

Table 1902 Break in series 1988
- a Includes Luxembourg
- b Data are year ending mid-1981 = 100

Table 1903 a Includes Luxembourg

Table 1904 a Includes Luxembourg

Table 1905 a Includes Luxembourg

Table 1906 a Includes Luxembourg

Table 1907 a Includes Luxembourg

Table 1908 0 = less than 500 metric tonnes
- a Includes Luxembourg

Table 1909
- A Roundwood '000m3
- B Fuelwood and charcoal '000m3
- C Sawnwood and sleepers '000m3
- D Wood pulp '000 MT
- E Paper and paperboard '000 MT
- F Printing and writing paper '000 MT
- G Household and sanitary paper '000 MT, figures are for 1989
- H Newsprint '000 MT
- a Includes Luxembourg
- b Data refer to 1989
- c Roundwood and fuelwood data refer to 1989
- d Sawnwood figure refers to 1989
- e Sawnwood and wood pulp data refer to 1989

Table 1910
- A Fish, crustaceans, molluscs (nominal catch)
- B Fresh, chilled or frozen fish
- C Dried, salted or smoked fish
- D Fish products and preparations
- E Oils and fats of aquatic animal origin
- F Meals, solubles etc of animal origin

- a Includes Luxembourg

Section Twenty

Communications

Table No: 2001

TELEPHONES

Trends in Number of Telephones in Use 1977-1990

'000

	1977	1980	1982	1983	1984	1985	1986	1987	1988	1989	1990
EC members											
Belgium	3100	3636	3959	4111	4243	4346	4556	4719	4925	5138	
Denmark	2718	3283	3595	3676	3828	4005	4195	4434	4509	4398	
France	17635	24859	29594	31483	33002	34346					
Germany: East	2860	3156	3344	3441	3527	3630	3755	3875	3977		
Germany: West	22932	28554	31370	35137	36582	37899	39128	40288	41735	43095	
Greece	2320	2796	3113	3313	3529	3721	3920	4125	4303	4522	
Ireland	519	650	779	824	894	942			1200		
Italy	16125	19277	21680	22992	24331	25615	26874	28052	29299	30715	
Luxembourg	186	207	220	226	234	241	250	257	266		
Netherlands	5845	7357	8023	8272	8544	8785	9080	9410	9750		
Portugal	1199	1372	1567	1685	1764	1835	1936	2072	2258	1109	
Spain	9528	11845	12820	13345	13825	14259	14748	15477		17072	
United Kingdom	21672	26651	28632	29062	29518					43599	45600
EFTA members											
Austria	2443	3010	3330	3469	3594	3720	3843	3979	4128	4310	
Finland	2032	2374	2644	2777	2899	3028	3423	3622			
Iceland	95	109	117	125	130	138	149	153	170		
Liechtenstein	9	11	11	11	12	13	13				
Norway	1571	1881	2204	2395	2579	2950	3130	3230			
Sweden	5930	6621	7132	7410	7669	7270	8000	8151	8300		
Switzerland	4145	4612	4955	5113	5270	5436	5623	5783	5879	6051	
Eastern Europe											
Albania											
Bulgaria	946	1255	1514	1790	1930	1980	2000	2010	2387	2515	2635
Czechoslovakia	2863	3150	3306	3402	3499	3591	3707	3838	3980	4132	
Hungary	1104	1261	1338	1383	1433	1485	1541	1609	1674	1770	1872
Poland	2925	3387	3648	3846	4028	4215	4418	4618	4830	4965	5137
Romania											
USSR	19600	23707	26667			31100	33000	35300	37532	40000	48500
Yugoslavia	1556	2139	2541	2795	3031		3598	3909	4243	4550	
Others											
Cyprus	83		143	164	196	220	244	272	304		
Gibraltar	9	10	10	11	11	11	11	13	14		
Malta	55	79	98	113	115	122	140	155	164	173	
Monaco	27	30	32	35	35	37			47		
Turkey	1379	1902	2368	2665	3091	3455	4222	4827	6387	7467	

Sources: International Telecommunication Union (ITU)/national statistical offices/Euromonitor

Table No: 2002

TELEPHONES

Trends in Total Telephone Traffic 1977-1989

Million calls

	1977	1980	1982	1983	1984	1985	1986	1987	1988	1989
EC members										
Belgium	1621	1917	2375	2570	2728	2891			5669	
Denmark	2791	3140	3404	3528	3556	4010	4209	4418	4655	4722
France[a]	37590	56486	68070	74489	78920	82897	86957	94564	98161	98998
Germany: East	1849	1960	2015	2070	2141	2082	2141	2220	2300	
Germany: West	16267	21193	24164	25408	26432	27616	28989	30326	30410	
Greece	2571	3763	3583	4784	5437	6921	8437	6611		
Ireland[a]	772	1615	1615	1977	2207	2298	2700	2799	3379	
Italy	11378	13502	14678	15529	17022	17706	18592	19828	21296	23774
Luxembourg[a,b]	97	139	127		150	166	173	174	181	
Netherlands	3946	4935	5329	5538	5785	6007	6240	6401	6609	
Portugal[a,b]	2822	3521	4288	4444	4646	6641	7301	8329	9401	
Spain[b]	1496	2072	2321	2415	2566	2819	2998	3312	3665	
United Kingdom	16011	19963	20937	21551	22976	24842				
EFTA members										
Austria[c]	19620	25755	24873	26847	25085	26371	27015			
Finland		1641	1807	1957	2185	2349	2487	3250	3472	3661
Iceland[a,b]	394	446	442	491	523	552	579	637	1076	
Liechtenstein	8	10	11	11	11	12	13			
Norway[a,b]	2979	3856	4622	4977	5400	6138	6745	7607		
Sweden[a]	20191	23010	24822	25767	26984	28882	33031	35854	37123	39961
Switzerland	8319	9451	10381	10919	11175	11650	12243	12937	13908	14676
Eastern Europe										
Albania										
Bulgaria	44	41	31	33	35	37	38			
Czechoslovakia	4154	3459	4101	4474	4916	5472	6074	6742		
Hungary[a]	1015	1644	2006	2230	2574	2950	3199	3475	3884	4982
Poland	787	1011	894		1142	1239	1309	1386		
Romania										
USSR[b,d]	963	1267	1457			1824	1994	2218	2396	
Yugoslavia[a]	8761	14369	17842	20788	22000		33463	37169	37982	39651
Others										
Cyprus[e]	7	12	1103	1316	1558	1746	1896	2182	2485	3049
Gibraltar[c,f]	0	0	2	2	2	3				
Malta	35	43	62	65	127	74	77		108	234
Monaco[a]	86	139	163	179	191	222			272	
Turkey[a,b]	1204	1926	3150	4535	5332	6957	8946	12665	15429	

Sources: ITU/national statistical offices
Notes: See end of section

Table No: 2003

TELEX

Trends in Number of Telex Lines 1977-1989

Number

	1977	1980	1983	1984	1985	1986	1987	1988	1989
EC members									
Belgium	17500	20700	23970	25379	26464	27570	27620	25027	20898
Denmark	8007	9456	11414	12700	13307	13367	13042	12000	10000
France	65884	83211	104986	114008	124515	134293	143916	150010	147429
Germany: East	12000	15000	15957	16200	16476	16724	17020	17363	
Germany: West	114000	137000	152826	157093	161482	164952	165246	155831	
Greece	8000	12200	15178	18232	20202	21643	23605	24329	24476
Ireland	3900	5300	7000	7255	7269	7143	6637	5371	4500
Italy	27800	40900	55746	61222	65416	69363	74406	72769	67904
Luxembourg	1205	1672	2089	2257	2391	2576	2731	2737	
Netherlands	27270	33178	36616	38114	39306	40200	38600	33100	
Portugal	3957	7581	14412	16528	18427	20898	24339	27651	28393
Spain	15500	23300	31443	33845	36910	39958	41956	41185	36876
United Kingdom	64800	85800	92600	95115	98975	104886	111505		
EFTA members									
Austria	16000	19000	22928	24321	25015	25774	25954	25032	21435
Finland	5400	6400	7500	7700	8400	8300	7800	7100	6500
Iceland	250	320	320	340	442	520	576	570	550
Liechtenstein		366	426	438	447	468			
Norway	6200	7300	9195	10197	10817	11026	10731	9540	7939
Sweden	11895	14678	16156	17387	18174	18408	19660	18320	16600
Switzerland	27960	30665	35953	37385	39011	40129	39318	35281	29572
Eastern Europe									
Albania									
Bulgaria	4399	5356	6030	6060	6120	6140			
Czechoslovakia	8010	9340	10170	10499	10818	11119	11395	11700	11980
Hungary	6699	8132	9761	10289	10782	11345	11960	12614	13480
Poland	17300	25000	27858	28737	29606	30733	31920	33544	
Romania									
USSR	930	1226	1512	1611	1704	1836	2072	2553	
Yugoslavia	7000	9000	12000	11462	12262	12999	13837	14682	14993
Others									
Cyprus	1038		2581	3013	3344	3479	3752	3913	3769
Gibraltar	76	135	155	163	188			224	
Malta	312	537	747	787	832	928	992	1043	1088
Monaco	310	450	597	630	672			737	
Turkey	3835	6344	8048	8262	14775	17550	20491	22225	22127

Sources: ITU/national statistical offices

Table No: 2004

TELEX

Trends in Total Telex Traffic 1977-1989

'000 minutes

	1977	1980	1982	1983	1984	1985	1986	1987	1988	1989
EC members										
Belgium[a]	81308	95517	103539	110385	117530	128264	135863	134029	120042	102183
Denmark	31425	37984	43451	45463	48694	55673	59611	70013	51158	40570
France	246004	328253	374856	413153	474550	519886	541612	571979	570018	528339
Germany: East[b]		228816	255956	262088	279428	297248	299336			
Germany: West			532114	557205	565883	572856	561961	528145	459020	
Greece	30725	40806	47531	48540	52964	55354	54923	56700		
Ireland	10250	18552	18867	18305	29900	31097	34319	31695	27308	1550
Italy	162597	222197	257431	278338	305000	362689	336146	334407	307551	252217
Luxembourg	5201	7709	9034		10110	10474		12079	11956	
Netherlands[a]	53626	71782	78586	82957	86009	88080	88064	82600	71900	
Portugal	15095	31665	49044	57024	64360	70927	77070	84806	91737	90151
Spain	49142	70600	86450	94823	102570	109622	117222	119755	107341	96723
United Kingdom[c]	124729	168264	186220	202007	218746					
EFTA members										
Austria	101341	115840	102579	105324	110514	113344	124700	127900		
Finland		22074	25018	25808	25988	26099	25150	22413	18164	14314
Iceland[a]	671	905	996	1048	1593	1730	1685	1821	1630	1165
Liechtenstein	450	645	687	719	753	787	835			
Norway	24404	27008	33343	36034	37755	40217	40009	37612	30601	27007
Sweden[a]	22690	27926	31311	32770	46643	48548	48649	44047	36880	28930
Switzerland	94889	111558	128082	139426	147414	157425	159146	151492	128325	106175
Eastern Europe										
Albania										
Bulgaria	30659	35917	30145	30732						
Czechoslovakia[a]	6137	5881	5865	5997	6174	6309	6481	6810	6948	6687
Hungary[b]	143278	172017	160819	200391	213097	226573	211885			
Poland[a]	9308	10475	7040	9050	9574	10098	9236	9427	14452	
Romania[a]										
USSR[a]	6896	8157	8458	9580	9580		11589	12398	13241	
Yugoslavia[a]	14054	13110	13380	13500	15004	18052	17344			
Others										
Cyprus[c]	2014		4436	5449	6257	6660	6689	6789	6643	6248
Gibraltar	184	294	292	333	363	436				
Malta	788	1649	1573	2038	2135	2440	2692		3113	2918
Monaco[a]	911	1409	4415	4254						
Turkey[a]	5233	5818	8078	10945	10434	14022	18204	20715	21255	17194

Sources: ITU/national statistical offices
Notes: See end of section

Table No: 2005

TELECOMMUNICATION

Penetration of Cellular Radio Telephones 1985-1991

User base

	1985	1986	1987	1988	1989	1990	1991
EC members							
Belgium			4251	19154	30791	42880	
Denmark	44900	57600	77400	101700	123800	148200	
France	4000	6500	35800	91800	173700	245900	
Germany: East							
Germany: West		50310	74182	123145	185508	291379	
Greece							
Ireland	100	600	2900	6300	13800	25000	
Italy	1900	9044	16534	33609	66010	265962	
Luxembourg	100	100	200	300	400	600	
Netherlands	6000	15300	24200	33000	56000	79000	
Portugal							
Spain	1000	1700	4200	11600	29800	54700	
United Kingdom	62300	101900	64000	130000	258000	429000	509000
EFTA members							
Austria	9700	19104	27800	38231	52017	64535	
Finland	31100	49700	71600	104600	190000	257800	
Iceland		1200	4900	6400	7800	8900	
Liechtenstein							
Norway	44900	106178	136069	163298	174992	196885	
Sweden	110000	113000	160000	229000	333000	461000	
Switzerland		10062	11100	11008	9917	8324	
Eastern Europe							
Albania							
Bulgaria							
Czechoslovakia							
Hungary							
Poland							
Romania							
USSR							
Yugoslavia							
Others							
Cyprus					1300	3200	
Gibraltar							
Malta							
Monaco							
Turkey		200	5100	10200	21000	34000	

Source: Industry estimates

Table No: 2006

TELECOMMUNICATION

Availability of Cellular Radio Telephone Systems 1991

	Systems	Users	Per '000 inhabitants
EC members			
Belgium	1	45204	4.6
Denmark	2	163066	31.7
France	2	332023	5.9
Germany: East			
Germany: West	1	369985	5.8
Greece	0		
Ireland	1	27200	7.8
Italy	2	433849	7.5
Luxembourg	1	767	2.0
Netherlands	2	100800	6.7
Portugal	1	9705	0.9
Spain	2	78565	2.0
United Kingdom	2	1196000	20.8
EFTA members			
Austria	2	92446	11.8
Finland	2	262059	51.4
Iceland		10896	41.9
Liechtenstein			
Norway	2	218801	51.5
Sweden	3	544712	63.3
Switzerland	1	150767	22.3
Eastern Europe			
Albania			
Bulgaria			
Czechoslovakia			
Hungary		4600	0.4
Poland			
Romania			
USSR			
Yugoslavia			
Others			
Cyprus	1	3929	5.2
Gibraltar			
Malta		1707	4.8
Monaco			
Turkey[a]	1	34000	0.6

Sources: Industry estimates/trade press/Euromonitor
Notes: See end of section

Table No: 2007

TELECOMMUNICATION

Fax systems 1986-1990

Number in use at end of year

	1986	1987	1988	1989	1990
EC members					
Belgium					
Denmark					
France	54000	106000	180000	350000	580000
Germany: East			10	256	14061
Germany: West	43799	84125	197245	411095	682168
Greece			2800		5600
Ireland				10000	32000
Italy	25203	47967	92413	135169	170450
Luxembourg					
Netherlands					719000
Portugal					17500
Spain			120000	200000	
United Kingdom	86000	173000	370000	556000	750000
EFTA members					
Austria			35000	70000	140000
Finland		990	1660	2600	7500
Iceland					
Liechtenstein					
Norway					
Sweden					
Switzerland			40000	68000	
Eastern Europe					
Albania					
Bulgaria					
Czechoslovakia				1000	
Hungary					
Poland					3300
Romania					600
USSR					
Yugoslavia					
Others					
Cyprus					2400
Gibraltar					
Malta				300	700
Monaco					
Turkey		8300	18100		40000

Source: Industry estimates

Notes to Tables in Section Twenty:

Table 2002 0 indicates less than 0.5 million
- a Million pulses
- b National traffic only
- c Million minutes
- d Long-distance calls only
- e 1977-1980 data refer to million minutes, and to international traffic only; 1981-1989 data refer to million pulses
- f International traffic only

Table 2004
- a International traffic only
- b '000 pulses
- c '000 calls

Table 2006 As at July
- a Data refers to 1990

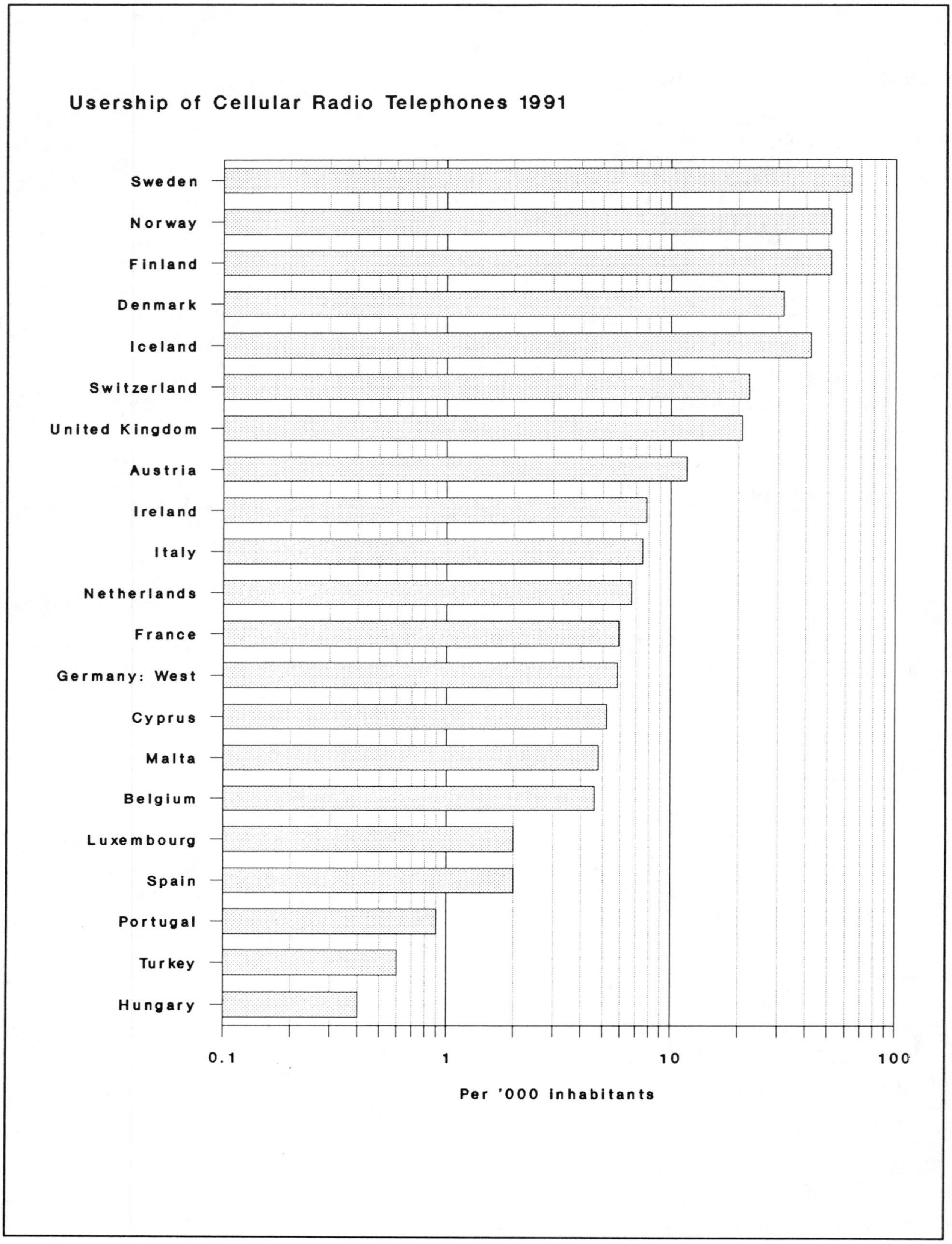
Usership of Cellular Radio Telephones 1991
Sweden
Norway
Finland
Denmark
Iceland
Switzerland
United Kingdom
Austria
Ireland
Italy
Netherlands
France
Germany: West
Cyprus
Malta
Belgium
Luxembourg
Spain
Portugal
Turkey
Hungary
0.1
1
10
100
Per '000 inhabitants

Section Twenty-One

Automotives

Table No: 2101

REGISTRATIONS

New Registrations of Passenger Cars 1977-1991

'000

	1977	1980	1983	1984	1985	1986	1987	1988	1989	1990	1991
EC members											
Belgium[a]	428.8	407.2	356.5	370.0	378.2	395.0	406.3	427.2	461.0	473.5	
Denmark[a]	141.2	73.8	116.2	134.3	157.5	169.4	129.4	88.6	78.0	80.9	84.1
France[a]	1907.0	1873.2	2017.6	1757.7	1766.3	1911.5	2105.2	2217.1	2274.0	2309.1	
Germany: East											
Germany: West[a]	2561.3	2426.2	2426.8	2393.9	2379.3	2829.4	2915.7	2807.9	2832.0	3040.8	3428.6
Greece			75.2	85.9	109.4	65.2	50.5	57.6	85.7	115.3	167.7
Ireland[b]	82.3	91.7	61.1	55.9	60.4	59.8	55.7	60.8	78.0	81.2	66.8
Italy[a]	1291.2	1530.5	1581.0	1634.9	1745.9	1825.4	1976.5	2184.3	2362.4	2348.3	
Luxembourg			26.1	26.4	26.9	29.1	29.8	30.7	30.1	34.4	39.1
Netherlands[a]	551.9	450.1	459.4	461.4	495.7	560.5	555.7	482.6	496.0	502.7	
Portugal[a]	76.5	58.4	92.3	85.6	104.2	114.2	129.2	227.1	193.0	212.7	231.4
Spain[b,c]	662.9	574.1	550.4	522.2	575.1	689.1	796.0	998.0	1095.7	963.4	869.9
United Kingdom[a]	1323.5	1513.8	1791.7	1749.6	1832.0	1882.5	2013.7	2215.6	2301.0	2008.9	
EC total	9026.6	8999.0	9554.3	9277.8	9630.9	10531.1	11163.7	11797.5	12286.9	12171.2	
EFTA members											
Austria[b]	295.9	227.5	256.7	215.6	242.7	262.2	243.2	253.1	276.0	288.6	303.7
Finland[a]	90.1	103.2	119.4	127.0	138.3	143.2	152.3	173.5	177.0	139.0	92.5
Iceland[d]			4.7	7.1	5.7	13.4	22.3	14.3	6.5	6.8	
Liechtenstein											
Norway[a]	145.2	95.6	109.7	107.2	159.1	167.4	115.1	67.8	55.0	61.9	53.4
Sweden[a]	241.4	192.6	217.1	231.1	263.0	271.1	316.0	344.0	307.1	229.9	
Switzerland[b]	234.2	280.5	273.9	267.5	265.5	300.2	303.3	319.4	320.0	323.0	310.2
EFTA total	1006.8	899.4	981.5	955.5	1074.3	1157.5	1152.2	1172.1	1141.6	1049.2	
Eastern Europe											
Albania											
Bulgaria					48.0		61.7	57.2	48.9		
Czechoslovakia							143.2	144.5	163.0	156.1	
Hungary[d]			89.1	92.0	101.3	121.1	147.1	128.3	137.6	141.4	
Poland			292.2	274.1	259.9	263.7	260.7	268.7	300.8	358.1	
Romania											
USSR											
Yugoslavia[e]			190.8	207.6	151.4	138.9	159.5	190.1	250.3	269.2	
E European total			572.1	573.7	560.6	523.7	772.2	788.8	900.6	924.8	
Others											
Cyprus			12.0	10.8	12.2	10.2	8.5	11.8	14.8	16.9	
Gibraltar					2.0	2.3	2.2	2.5	2.5	2.1	
Malta			3.1	2.3	4.1	4.0	5.6	9.2			
Monaco											
Turkey					63.9	103.8	105.8	116.5	124.6	215.0	
Total			15.1	13.1	82.2	120.3	122.1	140.0	141.9	234.0	
European total	10033.4	9898.4	11123.0	10820.1	11348.0	12332.6	13210.2	13898.4	14471.0	14379.2	

Sources: Society of Motor Manufacturers & Traders Ltd (SMMT), World Automotive Statistics/motor trades organisations
Notes: See end of section

Table No: 2102

REGISTRATIONS

New Registrations of Commercial Vehicles 1977-1991

'000

	1977	1980	1983	1984	1985	1986	1987	1988	1989	1990	1991
EC members											
Belgium[a]	28.4	32.5	27.3	26.8	31.9	36.4	41.0	42.0	50.7	49.5	
Denmark[a]	34.9	19.5	22.2	32.2	38.5	44.7	38.0	23.0	21.6	23.0	23.4
France[a]	298.4	323.3	346.3	316.1	342.2	390.6	418.0	429.0	448.4	447.0	
Germany: East											
Germany: West[a]	138.0	175.5	144.1	130.5	134.6	143.3	153.0	161.0	173.1	203.4	246.9
Greece			32.0	23.2	19.0	14.8	16.0	20.0	26.1	30.1	23.8
Ireland[b]	9.5	12.2	12.0	13.7	16.2	14.8	13.0	15.6	22.3	28.3	18.6
Italy[a]	110.1	122.3	101.9	97.6	100.7	105.4	124.0	144.0	157.2	159.5	
Luxembourg			1.3	3.0	3.4	3.9	5.0	5.0	6.6	7.1	8.1
Netherlands[a]	43.3	48.0	38.8	48.9	63.1	80.2	85.0	60.0	59.5	68.9	
Portugal[a]	32.8	47.0	27.2	21.5	23.1	32.1	50.0	57.0	70.6	75.8	73.9
Spain[b,c]	101.3	104.5	111.4	98.0	122.0	147.0	204.6	225.1	253.3	245.0	222.1
United Kingdom[a]	230.9	272.0	267.8	269.0	286.7	293.3	315.1	360.0	373.7	296.8	
EC total	1027.6	1156.8	1132.3	1080.5	1181.4	1306.5	1462.7	1541.7	1663.1	1634.4	616.8
EFTA members											
Austria[b]	18.7	21.8	20.3	21.1	22.3	23.4	26.0	29.7	26.9	30.9	31.5
Finland[a]	13.2	17.7	18.7	18.1	19.0	20.1	23.1	27.9	37.8	32.2	16.8
Iceland[d]			0.8	0.8	0.8	0.5	0.5	0.5	0.4	1.6	
Liechtenstein											
Norway[a]	17.2	15.1	25.2	28.0	42.5	43.1	31.5	22.5	17.6	23.0	17.6
Sweden[a]	19.9	19.7	18.1	20.3	22.9	24.6	30.5	37.0	44.4	33.1	
Switzerland[b]	10.8	22.4	18.6	19.5	20.5	23.6	25.0	28.1	26.8	28.9	23.3
EFTA total	79.8	96.7	101.7	107.8	128.0	135.3	136.6	145.7	153.9	149.7	89.2
Eastern Europe											
Albania											
Bulgaria											
Czechoslovakia							28.4	25.1	37.4	27.8	
Hungary[d]			23.0	25.0	27.0	26.8	24.2	25.1	27.0	21.5	
Poland			47.0	58.0	39.0	50.0	51.0	54.0	56.1	62.5	
Romania											
USSR											
Yugoslavia[e]			24.6	22.4	23.8	24.4	23.6	23.0	24.9	19.5	
E European total			94.6	105.4	89.8	101.2	127.2	127.2	145.4	131.3	
Others											
Cyprus			8.0	5.2	5.4	4.0	4.6	6.4	7.8	9.3	
Gibraltar							0.3	0.2	0.2	0.2	
Malta			0.6	0.6	0.6	0.3	0.5	0.5			
Monaco											
Turkey					25.2	25.4	16.8	15.4	12.7	17.1	
Total			8.6	5.8	31.2	29.7	22.2	22.5	20.7	26.6	
European total	1107.4	1253.5	1337.2	1299.5	1430.4	1572.7	1748.7	1837.1	1983.1	1942.0	

Sources: SMMT/motor trades organisations
Notes: See end of section

Table No: 2103

VEHICLE PRODUCTION

Production of Passenger Cars 1977-1991

'000

	1977	1980	1983	1984	1985	1986	1987	1988	1989	1990	1991
EC members											
Belgium	1053.6	882.0	972.3	865.3	986.2	1021.6	1123.4	1137.6	1143.7	1160.4	
Denmark											
France	3092.4	2938.6	2960.8	2713.3	2632.4	2773.1	3051.8	3224.0	3409.0	3294.8	3187.6
Germany: East	167.0	176.8	188.3	202.0	210.4	217.9	217.1	218.0	217.0	143.1	
Germany: West	3790.5	3520.9	3877.6	3790.2	4166.7	4310.8	4373.6	4346.3	4563.7	4660.7	4659.5
Greece											
Ireland	49.9	44.6	23.0								
Italy	1440.5	1445.2	1395.5	1439.3	1389.2	1652.5	1713.3	1884.3	1972.0	1874.7	1632.9
Luxembourg											
Netherlands	53.4	80.8	105.6	108.6	108.1	119.0	125.2	119.8	135.0	121.3	
Portugal	72.6	45.5	65.9	61.2	61.0	62.1	70.8	71.1			
Spain	989.0	1028.8	1141.6	1176.9	1230.1	1281.9	1402.6	1498.0	1638.6	1679.3	1773.8
United Kingdom	1327.8	923.7	1044.6	908.9	1048.0	1019.0	1143.0	1226.8	1299.1	1295.6	1236.9
EC total	12036.7	11086.9	11775.2	11265.7	11832.1	12457.9	13220.8	13725.9	14378.1	14229.9	12490.7
EFTA members											
Austria		7.5	6.1	5.6	7.1	6.8	7.0	7.3	6.6	14.7	
Finland	23.0	21.5	33.6	33.3	38.7	43.0	45.9	42.5	36.4	30.2	
Iceland											
Liechtenstein											
Norway											
Sweden	235.4	235.3	344.7	352.6	400.7	421.3	431.8	407.1	384.2	335.9	269.4
Switzerland											
EFTA total	258.4	264.3	384.4	391.5	446.5	471.1	484.7	456.9	427.2	380.8	269.4
Eastern Europe											
Albania											
Bulgaria					15.0	20.0	20.0	14.7	14.2	14.6	
Czechoslovakia	159.0	185.0	177.5	173.7	177.1	184.7	172.4	163.8	183.6	187.8	
Hungary											
Poland	296.2	364.5	270.2	279.1	283.0	295.3	296.8	296.3	288.7	266.4	
Romania	68.1	79.3	90.2	107.2	114.4	105.4	129.3	141.1	143.6	100.0	
USSR[a]	1280.0	1327.0	1317.7	1300.0	1305.0	1300.0	1307.0	1319.0	1300.0	1300.0	
Yugoslavia	231.1	255.2	210.1	236.0	217.8	239.8	288.1	294.1	308.5	289.4	
E European total	2034.4	2211.0	2065.0	2095.6	2112.3	2145.2	2213.6	2229.0	2238.5	2158.2	
Others											
Cyprus											
Gibraltar											
Malta											
Monaco											
Turkey		31.5	42.5	54.8	60.4	82.0	107.2	118.3	167.6		
Total		31.5	42.5	54.8	60.4	82.0	107.2	118.3	167.7		
European total	14329.5	13593.7	14267.1	13807.6	14451.3	15156.2	16026.3	16530.1	17211.5	16768.9	

Sources: SMMT/motor trades organisations
Notes: See end of section

Table No: 2104

VEHICLE PRODUCTION

Production of Commercial Vehicles 1977-1991

'000

	1977	1980	1983	1984	1985	1986	1987	1988	1989	1990	1991
EC members											
Belgium	80.1	47.0	36.5	52.1	48.7	73.2	72.3	92.6	104.2	91.8	
Denmark											
France	415.4	439.9	375.0	348.9	383.7	421.5	441.4	474.5	510.8	474.2	423.1
Germany: East	37.2	39.8	41.2	44.8	47.3	46.5	43.7	41.5	40.8	29.1	
Germany: West	313.7	357.6	276.8	255.3	279.2	286.1	260.4	279.0	288.0	315.9	355.5
Greece											
Ireland	2.5	2.6									
Italy	144.1	165.1	179.6	161.9	183.8	179.2	199.3	226.7	248.8	246.2	245.4
Luxembourg											
Netherlands[a]	34.5	32.1	11.8	13.6	14.3	15.4	17.6	19.3	21.5	17.3	
Portugal	33.5	58.4	29.1	23.1	26.5	33.9	53.1	65.4	73.0	77.5	
Spain	140.7	152.8	147.1	131.9	187.5	250.7	301.9	368.5	406.9	374.0	308.0
United Kingdom	386.4	389.2	244.5	224.8	266.0	228.7	246.7	318.0	326.6	270.3	217.1
EC total	1588.1	1684.5	1341.6	1256.4	1437.0	1535.2	1636.4	1885.5	2020.6	1896.3	1549.1
EFTA members											
Austria	8.2	8.5	6.1	5.4	11.2	11.9	10.3	10.6	11.8	17.0	
Finland		1.1	0.7	0.7	0.8	0.7	0.8	0.8	0.8	0.9	
Iceland											
Liechtenstein											
Norway											
Sweden	51.5	63.1	52.0	59.0	60.3	65.9	70.0	76.5	81.7	74.4	75.3
Switzerland	1.3	1.2									
EFTA total	61.0	73.9	58.8	65.1	72.3	78.5	81.1	87.9	94.3	92.3	75.3
Eastern Europe											
Albania											
Bulgaria						9.4	10.1	9.2	10.0	8.3	
Czechoslovakia	44.9	53.0	52.7	55.5	57.7	50.2	62.1	63.6	61.2	55.7	
Hungary	14.0	15.2	13.3	15.2	14.0	16.1	14.6	14.5	13.0	8.5	
Poland[a,b]	113.5	116.0	51.4	55.1	57.1	59.4	60.8	61.8	57.6	42.8	
Romania	46.4	49.1	18.2	17.9	19.8	19.0	17.1				
USSR[c]	808.0	872.0	860.4	600.0	610.0	600.0	610.0	600.0	600.0	600.0	
Yugoslavia	26.6	28.5	37.9	36.4	40.5	41.9	36.4	36.3	34.2	29.8	
E European total	1007.0	1133.8	1033.9	780.1	799.1	796.0	811.1	785.4	776.0	745.1	
Others											
Cyprus											
Gibraltar											
Malta											
Monaco											
Turkey		19.4	34.4	36.8	37.3	30.9	31.7	28.9	27.1	41.6	
Total		19.4	34.4	36.8	37.3	30.9	31.7	28.9	27.1	41.6	
European total	2656.1	2911.6	2468.7	2138.4	2345.7	2440.6	2560.3	2787.7	2918.0	2775.3	

Sources: SMMT/motor trades organisations
Notes: See end of section

Table No: 2105

CIRCULATION

Passenger Cars in Use 1977-1990

'000

	1977	1980	1985	1986	1987	1988	1989	1990	% growth 1977-90	% share 1977	% share 1990
EC members											
Belgium	2871.3	3158.7	3342.7	3360.3	3497.8	3573.3	3697.4	3833.3	33.50	2.7	2.1
Denmark	1374.9	1389.5	1500.9	1557.9	1587.6	1596.1	1597.3	1590.6	15.69	1.3	0.9
France	16990.0	19150.0	20940.0	21250.0	21970.0	22520.0	23010.0	23550.0	38.61	16.1	12.9
Germany: East[a]	2236.7	2532.9	3306.2	3722.0	3462.2	3743.6	3750.0	3898.9	74.31	2.1	2.1
Germany: West	20377.2	23236.1	26099.3	27223.8	28304.2	29190.3	30152.4	30695.1	50.63	19.3	16.9
Greece	618.8	879.8	1188.0	1301.1	1378.5	1437.7	1532.9	1550.0	150.48	0.6	0.9
Ireland	572.7	734.4	709.5	711.1	736.6	749.5	773.4	796.4	39.06	0.5	0.4
Italy	16466.2	17686.2	21500.0	22000.0	22500.0	23500.0	24300.0	27500.0	67.01	15.6	15.1
Luxembourg	141.4	147.4	152.0	156.0	162.5	162.5	177.0	180.0	27.30	0.1	0.1
Netherlands	3851.0	4515.0	4901.0	4950.0	5117.7	5250.6	5371.4	5509.2	43.06	3.7	3.0
Portugal	862.0	941.0	1185.0	1236.0	1290.0	1427.0	1474.3	1650.0	91.42	0.8	0.9
Spain	5944.9	7556.5	9273.7	9643.4	9750.0	10500.0	11467.7	11995.6	101.78	5.6	6.6
UK	14372.8	15437.7	19458.2	19390.2	20605.5	21437.7	22427.7	23123.4	60.88	13.6	12.7
EC total	86679.9	97365.2	113556.5	116501.8	120362.6	125088.3	129731.5	135872.5	56.75	82.2	74.6
EFTA members											
Austria	1965.3	2247.0	2530.8	2609.4	2684.8	2784.8	2902.9	2991.3	52.21	1.9	1.6
Finland	1075.4	1225.9	1546.1	1619.8	1698.7	1795.9	1909.2	1926.3	79.12	1.0	1.1
Iceland	67.0	80.0	100.0	104.4	105.0	133.7	124.3	121.1	80.75	0.1	0.1
Liechtenstein											
Norway	1106.6	1233.6	1514.0	1592.2	1623.1	1622.0	1612.7	1613.0	45.76	1.0	0.9
Sweden	2857.1	2883.0	3151.2	3253.6	3366.6	3482.7	3678.0	3600.5	26.02	2.7	2.0
Switzerland[b]	1932.8	2246.8	2617.2	2678.9	2732.7	2745.5	2900.3	2993.5	54.88	1.8	1.6
EFTA total	9004.2	9916.3	11459.3	11858.3	12210.9	12564.6	13127.4	13245.7	47.11	8.5	7.3
Eastern Europe											
Albania											
Bulgaria[a]	480.0	500.0	600.0	750.1	775.0	1000.0	1100.0	1200.0	150.00	0.5	0.7
Czechoslovakia	1560.0	1950.0	2575.0	2700.0	2700.0	2750.0	3122.3	3175.0	103.53	1.5	1.7
Hungary	738.0	925.0	1435.9	1510.0	1660.3	1789.6	1848.2	1943.9	163.40	0.7	1.1
Poland	1290.1	2269.9	3450.0	3600.0	3650.0	4519.0	4525.0	5260.0	307.72	1.2	2.9
Romania[a]	200.0	250.0	250.0	260.0			280.0	280.0	40.00	0.2	0.2
USSR[a]	3000.0	7000.0	11000.0	11500.0	11750.0	12500.0	13500.0	16000.0	433.33	2.8	8.8
Yugoslavia	1923.9	2416.9	2849.4	2935.3	2972.8	3023.7	3105.3	3339.4	73.57	1.8	1.8
E European total	9192.0	15311.8	22160.3	23255.4	23508.1	25582.3	27480.8	31198.3	239.41	8.7	17.1
Others											
Cyprus	71.5	92.0	120.0	125.0	130.0	164.7	179.8	180.0	151.75	0.1	0.1
Gibraltar[a]	5.6	6.5	8.7	9.0	9.5	11.0	11.0	11.3	101.79	0.0	0.0
Malta	56.0	66.2	75.0	80.0	80.0	89.5	97.6	114.7	104.82	0.1	0.1
Monaco											
Turkey	471.5	700.0	983.4	1052.0	1087.8	1175.0	1180.0	1434.8	204.31	0.4	0.8
Total	604.6	864.7	1187.1	1266.0	1307.3	1440.2	1468.4	1740.8	187.93	0.6	1.0
European total	105480.7	123458.0	148363.2	152881.5	157388.9	164675.4	171808.1	182057.3	72.60	100.0	100.0

Sources: SMMT/motor trades organisations
Notes: See end of section

Table No: 2106

CIRCULATION

Commercial Vehicles in Use 1977-1990

'000

	1977	1980	1985	1986	1987	1988	1989	1990	% growth 1977-90	% share 1977	% share 1990
EC members											
Belgium	330.1	354.5	356.1	353.1	382.7	363.2	383.0	401.9	21.8	1.9	1.2
Denmark	268.8	260.1	267.4	283.1	294.6	301.7	302.7	302.1	12.4	1.6	0.9
France	2340.0	2570.0	3980.0	4200.0	4370.0	4570.0	4748.0	4910.0	109.8	13.5	14.6
Germany: East[a]	570.0	613.2	416.5	420.0	449.1	510.2	515.0	450.0	-21.1	3.3	1.3
Germany: West	1412.7	1616.7	1722.6	1759.9	1813.8	1858.9	1927.2	2002.7	41.8	8.2	6.0
Greece	276.1	418.7	565.0	600.0	627.2	675.0	697.9	700.0	153.5	1.6	2.1
Ireland	59.5	70.2	101.0	109.6	119.4	127.4	138.9	152.2	155.8	0.3	0.5
Italy	1283.3	1428.8	1824.0	1856.0	1916.0	2000.0	2082.0	2429.0	89.3	7.4	7.2
Luxembourg	15.3	15.5	14.0	14.1	14.9	15.0	16.8	17.0	11.1	0.1	0.1
Netherlands	337.0	376.0	428.0	464.0	506.5	538.2	556.8	582.1	72.7	2.0	1.7
Portugal	198.5	264.0	356.0	369.0	393.5	422.0	434.0	593.0	198.7	1.1	1.8
Spain	1157.7	1380.9	1570.9	1720.4	1750.0	1975.0	2207.6	2378.7	105.5	6.7	7.1
United Kingdom	1911.7	1912.8	1650.0	1700.0	2915.0	3151.9	3309.7	3288.4	72.0	11.1	9.8
EC total	10160.7	11281.4	13251.5	13849.2	15552.7	16508.5	17319.6	18207.1	79.2	58.8	54.3
EFTA members											
Austria	176.6	208.2	232.3	244.6	255.4	271.8	286.9	295.0	67.0	1.0	0.9
Finland	152.2	166.9	200.3	209.1	221.0	235.9	274.5	270.8	77.9	0.9	0.8
Iceland	8.5	9.0	12.7	13.5	13.0	16.8	13.5	13.1	54.4	0.0	0.0
Liechtenstein											
Norway	153.2	164.5	249.7	282.8	303.2	313.9	230.4	329.5	115.1	0.9	1.0
Sweden	181.9	194.4	231.4	243.7	259.6	281.4	309.4	324.1	78.2	1.1	1.0
Switzerland[b]	151.7	180.5	211.3	217.8	228.8	250.8	261.0	303.7	100.2	0.9	0.9
EFTA total	824.1	923.5	1137.7	1211.5	1281.0	1370.6	1375.7	1536.2	86.4	4.8	4.6
Eastern Europe											
Albania											
Bulgaria[a]	110.0	130.0	150.0	150.0	150.0	150.0	150.0	800.0	627.3	0.6	2.4
Czechoslovakia[a]	290.0	370.0	405.0	425.0	425.0	425.0	327.5	335.0	15.5	1.7	1.0
Hungary	146.0	190.0	216.0	220.0	175.0	179.2	181.1	289.2	98.1	0.8	0.9
Poland[a]	524.2	650.0	815.0	825.0	850.0	1012.0	1015.0	1044.0	99.2	3.0	3.1
Romania[a]	100.0	130.0	150.0	155.0	250.0	250.0	170.0	170.0	70.0	0.6	0.5
USSR[a]	4500.0	6500.0	9000.0	9500.0	9500.0	9000.0	9000.0	9500.0	111.1	26.1	28.3
Yugoslavia[c]	276.6	237.6	299.3	301.2	789.4	831.5	846.0	881.3	218.6	1.6	2.6
E European total	5946.8	8207.6	11035.3	11576.2	12139.4	11847.7	11689.6	13019.5	118.9	34.4	38.8
Others											
Cyprus[a]	17.4	25.2	45.0	45.0	47.0	65.0	74.7	75.0	331.0	0.1	0.2
Gibraltar[a]	0.6	0.7	1.0	1.1	1.0	1.3	1.3	1.5	150.0	0.0	0.0
Malta[a]	15.5	14.2	17.5	19.0	19.0	17.2	19.3	21.2	37.0	0.1	0.1
Monaco											
Turkey	307.7	400.0	500.0	525.0	590.6	550.0	550.0	666.8	116.7	1.8	2.0
Total	341.2	440.1	563.5	590.1	657.6	633.5	645.3	764.5	124.1	2.0	2.3
European total	17272.8	20852.6	25988.0	27227.0	29630.7	30360.3	31030.2	33527.3	94.1	100.0	100.0

Sources: SMMT/motor trades organisations
Notes: See end of section

Table No: 2107

REGISTRATIONS

New Registrations of Diesel Cars 1981-1990

'000

	1981	1982	1983	1984	1985	1986	1987	1988	1989	1990
EC members										
Belgium[a]	63.3	63.5	83.5	103.6	95.0	104.0	109.3	132.3	154.7	155.4
Denmark	2.5	4.1	7.4	10.3	10.4	9.6	6.4	4.1	4.4	3.6
France	215.3	221.3	192.8	240.4	264.8	299.4	384.1	522.4	678.1	762.1
Germany: East										
Germany: West	335.0	326.2	270.5	321.8	530.7	775.6	567.5	382.5	294.2	337.6
Greece										
Ireland[b]				7.1	8.6	8.6	7.2	7.6	11.4	12.2
Italy[a]	260.8	327.9	295.2	425.9	438.7	449.0	483.5	404.8	295.5	171.0
Luxembourg	2.8	3.0	3.5	3.6	3.5	3.6	3.4	4.2	5.3	6.4
Netherlands	36.9	37.2	43.7	60.9	71.3	73.6	72.2	66.6	66.9	54.8
Portugal[a]	6.9	5.5	2.2	1.5	2.3	2.4	3.9	8.1	9.1	10.3
Spain	44.9	63.6	102.7	123.5	125.2	95.1	118.2	126.0	133.3	136.2
United Kingdom	9.7	14.5	24.5	45.4	66.2	77.5	93.2	101.1	123.3	128.6
EFTA members										
Austria	8.0	10.9	11.5	13.8	32.2	40.9	52.8	62.3	67.9	66.3
Finland	11.2	13.4	15.0	14.1	14.4	12.7	11.4	10.1	9.2	7.2
Iceland[c]	0.3	0.3	0.3	0.4	0.4	0.4	0.5			
Liechtenstein										
Norway	7.4	6.1	4.7	2.7	1.7	1.4	1.0	0.8	1.0	2.2
Sweden	12.6	13.5	11.7	9.5	5.7	3.4	4.0	3.0	1.8	1.4
Switzerland	3.9	4.8	4.6	7.1	9.3	12.0	17.6	12.1	8.5	9.0
Eastern Europe										
Albania										
Bulgaria										
Czechoslovakia										
Hungary										
Poland										
Romania										
USSR										
Yugoslavia										
Others										
Cyprus										
Gibraltar										
Malta										
Monaco										
Turkey										

Sources: SMMT/motor trades organisations
Notes: See end of section

Table No: 2108

TWO-WHEELER PRODUCTION

Production of Two-Wheelers 1982-1990

'000

	1982	1983	1984	1985	1986	1987	1988	1989	1990
EC members									
Belgium		53.2	55.8	58.3	47.0	48.7	42.1	39.2	61.3
Denmark									
France	503.5	578.5	449.3	448.4	291.2	280.0	311.6	320.5	338.2
Germany: East									
Germany: West	70.2	136.8	115.3	84.9	63.6	59.8	49.1	47.7	55.3
Greece									
Ireland									
Italy	596.5	529.0					913.5		
Luxembourg									
Netherlands	6.1	8.0	6.5	7.4	28.9	28.9	18.5	21.7	26.5
Portugal									
Spain	166.5	179.2	177.2	173.5	182.6	255.4	265.7	355.9	384.6
United Kingdom									
EFTA members									
Austria	123.4	124.8	134.4	148.7	98.7	55.7	23.0	16.4	20.9
Finland	16.3	15.4	15.0	14.8					
Iceland									
Liechtenstein									
Norway									
Sweden									
Switzerland									
Eastern Europe									
Albania									
Bulgaria	130.6	103.8	94.4						
Czechoslovakia				218.9	201.1				
Hungary									
Poland	150.0	162.0	155.0	142.5	113.0	117.0	106.0	101.8	17.9
Romania				2.0	0.4	6.0	3.9	4.1	4.1
USSR				297.9	313.9	333.1			
Yugoslavia				76.0	79.0	87.1	68.6	66.5	
Others									
Cyprus									
Gibraltar									
Malta									
Monaco									
Turkey									

Source: International Road Federation (IRF)
Note: See end of section

Table No: 2109

CIRCULATION

Two-Wheelers in Use 1982-1990

'000 in use at 31 December

	1982	1983	1984	1985	1986	1987	1988	1989	1990
EC members									
Belgium[a]	401.6	183.1	124.8	124.3	130.2	131.1	131.3	134.2	139.2
Denmark	207.8	209.4	199.2	186.4	191.3				
France	5250.0	5150.0	5065.0	4030.0	3675.0	3370.0			
Germany: East									
Germany: West	2882.2	2949.8	2894.7	2868.3	2688.7	2519.9	2429.9	2381.2	2368.1
Greece	164.7	163.7	153.5	169.0	179.3	188.8	203.6		
Ireland	25.7	25.2	26.3	26.0	25.7	25.8	24.9	24.5	22.8
Italy	4523.2	5231.5	5464.0	5673.0	5799.4	5861.5	6622.6		
Luxembourg	2.0	2.2	2.5	2.6	2.8	2.8	2.8	3.0	3.3
Netherlands			784.0	662.0	691.0	695.0	644.0	610.0	650.7
Portugal	97.9	100.1	101.8	103.1	106.9				
Spain	1282.9	1310.0		1389.1	2339.1	2621.3	2656.2	2575.8	3073.6
United Kingdom	1370.0	1290.0	1225.0	1048.0	1065.0	978.0	912.0	875.0	833.0
EFTA members									
Austria	634.8	638.5	645.7	648.3	629.1	610.1	601.3	589.5	548.0
Finland	208.9	205.2	200.8	196.0	182.0	181.0	177.0		
Iceland[b]	0.8	0.8	0.8	0.9	0.9	0.9	1.0	1.1	1.1
Liechtenstein									
Norway	164.1	167.6	176.1	186.6	199.0	199.1	202.9	202.2	203.5
Sweden[b]	16.8	19.0	22.0	26.3	29.0	31.0	32.5	36.5	
Switzerland	834.5	861.8	846.7	862.1	853.2	853.2	834.1	813.6	764.6
Eastern Europe									
Albania									
Bulgaria	423.0	422.8	420.0	469.0	406.0	478.2	490.2	500.5	481.7
Czechoslovakia				1481.6	1457.4	1440.1	1430.9	1441.9	1458.9
Hungary	630.1	422.0		395.6		405.7	412.4	381.4	
Poland	1616.2	1624.2	1664.0	1546.5	1515.2	1470.1	1464.1	1410.9	1356.6
Romania				297.5	293.8	298.1	297.2	294.6	311.6
USSR									
Yugoslavia	167.1	158.3	157.8	112.7	102.2	96.2	88.2	90.0	
Others									
Cyprus	39.5	40.8	43.3	40.0	41.4	43.4	44.8	47.2	
Gibraltar	1.2	1.3	1.4	1.5	1.8				
Malta									
Monaco	4.0	4.1	4.1	4.0	4.2				
Turkey						354.1	411.1	471.1	536.2

Source: IRF
Notes: See end of section

Table No: 2110

TWO-WHEELER REGISTRATIONS

New Registrations of Two-Wheelers 1982-1990

'000

	1982	1983	1984	1985	1986	1987	1988	1989	1990
EC members									
Belgium	11.0	10.6	8.5	7.5	6.6	6.5	6.8		
Denmark	2.8	3.8	3.2	2.6	2.0	2.0			
France[a]	116.9	98.3	78.6	71.6	84.7	91.8	102.4	111.1	123.1
Germany: East									
Germany: West		128.5	104.0	84.4	81.3	86.9	85.5	89.1	102.4
Greece	19.0	18.5	14.9	14.6		9.6	14.7		
Ireland	4.2	4.0	4.1	4.1	3.5	3.2	2.7	2.7	3.2
Italy	762.0	635.1			542.0	428.0	503.0		
Luxembourg				0.5					
Netherlands	54.6	51.3	58.1	54.0	65.3	71.3	76.3	69.9	74.4
Portugal[a]			1.8	1.4	3.8	6.1	6.4	6.7	7.3
Spain[a]					45.2	60.2	63.2		
United Kingdom					126.0	91.0	90.0	90.0	
EFTA members									
Austria	56.1	56.5	42.9	38.2	37.2	29.6	26.9	24.6	20.1
Finland[a]	4.0	4.9	4.5	4.4	3.6	3.3	3.7	4.5	5.1
Iceland[a]								0.1	0.1
Liechtenstein									
Norway	16.8	11.6	14.3	23.6	26.5	19.9	14.7	11.7	10.2
Sweden[a]	31.5	28.1	22.2	11.3	8.1	7.3	7.3	7.2	
Switzerland	31.2	29.9	31.2	31.2	33.0	29.8	28.6	31.5	31.1
Eastern Europe									
Albania									
Bulgaria				16.0		17.5	8.6	13.6	
Czechoslovakia									
Hungary									
Poland	78.7	104.6	76.9	50.0	48.0	47.4	42.6	49.0	31.4
Romania									
USSR									
Yugoslavia			14.3	12.3	7.0	7.6	12.2		
Others									
Cyprus	5.0	4.8	4.8	4.3	3.2	4.1	5.6	7.1	
Gibraltar									
Malta									
Monaco									
Turkey	22.2	12.4					57.0	59.9	65.2

Source: IRF
Notes: See end of section

Table No: 2111

AUTOMOTIVES FUEL USAGE

Penetration of Unleaded Petrol 1990

million tonnes/% share

	Total Petrol Consumption	Unleaded Petrol Consumption	Unleaded as % of total
EC members			
Belgium	2.68	0.72	26.9
Denmark	1.56	0.91	58.3
France	17.99	2.52	14.0
Germany: East	3.90	1.35	34.6
Germany: West	26.50	20.16	76.1
Greece	2.44	0.07	2.9
Ireland	0.89	0.18	20.2
Italy	13.63	0.66	4.8
Luxembourg	0.41	0.13	31.7
Netherlands	3.44	1.68	48.8
Portugal	1.37	0.01	0.7
Spain	8.14	0.06	0.7
United Kingdom	24.32	8.26	34.0
EC total	107.27	36.71	34.2
EFTA members			
Austria	2.53	1.31	51.8
Finland	1.96	0.95	48.5
Iceland			
Liechtenstein			
Norway	1.78	0.64	36.0
Sweden	4.15	2.21	53.3
Switzerland	3.69	1.88	50.9
EFTA total	14.11	6.99	49.5
Eastern Europe			
Albania			
Bulgaria			
Czechoslovakia			
Hungary			
Poland			
Romania			
USSR			
Yugoslavia			
East European total			
Others			
Cyprus			
Gibraltar			
Malta			
Monaco			
Turkey			
Total			
European total	121.38	43.70	36.0

Source: Institute of Petroleum, Petroleum Review

Notes to Tables in Section Twenty-One:

Table 2101
- a From trade association
- b From national statistics
- c Includes Canary Is., Ceuta, Melilla
- d Figures refer to new imports
- e Sales of domestic production/ assembly only

Table 2102
- a From trade association
- b From national statistics
- c Includes Canary Is., Ceuta, Melilla
- d Figures refer to new imports
- e Sales of domestic production/ assembly only

Table 2103 Includes vehicles assembled in each country
- a Estimated production figures

Table 2104
- a New series starting 1981
- b Includes agricultural tractors
- c Data from 1984 are estimated

Table 2105
- a Data are SMMT estimates and may refer only to some years in each country
- b Includes Liechtenstein

Table 2106
- a Data are SMMT estimates and may refer only to some years in each country
- b Includes Liechtenstein
- c New series starting 1987

Table 2107
- a Sales figures
- b Data not collated separately prior to 1984
- c Imports

Table 2108 Two-wheelers consist of motorcycles and mopeds

Table 2109 Two-wheelers consist of motorcycles and mopeds
- a New series starting 1983
- b Excludes mopeds

Table 2110 Two-wheelers consist of motorcycles and mopeds
- a Excludes mopeds

Growth in Number of Passenger Cars in Use 1977-1990: Selected countries

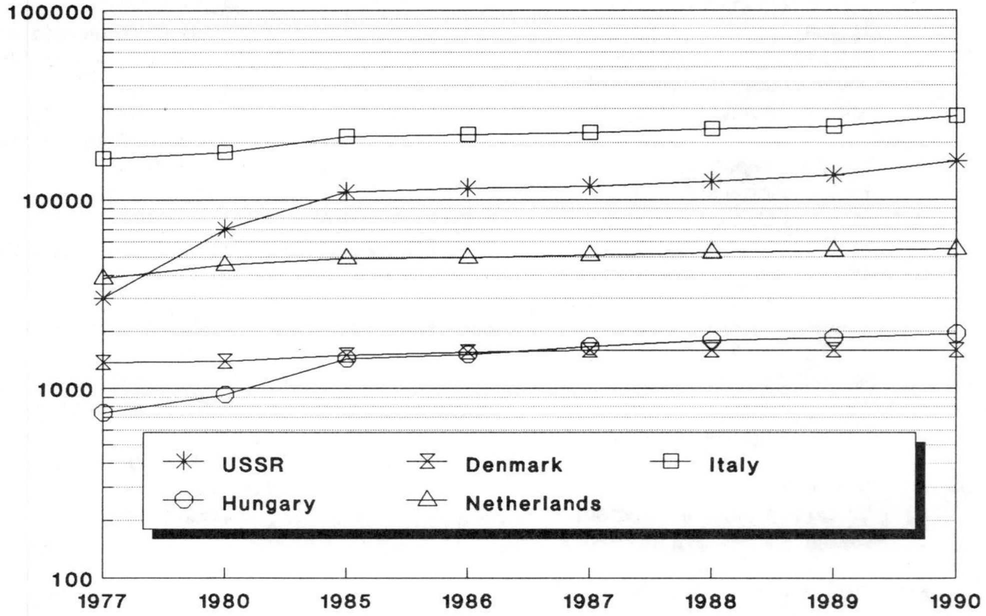

Penetration of Unleaded Petrol 1990: Selected countries

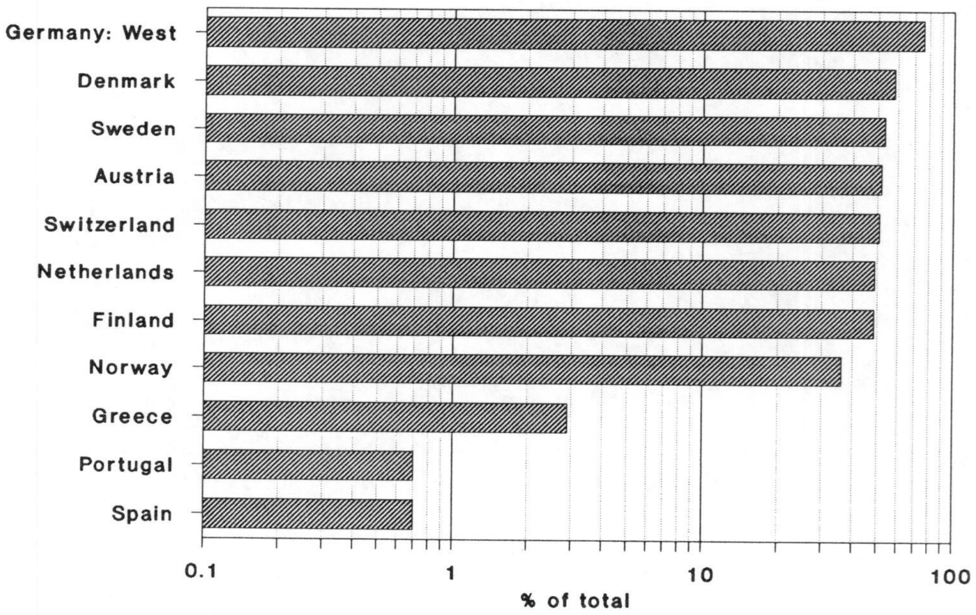

Section Twenty-Two

Transport Infrastructure

Table No: 2201

ROAD TRANSPORT

Road Network 1990 (End of Year)

Kilometres

	Total	Motorway	Highway (National)	Secondary (Regional)	Others (Local)	% paved	Density (km per km^2 of land area)
EC members							
Belgium	137876	1631	12885	1360	122000	94.0	4.50
Denmark	71065	650	3905	7110	59400	100.0	1.65
France[a]	805600	7100	28500	350000	420000	100.0	1.46
Germany: East[b]	124610	1855	11330	34025	77400	100.0	1.15
Germany: West[c]	496652	8721	31108	63441	393382	99.0	1.98
Greece	129990	190	8800	31000	90000	79.0	0.98
Ireland	92303	8	5255	10566	76474	94.0	1.31
Italy[c]	303007	6695	44753	109893	141666	100.0	1.00
Luxembourg	5092	79	869	1828	2316	99.1	1.97
Netherlands	115484	2094	2203	8692	102495	88.0	2.83
Portugal	70176	259	9071	35568	25278	86.00	0.79
Spain	324166	2368	18661	134667	168470	74.00	0.64
United Kingdom	356516	2993	12715	35034	305774	100.00	1.55
EC total							
EFTA members							
Austria	107838	1470	10269	25439	70660	100.00	1.30
Finland	76406	225	11265	29399	35517	61.00	0.22
Iceland	11378		3800	4454	3124	19.90	0.11
Liechtenstein							
Norway	88922	75	26146	26974	35727	69.00	0.27
Sweden	134003	830	13798	84375	35000	71.00	0.40
Switzerland[a]	71099	1495	18407	51197			1.70
EFTA total							
Eastern Europe							
Albania							
Bulgaria	36922	273	2933	3798	29918	91.60	0.33
Czechoslovakia	73751	548	9588	18080	45535	13.30	0.57
Hungary[d]	105397	311	6380	23023	75683	50.80	1.13
Poland	363116	257	45280	128854	188725	61.60	1.16
Romania	461882	113	14570	26967	420232	49.00	1.95
USSR[b]	1687000	3800	99700	170000	1413500	75.00	0.08
Yugoslavia[d]	122571		17470	32229	72872	73.00	0.48
East European total							
Others							
Cyprus[e]	9824		2138		7686	43.30	1.06
Gibraltar							
Malta[c]						92.00	4.64
Monaco[c]	50		50			100.0	25.26
Turkey	367409	281	31149	27979	308000		0.47
Total							
European total							

Sources: International Road Federation (IRF)/national statistical offices
Notes: See end of section

Table No: 2202

ROAD TRANSPORT

Trends in Car Traffic Volume 1978-1990

Million car kilometres

	1978	1980	1983	1984	1985	1986	1987	1988	1989	1990
EC members										
Belgium	38400	40861	41632	41745	42101	43348	45050	47611	49445	
Denmark	23800	21800	22000	23100	24200	25300	26800	28200	29100	29900
France	235800	240000	255000	256000	262000	275000	292000	305000	310000	314000
Germany: East										
Germany: West	279300	297400	304400	314000	313400	338300	356900	376500	385500	401600
Greece	10300							9392		
Ireland	13350	14798						16939	18366	19271
Italy	182700	190608	199280	205336	213543	219097	230920	244963		
Luxembourg		1382	1539	1999	2191	2438	2500	2613	2901	
Netherlands	55500	61400	63100	65300	65000	68100	71230	75530	77260	76960
Portugal			20300	21200	22500					
Spain	48525	52780	55750	56582	56300	61930	64407	69559		
United Kingdom[a]	220300	201100	213170	221790	228000	236000	257000	270000	294440	329700
EFTA members										
Austria	25095	25840	26200	27150	27500		41900			
Finland	21400	22200	24200	24900	25970	26840	28640	30730	32680	33430
Iceland	988	986								
Liechtenstein										
Norway	14221									
Sweden					52900			53000		
Switzerland										
Eastern Europe										
Albania										
Bulgaria								10302	11323	10597
Czechoslovakia										
Hungary	12431					11935				
Poland	16519	20494	17484	18842	20193	21790	23274	27115	29078	34194
Romania										19681
USSR										
Yugoslavia					24000	25135				
Others										
Cyprus										
Gibraltar										
Malta										
Monaco										
Turkey	11300	7444	8800			7961	9415	10254	12870	13730

Source: IRF
Notes: See end of section

Table No: 2203

ROAD TRANSPORT

Trends in Average Annual Distance Travelled (Cars) 1978-1990

Kilometres

	1978	1980	1983	1984	1985	1986	1987	1988	1989	1990
EC members										
Belgium	12914	12743	12760	12649	12595	12900	13030	13324	13373	
Denmark	15700	14000	14700	15100	15200	15700	16290	17048	17600	
France	13305	13000	12400	12300	12500	13000	13600	13500	13600	13600
Germany: East										
Germany: West	14700	14300	13800	14000	13600	14100	14300	14600	14500	14500
Greece	13700				16500					
Ireland										
Italy	12600	11400	10000	9900	9900	9900	10000	10200		
Luxembourg		10744	10880							
Netherlands	13700	13800	14220	14460	14680	14830	14980	15350	15190	14810
Portugal										
Spain[a]	7431	6985	9500	9100	9100	9100	9100	9100		
United Kingdom[b]	15400	13200	13000	13000	14000	14000	14800	14648	15282	16700
EFTA members										
Austria	12300	11500	11000	11000	11000		15600			
Finland	19500	18500	17500	17300	17200	17000	17300	17600	17700	17500
Iceland	13600	11800								
Liechtenstein										
Norway	12400		12900	13200	13500	13900	14000	14100		
Sweden	12800	12000	12000	12000	12000	12000	12500	12500	12000	
Switzerland										
Eastern Europe										
Albania										
Bulgaria								8700	9200	8300
Czechoslovakia										
Hungary	15800					10600				
Poland	9000	8600	5500	5500	5500	5500	5500	6000	6000	6500
Romania										
USSR										
Yugoslavia	15000	15000	12500	12500	8500	8500				
Others										
Cyprus										
Gibraltar										
Malta										
Monaco										
Turkey										

Source: IRF
Notes: See end of section

Table No: 2204

ROAD TRANSPORT

Trends in Total Goods Transported by Road 1977-1990

Million metric-tonne-kilometres

	1977	1980	1983	1984	1985	1986	1987	1988	1989	1990
EC members										
Belgium	14435	16738	17324	19046	19124	20261	21348	24103	25071	
Denmark	11800	9600	8300	8800	9500	10100	10100	10400	10600	10600
France	100100	115500	103000	105000	112000	116600	124400	137600	143800	147000
Germany: East[a]	20048	21020	15378	14491	15056	15293				
Germany: West	106900	124400	125300	128400	134100	140300	144600	153500	163100	
Greece										
Ireland										
Italy	74361	119629	143441	140494	144129	150648	157360	162847		
Luxembourg	255	278	198			239				
Netherlands	17184	17663		18366	18431	19249	20225	22214	22111	22091
Portugal		11800	7220					9370	10051	
Spain[b]	84800	94800	92400	111500	108100	116800	118891	124241		165580
United Kingdom[c]	98000	95900	100400	106900	102100	104100	113300		130200	137400
EFTA members										
Austria	6238	7931	7264	8685						
Finland		17900	21000	20700	22000	20100	22700	23500	25800	26300
Iceland										
Liechtenstein										
Norway	4894	5252	5695	6022	6418	7069	7487	7917	7981	
Sweden	19940	21362	21105	22986	21177		22611	25000	26000	
Switzerland		5689	6140	6337	6646					
Eastern Europe										
Albania										
Bulgaria	9449	10078	7193	7262	7082	7495	7556	14725	15148	13823
Czechoslovakia[a]	17305	21335	20646	20919	11729	12201	12533	13079	13247	11881
Hungary	9550	10258	11951		9716	12175	12765	13120		
Poland	40277	44546	35472	36577	36593	37029	37183	38796	38448	
Romania		11756	8260	7300	5388	5520	4851	4929	5070	
USSR[d]		131000	142000	138000	476366	489811	491955			
Yugoslavia	12510	18997	20528	21540	21184	22342	22416	20882		21796
Others										
Cyprus										
Gibraltar										
Malta										
Monaco										
Turkey	35861	37507	42678			54018	58831	62480	68239	65710

Source: IRF
Notes: See end of section

Table No: 2205

RAIL TRANSPORT

Length of Public Railway Network Operated (End of Year) 1977-1990

Kilometres

	1977	1980	1983	1984	1985	1986	1987	1988	1989	1990
EC members										
Belgium	4003	3971	3842	3741	3667	3618	3568	3554	3501	3479
Denmark	2498	2461	2448	2448	2471	2471	2476	2476	2476	2344
France	34150	33886	34193	34688	34676	34663	34646	34563	34420	34070
Germany: East	14215	14248	14226	14226	14054	14005	14008	14024	14020	13757
Germany: West	31721	28497	28039	27993	27628	27484	27421	27287	27105	26943
Greece	2479	2479	2479	2479	2479	2461	2461	2479	2480	2484
Ireland	2004	1987	1944	1944	1944	1944	1944	1944	1944	1944
Italy	19890	16480	16404	16349	16114	16068	15983	16015	16031	16066
Luxembourg	274	270	270	270	270	270	270	272	272	271
Netherlands	2850	2880	2852	2852	2824	2817	2809	2828	2798	2798
Portugal	3592	3588	3614	3614	3603	3603	3608	3608	3451	3064
Spain	15799	13431	13464	13466	12710	12721	12686	12550	12550	12560
United Kingdom	17973	17645	16964	16816	16752	16670	16630	16599	16591	16584
EC total	151448	141823	140739	140886	139192	138795	138510	138199	137639	136364
EFTA members										
Austria	5857	5847	5753	5756	5766	5745	5747	5630	5630	5624
Finland	6089	6096	6090	5998	5900	5899	5884	5884	5884	5867
Iceland										
Liechtenstein										
Norway	4241	4242	4242	4242	4242	4216	4217	4175	4106	4044
Sweden	12077	12006	12323	12063	11745	11715	11194	11076	10996	10801
Switzerland	4995	2926	2960	2969	2969	2969	2990	2990	2990	2987
EFTA total	33259	31117	31368	31028	30622	30544	30032	29755	29606	29323
Eastern Europe										
Albania	330	330	330	330	330	330	500	509		
Bulgaria	4295	4267	4278	4279	4297	4297	4297	4300	4300	4299
Czechoslovakia	13190	13131	13141	13114	13130	13116	13102	13104	13106	13111
Hungary	8063	7826	7824	7830	7837	7836	7628	7614	7616	7618
Poland	23953	24356	24329	24353	24361	24333	24241	26545	26371	26228
Romania	11127	11110	11106	11169	11269	11221				11348
USSR	228800	239400	244200	246400	247200					
Yugoslavia	9967	9465	9409	9279	9283	9246	9270	9349	9401	9490
E European total	299725	309885	314617	316754	317707	70379	59038	61421	60794	72094
Others										
Cyprus										
Gibraltar										
Malta										
Monaco										
Turkey	8139	8193	8169	8169	8169	8170	8169	8164	8255	8429
Total	8139	8193	8169	8169	8169	8170	8169	8164	8255	8429
European total	492571	491018	494893	496837	495690	247888	235749	237539	236294	246210

Sources: UN/Union Internationale des Chemins de Fer (UIC)

Table No: 2206

RAIL TRANSPORT

Trends in Railway Passenger-Kilometres 1977-1990

Million passenger-kilometres

	1977	1980	1983	1984	1985	1986	1987	1988	1989	1990
EC members										
Belgium	7668	6963	6624	6456	6552	6096	6270	6348	6396	6539
Denmark		4456	4391	4421	4508	4536	4782	4797	4802	4855
France	51828	54492	58428	60276	60780	59904	59732	63300	63288	63761
Germany: East	22356	23136	22608	22920	22452	22356	22522	23064	23808	
Germany: West	36540	41352	39336	38616	41208	41724	39174	44208	57372	61752
Greece	1620	1392	1560	1536	1500	1668	1973	1968	1536	1977
Ireland	876	1032	756	816	948	1008	1196	1092	1140	1226
Italy	38364	39492	36132	39048	37404	40500	41395	43344	44328	45512
Luxembourg	300	300	300	288	288	273	264	276	276	264
Netherlands	8016	8916	9048	8940	9228	8916	9396	9660	10224	11060
Portugal	5232	6072	5196	5448	5724	5808	5907	6036		5664
Spain	13104	13524	15096	15567	15972	15600	15394	15720	14712	15476
United Kingdom[a]	29304	31704	30156	30084	29688	30780	33140	34404	34140	33191
EC total	215208	232831	229631	234416	236252	239169	241145	254217	262022	251277
EFTA members										
Austria		8643		7212	7500	7536	7572	7788	8448	8575
Finland	2976	3216	3336	3276	3228	2676	3106	3204	2616	2736
Iceland										
Liechtenstein										
Norway	2004	2400	2172	2184	2232	2220	2187	2112	2124	2104
Sweden	5586	7019	6688	6690	6803	6363	6013	5964	5856	6076
Switzerland	9240	9179	9313	9554	9703	9653	10050	10848	10884	11049
EFTA total	19806	30457	21509	28916	29466	28448	28928	29916	29928	30540
Eastern Europe										
Albania										
Bulgaria	7344	7056	7260	7536	7788	8040	8076	8148	7596	7793
Czechoslovakia	19176	18048	18792	19320	19836	19836	20029		19572	19335
Hungary	13020	12372	10392	10512	10464	10452	10488	10764	9612	9060
Poland	44316	46320	50148	53184	51984	48528	48285	52128	55884	50373
Romania										30582
USSR	322200	332064								
Yugoslavia	10464	10272	11592	11736	12216	12384	11827	11568	11748	11325
E European total	416520	426132	98184	102288	102288	99240	98705	82608	104412	128468
Others										
Cyprus										
Gibraltar										
Malta										
Monaco										
Turkey	5088	6012	5760	6276	6492	6060	6174	6708	6840	6410
Total	5088	6012	5760	6276	6492	6060	6174	6708	6840	6410
European total	656622	695432	355084	371896	374498	372917	374952	373449	403202	416695

Sources: UN/UIC
Note: See end of section

Table No: 2207

RAIL TRANSPORT

Trends in Railway Freight Carried 1977-1990

Million net tonne-kilometres

	1977	1980	1983	1984	1985	1986	1987	1988	1989	1990
EC members										
Belgium	6492	8004	6864	7884	8256	7416	7272	7692	8052	8354
Denmark		1619	1627	1715	1649	1791	1748	1722		1637
France	66216	69468	59376	60120	58488	51684	51324	52284	53268	49677
Germany: East	58224	56400	54888	67008	69216	68952	68976	60360	58992	39591
Germany: West	55752	65292	55920	59844	63876	60468	59331	59916	56988	60329
Greece	852	816	672	768	732	708	600	600	660	600
Ireland	600	576	540	600	600	576	564	480	516	589
Italy	17580	18384	16752	17868	17964	17472	18432	19560	20856	19372
Luxembourg	564	660	504	588	648	600	588	636	672	615
Netherlands	2808	3468	2784	3120	3276	3048	3000	3204	3108	3070
Portugal	888	996	1044	1236	1308	1452	1648	1704		1442
Spain	11424	10528	10210	11820	11652	11304	11472	11712	11616	10555
United Kingdom[a]	20112	17640	17148	12720	16044	16560	17364	18216	15096	15986
EC total	241512	253851	228329	245291	253709	242031	242319	238086	229824	64248
EFTA members										
Austria		11002	10230	11247	11903	11599	11387	11208	11844	11983
Finland	6408	8340	8088	7980	8064	6948	7481	7812	7956	7877
Iceland										
Liechtenstein										
Norway	2628	3084	2460	2652	2928	3036	2822	2616	2712	2559
Sweden[b]	14782	16648	15445	16944	17592	17760	17628	18168	18888	18435
Switzerland[b]	6324	7752	6408	6888	7044	6972	6812	7500	8160	8127
EFTA total	30142	35824	32401	34464	35628	34716	34743	36096	37716	18264
Eastern Europe										
Albania										
Bulgaria	17076	17676	18060	18132	18168	18324	17844	17580	17040	14132
Czechoslovakia	71544	72636	73068	73992	73596	75156	67985	75288	71976	64260
Hungary	23556	23868	22560	22308	21816	22092	21387	20568	19368	16214
Poland	135408	134736	118032	123504	120648	121776	121425	122208	110208	81637
Romania										48540
USSR	3330900	3439860	3600000							
Yugoslavia	22224	24996	27564	28476	28320	27564	26071	25416	25800	23027
E European total	3600708	3713772	3859284	266412	262548	264912	254712	261060	244392	178692
Others										
Cyprus										
Gibraltar										
Malta										
Monaco										
Turkey	6348	5028	6120	7680	7956	7224	7260	8004	7572	7759
Total	6348	5028	6120	7680	7956	7224	7260	8004	7572	7944
European total	276408	291627	268421	288335	297029	283791	282462	279006	271356	72192

Sources: UN/UIC
Notes: See end of section

Table No: 2208

RAIL TRANSPORT

Railway Statistics of Major National Carriers 1990, Annual Average

	No. of Locomotives (units)	Rail Motor Vehicles (units)	Passengers Carried (million)	Average Length of Journey (km)	Total Goods Carried (million tonnes)
EC members					
Belgium	1040	687	142.4	45.9	79.5
Denmark	328	424	146.3	33.2	8.0
France	5654	1750	834.2	76.4	140.7
Germany: East	5893	724	470.9	37.1	224.0
Germany: West	5952	1270	1043.4	41.7	275.1
Greece[a]	232	168	12.1	163.8	3.7
Ireland	126	40	25.0	49.0	3.3
Italy	3165	1627	429.4	106.0	65.4
Luxembourg	80	19	10.0	20.7	17.5
Netherlands	522	722	255.7	43.3	18.4
Portugal	320	273	225.9	25.1	6.7
Spain	1287	785	274.4	56.4	33.2
United Kingdom[a,b]	2227	9384	762.4	43.5	138.1
EFTA members					
Austria	1231	322	168.4	50.9	62.6
Finland	562	100	46.0	72.4	34.6
Iceland					
Liechtenstein					
Norway	326	160	34.5	61.1	21.3
Sweden	1124	289	77.4	78.5	53.7
Switzerland[a]	1435	252	263.2	42.0	51.8
Eastern Europe					
Albania					
Bulgaria	962	95	102.4	76.1	63.3
Czechoslovakia	4623	1345	407.9	47.4	253.0
Hungary			169.9	53.3	84.7
Poland[a]	7125	1451	789.9	63.8	271.5
Romania	4293	151	407.9	75.0	217.8
USSR					
Yugoslavia[a]	1372	457	108.8	104.1	77.4
Others					
Cyprus					
Gibraltar					
Malta					
Monaco					
Turkey	763	138	139.1	46.1	13.4

Source: UIC
Notes: See end of section

Table No: 2209

CIVIL AVIATION STATISTICS

Trends in Total Distance Flown (Scheduled) 1977-1990

Million kilometres

	1977	1980	1983	1984	1985	1986	1987	1988	1989	1990
EC members										
Belgium	48.2	54.8	48.6	49.6	52.5	52.8	57.3	60.7	69.1	80.6
Denmark	38.4	33.0	32.0	35.9	39.4	42.2	45.0	46.0	53.5	58.3
France	270.0	276.3	275.2	270.8	275.8	288.1	318.3	287.2	348.1	367.2
Germany: East										
Germany: West	181.5	196.2	208.1	215.3	228.5	253.5	289.6	307.2	338.8	397.1
Greece	39.2	40.1	41.7	47.5	52.8	48.6	51.3	52.0	53.8	55.6
Ireland	20.0	21.9	19.1	20.5	21.1	20.9	23.0	35.9	41.5	45.3
Italy	137.9	139.2	128.9	132.6	142.8	139.3	145.6	120.9	175.4	196.1
Luxembourg	3.8	2.7	2.5	2.6	2.9	3.5	4.0	4.1	4.2	5.6
Netherlands	99.4	108.8	115.6	118.4	121.8	128.6	141.8	140.8	157.7	164.9
Portugal	34.6	39.2	38.0	37.2	37.8	39.7	41.8	47.4	52.3	56.3
Spain	139.8	164.3	158.0	156.5	157.2	154.9	158.1	175.8	187.6	200.0
United Kingdom	335.7	426.3	355.5	387.3	414.5	444.3	474.0	481.1	577.6	638.3
EC total	1348.5	1502.8	1423.2	1474.2	1547.1	1616.4	1749.8	1759.1		2265.3
EFTA members										
Austria	17.7	22.0	23.2	23.0	23.1	23.2	27.1	25.7	37.4	42.3
Finland	28.3	35.5	36.6	37.0	38.4	38.1	43.4	48.3	55.4	60.6
Iceland	14.3	11.1	13.6	16.5	17.0	16.9	20.3	20.1	15.5	18.3
Liechtenstein										
Norway	53.9	58.1	59.6	59.0	63.7	70.7	75.4	78.4	81.9	91.3
Sweden	62.6	66.2	74.2	78.8	80.0	90.7	95.1	64.9	113.9	121.3
Switzerland	89.3	97.8	106.0	103.6	106.4	113.4	117.9	124.6	134.2	143.0
EFTA total	266.1	290.7	313.2	317.9	328.6	353.0	379.2	362.0		476.8
Eastern Europe										
Albania										
Bulgaria	10.6	12.7	24.1	25.8	28.4	28.5	30.4	32.4	32.0	31.4
Czechoslovakia	26.8	24.7	20.7	21.6	23.4	23.5	24.3	25.7	24.6	23.9
Hungary	12.4	16.2	16.6	17.6	18.5	18.2	18.2	17.8	20.3	19.0
Poland	29.4	35.1	19.0	22.8	26.2	27.7	27.4	30.1	37.8	39.2
Romania	19.4	19.7	17.7	19.5	20.3	21.0	21.3	21.9	22.5	22.9
USSR			122.9	125.0	114.0	113.0	125.0	155.2	146.8	161.0
Yugoslavia	31.9	34.8	27.5	29.8	36.0	39.3	43.5	46.4	47.4	47.5
East European total	130.5	143.2	248.5	262.1	266.8	271.2	290.1	329.5	331.4	344.9
Others										
Cyprus	7.0	9.5	9.3	10.2	10.3	11.0	11.6	11.8	12.0	13.6
Gibraltar										
Malta	3.6	6.0	5.7	5.1	5.4	6.4	6.5	7.3	8.4	9.4
Monaco			0.2	0.3	0.3	0.4	0.4	0.4	0.4	0.4
Turkey	23.1	14.5	21.6	25.1	27.1	29.0	31.6	35.9	39.9	44.4
Total	33.7	30.0	36.8	40.7	43.1	46.8	50.1	55.4	60.7	67.8
European total	1778.8	1966.7	2021.7	2094.9	2185.6	2287.4	2469.2	2506.0	2890.0	3154.8

Source: International Civil Aviation Organisation (ICAO)

Table No: 2210

CIVIL AVIATION

Trends in Passenger-Kilometres 1979-1990

Million passenger-kilometres

	1979	1980	1983	1984	1985	1986	1987	1988	1989	1990
EC members										
Belgium	4824	4848	5292	5652	5664	5556	5973	6528	6761	7572
Denmark	3060	3048	3000	3072	3120	3204	3748	3869	4309	4671
France	32784	34128	38316	38472	39252	39240	44443	47799	51533	52525
Germany: East										
Germany: West	19848	21048	22704	24276	24432	26640	31810	34097	36316	42387
Greece	5136	5064	5328	6300	7464	6384	7122	7531	8015	7764
Ireland	2220	2052	2124	2196	2460	2496	2737	3567	4299	4567
Italy	11508	12396	12612	13644	14580	13992	18647	16260	21493	23768
Luxembourg			100	108	111	115	128	139	138	253
Netherlands	14016	14196	16068	17004	18240	19236	22605	24144	25896	29036
Portugal	3924	3432	3960	4236	4236	4476	5014	5673	6272	6881
Spain	15180	15516	16332	17460	18816	19152	20409	22272	22848	24157
United Kingdom	47004	50160	44448	45048	51228	51012	77161	83042	92283	105442
EC total	159504	165888	170284	177468	189603	191503	239797	254921	280163	309023
EFTA members										
Austria	1092	1116	1296	1404	1428	1380	1691	2031	3020	3799
Finland	1980	2136	2616	2676	2928	2916	3587	4034	4625	4859
Iceland	1992	1296	1680	2400	2400	2268	2586	2342	1631	1714
Liechtenstein										
Norway	3912	4068	3552	3744	3864	3960	5389	5632	5912	6502
Sweden	5298	5342	5877	6230	6365	6810	7275	6120	8497	9118
Switzerland	10332	10836	12204	12060	12612	12876	13834	14525	15536	16016
EFTA total	24606	24794	27225	28514	29597	30210	34362	34684	39221	42008
Eastern Europe										
Albania										
Bulgaria							2100	2279	2334	2313
Czechoslovakia	1740	1536	1632	1692	1860	1872	2063	2242	2195	2030
Hungary	960	1020	1140	1200	1284	1092	1181	1178	1379	1503
Poland	2316	2352	1308	1776	2232	2196	2301	2701	3734	3479
Romania	1179	1209	1223	1372	1462	1427	1544	1669	1646	1834
USSR	150708	160296	176484	183276	187608	194352	200123	213169	226734	240802
Yugoslavia					3845	4284	5229	3245	5123	5678
E European total	156903	166413	181787	189316	198291	205223	214541	226483	243145	257639
Others										
Cyprus	684	792	924	1128	1320	1404	1586	1629	1664	1861
Gibraltar										
Malta	588	600	564	564	660	744	633	698	737	903
Monaco										
Turkey							3269	3497	4254	4829
Total	1272	1392	1488	1692	1980	2148	5488	5824	6655	7593
European total	342285	358487	380784	396990	419471	429084	494188	521912	569184	616263

Source: ICAO

Table No: 2211

CIVIL AVIATION

Trends in Freight-Tonne/Kilometres 1979-1990

Million tonne-kilometres

	1979	1980	1982	1983	1984	1985	1986	1987	1988	1989	1990
EC members											
Belgium	411.1	405.8	492.2	503.0	541.7	583.4	594.0	535.5	650.5	660.7	663.2
Denmark	131.7	128.5	128.6	123.1	127.4	127.7	129.3	108.0	114.4	121.8	123.9
France	2031.3	2092.9	2297.8	2596.6	2893.9	2980.5	3195.5	3385.6	3681.6	3819.3	3990.8
Germany: East											
Germany: West	1585.7	1584.5	1687.6	2041.6	2345.3	2498.5	2958.9	3247.7	3470.0	3840.3	3994.2
Greece	68.0	68.1	66.4	74.1	79.1	114.9	101.4	104.3	101.9	103.1	112.7
Ireland	99.3	91.9	79.4	91.3	104.4	86.7	79.0	80.8	102.5	117.5	128.3
Italy	496.2	542.1	582.0	633.4	710.1	780.0	859.9	911.6	1029.2	1118.7	1172.3
Luxembourg								0.4	0.5	0.5	0.5
Netherlands	912.9	995.5	1086.2	1244.9	1455.9	1484.8	1595.8	1734.3	1881.8	2002.9	2129.1
Portugal	122.6	111.8	106.7	105.3	125.6	142.9	133.0	124.6	141.4	160.3	167.0
Spain	404.8	417.6	482.2	477.1	517.2	556.8	568.5	564.2	597.9	732.6	760.7
United Kingdom	1247.6	1369.6	1225.5	1355.4	1648.0	1757.6	1878.8	2362.5	3142.3	3446.8	3973.7
EC total	7511.2	7808.3	8234.6	9245.8	10548.6	11113.8	12094.1	13159.5	14914.0	16124.5	17216.4
EFTA members											
Austria	14.5	14.6	20.3	21.3	23.5	23.4	23.5	23.4	22.9	41.6	54.4
Finland	46.0	52.8	66.9	77.2	79.4	84.3	92.9	97.8	100.1	129.4	135.1
Iceland		23.6	23.7	27.0	28.6	22.4	25.0	25.8	34.3	33.1	22.8
Liechtenstein											
Norway	141.1	132.6	139.1	129.9	134.1	135.1	137.3	115.9	120.8	127.6	129.6
Sweden	201.5	195.8	194.9	188.2	195.7	193.4	195.7	169.2	175.0	185.3	191.1
Switzerland	434.3	453.2	500.7	565.8	680.2	685.9	722.3	784.5	813.7	888.7	928.5
EFTA total	837.4	872.6	945.6	1009.4	1141.5	1144.5	1196.7	1216.6	1266.8	1405.7	1461.5
Eastern Europe											
Albania											
Bulgaria								9.6	9.0	7.7	8.0
Czechoslovakia	18.0	14.6	17.1	17.4	16.9	21.2	21.0	20.7	17.2	17.3	15.0
Hungary	7.8	9.2	9.2	8.8	8.6	10.3	9.4	7.3	5.8	5.8	5.5
Poland	18.4	18.8	6.4	8.0	9.3	10.8	12.0	10.3	13.5	28.8	48.9
Romania	11.9	10.0	9.0	6.1	11.2	9.7	10.1	11.6	12.8	14.5	12.8
USSR	2099.0	2151.8	2185.7	2648.2	2744.9	2688.3	2650.4	2827.2	2720.8	2644.5	2545.3
Yugoslavia			53.6	58.1	81.4	81.9	100.2	99.1	124.4	135.5	135.3
E European total	2155.1	2204.4	2281.0	2746.6	2872.3	2822.2	2803.1	2985.8	2903.5	2854.1	2770.8
Others											
Cyprus	26.7	19.8	19.9	19.1	26.6	25.8	28.1	30.4	26.6	33.0	34.3
Gibraltar											
Malta	5.4	4.5	3.8	3.6	3.9	4.8	4.5	4.7	4.7	5.5	4.8
Monaco											
Turkey								46.9	52.7	81.8	101.3
Total	32.1	24.3	23.7	22.7	30.5	30.6	32.6	82.0	84.0	120.3	140.4
European total	10535.8	10909.6	11484.9	13024.5	14592.9	15111.1	16126.5	17443.9	19168.3	20504.6	21589.1

Source: ICAO

Table No: 2212

CIVIL AVIATION

National Airlines: Kilometres Flown, Passengers, Goods Carried 1990

	Aircraft Kilometres ('000)	Aircraft Departures (units)	Aircraft Hours (units)	Passengers Carried ('000)	Freight Carried ('000 tonnes)	Passenger Load Factor (%)	Weight Load Factor (%)
EC members							
Belgium	57907	48833	99747	2339	90	67	71
Denmark[a]	47337	58832	86796	3763	30	64	60
France[b]	276971	206818	445502	15720	518	69	65
Germany: East							
Germany: West	383032	316585	658688	698	65	65	67
Greece	56961	82413	112671	6178	55	64	48
Ireland	31425	51616	70458	3206	37	72	68
Italy	145184	131947	259943	11721	220	65	67
Luxembourg							
Netherlands	151806	80398	217282	6917	342	75	71
Portugal	55395	36781	86274	3258	59	70	61
Spain	160920	156577	268076	15073	225	70	61
United Kingdom[c]	253567	181796	415701	16918	261	73	68
EC total	1620505	1352596	2721138	85791	1902		
EFTA members							
Austria	35806	35805	68560	2261	25	60	53
Finland	75219	74642	127222	5217	40	72	62
Iceland	4418	4856	7852	181	4	60	60
Liechtenstein							
Norway[a]	61890	88143	119133	4697	37	64	61
Sweden[a]	79684	93583	144013	6494	46	65	61
Switzerland	133216	118412	228610	8036	219	65	66
EFTA total	390233	415441	695390	26886	371		
Eastern Europe							
Albania							
Bulgaria[d]	31442	37150	49466	1907	5	68	48
Czechoslovakia	27288	25340	37032	1249	7	67	62
Hungary[d]	18998	18974	34703	1363	5	66	54
Poland	9884	7300	14759	314	2	55	45
Romania	22886	22028	36474	1322	6	65	42
USSR	188600	74701	237046	137191	2938	87	71
Yugoslavia	51271	57375	96821	3827	34	68	66
East European total	350369	242868	506301	147173	2997		
Others							
Cyprus	16845	8742	25920	978	12	74	66
Gibraltar							
Malta	17370	10259	28566	1016	3	77	73
Monaco							
Turkey[d]	44353	40983	85741	4138	51	62	53
Total	78568	59984	140227	6132	66		
European total	2439675	2070889	4063056	265982	5336		

Source: ICAO
Notes: See end of section

Table No: 2213

MERCHANT SHIPPING

Size of Fleet 1977-1991

'000 gross tons

	1977	1980	1985	1986	1987	1988	1989	1990	1991
EC members									
Belgium	1595.5	1809.8	2400.3	2419.7	2268.4	2118.4	2043.6	1954.5	314.2
Denmark	5331.2	5390.4	4942.2	4651.2	4873.5	4501.7	4962.8	5188.1	5870.6
France	11613.9	11924.6	8237.4	5936.3	5371.3	4506.2	4413.5	3832.4	3988.1
Germany: East	1486.8	1532.2	1434.4	1518.9	1494.0	1442.8	1499.9	1437.0	
Germany: West[a]	9592.3	8355.6	6177.0	5565.2	4317.6	3917.3	3966.6	4300.8	5971.2
Greece	29517.1	39471.7	31031.5	28390.8	23559.9	21978.8	21324.3	20521.6	22752.9
Ireland	211.9	209.0	194.0	149.3	153.6	172.8	167.1	180.8	195.1
Italy	11111.2	11095.7	8843.2	7896.6	7817.4	7794.2	7602.0	7991.4	8121.6
Luxembourg						1.7	3.5	3.3	1703.5
Netherlands	5290.4	5723.8	4301.3	4324.1	3908.2	3726.5	3655.0	3784.8	3872.3
Portugal	1281.4	1356.0	1436.9	1114.4	1048.2	988.8	762.1	853.8	890.8
Spain	7186.1	8112.2	6256.2	5422.0	4949.4	4415.1	3961.9	3807.1	3617.2
United Kingdom	31646.4	27135.2	14343.5	11567.1	8405.6	8206.4	7645.8	6716.3	6610.6
EC total	115864.2	122116.2	89597.9	78955.6	68167.1	63770.7	62008.1	60571.9	63908.1
EFTA members									
Austria	53.3	88.8	134.2	124.8	193.5	201.3	204.1	139.3	139.3
Finland	2262.1	2530.1	1974.0	1469.9	1122.2	838.0	944.2	1069.0	1053.0
Iceland	166.7	188.2	180.3	176.4	173.6	174.6	183.4	176.6	167.6
Liechtenstein									
Norway	27801.5	22007.5	15338.6	9294.6	6359.3	9350.3	15596.9	23429.0	23585.7
Sweden	7429.4	4234.0	3161.9	2516.6	2269.5	2116.1	2166.9	2774.8	3174.3
Switzerland	252.7	310.8	342.0	346.2	354.6	259.4	220.1	287.5	285.7
EFTA total	37965.7	29359.4	21131.0	13928.5	10472.7	12939.7	19315.6	27876.2	28405.6
Eastern Europe									
Albania	55.9	56.1	56.1	56.1	56.1	56.1	56.1	55.8	59.1
Bulgaria	964.2	1233.3	1322.2	1385.0	1551.2	1392.4	1375.4	1360.5	1366.8
Czechoslovakia	148.7	155.3	184.3	197.9	157.0	157.9	190.7	325.8	360.7
Hungary	63.0	75.0	77.2	86.4	77.3	76.1	76.1	98.3	103.9
Poland	3447.5	3639.1	3315.3	3457.2	3469.7	3849.4	3416.0	3369.2	3348.4
Romania	1218.2	1856.3	3023.8	3233.9	3263.8	3560.7	3783.4	4004.6	3828.0
USSR	21438.3	23443.5	24745.4	24960.9	25232.0	25784.0	25853.7	26737.4	26405.0
Yugoslavia	2284.5	2466.6	2699.3	2872.6	3164.9	3476.4	3680.7	3816.0	3293.4
E European total	29620.3	32925.2	35423.6	36250.0	36972.0	38353.0	38432.1	39767.6	38765.3
Others									
Cyprus	2787.9	2091.1	8196.1	10616.8	15650.2	18390.6	18134.0	18335.9	20297.7
Gibraltar	10.5	2.3	583.3	1612.9	2827.1	3041.8	2611.3	2008.5	1410.3
Malta	100.4	132.9	1855.8	2014.9	2140.4	2148.5	3239.1	4518.7	6916.3
Monaco									
Turkey	1288.3	1454.8	3684.4	3423.7	3336.1	3281.2	3239.8	3718.6	4107.1
Total	4187.1	3681.1	14319.6	17668.3	23953.8	26862.1	27224.2	28581.7	32731.4
European total	187637.3	188081.9	160472.1	146802.4	139565.6	141925.5	146980.0	156797.4	163810.4

Source: Lloyd's Register of Shipping, Statistical Tables 1991
Note: See end of section

Table No: 2214

SHIPPING

Goods Loaded in International Seaborne Trade 1977-1991

Million tonnes

	1977	1980	1983	1984	1985	1986	1987	1988	1989	1990	1991
EC members											
Belgium	38.7	42.8	39.0	47.1	49.5	45.8	45.5	45.7	48.7	50.0	
Denmark	7.2	7.8	8.9	11.8	11.0	11.2	12.4	13.5	13.9	14.7	
France	58.7	54.1	52.2	52.3	55.0	56.0	57.1	55.6	60.1	61.8	
Germany: East	3.5	5.6	9.0	10.6	12.0	13.3	10.3	10.5			
Germany: West	32.4	35.1	40.8	43.6	44.5	40.1	42.6	44.0	47.3	47.5	
Greece	14.6	21.4	19.7	20.2	21.4	22.9	23.9	24.4	25.7		
Ireland	8.7	3.5	3.6	5.2	5.4	6.3	5.8	6.0			
Italy	36.4	35.0	34.5	35.0	35.3	38.8	36.9	38.5	38.2	41.8	
Luxembourg											
Netherlands	77.0	78.0	75.0	80.7	78.7	79.5	82.7	87.9	92.7	91.8	
Portugal	2.9	4.5	4.7	5.8	6.2	7.0	7.1	7.3			
Spain	26.1	33.2	44.0	44.7	46.8	45.1	40.3	41.3	39.7		
United Kingdom	77.6	100.8	129.7	136.1	143.8	153.7	148.1	129.1	114.8	124.4	128.3
EFTA members											
Austria											
Finland	14.1	17.9	17.8	20.7	20.3	20.2	22.4	23.4	22.4	24.0	26.6
Iceland	0.5	0.7	0.6	0.7	0.8	1.0	1.2	1.2			
Liechtenstein											
Norway	29.8	37.1	39.6	47.1	63.5	58.4	57.4	63.7	82.9	89.1	
Sweden	30.8	34.9	40.7	42.9	42.4	41.8	43.5	44.6	44.1	44.6	45.5
Switzerland											
Eastern Europe											
Albania		1.0	1.2	1.2	1.1	1.1	1.1	1.1			
Bulgaria	3.1	3.6	5.6	3.8	5.5	3.8	5.7	5.5			
Czechoslovakia											
Hungary											
Poland	37.8	28.1	30.6	39.4	33.0	29.9	31.6	32.0	27.3	30.7	
Romania			8.6	8.6	11.9	13.6	13.7	13.8	13.3	12.1	8.7
USSR			165.6	166.5	154.0	155.6	157.2	160.6			
Yugoslavia	4.7	5.2	6.3	6.5	6.7	7.5	9.9	8.5	8.1	7.3	
Others											
Cyprus	1.8	1.9	1.5	1.8	1.3	1.9	1.8	1.9	2.6	2.8	1.9
Gibraltar											
Malta	0.2	0.3	0.4	0.2	0.3	0.4	0.2	0.1			
Monaco											
Turkey	4.8	22.2	33.8	45.1	54.7	58.5	77.0	85.2	138.2	63.3	

Source: UN Monthly Bulletin of Statistics

Table No: 2215

SHIPPING

Total Goods Unloaded in International Seaborne Trade 1977-1991

Million tonnes

	1977	1980	1983	1984	1985	1986	1987	1988	1989	1990	1991
EC members											
Belgium	57.8	69.5	65.9	72.1	73.7	76.2	82.4	84.5	78.0	88.7	
Denmark	33.4	35.6	29.8	31.0	33.3	33.0	34.0	30.5	30.7	29.5	
France	231.4	219.6	167.9	172.3	170.9	177.3	172.0	177.0	178.5	177.0	
Germany: East		14.8	12.7	14.1	13.1	13.8	14.5	15.0			
Germany: West	104.2	114.0	80.8	85.0	91.9	93.2	89.7	94.2	93.0	97.5	
Greece	24.1	33.3	27.1	27.7	26.3	29.5	31.4	31.6	32.4		
Ireland	16.9	12.5	12.4	12.8	13.3	14.5	15.9	16.4			
Italy	217.6	225.4	187.6	194.7	193.4	208.8	199.2	199.2	213.0	226.7	
Luxembourg											
Netherlands	248.1	268.6	229.0	244.1	249.7	257.5	249.6	266.5	280.5	281.3	
Portugal	14.1	24.0	23.9	18.3	18.6	18.5	18.4	19.0			
Spain	84.0	94.3	92.6	88.8	91.5	97.4	97.0	105.6	119.9		
United Kingdom	158.2	132.5	117.2	136.1	139.9	147.5	149.8	159.7	168.3	170.1	171.6
EFTA members											
Austria											
Finland	25.6	31.5	30.9	29.4	31.6	30.0	31.3	31.9	33.6	34.8	35.5
Iceland	1.3	1.4	1.4	1.4	1.6	1.6	1.7	1.8			
Liechtenstein											
Norway	21.8	22.4	16.4	17.6	18.1	17.6	20.5	18.9	18.1	18.9	
Sweden	52.8	55.0	48.2	48.8	52.3	55.8	59.5	55.2	56.0	55.0	53.5
Switzerland											
Eastern Europe											
Albania		0.5	0.6	0.6	0.6	0.6	0.6	0.6			
Bulgaria	24.8	28.1	24.7	25.3	27.5	25.6	25.3	22.0			
Czechoslovakia											
Hungary											
Poland	24.0	22.8	14.9	15.9	15.9	14.8	17.4	18.2	17.0	12.5	
Romania			28.5	28.6	31.1	32.0	33.3	33.3	41.0	33.7	21.4
USSR			63.9	75.9	77.1	80.4	83.7	85.6			
Yugoslavia	16.5	23.1	22.1	22.3	24.0	24.9	25.4	25.5	25.3	26.8	
Others											
Cyprus	1.8	2.2	2.6	3.2	2.8	3.2	3.6	4.0	4.6	4.4	4.3
Gibraltar											
Malta	1.1	1.4	1.5	1.4	1.5	1.9	1.7	1.8			
Monaco											
Turkey	21.4	21.1	35.5	36.3	36.9	37.7	44.5	45.9	43.5	55.1	

Source: UN Monthly Bulletin of Statistics

Table No: 2216

MERCHANT SHIPPING

Shipping Fleets by Principal Types of Vessel 1991

'000 gross tonnes	Oil Tankers	Oil/ Chemical Tankers	Chemical Tankers	Liquid Gas Carriers	Ore & Bulk Carriers	General Cargo Single Deck	General Cargo Multi-Deck	Container Ships
EC members								
Belgium	7.1	5.1	4.7	21.8	0.0	2.4	2.9	30.5
Denmark	1537.4	523.9	24.2	220.0	525.5	54.8	197.8	1612.4
France	1659.8	13.9	12.0	201.0	405.8	18.0	75.0	609.9
Germany: East								
Germany: West[a]	100.7	147.8	27.9	145.8	527.1	275.5	1144.6	2341.0
Greece	8819.5	275.8	111.2	67.9	8748.1	191.4	1018.3	274.9
Ireland	6.9	12.2	0.0	0.0	9.1	52.2	5.4	23.0
Italy	2616.0	69.2	120.6	235.5	1802.5	171.5	132.2	393.0
Luxembourg	105.6	159.2	0.0	213.9	696.1	0.0	33.2	169.5
Netherlands	364.4	253.2	85.4	28.5	359.0	313.4	449.0	589.1
Portugal	460.3	0.0	4.6	7.6	195.6	26.3	31.2	12.0
Spain	1474.7	13.8	54.5	29.7	732.4	169.3	81.5	76.4
United Kingdom	2299.8	16.6	15.7	141.7	500.3	113.0	82.7	1091.3
EC total	19452.2	1490.7	460.8	1313.4	14501.5	1387.8	3253.8	7223.9
EFTA members								
Austria	0.0	0.0	0.0	0.0	71.4	45.9	21.9	0.0
Finland	124.9	83.7	8.8	20.8	89.2	36.4	38.6	0.0
Iceland	0.1	1.2	0.0	0.0	0.0	0.2	12.1	0.0
Liechtenstein								
Norway	10084.8	818.8	767.6	1468.3	5679.0	148.9	512.0	139.5
Sweden	691.1	171.1	92.0	0.0	161.5	57.8	48.5	86.7
Switzerland	0.0	0.0	10.9	0.0	251.9	12.2	1.6	0.0
EFTA total	10900.9	1074.8	879.3	1489.1	6253.0	301.4	634.7	226.2
Eastern Europe								
Albania	0.0	0.0	0.0	0.0	0.0	18.8	38.8	0.0
Bulgaria	292.5	0.0	8.2	0.0	601.2	86.2	191.4	19.1
Czechoslovakia	0.0	0.0	0.0	0.0	276.2	3.6	81.0	0.0
Hungary	0.0	0.0	0.0	0.0	17.3	18.9	67.7	0.0
Poland	107.7	27.8	0.0	0.0	1636.5	201.6	624.5	113.6
Romania	678.8	0.0	0.0	0.0	1697.9	227.9	818.7	15.2
USSR	3925.0	143.5	7.5	125.3	2863.4	2322.2	3057.4	636.8
Yugoslavia	264.1	0.0	8.1	0.0	1492.3	336.8	672.9	130.6
East European total	5268.1	171.3	23.8	125.3	8584.8	3216.0	5552.4	915.3
Others								
Cyprus	5828.2	168.2	86.3	37.1	8384.1	593.6	2196.7	378.0
Gibraltar	1110.6	12.5	0.0	0.0	71.4	0.6	65.5	0.0
Malta	2377.9	33.8	8.8	29.5	2317.1	357.0	941.7	74.8
Monaco								
Turkey	765.6	6.2	13.3	4.9	1751.5	413.8	353.3	0.0
Total	10082.3	220.7	108.4	71.5	12524.1	1365.0	3557.2	452.8
European total	45703.5	2957.5	1472.3	2999.3	41863.4	6270.2	12998.1	8818.2

Source: Lloyd's Register of Shipping, Statistical Tables 1991
Notes: See end of section

Notes to Tables in Section Twenty-Two:

Table 2201	a	Total and others exclude 700,000 km rural roads
	b	Data refer to 1987
	c	Data refer to 1988
	d	Data refer to 1989
	e	Highways includes motorways and secondary
Table 2202	a	Great Britain only
Table 2203	a	National roads only
	b	Great Britain only
Table 2204	a	Public and works goods transport only
	b	National roads only
	c	Great Britain only
	d	New series starting 1985
Table 2206	a	Great Britain only
Table 2207	a	National railway (Great Britain only)
	b	National railway only
Table 2208	a	End of year
	b	Great Britain only, excludes parcels
Table 2212	a	Data refer to Scandinavian Airlines System
	b	Air France only
	c	British Airways only
	d	Data refer to 1989
Table 2213		Ships of 100 gross tons or more Gross tonnage (gt) is a measure of the total volume within the hull, and above deck, available for cargo, passengers, crew, fuel, stores etc. 1 gt = 100 ft3
	a	Data for 1991 include former East Germany
Table 2216		0.0 = less than 500 gross ton
	a	Includes former East Germany

Section Twenty-Three

Tourism and Travel

Table No: 2301

TOURISM RECEIPTS

Trends in Tourism Receipts 1977-1990

Current US dollars (millions)

	1977	1979	1980	1981	1982	1983	1984	1985
EC members								
Belgium	1107	1629	1810	1585	1330	1450	1664	1663
Denmark	940	1312	1337	1239	1305	1308	1292	1326
France	4384	6826	8197	7193	6991	7226	7598	7942
Germany: East	120	150	150	150	245	250	260	270
Germany: West	3972	5741	6565	6279	5392	5453	4299	4748
Greece	981	1668	1734	1881	1527	1176	1313	1428
Ireland	322	527	574	537	477	409	461	531
Italy	4762	8218	8213	7554	8339	9034	8595	8758
Luxembourg							104	147
Netherlands	1110	1325	1662	1571	1545	1470	1694	1661
Portugal	405	942	1147	1023	859	819	960	1137
Spain	4003	6484	6968	6716	7126	6836	7717	8151
United Kingdom	4104	5996	6922	5931	5531	6083	6119	7120
EC total	26210	40818	45279	41659	40667	41514	42076	44882
EFTA members								
Austria	3748	5610	6442	5690	5695	5255	5049	5084
Finland	377	533	677	690	579	497	489	501
Iceland	15	22	23	22	25	27	34	41
Liechtenstein	13	15	16	17	18	19	19	20
Norway	485	635	751	758	733	673	660	755
Sweden	648	890	962	963	1005	1080	1128	1190
Switzerland	1943	2568	3149	3035	3015	3147	3163	3145
EFTA total	7229	10273	12020	11175	11070	10698	10542	10736
Eastern Europe								
Albania	5	7	8	9	10	10	10	10
Bulgaria	235	250	260	269	265	271	288	343
Czechoslovakia	184	385	338	252	268	299	328	307
Hungary	320	452	504	452	411	426	452	512
Poland	170	261	282	116	65	85	101	118
Romania	118	125	136	303	203	202	209	182
USSR	250	300	325	325	330	160	160	163
Yugoslavia	841	825	1115	1350	844	929	1054	1061
East European total	2123	2605	2968	3076	2396	2382	2602	2696
Others								
Cyprus	58	141	203	244	292	332	361	380
Gibraltar	5	5	6	7	9	10	10	15
Malta	81	206	329	265	185	152	130	149
Monaco	230	250	260	270	280	280	290	300
Turkey	205	281	327	381	600	800	1100	1482
Total	579	883	1125	1167	1366	1574	1891	2326
European total	36141	54579	61392	57077	55499	56168	57111	60640

Table No: 2301 (cont'd)

TOURISM RECEIPTS

Trends in Tourism Receipts 1977-1990

Current US dollars (millions)

	1986	1987	1988	1989	1990	% growth 1977-1990	% share 1977	% share 1990
EC members								
Belgium	2271	2980	3438	3064	3575	222.94	3.06	2.60
Denmark	1759	2219	2423	2311	3322	253.40	2.60	2.41
France	9724	11870	13786	16245	20187	360.47	12.13	14.67
Germany: East	350	420	470	520			0.33	
Germany: West	6294	7678	8449	8658	10683	168.96	10.99	7.76
Greece	1834	2268	2396	1976	2575	162.49	2.71	1.87
Ireland	639	839	997	1070	1447	349.38	0.89	1.05
Italy	9855	12174	12403	11984	19738	314.49	13.18	14.34
Luxembourg	193	201	238	286				
Netherlands	2229	2695	2899	3052	3615	225.68	3.07	2.63
Portugal	1533	2145	2402	2685	3556	778.02	1.12	2.58
Spain	12058	14760	16686	16174	18593	364.48	11.08	13.51
United Kingdom	8163	10225	11008	11182	15000	265.50	11.36	10.90
EC total	56902	70474	77595	79209	102291	290.27	72.52	74.32
EFTA members								
Austria	6954	8863	10090	10717	13017	247.31	10.37	9.46
Finland	598	823	983	1013	1169	210.08	1.04	0.85
Iceland	60	86	108	108	122	713.33	0.04	0.09
Liechtenstein	26	31	35	39			0.04	
Norway	1059	1255	1466	1336	1506	210.52	1.34	1.09
Sweden	1552	2033	2346	2543	2895	346.76	1.79	2.10
Switzerland	4227	5345	5720	5543	6839	251.98	5.38	4.97
EFTA total	14476	18436	20748	21299	25548	253.41	20.00	18.56
Eastern Europe								
Albania	13	16	17	17			0.01	
Bulgaria	356	357	359	362			0.65	
Czechoslovakia	383	493	608	581	470	155.43	0.51	0.34
Hungary	592	784	758	798	1000	212.50	0.89	0.73
Poland	136	184	206	202	266	56.47	0.47	0.19
Romania	178	176	171	167	106	-10.17	0.33	0.08
USSR	163	198	216	250			0.69	
Yugoslavia	1337	1668	2024	2230	2774	229.85	2.33	2.02
East European total	3158	3876	4359	4607	4616	117.43	5.87	3.35
Others								
Cyprus	497	666	782	990	1258	2068.97	0.16	0.91
Gibraltar[a]	41	53	66	91	112	2140.00	0.01	0.08
Malta	203	327	382	372	496	512.35	0.22	0.36
Monaco	380	470	560	630			0.64	
Turkey	1215	1721	2355	2557	3308	1513.66	0.57	2.40
Total	2336	3237	4145	4640	5174	793.61	1.60	3.76
European total	76892	96023	106847	109755	137629	280.81	100.00	100.00

Sources: World Tourism Organisation (WTO), Yearbook of Tourism Statistics/OECD/national reports/International Passenger Survey/Euromonitor

Note: See end of section

Table No: 2302

TOURISM RECEIPTS

Trends in Tourism Expenditure 1977-1990

Current US dollars (millions)

	1977	1979	1980	1981	1982	1983	1984	1985
EC members								
Belgium[a]	1583	2969	3272	2644	2190	2095	1953	2050
Denmark	942	1542	1560	1269	1330	1212	1227	1410
France	3923	5193	6027	5752	5157	4281	4271	4557
Germany: East	200	250	270	270				
Germany: West	10984	17754	20599	17853	16223	13274	12423	12809
Greece	89	202	190	249	231	362	339	368
Ireland	237	518	535	513	454	453	411	429
Italy	894	1507	1907	1664	1731	1822	2098	1880
Luxembourg								
Netherlands	2454	4804	4664	3648	3406	3289	3277	3416
Portugal	135	247	290	247	247	229	222	235
Spain	533	922	1229	1008	1008	894	835	1010
United Kingdom	1909	4497	6410	6478	6237	6223	6197	6369
EC total	23883	40405	46953	41595	38214	34134	33253	34533
EFTA members								
Austria	2098	2966	2847	2788	2744	2898	2624	2723
Finland	377	505	544	536	630	622	681	777
Iceland	27	38	42	53	54	66	85	94
Liechtenstein	3	3	3	3				
Norway	861	1189	1310	1433	1641	1587	1488	1722
Sweden	1412	2022	2235	2239	1895	1619	1713	1967
Switzerland	1114	2030	2357	2122	2216	2296	2282	2399
EFTA total	5892	8753	9338	9174	9180	9088	8873	9682
Eastern Europe								
Albania	3	4	4	3				
Bulgaria	33	38	40	40				
Czechoslovakia								
Hungary	167	190	196	164	142	152	157	208
Poland	256	352	380	289	111	195	225	184
Romania								
USSR					140	140	140	150
Yugoslavia	98	155	130	143	107	86	85	110
East European total	557	739	750	639	500	573	607	652
Others								
Cyprus[b]	29	45	56	57	66	68	71	78
Gibraltar								
Malta	23	21	41	50	57	53	50	50
Monaco	6	6	6	6				
Turkey	268	95	115	103	109	127	277	324
Total	326	167	218	216	232	248	398	452
European total	30658	50064	57259	51624	48126	44043	43131	45319

Table No: 2302 (cont'd)

TOURISM RECEIPTS

Trends in Tourism Expenditure 1977-1990

Current US dollars (millions)

	1986	1987	1988	1989	1990	% growth 1977-1990	% share 1977	% share 1990
EC members								
Belgium[a]	2889	3881	4428	4272	5664	257.80	5.16	4.44
Denmark	2119	2860	3087	2932	3676	290.23	3.07	2.88
France	6513	8493	9715	10031	12424	216.70	12.80	9.73
Germany: East							0.65	
Germany: West	18000	23341	25036	23727	29836	171.63	35.83	23.37
Greece	494	508	735	816	1088	1122.47	0.29	0.85
Ireland	685	839	961	989	1159	389.03	0.77	0.91
Italy	2758	4536	5989	6772	13826	1446.53	2.92	10.83
Luxembourg								
Netherlands	4901	6408	6750	6481	7340	199.10	8.00	5.75
Portugal	329	421	533		867	542.22	0.44	0.68
Spain	1513	1938	2440	3080	4254	698.12	1.74	3.33
United Kingdom	8942	11939	14624	15111	19106	900.84	6.23	14.96
EC total	49143	65164	74298	74211	99240	315.53	77.90	77.72
EFTA members								
Austria	4016	5592	6307	6266	7476	256.34	6.84	5.85
Finland	1060	1512	1842	2047	2765	633.42	1.23	2.17
Iceland	129	213	200	176	218	707.41	0.09	0.17
Liechtenstein							0.01	
Norway	2511	3067	3442	2855	3413	296.40	2.81	2.67
Sweden	2819	3784	4572	4966	6066	329.60	4.61	4.75
Switzerland	3368	4339	5019	4907	5989	437.61	3.63	4.69
EFTA total	13903	18507	21382	21217	25927	340.04	19.22	20.30
Eastern Europe								
Albania							0.01	
Bulgaria							0.11	
Czechoslovakia	349	409	399	431	636			0.50
Hungary	225	250	647	1008	600	259.28	0.54	0.47
Poland	186	203	251	215	220	-14.06	0.84	0.17
Romania	22	30	33	35	103			0.08
USSR	175	175	175					
Yugoslavia	132	90	109	131	149	52.04	0.32	0.12
East European total	1089	1157	1614	1820	1708	206.64	1.82	1.34
Others								
Cyprus[b]	54	68	81	133	162	458.62	0.09	0.13
Gibraltar								
Malta	69	102	120	107	134	482.61	0.08	0.10
Monaco							0.02	
Turkey	314	448	358	565	520	94.03	0.87	0.41
Total	437	618	559	805	816	150.31	1.06	0.64
European total	64572	85446	97853	98053	127691	316.50	100.00	100.00

Sources: WTO, Yearbook of Tourism Statistics/OECD/International Passenger Survey/Euromonitor
Notes: See end of section

Table No: 2303

TOURIST ARRIVALS

Foreign Tourist Arrivals at Frontiers 1977-1990

'000	1977	1980	1983	1984	1985	1986	1987	1988	1989	1990
EC members										
Belgium				2237	2460	2454	2516	2643	3018	3163
Denmark				1300	1281	1216	1171	1150	1218	
France	26265	30100	34018	35429	36748	36080	36974	38288	49549	51462
Germany: East	2000	2100	2500	1508	1555	1950	2102	2231	3102	
Germany: West[a]				11942	12686	13458	14045	14501	16115	17045
Greece	3961	4796	4778	5523	6574	7025	7564	7778	8082	8873
Ireland	1963	2258	2257	2514	2529	2464	2664	3007	3484	3666
Italy	17549	22087	22140	23043	25047	24762	25749	26155	25935	26679
Luxembourg				594	622	616	645	760	875	820
Netherlands				3218	3329	4829	4922	4876	5206	5795
Portugal	1347	2730	3714	4119	4989	5409	6102	6624	7116	8020
Spain	21000	22500	25583	27176	27477	29910	32900	35000	35350	34300
United Kingdom[b]	12281	12421	12464	13644	14449	13897	15566	15798	17338	18021
EC total	86366	98992	107454	132247	139746	144070	152920	158811	176388	177844
EFTA members										
Austria[c]				15110	15168	15092	15761	16571	18202	19011
Finland	259	365	451	489	543	598	823	877	882	
Iceland	73	66	78	85	97	114	129	129	131	142
Liechtenstein	80	73	90	88	91	76	75	72	77	78
Norway				1745	1933	1637	1782	1704	1867	1955
Sweden				839	853	824	814	830	837	
Switzerland	8341	8872	11490	11900	11900	11400	11600	11700	12600	13200
EFTA total	8753	9376	12109	30256	30585	29741	30984	31883	34596	34386
Eastern Europe										
Albania	30	32	40	45	50	55	60	60	60	60
Bulgaria					3427	3506	3604	3967	4316	4500
Czechoslovakia	6821	5055	5007	5208	4869	5330	6126	6886	8036	8100
Hungary[d]	7194	9413	6764	8731	9724	10613	11826	10563	14490	20510
Poland	4700	5664	1920	2398	2749	2500	2484	2495	3293	3400
Romania[b]	3685	6742	5802	6584	4772	4535	5142	5514	4852	6533
USSR[b]	4400	5900	3930	4203	4340	4309	5246	6007	7752	7204
Yugoslavia	5621			7224	8436	8464	8907	9018	8644	7880
East European total	32451	32806	23463	34393	38367	39312	43395	44510	51443	58187
Others										
Cyprus	178	353	600	666	770	828	949	1112	1378	1561
Gibraltar	54	75	63	65	86	90	123	156	162	132
Malta	362	729	491	480	518	574	746	784	828	872
Monaco	450		260	240	242	211	214	232	245	245
Turkey	1268	902	1288	1727	2230	2079	2468	3715	3921	4799
Total	2312	2059	2702	3178	3846	3782	4500	5999	6534	7609
European total	129882	143233	145728	200074	212544	216905	231799	241203	268961	278026

Sources: WTO, Yearbook of Tourism Statistics/national reports/International Passenger Survey/Euromonitor
Notes: See end of section

Table No: 2304

TOURIST ARRIVALS

Foreign Tourist Arrivals at Registered Accommodation Units 1977-1990

'000

	1977	1980	1983	1984	1985	1986	1987	1988	1989	1990
EC members										
Belgium	1500	1900	2234	2237	2460	2454	2516	2643	3018	3163
Denmark[a]	3406	3500	1218	1300	1281	1216	1171	1150	1218	
France[b,c]		5664	6120	6523	6928	5829	5962	7421	10103	
Germany: East	1101	1067	1500	1500	1500					
Germany: West	9793	10356	11328	11942	12686	12217	12780	13113	14653	
Greece	5049	5850	5725	6864	7056	6415	6490	6500		
Ireland	1470	1650	1715	1838	2450	2367	2095	2436	2814	
Italy	14836	18137	18483	19279	19789	19096	21349	20613	20585	
Luxembourg			586	688	689	616	645	760	875	820
Netherlands[d]		4168	4459	4933	4992	4829	4922	4876	5206	5795
Portugal	1479	2283	2554	2805	3294	3551	3829	3988	4243	
Spain	11785	9228	11728	12908	12442	13587	14886	14302	13966	
United Kingdom	10118									
EFTA members										
Austria	11748	13879	14482	15110	15168	15092	15761	16571	18202	19011
Finland[e]					2487	2294	2486	2611	2846	
Iceland	66	68								
Liechtenstein[f]			84	88	91	81	75	72	77	
Norway[f,g]	1238	1252	1272	1745	1933	1637	1782	1704		
Sweden			807	839	853	824	814	800		
Switzerland	8341	8872	9200	9482	9528	9157	9324	9359	10103	
Eastern Europe										
Albania	10	10								
Bulgaria			2767	2790	2833	2659	3052	2612	2776	2161
Czechoslovakia	2696	4236	2276	3139	3204	3543	3822	4167		
Hungary	2357	2448	3115	3549	3656	3571	4052	3628	4099	3526
Poland[a]	1865	1843	615	755	896					
Romania	1737	1997	1291	1434	1598	1358	1460	1344		
USSR										
Yugoslavia	6116	6410	5947	7224	8436	8464	8907	9018	8644	7880
Others										
Cyprus	126	254	437	517	567	586	731	950		
Gibraltar	105	33								
Malta	356	675			567	574	746	784	828	872
Monaco[f]	225	240	200	200	242	211	214	232	245	245
Turkey	531	413	1094	1582	1733	2011	2662	3412	3784	

Sources: WTO, Yearbook of Tourism Statistics/OECD/National Passenger Survey/Euromonitor
Notes: See end of section

Table No: 2305

TOURIST ARRIVALS

Method of Arrival 1990

'000

	Air	Road	Rail	Sea	Total	% by air
EC members						
Belgium						
Denmark						
France[a]	9439	32913	4793	2355	49500	19.1
Germany: East[b,c]	407	9134	3897	107	13545	3.0
Germany: West						
Greece	6305	1316	280	1410	9311	67.7
Ireland[c,d]	1347		724	936	3007	44.8
Italy[d]	6849	46823	5203	1426	60301	11.4
Luxembourg[a]	457					
Netherlands						
Portugal[d]	3094	14916	153	259	18422	16.8
Spain[d]	16739	30992	2524	1789	52044	32.2
United Kingdom[d]	12814			5207	18021	71.1
EFTA members						
Austria[b,c]	1422	147556	7759		156737	0.9
Finland						
Iceland	135			7	142	95.1
Liechtenstein						
Norway						
Sweden						
Switzerland						
Eastern Europe						
Albania						
Bulgaria	718	8612	922	78	10330	7.0
Czechoslovakia[a,b]	429	21758	7450	47	29684	1.4
Hungary[b]	597	30696	6236	103	37632	1.6
Poland						
Romania	223	3081	2130	193	5627	4.0
USSR[e]	4984		210			
Yugoslavia[d]	1591	35390	1821	771	39573	4.0
Others						
Cyprus[b]	1326			274	1600	82.9
Gibraltar	132	4156		85	4373	3.0
Malta	827			45	872	94.8
Monaco						
Turkey[f]	2559	1928	145	757	5389	47.5

Sources: WTO, Yearbook of Tourism Statistics/national reports/Euromonitor
Notes: See end of section

Table No: 2306

ACCOMMODATION

Use of Tourist Accommodation 1990

	Stay in Accommodation ('000 nights): International	Stay in Accommodation ('000 nights): Domestic	Hotel Bed Occupancy Rate %	Average Stay (nights): In an Accommodation Establishment	Average Stay (nights): In the Country
EC members					
Belgium[a,b]	12886	23953	23.0	3.2	4.5
Denmark[a,b]	9338	13334	35.0	2.5	4.1
France[a,c]	339273	725300		2.8	7.1
Germany: East					
Germany: West[b]	39146	234579	42.8	2.2	4.0
Greece[b,d,e]	11346	11396		5.0	14.0
Ireland[a,f,g]	8277		39.0	4.5	9.2
Italy[b]	84720	167496	41.5	4.3	7.0
Luxembourg[b,h,i]	30	301	41.1	3.2	3.0
Netherlands[b]	16459	39368	38.5	3.7	4.5
Portugal	19349	13206	32.4	4.6	7.4
Spain[i]	68630	64748	54.3	5.6	11.4
United Kingdom	196400	399000	46.0		10.9
EFTA members					
Austria[b]	94788	28841	31.8	4.9	7.0
Finland[b,g]	2830	10261	49.9	2.0	5.0
Iceland[b,i,j]	380	224	39.0		8.0
Liechtenstein[k]	149	1	31.5		1.9
Norway[b]	5840	11579	35.4	1.7	5.0
Sweden[e,l]	6575	27112	31.0	8.7	6.0
Switzerland[b]	36876	38935	44.0	3.5	4.5
Eastern Europe					
Albania					
Bulgaria	12759	17798	43.5	6.0	2.4
Czechoslovakia[c,i]	9350	25390	50.5	2.4	3.3
Hungary[h,m]	13618	8768	55.3	4.4	6.3
Poland	5350				
Romania[n,o]	5323			3.7	
USSR[i,p]			57.6		6.4
Yugoslavia[b]	43370	45003	42.9	5.5	7.0
Others					
Cyprus[o]	9426	178	62.3	13.3	14.8
Gibraltar[g,q]	278		52.3		4.3
Malta	9604		56.5		9.3
Monaco[b]	726		55.7	3.0	4.0
Turkey	13271	6878	48.2	3.4	8.3

Sources: WTO, Yearbook of Tourism Statistics/OECD/national reports
Notes: See end of section

Table No: 2307

TOURIST ARRIVALS

Principal Countries of Origin of Foreign Tourists 1989

% total tourist arrivals

	No. 1	%	No. 2	%	No. 3	%	No. 4	%
EC members								
Belgium	Netherlands	37.1	W.Germany	16.2	France	10.0	UK	9.8
Denmark[a]	W.Germany	35.2	Sweden	20.7	Norway	12.3	Netherlands	6.4
France[b]	W.Germany	20.9	UK	14.3	Belgium	13.2	Italy	10.8
Germany: East	Czechoslovakia	3.9	USSR	3.8	Poland	1.1	Bulgaria	0.7
Germany: West[a]	USA	14.3	Netherlands	14.3	UK	9.0	Sweden	6.2
Greece	W.Germany	20.2	UK	20.2	Italy	7.0	France	5.9
Ireland	UK	61.1	USA	13.9	W. Germany	5.5	France	5.0
Italy[c]	Switzerland	18.5	W.Germany	18.4	France	17.0	Austria	11.0
Luxembourg[a]	Belgium	27.2	W.Germany	14.6	Netherlands	13.7	France	9.8
Netherlands[a]	W.Germany	20.0	UK	18.2	USA	11.5	France	7.8
Portugal	Spain	42.6	UK	15.5	France	8.6	W.Germany	7.9
Spain[c]	France	22.2	Portugal	18.6	UK	13.6	W.Germany	12.5
United Kingdom[c]	USA	16.4	France	13.0	W.Germany	11.7	Ireland	7.5
EFTA members								
Austria	W.Germany	53.1	Netherlands	7.7	Italy	6.1	UK	4.7
Finland[a]	Sweden	24.3	USSR	19.3	W. Germany	14.0	USA	8.8
Iceland	USA	17.6	W.Germany	14.0	Sweden	12.6	Denmark	12.4
Liechtenstein[d]	W.Germany	27.9	Switzerland	21.5	USA	14.4	Italy	4.8
Norway[a]	Denmark	19.2	Sweden	17.2	W.Germany	16.1	USA	10.4
Sweden[a]	Norway	32.1	W.Germany	19.4	Denmark	9.1	Finland	8.3
Switzerland[a]	W.Germany	33.4	USA	10.7	France	7.7	UK	7.1
Eastern Europe								
Albania								
Bulgaria[c]	Turkey	36.1	Yugoslavia	14.9	Poland	10.8	Hungary	7.6
Czechoslovakia[c]	Poland	38.3	E.Germany	25.4	Hungary	18.6	Yugoslavia	4.3
Hungary	Poland	23.4	Czechoslovakia	16.6	USSR	11.4	W.Germany	10.1
Poland[c]	USSR	35.2	Czechoslovakia	18.3	E.Germany	14.5	Hungary	8.5
Romania[c]	USSR	19.6	Poland	18.6	Bulgaria	15.6	Czechoslovakia	9.8
USSR[c]	Finland	18.8	W.Germany	3.0	USA	2.3	Italy	1.3
Yugoslavia[a]	W.Germany	30.5	Italy	13.7	Austria	8.9	UK	7.5
Others								
Cyprus	UK	39.9	Sweden	8.3	W.Germany	7.9	Finland	6.3
Gibraltar								
Malta[b]	UK	59.5	W.Germany	11.1	Italy	6.4	France	3.4
Monaco[a]	Italy	25.4	France	22.2	USA	14.1	UK	9.1
Turkey[c,e]	W.Germany	20.1	UK	18.1	France	6.4	Greece	6.2

Sources: WTO, Yearbook of Tourism Statistics/OECD Tourism Policy and International Tourism
Notes: See end of section

Table No: 2308

ACCOMMODATION

Hotels and Similar Establishments: Available Capacity by Type 1990

'000 beds/places

	Hotels	Apartment Hotels	Motels	Inns	Guest and Boarding Houses	Holiday Villages	Other	Total
EC members								
Belgium	94							94
Denmark	88							88
France[a]	882					206		1088
Germany: East[b]	218							218
Germany: West	527			226	128		229	1110
Greece	373		3	5	20		37	438
Ireland[b]	41						4	45
Italy	1704							1704
Luxembourg[c]	16							16
Netherlands	111							111
Portugal	86		1	4	48		40	179
Spain	713		213		81		95	1102
United Kingdom[d,e]	873				120			993
EFTA members								
Austria	651							651
Finland	81				16			97
Iceland[a]	6							6
Liechtenstein	1							1
Norway	113							113
Sweden	114				48			162
Switzerland	235		6	30				270
Eastern Europe								
Albania								
Bulgaria[f]	114							114
Czechoslovakia	118		3	21		33	49	224
Hungary	34			19	7		7	57
Poland	49		2	30	7	460		548
Romania[a]	168			8				176
USSR[g]	64							64
Yugoslavia[a]	262		11	2	11	74	2	362
Others								
Cyprus	27	20					5	52
Gibraltar[c]	2							2
Malta	22				1	19		42
Monaco								
Turkey	148		4	3	6		4	165

Sources: WTO/OECD
Notes: See end of section

Table No: 2309

ACCOMMODATION

Bed Capacity for Tourists in Supplementary Accommodation Licensed/Reporting 1989

'000 beds/places

	Youth Hostels	Caravan/ Camp Site Places	Recreation/ Holiday Centres	Rented Accomm.	Health Estab.	Other	Total
EC members							
Belgium		357	24		4	67	451
Denmark	10						10
France[a,b]		2452				178	2629
Germany: East[b]	24	385			553		963
Germany: West	94		24	205	127	162	610
Greece		80		220		7	307
Ireland							
Italy[b]	6	1173		156		185	1520
Luxembourg[b]		51			0	4	55
Netherlands[c]	6		540			2	549
Portugal		257	12				269
Spain		470		336		10809	11615
United Kingdom[a,d]		355	37			20	411
EFTA members							
Austria	12		139	314	18	32	515
Finland[b]	3	23					26
Iceland							
Liechtenstein							
Norway	6						6
Sweden	15	395	46				456
Switzerland	8	270		360	7	228	873
Eastern Europe							
Albania							
Bulgaria		13		149	134	28	324
Czechoslovakia[b]		229		52			282
Hungary[b]		88		146			234
Poland[b]	41	418		66	22	19	566
Romania[b]		47		21	46	12	126
USSR							
Yugoslavia	59	372	112	455	17	24	1039
Others							
Cyprus[b]	0	1		6			7
Gibraltar							
Malta[b]				8			8
Monaco							
Turkey		9	19				28

Sources: WTO, Yearbook of Tourism Statistics/OECD
Notes: See end of section

Table No: 2310

HOLIDAYS

Adults Taking a Holiday (6 days or over) by Country 1990

% total adults	All Holidays	Own Country	Only in Own Country	Taking Domestic Holidays	Taking only Domestic Holidays
EC members					
Belgium	47	17	11	36	23
Denmark	62	37	23	60	37
France[a,b]	56	48	37	86	66
Germany: East[b]					
Germany: West	50	23	14	46	28
Greece	51	46	38	90	74
Ireland	40	21	19	52	47
Italy[b]	46	39	34	85	74
Luxembourg[b]	61	3	2	5	3
Netherlands[c]	63	31	17	49	27
Portugal	41	38	35	93	85
Spain	39	35	33	90	85
United Kingdom[a,d]	58	36	26	62	45
EC total	51	3	27	69	53
EFTA members					
Austria	54	32	17	59	31
Finland[b]	58	32	14	55	24
Iceland					
Liechtenstein					
Norway	58	40	29	69	50
Sweden	70	50	28	71	40
Switzerland	70	37	19	53	27
Eastern Europe					
Albania					
Bulgaria					
Czechoslovakia[b]					
Hungary[b]					
Poland[b]					
Romania[b]					
USSR					
Yugoslavia					
Others					
Cyprus[b]					
Gibraltar					
Malta[b]					
Monaco					
Turkey					

Sources: WTO, Yearbook of Tourism Statistics/OECD
Notes: See end of section

Notes to Tables in Section Twenty-Three:

Table 2301
- a New series starting 1986

Table 2302
- a Includes Luxembourg
- b New series starting 1986

Table 2303
- a Data for West Berlin included from 1986
- b Data from 1986 not comparable with previous series
- c Includes day-trippers
- d Arrivals at all accommodation
- e 1988 excludes residents of Eastern Europe

Table 2304
- a New series starting 1983
- b Arrivals at hotels; Ile de France (Paris) region only
- c New series starting 1985 and 1988
- d New series starting 1988
- e Tourist nights
- f Arrivals at hotels
- g New series starting 1984

Table 2305
- a Data refer to 1989
- b Includes all arrivals regardless of purpose of visit
- c Data refer to 1988
- d Visitor arrivals
- e Data refer to 1987
- f Traveller arrivals

Table 2306 West German data refer to unified country
- a Data for average stay in accommodation refer to 1983
- b Data for average stay in the country refer to 1987
- c Data for average stay in the country refer to 1989
- d Data for total domestic stay in accommodation refer to 1989
- e Data for average stay in accommodation refer to 1986
- f Hotel bed occupancy rate refers to 1987
- g Data for average stay in accommodation refer to 1987
- h Data for average stay in accommodation refer to 1988
- i Hotel bed occupancy rate refers to 1989
- j Data for total stay in accommodation (international and domestic) refer to 1989
- k Hotel bed occupancy rate refers to 1988
- l Data for average stay in the country refer to 1986
- m Data for average stay in the country refer to 1988
- n Data for total international stay in accommodation refer to 1989
- o Data for average stay in accommodation refer to 1989
- p Hotel bed occupancy rate refers to 1986
- q Data for total international stay in accommodation refer to 1987

Table 2307
- a Data refer to 1988
- b UK includes Ireland
- c All visitor arrivals
- d Data refer to 1987
- e Includes travellers for employment

Table 2308
- a Data refer to 1989
- b Data refer to 1988
- c Data refer to 1987
- d England and Wales only
- e Hotels include motels, inns and guest houses
- f Hotels include motels
- g Data refer to 1986

Table 2309 0 = less than 500
Some holiday villages are classified by WTO as hotels and similar establishments, but by OECD as supplementary
- a "Other" includes farms
- b Data refer to 1988
- c Data refer to 1986
- d England only (1988)

Table 2310 0 = less than 500
Some holiday villages are classified by WTO as hotels and similar establishments, but by OECD as supplementary
- a "Other" includes farms
- b Data refer to 1988
- c Data refer to 1986
- d England only (1988)

Section Twenty-Four

Cultural Indicators

Table No: 2401

LIBRARY STATISTICS

Selected Data on Libraries: Latest Year

	Year	Public Libraries	Service Points	Book Stocks (million volumes)	Book Stocks per inhabitant	Borrowers ('000)
EC members						
Belgium	1985	2351	717	21.8	2.2	1731
Denmark	1989	250	1054	34.7	6.8	1990
France	1983	1141	2422	64.4	1.2	6094
Germany: East	1986	8919	18868	52.0	3.1	4863
Germany: West	1989	12275	10929	92.9	1.5	6567
Greece	1986	615	615	8.3	0.8	1399
Ireland	1986	31	387	10.9	3.1	668
Italy	1985	47		16.1	0.3	2688
Luxembourg						
Netherlands	1986	473	988	39.6	2.7	4182
Portugal	1983	178	454	7.5	0.7	2304
Spain	1986	2307	2564	19.7	0.5	3044
United Kingdom	1989	165	5270	156.7	2.7	
EFTA members						
Austria	1987	2081	2313	7.4	1.0	802
Finland	1989	460	1429	34.9	7.0	2356
Iceland	1986	234	241	1.6	6.6	81
Liechtenstein[a]	1989	3	3	0.0	0.7	1
Norway	1989	446	1290	18.5	4.4	1100
Sweden	1987	382	2096	45.7	5.4	
Switzerland	1986			24.2	3.7	
Eastern Europe						
Albania	1988	45	3633	4.0	1.3	228
Bulgaria	1989	5356		46.0	5.1	1609
Czechoslovakia	1986	9453	11852	56.6	3.6	2908
Hungary	1987	4503	9049	51.8	4.9	2207
Poland	1987	10129	23286	129.7	3.4	7795
Romania	1987	7181		69.6	3.0	5094
USSR	1987	11822	296454	1523.1	5.4	106980
Yugoslavia	1989	808	1937	30.2	1.3	19548
Others						
Cyprus	1981		103	0.2	0.3	
Gibraltar[a]	1989	1	1	0.0	0.6	5
Malta	1988	1	56	0.3	0.9	91
Monaco						
Turkey	1986	206	836	6.6	0.1	655

Table No: 2401 (cont'd)

LIBRARY STATISTICS

Selected Data on Libraries: Latest Year

	Year	National Libraries	Higher Education Libraries	School Libraries	Special Libraries	Non-Specialised Libraries
EC members						
Belgium	1985	1			717	
Denmark	1989	1	17		13	5
France	1983	1	63			
Germany: East	1986	2	28			3
Germany: West	1989	7	201		628	36
Greece	1986	1			100	
Ireland	1986	1	8		21	758
Italy	1985	2	11		700	34
Luxembourg	1986	1	1			
Netherlands	1986	1	561		704	5
Portugal	1983	3	191	635	202	22
Spain	1986	1	408	626	435	
United Kingdom	1989	2	554			
EFTA members						
Austria	1987	1	796		1434	9
Finland	1989	1	28	5200	19	
Iceland	1986	1	1	48	52	
Liechtenstein[a]	1989	1	1	7		
Norway	1989	1	85	3521	172	20
Sweden	1987	1	15	5387	38	51
Switzerland	1986	1	13			33
Eastern Europe						
Albania	1988	1	2	1847		40
Bulgaria	1989	1	50	3446	673	27
Czechoslovakia	1986	19	1727			
Hungary	1987	1	221	3913		1
Poland	1987	1	956	19868	4254	124
Romania	1987	2	43	10984	3158	
USSR	1987	1		154000		450
Yugoslavia	1989	8	426	8263	1038	19
Others						
Cyprus	1981				68	
Gibraltar[a]	1989		1		1	
Malta	1988	1		51	9	
Monaco	1986	1				
Turkey	1986	1	139			

Sources: UNESCO/national statistical offices
Note: See end of section

Table No: 2402

BOOK PUBLISHING

Book Titles Published 1977-1989

Number of titles	1977	1980	1983	1984	1985	1986	1987	1988	1989
EC members									
Belgium	5964	9009	8065	6527	8327		7091	8289	6822
Denmark	8021	9256	9460	10660	9554	10957	11129	10584	10762
France	31673	32318	37576	37189	37860	32934	43505	39026	40115
Germany: East	5844	5915	6175	6175	6218	6486	6515	6526	6018
Germany: West	48736	64761	58489	48836	54442	63724	65670	68611	65980
Greece	4981	4048			4651				
Ireland	500	696	672	799	2679				
Italy	10116	12029	13718	14312	15545	16297	17109	19620	22647
Luxembourg	250	297	359	341	297	367	355	343	520
Netherlands	13111	14591		13209	12629	13368	13329	13845	15392
Portugal	6122	6085	8647	9041	10293	10782	7733		
Spain	24896	28195	32457	30764	34684	38405	38302	35426	38353
United Kingdom	36196	48069	50981	51411	52861				
EFTA members									
Austria	6800	7098	9374	9059	8440	9560	8910	8360	9462
Finland	3679	6511	8594	8563	8930	8694	9106	10386	10097
Iceland	801	1193	1121				1231	1244	1250
Liechtenstein			278						
Norway	4823	5578	5540	2653	3559	3284	6757	4894	5331
Sweden	6009	7598	8036	10373	9532	10587	11516	11794	11197
Switzerland	9894	10362	11355	11806	11822	11626	12410	12698	13270
Eastern Europe									
Albania		948	997	1130	959	959			4543
Bulgaria	4088	4681	4924	5367	5171	4924	4583	4379	9294
Czechoslovakia	9568	11647	9574	9911	9844	10020	10565	9558	8631
Hungary	9048	9254	8469	10421	9389	9857	9111	8621	10286
Poland	11552	11919	8789	9195	9649	9881	10416	10728	3867
Romania	7218	7350	5771	5632	5276				
USSR	85395	80676	82589	82790	83976	83472	83011		11339
Yugoslavia	10418	11301	10931	10918	11175	10374	10619	12100	47960
Others									
Cyprus	570	1137						488	561
Gibraltar									
Malta	120	110		313	357	346	421	390	386
Monaco	86	109					123	147	48
Turkey	6830	4318	7180	7224	6685				

Sources: UNESCO/national statistical offices

Table No: 2403

BOOK PUBLISHING

Books Published by Subject 1989

Number of titles

	General	Philosophy	Religion	Social Sciences	Philology	Pure Sciences
EC members						
Belgium	200	186	237	1178	143	244
Denmark	197	391	284	2058	284	718
France	725	1397	1001	10426	848	1886
Germany: East	87	103	281	702	287	458
Germany: West	5511	2890	3709	14568	2894	1958
Greece[a]	70	128	170	1061	226	267
Ireland[a]	3		47	270	11	36
Italy	611	1190	1444	4994	494	715
Luxembourg	22	6	16	178	9	12
Netherlands	118	619	806	1690	280	361
Portugal[b]	935	192	415	1445		604
Spain	995	1527	1674	5931	2166	2455
United Kingdom[a]	2178	1497	2179	9420	1234	4442
EC total	11652	10126	12263	53921	8876	14156
EFTA members						
Austria	225	388	371	2078	317	1422
Finland	397	165	326	2661	154	900
Iceland	41	23	31	189	82	95
Liechtenstein						
Norway	264	104	217	1522	127	315
Sweden	287	233	385	1864	309	688
Switzerland	213	627	728	2799	213	1002
EFTA total	1427	1540	2058	11113	1202	4422
Eastern Europe						
Albania[c]	5	8		175		185
Bulgaria	178	67	9	1235	140	461
Czechoslovakia	537	117	69	1809	334	920
Hungary	174	125	184	1667	355	636
Poland	171	206	478	1948	389	929
Romania	84	45	49	389	152	502
USSR	2244	1596	299	19676	1933	6425
Yugoslavia	492	239	369	3169	23	413
East European total	3885	2403	1457	30068	3326	10471
Others						
Cyprus	23	4	26	116	72	26
Gibraltar						
Malta	10	1	60	180	13	9
Monaco	12	1	1	5	1	4
Turkey[a]	86	96	522	1670	152	184
Total	131	102	609	1971	238	223
European total	17095	14171	16387	97073	13642	29272

Table No: 2403 (cont'd)

BOOK PUBLISHING

Books Published by Subject 1989

Number of titles	Applied Sciences	Arts	Literature	Geography/ History	Total, including others
EC members					
Belgium	779	459	2870	526	6822
Denmark	2543	703	2595	989	10762
France	4983	3029	10911	4909	40115
Germany: East	910	448	1399	287	4962
Germany: West	9048	5296	11806	8300	65980
Greece[a]	468	257	1569	435	4651
Ireland[a]	51	44	141	214	817
Italy	3115	2594	5260	2230	22647
Luxembourg	28	100	68	81	520
Netherlands	2367	899	3048	1189	11377
Portugal[b]	939	458	2053	692	7733
Spain	4615	3097	11859	4034	38353
United Kingdom[a]	6695	2836	11917	5651	48049
EC total	36541	20220	65496	29537	262788
EFTA members					
Austria	1794	836	1256	775	9462
Finland	2677	543	1772	502	10097
Iceland	131	77	444	137	1250
Liechtenstein					
Norway	705	312	1413	352	5331
Sweden	2397	793	3236	1005	11197
Switzerland	2839	1418	1667	1008	12514
EFTA total	10543	3979	9788	3779	49851
Eastern Europe					
Albania[c]	279	16	254	36	958
Bulgaria	1146	159	829	319	4543
Czechoslovakia	2951	742	1454	361	9294
Hungary	2136	683	1996	675	8631
Poland	2827	564	1888	886	10286
Romania	1322	136	1042	146	3867
USSR	27458	2655	11692	2219	76711
Yugoslavia	1712	1197	3171	554	11339
East European total	39831	6152	22326	5196	125629
Others					
Cyprus	109	14	113	58	561
Gibraltar					
Malta	12	38	32	31	386
Monaco	2	12	5	5	48
Turkey[a]	990	222	1294	326	5542
Total	1113	286	1444	420	6537
European total	88028	30637	99054	38932	444805

Sources: UNESCO/national statistical offices
Notes: See end of section

Table No: 2404

BOOK PUBLISHING

Books Published by Subject 1989

% of all published titles

	General	Philosophy	Religion	Social Sciences	Philology	Pure Sciences
EC members						
Belgium	2.9	2.7	3.5	17.3	2.1	3.6
Denmark	1.8	3.6	2.6	19.1	2.6	6.7
France	1.8	3.5	2.5	26.0	2.1	4.7
Germany: East	1.8	2.1	5.7	14.1	5.8	9.2
Germany: West	8.4	4.4	5.6	22.1	4.4	3.0
Greece[a]	1.5	2.8	3.7	22.8	4.9	5.7
Ireland[a]	0.4		5.8	33.0	1.3	4.4
Italy	2.7	5.3	6.4	22.1	2.2	3.2
Luxembourg	4.2	1.2	3.1	34.2	1.7	2.3
Netherlands	1.0	5.4	7.1	14.9	2.5	3.2
Portugal[b]	12.1	2.5	5.4	18.7		7.8
Spain	2.6	4.0	4.4	15.5	5.6	6.4
United Kingdom[a]	4.5	3.1	4.5	19.6	2.6	9.2
EC total	4.4	3.9	4.7	20.5	3.4	5.4
EFTA members						
Austria	2.4	4.1	3.9	22.0	3.4	15.0
Finland	3.9	1.6	3.2	26.4	1.5	8.9
Iceland	3.3	1.8	2.5	15.1	6.6	7.6
Liechtenstein						
Norway	5.0	2.0	4.1	28.5	2.4	5.9
Sweden	2.6	2.1	3.4	16.6	2.8	6.1
Switzerland	1.7	5.0	5.8	22.4	1.7	8.0
EFTA total	2.9	3.1	4.1	22.3	2.4	8.9
Eastern Europe						
Albania[c]	0.5	0.8		18.3		19.3
Bulgaria	3.9	1.5	0.2	27.2	3.1	10.1
Czechoslovakia	5.8	1.3	0.7	19.5	3.6	9.9
Hungary	2.0	1.4	2.1	19.3	4.1	7.4
Poland	1.7	2.0	4.6	18.9	3.8	9.0
Romania	2.2	1.2	1.3	10.1	3.9	13.0
USSR	2.9	2.1	0.4	25.6	2.5	8.4
Yugoslavia	4.3	2.1	3.3	27.9	0.2	3.6
East European total	3.1	1.9	1.2	23.9	2.6	8.3
Others						
Cyprus	4.1	0.7	4.6	20.7	12.8	4.6
Gibraltar						
Malta	2.6	0.3	15.5	46.6	3.4	2.3
Monaco	25.0	2.1	2.1	10.4	2.1	8.3
Turkey[a]	1.6	1.7	9.4	30.1	2.7	3.3
Total	2.0	1.6	9.3	30.2	3.6	3.4
European total	3.8	3.2	3.7	21.8	3.1	6.6

Table No: 2404 (cont'd)

BOOK PUBLISHING

Books Published by Subject 1989

% of all published titles

	Applied Sciences	Arts	Literature	Geography/ History	Total, including others
EC members					
Belgium	11.4	6.7	42.1	7.7	100.0
Denmark	23.6	6.5	24.1	9.2	100.0
France	12.4	7.6	27.2	12.2	100.0
Germany: East	18.3	9.0	28.2	5.8	100.0
Germany: West	13.7	8.0	17.9	12.6	100.0
Greece[a]	10.1	5.5	33.7	9.4	100.0
Ireland[a]	6.2	5.4	17.3	26.2	100.0
Italy	13.8	11.5	23.2	9.8	100.0
Luxembourg	5.4	19.2	13.1	15.6	100.0
Netherlands	20.8	7.9	26.8	10.5	100.0
Portugal[b]	12.1	5.9	26.5	8.9	100.0
Spain	12.0	8.1	30.9	10.5	100.0
United Kingdom[a]	13.9	5.9	24.8	11.8	100.0
EC total	13.9	7.7	24.9	11.2	100.0
EFTA members					
Austria	19.0	8.8	13.3	8.2	100.0
Finland	26.5	5.4	17.5	5.0	100.0
Iceland	10.5	6.2	35.5	11.0	100.0
Liechtenstein					
Norway	13.2	5.9	26.5	6.6	100.0
Sweden	21.4	7.1	28.9	9.0	100.0
Switzerland	22.7	11.3	13.3	8.1	100.0
EFTA total	21.1	8.0	19.6	7.6	100.0
Eastern Europe					
Albania[c]	29.1	1.7	26.5	3.8	100.0
Bulgaria	25.2	3.5	18.2	7.0	100.0
Czechoslovakia	31.8	8.0	15.6	3.9	100.0
Hungary	24.7	7.9	23.1	7.8	100.0
Poland	27.5	5.5	18.4	8.6	100.0
Romania	34.2	3.5	26.9	3.8	100.0
USSR	35.8	3.5	15.2	2.9	100.0
Yugoslavia	15.1	10.6	28.0	4.9	100.0
East European total	31.7	4.9	17.8	4.1	100.0
Others					
Cyprus	19.4	2.5	20.1	10.3	100.0
Gibraltar					
Malta	3.1	9.8	8.3	8.0	100.0
Monaco	4.2	25.0	10.4	10.4	
Turkey[a]	17.9	4.0	23.3	5.9	100.0
Total	17.0	4.4	22.1	6.4	100.0
European total	19.8	6.9	22.3	8.8	100.0

Sources: UNESCO/national statistical offices
Notes: See end of section

Table No: 2405

MUSEUMS

Museums, Museum Visitors: Latest Year

	Year	General	Specialised	Regional	Total, including others	Visitors (millions)
EC members						
Belgium	1976				137	4.6
Denmark	1985		69	125	280	8.5
France	1987		22		1200	12.4
Germany: East	1984		45	367	684	33.7
Germany: West	1987	58		1144	2314	66.3
Greece	1987				267	3.3
Ireland	1979				49	0.8
Italy[a]	1984				309	6.3
Luxembourg[b]	1987	1			1	0.1
Netherlands	1984	22			548	16.0
Portugal	1987	30	27	18	215	3.1
Spain	1979				610	13.9
United Kingdom	1985					18.0
EFTA members						
Austria	1987	16	47	42	179	12.2
Finland[c]	1984			501	572	2.9
Iceland	1982	3		11	14	0.1
Liechtenstein[d]	1986					0.0
Norway	1986	60			421	5.0
Sweden	1983	19	37		167	12.2
Switzerland	1985		270	10	620	9.0
Eastern Europe						
Albania						
Bulgaria	1984	24	23		206	15.5
Czechoslovakia[e]	1987		29	199	350	18.0
Hungary	1987	2	49	98	541	15.9
Poland	1987			158	545	22.4
Romania	1987				436	17.9
USSR[e]	1984		51	753	1479	174.4
Yugoslavia	1988	192	10		565	9.8
Others						
Cyprus	1979				26	0.1
Gibraltar	1984			1	1	
Malta	1986				22	0.6
Monaco	1979				4	1.6
Turkey	1984				127	5.4

Sources: UNESCO/national statistical offices
Notes: See end of section

Table No: 2406

CINEMAS

Cinema Statistics: Latest Year

	Year	A	B	C	D	E
EC members						
Belgium[a,b]	1988	407	16	16	2	
Denmark[c]	1988	381	10	12	2	128
France[c]	1987	5063	137	133	37	207
Germany: East[d]	1987	2064	58	16	1	126
Germany: West[c,e]	1988	3246	109	57	18	260
Greece[f]	1987			22	0	245
Ireland[f,g]	1987	125	12	1	0	161
Italy[c]	1988	3871	93	134	16	374
Luxembourg						
Netherlands[c,h]	1987	445	16	18	0	332
Portugal[d,i]	1987	358	17	5	2	235
Spain[f,i]	1986	2234	86	69	7	344
United Kingdom[j]	1987	1226	75	51	0	265
EFTA members						
Austria[c]	1987	444	5	12	3	339
Finland[c,k]	1988	344	7	14	3	195
Iceland[c,k]	1988	19	1	2	0	231
Liechtenstein	1987					
Norway[c,f]	1988	419	12	9	0	240
Sweden[c,e]	1988	1112	18	21	5	234
Switzerland[d,l]	1988	431	16	20	0	421
Eastern Europe						
Albania[h]	1987	103		14		10
Bulgaria	1987	3028	84	35	1	300
Czechoslovakia[c]	1987	2643	74	44	3	395
Hungary[d]	1987	1057	56	26	0	162
Poland[c]	1987	1704	89	39	6	154
Romania[c]	1987	625	161	26	0	95
USSR[m]	1987	121900	3800	156	7	
Yugoslavia[d]	1987	1174	70	30	3	166
Others						
Cyprus	1987					93
Gibraltar	1987	4	0			
Malta	1987	16	1			
Monaco	1987	3	0			
Turkey[f]	1987	576	26	96		640

Sources: UNESCO/national statistical offices
Notes: See end of section

Notes to Tables in Section Twenty-Four:

Table 2401 a Book stocks: 0.02 million

Table 2403 a Data refer to 1985
b Data refer to 1987
c Data refer to 1986

Table 2404 a Data refer to 1985
b Data refer to 1987
c Data refer to 1986

Table 2405 a Government institutions only
b State museum in Luxembourg-Ville only
c Regional museums includes general and specialised museums
d 0.0 = less than 500,000
e Regional museums includes general museums
f Specialised museums includes others

Table 2406 A Number of fixed cinemas (35mm+)
B Annual attendance (millions)
C Number of long films produced
D Of which co-productions
E Number of long films imported

a Columns A,B refer to 1987
b Column E other criteria than listed in notes c,d,f
c Column E shown commercially for first time in year indicated
d Column E imported in year indicated
e Columns D,E refer to 1987
f Column E approved by censor for public showing in year indicated
g Columns A,B refer to 1985
h Column E refers to 1982
i Column E refers to 1985
j Column E refers to 1983
k Column E refers to 1987
l Columns A,B,E refer to 1987
m Columns C,D refer to 1987

Library Book Stocks per Inhabitant: Latest Year (selected countries)

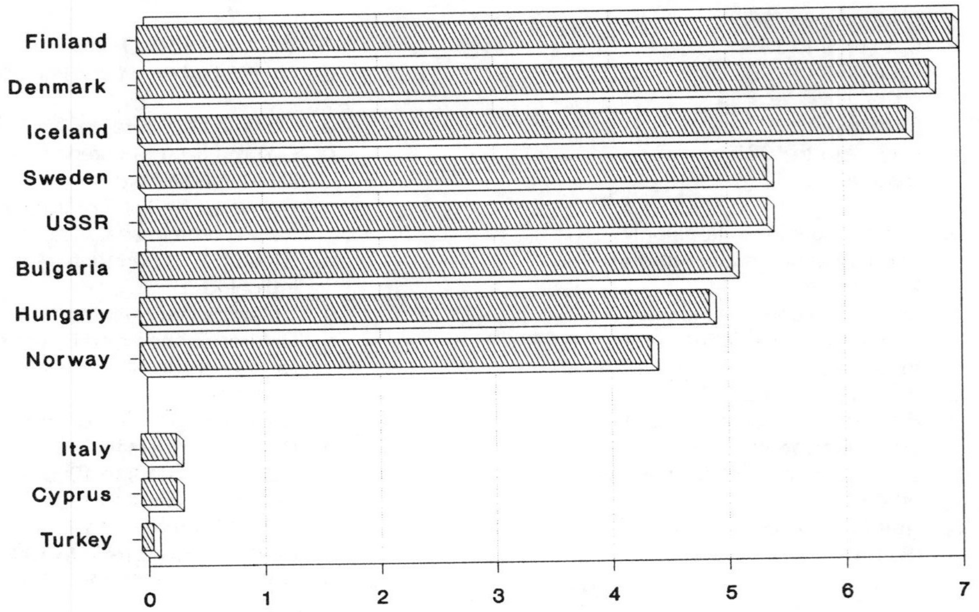

Total Books Published 1989 (selected countries)

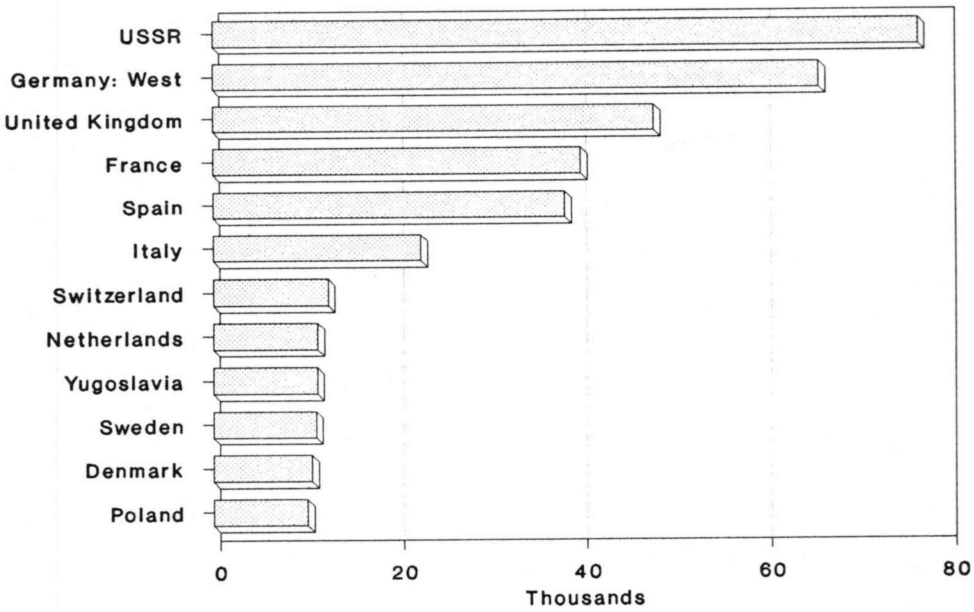

Index